CHURCHILL AS WAR LEADER

CHURCHILL AS WAR LEADER

RICHARD LAMB

Carroll & Graf Publishers, Inc.
New York

Photographs reproduced with permission of the Trustees of the Imperial War Museum, with the exception of nos. 1, 6, and 10.

Published by arrangement with Bloomsbury Publishing Limited.

First Carroll & Graf edition 1993

Carroll & Graf Publishers, Inc.
260 Fifth Avenue
New York, NY 10001

Library of Congress Cataloging-in-Publication Data

Lamb, Richard.
    Churchill as war leader / Richard Lamb.—1st Carroll & Graf ed.
      p.   cm.
    Includes bibliographical references and index.
    ISBN 0-88184-937-5 : $22.95
    1. Churchill, Winston, Sir, 1874–1965—Military leadership.
  2. World War, 1939–1945.   3. World War, 1939–1945—Great Britain.
  I. Title.
  D743.L25 1993
  941.084'092—dc20   92-38237
                                              CIP

Manufactured in the United States of America

Contents

	Introduction	1
1	Churchill out of favour	3
2	Churchill at Admiralty in phoney war	15
3	Norwegian disaster	22
4	Churchill takes over: peace feelers banned	43
5	The French collapse and surrender	53
6	Undeclared war with France after Britain sinks the French fleet	63
7	Britain stands alone: Churchill and Roosevelt June 1940–June 1941	74
8	The Middle East and the Balkans disaster 1940–41	82
9	Keyes, Turkey and Iraq	98
10	October 1940–June 1941: Churchill, Vichy and Syria	111
11	Wavell and Auchinleck under the lash	126
12	The USA and Japan in the war	147
13	Roosevelt and Churchill hand in hand	163
14	Singapore falls	178
15	Churchill and India 1942–45	197
16	North Africa and Casablanca	207
17	The Italians surrender, 1943	227
18	Eastern Aegean frustrations	237
19	Tito and Mihailovic blunder	250
20	D-Day to long-delayed German surrender	276
21	Invasion worries: gas, anthrax and de Gaulle	307
22	Potsdam and atom bombs	319
	Conclusion	339

Source notes   349
Bibliography   366
Selective chronology of the Second World War   370
War Cabinet, May 1940   374
Some members of the Roosevelt administration, 1940–45   374
Major figures in the Second World War   376
Index   383

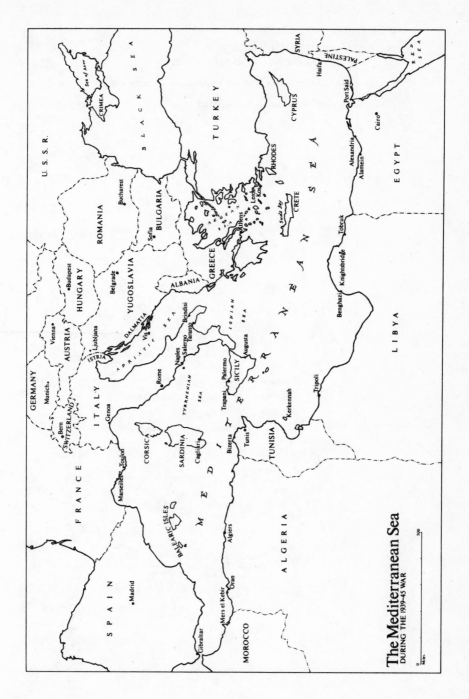

The Mediterranean Sea
DURING THE 1939–45 WAR

Europe 1942–45

INTERNATIONAL BOUNDARIES IN 1945

▲▲▲▲▲▲ Furthest extent of German Advance to December 1941

0 _____ 500
Miles

European Boundaries 1940

German Territory
Soviet Territory
Neutral

NORWAY
SWEDEN
FINLAND
German ally after 1940
DENMARK
UNITED KINGDOM
EIRE
BALTIC STATES
NETHER-LANDS
GERMANY
POLAND
U.S.S.R.
FRANCE
SLOVAKIA
SWITZ. AUSTRIA HUNGARY
ITALY
YUGOSLAVIA
ROMANIA
SPAIN

Lake Ladoga
Leningrad
Vologda
Kazan
Gorky
Moscow
Kuybyshev
Smolensk
Vitebsk
Tula
Katyn Forest
U.
Minsk
Orel
S.
Saratov
S.
R.
Bobruisk
Voronezh
Gomel
Kursk
Volga
Korosten
Kharkov
Stalingrad
Kiev
Zhitomir
Astrakhan
CASPIAN
UKRAINE
Taganrog
Mariupol
Odessa
Kerch
Mineralne Vody
Maykop
Novorossiysk
CRIMEA
Kislovodsk
Makhach Kala
ANIA
Sevastopol
Yalta
Vladikavkaz
Bucharest
BLACK
SEA
Batumi
GARIA
SEA
Istanbul
TURKEY

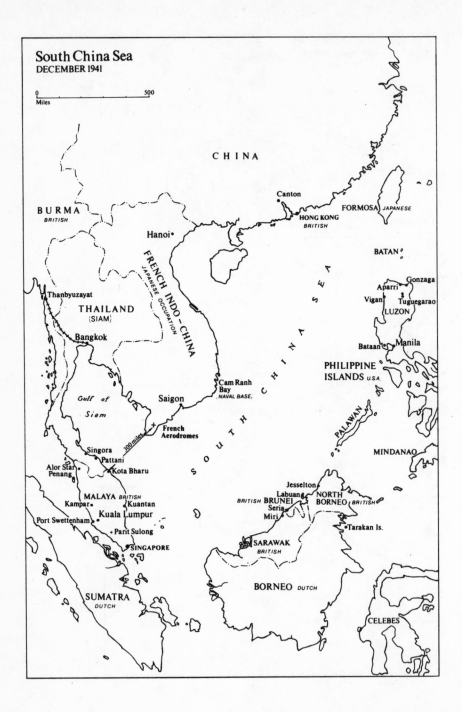

South China Sea
DECEMBER 1941

0   500
Miles

C H I N A

BURMA
BRITISH

Canton

FORMOSA *JAPANESE*

HONG KONG
BRITISH

Hanoi

BATAN

FRENCH INDO – CHINA
JAPANESE OCCUPATION

Thanbyuzayat

THAILAND
(SIAM)

Bangkok

Gonzaga
Aparri
Vigan   Tuguegarao
LUZON

Bataan   Manila

Cam Ranh
Bay
NAVAL BASE

Saigon

Gulf
of
Siam

PHILIPPINE
ISLANDS *U.S.A.*

S
O
U
T
H
   C
H
I
N
A
   S
E
A

300 miles
French
Aerodromes

Singora
Pattani
Alor Star
Penang   Kota Bharu

PALAWAN

MINDANAO

MALAYA *BRITISH*

Kampar   Kuantan
Kuala Lumpur
Port Swettenham
Parit Sulong

Jesselton
Labuang   NORTH
BRITISH   BRUNEI   BORNEO *BRITISH*
Seria
Miri

Tarakan Is.

SINGAPORE

SARAWAK
BRITISH

SUMATRA
DUTCH

BORNEO *DUTCH*

CELEBES

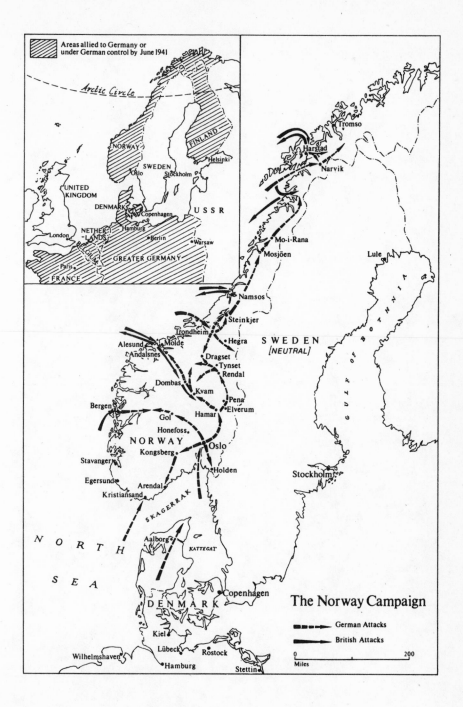

Areas allied to Germany or
under German control by June 1941

Arctic Circle

NORWAY

FINLAND

Helsinki

SWEDEN

Oslo   Stockholm

UNITED
KINGDOM

DENMARK

Copenhagen

NETHER-
LANDS

Hamburg

London

Berlin   Warsaw

GREATER GERMANY

Paris

FRANCE

U S S R

Tromso

Harstad

Narvik

Mo-i-Rana

Mosjöen

Lule

Namsos

Steinkjer

SWEDEN
[NEUTRAL]

Trondheim   Hegra

Alesund   Molde

Andalsnes

Dragset

Tynset

Rendal

Dombas

Kvam

Pena

Elverum

Bergen

Gol

Hamar

Honefoss

NORWAY

Kongsberg   Oslo

Stavanger

Holden

Egersund

Arendal

Kristiansand

Stockholm

SKAGERRAK

N O R T H

Aalborg   KATTEGAT

S E A

Copenhagen

DENMARK

Kiel

Wilhelmshaven

Lübeck   Rostock

Hamburg   Stettin

GULF OF BOTHNIA

The Norway Campaign

German Attacks

British Attacks

0   200
Miles

Introduction

I AM an admirer of Winston Churchill, and in my previous book *The Drift to War 1922–1939* I described how he spearheaded the opposition to Hitler's remilitarization of the Rhineland and his rearming of Germany, which resulted in France and Britain meekly allowing Germany to annex Austria. With at first almost derisory support Churchill denounced Munich as bluff on Hitler's part and demanded urgent rearmament; after Czechoslovakia had fallen he fearlessly advocated a military alliance with Russia as the only means of averting a second World War. Thus, when war began in September 1939, Churchill alone amongst the leading British politicians had clean hands over appeasement and his inclusion in Chamberlain's War Cabinet was inevitable. At this point I take up the story afresh.

I have based this book as far as possible on first hand evidence from archives, and interviews with survivors. Many archives quoted have been hitherto unknown and must cause accepted views on important war issues to be revised. I have found no archives in the Public Record Office which support the wild claims that Churchill deliberately sacrificed Coventry to prevent the Ultra secret being uncovered, nor that he was involved in Sikorski's death. I have omitted these two items.

I am most grateful for the help given to me by the Italian historians Antonio Varsori and Alberto Santoni, and to the French historians Capitaine de Vaisseau Claude Huan and Admiral Jacques Zang.

I am much indebted to the following: Nora Beloff, Mia Berner, Tom Braun, the late Roger Bullen, Axel van der Bussche, the late Sir Hugh Carleton-Green, Field Marshal Carver, Robert Craigie, the late Charles Cruickshank, Sir William Deakin, Captain Henry Denham RN, David Dilks, Elizabeth Evans, Robin Farquharson, Dominic Flessati, Lord Gladwyn, Admiral John Grant, the late Field Marshal Harding, Robert Harris, the late Sir Geoffrey Harrison, Sir William Hayter, Sir Nicholas Henderson, Hugh Humphrey, Helmut Krasnick, Michael Lees, Admiral Sir Hector Maclean, the late General Sir James Marshall-Cornwall, T. B. Martin, Karl Müller, George Newsom, Sir Godfrey Nicholson, the late Sir Con O'Neill, John Pritchard, Sir Frank Roberts, General Pip Roberts, the Earl of Selkirk, Christopher Seton-Watson, Lord Sherfield, the late General Sir Frank Simpson, Peter Solly-Flood, Lord Strauss, Philip Warner, Brigadier Sir Edgar Williams, Philip Ziegler.

I thank the staff of the Public Record Office, the London Library, Chatham House Library, the Wiltshire County Library and the Librarian of the United Oxford and Cambridge Club for their help and unfailing courtesy. Transcripts of the copyright material in the Public Records Office appear by kind permission of the Controller of Her Majesty's Stationery Office. I give warm thanks to Nigel Newton and Kathy Rooney of Bloomsbury for their encouragement; also to Kate Newman of Bloomsbury and Esther Jagger for their meticulous editing. Finally I am most grateful to Joan Moore and John Mark for secretarial help, and to my wife.

Richard Lamb
April 1991

CHAPTER ONE

Churchill out of favour

WHEN THE Second World War began in September 1939 Winston Churchill was immediately recalled to the Cabinet by Neville Chamberlain as First Lord of the Admiralty, but he did not seem to many a potential Prime Minister. His reputation was low. Churchill had been Chancellor of the Exchequer in the Baldwin Government, which was defeated by Labour in the 1929 General Election. The Ramsay MacDonald Government fell because of internal dissensions in 1931 and was replaced by the so-called 'National' Government, with MacDonald as nominal Prime Minister but with the real power held by Stanley Baldwin. In order to give the image of being a National Government, Cabinet places had to be found for Liberal and Labour ministers, and Baldwin could not find room for Churchill. When Baldwin was replaced as Prime Minister by Neville Chamberlain in the summer of 1937 Churchill had high hopes of office, but these were dashed.

In June that year the *Spectator* wrote that, in spite of Churchill's intellectual brilliance and executive ability, 'Cabinet restrictions would sit ill upon him after a period of unrestricted freedom and he may himself prefer his unchallenged domination of the back benches. If he did not join the Cabinet last week there is no particular reason why he should in the next year.' The *Spectator* was wrong. Churchill was desperately anxious for office, and at first did all he could to ingratiate himself with Chamberlain. When this had no effect he changed his attitude to one of hostility. The *Spectator* commented aptly in August 1938 that Churchill had at first appeared a friend of Chamberlain and had been full of helpfulness. 'Now his attitude has changed and his shafts against the Government have been as barbed as in the Baldwin days. His entourage is not large.'[1] During this period of political exile Churchill's public image had slumped disastrously and Chamberlain would not rescue him, feeling he would be an embarrassment in Cabinet.

Although he had been a relatively popular Chancellor of the Exchequer, Churchill had appeared completely out-of-date and made himself almost a figure of fun by his vehement opposition to any form of independence for India. In January 1931 he expressed himself intemperately in the Commons, making a passionate assault on the policy of yielding to Indian demands, and on the same day resigning from the Shadow Cabinet because Baldwin took a more moderate line.

In February 1935 Churchill carried seventy-five Conservative MPs with him into the Lobby to vote against the Baldwin Government's proposals for India. His son Randolph insisted on fighting his father's battle over India by standing as an Independent Conservative in the Wavertree by-election and scoring a surprisingly high 23.9 per cent of the votes, thus making Labour the victor with only 35.4 per cent in what had been a safe Conservative seat.

Surprisingly, Randolph was forgiven by the Tory hierarchy and for the November 1935 General Election was adopted as official Conservative candidate for Toxteth, next door to the Wavertree constituency. However, Randolph was incorrigible. Defeated at Toxteth he stood as unofficial Conservative candidate (against his father's wishes) in the February 1936 Ross and Cromarty by-election against Malcolm MacDonald, Ramsay's son, who was in the Cabinet but had been defeated in the General Election.

Winston's standing slumped again during the Abdication crisis later in 1936, when he attempted to form a King's Party with his close friend Lord Beaverbrook and a small group of around forty MPs. Unfortunately the King decided to abdicate, and Churchill was discomfited. Beaverbrook had told him that 'our cock won't fight', but Churchill unwisely ignored this advice. Sir Oswald Mosley, the former Labour Minister, wanted to use his Blackshirt Movement to 'save the King from Baldwin'; Churchill was paddling in dangerous waters. In the debate on the Abdication on 8 December 1936 he was howled down. Baffy Dugdale, the astute political commentator, recorded in her diary that he was 'done for. In three minutes his hopes of a return to power and influence are shattered.'[2]

Surviving backbench Conservative MPs from the Parliaments of the thirties are scarce, but the author's conversations with some reveal that Churchill was considered 'wild', and the Conservative Whips told any young Tory MP who felt like siding with him that he was an 'alcoholic' who invariably spoilt his own case by personal abuse.[3]

After Hitler came to power in Germany in 1933 Churchill exposed the dangers of Germany's rapid illegal rearmament. Both he and Sir Austen Chamberlain, Baldwin's former Foreign Secretary, made forceful speeches in the Commons condemning the rapidly rising imbalance between Germany and Britain's armed strength, and the need to keep in step with France. However, Austen's clothes and manner of speaking were Edwardian and dated, and neither he nor Churchill had much influence on Conservative MPs, who were mainly pacifist-minded.

In 1935 and 1936, during the crisis over the Abyssinian war, when Mussolini had ignored the Covenant of the League of Nations and invaded another member state, Churchill argued with passion for League of Nations sanctions against Italy because Mussolini had violated the Covenant of the League by attacking another League member. Winston had not previously been a strong supporter of the League, and was cynically welcomed by Attlee as a 'late convert'.

Opponents recalled that in the late twenties, as Chancellor of the Exchequer, Churchill had been an enthusiast for Mussolini. In 1925 the Chancellor had negotiated a most generous settlement of Italy's war debts to Britain. Two years later he made an official trip to Genoa and Rome, where he told journalists that he could not help being charmed by the Italian dictator, and said publicly to Mussolini: 'If I had been an Italian I am sure I would have been with you wholeheartedly from the start . . . your Movement has rendered service to the whole world.' This praise from the Chancellor of the Exchequer for a Fascist leader who had battered the Italian trade unions and imprisoned their members was ill received in Labour circles. Again in 1933 Churchill praised Mussolini as 'the Roman genius' and 'the greatest lawgiver amongst living men'. His sudden conversion to anti-Fascism was commented on critically. (When Mussolini was captured and assassinated by the partisans in 1945 he was carrying letters from Churchill for use if he was tried as a war criminal. They have not survived.)

Churchill felt strongly that the moment to stop Hitler dead in his tracks was when he breached the terms of the Locarno and Versailles treaties by occupying the demilitarized zone of the Rhineland in March 1936. The French Cabinet, if Britain had supported them, would have thrown the German Army out by force; but Baldwin and his Foreign Secretary, Anthony Eden, turned down out of hand any suggestions of military action and acquiesced in Hitler's aggression – to the disgust of the French. Neville Chamberlain told Parliament, to Churchill's indignation, 'the German Chancellor has declared he has no intentions other than peaceful intentions at the moment. Personally I believe that.' Winston spoilt his case by suggesting implausibly during the debate that Britain should remove sanctions against Italy and impose them on Germany. He suggested a mixed British, French and Italian force on German territory; Hugh Dalton, from the Opposition front bench, described this as 'fantastic and absurd'.

With hindsight we know that Churchill was completely justified in his stance over the Rhineland, and Hitler would have withdrawn from the Rhine if the French had used force; but the country was in a pacifist mood, and the majority of MPs and the nation supported Eden and Baldwin in what amounted to a pro-Hitler and anti-French attitude. The Franco–Soviet Pact of 1936, which Hitler used as his excuse for his Rhineland adventure, had aroused fears in right-wing circles of the spread of Bolshevism into eastern Europe, while many on the left resented France's lack of enthusiasm for sanctions against Italy. The prevalent feeling was that, as Germany had only marched into her own back yard, there was little to worry about, and Churchill's vigorous opposition aroused little popular spark; it diminished rather than enhanced his popularity. When Hoesch, the German Ambassador, went to see Austen Chamberlain at the House of Lords, Austen became so heated that he shouted at the German about Hitler's disgraceful behaviour. Austen was Churchill's most powerful ally, and one can only wring one's hands that Baldwin did not make him Foreign Secretary, as he so nearly did, instead of Eden in 1935.

Lord Home, then a Commons Government Whip, reported that at the Conservative Parliamentary Foreign Affairs Committee Churchill had made little impression when he had declared 'all the countries of Europe would hurry to assist France and ourselves against Germany'. This type of overstatement was typical of Churchill at that period, and did him harm.[4]

In 1937, after Austen's death, Winston became the main spokesman for those opposed to Hitler's obvious rapid rearmament, which was producing a strong and growing demand for a single Minister for Defence. Although Churchill was the popular choice, especially outside Parliament, soon after he succeeded Baldwin as Prime Minister, Chamberlain appointed Sir Thomas Inskip, who was easy-going and amiable and at the time Solicitor General. In his diary Chamberlain noted that Inskip would create 'no jealousies, although he would excite no enthusiasm', while appointing Churchill – with his known views on Europe – would be 'dangerous for the Cabinet'. Macmillan wrote that the appointment was astonishing and recalled that the common phrase was that nothing like it had been known since Caligula made his horse Consul.[5]

If Churchill had joined the Cabinet he would have been muted, but he would not have acquiesced in the appeasement policy and failure to rearm. Almost certainly it would have resulted in a dramatic resignation – although he would have been impotent to topple Chamberlain, who was then very popular.

In February 1938 rows arose between Chamberlain and Eden over Mussolini. Eden, both in Cabinet at the time and later in his memoirs, emphasized his almost exclusive concern with Mussolini's behaviour in intervening on the Franco side in the Spanish Civil War (a side issue), and did not appreciate the danger to European peace from the threats of Germany annexing Austria (Anschluss). Oliver Harvey, his close confidant and adviser, reflected Eden's views when he wrote in his diary: 'The prohibition on the Anschluss has been wrong from the start . . . I can't believe the absorption of Austria will strengthen Germany; it should put water in the Nazi wine.'[6]

Chamberlain, on the other hand, saw clearly that the Anschluss would render Czechoslovakia almost indefensible, because her defence plans were based on fortifications along the well-fortified hilly and narrow frontier with Germany; once the German Army could attack over the Austrian frontier, Czechoslovakia was dangerously vulnerable. Accordingly he insisted that Eden should mend fences with Mussolini and try to persuade the Italian dictator to prevent Hitler taking Austria. Chamberlain therefore wanted his Foreign Secretary to give immediate *de jure* recognition of the conquest of Abyssinia by Italy. Eden refused point blank, and he and the Prime Minister had a violent quarrel. The Cabinet backed Chamberlain, and Eden was forced to go. Within weeks Hitler invaded Austria; there was neither resistance nor protest from Mussolini, and little from Britain.

Eden, with more reticence than is shown by front bench politicians nowadays, did not reveal the true reasons why he had resigned. Churchill, ignorant of the facts, believed that he had resigned as a gesture against the appeasement of Hitler and the failure of Britain to rearm, and he sent him an enthusiastic letter of support stating that 'his cause was the cause of England'. Eden's view that Spain was more important than Austria was shared by Sir Alec Cadogan (Permanent Under Secretary Foreign Office), who wrote in his diary after the Anschluss;

'Thank goodness Austria is out of the way . . . we only forbade the Anschluss to spite Germany.'[7]

Churchill's stance over Austria was fundamentally different from Eden's; he said in the Commons that Britain could not afford to accept the Anschluss, and called for urgent discussions with 'our' Allies and the League of Nations – emphasizing that Czechoslovakia was now isolated economically and militarily, so that Hitler was in a position to dominate the whole of south-west Europe. Churchill also declared that he wanted better relations with Italy.

Thus the impression was given that Churchill and Eden were in agreement in resisting appeasement of Hitler, and the myth has been perpetuated. In fact Eden wanted to appease Hitler and take a firm stand against Italy, while Churchill wanted overtures to Mussolini and a firm stand against Hitler. Churchill even stated that he now regretted having supported sanctions against Italy in 1936.[8] Many historians have expressed surprise that the Eden–Churchill political co-operation did not bloom after the Anschluss, but there was no real meeting of minds and Eden did not want to become close to Churchill as he hoped to be included again in Chamberlain's Cabinet – Churchill had already burnt his boats with the Prime Minister by his all-out opposition to appeasement. Eden was encouraged to think he would soon achieve high office again, because Chamberlain had brought Sam Hoare back into the Cabinet soon after his resignation following the fiasco over the Hoare–Laval attempt to appease Mussolini in 1935. If Eden had thrown in his lot wholeheartedly with Churchill after his resignation, Churchill's position would have been enormously strengthened. Eden was very popular, and Chamberlain might well have been forced to abandon his appease-ment policy which culminated in the Munich Agreement in September 1938, so that the course of history might have been different. In his memoirs Churchill dramatized Eden's resignation, writing that Eden had resigned as a gesture against appeasement, and that he himself was deserted by sleep at night. 'From midnight to dawn I lay on my bed consumed by emotions of fear and sorrow. There seemed one young man standing up against long dismal drawling tides of drift and surrender . . . he seemed to me at this moment to embody the life hope of the British nation.' This was a total misconception, because Eden was just as appeasement-minded as Chamberlain, and complacent over Austria being annexed.[9]

Because the Anschluss had left Czechoslovakia with her fortifications out-flanked, and therefore vulnerable to a German attack, Churchill argued for faster rearmament and a Grand Alliance of France, Britain, Russia, Poland and Romania to defend her. But Chamberlain refused to believe that Hitler's ambitions were insatiable, instead he stepped up his appeasement policy and eschewed any alliance with Russia.

Eden would not co-operate with Churchill on the anti-Nazi group known as Focus: Leo Amery was Churchill's most influential supporter in it; other MP members included General Spears, Brendan Bracken, Robert Boothby, Harold Macmillan and Harold Nicolson. Focus had been formed in 1936 with money from wealthy and influential British and American Jews as a counter-move to

Hitler's persecution of German Jews. Churchill, who was quickly recruited, addressed mass rallies at the Albert Hall, spoke at lunches for important people and became its driving force. A manifesto was issued, with great publicity, and Focus developed into an important political pressure group opposing the Government's appeasement and calling for immediate rearmament, for which Churchill argued vehemently. Violet Bonham Carter, Sinclair, the Liberal leader, and the trade unionists Citrine and Bevin helped to give the group credibility.

Once involved in Focus, Churchill became 100 per cent pro-Zionist. He testified to the Peel Commission on Palestine that all Palestine should be handed over to the Jews regardless of Arab interests, which was in sharp contrast with his views on Palestine when he had been Colonial Secretary in 1922. Then he had been parsimonious about the number of Jews to be admitted, and said that only 'good citizens' amongst the Jews should be allowed in: 'We cannot have a country inundated by bolshevik riff-raff who would seek to subvert institutions in Palestine as they have done in the land from which they came.' In office he had twice suspended Jewish immigration and favoured abandoning Britain's Palestine mandate from the League of Nations under which Britain garrisoned and governed Palestine in the 1920s and 30s.[10]

The Peel Commission in 1937 recommended limitations on Jewish immigration; its report coincided with an escalation of Hitler's persecution of Jews inside Germany, which was creating an urgent demand for a vast increase in the numbers of Jews to be allowed to enter Palestine. Yet the Chamberlain Government imposed quotas on German Jewish immigration both to Palestine and to Britain. As the USA also restricted Jewish immigration, great numbers of fugitives from Nazi tyranny had nowhere to go, and after an abortive London Conference of Jews and Arabs, a White Paper in 1939 stated that no further Jewish immigration into Palestine should be allowed against Arab wishes. It was a British rejection of the Balfour Declaration of 1917 establishing Palestine as a national home for Jewish people, at a moment when European Jewry faced disaster. The Commons divided on non-party lines, with Churchill opposing the White Paper strongly; the Government majority sank to 89 against its normal 240.[11]

Voices hostile to Churchill alleged that his pro-Zionist stance was the result of gifts to him from rich Jews. Certainly he suffered a financial crisis in 1937. His lifestyle was extravagant and his love of gambling and Stock Exchange speculation cost him dear. His wife Clementine constantly complained about his extravagance. He loved his spacious country home, Chartwell, where he would keep open house for his many friends and his children. Winston insisted, against Clemmie's advice, on keeping nine indoor servants and three gardeners plus a groom.

The marriage was stable and a support to Winston in that he never committed adultery. But he was affectionate and mildly flirtatious with his old flames. Clemmie, an insecure character and the daughter of unmarried parents, became madly jealous. Churchill adored his erratic son Randolph, but his mother disliked him for his brashness, conceit and drinking habits. Clemmie also disliked Churchill's closest men friends, Beaverbrook and Brendan Bracken. She had strong but irrational views on most political problems, which cannot have been helpful to Winston when he was worried as to whether he had made the right decision. Undoubtedly they got on each other's nerves – especially when Churchill's political fortunes were at a low ebb in the thirties. But she rallied to his support like a bulldog when social acquaintances criticized him. Fortunately, perhaps, they went on separate holidays. Churchill liked riding horses and painting; she adored skiing and travel, and went on long sea cruises where she made friends outside Churchill's circle, so that when they came together again the strain was relieved.

The financial crisis so dreaded by Clemmie came to a head in 1938 when Beaverbrook, without notice, terminated Churchill's well-paid contract to write for the *Daily Express*. Churchill had just lost large sums by gambling in shares on Wall Street and the London Stock Exchange. So Chartwell was put up for sale, for £25,000. Bernard Baruch, a multi-millionaire American Jewish friend of Churchill's, bailed him out from his Stock Exchange losses. (They had become friends when Woodrow Wilson brought Baruch to the Peace Conference in Paris in 1919.) Now, in 1938, another close Jewish friend and a prominent member of Focus, Sir Henry Strakosch, Chairman of Union Corporation, who had made an immense fortune in South African gold, rescued Churchill for the second time. Chartwell was saved, and Strakosch continued to visit Churchill at Chequers throughout the war.

Churchill's financial problems were widely known; so was the fact that Baruch and Strakosch had bailed him out. Thus in addition to Chamberlain's supporters declaring again and again that Churchill had been crying wolf too often about Hitler, rumours spread that his policy statements on Palestine were dictated by his dependence on Jewish money.

How true this is must be a matter of opinion, but when Chamberlain surrendered to Hitler at Munich in September 1938 and effectively ordered the Czechs to abandon their fortifications on the German frontier and hand over the Sudetenland to Germany without notice, Churchill's protests rallied a strong section of public opinion to his side. At the height of the Munich Crisis Churchill, with Violet Asquith and others in the Focus group, tried to persuade Attlee, Eden and Sinclair to send a telegram to Chamberlain declaring that, if he imposed onerous terms on Czechoslovakia, he would be fought in the House. Eden refused: his sights were set on being recalled to Chamberlain's Cabinet. Attlee dilly-dallied. As a result the telegram was not sent. Soon afterwards Eden cancelled an engagement to speak at a League of Nations Union meeting because he would have to share the platform with Sinclair and Attlee – a clear sign he expected to rejoin the Cabinet. But Churchill and thirty other dissident Conservatives abstained from voting after the Commons debate on Munich.[12]

At Chamberlain's request the *Times* and other newspapers promoted the case for abandoning Czechoslovakia, and most of the photographs published showed Nazi soldiers being welcomed by the Sudeten population. The Nazis maltreated the non-Germans in the Sudetenland, but this was little reported in London. Churchill argued vigorously for conscription and the creation of a Ministry of Supply. Chamberlain rejected his calls out of hand.

However, Churchill's case was reinforced when, after Halifax had told the German Ambassador that he was concerned at reports of ill-treatment of non-German residents in the Sudetenland, Hitler replied: 'We cannot tolerate the tutelage of governesses. Inquiries by British politicians concerning the acts of Germans within the frontier of the Reich are out of place.'

At first the Munich Agreement was very popular. Forty thousand letters of support came to the Prime Minister as the public heaved a sigh of relief at having avoided war. Chamberlain was looked on generally as an apostle of peace, and Churchill as a warmonger. There was a move to deselect Churchill in his Epping constituency. For the first few months after Munich, the easiest way to arouse applause at a Conservative Party meeting was to say that, but for Chamberlain and Munich, Britain would be at war. Churchill, loyally backed by Leo Amery, managed to sow the seeds of distrust within some Conservative associations, but if a General Election had been held immediately after Munich Chamberlain would have won hands down. Indeed, there were press rumours of a 'snap' General Election.

The Oxford by-election on 27 October showed how popular Munich was. Quintin Hogg (now second Lord Hailsham) campaigned in support of Chamberlain's Munich policy, while his opponent, A. T. Lindsay, Master of Balliol College, who had both Liberal and Labour support, made opposition to Munich almost his sole argument. Churchill, Duff Cooper and Harold Macmillan sent letters of support to Lindsay, but Churchill refused to speak against his party at a by-election. In a turn-out higher than in the General Election, Hogg obtained 56.1 per cent of the vote – a sign of great support for Chamberlain's appeasement policy. Lord Hailsham told the author that Lindsay was an appallingly bad candidate, which made his task easier.

However, in the Bridgwater by-election in the middle of November the Independent Vernon Bartlett, who had his candidature endorsed by Churchill and the Liberal and Labour Parties, concentrated on attacking Chamberlain's 'weak and vacillating foreign policy'. He won a spectacular victory in a safe Conservative seat.

Disquieting news from Germany, especially the deportation of thirteen thousand Polish Jews without their property and money, and the Kristallnacht pogrom in Berlin on 6 November 1936, had some effect on public opinion. In certain Conservative circles Chamberlain began to be called the 'undertaker', not the 'apostle of peace', and Churchill's popularity increased.

Meanwhile, expert opinion was horrified when it was reported from America that the Runciman Report, which Chamberlain alleged recommended secession of the Sudetenland to Germany as the only solution, had been rigged. Apparently Runciman had originally proposed a federal solution, with the Sudetenland remaining within the Czech frontiers. For the report, and his part in altering it, Runciman was rewarded by a place in the Cabinet from Chamberlain.

In addition, Professor Seton-Watson, the eastern European expert, produced an authoritative and widely circulated pamphlet which showed that the actual Munich settlement and the way in which it was being interpreted was far worse for the Czechs than Hitler's Godesberg ultimatum, which Chamberlain had rejected with Cabinet approval after his previous meeting with Hitler. In the Commons Munich debate Chamberlain had staked his reputation on the argument that he had persuaded Hitler to tone down his Godesberg threats, which he claimed was proof of Hitler's sincerity and desire for peace. Churchill's prestige amongst MPs rose. Hugh Dalton, the Opposition spokesman on foreign policy, and other intelligent Labour MPs knowledgeable about foreign policy, began to co-operate with Churchill; there was even talk of an electoral pact, with Labour not opposing Conservative candidates who took the Churchill line.[13]

But this came to nothing. Eden again refused to co-operate, and apart from Dalton the Labour leaders were unresponsive. Attlee and Morrison would not enter into discussions with Churchill. Unlike Churchill, during the autumn of 1938, the Labour hierarchy failed to realize the inevitability of war. Churchill, not Baldwin, had been responsible in 1924 for crushing the General Strike and causing much damage to the trade unions, and left-wing trade unionists were unforgiving.

Not surprisingly, opinion polls which had originally shown a large majority in favour of the Munich settlement and Chamberlain's policy recorded a sharp dwindling in the popularity of Munich as 1939 dawned. Churchill's all-out opposition to Munich was dramatically vindicated when on 15 March, without warning, German troops occupied Prague and the rump of Czechoslovakia. The Government's appeasement policy lay in ruins. Chamberlain had to reorientate his plans, and in a panic he and Halifax offered to give Poland a guarantee as that country was clearly Hitler's most likely next victim; temporarily they embraced Churchill's policy of a Grand Alliance with Russia and the states surrounding Germany in order to hem in Hitler.

In spite of the shock of Hitler breaking his solemn promise given at Munich, in his speeches Chamberlain continued to argue against Churchill that Munich was a victory because Britain had immediately recognized her vulnerability and used the respite to take measures to correct her military deficiencies. Chamberlain became less and less plausible, and there was fierce criticism from his outraged opponents in Parliament and in sections of the press. However, the nation was still appeasement-minded and Chamberlain's position as Prime Minister remained unassailable. To the end of his life Chamberlain believed he had been right at Munich and Hitler had 'missed the bus' there. Even today some historians defend Chamberlain and argue on flimsy evidence that a year's respite from war strengthened Britain and France vis-à-vis Germany. This is untenable.

Britain built Hurricanes and Spitfires without which the Battle of Britain would not have been won, but other resources were concentrated on AA guns and radar, not on equipment for the field army. After Munich the Czechoslovak Skoda works made arms for the Germans instead of for the Allies, and produced in the twelve months between August 1938 and September 1939 as much as the total output of British factories. French arms production was sluggish, whereas German factories went ahead at full steam to produce tanks and armoured cars for the Panzer divisions. In addition, Germany collected in Czechoslovakia six hundred tanks and over two thousand field guns. Along her borders with Germany Czechoslovakia had extremely well-built fortifications, and developed a well-trained and well-equipped army of thirty-five divisions. Had it not been for the Munich Agreement, Russia would have helped Czechoslovakia, and had in fact sent military aircraft there before Munich.

General Keitel, Hitler's Chief of Staff, said in his evidence at Nuremberg: 'We were extraordinarily happy that it had not come to a military operation because our means of attack against the frontier fortifications of Czechoslovakia were insufficient and the Czechs could have deployed an equal number of divisions to us.' In his evidence, General Jodl stated that at the time of Munich: 'War was out of the question because there were only five German fighting divisions on the western fortifications [Siegfried Line] which were nothing but a large construction site to hold out against 100 French divisions. This was militarily impossible.'

Churchill held strongly to the view that if Hitler's bluff had been called at Munich the French Army, which he so admired, could have advanced into Germany with little opposition. The German commander on the Siegfried Line, General Wilhelm Adam, wrote in his memoirs that the troops under his command were 'completely inadequate to withstand a French invasion'; he thought a war with France and Britain in September 1938 would have been 'sheer lunacy'. He also revealed the poor state of the partly built Siegfried Line fortifications.[14]

German survivors of the Resistance have shown that dissident German generals and politicians would have tried to overthrow Hitler in September 1938 if he had given the order to attack Czechoslovakia. Post-war evidence entirely vindicates Churchill's claim that the military situation in 1938 was such that it was folly to capitulate to Hitler at Munich. However, in 1939 the majority of the nation continued to side with Chamberlain.

Even so, Churchill's opposition to appeasement and his call for faster rearmament in the spring and summer of 1939 attracted more and more support and his popularity rose. As he reiterated his call for a Grand Alliance involving the Soviet Union, public opinion began to swing his way and a press campaign for his inclusion in the Government came to a crescendo. Churchill's reputation, which had sunk to its nadir after the Abdication Crisis, was higher with the public, but he failed to attract the support of many Tory MPs. Eden and his tiny group still fought shy of him. Both Churchill and Eden were considering standing as Independent Conservatives in the General Election in opposition to Chamberlain, but their plans never coalesced. Chamberlain, much concerned at the threat from Churchill and Eden, spread rumours that Churchill illicitly obtained Government papers and leaked what had happened in the Cabinet in a way which was undignified for a former Chancellor of the Exchequer. He went further, and commissioned Sir Joseph Ball, former head of the Conservative Central Office, to discredit Churchill by lampooning attacks in *Truth* (the political weekly) and other underhand methods, so that doubts about Churchill's age, his lack of judgement and impetuosity surfaced in the national newspapers.[15]

Chamberlain hoped until the end to avert war, and until it came he was determined to exclude Churchill from his Government. Churchill was delighted when Chamberlain reluctantly agreed to allow a military mission to go to Moscow to begin staff talks with the Soviets on how to defend Poland. But Stalin got wind that Chamberlain was double-crossing him by sending secret messages to Hitler, indicating that Britain was willing to negotiate the return to Germany of the Polish Corridor and Danzig, conceded to Poland at the expense of Germany in the Treaty of Versailles.

Despairing of Britain, Stalin decided on a deal with Hitler, and on 23 August, to the horror of Chamberlain and amid almost universal surprise, the Ribbentrop–Molotov non-aggression pact was announced. This put Hitler in an overwhelmingly strong position to attack Poland. Churchill feared that Chamberlain would then sell out the Poles (as Chamberlain, Halifax and Butler wanted), and in frenzied negotiation in Berlin this nearly occurred. Goering, who commanded the Luftwaffe, wanted to prevent war, and secretly sent as emissary to London a violently anti-Polish Swede called Dahlerus who was twice received by Chamberlain and Halifax at 10 Downing Street. Hitler actually counter-manded his orders for an attack on Poland, but finally the Poles refused to send a plenipotentiary to Hitler to negotiate away Danzig and the Polish corridor. If the plenipotentiary had come, as Chamberlain wanted, there would have been another Munich, as Churchill feared.

On 1 September, Hitler sent his troops into Poland on the trumped up excuse that Polish soldiers had attacked a German border post, and Britain's guarantee to Poland became operative. That morning Chamberlain told Winston he was forming a small War Cabinet in which Churchill would be included. Yet Chamberlain procrastinated and Churchill, who had agreed to take office, was perforce muted. We will never know if Chamberlain had invited Churchill into the Cabinet in order to stifle his criticism if war was averted after Hitler's unprovoked aggression.

Churchill heard no more from Chamberlain for forty-eight hours, while Halifax beavered away in an effort to get Mussolini to call another Munich-style conference. As Hitler bombed Polish towns and cities and his armoured divisions drove deep into the country, Chamberlain ignored the Poles' request for RAF intervention and Halifax told Mussolini that if Hitler would withdraw his troops they were willing to hold an international conference to rewrite the Treaty of Versailles. Sir Horace Wilson, Chamberlain's most intimate civil servant, told Hitler's emissary in London the same.[16]

But Hitler would not withdraw his troops, and after an agonizing two days Britain and France declared war on Germany on 3 September. The Commons, furious at the delay, had forced Chamberlain's hand. One can imagine what Churchill's reactions would have been if the Mussolini-inspired conference had taken place. Chamberlain had told Churchill on 1 September that 'The die was cast', and as peace negotiations appeared to be hanging in the balance, at midnight on 2 September Churchill wrote to the PM: 'I have not heard anything from you since our talks on Friday, when I understood that I was to serve as your colleague, and when you told me that this would be announced speedily. I really do not know what has happened during the course of this agitated day, though it seems to me that entirely different ideas have ruled from those which you expressed to me when you said "the die was cast." '[17]

The die was cast the next morning; Britain and Germany were at war and on Sunday, 3 September, Chamberlain told Winston he was to have the Admiralty. The long-standing breach between the two was healed. Winston was happy. He had been at the Admiralty at the start of the First World War, but had been dismissed by Asquith for his mishandling of the Gallipoli campaign. Now he felt he could make up for his mistakes of twenty-five years before and re-establish his reputation as a great statesman.

CHAPTER TWO

Churchill at Admiralty in phoney war

AT 11.15 a.m. on 3 September 1939 Chamberlain made a sad and uninspired broadcast to tell the nation they were at war. In place of promising speedy help to Poland, the ally on whose behalf war was being declared, he spoke of his personal sadness. In Warsaw the Poles were delighted and cheered the British Military Mission of thirty led by Carton de Wiart and Colin Gubbins, who changed into military uniform on hearing of the declaration of war. Not until 9 September did a Polish Military Mission arrive in London, and they found the British Government had no plan to aid Poland. All the War Office could offer was a few thousand old rifles, and the members of the Mission were advised to try and buy arms from neutral Spain and Belgium.

The French were treacherous, because on 19 May 1939 General Gamelin had signed a military agreement with the Polish General Kasprzycki in which he promised to launch an offensive against the Siegfried Line fifteen days after war was declared. But now, Gamelin had no intention of doing so. Nor would Britain and France bomb the Germans to help Poland. Hitler was engaged in terror bombing of Polish cities, but the British War Cabinet refused to believe this until a member of the British Military Mission to Poland returned to London and told the Chief of Air Staff, Air Marshal Newall, that he had actually been present during the Luftwaffe's indiscriminate bombing of Polish towns. Newall advised the War Cabinet that the RAF should launch retaliatory attacks on German industrial centres, but not even Churchill in the War Cabinet supported this.

At his Nuremberg trial General Jodl stated that at the outbreak of war 110 French divisions faced twenty-three German divisions on the Siegfried Line, and it was only 'the inactivity of the Allies that saved Germany from defeat'. In his evidence Keitel declared that there were only twenty German divisions, including reserves, in the Rhineland in September 1939 (against six in 1938), and 'A French attack during the Polish campaign would have encountered only a German military screen, not a real defence . . . we soldiers thought the Western powers had no serious intentions because they did not take advantage of the extremely favourable situation'. Keitel's assessment of British and French intentions proved correct.[1]

In face of Chamberlain's and Gamelin's timidity Churchill was not able to demand the French advance into Germany which might also have spurred the

German dissident generals into action against Hitler; he acquiesced in the inertia, although from his temperament he wanted to act and seize the initiative from Hitler. He could do nothing because the Prime Minister wanted to negotiate peace, not to escalate the war, and refused to believe that Hitler had decided on all-out war against Britain and France. Eden, who had been made Secretary of State for War, was not a member of the War Cabinet. Chamberlain and the old gang still ruled the roost, and Churchill must have felt his position was not yet strong enough to demand that Britain and France engaged immediately in aggressive fighting.

At the second meeting of Chamberlain's War Cabinet, on 4 September, Churchill suggested that 'every means possible should be employed to relieve the pressure on Poland', and suggested an attack against the Siegfried Line by the French Army supported by the RAF. (The small British Army was in no position to offer real help in such an attack.) The War Cabinet agreed that a combined plan of action was 'a vital necessity'. When, however, the French made no move, Churchill did not protest in Cabinet. On the fifth day of war the War Cabinet received a report that 'we should assume the war will last three years and the French army would need assistance in equipping itself after the first four months'. Churchill, like Chamberlain, soon gave up hope that a French advance into Germany could produce the quick victory which Jodl and Keitel feared.

Indeed, on 10 September Churchill wrote to Chamberlain that 'we should not take the initiative in bombing' except to help the French Army. Apparently he was reconciled to Chamberlain's view that an economic blockade would eventually topple Hitler, and on 21 September the Chiefs of Staff reported that no bombing operations had taken place for a week except against submarines. They advised that there should be no bombing attacks on Germany except on military targets because of the risk of reprisals against armaments factories in France and Britain, and that the RAF could have no effect on relieving pressure on Poland, so the planes should be kept for supporting a French offensive: 'If we go beyond the limits of our present attacks on military targets this country will be subject to air attack.' No change was asked for by either Churchill or other members of the War Cabinet, even when on 14 September the War Cabinet agreed that Germany had violated the principles of warfare. On the 15th the War Cabinet decided that no more ships should be loaded with military supplies for Poland because the Germans were winning so easily. The French had been more generous and made fifty aeroplanes available at Marseilles, and 1000 tons of bombs at Dunkirk.[2]

The Chiefs of Staff agreed with Gamelin over abandoning plans for an autumn offensive against the Siegfried Line, and at the meeting of the Supreme War Council in Paris on 12 September Neville Chamberlain said that the decision not to undertake large operations as yet in France had been 'wise. In his view there was no hurry.' Chamberlain had been accompanied only by the insignificant Lord Chatfield, Chairman of the Committee for Co-ordination of Defence. Daladier said 'the situation might have been different if Belgium were not neutral'. Chatfield then asked Gamelin whether he contemplated any change in his plan in the West if Poland managed to hold out longer than envisaged. Gamelin replied: 'No. Britain and France needed longer time to prepare.' Winston saw the minutes of the meeting and expressed no objection. All this, of course, delighted Hitler, whose armies were becoming stronger every week as he got ready to launch a devastating attack in the West.[3]

In a speech at Danzig on 29 September, and again in a speech to the Reichstag on 6 October, Hitler held out an olive branch. In the Reichstag he asked: 'Why war in the West?' and declared that the future of Poland must be settled by Germany and Russia alone, but promised to respect the frontiers of Denmark, Holland and Belgium, stating that he had no claims on France and only wanted to bury the hatchet. He asked for a peace conference at which European disarmament, currencies and raw materials could be considered, and finished up with words of seeming sweet reason: 'Churchill and his friends will look on my offer as cowardice, but never in the history of the world have there been two victors although often, as in the last war, two vanquished.'

Draft replies were prepared for the Prime Minister by Halifax, Cadogan, Vansittart and Butler. On reading these drafts, which Halifax had obligingly shown to him, Churchill was alarmed, and wrote to Chamberlain that they were too 'defensive in tone'; he sent his own draft, adding: 'I think opinion is hardening against Hitler's terms and the Press seems unanimous, so does the Empire.'

But the Empire was not unanimous. Mackenzie King, on behalf of Canada, suggested a committee of neutrals to mediate, and urged that everything must be done to stop the war before the slaughter began. Menzies of Australia wanted definition of Allied war aims, as did Smuts from South Africa, who added that there was 'a universal demand for them'. New Zealand wanted 'no door closed' that might lead to a peaceful solution.

Winston's draft contained typical Churchillian flourishes which would have made headlines in the world press but languishes unread in the archives of the Public Record Office. Chamberlain borrowed only one Churchill phrase for his Commons reply to Hitler: 'Acts, not words, must be forthcoming before we, the British peoples and France, our gallant and trusted ally, would be justified in ceasing to wage war to the utmost of our strength', but it had taken four Cabinet meetings to decide on the final draft.[4]

Hitler continued to put out peace offers, and Goering, sometimes behind the Führer's back, was also active. Hitler, intoxicated by the success of his armies in Poland, was torn between consolidating his victories by a deal with France and Britain, and launching a lightning autumn campaign through the Low Countries which would culminate in the over-running of France. Halifax wrote to Lothian: 'Peace feelers come almost every day'; and to Gort: 'A good many peace feelers being put out, all of them tracing to Goering.' Dissident Germans hoped that Goering, who was against war, would replace Hitler, and many German generals at this period, apprehensive that an attack on the Low Countries might end in disaster, were discussing with the politicians of the Resistance a coup to overthrow Hitler.[5]

Churchill was scornful of suggestions of a negotiated peace. His great friend, the flamboyant, charming and handsome Bendor, Duke of Westminster, had held a meeting with the Duke of Buccleuch, Lord Rushcliffe and the influential Tory MP Sir Arnold Wilson, noted for his support of appeasement. Bendor said Britain need not be at war with Germany, and that 'the war was part of a Jewish and Masonic plot'. Churchill immediately wrote a bitter letter to his friend and told him to come and see him; the meeting was reported to several members of the War Cabinet, and Neville Chamberlain sent Sir Joseph Ball, former head of the Conservative Central Office, to see Bendor.

Early in November Queen Wilhelmina of Holland and King Leopold of Belgium made a joint offer to King George VI to mediate. Churchill was alarmed, because the offer was applauded by a large section of the press and public. Twenty Labour MPs led by George Lansbury, who had resigned as leader of the opposition because of his pacifist views, and including Alfred Salter, David Kirkwood, Fred Messer, John Rhys Davies, Sydney Silverman, Reginald Sorenson, Commander Reginald Fletcher and the charismatic Dick Stokes, signed a memorandum to Chamberlain calling for a conference with Germany, Russia, Italy and France because 'the future of Poland, Austria and Czechoslovakia was a matter for Europe as a whole, not solely for Great Britain and France'.

In reply, Chamberlain asked Lansbury to let him know what support there was: Lansbury stated that fourteen thousand individuals and numerous organizations had expressed support, and that if his campaign had been properly organized and publicized the replies would have run into millions. Lansbury may well have been correct, such was the pacifist mood of the country.

Chamberlain asked Keyes, who was a close friend of King Leopold, to send an unofficial reply to the King of Belgium stating that the Prime Minister 'would wholeheartedly welcome any steps taken by you which might avert or even postpone the outbreak of warfare'. Keyes took the letter round to the Admiralty to be typed, which made Churchill aware of it. He was dismayed by both Keyes' and the Prime Minister's draft reply, and wrote to Chamberlain that it was nothing less than 'the authorisation to King Leopold to open another channel of communication with Hitler. The King will be entitled to act upon this, and say he had your hearty concurrence. Nothing like this has been put to the Cabinet and as the matter is full of danger I venture to hope that you will allow us to consider them [the draft replies] before they are sent.'

Chamberlain was obliged to toughen up both his reply and Keyes' letter. Meanwhile arch-appeasers in the Conservative Party – Lord Brockett, the Duke of Buccleuch, the Earl of Londonderry, Lord Ponsonby and the Earl of Darnley – bombarded Chamberlain and Halifax with long letters pointing out how badly Germany had been treated at Versailles.[6]

Chamberlain and Halifax paid a surprising amount of attention to this aristocratic Conservative peace lobby, replying to all the letters and inviting the authors to lunch. Probably Chamberlain felt he might need this influential Conservative support if he negotiated with Hitler or Goering, because Churchill would sharply oppose such a move.[7]

President Roosevelt now sent his Under Secretary for Foreign Affairs, Sumner Welles, to Europe to try and find a basis for a negotiated peace. On 13 March 1940 Welles held a conference with Chamberlain, Halifax and the US Ambassador in London, Joseph Kennedy. When asked by Welles if he would deal with the present German regime, Chamberlain replied: 'Any settlement should not be such that Hitler could represent it as having been able to get away with it . . . if there was complete reversal of Hitler's policy and the freedom of the German people from the Gestapo then we should not be justified in refusing a discussion. But this would be a miracle'; and 'We could not be satisfied with any settlement from which it did not clearly emerge that Herr Hitler's policy had been a failure', but there would be no difficulty in giving some sort of preferential economic position to countries adjoining Germany. Halifax said that Britain would require evidence of German co-operation in Europe, whether through the League of Nations or some other organization. Chamberlain wrote to his sister that: 'if Hitler did not disappear he would have to agree to give up most of what Nazidom stands for', although he thought there was one chance in ten thousand that this might occur, and the way in which Hitler had talked to Welles 'seems significant of a lurking want of confidence at the bottom of his mind'. The record of the Chamberlain and Halifax talk with Welles was written by Cadogan and kept a close secret. Churchill was not aware of what transpired, and if he had been, he would have been extremely provoked.[8]

Churchill would have been even more angry if he had known what his friend Lord Beaverbrook was up to. In January 1940, when Richard Stokes had published a well-argued pamphlet making the case for an agreed peace, Beaverbrook wrote to say how much he agreed with him, and promised that if Stokes put his case at the Labour Party Conference in May the *Daily Express* would be told to report him fully. Beaverbrook then decided to promote and finance a campaign for a speedy peace on a compromise basis, and invited to dinner three MPs of the Independent Labour Party (Maxton, MacGovern and Campbell Stevens), telling them there was widespread support for a negotiated peace. The Foreign Office learnt of this, and Vansittart recommended that the Prime Minister and Halifax should send for Beaverbrook and ask him to drop it 'both as a matter of patriotism and commonsense, for the peace he has in mind would only result without fail in our having our throats cut in a couple of years'. Halifax funked having a heart-to-heart talk with Beaverbrook on such a sensitive subject; his and Chamberlain's view were too close to Beaverbrook's. Instead he minuted that the best person to talk to Beaverbrook would be Churchill, but the matter was allowed to drop in the office. Thus Churchill never heard of Beaverbrook's flirtation with the ILP over a negotiated peace. Had Winston been consulted, it is almost impossible that he would have made Beaverbrook Minister of Aircraft Production immediately after becoming Prime Minister on 12 May.[9]

In a by-election speech in May 1941 MacGovern argued for a negotiated peace; he claimed that Beaverbrook had been carrying on his own peace campaign only weeks before he became Minister of Aircraft Production, and revealed the details of the dinner of 1940. In Parliament on 28 June that year Churchill defended Beaverbrook against MacGovern's charges. Colville told the author that after the debate Churchill said, 'Most people will believe Maxton, not Beaverbrook.' Beaverbrook, taxed by Churchill, replied that he could not remember the episode.[10]

From the moment he joined Chamberlain's War Cabinet, Churchill felt continually frustrated by what he considered the apathy of his colleagues and the civil servants who were digging in for a long war of economic attrition with Germany and were unrealistic about fighting. He considered it his duty to spur on his colleagues and to send them memoranda on how to conduct their Departments' business. This was often ill received, as was his insistence that his scientific advisor, Professor Lindemann, attended nearly all the Admiralty Scientific Committees although his previous knowledge of battleships was zero.

He was particularly annoyed by a paper on Economic Co-ordination by Lord Stamp which was critical of 'excessive expenditure' on the Army, and let the Cabinet know how displeased he was. However, Winston was careful not to antagonize Chamberlain, and refused to talk to the small clique of Tory MPs led by Leo Amery who wanted to oust the Prime Minister.[11]

Winston accepted the Russian invasion of the rump of Poland with equanimity. On 17 September, as the rains started and remnants of the Polish Army in the Romanian corner of Poland were at last having minor successes, the Red Army crossed the frontier and occupied the parts of Poland agreed as theirs in a secret annex to the Ribbentrop–Molotov Pact. Poland ceased to exist and, also by agreement with Hitler, Stalin callously obliterated the Baltic states of Estonia, Latvia and Lithuania.

The Foreign Office pointed out to the War Cabinet that the British treaty with Poland only covered aggression by Germany and excluded a Russian attack. Chamberlain was much relieved, and Churchill did not demur. The Foreign Office also pointed out that the Russians would occupy the Polish–Romanian border, so Germany could now only attack Romania via Hungary. A cynical Foreign Office note approved by Halifax said that: 'We should stand for an ethnographical and cultural Poland without treading on Russian toes, and the predominantly Polish population was in the German section'.

On 18 November Churchill approved the War Cabinet decision to exclude the Poles from the Supreme War Council, and the Foreign Office minuted: 'We have been very careful to avoid committing ourselves to any guarantee to restore Polish frontiers.' It was abundantly clear now that Chamberlain rued his guarantee to Poland and would go to extreme lengths to get out of the war. Churchill, although he showed signs of expecting war with Russia, did not oppose the policy of abandoning Poland to the Russians.[12] As early as 18 September he minuted that he was hopeful that Turkey would come in on the Allied side, and he pursued this will o' the wisp until the end of the war.

Fast-changing instructions to the Admiralty flowed from Churchill. He asked for plans to make liners impregnable to air attack, but as soon as he was told that the cost of the iron plating would be sky-high and would take years in the shipyards he forgot about it. The same occurred with his minute that the Admiralty should examine the consequences of suspending for one year all work on battleships which could not come into action before the end of 1941. The Admiralty, with good reason, would not consider it. Then he wanted designs for a small aircraft carrier to carry six planes and to work with cruiser squadrons in 'our seas'. His advisers told him that no small aircraft carriers could be designed and built in under three years, and then only at great expense in labour and materials. Once his impromptu plans had been properly considered and rejected by experts, Churchill put them out of his mind.[13]

CHAPTER THREE

Norwegian disaster

CONSIDERABLE CRITICISM has been levelled at Churchill over Norway while he was First Lord of the Admiralty. It is impossible to brush this aside. From the start Churchill turned his mind to blocking the supplies of iron ore from Sweden and Norway which were vital for German steel production. This issue had also been raised during the First World War. Now, in the Second World War, he was convinced that depriving Germany of iron ore would be a swift and dramatic contribution to the early defeat of Hitler.

The bulk of the Scandinavian iron ore was produced near Lulea in north-west Sweden. However, the port of Lulea in the Gulf of Bothnia was icebound all winter; during this period the ore was transported by railway to Narvik in north-west Norway and thence by sea to German ports. German supplies of Scandinavian iron ore could be cut off by blocking the ports of Narvik and Lulea. Pre-war from Narvik the Germans were obtaining 1¾ million tons, while the British drew 850,000 tons. In 1939 the Ministry of Economic Warfare (MEW) informed the War Cabinet that, if Germany was cut off completely from Swedish iron ore, after twelve months she would be unable to wage war due to lack of ammunition, because her steelmaking capacity would be drastically reduced.

After the war the United States Strategic Bombing Survey (USSBS) established that in 1939 Germany had a steelmaking capacity of 23 million tons annually, and in spite of great efforts to develop low-grade and medium-grade ores at home, Germany was dependent on Sweden for 70 per cent of her supplies. Of course, after Hitler's victories in 1940 France and Luxembourg provided all the steel and iron ore needed, but it is correct that in September 1939 Swedish/Norwegian iron ore was vital for Germany's steelmaking capacity, and that if the flow could be stopped Hitler would be tremendously disadvantaged.

Immediately on assuming office in September Churchill asked his Admiralty staff for an urgent appreciation of the possibility of the Fleet forcing an entrance into the Baltic. He named the plan Catherine, and the Admiralty thought it possible. By 12 September the plan had taken shape. It consisted of sending into the Baltic a self-supporting force of two or three battleships, an aircraft carrier, five cruisers, two destroyer flotillas, submarines, supply ships and tankers. The battleships were to be strengthened by anti-torpedo bulges, and defended from air attack by stronger armoured decks and extra AA guns. Twelve specially prepared vessels equipped as mine 'bumpers' were to precede the Fleet into the Baltic.

Churchill agreed to the project enthusiastically and insisted that planning for it should have absolute priority. At first he fixed 15 February 1940 as D-Day for Catherine; however, the alterations to the ships were more time-consuming than had been anticipated and many of the ships earmarked could not be spared from convoy duties. On 22 November Churchill agreed to postpone Catherine until 30 April 1940.[1]

The original plan agreed by Churchill and Admiral the Earl of Cork (Director of Plans) in October 1939 was that on 15 February 1940 an attacking fleet was to pass through the Kattegat in thick fog at dawn; then to pass the German coast batteries at Fehmarn on the southern coast of the island of Lolland at 20.00 in the dark and to reach the Bornholm Channel by 06.00 the next day. Then Gävle on the Swedish coast or Mariehamn on the Aaland Islands were to be used as anchorages. Gävle was described as having ship repairing facilities and ample oil, and from there the fleet would carry out the 'offensive action necessary to obtain control of the Baltic'. This, of course, involved blatant violation of Sweden's neutrality. The Foreign Secretary, Halifax, was entirely opposed to this, and Lothian, the British Ambassador in Washington, had warned that the plan would be very badly received by Roosevelt.

On 23 October Cork minuted to Winston with a revised plan: 'It is necessary to make a decision and give the required orders now', and on the 28th he gave a summary of the arguments he had used in favour of it in a conversation with John Simon, the pacifist Chancellor of the Exchequer. Churchill replied: 'It is not possible to express the objects [sic objectives] more clearly. I trust the results were satisfactory.' On 6 November the First Sea Lord, Dudley Pound, minuted to Churchill that Cork wanted all ships for Catherine to be ready by 10 January, but he (Pound) 'could not see the slightest hope of the operation being possible, and that four months would be needed from the word "go".' The following day Cork told Churchill: 'It is questionable whether the operation should be proceeded with unless the Force can be got away before the end of March', because after that there would be insufficient hours of darkness. On 17 November Cork told Churchill that there was a feeling '(though not often expressed at the Conferences held in your room) that it will be impossible to spare ships for the proposed Operation'.

On 7 December Cork received a personal minute from Churchill to fix the date for the assembly of the Force as 31 March, with a view to sailing on 30 April. Cork replied that this was too late; and anyway enthusiasm in the Admiralty for the project had declined, so that only energetic orders from the top 'will get this Expeditionary Force ready by 31 March – or even by some later date'.

A Baltic expedition had been the brainchild of Admiral Fisher in the First World War, and Churchill, as First Lord of the Admiralty then, had been enthusiastic for it. At that time there would have been the inestimable advantage of Russian co-operation. Once the Fleet had command of the Baltic, a large Allied Expeditionary Force, mainly Russian, would have landed on the unde-

fended coast of Northern Pomerania and started a drive on Berlin by the shortest
route. The Kaiser's armies would have had great difficulty in stopping them
without withdrawing troops and therefore dangerously weakening the Western
front. On 22 December 1914 Winston had written to Fisher: 'I am wholly with
you about the Baltic . . . The Baltic is the only theatre in which naval action can
appreciably shorten the war. Denmark must come in, and the Russians let loose
on Berlin'.[2]

In 1939 Churchill emphasized to his Cabinet colleagues and the Admiralty
that a successful Catherine would isolate Germany from Scandinavia, thus
cutting off her vital iron ore supplies; it might bring in the Scandinavian states on
the Allied side, and conceivably could cause Russia to abandon her neutrality. A
further argument was advanced, that the operation might produce a clash with
the German Fleet which, whatever the result, would afterwards be 'in no
condition for further service'; for the Germans it would be 'the disablement of all
their fleet', while for Britain at worst merely a detachment would be involved.

With hindsight Catherine appears a wildcat scheme, and in his memoirs
Churchill gives a woefully inadequate description of his activities and enthusiasm
for it. In fact he became so obsessed with it that it occupied a great deal of his time
and put an enormous strain on the Admiralty's planning staff. To avoid the
ghastly mistakes made at the Dardanelles Churchill insisted that Catherine must
be planned in meticulous detail – a great contrast to the way in which the
Norwegian Expeditionary Force was thrown together at the last moment in the
spring of 1940.

Dudley Pound always doubted if Catherine was practical, but did not dare
confront Winston. In a memorandum on 26 September he laid down formidable
preconditions: Russia must not join Germany, and Swedish 'active co-operation'
must be forthcoming soon after 'our arrival in the Baltic and the plan must deal
with the air menace'. Churchill minuted that he agreed with all Pound's remarks,
and the next day appointed Admiral Earl Cork to plan the operation with a special
staff.

Pound had put his finger on the essential weakness of Catherine: the Fleet in
the Baltic would be destroyed by land-based German aircraft. At that time
Churchill and some of the admirals completely underestimated the power of
shore-based aircraft to sink ships. Later experience with the Archangel convoys
and with the *Repulse* and *Prince of Wales* in the Gulf of Siam showed that naval AA
guns were impotent to protect ships from dive bombing attacks. Churchill
blithely assumed that the Fleet, unprotected by fighter cover, could cope with
German dive bombers. He wrote to Roosevelt on 16 October: 'We have not been
at all impressed with the accuracy of the German air bombing of our warships.
They seem to have no effective bomb sights.' However in his memoirs Churchill
admitted he was wrong, writing that in common with 'prevailing Admiralty belief
I did not feel sufficiently the danger to British warships from air attacks'. He also
did not realize that Hitler would immediately invade southern Denmark, so that
the Fleet would be subject to artillery fire as well as to non-stop air attack from
bombers stationed at aerodromes on the Baltic coast.[3]

Cork, then aged sixty-six, was an old friend of Churchill's and during the First World War had commanded the *Repulse* with distinction; he immediately became enthusiastic for Catherine. However, he insisted that a Swedish base must be found in the Gulf of Bothnia. It was taken for granted that this would be forthcoming, but the Swedes would never have agreed to such a gross breach of their neutrality.[4] The aircraft carrier *Ark Royal* was to try to provide fighter coverage from the North Sea, and if its hundred Spitfires were to be effective, a landing ground for them in Sweden was vital. The iron ore was shipped from both Narvik in Norway and Lulea in Sweden to Germany. Supplies from the Swedish port of Lulea could only be stopped by sending the British Fleet into the Baltic Sea and the Gulf of Bothnia – considered by Chamberlain a wild operation, but one which Churchill seriously contemplated. But Pound became resolutely opposed to Catherine; Cork's planning committee was so large that it was tying up numbers of officers urgently required for other duties, and Pound wanted it disbanded. He also pointed out that the necessary ships could not be spared. Churchill was displeased, but by now the War Cabinet were contemplating aid to Finland through a landing at Narvik and then pushing through Swedish territory to Lulea. Russia had attacked Finland, and there was strong French and British public support for aid to that country.

Churchill hoped while the Russo–Finnish War continued that British troops might be able to occupy Narvik and Lulea under the pretext of helping Finland against the Russians, with the co-operation of Sweden and Norway. But even without the support of these neutral nations he hoped to execute a smaller plan of occupying Narvik and driving through to Lulea without the permission of the neutral powers, telling the Chiefs of Staff on 31 December 1939: 'This causes little injury to Norway and Sweden and is the minimum violation of their neutrality. It is not comparable to an act of invasion of their soil.'[5]

This was strange reasoning. During the Nuremberg Trials Admiral Raeder was accused and convicted of waging a war of aggression because he planned the invasion of Norway in 1940. Halifax and Chamberlain were opposed to any violation of Norwegian neutrality. But approval was given by the War Cabinet to the preparation of assault plans in the hope that Finland would ask for help and Norway and Sweden would agree to the landings.

Churchill agreed that no date for Catherine could be fixed, but instructed Cork: 'The study of the project is to continue and all preparations are to be pressed forward subject to the inevitable demands of the naval war from day to day; but that neither this study nor these preparations in any way commit the Admiralty or HMG to authorise action. The position remains as I said "the gun is to be loaded for firing." This and no more.' Cork was ordered to recast Catherine on the basis that an attack had been made at Narvik so that British troops held Lulea and Gävle with adequate airpower for protection, and that Russia was not actually at war with Britain.

Pound replied firmly and bluntly on 31 December 1939, and gave expression to his grave misgivings.

I simply cannot visualise that a Fleet whose position would always be known whether at sea or in harbour and which would be continually under attack from the air and under water and when at sea exposed to mines also could achieve any useful purpose before it was itself reduced to impotence. It must be remembered also that if any ship gets badly damaged all that we could do would be to beach her . . . Apart from the feasibility of the plan it is quite certain that we could not spare the necessary force for the operation.

Catherine is a great gamble even if there were adequate fighter protection for the Fleet, and if Russia were on our side and we had the use of Russian bases. As neither of these conditions will be present I consider that the sending of a fleet of surface ships into the Baltic is courting disaster . . .

I do represent most strongly however that all preparations apart from planning are discontinued except for alterations to ships as will make them more efficient for their normal duties.

All Pound would agree to was the despatch of a strong submarine force into the Baltic if the Germans landed or declared war on Sweden.[6]

Although Churchill writes in his memoirs that he was now 'increasingly convinced there could be no "Operation Catherine" in 1940' he did not yield readily, replying to Pound with surprising optimism they would soon master the U-Boats and surface raiders and thus have 'a superfluity of force for the Baltic'; in addition, Russia might veer towards the Allies at any moment, although it would be 'wrong to try it (Catherine) unless we can see our way of maintaining it under air attack'.[7] Cork made it clear on 10 January 1940 that it had not been possible to make adequate progress with preparations and modifications to ships, and finally Churchill climbed down. The duty of a First Sea Lord is to prevent the temporary occupant of the post of First Lord of the Admiralty from risking the Fleet with the authority of the Cabinet in any action which did not constitute proper operations of war. Pound did his job correctly. On 15 January Churchill reluctantly agreed that Catherine would not be practicable in 1940, but stated that preparations for the operation were to be kept under continuous review by a reduced Committee.

The author showed Admiral Sir Hector Maclean, who joined the Navy in 1926, copies of the Admiralty papers about the plans for Catherine. He wrote:

I never heard of Catherine at the time. I am astonished at Lord Cork – my naval hero at that period. He was always one for forward strategy, in this case to the point of madness. My generation had little confidence in the AA armament of our ships in being able to withstand enemy bombers, but we all underestimated air power against warships until the Norwegian campaign.

Catherine would have been military madness, and I thank God for Dudley Pound, the First Sea Lord, who put the case against Catherine so clearly.

Admiral John Grant also joined the Navy in 1926 and had been attached to Dudley Pound's staff in the late twenties. After reading the papers he wrote that he fully agreed with Maclean, and he too 'thanked God' for the First Sea Lord's lucid exposure of the madness of Catherine.

The Earl of Selkirk, a former First Lord and a member of Churchill's post-war

Cabinet, told the author he agreed entirely that it was 'virtually a mad expedition'. Selkirk's mother, the Duchess of Hamilton, was one of Lord Fisher's closest friends; Selkirk wrote to the author that he had had one or two talks with Fisher about his proposal to land in Pomerania in 1915. In his view Fisher's plan was a totally different proposition, not so much because with Russia as an ally the British had complete command of the sea, but because there was then no likelihood of the Germans getting control of Norway or even Denmark. He wrote: 'Churchill was always a great adventurer in war, and my reading of 1939–40 is that an expedition to Norway, while of value politically, was strategically useless and should never have been attempted. Churchill just felt something must be done.'[8]

Arthur Marder wrote that 'the cost of Catherine in wasted hours had been prodigious'.[9] Fortunately the £12 million invested in equipping special craft for the operation was not wasted. After Fisher's abortive Baltic scheme in the First World War self-propelled lighters were built and played an important role in the Dardanelles; now four Glen Line cargo ships converted for Catherine in 1939 to carrying 5000 tons of fuel and 2000 tons of ammunition, and provided with special protection against torpedoes and bombs, would be put to excellent use in supplying Malta and Crete in 1941–2. However, the tremendous congestion in the shipyards had made it impossible to carry out Churchill's 1939 plan to give the battleships special deck protection against bombs and 'super blisters' against torpedoes.

In December, as Pound and his Admiralty colleagues – apart from Cork – objected ever more strongly to Catherine, Churchill realized it could not be carried out. As an alternative he became enthusiastic for stopping German supplies of iron ore from Narvik either by mining the sea routes (the Leads, a chain of outlying islands) or by a military landing at Narvik. As the Russo–Finnish War developed and the Finnish appeal to the League of Nations became abortive, arguments about a Narvik landing were entangled with those of sending a large Anglo–French Expeditionary Force to Sweden via Narvik and Lulea (the sea route to Petsamo was icebound). As early as 19 September 1939 Churchill had suggested to the War Cabinet the mining of the Leads, and he had returned to this idea several times without making headway with his colleagues.

On 14 December Churchill told the War Cabinet that Germany had sunk three ships within Norwegian territorial waters, and that this 'gave Britain the strongest possible case for retaliatory action'. Therefore he asked for permission to send four or five destroyers to arrest all ships carrying ore to Germany and take them as prizes. But John Simon, the Chancellor of the Exchequer, objected and consent was not given.

On the 16th Churchill brought to the War Cabinet a memorandum from the Admiralty urging a plan to mine Norwegian waters. During the discussion Churchill reiterated if the British could stop the movement of iron ore from Narvik and Lulea 'we should shorten the war and save many thousands of lives'. (He overlooked the fact that the ore from Lulea could alternatively be shipped from non-icebound southern Swedish ports.) According to the memorandum, stopping iron ore would rank as 'a major offensive operation of war which would be equal to a first class victory in the field without any serious sacrifice of life. It might be decisive'. If war spread to Norway, he wanted to occupy Narvik and Bergen; urging the laying of a minefield by submarines in the Gulf of Bothnia, he was ready to abrogate some of the rules of warfare and said that 'humanity, not legality, must be our guide.' Cyril Newall, Chief of the Air Staff, pointed out that the War Cabinet had prohibited bombing which might cause loss of civilian life, and Kingsley Wood (Lord Privy Seal, later Chancellor of the Exchequer) thought it unwise to disturb the present situation 'since by doing so we might lose more than we gain'.[10]

A War Cabinet decision was deferred. Meanwhile at the Supreme War Council on 19 December the French proposed action at Narvik. At the War Cabinet on the 22nd Churchill produced a summary of views from Thyssen, the German steel tycoon, then in Switzerland, claiming that victory in the war would go to the side which obtained control of Swedish ore. Winston suggested the Government should urge Sweden and Norway to give all possible help to Finland, and also tell Norway that the British proposed to mine her waters. Halifax poured cold water on the proposals, saying that if the British were to adopt them they would have to land a force at Narvik and send it to the Swedish ore fields. The Prime Minister agreed with Halifax that the agreement of Sweden and Norway must be obtained before taking such drastic action, and the War Cabinet decided to ask Halifax to approach the Norwegian and Swedish Governments in London.

On 22 December, discussing the landing at Narvik, the War Cabinet would not go further than inviting the Chiefs of Staff to report on the military implications of a policy designed to bring a halt to all the ore traffic. On Christmas Day Churchill sent a minute to Pound, asking what the Navy could do if British troops occupied the Gallivare ore fields and Germany attacked with a large army 'as it certainly would' as soon as the port of Lulea was no longer icebound. Pound's minute restated the case against Catherine; he asserted that sending the British Navy into the Gulf of Bothnia (the only possible counter-stroke) would subject it to 'great hazards' and the Government would have to be prepared to 'write off this force'. This important minute by Pound was not discovered and read by the official historians, Woodward, Derry and Butler, nor by Churchill's biographers Gilbert and Irving. The advice made Churchill less enthusiastic for an adventure in the Gallivare region, and he gave up his pet plan of sending the Fleet into the Baltic. This change of mind explains alleged inconsistencies in his approach to the Scandinavian problem, for which he has been criticized by certain historians.

On 27 December Churchill, obviously disconcerted by Pound's firm minute, denied that he wanted to land troops at Narvik or occupy the ore fields 'at this stage'. He only wanted to send destroyers to intercept the chain of cargo ships taking ore from Narvik to Germany. However, the Chiefs of Staff responded to the War Cabinet request of 22 December by stating that 'the only way' to stop the export of iron ore from Gallivare was to despatch an expedition in the early spring via Narvik into Sweden, and the gains justified the risk because the seizure of Gallivare 'could be decisive'.

At War Cabinets on 2 and 3 January the Chiefs of Staff opposed Churchill's 'half cock scheme' of naval action alone, which in their view would antagonize the Norwegians and Swedes and lessen their chances of co-operation in the larger scheme. Churchill fought hard for his 'limited operation', showing how much he respected Pound's opinion. The War Cabinet approved Churchill's 'limited scheme', and authorized Halifax to inform Norway that in connection with German violation of Norway's territorial waters British ships would 'at times enter and operate in Norwegian territorial waters'.[11]

The Norwegian reaction was a violent protest, as was the Swedish. This was reported to the War Cabinet on 10 January. Churchill, however, was all for going on anyway, and thought that Norway and Sweden would be more inclined to co-operate with an expedition to Lulea if they were 'more frightened of us than Germany'.[12] On 12 January he pleaded again for his scheme, saying 'he was not impatient for action merely for action's sake, but ever since the beginning of the war we had let the initiative rest with Germany'. However, to Churchill's dismay the War Cabinet decided to do nothing for the time being, having been shaken by the violence of the Scandinavian Governments' protests. This led Churchill to protest that 'the discussion of this subject had now been proceeding for six weeks and every argument had been brought up in favour of doing nothing'. Churchill was finding himself in the position of being able to change military strategy but unable to initiate action, because Chamberlain and his pre-war appeasement colleagues were opposed to anything which might escalate the cold war into a shooting war.

Chamberlain again employed delaying tactics by suggesting that a mission under Hoare (the former Foreign Secretary, Secretary of State for Air) should be sent to Sweden to invite their active co-operation. This was discussed on 17 January; Lord Halifax said he could not contemplate war with Norway to capture Narvik. Churchill argued it would be better to take naval action first and then send the mission; he was also angered because Chamberlain said it was necessary to consult with the Dominions before any action was taken. Intensely frustrated, Churchill wrote to Halifax about the 'awful difficulties which our machinery of war conduct presents to positive action. I see such immense walls of prevention all built and building that I wonder whether any plan will have a chance of climbing over them.' He referred to the seven weeks of argument over a Narvik operation, and went on: 'one thing is absolutely certain, namely that victory will never be found by taking the line of least resistance'.

Churchill was almost in despair; Chamberlain occasionally supported his arguments, but always with heavy reservations. Halifax always sided with the Prime Minister because he believed a negotiated peace through Goering was possible. On 13 March Halifax discussed such a negotiated peace with Rab Butler, his Under Secretary. When Butler said he would not 'exclude a truce if Mussolini, the Pope and Roosevelt would come in', Halifax replied: 'That is a challenging statement, but I agree with you.'[13]

Sir John Colville was Chamberlain's private secretary in 1940. He told the author the feeling amongst those who worked at No. 10 was that there would be no 'real war', and Chamberlain said to him several times that it must stop before the shooting began. Colville felt Chamberlain was confident the Germans would have to negotiate a peace because the economic blockade would make it impossible for them to hold out. According to Colville, Chamberlain made no secret that he was ready to do a deal with anyone in power in Germany, although perhaps because of vanity he could not forgive Hitler for breaking his promise at Munich. Colville said Chamberlain would have done a deal with Goering, although he added that the Prime Minister did not have the same confidence in Goering as Halifax did. According to Colville, Chamberlain used to say to him, 'We must call a halt before the blood bath starts', and this was apparently also Halifax's line.[14]

As has been seen, in March Chamberlain told Sumner Welles that under certain circumstances he might negotiate with Hitler. Thus Churchill was up against a brick wall in his efforts to persuade the War Cabinet to take vigorous action in Scandinavia because Chamberlain, Halifax and Kingsley Wood were opposed to anything which might provoke German retaliation and worsen the prospects for a negotiated peace. As a result, abortive discussions about action against Narvik continued, with Churchill getting more and more desperate.

On 5 February Churchill accompanied Chamberlain to Paris for the Supreme War Council. It was agreed to prepare three or four divisions for Finland, send them via Narvik and take control of the Gallivare ore fields. The French Prime Minister Daladier and his colleagues were keen on this operation because they were eager there should be a major encounter with German troops away from French soil. By 17 February the Chiefs of Staff had a plan of action and a timetable. The earliest date for the landing at Narvik would be 20 March, but the last possible date was 3 April if they were to reach Lulea before the ice melted. Finland was to be asked to make an appeal for help to France and Britain.

With hindsight it is astonishing how lightly the French treated the risk of Russia reacting by declaring war on Britain and France. The attendant dangers for France were less serious than for Britain, because France would not be involved in any Russian action against India. French enthusiasm was based on the hope that bombing the Russian oilfields at Baku on the Caspian Sea would deprive Germany entirely of Russian oil. The fact Chamberlain was prepared to risk war with Russia shows how little he had moved from his previous year's position that the Nazis ought to be a bulwark against the spread of Bolshevism. Churchill opposed the Finnish expedition because, being more realistic, he understood how essential it was to stop Hitler and Stalin operating together militarily, and that in the end Russian help would be needed to defeat Germany. Churchill told the War Cabinet that the Finnish war could not be a profitable diversion since German forces were not engaged, and he deprecated weakening Britain by sending aeroplanes to the Finns. When on 5 December Cork had written to Churchill that the Russian attack on Finland offered a wonderful chance of mobilizing the anti-Bolshevik forces on the British side, and wanted Catherine accelerated, Winston had replied coldly: 'It is my policy to avoid war with Russia', and he stuck to this line.

Chamberlain told the 5 February Supreme War Council that the Finnish Expeditionary Force must consist of regular divisions although they would go as volunteers, and strangely argued that because the troops were volunteers Russia need not declare war unless she wished to do so.[15] However, the stumbling block was the impossibility of obtaining Norwegian and Swedish consent. With unjustifiable optimism, Chamberlain stated that he doubted whether Norway and Sweden could resist appeals for action to save Finland. When Daladier asked Chamberlain what the Allies would do if the Scandinavian countries refused rights of passage, Chamberlain replied that refusal was unlikely and there would be nothing more than protests.

It is surprising that the War Cabinet agreed to the Finnish Expeditionary Force with its attendant risk of reprisals from both Germany and Russia, because the military prospects of the Finns were already poor and deteriorating rapidly. As ought to have been anticipated, Norway and Sweden were adamant in refusing rights of passage, and Halifax informed the War Cabinet of this on 12 February.

The general attitude of the Scandinavian Governments became clear from the *Altmark* incident of 16 February, when the Norwegian Government protested vigorously because the British had boarded this ship in Norwegian waters although it was carrying British prisoners. All hope of a change in Swedish policy was ruled out on 19 February when the King of Sweden announced that he had refused the Finnish request for aid.

Faced with this impasse after two months of discussions and procrastinations over Narvik, on 29 February the War Cabinet again discussed laying mines off Narvik. Chamberlain had consulted Sinclair, Attlee and Greenwood and the Dominion Governments; because of their opposition, and the USA attitude, Chamberlain said it would be 'advisable' to postpone action. Churchill argued vehemently that the mine laying was 'justified', and 'would do more to hasten the defeat of Germany than any other single measure within our power'. He added 'it would have been even more effective if it had been carried out three months before as he had originally proposed'. However, despite their hesitations the War Cabinet did agree to Churchill's proposal that the Stratford force – the troops to occupy Bergen, Trondheim and Stavanger, authorized by the War Cabinet on 16 February – should be fully mobilized and ready to move.[16]

On 1 March Churchill argued to the Cabinet that Britain should make a strong request for passage of the Finnish Expeditionary Force across Norway and Sweden to Lulea, and back up the demand with the arrival off Narvik of an Expeditionary Force. Churchill was not so much interested in relieving Finland, whose position was by now almost hopeless, as of getting a foothold at Narvik. He told his colleagues that if the Norwegians resisted, the British force would probably have to return without landing, but 'at the same time he would not entirely exclude at this stage the use of some force to make our way through'. Once again the War Cabinet procrastinated and made no decision.[17]

On 11 March Churchill tried hard, but again, in vain, to ginger his colleagues into action. He reiterated that the Norwegians would not oppose a Narvik landing vigorously, and the Chiefs of Staff reported it was 'most desirable' to secure a footing at Trondheim as well as Narvik. Next day the British Minister to Norway, Sir C. Dormer, reported that in his view he did not expect the Norwegians to put up any serious resistance or obstruction to a landing at Narvik, and the War Cabinet agreed to it. At last Churchill had overcome his weaker colleagues and got authorization for action. But once again he was disappointed, because on the 13th the Finns capitulated to the Russians.

However the French Government, intent on diverting the Germans into battle away from French soil, would not give up the Narvik landing plan. They proposed mining the Narvik waters (Operation Wilfred); if the Germans reacted as was probable, the Allies would be able to take control of the ore fields. On 19 March the British War Cabinet rejected the French proposal, again over-riding Churchill.

Unexpectedly the Daladier Government resigned next day; Reynaud became Prime Minister and also Minister for Foreign Affairs, while the cowardly Daladier took over the job of War and Defence. Churchill was delighted because Reynaud, like him, had been in favour of fighting at the time of Munich and the two had collaborated before the war. Churchill anticipated a firmer line from the new Government, and he did not have long to wait. On 26 March Reynaud sent a memorandum advocating immediate mining of the Leads, and using the probable German retaliation as an excuse to occupy the ore fields. Reynaud also reiterated Daladier's suggestion of bombing the Baku oil fields. The War Cabinet did not even discuss the French proposals for bombing Russia because Anglo–Russian relations had suddenly taken a turn for the better. At his own suggestion Sir Stafford Cripps, the Labour MP, had flown to Russia to see Molotov, the Soviet Foreign Minister, and reported that Russia was ready for a trade agreement with Britain. Maisky, Russian Ambassador in London, had confirmed this to Halifax and emphasized that there was no question of a Russo–German military alliance; Russia would remain independent.

For some months Churchill had shown great enthusiasm for Operation Royal Marine, whose purpose was to drop floating mines by air and manually from the French bank into the Rhine and adjoining rivers. Daladier disapproved because he thought it would lead to retaliatory air raids on French aircraft factories. Churchill insisted that the plan had prominence in Anglo–French discussion because he wanted the Allies to take the initiative. It is extraordinary that, although the French Government was ready to risk war with Russia, they would not provoke the Germans with mines on the Rhine. Already the German behaviour at sea in sinking passenger ships proved that if they thought it worthwhile to bomb French factories involved in the war effort they would do so regardless. Churchill was justified in his enthusiasm for Royal Marine, because when it was carried out in June it completely closed part of the Rhine waterways.

After the mines were deployed on 10 June there were only eight barges moving between Karlsruhe and Mainz; all traffic from Karlsruhe to Mainz was forbidden; the Karlsruhe barrage was broken up and the permanent bridge at Germersheim broken; and no bathing was allowed.[18]

At the Supreme War Council on 28 March Chamberlain urged Royal Marine should be put into operation, but he opposed the bombing of Russian oil fields. He also said there were no short cuts to winning the war and that the main Allied weapon was the economic blockade. Reynaud said the French Military Committee would not accept Royal Marine unless it was accompanied by attacks on Baku, but wanted the minefield in the Leads – Operation Wilfred – laid immediately; he also wanted bombs for Russia to be sent to Syria at once to be ready for use. The Council also made the momentous decision that neither France nor Britain would conclude an armistice or treaty of peace except 'by mutual agreement'.

Chamberlain sensibly refused to commit Britain to an attack on Baku and asked whether it was in British interests that the war should spread to Russia; he also reported signs that Russia wanted to improve relations with the Allies. Irrationally, Reynaud replied that an attack on Baku oil supplies would disorganize Russian agriculture and might even help to bring Russia in on the side of the Allies. Reynaud was not proving quite the bold man that Churchill expected, and a Foreign Office study revealed that Germany had oil supplies for several months; the Baku plan faded out.[19]

However, to Churchill's joy the Supreme War Council agreed that Royal Marine should begin on 4 April and that minefields should be laid in Norwegian waters on 5 April. The next day the War Cabinet accepted these decisions. At last Churchill had his way, and to tackle the German reaction the Chiefs of Staff assigned one British brigade of three battalions and a French force for Narvik, and five British battalions for the southern operation. Infantry embarked on cruisers ready for an unopposed landing at Narvik, Stavanger and Bergen, where they would be ready to deal with a German riposte. But to Churchill's intense irritation, just as all arrangements were complete to launch the floating mines on the German Rhine waterways the French War Committee decided to postpone Royal Marine for three months 'for fear of reprisals'. On 31 March Corbin, the French Ambassador, called on Churchill to deliver this news. Daladier, he said, had objected to the plan. Corbin told Chamberlain that Reynaud was 'extremely disappointed and it was very embarrassing for him'. With evident pride, Chamberlain recorded for his colleagues that he replied: 'No mines – no Narvik.' If one was adjourned, the other must be too. Corbin said that if both were abandoned the Allies would be doing exactly nothing, to which Chamberlain responded: 'Precisely, that is why it seems to me that the decision is awkard for Monsieur Reynaud.' Chamberlain refused Corbin's suggestion that he fly to Paris to get the decision reversed.

It is inexplicable how the British Prime Minister should have been so petty as to say that without Royal Marine Wilfred must be cancelled. Possibly he was so opposed to escalation of the war that he snatched at any straw to postpone the operation. What makes it even more surprising is that the Secret Service and Admiralty were reporting signs of an imminent large-scale German invasion of Norway.

Reynaud told Campbell, the British Ambassador in Paris, that on his way back in the aeroplane from London he had begun to have doubts about Royal Marine because Hitler 'for internal reasons would be bound to take some drastic action in reply, and we should find ourselves plunged into unrestricted aerial warfare'. It was Churchill, not Chamberlain, who went to Paris. He was furious at Chamberlain's postponing of Wilfrid, and insisted to the Prime Minister that, whatever the French did over Royal Marine, 'the sooner the mining of Norwegian territorial waters took place, the better'. As a sop to Churchill Chamberlain agreed that Operation Wilfred should now start on 8 April instead of the 5th, even if the French still denied Royal Marine. This delay was entirely due to Chamberlain's off-the-cuff petulant response to Corbin's unexpected declaration, and it had dire consequences. Churchill told his colleagues, 'I might be able to do some good with Daladier', and went to Paris on 4 April determined 'to do his best to bring Daladier round'.

That evening Churchill and Reynaud dined alone at the British Embassy with only the Ambassador present. Daladier had churlishly refused the invitation. Churchill explained to Reynaud 'with great force' the argument in favour of putting Royal Marine into execution at once. Reynaud replied that he had tried for three hours in the War Committee to overcome Daladier's opposition – but he had only done this out of loyalty to the decision of the Supreme War Council, because 'he had come round to the view there was much to be said' for postponement. Churchill was gravely disappointed in the new French Premier, upon whose resolution and desire for active prosecution of the war he was pinning great hopes. He was to be even more disappointed in Reynaud in the coming weeks.

Reynaud emphasized that he could not over-rule Daladier, his Minister of War, on a point of strategy, and Churchill formed the impression that the Reynaud Government might fall if Britain insisted on an immediate Royal Marine. In that case, the British Ambassador felt, 'Reynaud's days were numbered.' The next day Daladier again refused Churchill's invitation to dine at the Embassy; they met in Daladier's office and Churchill accepted the cancellation of the Rhine operation with good grace.

Reynaud insisted, however, that Wilfred was essential and must not be abandoned. He and Churchill were in agreement, and on 6 April Churchill telephoned Chamberlain to the effect that 'It would be a great mistake to force the French to fall in with our wishes' over Royal Marine. Chamberlain then withdrew his objection to Wilfred and the War Cabinet authorized it for 8 April, while Admiral Phillips gave them details of the ships held in readiness for British landings at Narvik, Stavanger, Bergen and Trondheim if there was a German reaction. As soon as he got back to London Churchill wrote happily to Chamberlain: 'All is moving.' By dawn on 8 April the minefields around Narvik had been laid by four British destroyers. But Chamberlain's pique during his interview with Corbin had resulted in fatal delay, and on that day the Germans arrived in Narvik first.[20]

In the early hours of 8 April strong German forces landed at Oslo, Trondheim, Bergen and Narvik. Britain was taken by surprise. She should not have been. As early as 6 April the Admiralty had been informed by Denham, the Naval Attaché in Copenhagen, that he had seen through his binoculars the German Battle Fleet proceeding towards the Skagerrak. This news was disregarded. Additionally, the Secret Service reported large numbers of troops embarking on transports in Baltic ports. This too was disbelieved. At 09.00 on 7 April RAF planes reported German battleships north of Heligoland and off Jutland Bank, sailing north or north-west at high speed. Churchill would not believe that Hitler was sending an invasion force to Norway. Denham was convinced the German Battle Fleet was breaking out into the Atlantic.[21]

So on the night of 7 April Churchill ordered the Home Fleet to sail north–east from Scapa Flow. The *Rodney*, *Valiant* and *Repulse* all went under Admiral Sir Charles Forbes in the wrong direction. During 7 April troops for plan R4, the seizure of Stavanger and Bergen, had been boarding four cruisers at Rosyth to make landings if the Germans responded to the minelaying in the Leads by violating Norwegian neutrality. On his own initiative Churchill ordered the troops ashore, and the four cruisers followed Forbes with the soldiers' equipment still aboard. Thus four battalions were immobilized.

Hitler had planned the invason of Norway for several months; every detail had been prepared with meticulous German precision and all went according to plan; whereas on the British side, as a result of divided counsels and contradictory plans, all had to be improvised. At first Churchill was optimistic, telling the Cabinet that 'we were in a far better position . . . our hands are now free, and we could apply our overwhelming sea power on the Norwegian coast'. His first reaction was to embark immediately on Rupert – the capture of Narvik – without dissipating his forces by attempting to recapture Bergen and Trondheim.[22]

Chamberlain had now reshuffled his Cabinet. Chatfield, the Minister of Defence, was retired and not replaced. Instead Churchill was made Chairman of the Military Co-ordination Committee. This was an unsatisfactory halfway house for him: he did not have the authority of a Minister of Defence, although the main responsibility for military decisions fell on him. He immediately persuaded the War Cabinet to approve the capture of Narvik.

The invasion forces sailed for Narvik on 11 April but could not assault the port as the ships were not loaded for an immediate offensive. The Norwegian Army, although taken completely by surprise, was resisting and holding up the German overland advance from Oslo to Trondheim. The British Minister, Dormer, had left Oslo with the King and the Norwegian Government and on 13 April one of his staff cabled London:

I have had conversation with the Commander-in-Chief, who takes an optimistic view of the situation provided he can get assistance at once, i.e. today or tomorrow.

He is of the opinion that if the British do not help him now the war will be ended in a very few days.

The Norwegian Government went to war on the promise of Dormer that Britain would act at once. The former Commander-in-Chief resigned two days ago because he did not believe the British would act quickly enough. The present Commander-in-Chief, who trusted the British word, must not be let down. [General Ruge had replaced General Laake on 1 April].

Chamberlain, buoyed up by Churchill's energy and optimism, and by the brilliant victory of the Navy that day when all the German ships in the Narvik fjord had been sunk, replied:

We are coming as fast as possible and in great strength. Further details later. Meanwhile use every effort at all costs to cut railway communications so that neither Bergen nor Trondheim can be reinforced by land. We are preventing enemy reinforcements arriving by sea. We are inspired by your message and feel sure that you have only to hold on until we arrive for both our countries to emerge victorious.

On the same day the War Office sent Ruge a futile request to capture Bardufoss aerodrome near Narvik, not realizing that there were no Norwegian forces anywhere near. Ruge replied with a cable to Chamberlain, stating that British action was necessary 'both to make further resistance possible and to make the Norwegian people and army understand England really means business . . . Trondheim must be taken while I am able to help you and I shall not be able to do so unless you attack at once.' Chamberlain promised to send five divisions immediately; nothing like this strength was available.[23]

However, the War Cabinet then decided to tell the Norwegians that they intended to take Trondheim, as the Norwegian Commander-in-Chief was sending repeated signals to London urging its immediate recovery. Ironside, the Chief of the Imperial General Staff (CIGS), was opposed; and Churchill, at first contrary, suddenly changed his mind and backed Hammer – a direct amphibious assault on Trondheim now favoured by the Admiralty. For this sudden change of mind Churchill has been much criticized. According to the *Ironside Diaries*,

At 2 a.m. on the morning of 14 April, Mr Churchill, accompanied only by the Deputy Chief of the Naval Staff, Admiral Tom Phillips, came to Ironside's room at the War Office. 'Tiny, we are going for the wrong place. We should go for Trondheim,' said the First Lord. 'The Navy will make a direct attack on it and I want a small force of good troops, well led, to follow up the naval attack. I also want landings made north and south of Trondheim, one at Nemsos and the other at Aandalsnes, to co-operate with the assault when it comes off by a pincer movement on Trondheim.' Mr Churchill was unable to give any date for the naval attack.

Ironside protested that he had no troops available for Trondheim until Narvik had been taken. Mr Churchill then insisted that the rear half of the Narvik convoy, which was carrying the 146 Territorial Brigade, should be diverted to Namsos. Ironside again protested, this time with some heat, that Mr Churchill at least should know how impractical such a diversion would be. If half the Narvik force were removed, the Narvik operation would be ruined. The troops and their equipment had been loaded and the administration organized for a single operation, and everything would be upset if half the convoy was dispatched. It would be better, said Ironside, to abandon Narvik altogether, or at most, to invest it. He was overruled.'

Churchill made a horrendous mistake by over-ruling the CIGS and bowing to his colleagues and the French wish for the Trondheim operation; the result was that the Narvik expeditionary force became too weak and the troops sent to the Trondheim area met with disaster.

On 14 April Churchill told the War Cabinet that, because of the naval victory at Narvik, the risks of landing at Trondheim were 'not unjustifiable'. The next day he was less optimistic, but was subject to severe pressure from his colleagues to undertake the operation. As a result landings were made at Namsos, 80 miles from Trondheim, and Aandalsnes, 150 miles away, on 17 and 18 April. In his memoirs Churchill wrote: 'I now looked forward to this exciting enterprise to which so many staid and cautious Ministers had given their strong adherence, and which seemed to find much favour with the Naval Staff and indeed among all our experts. Such was the position on the 17th.'[25]

At their meeting on 19 April the Chiefs of Staff categorically opposed a direct frontal assault on Trondheim; instead they recommended a pincer movement on the town by the forces already landed at Namsos and Aandalsnes. This was a bitter pill for Churchill after his recent enthusiastic conversion to Hammer. The Military Co-ordination Committee agreed with the Chiefs of Staff, and on 20 April the War Cabinet declared Hammer dead. A warning note was struck by Ironside, who told the War Cabinet that the troops at Dombás, near Trondheim, 'had no guns or transport' and were 'not in condition to fight a serious action'. Neither the British general commanders in the field nor the Norwegians and French were told of the change of plan.[26]

At the Supreme War Council in Paris on 22 and 23 April the French urged concentration on Norway, and offered to put the Chasseurs Alpins and other French troops under British command. Hopes were high not only that Trondheim would fall, but also that an advance would be made from Narvik through the Swedish frontier to the Gulf of Bothnia at Lulea. However, it was pointed out that there was only a fortnight before Lulea would be ice-free and the Allies would need to land at Narvik in great force to reach the iron ore fields before the Germans landed troops by sea at Lulea.

Reynaud urged the deployment of more troops around Trondheim and the capture of Narvik at whatever cost. Chamberlain deceived the French by describing a plan for the naval attack on Trondheim, although the War Cabinet had already cancelled Operation Hammer. Churchill realistically explained the grave difficulties of the Allied forces at Namsos and Aandalsnes – no adequate port, lack of AA and artillery, and the deadly effects of German bombing. Reynaud finished the meeting by declaring that 'the main thing was to take Trondheim and turn it into a strong base for future operations'. His faith in Churchill and Chamberlain must have been badly shaken when he learnt that Hammer had already been abandoned. On his copy of the minutes Daladier wrote 'farcical'. Daladier may have been better informed of British intentions than Reynaud was.[27]

All this soon became wishful thinking. Narvik could not be assaulted for lack of guns and troops, and the landings at Namsos and Aandalsnes ran into dire trouble. The Germans completely destroyed the town and port of Namsos by air raids, thus proving how nonsensical it was for Kingsley Wood and other ministers to cling to the idea that Hitler might not indulge in air raids causing civilian casualties, and therefore should not be provoked: he was ruthless in killing civilians whenever it suited his book. Around Trondheim, with the aerodrome in German hands, the Luftwaffe ranged in overwhelming strength and almost without interference over the British land positions, and at the same time inflicted serious damage and losses on British ships.

By 26 April the port at Aandalsnes, like that at Namsos, had been devastated by German bombing; the Allied forces were in danger of being encircled by the Germans, and the generals reported that there was no alternative to evacuation. On the 27th the War Cabinet agreed (although their written conclusions are inexcusably ambiguous). Churchill argued that the Government should leave the troops 'now in Norway to put up the best fight they could in conjunction with the Norwegians', and reminded his colleagues that Admiral Sir Roger Keyes, MP, the First World War hero, was making urgent appeals for a Hammer-type operation. Keyes' plan always had an emotional and illogical appeal for Churchill. Ironside made it clear that the alternative to evacuation was military disaster. The Supreme War Council met in London two hours later. Gamelin and Reynaud made appeals for 'face saving' by leaving 'some elements of resistance around Trondheim'. Again Chamberlain was far from frank and did not reveal that a firm decision to evacuate had been taken by the British.

Reynaud, misled by Chamberlain, went back to Paris confident that the British would continue the Trondheim operations; two hours after he left London urgent orders were sent from the War Office for the immediate evacuation of Namsos and Aandalsnes, thus flouting the Supreme War Council. Fortunately, bad weather prevented the Luftwaffe interfering too much with the evacuation. On 2 May French and British ships took off 4200 men from Namsos, and over 2000 from Aandalsnes. Reynaud and Gamelin were furious, but the military situation was so bad that nothing else was feasible.[28]

Meanwhile Churchill was being heavily criticized by the Service Chiefs. Ironside complained that Winston wanted to divert troops to Narvik from all over the place: 'He tires of a thing, and then wants to hear no more of it. He was mad to divert the Brigade from Narvik to Namsos . . . Now he is bored with the Namsos operation and is all for Narvik again. It is most extraordinary how mercurial he is.'[29]

The trouble with the Narvik operation was that the ships had not been loaded for assault landings. The troops required several days to unload their guns and equipment before they became fully operational. This was exactly the mistake which Churchill had allowed to happen with the Dardanelles landings twenty-five years before. There the original assault, on 18 March 1915, was chaotic:

units on one ship, their guns on another and ammunition on a third, so that the ships had to return to Alexandria to be reloaded for assault landings. As a result, the Turks knew from their spies in Egypt exactly what was planned and on what date, so that they were ready when the British force returned to the Dardanelles a month later. The result was a costly failure. In Whitehall in 1940 memories of the Dardanelles were vivid, and anger against Churchill boiled up over the military blunders of the Norwegian campaign. Always highly sensitive, Churchill was aware of this and asked Chamberlain to take over the chairmanship of the Military Co-ordination Committee because he did not want to be looked on as the architect of disaster.

The Chiefs of Staff were particularly concerned because Churchill was continually summoning them to the Military Co-ordination Committee to consider problems before they had 'an opportunity of meeting together to discuss them amongst themselves' or with their staffs. They also complained that the Joint Planning Staffs were being squeezed out of the picture. General Ismay went so far as to tell the Secretary to the Cabinet that there was 'every chance of a first class row if Churchill took the chair at the key meeting on 16 April of the Military Co-ordination Committee to discuss the projected attack on Trondheim', and before it Ismay implored the Chiefs of Staff in private 'to exercise the most rigid self control over themselves and at all costs to keep their tempers, saying if there was a row he was afraid of a first class political crisis'.[30]

It was apparent in Whitehall that the Norwegian campaign was in many ways a repeat of Gallipoli. Then Churchill had been forced to resign because of incompetence, and from that time on he had not been trusted by military experts. In 1940, to his horror, Churchill found that the Norway orders were being so altered as to be almost worthless. Originally on 6 April as part of the Stratford plan 148 Brigade had been put aboard two cruisers to carry out an unopposed landing at Stavanger; then the brigade was put ashore and in the confusion much equipment was lost or destroyed. On 13 April the brigade was ordered to land at Namsos, but three days later was diverted to Aandalsnes after the whole brigade had embarked on the Namsos-bound *Orion*. That night the troops were taken off the *Orion* and reloaded on five warships, with more damage and loss of equipment. Then, through an oversight, half a battalion was left behind, as were the rangefinders and searchlights for the AA batteries, all the mortar ammunition and motor transport except one truck; on top of that they had full sets of maps for Namsos but none for Aandalsnes.[31]

At Narvik it was a similar situation, and Churchill's worst fears were realized. He sent imperious orders to Cork, in charge of the naval side of the expedition, to launch an immediate amphibious attack on German-held Narvik. It was impossible. On 15 April, when Cork met the commander of the land force, General Mackesy, for the first time to plan the attack ordered by Churchill, Mackesy told Cork to his great surprise that 'his force was embarked as for a peaceful landing, and consequently was unready for immediate operations', and the orders he had received from the War Office 'ruled out any idea of attempting an opposed landing'. In addition Mackesy's force had almost no mortar ammunition, few grenades, no spare ammunition, no artillery or A A guns, and no tanks or landing craft. Churchill's hopes that well-defended Narvik could be taken immediately were a wild dream; he was so annoyed that he told Cork he could sack Mackesy and take sole charge of the operation. But Cork wisely decided otherwise. Instead of an amphibious assault, a naval bombardment of Narvik was carried out – fruitlessly – on 24 April.[32]

Perhaps the worst command omission was the failure to inform the British commanders at Namsos and Aandalsnes that the frontal attack on Trondheim had been abandoned. Left in ignorance, they made dispositions which produced needless casualties. When 146 Brigade landed at Namsos its commander, Brigadier Phipps, was on a ship proceeding to Narvik; the soldiers were separated from much of their equipment, and the gunners from their guns.

Typical was the tramp steamer *Lochmanar*, which arrived at Aalesund carrying 26 tons of petrol, to find the port awash with the stuff. This ship was then loaded with British wounded soldiers, but had no medical facilities at all. It had no charts, and carried no weapons. When the Sherwood Foresters and Leicesters lost 900 out of 1300 men, Churchill was unaware of the disaster. Rowland Kenny of the British Legation in Oslo gave a good picture of the situation in a report during the campaign:

> When the British military forces arrived at Aandalsnes, the Norwegian people and troops gave a profound sigh of relief, as they now regarded their early delivery from the German invader as certain. They had not, however, reckoned with the difficulties with which the British forces would obviously have to contend. German bombing was incessant for six or seven hours every day, and although anti-aircraft guns were landed and mounted, these did not prevent German attacks on the British ships, the quay and the railway station, and the town, by German bombers. The Norwegians had, of course, expected that the enemy would not leave Aandalsnes unmolested, but they appeared to be surprised at the persistence of German attacks from the air and the destruction achieved.
>
> Two things soon caused a certain reaction among the Norwegian troops and people: The first was the looting of the evacuated houses and shops by the British forces billeted in them. The second point which upset the Norwegians to some extent was the attitude towards the officers and men of the Norwegian forces of some of the British military forces. Norwegian troops were distressed and even dismayed at what they regarded as the 'Prussian' attitude of one or two of the British officers towards them . . . These remarks do not apply to the British naval personnel.
>
> When the first detachment of British troops went into action, some of the Norwegian officers expressed surprise and some bitterness at their lack of artillery and effective equipment. A wounded British sergeant who returned with me on the s.s. *Lochnagar* [sic] from Aalesund to Scapa Flow told me that they were not in any way armed to meet the heavily mechanised German forces. Even the anti-tank rifles they carried had a range of 200 yards less than the German tank guns, and were, therefore, quite ineffective. Norwegian disappointment was expressed in bitter terms by one or two Norwegiann staff officers about one particularly unfortunate factor in the problem. The British troops went into the line with four footballs and

50,000 cigarettes instead of the guns for which the Norwegians had hoped and prayed!

In conversation with British airmen at Kirkwall, I found them puzzled and irritated at the manner in which they were being used, or misused. The first British bombers over the aerodrome at Stavanger, I was told, had noted about 70 German bombers parked there, and a great destruction of enemy machines could have been achieved had the British airmen been allowed to bomb them; but their instructions were to engage only in reconnaissance work and photography! When next they appeared over the aerodrome, the German bombers had, of course, been scattered and camouflaged in the surrounding neighbourhood. Even recently Blenheim bombers were being sent to Norway ammunitioned with only a single burst of machine-gun fire.

The Norwegian naval authorities were bewildered at what they considered to be a lack of enterprise and understanding on the part of the British. The Germans in Bergen believed after the first shattering attack on them by the Fleet Air Arm that they were scuppered and had not long to last. To the south, the Hardanger Fjord was open for the first twelve days of the war; a small Norwegian gunboat made daily trips down the fjord into the North Sea on patrol work and returned safely. To the north of Bergen a number of units of the Norwegian fleet were there for at least a week after the war started, and no adequate contact was made with them by British naval forces. The Hardanger Fjord, the Sogne Fjord, and the Nord Fjord were open, and the Norwegians expected British forces to be landed here and join in an attack from inland on Bergen. The Norwegians believed that such an attack could have been carried out successfully in the first few days of the war, but nothing happened, and now Bergen is so strongly fortified as to resist any attack that may be made upon it.[33]

T. K. Derry's official history of the Norwegian campaign is over-favourable to those in charge in London. The Cabinet Committee responsible for the official histories recorded on 10 May 1950, when it was clear that Churchill was about to become Prime Minister again: 'The Norway operations could not in their nature have been successful, and probably all that was possible in the circumstances was achieved.'

This contradicts the view given by Sir Ian Jacob to the Cabinet Committee in 1955. He wrote:

The three Service Ministries were acting as independent HQs. The main lesson of the campaign which is not fully brought out by Derry (in his draft) is that any campaign must have a directing HQ which is not inside all the Service Ministries. I well remember the disastrous results of the arrival of signals from one or other of the local Commanders direct into Cabinet meetings or meetings of the Military Co-ordination Committee, and action being taken on them without knowledge of the general situation.

Professor Butler, Overseeing Editor of the War Histories, recorded: 'The story of the campaign is a depressing one for the British reader . . . the general impression can hardly fail to be one of incompetence at various levels'; while General Pownall, who had been charged by Churchill (when he became Prime Minister again in 1951) with the task of reading the drafts on his behalf, asserted

'Churchill's view should not be given unless the author is prepared to adopt it'.

Admiral Blake thought that 'Derry's account of naval operations was much too obviously the work of a layman . . . who didn't know the sharp end from the blunt'. Acheson, secretary to the Committee, counselled caution:

> If defects, particularly at the London end, to which much of the comments of the service members was directed are to be given the prominence which they seemed to suggest, the book may run into deep waters when it comes to be officially circulated . . . if an official history is written in such a way as to bear the appearance of being a strong attack on the Government of the day or on those in charge of the fighting services of the day, service departments may be disposed to object.

As a result Derry cast a veil over the glaring mistakes made in Whitehall, and not until the time when historians like Marder and Kersaudy saw the documents under the thirty-year rule, was the disarray revealed. The 'deep waters' to which Acherson referred were the rancorous eyes of Churchill as he read the drafts of anything unfavourable to him.[34]

Stephen Roskill, the official naval historian, did not criticize Churchill seriously in his official volume, but was more courageous many years later when Churchill was dead; then he accused Churchill of frequently interfering unreasonably in strategy and operations, claiming that this was made possible because 'he had a ready, indeed too ready, mouthpiece in the compliant Pound'. But Professor Marder in his book effectively disposes of Roskill's criticism of Pound and argues that as First Lord Churchill did not make 'forays into naval concerns except when political considerations were involved'.[35]

CHAPTER FOUR

Churchill takes over:
peace feelers banned

THE NATIONAL press made it abundantly clear that the Norwegian campaign was an expensive disaster, and public opinion was outraged at the ignominious withdrawal from Trondheim announced by the Prime Minister on 2 May. A Commons debate on Norway was fixed for 7 May. In the Cabinet there was concern about the bad publicity which would arise when the troops evacuated from Norway landed in Britain with stories of the muddles and mistakes which had cost the lives of so many.

In the Commons debate Sir Archibald Sinclair, the Liberal leader, complained that there had been 'no foresight' and the staffs 'were hastily improvising instead of working to long and carefully matured plans'. Admiral Sir Roger Keyes, in uniform with six rows of medals, made a devastating attack upon the naval conduct of the war and especially over Narvik and Trondheim, saying the naval staff had assured him that a naval action at Trondheim was easy but unnecessary owing to the 'success of the military'. Keyes received great applause. Leo Amery, an old colleague and friend of Chamberlain's, told the Prime Minister: 'You have sat too long for any good you have been doing. Depart, I say, and have done with you. In the name of God go.' These were the words that Cromwell had used to the Long Parliament, and they created a sensation coming from such an influential Conservative.

The next day, after an attack by Herbert Morrison, from the Opposition front bench, the Prime Minister made a grave tactical mistake by stating, 'I have friends in this House', which provoked Lloyd George into making an eloquent appeal for his resignation. Many Conservative MPs were chary of making too heavy criticisms of the Norway campaign for fear of damaging Churchill, who it was well known had been largely responsible for the disaster. When Churchill said, 'I take complete responsibility for everything that has happened', Lloyd George intervened, saying that Churchill 'must not allow himself to be turned into an air-raid shelter to keep the splinters from hitting his colleagues'. This devastating remark formed the final nail in Chamberlain's coffin.

Winston was far from convincing in the final speech; he had been given a bad brief, especially over the attack and withdrawal from Trondheim, and made a grave error in saying that the German invasion of Norway had been for Hitler 'a cardinal political and strategic error', whereas it was clear to the House that it had been a German victory. Churchill was badly heckled by Labour and did not make all the oratorial points he had prepared.

He was on the horns of a dilemma. He was desperately anxious for Chamberlain to resign so that he could take over the premiership, which he knew he could operate immeasurably more effectively. On the other hand, if he associated himself too deeply with the inefficiency which was causing such despair to the House he might ruin his chances of becoming Prime Minister. In the event he behaved with praiseworthy loyalty to Chamberlain, using his considerable powers of debate to rehabilitate the Prime Minister. However, they were insufficient.

Intense pressure was put on dissident Conservative MPs to support the Cabinet, and a three-line whip was imposed. Yet 41 Tory supporters voted with the Opposition, and a further 60 abstained, so that the Government majority in the division lobby was only 81 whereas it should have been 213. Chamberlain was doomed, but that evening told the King he would not resign as he hoped to form a National Government with Liberal and Labour support. But Attlee and Morrison would not join a National Government under Chamberlain, although they indicated they might under another leader. Chamberlain immediately decided to resign, hoping Halifax would succeed him.

The next morning, 10 May, the newspapers carried headlines that Hitler had invaded Holland and Belgium. For a moment Chamberlain thought that in view of this new crisis he should delay his resignation, but he was soon persuaded to change his mind. It was touch and go whether Churchill or Halifax became Prime Minister. Conservative MPs were overwhelmingly in favour of Halifax, and at first he was ready to serve. However, during a conversation between the Prime Minister, Halifax and Churchill at 10 Downing Street Chamberlain asked Churchill for his opinion as to whether a peer could be Prime Minister. If Churchill had said 'Yes', Halifax would have been Prime Minister. Instead, as Colville, private secretary to Chamberlain, told the author, Churchill walked to the window, looked out and refused to reply. This intransigence made Halifax realize how difficult it would be for him to be Prime Minister in the Lords with Winston in the Commons running Defence. Halifax recorded in his diary that he then told the others he would speedily become 'a more or less honorary Prime Minister living in a kind of twilight just outside the things that really matter'. Chamberlain reluctantly accepted this, although, according to Halifax, Winston showed a great deal less reluctance.[1]

Thus Churchill became Prime Minister as a result of the Norway fiasco, although he was the member of the Cabinet most responsible for everything which had gone wrong. It was paradoxical; the same thing happened in 1957 when Eden was forced out of Downing Street because of the Suez failure and Macmillan, who had been the most enthusiastic supporter of the Egyptian war in Eden's Cabinet, then took over as Prime Minister.

Churchill was the right choice. Alone amongst the front bench statesmen of the three parties his hands were clean of any stain of appeasement. Faced with the dire danger from Hitler's invasion of western Europe which Chamberlain and

Halifax had convinced themselves would never happen, he was the only man who could galvanize the nation into action.

During the phoney war Churchill had been frustrated. He drank too much; and at the Admiralty he had wild ideas and changed his mind frequently, as has been seen. Now the responsibility of ruling brought out all that was best in him. His powers of concentration and of quickly absorbing the import of Civil Service reports were almost unique. His energy was amazing, and instead of being a despised figure in Whitehall almost immediately he had aroused the admiration of all the civil servants and the Defence staff, and inspired enormous loyalty.[2]

John Colville remained as private secretary in 10 Downing Street. He told the author that during the evening of 10 May he had a drink with Rab Butler and they both agreed it was a national disaster that anyone as unreliable as Churchill should have become Prime Minister. Queen Mary wrote to Colville's mother, saying she hoped John 'would not stay with that dreadful Mr Churchill'. But Colville quickly changed his own view about Churchill, and has written:

> In May 1940 the mere thought of Churchill as Prime Minister sent a cold chill down the spines of the staff at 10 Downing Street . . . Churchill's impetuosity we thought had contributed to the Norwegian farce, and General Ismay told us in despairing tones of the confusion caused by his enthusiastic irruptions into the peaceful and orderly deliberations of the Military Co-ordination Committee and the Chiefs of Staff. His verbosity and restlessness made unnecessary work and prevented real planning and caused friction . . . Our feelings at Downing Street were widely shared in the Cabinet Offices and throughout Whitehall.
>
> However Government Departments which under Neville Chamberlain had continued to work at much the same speed as in peacetime, awoke under Churchill to the realities of war. A sense of urgency was created in the course of a few days and respectable civil servants were actually to be seen running along the corridors. No delays were condoned; telephone switchboards quadrupled their efficiency . . .
>
> Seldom can a Prime Minister have taken office with the Establishment so dubious of the choice and prepared to find its doubts justified. I doubt if there has ever been such a rapid transformation of opinion in Whitehall and of the tempo at which business was conducted . . .[2]

Lord Bridges[3] and Lord Normanbrook[4] have written similarly about the way in which Churchill galvanized the machinery of government into a spirit of urgency.

Eric Seal, another private secretary, remarked how much Churchill had changed since becoming Prime Minister: 'He has sobered down, becoming less violent, less wild and less impetuous.' Seal thought Winston believed 'in his mission to extricate this country from its present troubles, and he will certainly kill himself if necessary in order to achieve his object'.[5]

When on 11 May 1940 Churchill became Prime Minister, from that day onwards he was in direct control of the hour-to-hour conduct of the war. As Prime Minister of a coalition Government and his own Defence Minister, he was in a position of unique authority – virtually a dictator in moments of crisis. Yet he was careful to listen to the views of the Chiefs of Staff Committee whenever possible and relied heavily on General Pug Ismay, head of the Defence

Minister's office. Seldom did Churchill over-ride the views of this Committee, although he would have been free to do so. Nor did he always domineer in Cabinet, although Mrs Churchill wrote to her husband on 27 June:

> One of the men in your entourage (a devoted friend) has been and told me that there is a danger of your being generally disliked by your colleagues and subordinates because of your rough, sarcastic and overbearing manner . . .
>
>   Higher up if an idea is suggested (say at a conference) you are supposed to be so contemptuous that presently no ideas, good or bad, will be forthcoming . . . you won't get the best results by irascibility and rudeness.[6]

Churchill showed great tact in persuading Ernest Bevin, Secretary of the Transport and General Workers' Union and the most influential trade unionist of the time, to accept the post of Minister of Labour. Bevin was indispensable if the wholehearted co-operation of industrial workers in the war effort was to be obtained. Churchill promised Bevin he would deal with the 'present difficulties of the Trades Union Act' over opting out or in, or over picketing, and there would be no hanging on to the status quo over social services. This angered many Conservatives, but it was wise statesmanship. As a result the Beveridge Report, advocating family allowance and increased social security was produced.

Within forty-eight hours of forming his Government Churchill had to face the worst crisis of any Prime Minister of the twentieth century. On 13 May Ironside told the War Cabinet that 'strong German forces were advancing, and the situation in Holland and Belgium was deteriorating'. Even then Churchill would not authorize the bombing of the Ruhr. Worse news came twenty-four hours later. Reynaud reported that German troops had broken through the French frontier at Sedan and asked for the immediate despatch of ten more fighter squadrons to France.[7] Churchill was presented with two agonizing and momentous decisions: whether to risk sending more British fighter squadrons to France, and, shortly afterwards, whether or not to try and evacuate the BEF from France. In both instances he made the correct decision, proving his fitness to rule in Britain's blackest hour.

Gort, commanding the British Expeditionary Force (BEF), urged sending the ten fighter squadrons to France, but Newall, Chief of Air Staff, warned that the bulk of the squadrons would certainly be lost if they went to France, and Britain would then be almost defenceless against Hitler's bombers. Churchill adored France and temperamentally would have loved to make a quixotic gesture to save the French Army in its hour of need. He had always looked on it as Europe's chief bulwark against Communism and Fascism, and found it hard to believe that his romantic faith in it had been misplaced.

Air Chief Marshall Sir Hugh Dowding, C in C Fighter Command, advised that if more fighters were taken from him 'they would not achieve decisive results in France and he would be left too weak to carry on over here', and he was opposed to sending a single extra Hurricane to French aerodromes. Reluctantly but firmly, Churchill refused Reynaud's request for the fighters, and was to do the same when the French armies were disintegrating and the French made appeal after appeal for more fighter aircraft. The verdict of history must be that Churchill was 100 per cent correct.

General Kluge's Panzers, commanded by General Rommel, had by 19 May driven a long, narrow salient between the British and French armies: the BEF were in deadly danger of becoming trapped against the coast. Two plans were made. One was to attack to the south to link up with the French; the alternative was to withdraw to Dunkirk. Gort, C in C BEF, telephoned to Eden asking for an immediate decision. Churchill insisted to the War Cabinet that Gort must attack south to link up with the French.[8]

Accordingly the British 5th and 50th Divisions were assembled hastily at Arras, together with the 1st Army Tank Brigade (infantry tanks), while the French promised to co-operate with two mechanized divisions and two infantry divisions from the south. Their plan was to punch out Kluge's salient with a simultaneous tank attack from the south and the north. The French were taking longer to prepare for the attack than Churchill had anticipated. On 21 May came the dire news that Guderian's Panzer Corps had raced through Amiens and reached the sea near Abbeville, thus cutting the Allied armies completely in two; while to the north the Belgians had no stomach for the fight and indeed were to capitulate on 27 May. The British therefore decided to attack on 21 May without waiting for the French, although seventy French tanks co-operated on the right flank.

Just when the British attack looked like being a success, fourteen out of sixteen Matilda tanks broke down or caught fire and the scales were turned in the Germans' favour. Out of sixty-two British tanks, forty-six were lost in a nine-hour battle. With little artillery or RAF support, the British attack ground to a halt in face of Rommel's hastily established defence line and heavy Stuka bomber attacks. Apart from a counter-attack led by de Gaulle, this was the Allies' only serious counter-stroke in the campaign; Rommel had losses of several hundred men and described the battle as 'very heavy against hundreds of enemy tanks and following infantry' – a considerable exaggeration.

However it had favourable consequences. Kluge was so worried by it that he told the Führer if his Panzers advanced again they might be cut off before their infantry could arrive to support them. As a result Hitler gave an order on 24 May for Kluge's army to halt when German mechanized forward elements were only ten miles from Dunkirk, by then the only possible escape route for the British Army.[9]

It became clear to the generals and Churchill that there was no longer a reasonable chance of Gort linking up again with the French. Communication by line with Gort had been cut off and General Dill, who was soon to become CIGS, was sent to France by Churchill; when he returned he reported that if Gort made another abortive attack to link up with the French he would have insufficient strength to execute his only alternative, 'namely to cut his way north to the coast'. Without hesitation Churchill told the Defence Committee on 25 May that the BEF must be evacuated through Dunkirk; immediately, with tremendous vigour and authority, he gave the necessary orders to implement the decision, so that in the minimum time an armada of ships was sent to Dunkirk to bring the soldiers home.[10]

Churchill's decision to order a counter-attack at Arras had been proved correct, because it resulted in Hitler halting his armour. The later decision to evacuate through Dunkirk was also right; it was taken in the nick of time, and as a result the BEF was saved from what seemed to be unavoidable disaster.

The nation was appalled by the news of the complete defeat in such a short time of the French and British armies. It seemed that everything gained by the First World War had been thrown away through mismanagement, so that the tremendous sacrifices of 1914–18 were in vain. Veterans of the First World War could not understand how towns like Arras and Amiens, for which they and their comrades had fought for years, should have been defended so inadequately. There were recriminations about the poor equipment of the BEF (who used bayonets against tommy guns, and had very few anti-tank guns), and the false hopes placed in the strength of the French Army. Returning soldiers criticized the RAF for not doing more in France to stop the Germans bombing them. Fortunately for Churchill, he had only just assumed office and could not be made the scapegoat. Instead Stanley Baldwin, and to a lesser degree Chamberlain, became targets for abuse. Beaverbrook in the *Daily Express* made poisonous comments about Baldwin's responsibility for causing the war by not rearming when he was Prime Minister 1935–37; these articles produced a spate of abusive letters which Baldwin, without a secretary, had perforce to open himself. The nation needed a scapegoat, and Baldwin filled the bill. In addition there were calls for Chamberlain to resign from the Cabinet, which Winston ignored.

In contrast Churchill was able to trade on his impeccable pre-war record of opposition to the appeasement of Hitler and his campaign for more rearmament. In brilliant speeches and broadcasts he refused to admit the possibility of defeat, and became a national hero. France was crumbling and Britain stood alone, with little apparent chance of preventing Hitler from dominating western Europe. The most realistic assessment was that the war was a hopeless crusade even with the non-belligerent help of the USA. Yet Churchill refused to accept he was leading a lost cause, and inspired his colleagues and the nation. The way in which he maintained British morale was almost miraculous; no other British statesman could have done the same – Chamberlain or Halifax would have been impotent. Convincingly, in his speeches Churchill declared that Britain would win in the end, and convinced the bulk of the nation that this was so.

In Churchill's War Cabinet of five Halifax continued as Foreign Secretary; Chamberlain was Lord President of the Council, Attlee Lord Privy Seal, and Greenwood Minister without Portfolio. Winston had to contend with defeatism inside his Cabinet as well as in the country: Chamberlain and Halifax were still prepared to negotiate a compromise peace.

By 25 May France was beaten. General Weygand's defence line on the Somme had been pierced; there was no hope of a counter-attack; German tanks were speeding across France and the BEF was retreating towards Dunkirk. At the French War Committee in Paris that day an armistice was suggested by

Weygand. The next day Reynaud went to London – not to ask official permission from his ally to capitulate, but to obtain the support of the British Government 'for concessions to Mussolini in the hope of keeping Italy out of the war' and to explore the chance of mediation by the Italians.

At lunch with Churchill on the 26th Reynaud spoke of the possibility of cessation of hostilities, and got a dusty reply. Churchill said France must stay in the war. That morning he had received a depressing report from the British Chiefs of Staff on the situation which would arise if France dropped out of the conflict. Churchill did not show this to his War Cabinet, fearing the reaction of Halifax and Chamberlain.

The British Cabinet had already met before Reynaud arrived. Churchill had told them he 'doubted whether anything would come of an approach to Italy', but they should consider it after Halifax reported his conversation of the day before with the Italian Ambassador, Bastianini.[11]

On 24 May the War Cabinet had authorized Halifax to say that if Italy remained neutral Britain would take account of reasonable Italian claims at the peace conference, at which Italy would appear 'on an equal footing with the belligerents'. Halifax's talk to Bastianini was an attempt to bribe Italy to stay out of the war and importune Mussolini to persuade Hitler to hold a peace conference. But Halifax went further than Churchill intended, telling the Italian Ambassador that 'the Allies would be prepared to consider any proposals which might lead to peace'. Gibraltar, Malta and Suez might be sacrificed to Italy by Britain; Djibouti and Tunis by France. Halifax said the British and French were ready to 'internationalize' these possessions, which in effect meant handing them to Italy.

On the afternoon of 26 May Halifax saw Reynaud with Churchill. He told the French Prime Minister that, if Italy would collaborate in a peace which would safeguard the independence of France and Britain, the Allies would discuss all the claims of Italy in the Mediterranean – in particular 'the outlets of this sea'. Churchill did not dissent specifically. On his return to Paris Reynaud reported: 'Halifax agreed, but Churchill took refuge behind the War Cabinet.' On the 26th, with the fate of the BEF in France in the balance, Churchill was subdued. Yet as more and more troops from Dunkirk returned safely to England, he became more optimistic and less inclined to offer inducements to Mussolini or seek a compromise peace with Hitler.[12]

Fateful War Cabinet meetings took place on 27 and 28 May after Reynaud's departure. Over everything loomed the precarious position of the BEF. On the 27th Cadogan noted: 'I see no hope for more than a tiny fraction of them now that Belgium has capitulated.'[13]

Halifax argued that Mussolini was alarmed at Hitler's 'power', and the Government ought to approach him as the French suggested. Chamberlain supported Halifax, who defended himself against attacks by Churchill, saying: 'If we got to the point of discussing a general settlement and found we could obtain terms which did not postulate the destruction of our independence we should be foolish not to accept them.' Churchill reluctantly allowed a telegram to be sent to

Paris confirming that an approach would be made to Mussolini through the President of the United States.

At a second meeting on 27 May the War Cabinet learnt that Stanley Bruce, the Australian High Commissioner in London, had become defeatist, saying that Britain must mobilize Roosevelt and Mussolini before Paris fell. Chamberlain wanted to tell the Dominions 'we should fight on', but with the rider that 'if terms were offered we should consider them on their merit'.

Churchill said Britain could not get out of her difficulties by concessions to Italy in the Mediterranean and giving back Germany her African colonies, taken away by the treaty of Versailles; any terms offered by Hitler would prevent Britain continuing with rearmament, and the only thing to do was to show Hitler 'he could not conquer this country'. In his view, 'Even if we are beaten we would be no worse than if we abandoned the struggle now.' However, as a concession to Halifax and Chamberlain he agreed to some approach to Mussolini, although he thought talks with Hitler through Mussolini would be futile. Nevertheless he agreed that Britain must help her ally, France, to keep Italy out of the war.

Halifax now disagreed with Churchill and declared that there were 'profound differences' between him and the Prime Minister. Making an approach to Mussolini bore no resemblance to suing for terms, which the Prime Minister said would lead to disaster. The day before, the Prime Minister had been ready to discuss terms 'provided matters vital to our independence were unaffected', and the Prime Minister had agreed that 'we should be thankful to get out of our present difficulties even at the cession of territory'. Now the Prime Minister would contemplate 'no course but fighting to the finish'. Halifax said his own position was that if the country's independence was not at stake he thought it right to accept an offer 'which would save our country from unavoidable disaster'. The Prime Minister replied that he was talking in 'unreal terms'. Nettled, Halifax retorted: 'Suppose the French army collapsed and Hitler made an offer of terms, would the Prime Minister be prepared to discuss Hitler's terms?' Churchill said he would not ask for terms, but if he was told the terms he would be prepared to consider them.[14]

That was the nearest Churchill got to agreeing to negotiations. He was still poles apart from Halifax and Chamberlain, but fortunately for Churchill, Attlee and Greenwood backed him. Halifax was near to resignation, which would have produced grave political problems for Churchill in view of Halifax's popularity within the Conservative Party. The Foreign Secretary wrote in his diary: 'Winston talked the most frightful rot, and also Greenwood, and after hearing it all for some time I said exactly what I thought of them, adding that if that was really their view if it came to the point our ways must part.' The discussion was more acrimonious than the official minutes record.

Winston was surprised, and in the garden of 10 Downing Street soothed his Foreign Secretary by 'apologies and affection', with the result that Halifax withdrew his resignation threat. Before this conversation Halifax had said to Cadogan, 'I can't work with Winston any longer.' Cadogan replied: 'Don't do anything without consulting Neville.'[15] It must have been touch and go whether Halifax's or Churchill's view prevailed. If Halifax had had his way, European history would have been very different. On 27 May he was ready for overtures to Hitler.

The next day the War Cabinet met at 4.30 p.m. Chamberlain and Halifax again stated that they favoured an approach to Hitler through Mussolini, with a view to a conference. Halifax said that if Mussolini wanted to play the part of a mediator and could procure terms which would not affect Britain's independence, the Government should consider them: 'We might get better terms before France went out of the war and our aircraft factories were bombed than we might get in three months' time.'

Churchill would have none of it. He replied that Reynaud wanted Britain at a conference table with Hitler. If this happened, 'we should find that Hitler's terms infringed our independence and integrity and if we then left the conference table we should find our resolution to fight Hitler would have vanished'. Chamberlain and the Labour ministers tended to agree with Churchill, and Halifax was isolated. The Foreign Secretary reiterated that they should try out the possibilities of mediation 'which the Prime Minister felt was so wrong'. Halifax must have been again close to resignation once again.[16]

During an interval between 5.15 and 7 p.m. Churchill met in his room in the Commons the other ministers of Cabinet rank outside the War Cabinet. He said to them: 'I have thought carefully whether I should enter into negotiations with that man. But I am convinced that every man of you would rise up and tear me down from my place if I were for one moment to contemplate parley or surrender.' According to Hugh Dalton, 'there were loud cries of approval and no one expressed even the faintest flicker of dissent'.

Accounts by others present throw doubt on Dalton's assertion there was no 'dissent', but anyway, fortified by what he called 'enthusiastic support', Churchill told the War Cabinet later that evening that their colleagues had expressed the greatest satisfaction when he told them there was no chance of giving up the struggle. So Halifax was over-ruled. The War Cabinet agreed to telegraph Reynaud that this was 'not the right moment to approach the Italian dictator'.

Once the greater part of the BEF was safe, Churchill would not consider peace terms. From South Africa General Smuts weighed in with a telegram that 'we must fight alone'. Halifax argued in vain. There were to be no negotiations with Hitler then or in the future. The Foreign Secretary had shot his bolt.

On 2 June Oliver Harvey noted in his diary that 'Halifax was anxiously exploring possibility of peace proposals à la Lansdowne'; the Prime Minister had 'flatly turned them down'.[17] Surprisingly, Churchill made Lloyd George an offer of a place in his War Cabinet on 28 May and again on 19 June; Lloyd George was defeatist and wanted peace negotiations. According to Halifax's diary, Churchill intended to get an assurance from Lloyd George that he would never advocate any peace terms 'which would be destructive of our independence'. Another possibility is that Churchill feared he would be swept from office in the event of

Hitler triumphing, and he wanted an orderly transfer of power to an acceptable successor who would negotiate the peace.

For two days the fate of Europe had been in the melting pot. How close Halifax and Chamberlain were to carrying the day we shall never know. If the BEF had not returned from Dunkirk with fewer casualties than expected, the outcome could have been different. The minutes do not tell the full story, but enough can be pieced together to reveal the split. After he read these Cabinet minutes, Churchill ordered that no such full note of the discussions should be taken in future. For the rest of the conflict the War Cabinet minutes reveal less discord.[18]

CHAPTER FIVE

The French collapse and surrender

BY 31 MAY 133,878 British and 11,666 Allied troops, mostly French, had been safely evacuated from Dunkirk, although almost all their much-needed equipment had been lost. Churchill flew to Paris on that day, cheered by the news. He promised the French at the Supreme War Council that every effort would be made to get the French off first at Dunkirk. The Council agreed that Italy was certain to enter the war, and made plans to bombard from the air and sea those places on the Italian coast where her oil supplies were stored. This, said Admiral Darlan, Head of the French Admiralty, would cripple Italy 'seriously'. Churchill entertained the French leaders to dinner at the Embassy and uttered a typical Churchillian phrase: 'The partner that survives will go on.' According to Spears, 'Reynaud clutched at these words as if to a lifeline.'[1]

Churchill consistently opposed the French demand for more fighter aircraft and became annoyed with Reynaud for his importuning. Late on 1 June the Chiefs of Staff and the War Cabinet considered whether or not to send fresh troops to support the French, which Reynaud was also asking for. Churchill told the War Cabinet that 'French resistance might collapse', and 'if Paris fell they might be tempted to make a separate peace'. This would mean the establishment of a Government in France friendly to the Nazis, so that Britain might become faced with a regime 'not merely out of the war, but actually hostile to us'. Attlee was opposed to sending more aircraft to France, but wanted to send one or two divisions 'to hearten the French'. No decision was reached. Meanwhile on 3 June came news that the Dunkirk evacuation was over: 222,568 British troops and 70,000 French had been saved.[2]

On 24 May Churchill had told the Defence Committee firmly that 'in view of the danger of an invasion of Britain we could not possibly send any more troops to France, and Reynaud had been informed accordingly'. Unfortunately, in his anxiety to try and keep the French fighting the Prime Minister quickly changed his mind. On 29 May General Marshall Cornwall was ordered to France as head of a new No. 17 Military Mission with the French Tenth Army, to watch over the interests of the British 1st Armoured Division and the 51st Highland Division who had been cut off from Gort's beleaguered British Expeditionary Force at Dunkirk and were now south of the Somme.[3]

Instead of being given orders to evacuate these two valuable divisions to the

UK, Marshall Cornwall was told they must continue to fight in co-operation with the French, and arrangements were being made for more British troops to join them. Marshall Cornwall was told explicitly that the Prime Minister insisted British troops should continue to fight to the 'last extremity in order to give the French no excuse to abandon the struggle'.

On 3 June von Kluge's Fourth German Army attacked all along the Somme front. As 51st Highland Division was 'completely exhausted', Marshall Cornwall earnestly begged the French General Altmayer, under whose orders it had been placed, to relieve it and allow it to withdraw from the front. Marshall Cornwall signalled to the War Office:

> Situation of 51st Division is now serious. It has been fighting continuously for three days and has suffered heavy casualties . . . 51st Division is hardly fit for more fighting and may crack if seriously attacked . . . If politically undesirable to withdraw all British troops from that line I would urge that two more British Divisions with fighter support be sent urgently to France.[4]

Churchill told the Chiefs of Staff he was agreeable to sending two divisions, but he would not agree to Marshall Cornwall's plea to allow 51st Division to withdraw. On 6 June he sent out to France a new Corps Headquarters under General Brooke, together with the 52nd Lowland Division and the 1st Canadian Division; he was vehement that the British must fight on in support of the rapidly disintegrating French Army.

On 8 June the Defence Committee discussed the situation of the 51st Division, together with the news that Altmayer was no longer capable of exercising command 'as he had no communication with the troops under him', and that 51st Division under his command was in danger of having its communications cut. A telegram was received that day from Marshall Cornwall saying that 51st Division 'would probably have to be evacuated from Dieppe beach'. Churchill left the matter to his Staff.[5]

Meanwhile Weygand, the French Commander in Chief, had become hysterical and incoherent; after a futile conference with him on 8 June, Marshall Cornwall argued desperately with Altmayer to allow 51st Division to be withdrawn. At first Altmayer refused, but gave way later in the day.

On the 9th June Marshall Cornwall informed the War Office that he had been unable to send General Fortune, Commander of 51st Division, orders to withdraw (their cypher van had been destroyed by a bomb). It was essential, he said, to re-establish communication with Fortune – either by the destroyer which was operating off Le Tréport, or by an RAF plane to Dieppe airport; it was also essential that independent action was taken to extricate 51st Division, possibly from Le Havre. Obviously a joint RAF and RN action was desperately required. Churchill ignored this *cri de coeur*. His heart was set on inspiring the French to fight on, and he hoped 52nd Division could relieve 51st.[6]

Winston was also keen on the plan, concocted by himself and Reynaud, of forming in the Brittany peninsula an Anglo–French entrenched camp which would form a defensive bridgehead to be used as a springboard for future offensive operations. If attempted, this plan would have been disastrous, but Churchill was ready to play for high stakes to keep France in the war.

Against his better judgement Marshall Cornwall carried out Churchill's orders not to withdraw 51st Division towards Le Havre. By 10 June the division was in a hopeless position, hemmed in by Rommel's troops against the sea in the fishing port of St Valéry without reserve supplies, rations or ammunition. Late that evening Fortune asked for as much as possible of his division to be embarked from between St Valéry and the mouth of the River Durent. Churchill did not bestir himself over 51st Division's desperate plight. He was at work in London on the morning of 11 June, and did not leave for France until 2 p.m., which was a contrast to the way he had galvanized the Navy into Herculean activity to save the BEF from Dunkirk. In his memoirs Churchill writes: 'Fog prevented the ships reaching St Valéry.' This is incorrect.[7]

At 10.35 p.m. on 11 June the Admiralty at Portsmouth decyphered an urgent last-minute plea from Fortune, which said: 'Tonight [11–12 June] is the last possible chance of evacuation of 51st Division'; the French had given permission, and he requested ships and boats to embark ten thousand British and five thousand French troops from St Valéry. The Germans had installed batteries and machine gun posts on the cliffs overlooking the harbour, and no evacuation was possible during the day. No vessels came, and quite why this occurred remains a mystery. The Admiralty papers for Portsmouth of 11 and 12 June are missing, although there is a mass of messages about the evacuation from Dunkirk and Calais.

Despite this, 2137 British and 1184 French troops were safely embarked from a beach north of St Valéry. At 7.45 a.m. on 12 June Fortune cabled that some of his troops had waited all night on the beach, but many boats arrived too late because by the time they appeared the Germans had installed batteries and machine gun posts on the clifftops. He asked for ships to bombard the cliffs. Later Fortune signalled that the French had ordered him to cease fire, but he refused to comply until he was sure there was no possibility of evacuating his division, even though the French had put out white flags everywhere. At 10.35 Fortune surrendered to Rommel. Churchill had left a fine division to its fate.

It was ignominious. According to Colville, Winston described it as the 'most brutal disaster' the British had yet suffered. But it was his fault for not allowing them to retreat, as Marshall Cornwall had urged on 3 June.[8]

Meanwhile General Brooke had arrived in France on 12 June and set up his headquarters at Le Mans. He was to command the remnants of the BEF plus the fresh 52nd Division and 1st Canadian Division. Churchill's instructions were that he was to support the French Army and restore its shattered morale. It was an impossible task, and Brooke was in no doubt about its futility. Before he left London he had told Eden, Secretary of State, that 'the mission I was being sent on from a military point of view had no value and no possibility of accomplishing anything. Furthermore that we had only just escaped a major disaster at Dunkirk and were now risking a second.'

This finds no place in Eden's memoirs, and the author has been unable to trace whether or not Eden passed on this gloomy prognostication to the Prime Minister. If he had done so it would have been ill received. At the eleventh hour Churchill was still determined, come what may, to throw in everything available to prop up his tottering ally, despite continual reports from Brooke that the French Army was no longer able to offer organized resistance and was 'disintegrating into disconnected groups, and that to continue to support them could only lead to further losses of British troops without results'.

Brooke found when he consulted with Weygand and General Georges, who had commanded the French advance into Belgium, that all three thought the idea of a Brittany redoubt was absurd. Weygand described it as 'romantic' and Georges as 'silly', and anyway the French generals were adamant that there was no alternative to capitulation. However, Brooke was persuaded to sign an agreement to defend Brittany. After forty-eight hours in France Brooke informed the War Office that on no account should any more fresh troops be sent to France to reinforce him, and he was ordering evacuation of all the British forces.

Although Churchill had told Dill that the agreement to defend Brittany did not bind the Government, he was in fact furious. He telephoned Brooke on 14 June to say that he did not agree, and that Brooke had been sent to France to make the French feel the British were supporting them. Brooke replied: 'It is impossible to make a corpse feel, and the French Army is to all intents and purposes dead. To throw one division into an attack now would inevitably result in throwing away good troops with no hopes of achieving results.'[9]

Brooke has recorded that the conversation lasted over half an hour and that several times Churchill accused him of suffering from 'cold feet'. This so infuriated Brooke that he told the Prime Minister: 'You've lost one Scottish Division. Do you want me to lose another?' Finally Churchill caved in, realizing that as Prime Minister he could not interfere with the judgement of his commander in the field without risking grave political embarrassment if he was proved wrong. Brooke ordered Marshall Cornwall to take command of all the British forces still operating in France, and to organize their evacuation from Cherbourg.

Even on 17 June, when the French had rejected an offer of union with Britain and were negotiating an armistice with Germany, Churchill mysteriously was not reconciled to the recall of the BEF. He made Dill ring up Brooke and ask him to stay in France, because his presence and the use of his name was 'of great political importance' – although Dill added that it seemed silly from the military point of view. Dill told Brooke that Marshall Cornwall must fight on, but fortunately Brooke ignored this and told Dill: 'I hope you will not expect him to cling on here after they have disintegrated.' That is what Churchill seemingly wanted. The telephone call between Brooke and the CIGS took place at 10.30 in the morning; at 3.20 Eden told Brooke and Marshall Cornwall that the French Army had ceased fighting and the British force must withdraw to Cherbourg–by luck, exactly what Brooke and Marshall Cornwall were doing. Churchill was gambling with an important part of the British Army.

It was a crucial moment. Two Panzer divisions under Rommel were pushing through wide gaps in the French rearguard, but Marshall Cornwall managed to withdraw his forces intact into the Cotentin peninsula and immediately began embarking them on a fleet of transports which had arrived in Cherbourg. Embarkation began on 17 June and Marshall Cornwall hoped to continue it until the 21st, which would have enabled him to bring back to England the thousands of mechanized transport vehicles which had arrived in the port. However, Rommel was too close in pursuit because French resistance had crumbled, and by the afternoon of 18 June German armoured cars were on the outskirts of Cherbourg. At midday Marshall Cornwall had spoken on the telephone to Ironside and said: 'The Boche are within four miles of us. They have gone through the French like butter although five French battalions in the Cherbourg area are more or less co-operating.' Ironside said optimistically: 'Can you launch a counter-attack?' Marshall Cornwall replied: 'No! The time for that is gone.' He left Cherbourg in the last ship at 16.00 that afternoon. It was a splendid achievement: 160,000 British and Allied troops with more than 300 guns had been embarked, with minimal casualties.

Only one 3.7 AA gun was left behind in France together with two anti-tank guns, and they had been rendered unserviceable. Marshall Cornwall's report to the War Office made it clear that the two French armies were divided by a gap of 300 miles, which shows how reckless Churchill had been in trying to persuade Brooke not to withdraw the British troops. But although Marshall Cornwall was the most able and efficient senior general, he was not to be rewarded by a command in the field for his feat in bringing away the second B E F safely.[10]

The campaign in Normandy receives little space in Churchill's memoirs; an analysis would not be favourable to him. Nor did Marshall Cornwall find favour later with the Prime Minister. In his memoirs the General recorded that on 26 July 1940, when he was commanding 3 Corps, he was summoned to Chequers. Churchill was displeased when Marshall Cornwall told him before dinner that his divisions had nothing like the complement of weapons which the War Office had told the Prime Minister they possessed. Then after dinner Churchill asked Marshall Cornwall what plan he would make to capture Massawa, the Italian port on the Red Sea in Italian Somaliland. Marshall Cornwall wrote in his memoirs:

I saw Dill and Ismay watching me anxiously and felt that I was being drawn into some trap. I looked hard at the map for a minute then answered, "Well, Sir, I have never been to Massawa. I have only passed out of sight of it, going down the Red Sea. It is a defended port, protected by coast defence and anti-aircraft batteries. It must be a good 500 miles from Aden, and therefore beyond cover of our fighters. The harbour has a very narrow entrance channel, protected by coral reefs, and is certain to be mined, making an opposed landing impracticable. I should prefer to wait until General Wavell's offensive against Eritrea develops; he will capture it more easily from the land side. The P. M. gave me a withering look, rolled up the map and muttered peevishly, 'You soldiers are all alike; you have no imagination.'

We went to bed. I left the Wonderland of Chequers on the following afternoon, after a walk in the woods with Duncan Sandys, whom I have never found very communicative. On our way back to London Jack Dill said to me, 'I'm thankful, Jimmy, that you took the line you did last night. If you had shown the least enthusiasm for the project, I should have been given orders to embark your Corps for the Red Sea next week.[11]

All this was, of course, at the height of the invasion danger, when no troops could be spared from coast defence. In the event after only token resistance Massawa was surrendered to a small Free French detachment in April 1941. Churchill and Marshall Cornwall did not appreciate each other, and this encounter at Chequers probably prevented him achieving a high command, which was the nation's loss.

Winston tried desperately to keep France in the war as Hitler's Panzers drove at will through the demoralized and disorganized French divisions south of the Somme.

Although four hundred thousand French troops were in the north on the Maginot Line, they could play no part in saving France because they were unable to break out of the German encirclement once Besançon had fallen. They did not surrender until 30 June; then many of their forts were intact, and many units at their full complement, having done no fighting. Unfortunately Weygand, who had replaced Gamelin as French Commander in Chief, was a broken reed; he was the legendary hero general of the First World War, but quickly become defeatist when the BEF could not fill the yawning gap between them and the French Army.

Churchill flew to France four times: to Paris on 22 May, the day after Gort's counter-attack at Arras, on which Churchill had pinned great hopes, had failed; back to Paris on 31 May for a meeting of the Supreme War Council; to Briare near Orleans on the Loire on 11 June after the Government had left Paris, which fell to the Germans on 14 June; and finally to Tours on 12 June to be told that France would capitulate. These meetings have been overdramatized both by Churchill and by his official biographer.

Churchill pleaded in vain in his bad French and in English that the French Government should go to North Africa and continue the war with British help from their African colonies. But he was beating his head against a brick wall. The French Cabinet were determined to ask for an armistice and, rocked by the sudden catastrophe which had overtaken their Army, were anti-British. With some justification they blamed their army's defeat on the Baldwin and Chamberlain Governments, which they felt had undermined French military morale by emphasizing in public and private that in the event of war they expected the French Army to bear the lion's share of the fighting in the West. Even at the time of his reckless guarantee to Poland in April 1939, which made war almost inevitable, Chamberlain had only promised a BEF of four divisions to help the French. Deep-seated, too, was French anger with the British for legalizing Hitler's naval rearmament by the Anglo–German Naval Agreement of 1935. This breached the disarmament clauses of Locarno and Versailles and was concluded without consultation with the French. The reason, well known to the French, was that the British Admiralty wanted to be free to send more warships to the Far East to impress Japan with a powerful presence. In addition, the failure of

Baldwin and Eden to promise support to the French if they threw German troops out of the demilitarized Rhineland in March 1936 was a running sore. Churchill bore no responsibility for any of this, but in defeat the French talked more and more about *le perfide Albion*.

However, Churchill snatched at two straws, both of which proved non-runners. The first was an unguarded telegram sent on 13 June by Roosevelt in response to an eleventh-hour appeal from Reynaud in Tours 'to declare war if you can'. Roosevelt replied that he promised 'all material aid', which was optimistically interpreted as active assistance, plus a call to France to go on fighting. Churchill, suffering from strain, attached too much importance to the telegram and asked the President to allow it to be published immediately. Roosevelt replied that he could not allow the telegram to be published and, although he renewed his assurance of aid, said his message was in no sense a commitment to military participation because only Congress could make such a commitment.

Churchill should have known in his heart of hearts that there was no chance of America entering the war at this stage, no matter how much goodwill Roosevelt himself had towards France and Britain. But he told the War Cabinet that 'it came as near as possible to a declaration of war'. Colville recorded laconically: 'It seems that P. M.'s expectation last night of immediate American help was exaggerated.' Halifax, too, deceived himself, telegraphing to Campbell (British Ambassador to France) that 'it seemed very near to the definite step of a declaration of war'.[12]

The second false hope was a proposal for union between France and Britain, made when the French Government were seeking permission to make a separate armistice with Germany; they had a formal commitment not to do so without British consent. Churchill originally intended to stick to his line: 'Make peace if you like, but let us have the French fleet.' However Pleven (later French Prime Minister) and Monnet (the architect of the plan for the Common Market after the war), enthusiastically backed by General de Gaulle, who, after commanding a division had been made Under-Secretary for War, formulated a startling and romantic plan for declaring the political unity of France and Britain. According to Colville, Winston at first was bored and critical; Chamberlain was more enthusiastic, and brought to the War Cabinet on 15 June the dramatic memorandum proposing an Anglo–French union with joint Parliaments and a joint Cabinet. Halifax asked Vansittart (the former Permanent Under Secretary, Foreign Office) to draft a document in consultation with de Gaulle, Pleven and Monnet for a non-dissoluble union with common citizenship, and this was discussed in the War Cabinet the next day. Under it France and Great Britain 'would no longer be two nations but one'. Churchill has written that at first he was against the plan, but believed some dramatic announcement was clearly necessary to 'keep the French going'. The War Cabinet also had in front of them a message from de Gaulle that Reynaud had said he might be able to continue the resistance if Anglo–French union took place, but otherwise further resistance was impossible.[13]

While the War Cabinet discussed the project of union for two hours during the afternoon of 16 June, de Gaulle waited in an outer room for their decision. At 16.30 he was told the War Cabinet had agreed to it, and he immediately dictated the text to Reynaud in Bordeaux by telephone. Campbell and General Spears (Churchill's friend, head of the liaison mission to the French Government) were with the French Prime Minister and reported that it acted like a tonic on him; he immediately became enthusiastic, especially over the words 'in future Britain and France could be one nation with a single War Cabinet'. In an effort to inspire him, de Gaulle added that Reynaud would probably head the new joint War Cabinet. Churchill also spoke to Reynaud and the two heads of state were warm and optimistic. It was arranged that next day Churchill should go by battleship to Concarneau in southern Brittany and meet Reynaud there to speed on the union.[14]

Reynaud told Spears he was certain the French Cabinet would agree. However, this confidence did not last long because a few minutes later he told his Foreign Minister Baudouin there was a fear of his government falling and being succeeded by a Pétain government with Laval as Foreign Minister, which would mean a complete break with Britain.

At 17.30 the French Cabinet of twenty-five met in Bordeaux. Telegrams had come in to say that the Germans had reached Dijon and their armoured columns were rolling south almost unopposed. This cast a gloom over the meeting. Reynaud read the text of the Declaration twice and expressed enthusiasm, expecting it to be received with applause. He was grievously disappointed. Chautemps (Vice-President of the Council) voiced the feeling of many of those present by saying that France must not become a British colony. A surge of Anglophobia had swept France after the crushing defeat of their armies and the disclosure of the small contribution by the British in the fighting. Only President Albert Lebrun and radical socialist senator Alphonse Rio, Minister of Mercantile Marine, warmly welcomed the project, and the best estimates by French historians are that only four ministers were 100 per cent in favour. Halifax claimed there were fourteen against and ten for, but this has no confirmation from French sources. The forces of defeatism were too strong for Reynaud.

The meeting then discussed whether or not to continue the war, and a bitter debate ensued. Chautemps argued strongly that secret approaches should be made to Germany to ask for the terms of an armistice. Reynaud declared he would personally never consent to an armistice unless Britain formally released France from her undertaking of 28 February 1940 never to seek one separately.

Several Ministers stated there could be no simple '*oui*' or '*non*', and that the discussion should be adjourned until the German terms were available: if these were dishonourable, the Government must remain united so that it would be strong enough to continue the war from North Africa or England. After an 'interminable discussion', Reynaud declared there was a majority in favour of Chautemps' suggestion of finding out the German terms, and he adjourned the meeting until 10 p.m. when he said his Government would probably have resigned. Meanwhile he would consult with the President of the Republic. Again no vote was taken. According to the memories of several ministers after the Liberation, if a vote had been taken it would have been a close thing, but Reynaud affirmed after the war that he was in a minority.

French historians believe that if Reynaud had stood his ground he could have formed a fresh Government, with Pétain and his supporters excluded, and taken it overseas without enquiring from the Germans what their armistice terms would be. But with Pétain hostile and the Cabinet divided Reynaud found the burden of responsibility too heavy. Additionally, his domineering and very politically conscious mistress, Hélène les Portes, was completely defeatist and pro-Pétain. (She died in a motor accident a few days after the armistice.) Feeling desperate, Reynaud told Lebrun he must resign and Pétain must succeed. President Lebrun remonstrated and told Reynaud it was his duty to stay on and form a new Government, either in France or overseas. Reynaud then insisted on resigning. It was a bitter blow to Churchill. After Munich Reynaud, unlike Daladier, had taken Churchill's line and been his collaborator and confidant. He had been overjoyed when Reynaud replaced Daladier on 6 June as Prime Minister, and had faith that in Reynaud there was a strong man friendly to Britain who would hold out and fight to the last. At 22.30 on 16 June Reynaud, to the surprise of his colleagues, announced the resignation of his Cabinet. He was succeeded by Pétain, who was given a mandate by the President to seek an armistice. The Prime Minister was already on the train at Waterloo *en route* to Southampton with Attlee, Sinclair and the Chiefs of Staff when the news came through.

In the moment of crisis Reynaud was weak and lacking in resolution. He had been demoralized by his country's defeats in battle, and by Weygand and the other Service Chiefs' insistence that there must be an armistice. On top of this he had a reverence for Pétain, who he believed was the only leader who could hold a defeated France together and prevent chaos and revolution.[15]

The first act of the Pétain Government was to ask Germany for an armistice through Franco, the Spanish dictator; ignominiously they followed this up with an appeal through the Papal Nuncio in France for Italian terms to be transmitted. At midnight on 21 June the German terms were received by Pétain, and an armistice was signed on 22 June. A last-minute attempt by Reynaud and other ministers to form an alternative French Government in North Africa was frustrated by Pétain and Weygand, who gave orders not to allow them to land from their ship in Morocco.

The French Cabinet ministers were certain that Britain's surrender must follow automatically within a few weeks. Neither they nor the French generals could believe that after the large French Army, which they thought was the greatest in the world, had been completely defeated, the numerically tiny and ill-equipped British Army could hold out against the Germans.

Britain was alone. Italy had declared war on France and Britain on 10 June. Churchill had a sentimental love of Italy, and in his memoirs wrote romantically of how Britain had aided Garibaldi and Cavour during the Risorgimento. He loved Trevelyan's histories of this period and he adapted his most famous wartime phrase, 'I offer you nothing but blood, toil, sweat and tears', from the speech that Garibaldi made in St Peter's Square as Rome fell to the French in July 1849: 'I offer you not pay, quarters nor provisions. I offer hunger, thirst, forced marches, battles and death. Let him who loves his country with his heart, not with his lips only, follow me.' Similar words in the Commons by Churchill rallied the British nation at their darkest hour.[16]

CHAPTER SIX

Undeclared war with France after Britain sinks the French fleet

ON 11 JUNE 1940, when Churchill was in France desperately trying to prevent the French Government making a separate peace with Germany, Admiral Darlan assured him that he would never let the French Fleet fall into German hands, and informed him that on 28 May he had sent out orders that in the event of an armistice all French ships were to sail to British-held ports. On 13 June the French Government at Tours asked Churchill in person to relieve them of their obligation undertaken on 28 March not to make a separate armistice with Germany; Churchill returned to England without giving an answer, as both countries awaited Roosevelt's response to a desperate appeal for help. (As has been seen, Roosevelt turned the appeal down.)[1]

On 16 June Halifax sent telegrams to the French Government, stating that Britain would only agree to a separate armistice for France if the French Fleet was ordered to sail to British ports. These telegrams were immediately rescinded; instead Britain, as has been seen, made a dramatic but unsuccessful offer of union with France.

On the morning of 17 June, the day after Reynaud's resignation, Campbell, the British Ambassador, asked the new French Prime Minister, Pétain, whether in view of the negotiations for an armistice with Germany he would order the French Fleet to sail to British ports forthwith. Pétain refused, saying it was too late, but added that the ships would be scuttled rather than surrendered. On the 18th June the French Cabinet decided they would not sign the armistice if Germany demanded a single ship; accordingly Darlan sent orders that French ships were to be scuttled if the Germans tried to seize them. Thus he honoured his promise to Churchill.[2]

Churchill again visited the French Government in Bordeaux on 19 June. Baudouin (Pétain's Foreign Minister) assured him that a *sine qua non* of the armistice terms would be that no ship would be given up to Germany, and gave his word of honour that strict secret orders to this effect had been given to the Fleet. Admiral Pound and Alexander, First Lord of the Admiralty, who accompanied Churchill, met Darlan, who had been created Minister of Marine by Pétain. They did not ask the Frenchman to order his ships to British ports because they agreed that Darlan's orders (which they read) were satisfactory; they made no objections and asked for no conditions. The meeting was friendly and, having reported to Churchill, Alexander and Pound went back to London much relieved.

According to the French Admiral Auphan, who was present at the conference, Pound and Alexander were 'moved, warm and to all appearances entirely satisfied'. On the next day Lord Lloyd, the Colonial Secretary, who was accompanying Churchill, also talked to Darlan and told the French Admiral the British Government was satisfied with his orders to the French Fleet.[3]

Darlan recorded after the talks that the British were like the heirs to a dying man who came to make sure that the will had been drawn up in their favour. Nor was he pleased with a message received on that day from the American diplomat Biddle that if the French Fleet fell into German hands France would positively lose US goodwill.[4]

Darlan, who had commanded the French Navy from the beginning of the war, was now Minister of Marine. He was ambivalent. Unlike the French Army, on 10 June the Fleet was intact, loyal and would obey any orders he sent them. He was a strange character – secretive and surly, but with a clear mind; he was also a tremendous worker and loved the Navy with a father's passion. He abhorred the idea of the French Navy coming under either British or German command. Undoubtedly he was Anglophobe. The fact that at Dunkirk the British had begun the naval evacuation without consulting him, together with a dozen other incidents in the difficult days following Hitler's attack, made him forget the fraternal alliance between the French and the British Navy to such an extent that Admiral Odendhal reminded him in a minute of 5 June 1940: 'We are at war with the Boche, not with England; whatever the events of Dunkirk they must not be allowed to create bitterness.'[5]

After Darlan had emphatically told Churchill on 11 June that the French Fleet would never be surrendered to the Germans, and to prevent this would be sunk if necessary, he told several colleagues in Bordeaux that if there was an armistice he would end his career with a magnificent gesture of insubordination and sail with the fleet to Britain. If Darlan had done this he would automatically have become the much-hailed leader of the French Resistance. Churchill has written: 'Darlan had but to sail in any one of his ships to any port outside France to become the master of all French interests beyond German control . . . Darlan would have become the chief of the French Resistance with a mighty weapon in his hand . . . The whole French Empire would have rallied to him. Nothing could have prevented him from being the Liberator of France.'[6]

Why did Darlan change his mind? On 17 June Pétain had made him Minister of Marine. The explanation given to his son a few days after the armistice was: 'As Navy Minister I had no right to sail the Fleet away. France had put me in command of the Fleet but the Fleet belonged to France, not to me.' The truth also was that the French Government saw their Fleet as an important bargaining counter with the Germans over the terms of the armistice.[7]

To Churchill's intense anger the French Government refused to go to North Africa to continue the war, and in a broadcast to France he protested vehemently and demanded that the Fleet should sail to British ports. The President of the

Republic, Lebrun, then sent Britain assurances that the Germans would never take possession of the French Fleet.

Churchill would not believe this. Instead he became obsessed by a conviction that the Germans would capture the French Fleet and either find or train enough German sailors to man the newly acquired ships. This, he felt, was a potential disaster for the Royal Navy and merchant ships, which would be a decisive factor in the outcome of the war, and he considered Britain in this situation would lose. As a result he was belligerent at the War Cabinet on 22 June, dismissing out of hand a claim by Pound that Darlan was taking all possible steps to protect British interests and saying:

> In a matter so vital to the safety of the whole British Empire we could not afford to rely on the word of Admiral Darlan. However good his intentions might be, he might be forced to resign and his place taken by another Minister who would not shrink from betraying us. The most important thing to do was to make certain of the two modern battleships *Richelieu* and *Jean Bart*. If these fell into the hands of the Germans, they would have a very formidable line of battle when the [battleship] *Bismarck* was commissioned next August. Against these fast and powerful ships we should only have *Nelson*, *Rodney* and the older battleships like *Valiant*. *Strasbourg* and *Dunkirk* would certainly be a great nuisance if they fell into the hands of the enemy, but it was the two modern ships which might alter the whole course of the war . . . at all costs *Richelieu* and *Jean Bart*, particularly the former, must not be allowed to get loose . . . A strong force must be sent and *Richelieu* dealt with first. If the captains refuse to parley they must be treated as traitors to the Allied cause. The ships might have to be bombed by aircraft from *Ark Royal* or they must be mined into their harbours and naval forces stationed outside to prevent the minefields being swept up. In no circumstances whatever must these ships be allowed to escape.

That day Churchill could not persuade his colleagues to agree to force. Halifax suggested that 'all efforts should be made to make the parleys a success', and the other ministers concurred. Baulked, Churchill said finally: 'At all times we must keep in view our main object which is in no circumstances must we run the mortal risk of allowing these ships to fall into the hands of the enemy. Rather than that we should have to fight and sink them.'[8]

The Franco–German armistice was signed at 19.30 on 24 June. The Atlantic, but not the Mediterranean, ports were to be occupied by the Germans. At 6 p.m. a Cabinet meeting was held: the members were told that an armistice had been signed but no details were known. The Chiefs of Staff were asked for an urgent naval staff appreciation about using force against the French Fleet. This was completed within two hours: the naval experts advised against such action on the grounds that as soon as British forces attempted to take over or sink French naval units the crews of the remaining ships would become actively hostile, and this would reduce British chances of securing more than a small part of the French Fleet.

At 10.30 p.m. the War Cabinet met again, with the naval staff report before them. At the two previous meetings that day pessimistic reports had been given about the likelihood of the French captains agreeing to sail their ships to British ports. Pound told the late evening Cabinet: 'The only real chance of success lay in a surprise attack carried out at dawn . . . The operation might well result in the loss or partial disablement of both our battleships, and we should then in consequence be badly handicapped in dealing with the *Richelieu* and *Jean Bart.*' The First Sea Lord was extremely reluctant to take extreme measures saying:

> The probable loss of our two ships seemed a heavy price to pay for the elimination or partial elimination of Force de Rade [striking force]. Admiral Darlan and other French Admirals had maintained the consistent attitude that in no circumstances would the French Fleet be surrendered, and we would be more likely to achieve our object by trusting in these assurances. He did not, therefore, recommend the proposed operation.

Once again Churchill could not persuade his colleagues to agree to force and a decision was postponed, although the Cabinet agreed to detain French warships in British ports and at Alexandria. In his memoirs, and to the Commons at the time, Churchill claimed there was 'unanimity'.[9] The Cabinet and Chiefs of Staff records show that this was far from being the case.

Meanwhile the Admiralty made an all-out effort to discover the attitude of French naval officers towards handing their Fleet over to the British. Admiral North, the naval commander in Gibraltar, visited Admiral Gensoul, his French counterpart at Oran, and after the talk reported to the Admiralty that there was no doubt about French friendship; Gensoul told him that under no circumstances would he turn over his ships to the Germans, and showed him Darlan's specific orders to scuttle them if necessary. Part of Darlan's orders read: 'Make secret preparations for auto sabotage to prevent seizure of vessels.'

North and Somerville in Gibraltar called a conference of all flag officers; they all unanimously opposed the use of force. The general view was that the French would resist demands to surrender by force, and anyway there was little fear of the French allowing their ships to fall into German hands. All the British naval liaison officers in French ports in Africa were summoned to Gibraltar. They reported that in spirit the French Fleet was on the British side, and that under no circumstances should force be used; the threat of force would be 'disastrous'; while it might be possible to persuade the French to adopt one of the alternatives, 'a threat would antagonise them immediately', and no admiral, especially a French one with his sense of honour and dignity, could do anything but resist such an ultimatum. Somerville informed the Admiralty how 'impressed' he was with the unanimous opinion of all the officers.[10]

On 25 June Pound cabled to North: 'Do you consider there would be any prospect of French ships at Oran surrendering to us if British force arrived off port and summoned them to surrender?' North replied that from his interview he was sure 'they would not surrender'. Other reports confirmed this view.

Without consulting his Cabinet colleagues, Churchill rode roughshod over the opinions of these naval officers who knew and understood the French. At this stage of the war he was virtually a military dictator, and by 30 June he had bludgeoned the Chiefs of Staff into repudiating the opinion they had given on 24 June and to agree that an attack on French ships in Algerian waters should be carried out as soon as possible. The plan, known as Operation Catapult, went before the War Cabinet the next day, 1 July; this time, fortified by the military experts, Churchill was able to railroad the decision to attack the French Fleet if they would not surrender. Somerville was ordered to undertake Operation Catapult to sink or secure the surrender of the French ships at Mers-el-Kebir.

The Germans did not demand the surrender of the French Fleet. Hitler feared that if he insisted on seizing the Fleet France would go on fighting and hand over the ships to the British. Instead, under clause 8 of the armistice the ships were to be demobilized under German or Italian control, but the German word used for 'control' meant 'control' as for passports or railway tickets. This clause was more lenient than the French had expected. Darlan, much relieved, abandoned all idea of sending the Fleet to British ports and felt that by ordering his captains to sink the ships rather than surrender them to the Germans or Italians he had discharged his duty to Britain.[11]

The armistice came into operation at midnight on 24 June. At Brest, which was within the zone to be occupied by the Germans, five submarines and one destroyer unfit to sail were sunk, and the *Richelieu*, with twenty-four other ships, sailed for Casablanca in Morocco. From St Nazaire on the Atlantic Coast, also about to be occupied by the Germans, the *Jean Bart* too sailed for North Africa. At Lorient the French sank some of their ships and others sailed out of the German occupation zone. In fact the French Navy did not leave a single ship in the ports to be occupied by the Germans, and the harbour installations were blown up.[12]

Yet Churchill wrote in his memoirs that 'no French warship sailed away from German power', and misrepresented the evidence to justify his action on 3 July in bombarding the French Fleet at Oran. None of the French Fleet was left in ports occupied by the Germans; apart from the ships in England they were in the naval towns of Toulon, Oran, Mers-el-Kebir, Bizerta, Algiers and Alexandria. Churchill alleged that Darlan had broken his word by not ordering the French Fleet to sail to British ports, completely ignoring the fact that at Bordeaux Alexander, Pound and Lloyd had agreed Darlan's orders were 'satisfactory' if the Fleet remained in North Africa and ports in the unoccupied zone of France.

Somerville arrived with his ships off Mers-el-Kebir early on 3 July and Captain Holland, the former naval attaché in Paris, went into the harbour to negotiate. Gensoul refused to see him, and he returned to Somerville's flagship having delivered a written ultimatum that the French ships would be destroyed unless Gensoul agreed to scuttle them or sail them either to British ports or the West Indies. However at 14.42 Gensoul sent a signal: 'I am ready to receive your delegate for honourable discussion.' This was a great relief to Holland, who had been bobbing up and down in a small boat amid a hostile fleet for hours, with enormous responsibilities on his shoulders and grave fears for the safety of the RN liaison officers and their families in French territory.

Somerville immediately reported to Churchill 'Slight sign of weakening.'

Holland arrived on board Gensoul's flagship, the *Dunkerque*, at 16.15. Gensoul showed him orders he had received from Darlan to proceed to the USA if the Germans broke their armistice promises and demanded the ships. Holland remarked: 'If we had known this before it would have made all the difference.' Gensoul then told Holland that in order to reach a compromise he was ready to give an undertaking to disarm all his ships at Oran, even though it meant exceeding his instructions.

Meanwhile the Admiralty had intercepted a signal from the Vichy Government ordering French reinforcements to steam urgently to Oran. Churchill refused to delay, ordering Somerville to 'Settle everything before dark or you will have reinforcements to deal with.' The bombardment then began; one battleship and five destroyers escaped to Toulon, but the remainder of the French Fleet at Mers-el-Kebir was put out of action by the British guns; 1300 French seamen died.[13]

At the Baudouin trial in 1947 Admiral Gensoul testified that 'if the British proposals had been presented in another manner things would have been different', and that previous to Oran 'the French Fleet was 100 per cent pro-British'. In their official reports Somerville and Holland both emphasized that, given more time, a basis for agreement could have been reached.[14]

In *The War at Sea* S. W. Roskill, the official war historian, wrote, 'I had many interviews and much correspondence with Cunningham, North and Somerville, the three admirals concerned . . . None of them ever budged from the view that given more time for negotiations the tragedy could have been averted.'

The butchery was Churchill's doing, and Anglo–French relations sank to their lowest level, amounting to undeclared warfare. When he first heard of the Mers-el-Kebir tragedy de Gaulle was angry, and stated that it was so disastrous from his standpoint that he planned to retire to Canada and live as a simple individual. But he soon changed his mind, and declared in a broadcast to France on 8 July that he preferred French battleships stranded off Mers-el-Kebir to their being manned by Germans to fight the British. The Vichy Government broke off diplomatic relations with Britain. Ninety per cent of French sailors on ships in British ports refused to join de Gaulle; recruiting to his forces, which had been brisk, dwindled to a trickle all over the world – not helped by the British Treasury's stingy refusal to pay travel expenses.

Admiral Jacques Zang, the French naval historian, told the author that on 3 July he was a young officer on the *Richelieu* at Dakar; he and a friend had decided to abscond and cycle to Bathurst in British Gambia to join de Gaulle. But after Mers-el-Kebir they changed their minds, and not until after his ship had been scuttled at Toulon in 1942 did he cross Spain to join the Free French. This story could be multiplied many times over. Of the French servicemen evacuated from Dunkirk 31,000 applied to be repatriated, and at the time of Mers-el-Kebir there were around 115,000 French soldiers and sailors in Britain, including many who had been evacuated from Narvik. In Britain de Gaulle's recruits only totalled around two thousand, less than 2 per cent of those available.

Somerville declared it had been 'a bloody business', and for the French the tragedy of Mers-el-Kebir has never been expiated. There are many elderly former French naval officers today who still hate Churchill and the Royal Navy for carrying out his orders.[15]

Although Mers-el-Kebir made Churchill unpopular with the Navy, he used the battle to good account in the Commons debate, greatly improving his political standing both there and outside. He was, not surprisingly, very nervous, and before he rose the House was ashamed and in two minds. But he spoke so well about the 'mortal injury' which Britain would almost certainly have suffered otherwise that the whole House accepted his arguments and he was resoundingly cheered. Strangely, he managed to give the impression that, because he had been ruthless with his former ally, Britain at last had a leader with the necessary ruthlessness and determination to overcome Hitler. The consensus view in the national press, which had no idea of the promises made by Darlan and Pétain, was that it was the sad but inevitable consequence of Hitler's victory. The Government's callous refusal to allow the French in Britain to hold a memorial service for the dead went unnoticed.

Darlan's orders to sink the ships rather than allow the Germans or Italians to seize them would always have been carried out. After the battle Admiral Somerville wrote to his wife: 'I warned the Admiralty it was the biggest political blunder of modern times, and I imagine it will rouse the whole world against us.' Somerville's gloomy prediction was correct.[16]

There were two grave consequences. First, the Germans altered the armistice terms and allowed the French ships to be kept in battle condition so that they were used against the British when merchant ships were trying to evade the blockade and bring supplies to France. Secondly, when Churchill and de Gaulle conceived a plan, codenamed Menace, to occupy Dakar in Senegal and raise the Free French flag in the hope that all the French colonies in West and Equatorial Africa would rally to de Gaulle, the French Governor and garrison stayed resolutely loyal to Vichy. As a result the plans, which depended on de Gaulle being greeted sympathetically, misfired and ended ignominiously. The entire Board of Admiralty were opposed to the Dakar operation, but Churchill again railroaded it through, and on 18 September the War Cabinet approved it, albeit with reluctance.

Churchill was its enthusiastic chief sponsor, and it became his pet scheme as he breathed life into it with boundless energy and drive, although at one moment he changed his mind about carrying it out. The expedition was under the joint command of Admiral John Cunningham (no relation of Admiral Andrew Cunningham) and General Irwin, who had distinguished himself as a brigade commander in France and made no secret that he thought the operation unwise. Two battleships, three cruisers and the aircraft carrier *Ark Royal*, together with ten destroyers and twelve transports, carried 2400 Free French and 4270 British troops. At Churchill's insistence, Admiral Keyes had been made Director of Combined Operations, but his headquarters was not consulted. He told the Chiefs of Staff afterwards that the plan was 'fantastically foolish', and his offer to help was ignored.

The attack took place on 23 September in thick fog. De Gaulle demanded that he and the Free French should be allowed to take over the town. The Governor General, Boisson, refused point blank. There was considerable shelling from both sides, and 40 Free French and British were killed against 166 Vichy French. An attempted Free French landing at Rufisque was repulsed by native troops before the British contingent arrived in an unholy military muddle in the fog, and Admiral Cunningham and General Irwin, judging another landing impractical, called the operation off; Goebbels' propaganda machine had a field day. The battleships *Resolution* and *Barham* were both damaged by shells from the *Richelieu* which had been sealed to Dakar. The *Resolution* had a hole big enough to take 'a double decker bus'.[17]

Churchill had been elated by the nation's enthusiasm for the Mers-el-Kebir battle and was desperately anxious for a similar 'success' at Dakar. He pointed out to the War Cabinet on 17 September that they 'had lived to bless the day on which they decided upon the Oran operation'. As on other occasions, Churchill could over-rule the Chiefs of Staff. The following telegram, sent to Combined Command at the height of the Dakar action, shows how he interfered in the hour-to-hour running of the battle:

> Your signal gives no indication of your plans. We asked you particularly to be full and clear in your accounts. Why have you not sent two or three hundred words to let us know your difficulties and how you propose to meet them?
>
> We do not understand conditions under which bombardment proceeded for some hours at 10,000 yards without grave damage to ships or forts unless visibility was so bad as to make targets invisible. Also if visibility is bad why is it not possible to force a landing at beaches near Rufisque in spite of fire from Goree Island? Without this information we can only ask you why you do not land in force by night or in the fog or both on beaches near Rufisque and take Rufisque for a start observing that enemy cannot be heartwhole and force Rufisque is comprised largely of native troops. At the same time if the weather clears you could hold down batteries on Goree Island in daylight by long range sea fire and if there is fog you would not need to do so. It should be possible to feed the force once ashore by night. This force once landed ought to be able to advance on Dakar.
>
> More ammunition is being sent from Gibraltar but evidently supplies will not stand many days firing like today. Neither is there unlimited time as not only French but German submarines will probably arrive in six or seven days. Pray act as you think best, but meanwhile give reasoned answers to these points. Matter must be pushed to conclusion without delay.[18]

This is evidence of Churchill's frustration and the risks he was prepared to take, while clearly he was oblivious of the consequences of further alienating the Vichy Government.

Cunningham's staff were furious at Churchill's complaint that they had not sent 'two or three hundred words', according to one 'not being in the mood for composing a further powerful instalment and encyphering it'. After a 'sober discussion' the War Cabinet agreed that the operation should be abandoned, but not before the First Lord, A. V. Alexander, had declared he had opposed the operation from the beginning.[19]

Some compensation resulted when Libreville surrendered to de Gaulle. It enabled him to organize a Confederation of Free French Equatorial African States which became known as Free French Africa and was the foundation of Free France. This ensured de Gaulle's future.

Not until all the French survivors are dead will the agony of Mers-el-Kebir and the subsequent bitter French hatred for the British pass into history. The French have never forgiven Churchill, and the verdict of history must be that by ignoring Admiralty advice and provoking an undeclared war between France and Britain he prejudiced the Allied cause. His refusal to believe French promises that they would never allow the Germans to obtain the French Fleet was almost his biggest wartime error.

On the same day as the Mers-el-Kebir battle took place the Chiefs of Staff submitted plans for Operation Susan, later Catapult 2; its aim was to seize Casablanca from the Vichy French with two RAF fighter squadrons, one Polish and one French division, together with a British infantry brigade. Ten liners, three store ships and two petrol ships would be ready to arrive at Casablanca thirty-seven days after the Cabinet gave the decision to go ahead. However the anti-Vichy troops in Britain were not in good shape. Even before the news of Mers-el-Kebir was known the Foreign Legion was said to be disaffected, with poor morale, while the Chasseurs Alpins, who had recently returned from Norway, were not suitable for tropical warfare in midsummer, being equipped for snowy mountains. Churchill was keen on Susan, but it was overtaken by events and did not come to fruition.[20]

An interesting postscript to Mers-el-Kebir lies in the War History archives of the Cabinet Offices. Commander Stitt RN, a distinguished wartime naval officer and author of two important books, was commissioned to carry out the research on Mers-el-Kebir for the Mediterranean and Middle East volumes of the official War History to be written and edited by General Playfair. Stitt went to France to gather evidence from French sources and delivered his final manuscript in June 1951. The chief official historian, Sir Llewellyn Woodward, read his report and immediately commented to A. B. Acheson, Secretary of the Cabinet Office Historical Section, that Stitt's paper should be suppressed because it was too favourable to France and he wanted a meeting to discuss it. In the meantime Stitt died.

At that time it was clear that Churchill would soon be Prime Minister again in place of Attlee, and in October Winston returned to Downing Street. Stitt's draft contradicted the account in Volume II of Churchill's *Memoirs*, published in 1949. Stitt had written:

> Those in the Mediterranean, however, who had been in close contact with the French fleet and knew something of the spirit which animated the officers and men, felt confident that diplomatic handling of the situation would ensure that the French navy would not only be kept beyond the reach of the Germans and Italians but would preserve a loyalty to their British comrades in arms and a readiness to renew the struggle when opportunity again afforded.[21]

Stitt continued that Mers-el-Kebir 'alienated' the friendship of the French Navy and was directly responsible for the misfortunes which attended Dakar; neither Somerville nor Holland in their reports, he wrote, could 'understand the haste urged by the Government' and emphasized that, given more time, a basis of agreement could have been reached. Stitt thought that if Gensoul had received Holland in the morning of 3 July a solution would have been found, and concluded: 'if Somerville or North had been instructed to reach a satisfactory agreement with Gensoul and the question of force had been withheld a reasonable compromise might well have been reached'. He also pointed out correctly that Churchill's statement in his broadcast of 25 June – that agreement had been reached that the French Fleet should sail to British ports as a condition of Britain agreeing to a separate peace – was 'untrue', and that Admiral Cunningham had sent a message to the Admiralty to the effect that Churchill's charge that the Bordeaux Government had betrayed the country was causing bitter resentment amongst the French which in his opinion might result in complete non-cooperation.

As soon as Churchill became Prime Minister in 1951 he insisted he must approve all references to his decisions as wartime Prime Minister in the draft official histories. Accordingly he or his private secretaries carefully vetted anything controversial. Woodward and Acheson knew that Stitt's comments and report on Mers-el-Kebir would arouse Churchill, and as a result Stitt's account was ignored.

However in 1952 (when Churchill was Prime Minister), at a meeting of the panel to consider Playfair's draft for the official history of Mers-el-Kebir, Admiral Sir Geoffrey Blake pointed out that no account had been taken of Stitt's views. A letter from Admiral Cunningham was also considered; this suggested that Stitt's paper should be published separately 'as a means of removing the bitterness created by the Oran affair with the French', similar suggestions had been made by the French on the grounds that if an agreed account could be officially issued it might go a long way to counter-balance 'the accounts published in France with bitter comments on the actions taken by the Royal Navy'. But the committee ignored these reasonable suggestions on the grounds that Stitt's paper was not accepted by Playfair. It would have been more honest if they had recorded that they refused because it would result in a clash between Stitt's and Churchill's published version, so that the Prime Minister would have intervened angrily.[22]

There are many instances of Churchill, during his final term of office as Prime Minister from 1951 to 1955, sanitizing controversial pieces of official history. Students should treat with caution many accounts in the official histories of Churchill's controversial decisions because much which is derogatory to him is excluded. Anyone wanting a detailed acount of Mers-el-Kebir should send for Cab 101/95 in the Public Record Office; this contains nothing but Stitt's well-researched and authoritative fifty-page account based on the official secret documents available to him as an official historian, and on post-war interviews in France.

Both Woodward's and Playfair's accounts of Mers-el-Kebir in the official histories are untrustworthy. Woodward wrote that Gensoul 'refused to meet Holland', ignoring Stitt's account of the meeting on the *Dunkerque* at 16.15 when hopes of a compromise were strong, and referring to 'only the shadowy safeguard of a German promise'. This is supporting Churchill with a vengeance. And Playfair writes obsequiously and justifies the Prime Minister: 'The orders were entirely consistent with the decision to which the British Government had come for reasons which in the light of known facts seemed to be good and sufficient' – a far cry from the view of Stitt, the original official researcher of this controversial episode.[23]

CHAPTER SEVEN

Britain stands alone:
Churchill and Roosevelt
June 1940–June 1941

THE DARKEST days of the war were from the French surrender on 17 June 1940 until Hitler's attack on Russia on 21 June 1941. Churchill's own biographer writes that he was then close to despair with his knowledge of the truth, and he told Eden he woke up each morning 'with dread in his heart'.

When the RAF prevented German aircraft dominating the skies, Hitler called off his invasion plans; this was an immense relief to Churchill. The Chiefs of Staff had warned him that 'if German forces got a firm footing in Britain our land forces would be insufficient' and 'our conclusion is that *prima facie* Germany has most of the cards'.[1]

The Battle of Britain made Churchill immensely popular; a Gallup Poll in October 1940 showed 89 per cent for him. He loved power and gloried in his own popularity. With the German victory over France subjecting Britain to the gravest threat ever, Churchill's leadership had a magical quality. In his broadcasts and speeches to the Commons he radiated confidence in final victory. Anyone reading the Foreign Office papers cannot fail to be struck by the confidence expressed in final victory by the diplomats. This was due to Churchill. And we have already seen how Churchill galvanized Whitehall so that all the machinery of war was operated at maximum pressure and efficiency.

During a tour of coastal defences at Brighton, Churchill met for the first time General Bernard Montgomery, commanding the 3rd Division. During the course of a meal Montgomery convinced the Prime Minister that what was lacking was a mobile reserve; all the best fighting troops were on the beaches to repulse the first assault. Immediately Churchill over-rode his advisers and insisted that Montgomery's division and other regular divisions were provided with buses and motor transport so that they could be thrown into the battle wherever they were most needed. Churchill, typically, insisted on the changes being made at speed. This was sensible, although it was never put to the actual test because the German invasion did not happen.[2]

Realistically Churchill knew that Britain could not win without the United States, and he dwelt longingly on the possibility of America soon declaring war on Germany. But there was no real hope of this because in his presidential campaign in November 1940 Roosevelt had assured the nation that American troops would never fight in Europe again, and he had no intention of reneging on this pledge.

The friendship between Roosevelt and Churchill has been over-romanticized by historians; they have been seduced by the picture painted by Churchill in his memoirs. The Roosevelt–Churchill wartime correspondence began with a letter from Roosevelt on 11 September 1939, nine days after Churchill had become First Lord of the Admiralty, and it grew apace. Churchill's Cabinet colleagues and the Prime Minister tolerated the relationship, apart from Halifax who, like the Foreign Office, actively disliked the way in which Churchill bypassed the normal channels by sending messages direct through the US Embassy in London. This prevented the Foreign Office vetting them, although Churchill sent them copies, and it allowed the American Ambassador in London, Joseph Kennedy, to comment before his British counterpart in Washington, Lothian, had read them. When the Foreign Office protested that they should be able to exercise control over the exchanges, Churchill ignored them. The Foreign Office also pointed out that the American Ambassador was an 'undesirable channel' because of his defeatism; Churchill agreed to send his letters through Lothian, but did not do so.[3]

With the fall of France a new phase in the relationship began. The gist of all Churchill's messages became 'Help urgently'. When his hopes of immediate US intervention were dashed after his false interpretation of Roosevelt's message to Reynaud he was almost distraught, and warned Roosevelt that Great Britain could not be expected to fight on alone without hope of American intervention. Cunningly, he used the threat to push America into a fully-fledged alliance that if things continued to go wrong his Government might be replaced by one which would negotiate peace with Hitler. Churchill was bluffing, but there was substance in his threat, because a number of influential British MPs wanted a compromise peace.

As the official historian puts it: 'It was widely believed outside Great Britain that we were in imminent danger of defeat, while few people thought we could hope for more than a stalemate. In fact as long as enemy morale held it seemed hardly possible for us to defeat Germany by direct action on the Continent.' Churchill, sensitive to all shades of political opinion, knew well that the defeatist views expressed by Chamberlain and Halifax at the May Cabinets were shared by other ministers of lower rank; he issued a strong directive to all his ministers that they were at all times to show complete confidence and no signs of defeatism.

He was much put out when Rab Butler, Halifax's Under Secretary at the Foreign Office and the Commons spokesman on Foreign Affairs, breached his edict. On 17 June Butler met Bjorn Prytz, the much respected Swedish Minister, in St James's Park and brought him back to his room in the Foreign Office for a chat about the probable outcome of the war. Prytz reported to the Swedish Government that Butler 'told him no opportunity would be neglected for concluding a compromise peace if the chance was offered on reasonable conditions'; further, after being called away to see Halifax, Butler returned with a message from the Foreign Secretary to Prytz that 'commonsense, not bravado, would dictate the British Government policy' and that Halifax knew that such an attitude would be welcomed by Prytz although he 'must not interpret it as peace at any price'. In his report to Stockholm, Prytz added that many MPs expected Halifax to succeed Churchill as Prime Minister. This report was discussed by the Swedish Foreign Policy Committee under obligations of strict secrecy.

At the time Sweden was desperately anxious for a peace to be arranged as it was being faced with harsh demands from Germany for transit rights for troops and materials through Swedish territory, and the report was immediately leaked to the press. The Stockholm correspondent of the *News Chronicle* informed his paper on 20 June that Butler had said Britain would only fight on if sure of victory. Ribbentrop (German Foreign Minister) immediately made enquiries through Sweden as to whether Britain wanted to negotiate, and the British Minister in Stockholm reported this approach to the Foreign Office.

Churchill read the telegrams and was furious, telling Halifax that in the secret session of the Commons he had given assurances that the present Government and all its members were determined to fight to the death. Butler was close to being sacked; he wrote to Halifax that the report was not a true reflection of the conversation, but he agreed he should have been more cautious and apologised.[4]

Halifax wrote to Churchill that they should accept Butler's explanation, and Butler was saved. However, it became well known within the Conservative Party that Butler had expressed a wish for a negotiated peace, and the story was assiduously fanned by Randolph Churchill. As a result it was a factor in Butler failing to become Prime Minister both when Eden resigned in 1957 and when Macmillan resigned in 1963.

At first Churchill cunningly refused to give Roosevelt an iron-clad guarantee that if Britain was over-run by the Nazis the Fleet would be transferred to the United States. Undoubtedly this is what he planned, but he hoped the fear of the British Fleet falling into German hands would stimulate Roosevelt and his administration to action and perhaps to a firm alliance. Roosevelt frequently expressed deep concern about the future of the Fleet if Britain surrendered, and Churchill's tactics probably stiffened the President's support for Britain.

At the end of July Roosevelt agreed to offer Britain over-age destroyers in return for strategically important base rights in the Western Hemisphere. He stipulated that he must have an assurance that if Britain succumbed, the Fleet would be neither destroyed nor surrendered, but sailed to ports in the United States and the British Empire, in particular to Canada.

On 30 August Churchill wrote to Roosevelt that it was certainly the settled policy of His Majesty's Government never to surrender or scuttle her Fleet. Characteristically Churchill added to the President, 'I must observe that these hypothetical contingencies seem more likely to concern the German fleet or what is left of it, than ours.' On top of this assurance Churchill agreed to lease free of charge for ninety-nine years' naval and air base facilities for US defence in: Newfoundland, Bermuda, the Bahamas, Jamaica, Antigua, St Lucia, Trinidad and British Guiana. Roosevelt then firmed up his offer of ships and promised fifty old destroyers, MTBs and much other war material to Britain.[5]

Churchill negotiated with great skill. Unfortunately, owing to their age and lack of maintenance the American destroyers needed an unexpected amount of repairs and were of much less use than had been expected. Only nine were in use by the end of December 1941.

The presidential elections took place on 5 November. Roosevelt's opponent, Wendell Wilkie, was also a strong advocate of aid to what he called 'the heroic British people'. However, Churchill had carefully fostered the confidence and friendship of Roosevelt, which he expected to be a vital factor in winning the war, and he felt 'indescribable relief' when Roosevelt was re-elected by a resounding majority. Churchill refused to comment on the election while it was in progress. Some American historians claim that Roosevelt was piqued by Churchill's failure to support him. But the evidence is flimsy, and Churchill behaved with admirable correctness.

With generosity Roosevelt announced on 8 November, three days after his re-election, that as weapons came off the American production line they were to be divided roughly fifty-fifty between the US and the British and Canadian forces. Britain had taken over all the French armament orders.

There now emerged the grim problem of paying for this enormous quantity of armament. Britain had started the war with around $4\frac{1}{2}$ billion dollars in gold and US investments. The only way in which this sum could be increased was by the sale of newly mined gold from South Africa or other parts of the British Dominions, or by exports of British non-essential manufacture to the USA. The Chamberlain Cabinet had been gravely concerned by gloomy reports from John Simon, the Chancellor of the Exchequer, about the cost of US arms and the need to conserve British dollar balances. Immediately Churchill became Prime Minister he replaced Simon with Kingsley Wood and instructed him that everything possible should be ordered and the cash problem left 'on the lap of the Eternal Gods'. Until November 1940 Britain had paid for all she had received, but by then it was plain there was no possibility of paying for arms at the rate at which they were being bought.

After several drafts on 7 December, Churchill finalized and sent a brilliant letter to Roosevelt which he considered to be the most important one he had ever written. It gave a full statement of Britain's hopeless financial position, and was taken personally by Lothian to the President while Roosevelt was holidaying in the Caribbean aboard an American warship. In the letter Churchill stated that the moment had come when Britain could no longer pay cash for supplies and begged Roosevelt not to confine his 'help' which he had so generously promised to such munitions of war and commodities as could immediately be paid for.

Straightaway Roosevelt stated at a press conference that he would 'lease' material to Britain, get rid of the 'dollar sign' in relations between the two countries and substitute a gentleman's agreement. These words had immense significance and raised the curtain on the historic Lend Lease arrangement. Roosevelt continued: 'Emphatically we must get these weapons to them in sufficient volume and quickly enough so that we and our children will be saved the agony and suffering of war which others have had to endure.' Lord Lothian was carrying on important and delicate negotiations in Washington when he died suddenly of uraemic poisoning on 11 December. (To the consternation of the Foreign Office Churchill proposed Lloyd George as Lothian's successor. Roosevelt agreed reluctantly, commenting 'I hope he will in no way play into the hands of the appeasers.' Fortunately Lloyd George declined on health grounds. Instead Churchill appointed Halifax, much against the latter's will; Churchill wanted him as a former prominent appeaser, out of his Cabinet so that Eden could become Foreign Secretary.) In a fireside chat – the President's label for a talk to the nation – Roosevelt said on 29 December that America would become 'the great arsenal for democracy', and gave instructions for the Lend Lease Act to be drafted.[6]

The Lend Lease Bill was passed by Congress in January 1941, and Britain's financial worries were over. Although Churchill had not been able to persuade Roosevelt to bring America actively into the war, he had accomplished a magnificent stroke of diplomacy. No historian should fail to give great credit to Churchill for his negotiations over the bases, destroyers and Lend Lease. By showing imagination, diplomatic skill and a sensitive understanding of Roosevelt's psychological approach he was able to bring the negotiations to a triumphant conclusion.

In March 1941 Roosevelt sent Harry Hopkins, his principal adviser, to London to discuss with Churchill what further aid America could give after Lend Lease was ratified by Parliament. Hopkins arrived in London expecting not to like the Prime Minister; instead he was soon captivated by Churchill's charm and became a devoted admirer and loyal collaborator.

In the USA there had been a reaction to the Lend Lease Bill. It had been presented as an alternative to war, with America becoming the 'arsenal of democracy without making an active military intervention'. However, the iso- lationists made political capital by asserting that Lend Lease was camouflage and that Roosevelt intended to lead his country into war by a series of crab-like steps.

In the summer of 1941 the central issue was American intervention in the Atlantic. Through Hopkins Churchill tried to persuade Roosevelt to move forward, and he achieved partial success: in April the President consented to a plan that the position of any Axis ship spotted as far east as the 26th Meridian should be reported to the British. In September Roosevelt authorized American troops for Iceland, where they freed the British garrison for other duties, and all convoys going to Iceland were protected by the US Navy against German submarines. Two American flying schools trained British pilots.

When news came of the German attack on Russia later that year Roosevelt was sure in his own mind that aid should be given to Russia on the same terms as to Britain, but he bumped up against much opposition from Roman Catholics, and the extreme anti-Communists. Admiral Stark, his principal naval adviser, wanted Roosevelt to authorize the US Navy to escort convoys in the Western Atlantic. Roosevelt shilly-shallied over this.

In July Roosevelt suggested a personal meeting to Churchill, so that they could discuss these matters and use the occasion as a propaganda platform for American and British post-war aims. The President told the Prime Minister that the 'mere announcement' of Anglo–American post-war aims would give 'invaluable encouragement' to all those fighting against Hitler. Churchill eagerly agreed. He was hopeful that such a meeting would produce some immediate practical outcome, although his intimate talks with Hopkins had made it clear that an American declaration of war was still out of the question.[7]

Churchill had such high hopes that he brought with him a larger staff than Roosevelt. If he had known that Roosevelt was planning the conference in strict secrecy, not letting the public nor even his Secretaries of State known in advance, he would not have been so confident. The US Secretary of State, Cordell Hull, was – to his fury – neither informed nor invited, while Sumner Welles, the Under Secretary, played an important role.[8]

The venue was Argentia harbour in Newfoundland, where the United States was constructing one of the bases obtained in exchange for destroyers. On 9 August Churchill, on the newly commissioned battleship *Prince of Wales*, rendezvoused with the USS *Augusta*, which had the President on board. To Churchill's disappointment Roosevelt did not put on the agenda any new commitment which called for executive action. Instead Roosevelt only planned a propaganda move, which he put to Churchill at dinner on board the *Augusta* on the first night. A draft charter was ready, with pious declarations that America and Britain would 'concert' together to provide the means to resist Nazi aggression, and the two countries sought no territorial aggrandizement. After discussion the wording was agreed as 'they desire to see no territorial changes that do not accord with the freely expressed views of the people concerned', and 'they respect the right of all peoples to choose the form of Government under which they will live'. This right for nations to choose their own Government sounded fine, but Churchill later said it did not apply to India or the British Commonwealth, and when after their surrender the Italians asked if it could apply to them it was made clear that defeated nations were not included.

A minor disagreement came over a clause implying that free trade would be permitted by allowing all peoples free access on equal terms to the markets and raw materials of the world whenever it was necessary for 'economic prosperity'. Churchill, himself a free trader, knew that he would have no chance of persuading the British Conservative Party to renege on either the Commonwealth Preference of the Ottawa Agreement or the comprehensive import duties imposed by the Baldwin Government in 1932.

With his tongue in his cheek, Churchill reminded the Americans that Britain had adhered to free trade for eighty years in face of ever-mounting American tariffs. In the end the word 'trade' was substituted by 'markets' and the qualifying phrase 'with due respect for existing obligations' was added, thus making the free trade clause a non-event.[9]

In both Britain and America there was initial enthusiasm for the declaration which was given the high-sounding title of Atlantic Charter. But this feeling soon evaporated, as the meeting was not followed by any dramatic new American intervention in the war. The British general public took little interest in the declaration of post-war aims; they seemed too distant when Britain was fighting for survival.

The most revealing judgement on the Atlantic Charter comes from the diplomat Oliver Harvey, who recorded in his diary that it was

> a terrible woolly document full of the old clichés of the League of Nations period . . . There is obviously no alternative but to accept it woolly as it is. A. E. [Anthony Eden] considers that FDR has bowled the P.M. a very quick one – such a document might well have been communicated in advance. However I think it will go well in America where they like resounding phrases, and also in Liberal and Labour circles here – though A.E. said Bevin was very critical.[10]

At the Atlantic meeting discussions took place between the British and American Chiefs of Staff; these, too, were disappointing, and the British were 'distressed' to find that the allocation of heavy bombers to them had been reduced, which 'we consider a serious matter'. They were also concerned at the small numbers of Catalinas, the long-range flying boats which were of great value to Coastal Command, allocated during the next few months.[11]

Churchill reported on his Atlantic meeting to the War Cabinet as soon as he got back to London on 19 August. It was a period in the war when much had gone wrong for British arms in the Middle East and Far East. Probably in an attempt to buoy up his colleagues' spirits Churchill gave a misleading and over-optimistic report of his meeting with the President. His written account gives an impression of self-satisfaction. He claimed an astonishing depth to Roosevelt's intense desire for war, and said that if the American people, and especially Congress, were still determined to keep out of the conflict Roosevelt hoped to manoeuvre the Germans into giving the Americans no choice, and he made much of the fact that the US Navy was escorting convoys to Iceland. Churchill claimed the President had told him he would wage war but not declare it, and that he would become more and more provocative and 'he was obviously determined they should come in'.[12]

There is controversy over whether or not Churchill read too much into Roosevelt's words during their intimate conversations, but both he and his Cabinet colleagues were disconcerted when, at the President's first press conference after the meeting, Roosevelt stated: 'The conference involved no more than an exchange of views', and when asked 'if we were any closer to entry into the war' he responded with an emphatic 'No.' A further douche of cold water was poured on to the outcome of the Atlantic Conference by the Chiefs of Staff (COS) assessment: 'We neither expected nor achieved startling results. The American COS are quite clearly thinking in terms of the defence of the western hemisphere and have so far not formulated any joint strategy for the defeat of Germany.'[13]

Halifax summed up Roosevelt's stance after a candid interview with the President, writing:

Roosevelt told me what indeed we have always known, that his perpetual problem was to steer a course between the two factors represented by:

(1) The wish of 70 per cent of Americans to keep out of war;

(2) The wish of 70 per cent of Americans to do everything to break Hitler even if it means war.

He said that if he asked for a declaration of war he wouldn't get it, and opinion would swing against him. He therefore intended to go on doing whatever he best could to help us, and declarations of war were, he said, out of fashion.[14]

At the Atlantic Conference Roosevelt had given Churchill the impression he would order the US Navy to seek and attack German submarines, but he did not do so.

Fortuitously, America was soon drawn into the Atlantic war, as Churchill had hoped. In early September a British bomber radioed the position of a German submarine to the US destroyer *Greer* which was steaming towards Iceland. In accordance with instructions, the *Greer* tracked the submarine for four hours but did not attack it. When the pilot of the British bomber found that the *Greer* would not attack, it dropped depth charges and left. The German submarine, unaware of where the depth charges had come from or whether the *Greer* was British or American, fired a torpedo at the American ship, which dodged and fired depth charges. Roosevelt treated the *Greer* incident as an unprovoked attack; in a fireside chat he said it was 'piracy, legally and morally' – which was not strictly true – and gave the Navy an order to attack German vessels that were threatening convoys.

Hitler, who wanted to postpone war with America, did not give orders to retaliate, but on 16 October a German submarine torpedoed the US destroyer *Kearney*, with the loss of eleven lives. American public opinion was outraged, and Congress voted by 113 to 39 to arm merchantmen. Then, on 31 October, the Germans sank the US destroyer *Reuben James* with the loss of 100 sailors while it was protecting a convoy. These and other German attacks gave Roosevelt grounds to take up the position over Atlantic convoys into which Churchill had failed to persuade him in August.[15]

CHAPTER EIGHT

The Middle East and the
Balkans disaster 1940—41

IN THE late summer of 1940 Churchill had to deal with preparations to resist the German invasion of England, codenamed Sealion, the air 'Battle of Britain' and the Atlantic War. However the only point where land forces were engaged with the enemy was against Italy on the Egyptian–Libyan frontier. Churchill gave the Middle East his maximum concentration despite his other worries.

Italy had declared war on 10 June. In Libya and Tripoli the Italian forces under Marshal Graziani vastly outnumbered the British in Eygpt. Graziani's strength was 250,000. The British forces under General Wavell amounted to less than 90,000, including miscellaneous units in Sudan, Kenya and British Somaliland. Yet Wavell's 7th Armoured Division dominated the no man's land between the two armies and Graziani was too cautious to attack. Wavell sent to London long lists of deficiencies and requirements for his troops, and complained about 'sketchy' training and failure to comply with his requests. Churchill was dissatisfied with Wavell, especially over the dispersion of his troops; he yearned for a spectacular victory over the ill-trained and unenthusiastic Italian Army in the Western Desert, and was very critical of Wavell's troop dispositions, insisting that more divisions should be concentrated on the Libyan front.

Accordingly Winston summoned him to London after passing a tetchy minute to Ismay complaining of Wavell's inaction. Wavell arrived in London from Cairo on 8 August, and he and Churchill got on badly. Wavell wrote well but was a poor communicator, being taciturn in conversation. At their first meeting in Downing Street Churchill accused Wavell of contradicting himself over Graziani's intentions. Wavell replied firmly, 'I did not say that.' Churchill was furious, and with the Battle of Britain raging and a cross-Channel invasion probable he was at his most imperious and irascible.

Both Wavell and Churchill were wounded by the conversation; there were trivial faults on both sides, which became of great consequence. Afterwards Wavell told Dill that 'the Prime Minister had asked him down to Chequers for the weekend, but he would be damned if he would risk further treatment of the same kind'. Dill calmed him down, saying the Prime Minister carried an almost incredible burden and that 'although you have had unbearable provocation you can be replaced, whereas he cannot be. You must go to Chequers.' Wavell told Eden, the Secretary of State for War, that if Churchill did not approve his troops' dispositions he should appoint someone else. Churchill indeed asked Eden who could replace Wavell. Eden replied, 'Only Auchinleck', but managed to persuade the Prime Minister that a change of command in Cairo would have a very bad effect on Middle East morale.

It was sad that Churchill and Wavell got on so badly, because Churchill was full of ardour for an offensive in the desert and ready to the point of rashness to deprive the home army of tanks and equipment in order to make Wavell stronger. Churchill, whose temper was quick to flare, was seldom rancorous for long. Yet he never forgave or really trusted Wavell after their first encounter.[1]

In the London discussions Churchill expressed his grave disquiet at the large forces Wavell was keeping in Kenya, including the South African Brigade and West African Brigades which he considered ought to be valuable reinforcements for the Western Desert. Wavell replied that the South Africans were too short of training, which provoked the angry response from Churchill that they would be 'no inferior to British Territorial units. Anyhow they are good enough to fight Italians.' Churchill was also angry because Wavell kept Australians and New Zealanders for six months in Palestine instead of moving them to the key Egyptian frontier, saying, 'How disgraceful it would be if owing to our mis-handling of this important force only one Brigade took part' in the decisive Egyptian operations. Churchill put these comments into writing and then ordered Wavell to discuss them with him the same day. It was an unusual way to treat the country's most prestigious general.

However, as a result of Wavell's discussions at the War Office, Dill and Eden persuaded Churchill that over 150 tanks and 48 anti-tank guns should be sent to Wavell immediately. Churchill described this as 'a blood transfusion in face of a mortal danger', but it was of course weakening the home army who were desperately short of armour in the event of a German invasion. Churchill, however, had secret intelligence that this risk was diminishing. He wanted to send the tanks on a convoy through the Mediterranean, but Wavell objected that this was too risky and he would prefer to receive the armour intact and late. Churchill was again angry at this negative response, but as soon as Admirals Cunningham and Pound supported Wavell he gave way: the tanks went by the Cape and arrived safely with the minimum of delay.

In his memoirs Churchill wrote that he was grieved and vexed by Pound's caution, but he would not imperil his good relations with him by a formal appeal to the Cabinet to over-rule him.

It was a pity he did not have the same concern for Wavell's feelings. If he had, the course of the war in the Mediterranean in 1941 might have been more favourable. Wavell left London on 15 August, and on the 23rd in Cairo he received an unprecedented document of precise orders from Churchill. Wavell observed that this showed: 'Winston did not trust me to run my own show and was set on his own ideas.' In his memoirs Churchill records: 'While not in full agreement with General Wavell's use of the resources at his disposal I thought it best to leave him in command.'

The instructions forwarded to Wavell contained details of how the Prime

Minister thought his resources should be used; Wavell complied with the majority, and as result greatly improved his potential strength for an attack on Graziani's army. Churchill's main criticism was the gap between the ration strength and the fighting strength. Here Churchill was on strong ground, and Wavell remedied the deficiency.[2]

Not only did Churchill imperiously order Wavell to move specified units from Palestine and Kenya to Egypt, but in addition he gave detailed instructions to make the desert wells on the Italian side of the frontier undrinkable, and to make the tarmac coast road impassable. Many of Churchill's instructions were impracticable. In reply Wavell was statesmanlike. Much as he must have wanted to challenge head on this infringement of his authority he later decided, as he wrote, to 'carry out such parts of the directive as were practicable and useful, and disregard a great deal of it'. Tactfully he spread out his reply in four different cables between 23 and 27 August.

Churchill's brush with Wavell produced magnetic results. Taking to heart criticisms of his slackness and lack of drive, Wavell decided to launch an offensive against Graziani. Early in September, while his reinforcement of tanks was still rounding the Cape, he began plans for this operation, known as Compass. It was to be a dramatic success, shattering Mussolini's North African empire and setting Churchill temporarily aglow with praise for Wavell and his army.

Meanwhile Mussolini had prodded Graziani into an offensive against Egypt. Ciano, Mussolini's deputy Foreign Secretary, noted in his diary: 'Never has a military operation been undertaken so much against the will of the Commander.' Graziani's attack started on 13 September; but the Italians did not expect to drive Britain out of Egypt. Wavell allowed the Italians to advance, while he inflicted considerable casualties on them; Sollum and Sidi Barrani fell. Here Graziani halted and his offensive was over. No attempt was made to proceed the further 75 miles along the coast to Mersa Matruh.

On 24 September 1940 the convoy of tanks and guns sanctioned in August arrived in the Middle East. The heavy Matilda tanks of 7 Royal Tank Regiment had armour which the Italian guns could not penetrate. Wavell now planned his Compass counter-offensive in great secrecy, not even letting Churchill know; he was risking further rage from the Prime Minister who, Wavell noted: 'always liked to have one finger in any military pie, and I did not want to arouse premature hopes'. Cairo and Alexandria were, of course, leaking sieves for Italian spies. Meanwhile Eden arrived in Cairo on 15 October. In their first discussions Wavell did not tell him of his now advanced plans for Compass. However, on 28 October Mussolini attacked Greece. Eden, although War Minister, was always more interested in diplomacy than military affairs and began suggesting that Wavell should divert troops and supplies from the desert to Greece. Horrified at this prospect, although until then he had no intention of informing his masters, Wavell was forced to reveal his plans for Compass by *force majeure*. As soon as Eden got back in London with news of Compass, Churchill declared 'he was purring like six cats', saying that 'now we will wrest the initiative from the enemy and impose our will upon him'. He approved Compass without hesitation.

Wavell would not, however, reveal the D-Day for the operation. During a meeting of the Defence Committee on 4 December Churchill became angry over this refusal; he criticized Eden for not asking Wavell the date and made complaints against Wavell and the army as a whole. Eden replied that he did not believe in fussing Wavell, saying that 'he knew our view, he had best be left to get on with it'. In his memoirs Eden wrote, 'This did not suit W [Churchill]. Dill was angry at his attitude'.[3]

To Wavell's irritation, on 26 November Churchill told him he had instructed the War Office to prepare 'a staff study of possibilities open to us if all goes well for moving troops and also reserves forward by sea in long hops along the coast and setting up new supply bases to which pursuing armoured vehicles might resort'. Officially he asked Wavell if all this had been 'weighed, explored and as far as possible prepared'. This must have been excessively galling to Wavell, who was beset by all the problems of Compass and was also making plans which he kept secret from the Prime Minister, to capture Abyssinia and Somaliland. (British Somaliland had been taken by the Italians, to Churchill's extreme annoyance.)

In his final paragraph Churchill added, ominously for Wavell's plans for East Africa, 'One may indeed see possibility of centre of gravity in Middle East shifting suddenly from Egypt to the Balkans and Cairo to Constantinople. You are no doubt preparing your mind for this and we are also having a staff study made here.' As Wavell's inadequate forces were already stretched to the limit, this was a grave threat to his carefully worked out plans to attack the Italians both in the Western Desert and in East Africa.[4]

In this signal of 26 November Churchill wrote to Wavell: 'As we told you the other day we shall stand by you and Wilson [General Officer Commanding Cyrenaica] in any well conceived action irrespective of result because no-one can guarantee success in war, but only deserve it.' Unfortunately for Wavell, Churchill did not stand by his comforting words and, as will be seen when all went wrong, decided to jettison Wavell.

Churchill minuted to the Chiefs of Staff that they must attach 'greatest importance' to the paragraph in his message to Wavell about bringing up fresh troops by sea, and pointed out that Wavell's reply did not take 'any account of this; it would be a crime to have amphibious power and leave it unused'. He wanted the study, if favourable, to be telegraphed to Wavell urgently. The Chiefs of Staff, however, managed to spare Wavell a further irritation at the moment of tension before his big offensive.

Under pressure from Churchill to disclose D-Day for Compass, Wavell signalled to the War Office on 6 December, 'Feel undue hopes are being placed on this operation which was designed as raid only. We are greatly outnumbered on the ground, and in air have to move over seventy-five miles of desert and attack enemy who has fortified himself for three months. Please do not encourage optimism.'

Churchill showed his mistrust of Wavell by immediately minuting to the CIGS that 'naturally' he was shocked, and 'I trust your explanation of it will be realized. If with the situation as it is General Wavell is only playing small and is not hurling his whole valuable force with furious energy, he will have failed to rise to the height of circumstances. I never "worry" about action, but only about inaction.' Wavell's signal was purposefully misleading, and reveals the lack of understanding between him and the Prime Minister.[5]

Compass began at dawn on 9 December and was an undreamt of success. Within three days the whole Italian line from Sofafi to Sidi Barrani had been rolled up; by the evening of the 11th 38,300 POWs had been taken for a loss of 624 killed, wounded and missing. On 3 January Bardia was attacked; it fell after forty-eight hours, costing the Italians 40,000 men. Compass had eliminated eight enemy divisions in under a month. On 22 January the valuable harbour of Tobruk with its fresh water distillation plant was captured, along with another 25,000 POWs. Bardia gave Wavell the forward administration base he needed for a further advance. By 29 January Compass had succeeded far beyond any expectations because Benghazi fell; this was the end of the Italian desert army. During the progress of Compass a total of ten Italian divisions were eliminated and 130,000 POWs taken.

On 10 February Wavell told the War Office that he might be able to capture Tripoli. That would be the end of the Axis presence in North Africa, and Allied troops would be next to Darlan in Tunisia. But Churchill forbade the attack on Tripoli. He cabled Wavell on 12 February, ordering him to make his 'major effort to aid Greece and/or Turkey. This rules out any serious effort against Tripoli . . . you should therefore make yourself secure at Benghazi and concentrate all available forces in the [Nile] Delta for movement to Europe.'[6]

Hitler insisted on the Italians defending Sirte, but the Italian generals did not believe a stand could be made in front of Tripoli; all they could do was to turn the place into a fortified camp. However, German aircraft were making life difficult for the Allies, and on 12 February Rommel arrived in Tripoli with a Panzer division, so that the whole situation in North Africa was irretrievably altered to Britain's disadvantage.

General Sir John Kennedy, Director of Military Operations, has recorded that Wavell made a mistake in not sending a small force to Tripoli 'in a bold attempt to seize this great prize, and diversion of such a force would not have affected his ability to operate in Greece'. Kennedy's view was that, with Tripoli taken, the enemy could have been kept out of North Africa for the rest of the war, and occupation of the shore would have 'given us control' of the sea communications in the eastern Mediterranean. When Wavell's offensive had opened Churchill had cabled to him that his task was 'to rip the Italian army from the African shores'; now, with Tripoli nearly in Wavell's grasp, Churchill refused to listen to the arguments of Dill and Kennedy that it should be taken.[7]

Instead, Churchill told Wavell to make available for Greece four divisions out of his Middle East forces. As the desert army had already been depleted by the detachment of 4th Indian Division to Eritrea, Wavell had insufficient troops to advance on Tripoli and inadequate numbers to make Benghazi secure. In fact two Indian divisions had gone to Kenya and the Sudan for the East African expedition, and although this campaign quickly liquidated Eritrea and Italian East Africa in a victory as startling as his success in the Western Desert, they tied up those forces which could have taken Tripoli. For example, at Keren a hundred thousand shells were fired in the final stages of the battle, and a thousand trucks were needed for their transport. The Indian divisions would have been better employed in the Western Desert. Churchill was ambivalent and contradictory about the East African campaign when Wavell eventually let him hear about it. At first the Prime Minister said the Italians should have been 'allowed to rot' (as they would have done); then he demanded a quick victory to release troops for the Mediterranean. Even one of the Indian divisions would have enabled Wavell to capture Tripoli.[8]

To Churchill's surprise, in January 1941 Hiter decided to support the Italians in Greece with German troops from Romania and Bulgaria. The Italian invasion of Greece had been anything but successful. Instead of racing for the key port of Salonika, the Italians tried to fight their way south from Albania into the strategically worthless region of Epirus down to the Gulf of Arta; if they ever reached it their plan was to march on Athens. Their offensive got nowhere; torrential rain delayed them, and Mussolini had not provided the necessary engineers and bridging equipment. The outbreak of war between Greece and Italy had enabled the British to occupy Crete, and Churchill was overjoyed at the British Fleet being able to anchor in Suda Bay.

Hitler had two main objectives in entering Greece. The first was to prevent the British occupying air bases in Crete and Greece which would threaten the Italian route to Tripoli. This in turn would give Germany the necessary air bases for what became, as will be seen, his abortive plan to dominate Iraq and Syria which he wanted to secure before his invasion of Russia.[9]

If Churchill had decided only to occupy Crete and fortify it against German attack the island might have been successfully defended, but instead, after much heart-searching, Churchill plumped for an expeditionary force to go into Greece. The results were disastrous.

As early as 10 January Churchill instructed Wavell to give Greece the maximum possible assistance against Italy: 'nothing must hamper capture of Tobruk, but thereafter all operations in Libya are subordinated to aiding Greece'. On the 13th, before Tobruk had fallen, Wavell conferred with the Greek Government in Athens; he was much relieved when they turned down Churchill's proferred aid against the Italians for fear it would provoke the Germans to attack them. Then Churchill, faced with this ungracious reply to his offer, authorized Wavell to press on to Benghazi; however, for Wavell it was a foretaste of what was to come.

Meanwhile the War Office learnt from interrupted signals that Germany was preparing to invade Greece. On 10 February the War Cabinet recorded that they refused to allow Wavell to advance to Tripoli, and that because on 13 April 1939 Britain had given Greece a guarantee she must have precedence over Tripoli if Germany attacked. According to Dill, Churchill lost his temper with him at this meeting when the CIGS gave his view that 'all the troops in the Middle East are fully employed and none available for Greece'. Churchill retorted in a rage: 'What you need out there is a Court Martial and a firing squad. Wavell has 300,000 men, etc. etc.' This outburst is not recorded in the minutes. According to Kennedy, at this stage of the war, when Britain had lost almost all her battles, Churchill developed the idiosyncrasy of talking about 'shooting Generals'. It was a vent for his feelings, and no one took him seriously.

It was decided that Eden and Dill should fly out to the Middle East. Churchill ordered Wavell 'to get in a position . . . to offer to transfer to Greece the fighting portion of the army which has hitherto defended Egypt, and make every plan for sending and reinforcing it to the limit'.[10]

Churchill quickly had cold feet over this momentous decision. From Ultra he learnt that the Germans were landing in Tripoli, and he feared the Greeks would quickly make peace in the event of a German invasion. He told the War Cabinet on 18 February that if the Greeks made peace the British would have 'to content ourselves by making our position in the Greek islands as strong as possible, and the question of advancing into Tripoli would again arise'. He then cabled to Eden and Dill in Cairo: 'Do not feel obligated to the Greek enterprise if in your hearts you feel it will only be another Norwegian fiasco.' However, as Churchill turned dubious over the Greek adventure, Eden became optimistic.[11]

Eden flew to Athens, where the Greek commanding general repeated his misgivings that insufficient British military help would merely precipitate the German attack. However the King, the Prime Minister and General Papagos thought differently and the British and Greek Governments came to the conclusion that the seventy-mile 'Aliakhmon position', running from the sea west of the Vardar river north-west to the Yugoslav border, was the only possible line that could be held. This meant sacrificing Salonika, and it was agreed the Greeks should immediately withdraw from the Albanian front against the Italians to the Aliakhmon Line while British troops would move from Egypt to join them there. The Aliakhmon line had the great advantage of being short and naturally strong.

On 24 February a momentous meeting of the War Cabinet took place. Spread on the table were optimistic signals from Wavell and Dill, together with the COS assessment. They favoured going ahead. Churchill covered himself by emphasizing his telegram to Eden about avoiding 'another Norwegian fiasco, and that Wavell was in favour although he was inclined to understatement and so far had always promised less than he had performed and was a man who wished to be better than his word'. He also stressed the fact that Dill had changed his view and was now in favour, although he had previously doubted whether 'Germany would be successfully resisted'.

After much discussion, with Australian Prime Minister Menzies, who was visiting London, expressing doubts, Churchill asked the ministers to give their individual views; all were in favour of sending troops. Churchill cabled Eden that evening: 'Full steam ahead.' On 4 March the first detachments sailed from Cairo for Greece: Operation Lustre was in progress.[12]

In London Churchill faced another agonizing day of decision. There was still time to call Lustre off, as the troop ships would not arrive in Greece for four days. He told the War Cabinet:

> Bulgaria was now under German control. It looked as though Greece would have to fight for her life and as though Yugoslavia intended to take no action before she was surrounded . . . his doubts had returned but as General Dill and General Wilson wished the movement to proceed I would be most disinclined to give countermanding orders. Nevertheless I still think the Cabinet might wish to take a final view of the whole situation.[13]

The next day a long, alarming signal came from Eden in Athens. The Greeks had failed to withdraw and take up positions on the Aliakhmon line where the British troops were to be committed. Instead Papagos wanted to hold a line further forward near the Macedonian border, and there was no time to prepare fortifications there. Eden had been tempted to withdraw 'our offer of military support altogether'. It would have been much better if he had. Instead, he had agreed that the Aliakhmon line should be manned by the British with a few Greek troops in support. Churchill signalled to Eden asking for further information, failing which, he warned, the War Cabinet 'would probably seek to change Eden's decision'. Churchill went on: 'We must be careful not to urge Greece against her better judgement into a hopeless resistance alone when we have only a handful of troops which can reach the scene in time . . . we must liberate Greeks from feeling bound to reject a German ultimatum.' In conclusion he again warned Eden that the War Cabinet might cancel Lustre 'tomorrow'.

The Greeks had decided to fight, buoyed up by the promise of British support. Churchill's dilemma was that he now realized Lustre was a bad operation of war, but Britain had committed herself in honour to Greece. After further long and painful discussions in the War Cabinet Churchill cabled to Eden: 'We must not take on our shoulders responsibility of urging the Greeks against their better judgement to fight a hopeless battle, . . . if however knowing how little we can send at particular dates, they resolve to fight to the death, obviously we must, as I have already said, share their ordeal.'[14]

Churchill never received a purely military appreciation from either the Chiefs of Staff or Wavell, although he had called for one. All the Service advice had been coloured by political considerations – a dangerous procedure. Although Dill and Wavell had become converted in favour of the action in Greece the Director of Military Operations, Kennedy, who stayed in London, was opposed. While Dill was away in the Middle East, Kennedy attended the War Cabinet and Chiefs of Staff in his place; he pressed his objection as far as he could, but without avail. Pound now favoured Greece, and his view always had great influence on Churchill.

In the War Cabinet on 7 March after Pound had said 'our military advisers on the spot were convinced that the Greek campaign would not be a hopeless venture. The Chiefs of Staff are prepared to accept their judgement that the campaign should go ahead', Churchill listed the considerations which 'seemed to him important'. To the historian, with hindsight they seem frail.

We had a fair chance of reaching the Aliakhmon line in time to check the German advance. If so there might be a pause while the enemy brought up new forces. The Yugoslavs are adopting a cryptic attitude but we need not despair entirely of their entry into the war on our side. If the Anglo–Greek force were compelled to retire from the Aliakhmon line they would be retiring down a narrowing peninsula which contained a number of strong defensive positions. We should shortly have strong airforces in Greece. They would be outnumbered by the enemy's airforces but the odds would not be greater than they had been on many occasions in the last few months.

He went on that British policy could not be presented as having forced the Greeks into making hopeless resistance, and his view was: 'We should go forward with a good heart.'

In his memoirs Churchill does not quote the above words in Cabinet on 7 March. Within a few days his military appreciation, especially on the air situation, was proved nonsensical. However, that day he had managed to convince himself, probably against his better judgement. He concluded: 'The time has come for taking decisions. In his view it was our duty to go forward.' His colleagues, including Menzies, agreed, and he signalled to Eden: 'Cabinet decided to authorize you to proceed with the operation, and by doing so Cabinet accepted for itself the fullest responsibility.'

When the 7 March War Cabinet was over, a telegram arrived from Eden: 'We are all convinced not only that there is a reasonable fighting chance, but that we have here an opportunity if fortune favours of perhaps seriously upsetting the German plans. It very much depends on the air.' This was a false appreciation, especially over 'the air'. RAF strength in Greece was eighty operational aircraft: the Germans had eight hundred.[16]

Undoubtedly Churchill wanted to cancel Lustre at the eleventh hour but he did not, partly on account of honour and partly because of the misleading advice about its military potential received from Eden after Wavell and Dill, who had originally been strongly opposed, had changed their minds. Wavell's conversion is hard to explain. Perhaps he felt he could not stand up to any more hectoring from Churchill, who always wanted an attacking policy, and at first had too hastily jumped to the conclusion that Greece ought to have precedence over Tripoli. Dill summed it up: 'The Prime Minister had led the hunt before we left England . . . by the time he had begun to doubt, the momentum was too great. The offer had been made to the Greeks and the troops were in motion.'[17]

Had Wavell advised from Cairo against the Greek venture he could have killed it, despite Churchill's original enthusiasm. On 6 April a meeting was held with Wavell, Cunningham, Eden and Dill to discuss Lustre in light of Churchill's last-minute doubts. Eden turned to Wavell and said: 'It is soldiers' business; it is for you to say.' Wavell's reply was: 'War is an option of difficulties. We go.' Thus in the end neither Eden nor Churchill was primarily responsible for the disastrous decision. It was Wavell's responsibility. On the next day Eden cabled to Churchill: 'Situation Western Desert serious'.[18]

Yugoslavia had signed a tripartite pact with Germany and Italy in Vienna on

26 March. This was a blow to Churchill's hopes of Yugoslavia joining with Britain, but he suddenly became optimistic when the pro-Axis Yugoslav Government was unexpectedly overthrown in a coup in Belgrade the next day. For a few days Churchill saw a golden chance of uniting Greece and Yugoslavia with Britain, and thought this might deter Hitler from attacking Greece.[19] Instead Hitler flew into one of his most frenzied rages and ordered Yugoslavia to be destroyed as a nation, without warning and with 'merciless harshness'. The remains were to be tossed to Hungary, Romania and Italy.

General Simonovitch became President of the Yugoslav Council; he was ready to receive Dill in Belgrade, but not Eden because he was most anxious not to provoke Hitler into war. Nothing resulted from an abortive meeting between British, Greek and Yugoslav generals on 3 and 4 April near the Yugoslav–Greek frontier, and on the 6th the Germans attacked simultaneously both Greece and Yugoslavia in great strength and with barbarous bombing.

Wavell's approval of the Greek project had been based on the belief that not only would the Greeks supply a considerable number of infantry divisions on the agreed line, but that his western flank beyond Benghazi was secure. Regrettably he did not do his homework on the ground west of Benghazi. As a result of Lustre the Western Desert Force at Benghazi was shockingly weak in anti-tank weapons, and the R A F were completely outnumbered by Luftwaffe bombers from Sicily, the Dodecanese and Tripoli.

In mid-March there were signs of the growing German presence on the Cyrenaica frontier. It was thought they might be preparing a full-scale attack, although shortage of transport and administrative difficulties made it unlikely that it would be anything but a limited advance. But they reached Agheila on 25 March. On the 26th Churchill cabled to Wavell: 'We are naturally concerned at rapid German advance to Agheila . . . I presume you are only waiting for the tortoise to stick his head out far enough before chopping it off.'[20]

Wavell's response on the following day showed he was rueing his decision to go into Greece, and Churchill must have realized that the Government's plan to deplete Cyrenaica of troops for the benefit of Greece was a gamble which might turn into a disaster. Wavell replied:

I have to admit to having taken considerable risk in Cyrenaica after capture of Benghazi in order to provide maximum support for Greece . . . after we had accepted Greek liability evidence began to accumulate of German reinforcements which were coupled with attacks on Malta which prevented bombing of Tripoli upon which I had counted . . . result is I am weak in Cyrenaica at present and no reinforcements of armoured troops which are our chief requirement are at present available.

Happily on the same day Keren and Harare were captured from the Italians in East Africa, and Churchill was able to cable Wavell 'congratulations on his double success'.[21]

However by 4 April Rommel had forced the British out of Benghazi, and by the 11th he was on the Egyptian frontier except for an Australian garrison which was invested at Tobruk. This was the precise disaster which Wavell and Churchill had dreaded ever since it had been decided to transfer forces from the desert to Greece. Churchill sent a supportive message to Wavell: 'Press and public have taken evacuation of Benghazi well.'

Nevertheless Churchill administered an unkind snub to Wavell at the very moment when his worries over Cyrenaica and Greece were at their peak. On 7 April he instructed Wavell:

> Inconvenience is caused by your issue from Cairo of communiqués which some-times reverse what we have been told to say here, and which in other cases have not struck the right note for our public. London is the place where opinion has to be held. Actually there is more complaint today about a Cairo communiqué belittling the value of Benghazi than about its loss. I wish you therefore to send your communiqués to WO in plain language and let us handle them for all concerned including Egypt and Australia.[22]

The inference that he and his staff were incompetent in their press releases must have been a bitter pill for Wavell after all the other pinpricks he had suffered from Churchill. He meekly complied. His successor, General Auchinleck, would have none of it. On 20 November, at the height of the Crusader battle, Auchinleck curtly informed Churchill that no more press communiqués were to be issued in London because their editing in the War Office was 'dangerous'; he insisted that 'a communiqué is a weapon which can be used against the enemy'. In face of this Churchill had no option but to agree, but as always he itched to control all press releases.[23]

Alarmed at the loss of Benghazi, Winston wired to Eden, who was in Athens:

> Evacuation Benghazi serious as Germans once established in aerodromes there-abouts will probably deny us use of Tobruk. Find out what is strategic and tactical plan to chop the enemy . . . far more important than the loss of ground is the idea that we cannot face the enemy Germans and that their appearance is enough to drive us back many scores of miles. This may react most evilly throughout Balkans and Turkey. Pray go back to Cairo.

At that moment the New Zealand Division was following the British 1st Armoured Brigade into Greece, and the staff talks with Yugoslavia at Florina were getting nowhere. Churchill must already have been rueing the decision to go into Greece, but it was almost impossible to turn back, despite the fact that Wavell warned repeatedly that the desert situation was deteriorating fast and he was trying to withdraw his forces faster than Rommel was advancing.

Soon Rommel had bypassed Tobruk and was threatening the Egyptian frontier. Apart from Tobruk, Wavell was back to his start line against the Italians the previous December. Churchill signalled to Wavell on 7 April: 'You should surely be able to hold Tobruk'; Wavell replied: 'I propose to hold Tobruk . . . my resources are very limited especially of armoured troops and of anti-tank and AA guns. It will be a race against time.' Churchill attached much more importance to holding Tobruk than did Wavell, cabling from London to Cairo on 13 April: 'Tobruk seems to be an invaluable bridgehead for offensive punches against all passers by . . . This is one of the crucial fights in the history of the British army'; again that day the Prime Minister cabled: 'Bravo Tobruk. We feel it vital that Tobruk should be regarded as a sallyport and not please as an excrescence.'[24]

The War Office insisted on Wavell providing details of the disaster for the Prime Minister. He explained on 25 April that 3rd Armoured Brigade and Infantry Brigade near Benghazi 'had not settled down to desert fighting', and 3rd Armoured completely disappeared as a fighting force because they melted away from tank breakdowns and the 'unpractised Headquarters (sic) after they had gone the wrong way left 1 Independent Motor Brigade at Mechili without armoured support so that it was captured'. Wavell added he was 'not aware of the bad mechanical state of the Crusader tanks', and that the exploitation of the initial success by Rommel was 'unexpected' because captured documents showed at first that he did not intend it. Wavell was much distressed because Generals O'Connor and Neame, who had played a prominent part in the success earlier in the year, had been captured. He concluded 'the above is outline of the disastrous episode for which the main responsibility is mine'.[25] It is astonishing that Churchill was able to follow the minutiae of the battle with all his other occupations. He cabled back to Wavell: 'We seem to have had bad luck', but he felt Wavell had conducted the battle badly.

Lustre was an even worse military disaster than Cyrenaica. Within one and a half hours of declaring war mass German bombing formations destroyed Belgrade, while Hitler's armies rapidly overwhelmed the Yugoslavs, Greeks and British. On 16 April Papagos suggested the departure of the British force, and Wavell agreed with the full approval of the Greek Government, to evacuate on the 21st. Three days later embarkation began and continued until the night of 28–29 April. Fifty thousand out of sixty-two thousand troops engaged in Lustre were successfully evacuated, but the losses in tanks, guns, artillery and equipment were crippling.

During the evacuation from Greece twenty thousand troops were taken to Crete, mainly because it was nearer and there was a quicker turnround of ships. But Wavell had failed to make adequate preparations to defend Crete. There was a weak garrison of ten thousand troops already, but virtually no tanks, artillery or AA guns. Before the fall of France there was an Allied understanding that, if Italy declared war on Greece, French troops would garrison the island. Probably this was the reason why Wavell and his staff never saw the need to carry out a study of how the island ought to be defended.

As soon as Italy declared war on Greece in October 1940 Churchill, always enthusiastic over the prospect of the Royal Navy being able to use the Suda Bay anchorage off Crete, expressed his delight in various communications. On 26 November Churchill had written to Wavell that he rejoiced because the commanders in the Middle East felt Suda Bay 'an inestimable benefit'. And on 1 December he minuted to Dill: 'Possession of Suda Bay has made an enormous change in the Eastern Mediterranean', especially because it safeguarded Malta.[26] He also sent the War Office a succession of notes in which he directed them to give Wavell detailed instructions about the defence of the island, even specifying the number of battalions to garrison it. Dill objected strongly, saying it would be quite wrong for London to dictate to Cairo the strength of the garrison; and, after the Chiefs of Staff Committee had backed Dill, Churchill agreed that all that was necessary was a telegram to Wavell drawing his attention to the importance of securing Crete but making clear that the size of the garrison was his responsibility. Unfortunately Churchill, perhaps piqued at being over-ruled, never returned to the subject until Greece was evacuated seven months later.

Crete should have been turned into a fortress. Unfortunately the defence had low priority for Wavell amid the daunting tasks before his inadequate forces. Not even the usual naval defence was provided for Suda Bay. By 19 April there were only four Hurricanes and three Gladiators on the island (originally there had been six Hurricanes and seventeen obsolete aircraft). The Luftwaffe had overwhelming superiority in the air over Crete. Fighters based in Egypt could spare very little time over the island because of the distance, and the nearer air bases in Cyrenaica had been lost; the Germans, or the other hand, could operate at short range from the Greek mainland as well as Rhodes, Leros and Cos. Athens was only 200 miles from Crete, as were the newly captured German aerodromes on the Libyan coast, while Cos and Leros were 150 miles away.

Churchill made Wavell entrust the defence to the New Zealand General B. C. Freyberg V C. After visiting Crete on 30 April Wavell described its defence as 'a difficult and dangerous commitment'. Churchill did not see it like that, but on 1 May Freyberg signalled Wavell:

> Forces at my disposal are totally inadequate to meet attack envisaged. Unless fighter aircraft are greatly increased and naval forces made available to deal with seaborne attack I cannot hope to hold out with land forces alone . . . If for other reasons these cannot be made available at once, urge that question of holding Crete should be reconsidered. I feel that under terms of my charter it is my duty to inform New Zealand Government of situation.'

As a result the New Zealand Government urged London that either their troops should be supplied with sufficient means to defend the island, or the decision to hold it at all costs should be reviewed.[27]

Churchill replied firmly, pointing out the important contribution that the defence of Crete would make to Egypt's security. He thought a seaborne attack unlikely to succeed, and as for an airborne attack this should suit the New Zealanders down to the ground for 'they will then be able to come to close quarters man to man with the enemy who will not have the advantage of the tanks and artillery on which he so largely relies'. Churchill overlooked the fact that the defenders would have almost no tanks, although he admitted that the British air strength would be 'scant'.

On 20 May the Germans launched their airborne attack on Crete. The paratroopers were protected by masses of dive bombers, which made it imposs- ible for the British to launch counter-attacks in daylight. For two days Maleme airport, the main target of the attack, was denied to them, but on the third day

German troop carriers were using it and the rout began. Churchill was particularly concerned because tanks could not be used against the Germans on
Maleme aerodrome, and according to Colville lamented very strongly on 23 May
that the tanks which he had asked Wavell to send to Crete were not sent – 'they
might have made all the difference to the battle'. Again, at dinner on the 25th he
criticized Wavell very heavily 'about tanks for Crete', also complaining that 'the
Middle East had been very badly managed, and [he] thought Cunningham was
shirking his task of preventing a seaborne landing on Crete since he 'fears severe
losses from bombing'.

General Robert Laycock, later Chief of Combined Operations, had been in
charge of the commandos in Crete. He was a favourite of Churchill's and after his
return lunched with Churchill at Chequers, where he told the Prime Minister
that 'a dozen tanks could have saved Crete'. Churchill had besought Wavell
unavailingly to spare tanks for Crete, and Laycock sealed his fellow general's
fate.[28]

As the British defenders in Crete crumbled Churchill exhorted Wavell to
greater efforts with 'Crete battle must be won. Even if enemy secures good
lodgements fighting must be maintained indefinitely in the island with us keeping
enemy main striking force tied down . . . hope you will reinforce Crete every
night to fullest extent. Is it not possible to send more tanks and thus reconquer
any captured aerodrome?' He made the Chiefs of Staff signal to Wavell:
'Imperative that reinforcements in greatest strength possible should be sent as
soon as possible to island . . . the vital importance of the battle is well known to
you, and great risks must be accepted to ensure our success.'

The Navy was accomplishing wonders in preventing seaborne landings on the
north coast of Crete, in spite of continuous bombing by the Luftwaffe from their
nearby aerodromes. But, after Cunningham had lost two cruisers and four
destroyers sunk, plus one battleship put out of action for months and two other
cruisers and four destroyers considerably damaged, he could not allow the fleet to
operate to the north of the island in daylight. On 24 May he cabled the Admiralty
that he was forced to the 'melancholy conclusion that owing to our weakness in
the air we must admit defeat in the coastal area and the naval losses in preventing
German landings were not justified'. The Prime Minister refused to agree to this
and signalled Cunningham to take 'more drastic naval action'. The Fleet and the
RAF, he said, must 'accept whatever risk is entailed' in preventing the Germans
reaching Crete by sea by night or day, and 'it will be essential for the Fleet to
operate north of the island by day even though the losses incurred in doing so will
be considerable'.

Cunningham and his naval staff deeply resented this message. In a private
letter to Pound, Cunningham wrote that if the Prime Minister or the Admiralty
would like a change of command he would not feel 'in any way annoyed', while in
an official reply he reported that the 'effect of recent operations on personnel is
cumulative. Our light craft, officers, men and machinery alike are nearing
exhaustion. Since Lustre started at the end of February they have been kept
running almost to the limit of endurance and now, when work is redoubled, they

are faced with an air concentration beside which, I am assured, Norway was child's play.'[29]

Churchill had gone too far; his bullying of his Middle East commanders was demoralizing not only them, but also the Service Chiefs and staff in Whitehall as a result of his irresponsible orders and prodding. Kennedy recorded:

> at this time criticism of Churchill was 'bitter and general' because we were living from hand to mouth on a diet of improvisation and opportunism with no clear cut military appreciations laid before the War Cabinet, while military opinions were distorted by Churchill's formidable advocacy. Menzies while in London was the most formidable of his critics. But nearly all agreed Churchill's magnificcent and courageous leadership compensated for his deplorable strategy.[30]

Churchill's 'magnificent leadership and courage' was useless as far as Crete was concerned. The island was lost even before he signalled Cunningham, and Churchill's irresponsible exhortations only intensified the resentment felt towards him in the moment of defeat.

On 26 May Freyberg told Wavell: 'Our situation is hopeless. Provided a decision is taken at once a certain proportion of force might be embarked.' Wavell pressed Freyberg to make one more effort to drive the enemy back, and even if this failed not to evacuate immediately but to retire to new positions, adding that 'it should thus be possible to hold enemy for some time'. However, he sent a warning signal to Churchill: 'Matter is in balance and doubtful if we can retain permanent hold.' In the early hours of the 27th Churchill sent a last despairing signal back: 'Victory in Crete essential at this turning point in the war. Keep hurling in all aid you can.' But it was too late for exhortation.

Fortunately 18,000 UK, Australian and New Zealand troops were safely evacuated out of around 32,000. But British Army casualties amounted to 1800 killed and as many wounded, and 12,000 became POWs. Royal Navy casualties were over 1800 killed. On the other side of the account, German casualties were over 6000; and there were such heavy losses in planes that Hitler did not attempt another airborne operation during the war.

With hindsight Churchill's decision to defend Crete was clearly wrong, and Freyberg was correct. Even if the island had been held against the initial assault it could not have been held indefinitely. Naval losses from Luftwaffe bombing would have been unsustainable, and the RAF could do little from distant aerodromes in Egypt against the masses of German planes operating from nearby bases.

In the War Cabinet that morning Churchill told his colleagues that all chances of winning the battle in Crete had gone and Britain faced the prospect of the loss of most of its forces there. They then discussed how to present this dire news to the British public, and Churchill proposed a delay. His colleagues agreed he should only say to the Commons that 'hard fighting' was going on in Crete, and that the enemy had air superiority. Fortunately Churchill was able to announce in the House that afternoon that the *Bismarck* had been sunk, which produced wild cheers reminiscent of those that greeted Chamberlain's announcement of Hitler's invitation to come to Munich.

That evening at the meeting of the Defence Committee Churchill gave the news that Wavell had ordered evacuation, to which he had reluctantly concurred. However he showed the characteristic resilience which he always displayed after a disaster by turning to the wider Middle East situation, saying that 'the first essential was to defeat the German army in Libya'.[31] The evacuation meant that with Crete on one flank and Cyrenaica on the other, the British Mediterranean Fleet had to run the gauntlet of air attack every time it tried to send a ship to Malta or to venture into the central Mediterranean; whereas until Crete's fall the Malta and Alexandria convoys had been escorted through with minimum losses.

On 10 June the Commons debated Crete; it was comparable to the previous year's debate on Norway, but this time no one demanded a change of Premier and there was no division. Churchill argued that Crete was 'an extremely important salient in our line of defence'. Here he was on weak ground, but no one suggested it would have been better to evacuate it without fighting. In the Commons, the Prime Minister defended the actions of his commanders but in private he was gravely dissatisfied, feeling that Wavell had never had a real grip on the operation. He instructed the Chiefs of Staff to put in hand a detailed enquiry, and himself issued an elaborate questionnaire for Middle East Command to answer. The New Zealand and Australian Governments were perturbed at their troops' defeat and heavy losses, and their confidence in Churchill was shaken.

CHAPTER NINE

Keyes, Turkey and Iraq

ADMIRAL ROGER KEYES had a great influence on Churchill. Both were enthusiastic for dramatic amphibious landings. No one should stint their praise for Keyes' dash and gallantry especially when he commanded the raid on U-Boat bases at Zeebrugge and Ostend in 1918. He had any amount of drive and courage, but little modesty. As soon as the war began in 1939 he bombarded Churchill with demands for actions in which he would be the commander. Colville writes that he caused the maximum irritation in Whitehall with the minimum of useful results. For a time Churchill was blind to Keyes' faults, and it was only the solid opposition of the Chiefs of Staff and Ismay which finally dissuaded Churchill from making him, when Keyes was long past his prime, Chairman of the Chiefs of Staff Committee.[1]

After the fall of France Churchill enthusiastically endorsed the creation of raiding parties to land on the French coast, with the aim of forcing the Germans to disperse their troops and of raising morale in Britain. Churchill appointed General Alan Bourne, Adjutant General to the Royal Marines, to the post of 'Commander of Raiding Operations'. Bourne, who had charm and ability, did not get on with Churchill; he was too academic and intellectual. One evening in July 1940 at 10 Downing Street he gave Churchill a 'dissertation on strategy'. According to General Hollis, 'that was the end of Bourne as Commander of Raiding Operations'.[2]

While Churchill was still at the Admiralty Keyes continued to entreat him for an active command. Even though his proposal to lead a raid on Trondheim in April 1940 had been turned down out of hand, as late as 1 May he offered to lead another amphibious attack on that port and considerably upset Chamberlain by telling Churchill falsely that the Prime Minister was in favour.

On 17 July Churchill yielded to Keyes and appointed him Director of Combined Operations, to take over from Bourne. According to Hollis, 'combined operations began in an atmosphere of controversy and acrimony. They were hated by all three established Services and came in for special loathing from the Admiralty [who] . . . were traditionally jealous of what they imagined might become a rival concern.' Hollis also recorded that Keyes fell foul of the Naval High Command mainly because he was so much senior to Pound.[3]

Although the Chiefs of Staff disliked Keyes' operations and his strong personal influence over the Prime Minister, Churchill loved his Combined Operations baby, the parenthood of which he shared with Keyes. Keyes caught his fancy with a suggestion for a raid on Pantellaria, an island lying between Sicily and Tunisia, 140 miles south-east of Malta. It was small and rocky, seven miles by eight, and had been developed by the Italians as a base for E-Boats. It was important to the enemy because it lay on their sea route to Tripoli, and to Britain because it would help in the defence of Malta. The plan of attack proposed by Keyes was that two or three troop ships would follow a normal convoy to Malta and, in Churchill's words, 'while the main body was engaging the enemy's attention these would drop off in the dark and storm the island by surprise'.

The project was called Workshop; Keyes was so keen that he proposed to lead the attack in person, waiving his rank as Admiral of the Fleet. Churchill, too, became wildly enthusiastic for Workshop, ridiculously overemphasizing its importance. Pound, Cunningham and Dill were opposed. According to Kennedy, Churchill badgered Dill over Pantellaria night after night for many months.

Kennedy has summed up the collective view of the War Office and Admiralty by writing: 'It would be an embarrassment to the Navy to be saddled with the maintenance of a garrison in Pantellaria. Malta was as much as they could manage', and he has recorded Dill as saying that 'we should not risk failure for so small a prize'. But Churchill had set his mind on Pantellaria, and a vast amount of time and energy was wasted upon it. Kennedy also records that on 4 December, after Dill had had a long meeting with Churchill about Pantellaria, Dill had said to him: 'I cannot tell you how angry the Prime Minister has made me. What he said about the army tonight I can never forgive.'[4]

In Cairo Admiral Cunningham was strongly against it. Asked by the Chiefs of Staff for his view, he replied (perhaps as a sop to Churchill) that he 'admired the spirit of adventure, and had no reason to doubt it was feasible'. On the other hand he felt strongly that the Fleet already had heavy responsibilities in the Mediterranean; it was difficult to keep Malta supplied, and to attempt to supply Pantellaria as well would involve an unjustified diversion of effort from the Eastern Mediterranean. There were not enough aircraft or AA guns in Malta; how could it be right to spread our resources still wider? The Italians were not annoying us from Pantellaria; it was doubtful if we could annoy them from there. He preferred the plan of attacking similar Dodecanese islands near Rhodes, beginning with Scarpanto and Stampalia.[5]

This douche of cold water had no effect upon Keyes and Churchill. But to their extreme annoyance the Defence Committee on 5 December refused to approve Workshop. Pound said the COS, after further consideration, believed that 'it was their duty to report frankly their opinion of the unlikelihood of the success of the operation because of the lack of surprise and insufficiency of destroyers'. Eden, still Secretary of State for War, agreed with Portal (Chief of Air Staff) that the operation would only have a 'four to one chance'. Churchill said he regretted the COS view and added that 'there was, of course, no absolute guarantee of success in war . . . many of the greatest battles of history have been won with forces which before the event would have been considered hopelessly inadequate'.

However, the Chiefs were asked to see whether the plan could be improved. Much put out, Churchill asked Eden in private to go out to Command in the Middle East. Eden declined very firmly. Frustrated, Churchill returned to the attack and railroaded Workshop through the Defence Committee on 9 December.

Then Pound said that if the island was captured now the British would be faced with a considerable maintenance commitment without any immediate return, because fighter aircraft could not be installed until AA guns were in position (Malta was short of them) and captured guns and ammunition could not be relied on. The Chiefs of Staff felt the chances against success were three to one: 'Nevertheless if the political risk of failure could be accepted they felt that the operation could go ahead provided the C in C Mediterranean was satisfied that he could accept the commitment involved in the subsequent maintenance of the garrison.' Dill said the island might have 'a fair sized garrison. We would be unable to give any fire support to the landing.' A long discussion of details then took place with the aid of maps and models of the island. Beaverbrook, Attlee, Alexander, Eden and Sinclair gave cautious support to the operation, mainly on political grounds. Churchill then said he would be the first to call it off if, nearer the time, it were found that it did not fit harmoniously into 'the strategic plans, and the fact that the chances were judged by the Chiefs of Staff to be three to one against (odds which he personally did not accept) could not be admitted as valid argument against the operation'. The Committee then reversed their 5 December decision and approved Workshop, to Keyes' and Churchill's delight.[6]

Churchill was over-ruling his generals and admirals, dictating strategy at this stage of the war. He was very conscious that he alone had prevented a surrender after the fall of France, and that without his dynamism the air Battle of Britain and sea Battle of the Atlantic could not have been won, nor would Hitler have been deterred from invading Britain. He felt acutely that he alone had the courage to undertake an attacking policy. Later on, and especially after America came into the war, as will be seen, he bowed to the advice of the Chiefs of Staff in a more humble manner, although he never lost his faculty for suggesting bold enterprises.

Workshop never took place. False intelligence arrived that Hitler was intending to occupy Spain and attack Gibraltar. On 16 December the British operation was postponed for at least a month because the commandos had to be kept in Britain to be used against any such move by Hitler.

This aroused Keyes to fury. He wrote to Churchill on 17 December offering to resign and to find some other way of helping to win the war 'more speedily than your Chiefs of Staff and those dreadful Staff Committees will allow you to'. Keyes was annoyed because Churchill had refused a request for an interview, but went on that it was 'unwise to leave such a splendid striking force [the commandos intended for Pantellaria] and shining sword to rust and lose its temper in the Highlands'. Keyes had been to see Halifax and General Alexander

(GOC Southern Command), arguing that he should lead the Workshop expedition using the Glen Line cargo ships (those strengthened against sub-marines and air attacks in 1939 for the abortive Baltic expedition) to attack Pantellaria from Malta. He begged Churchill to 'get his force' to Malta by 1 January, as any further delay would take the heart out of his volunteer commandos.[7]

Churchill had acquiesced quietly to the postponement, but he was still fired by Keyes' enthusiasm (although he was irritated by the man's constant importuning and requests for talks). So he kept on prodding the Service Chiefs over Pantellaria, telling them that the Germans might get there first. At the Defence Committee on 13 January Admiral Tom Phillips, Vice Chief of Naval Staff, said that 'even if we had fighters in Malta and Pantellaria we still could not protect our convoys. The only method of gaining complete control in the Central Mediter-ranean would be to take Sicily.' Aroused, Churchill sprang to the attack:

We were open to very grave reproach for not having taken Pantellaria when we still had the opportunity. This would be classed as one of the capital errors of the war . . . We had missed the chance and now we would find that the Germans would occupy the island and probably a position on the coast and we should find the Mediterranean closed to us. The fate of Malta itself might be sealed. We ought now to see whether we could still take the island.

The Committee could not resist the force of Churchill's advocacy, and to Churchill's and Keyes' renewed delight the COS were asked to report on a plan for Workshop in a month's time. But by now fears of a German invasion of Greece dominated strategy, and it was obvious the overstretched forces in the Middle East could not undertake further tasks such as maintaining Pantellaria if it was taken. On 17 January Churchill very reluctantly agreed to postpone Workshop, and a few days later, as news of German plans to invade Greece became more ominous, it was abandoned.[8]

On 21 January 1941 Churchill forbade Keyes to go to the Middle East to command in person the attacks on Rhodes and the other islands; in the same document he gave orders for the three Glen Line ships and the commandos to sail via Cape Town to Suez with a view to the main Mandible operation, the capture of Rhodes, being carried out not later than 1 March. Wavell was ordered to make all preparations for the attack on Rhodes pending the arrival of the Glen Line ships.[9]

The Workshop deliberations show how at this stage of the war Churchill dominated Eden, his Secretary of State of War, Alexander, his First Lord of the Admiralty, a Labour member of the War Cabinet and the Chiefs of Staff. They also reveal how attracted he was by the ideas of the unreliable but attack-minded Keyes, which satisfied his continued urge for Britain to take the initiative somewhere.

Meanwhile, unknown to Churchill Wavell had planned a seaborne assault on the Italian-held island of Kasos, east of Crete. When Churchill heard of this he vetoed it a few hours before the assault was due because it would have meant

cancelling Workshop. Wavell argued that the possession of Kasos enabled the
Germans to shell the main Scarpanto airfield on Rhodes and its capture first
would be a great help in the attack on Rhodes, on which Churchill was very keen;
he also felt that Kasos could be taken as a preliminary to the attack on Rhodes
when the Glen Line ships and commandos arrived. Reluctantly Churchill
agreed. Kasos and the nearby island of Castelrizo were attacked unsuccessfully,
with ships and troops already in the Middle East, on 26 February 1941.

The Middle East handling of these operations was bad. The staff officers in
charge had not been inspired by Churchill and Keyes, so there was little
enthusiasm on the part of the commandos for daring amphibious assaults.
Encouraged by Churchill, Wavell had raised 50 and 52 Commando in the
Middle East from volunteers, and trained them at a Commando School set up on
the Great Bitter Lake. However 50 Commando, who assaulted Castelrizo,
lacked the vital long specialist training, as well as the weapons and equipment,
which Keyes was providing in full measure to his commandos in the Highlands of
Scotland. It was obvious that the Middle East had much to learn about
amphibious assaults. Churchill was furious at the failure, cabling Eden, who had
gone to Cairo:

> I am perplexed and somewhat unsettled by accounts which have so far reached us
> about Castelrizo. We did not understand why this island or indeed Casos were
> selected and timed so much in advance of main Mandibles. Story received about
> Casos seems to show lack of purpose and management and difficult to believe
> enemy not disturbed. Story about Castelrizo does not explain how many of our men
> landed; where they landed; how far they got; what they did; what prisoners they
> took; what losses they suffered. How was it that enemy could be reinforced by sea
> observing we had supposed we had local command of the sea. What was the Naval
> and Military force which relieved and reinforced enemy. Where did they come
> from; how did they get there. How was it that after island reported captured it was
> only discovered during evacuation that a considerable enemy ship was in the inner
> harbour. Did we ever take the inner harbour or the defences around it. Anxiety also
> arises from severity of air attack. Was this not foreseen. Where did it come from.
> Was it Italian or German. Please ascertain all these details.
>
> Importance of knowing these facts does not arise mainly through this particular
> operation for evidently the same conditions may be present in aggravated form
> when larger Mandibles is attempted. Pray endeavour reassure me on this.
>
> Largest project must certainly be affected if enemy air dominance can be
> maintained in these waters. Without certainty that we can take and hold main
> Mandibles whole question of communication of largest scheme seems challenged.
>
> For these reasons vitally important we should understand whole sequence of plan
> as you and our military friends foresee it.[10]

Eden instructed Cunningham to reply. The Admiral had to admit that the
officer commanding the Castelrizo attack, Admiral Renouf, was 'a sick man',
and the destroyers were short of fuel due to the high speed with which they had
come from Suda Bay, which resulted in the island being uncovered for two days
and nights. This was aggravated by 'inadequate communications' and the
'deplorable failure of HMS *Hereward* to attack the enemy ship in the harbour'.

There were, according to Cunningham, many military causes which contributed to the failure; the army held the view that since the island was so close to enemy air bases it could not have been held without many AA guns (this was not Cunningham's view), and 'the landing of such guns was never at any time contemplated in planning and indeed were not available'. But he and Wavell were adamant there would be no useful purpose in holding an enquiry, because the sequence of events was clear, as was the reason for the evacuation. Wavell added to Churchill: 'During 27 February the enemy landed a force greatly superior to our own; 26 February enemy air and naval action prevented our landing a force intended to relieve the raiding force and garrison the island; and an Italian ship was unexpectedly found in the harbour.'

Faced with this catalogue of errors, Churchill minuted to Alexander: 'What disciplinary measures or others are going to be taken upon this deplorable mismanagement occuring after we have already had eighteen months of war?' No more was heard of it, but the operation was described to the public as a 'raid' to avoid revealing its failure.

This episode shows Churchill interfering over a minor operation in a manner unusual for a Prime Minister. But as he was his own Minister of Defence and Britain had no ally, he was a virtual dictator over military matters. He felt overwhelmingly that only he himself by his own efforts could ensure a resolute and efficient performance in battle, and he was probably correct.[11]

In mid-March the Glen Line ships carrying commandos from the Highlands – but without Keyes – arrived in the Middle East via the Cape. By now the commitment in Greece meant that raids were out of the question, but the ships and their commandos were useful in Crete.

In February 1941, while Keyes was badgering him almost daily, Churchill wrote:

> My dear Roger,
> It is quite impossible for me to receive a letter of this character. I am sure it would do you a great deal of harm if it fell into unsympathetic hands. I therefore return it to you with the enclosures. If you wish to write on matters affecting the Commando pray do so to General Ismay.

As Keyes' letter and enclosures were not retained in the Prime Minister's office we do not know their contents, but judged by the rest of the correspondence they contained a tirade against the Chiefs of Staff for thwarting Keyes' plan for Workshop, Brisk (an invasion of the Azores), Pilgrim or Shrapnel (an invasion of Canary Islands) and other daring projects which Churchill had at first endorsed eagerly when Keyes had suggested them. They included capturing the Channel Islands and Casablanca, and towing concrete towers out to sea to act as anti-submarine forts. Previously Keyes had written: 'I suppose you realize that deprived of my support and leadership the Commando will disappear . . . I am afraid Pound and General Planning Staff are rocks on which any bold plans will founder.'

In June Churchill accepted Keyes' enthusiastic invitation to visit the

commando training depot in Scotland. It was a happy occasion. Both were fired
with ardour for dramatic exploits to come. Alas, it was the last time the two were
fully in accord. Ismay minuted to the Prime Minister that he had had several long
talks with Keyes about his grievances; 'but it had been impossible to make much
headway owing to the fact that there is a fundamental divergence of opinion
between Sir Roger Keyes on the one side and the Chiefs of Staff on the other, as
to the scope and character of Sir Roger Keyes' responsibilities'.[12]

In August Keyes was hankering after a wild scheme for the capture of Sardinia,
arguing to Churchill that the Sardinians 'have never been amenable to the Fascist
regime', and on 2 September he wrote a letter of complaint to Churchill about the
Chiefs of Staff:

> The COS were originally as keen as we were about the capture of Pantellaria and
> could easily have been roused to enthusiasms about the capture of Sardinia, but it
> was those 'marplots' the inner Service Committees who frightened the COS and
> arrayed every conceivable argument against any offensive action which could not
> have failed before we were forestalled by the Germans.
>
> If you had left me as Governor of Sardinia and its dependency Pantellaria I would
> not have lost them through sheer ineptitude as Crete was lost.
>
> I am so consistently discredited by your advisors that I have to blow my own
> trumpet and am tired of having to waste energy in trying to overcome the supine
> objections of our own people.[13]

During May and June 1941 the plan to attack the Canary Islands (Pilgrim) was
constantly debated by the War Cabinet. The standard of training needed to be
improved for it, so a full-scale exercise employing the whole force was ordered.
General Alexander was commander designate. The exercise, called Leapfrog,
was carried out on 10 August. The assault force sailed from the Clyde and carried
out a dress rehearsal, landing at Scapa Flow. Many mistakes which had occurred
on raids organized by Keyes on the French coast were repeated; movement from
the beaches was slow, and there were delays in landing vehicles. According to the
official report 'an important requirement' was for a Combined Headquarters so
that the force commanders and their staff could learn to work together. One staff
officer who took part described it to the author as a 'shambles'.

The inquest into Leapfrog produced a flaming row between Keyes and the
Chiefs of Staff, who as a result of their detailed enquiries into the shortcomings
of the exercise recommended to Churchill that Keyes should be issued with a
new directive limiting his responsibilities. Keyes reacted violently, and, although
the Prime Minister endeavoured to persuade him to agree, Keyes refused,
declaring that the terms were contrary to his 'own beliefs'.

After much importuning, Churchill gave Keyes a short interview on 5
September. Winston's patience had been sorely tried and they had a row. The
Chiefs of Staff had sent the Prime Minister a paper recommending Keyes'
elimination as a means of avoiding future miscarriages of the kind which had
occurred in Leapfrog. After the interview, Keyes wrote the same day to Churchill
that 'it was good of you to spare me those five stormy minutes during most of
which we were at cross purposes. Please try and read enclosed paper (re

Leapfrog). Leapfrog was a futile waste of time and effort which could have been avoided if I had been allowed any say in the preparation of the plan.'[14]

This was the end of the road for Keyes, who had tried Churchill's patience too far. With his great reputation for gallantry as a result of the Zeebrugge raid in 1918 he had at first seemed to Churchill the ideal romantic figure to lead a series of dramatic sea landings which would be a tonic to the morale of both the fighting forces and the nation. But repeated failures of raids on the French coast had made it clear to Churchill that Keyes was inefficient (although the raid on Lofoten had been a success). The Prime Minister was in addition fussed by the complaints which came from the Chiefs of Staff, and by the way in which Keyes attributed any disagreement with his views to prejudice and personal dislike.

At 11 p.m. on 11 October Churchill sent for Hollis, who was in bed, to come to 10 Downing Street. Churchill told him: 'I have complaints that Keyes is taking up too much time of the Chiefs of Staff. He is a man of vigour and gallantry but I am told they do not like his plans. What do you think?'

Hollis replied: 'Keyes is very gallant, but it is quite true he takes up far too much of the Chiefs' time. His plans are not feasible; yet he continually bombards them with new suggestions for landings, raids and attacks on remote unimportant places when they have more than enough to do coping with their own work. Then when his plans are turned down, as they invariably are, they all have to be reconsidered because he has your ear, Prime Minister; he refuses to take "No" for an answer. This is reacting badly on the staff in the Service Departments all down the line.'

Churchill said: 'This sounds serious. I see you are a hard man, Hollis. What would you do?'

Hollis drew a deep breath and replied: 'Since you ask me, Prime Minister, I suggest that you ask for his resignation.'

Churchill said: 'You *are* a very hard man.'

He did not like to sack his old friend, but realized it was inevitable. He sent for a shorthand writer and dictated a letter of dismissal. Hollis knew that Churchill hankered after the many fighting schemes that Keyes produced, and might suddenly change his mind if the letter was not signed immediately, so he said, 'Would you sign it now, Prime Minister?' Slowly Churchill took out his gold pen and signed it. Hollis said, 'I will take this with me.'

The next morning Churchill rang up Hollis: 'You did not send that letter, I hope. I feel that we have been too hard – much too hard. I do not want it to go.'

'I am sorry sir,' replied Hollis. 'It is already on Keyes' desk.'[15]

Keyes wanted to come to Chequers to complain against his unfair dismissal. But Churchill refused, writing on 16 October:

I am quite sure you have not been the victim of intrigue although, of course, there is widespread prejudice against bringing back retired officers to executive positions and retaining them when they verge on 70. Your very high rank and personal association with me also caused embarrassment and friction . . . in regard to what you say about people begging you to continue 'to fight for the protection of offensive warfare' I can only say that I am sure you will most scrupulously respect the many secret matters with which you have been brought into contact as the slightest leakage may cause disaster and loss of life in the various operations which are impending.

Lord Louis Mountbatten, Captain of the Fifth Destroyer Flotilla on HMS *Kelly*, was appointed to succeed Keyes. When they met, Keyes told Mountbatten: 'The trouble is that the British have lost their will to fight. There is no spirit of attack any more. The Chiefs of Staff are the greatest cowards I have ever met.' This was also Churchill's view, and explains why he put up with so much annoyance from his old friend.[16]

Churchill was convinced that it was essential to secure Turkey as an ally in order to safeguard the northern flank of Egypt and to keep the Balkans out of Hitler's hands. As early as 22 May 1940 he had minuted to Dill: 'We must now call on Turkey to come in or face the consequences. A British victory in Libya would turn the scale, and then we could shift our forces to the new theatre . . . all his [Wavell's] troops except the barest defensive minimum will be drawn out of him before long.' To Wavell he telegraphed later: 'Importance of getting Turkey in and perhaps Yugoslavia far outweighs any Libyan operation and you would be relegated to the very minimum defensive role in Egypt . . . we may be forced to abandon Compass altogether.' This was not Wavell's policy. As we have seen, he was carefully planning his Compass offensive in the Western Desert, which he knew would make the best use of the troops under his command in the Middle East.[17]

On 25 November 1940 Churchill decided to send a military mission to Turkey to try and secure it as an active ally. Marshall Cornwall, as the only senior general with a first-class interpreter's qualification in Turkish, was put in command of the mission. He was wrenched out of the command of 3 Corps (who were in a key role in the defence of the British south coast) and sent off to Cairo, where he stayed with his friend Wavell and rode his polo ponies. Marshall Cornwall had discovered in London that Pound was not enthusiastic about bringing the Turks into the war because it would greatly complicate his problems with Mediterranean convoys. Dill informed Marshall Cornwall that if the Turks came into the war Churchill had agreed Britain would reinforce them with an armoured Division and a motorized infantry division. How these troops were to be spared from the forces in the Middle East under Wavell's command Churchill never explained.

In Cairo Marshall Cornwall found Wavell, Cunningham and Longmore, the Air Chief, frigid about his mission. Not until 13 January did he reach Ankara, where he stayed with the Ambassador, Sir Hugh Knatchbull-Huggesen, whose valet was later discovered to be the notorious spy Cicero.

The Turkish Commander in Chief was, according to Cornwall, unenthusiastic and 'obsessed with the military strength of the Germans'. The Turks agreed to start military talks, but were solely interested in obtaining possession of Syria and the Dodecanese. On 31 January Churchill sent a personal appeal to the Turkish President, asking him to join Britain in the war and promising ten squadrons of fighter and bomber planes to bomb the Romanian airfields if the Germans moved into Bulgaria, and a hundred A A guns complete with gunners. This message coincided with Wavell's spectacular victories over the Italians in the desert, and Churchill concluded: 'The victories we have gained in Libya will enable us to give a far more direct and immediate measure of aid to Turkey in the event of our two countries becoming allies.' However, Winston's offer was politely rejected, and Marshall Cornwall returned to Cairo. Being convinced that Turkey would be more use as a benevolent neutral he had not urged Churchill's case strenuously, although he made himself popular with the Turkish General Staff.

Marshall Cornwall's military appreciation was that the Turkish Army would stand no chance against a German invasion, and far from being a worthwhile ally, Turkey would be an expensive drain on Middle East resources. German Panzer divisions could quickly over-run Thrace, which was ideal fighting ground for tanks, and Istanbul being largely built of wood, would be reduced to ashes in a few hours by German bombers. Although they were tough infantry fighters, as proved in the first World War, the Turks had little armour or A A defence and their field artillery was all horse-drawn – 'a bow and arrow army' compared with the Germans.

Until the end of the war Churchill pursued this will-o'-the-wisp of making Turkey a military ally. He even forced Eden to make two fruitless visits to talk to the Turks in the spring of 1941. Although the Turks were anti-German they had no intention of fighting – least of all in 1941 when the attitude of Russia was still unknown, and British prospects of defeating Germany poor. And only by promises, which would have been difficult or impossible to redeem, of extra territory at the expense of Greece and Italy would they have come in later, in 1944, when it was clear that the Allies were poised for victory.

Cadogan told Churchill on 6 April 1941 that Turkey had an obligation under the Balkan Pact to come to the assistance of Yugoslavia if she was attacked by Germany, but if Turkey did not look on this as a '*casus belli*' it was 'not worth while trying further'.[18]

Knatchbull-Huggesen stated that Marshall Cornwall had informed the Turkish General Staff that he and Wavell thought on military grounds Turkey should keep out of war with Germany; he as Ambassador agreed, and thought Britain should not push Turkey any further. Nevertheless Churchill insisted on one more try and Marshall Cornwall was sent back to Ankara where he and Knatchbull-Huggesen saw President Ismet Inonu on 9 April. Unfortunately Rommel's Panzers had just recaptured Benghazi. Marshall Cornwall had been told by Churchill to promise Inonu that Britain would hand over a hundred Hurricanes and a hundred A A guns on the day Turkey declared war. When he gave this message Inonu only laughed and said: 'You know as well as I do you could not spare them for us; you would be completely lost without them. No, we are far more useful to you as a neutral country.' Marshall Cornwall inwardly agreed.[19]

On receiving Knatchbull-Huggesen's report of the conversation the first official in the Foreign Office, Sargent (later P U S) minuted that Marshall Cornwall's remarks to the Turks had had 'an unfortunate effect'; while the second, Nicholls, later Ambassador to the Netherlands, pointed out that Eden's visit to Cairo had been to ensure that military and foreign policy went hand in hand. Wavell and Marshall Cornwall had wrecked this over Turkey. Eden minuted: 'General Marshall Cornwall is too apt to step out of the military sphere', a remark with which Churchill thoroughly agreed.

Of course Wavell, who fiercely disagreed with Churchill's aim of involving Turkey in war with Germany, was responsible for Marshall Cornwall's behaviour, and Churchill knew this well. The divergence of views over Turkey widened the breach between Wavell and Churchill. And Churchill and Wavell were soon in conflict again, this time over Iraq.

Iraq was immensely important to Britain – not only for her own oil supplies but also for those of Iran, whose pipelines crossed Iraq and were indispensable. Iraq was bound to Britain by the Treaty of 1930. Then Britain gave up her mandate, and both parties promised to come to the aid of the other as an ally in the event of war.

For several years the Germans had tried to win over Iraqi opinion, and their successes in Europe, Greece and Crete had made a deep impression. Although the Regent, Amir Abdullah, and General Nuri, the Prime Minister, were friendly to Britain, Rashid Ali, a prominent politician, and the influential Mufti of Jerusalem were violently anti-British, as were the army leaders known as the 'Golden Square'. In March 1940 Rashid Ali replaced Nuri. The British victories over the Italians in the desert in December 1940 produced a favourable reaction and Rashid Ali was forced to resign, but the new Prime Minister, Taha Pasha, was not co-operative. On 1 April 1941 Rashid Ali and the military clique carried out a coup and established themselves in power. The British refused to recognize the new regime. The British Ambassador, Sir K. Cornwallis, wanted Wavell to intervene with force immediately, but because of the critical situation in the desert and the Greek campaign he would not comply and thought the British must risk a hostile government.

This was not Churchill's view. He immediately asked for troops from India to be sent to Baghdad, and Auchinleck, who was commanding the Army in India, sent a brigade group to the port of Basra. More Indian Army troops were on their way, but Rashid Ali said he would not allow them to land. He was counting on the assistance of German troops and especially of Student's airborne division. Fortunately the British had inflicted such heavy casualties on the German airborne troops in Crete that Hitler would not risk this kind of operation again; otherwise the Germans might have launched a successful airborne assault on Iraq from the Dodecanese islands.

Rashid Ali's troops attacked the large British base at Habbaniya on 30 April and he appealed to Hitler for immediate aid. The Germans demanded from Vichy France the use of the Syrian and Lebanese aerodromes as staging posts for German squadrons flying to Iraq. They also ordered military supplies to be sent from the French Syrian military depots to the Iraqi rebels. Vichy acquiesced, and thus, as will be seen in the next chapter, Pétain abrogated the agreement he had made with Churchill the previous October.

Churchill was angered because Wavell cabled to London he could not commit any of his troops to Iraq, and any force he could make available would be 'inadequate and too late'. Wavell stated: 'I have consistently warned you that no assistance could be given to Iraq from Palestine in present circumstances and have always advised that a commitment in Iraq should be avoided . . . My forces are stretched to the limit everywhere and I simply cannot afford to risk part of them on what cannot produce any effect.' At this moment Crete was threatened, and Rommel was advancing in the desert.

An angry Churchill ordered Wavell to send troops. Wavell obeyed under protest, cabling: '5 May. Your message takes little account of realities. You must face facts.' He did not believe that the forces he was gathering were strong enough to relieve Habbaniya, or indeed whether Habbaniya could hold out until they arrived. To Churchill's further irritation he cabled:

> I feel it is my duty to warn you in the gravest possible terms that I consider the prolongation of fighting in Iraq will seriously endanger the defence of Palestine and Egypt. The political consequences will be incalculable and may result in what I have spent nearly two years trying to avoid, namely, serious internal trouble in our bases. I therefore urge again most strongly that a settlement should be negotiated as early as possible.

This produced a furious minute from Churchill to Dill that Wavell's proposed available force should be strong enough, and

> Fancy having kept the Cavalry Division in Palestine all this time without having the rudiments of a mobile column organized!
> I am deeply disturbed at General Wavell's attitude. He seems to have been taken as much by surprise on his eastern as he was on his western flank, and in spite of the enormous number of men at his disposal and the great convoys reaching him, he seems to be hard up for battalions and companies. He gives me the impression of being tired out.

Urgent orders were sent to Wavell that the Chiefs of Staff accepted responsibility for a force being sent from Wavell's command 'at the earliest possible moment'.[20]

In his memoirs Ismay wrote that the order to Wavell on 6 May to attack the Iraqis 'was the first occasion in the war on which the Chiefs of Staff overruled the commander on the spot, and took full responsibility for the consequences'. Of course it was entirely Churchill's doing. That morning Churchill told Dill he wanted to sack Wavell and replace him with Auchinleck.[21]

On 9 May Churchill told Wavell: 'Our information is that Rashid Ali and his partisans are in desperate straits. However this may be, you are to fight hard against them . . . there can be no question of negotiation with Rashid Ali unless he immediately accepts terms. Negotiations would only lead to delay during which the German air force would arrive.' On the 12th the Prime Minister ordered Wavell to march on Baghdad: 'About Iraq you do not need to bother too much about the long future. Your immediate task is to get a friendly Government set up in Baghdad and to beat down Rashid Ali's force with the utmost vigour. What matters is action – namely the swift advance of the mobile column to establish contact between Palestine and Baghdad. Every day counts for the Germans may not be long.'

Wavell refused, cabling in a mood of insubordination: 'Force from Palestine . . . is not capable of entering Baghdad against opposition or maintaining itself there . . . in order to avoid a military commitment in a non-vital area I still recommend that a political settlement be sought.' Churchill ignored Wavell's protest and ordered him to break into Baghdad 'even with quite small forces and running the same kind of risks as the Germans are accustomed to run and profit by'; he ruled out any negotiations with Rashid Ali. Churchill knew from intercepted German signals that Hitler was on the brink of intervening in Iraq, and he scented the grave danger of Student's airborne troops being flown in from the Dodecanese islands. If they were used in Iraq, as Hitler was considering , Britain's oil supplies would be in the utmost danger.

Wavell complied with Churchill's orders and, despite interference by German aircraft, on 30 May Baghdad was taken. Rashid Ali fled; the Regent was reinstalled and Churchill's desired 'friendly Government' took office.[22]

Churchill had taken command out of Wavell's hands by ordering him to attack Habbaniya and then to advance to Baghdad. How right he was to do so is proved by the resulting success. But the relationship between Wavell and Churchill had reached a new low.

CHAPTER TEN

October 1940–June 1941
Churchill, Vichy and Syria

AFTER THE failure of the Dakar expedition Churchill had doubts whether de Gaulle and his Free French were an asset or a liability. He remained on friendly terms with de Gaulle and even asked him to stay at Chequers. But he feared that Vichy might declare war on Britain; Laval, who was head of Pétain's Government until December 1940, was pro-German and a violent enemy of Britain.

Churchill was trying to ride two horses at the same time. While he was encouraging de Gaulle to raise forces and take over French colonies, he also had to prevent Vichy France declaring war. Meanwhile de Gaulle was regarded as public enemy number one in Vichy, and had been condemned to death. Everything Churchill did to encourage the Free French antagonized Vichy. Churchill decided he must throw a lifeline to Pétain and mend his fences with Vichy.

Accordingly, in October Churchill agreed that Pétain could send an emissary to London. He was Professor Louis Rougier, rather anti-British and a strong supporter of Pétain, but sincere and honest. He held the Chair of Philosophy at Besançon University. Churchill saw him twice at 10 Downing Street. At a preliminary meeting on 24 October Halifax proposed a 'gentleman's agreement' or protocol under which food ships from French colonies could pass through the blockade to southern French ports, so that Britain could not be blamed for French hunger. Halifax suggested to Rougier sending a Vichy economic expert to Madrid, and it was agreed that personal attacks on Pétain on the BBC would cease.

The next day, when Rougier and Churchill met for the second time, the world press was full of alarm because it was feared that at a meeting at Montoire the day before Pétain, Laval and Hitler had agreed a peace treaty under which France would cede her Fleet and naval bases to Germany. Churchill told Rougier excitedly that if Pétain's Government participated in the war effort he would bomb Vichy. Rougier calmed him down by explaining that, although Laval wanted to bring France into the war on the side of Germany, Pétain and Weygand were strongly opposed and were determined to keep the French Fleet and colonies out of German hands. Rougier suggested that Weygand should send a liaison officer to Tangier to 'concert' with the British consul, Gascoigne, a list of the tanks, anti-tank guns and other military material which Weygand would need if he were to take up arms on the side of Britain. The meeting was friendly and a protocol was agreed to be sent to Pétain. On 28 October, at the Foreign Office, Rougier was given a copy of the protocol with amendments in Churchill's handwriting. France would promise not to try to recapture by force colonies which de Gaulle had taken over, and not to cede to Germany ports in Provence, North Africa, Morocco or West Africa. Britain agreed not to take French possessions by force. France would agree that her Empire would resume the war against Germany when Britain was in a position to equip the French colonial troops with anti-tank guns and necessary heavy equipment. France would also sabotage all her Fleet rather than allow the ships to fall into German or Italian hands. Weygand, who had originally been Defence Minister in Pétain's Government, was now in Algiers.

The diplomat Sir William Strang, with Churchill's approval, added in his handwriting: 'If General Weygand will raise the standard in North Africa he can count on the renewal of the whole-hearted collaboration of the Governments and peoples of the British Empire and on a share of the assistance afforded by the United States.' While Rougier was at the Foreign Office on 28 October Cadogan congratulated him, saying, 'Never has an Ambassador succeeded in as difficult a negotiation as you have just done.'[1] At this stage Churchill and the Foreign Office were doubtful whether it was worth backing de Gaulle any further in his efforts to take over French overseas possessions, unless he would co-operate with or act under Weygand's orders. Rougier took his copy of the protocol with the handwritten amendments to Pétain in Vichy. On 11 November he had a long talk with Pétain in the presence of Admiral Fernet, and the next day Pétain told Rougier that he had ratified the protocol through his diplomatic representatives. Cadogan had asked Rougier to go on to Geneva, where on 21 November he was sent a telegram from the Foreign Office stating:

The Vichy Government have assured us that they will make no unjustified attack on us and have declared their determination to retain control of their Colonial Empire and Fleet. We have asked them that they should for the time being tacitly refrain from active operations against the free French Colonies, that they will resist German or Italian attack on, or infiltration into, those territories which have remained loyal to Vichy, and that they will effectively prevent their ports or territories being used as bases for Air or U-Boat attack on us.

On our side we do not covet or seek to acquire any French territory and would be prepared to help any French resistance to German or Italian designs to the best of our ability.

If, however, in present circumstances, any part of the French Empire should spontaneously declare for General de Gaulle, we would recognise its accession to his cause and would defend it from the sea in accordance with the undertaking we have already given to General de Gaulle.

We have already declared our intention, when victory is achieved, to restore the greatness and independence of France and this covers those parts of the French Empire which have declared or may declare for General de Gaulle.

The conditions outlined above would constitute merely a provisional arrangement whereby the situation might be held while means are sought of reaching a *modus vivendi*.

On this understanding we are prepared to begin economic discussions with the Vichy Government at Madrid, trade between French North Africa and Ports in unoccupied France being first reviewed, and are prepared to send a representative from this country to meet a representative from Vichy at Madrid.[2]

Rougier was delighted, and went back to Vichy to see Pétain again.

On 5 December Rougier wrote to Churchill and Halifax from the British Embassy in Lisbon that Pétain had promised not to surrender air or naval bases or the French Fleet to the Axis powers, and accepted as a *fait accompli* until the end of hostilities 'the subjection of French Equatorial Africa to de Gaulle on the understanding that no fresh operations would be directed (by de Gaulle) against French West Africa, Morocco or North Africa.' Rougier said the acceptance of the *fait accompli* had been difficult to secure, because Darlan and Laval wanted to send the French Fleet to recapture Libreville the capital of Gabon in French Equatorial Africa. Rougier also sent a series of notes from the Vichy Government about relaxing the blockade, the attitude to be adopted towards Weygand and the position of Morocco. This was the confirmation of an agreement between Churchill and Pétain.[3]

Significantly, Cadogan minuted on 12 December about the Rougier protocol: 'We have already got more than we expected out of the French, and consequently we need not perhaps at present go further and promise to restrain de Gaulle from further adventures. Evidently de Gaulle should be encouraged to occupy his troops against the Italians (if we welcome them; the Greeks evidently don't).' On the same file Strang minuted:

> If we could give Vichy some kind of assurance about de Gaulle's future actions, it would be useful to us as a means of establishing this *modus vivendi* [the Rougier Protocol]. We have already twice in our draft telegrams to Madrid suggested the inclusion of sentences for a communication to Vichy to the effect that we would restrain de Gaulle from any further adventure for the present, but this sentence has twice been struck out by the Prime Minister.[4]

By twice striking out the reference to 'restraining' de Gaulle Churchill showed he had qualms about backtracking on the General, but he had written in his own hand on a document given to Rougier with regard to de Gaulle coming under Weygand's orders: 'We shall do our best in this sense but we cannot speak definitely for de Gaulle.' At an informal meeting with Churchill and Attlee on 31 October Halifax said he thought 'it would be unwise to prejudice the approach being made to Weygand' after Churchill had drawn attention to telegrams from de Gaulle stating he was anxious to press on with operations in West Africa. Churchill then said the British would be reluctant to take part in these operations until 'we knew more definitely how we stood with Vichy'.[5]

De Gaulle's headquarters in Carlton Gardens tried to blacken Rougier's character. On 23 November Speaight of the Foreign Office French department minuted that their grounds were 'very thin', the British Government gave financial assistance to Rougier in Lisbon and also asked Lothian to give him money later in Washington.[6]

At the end of October Churchill instructed the BBC that anti-Pétain broadcasts by de Gaulle's supporters in London were vetoed. De Gaulle, who was in Brazzaville, protested; he also objected to any agreement between London and Pétain without the consent of his Free French Council, which he had just set up. This resulted in a Foreign Office minute for Churchill that de Gaulle goes 'much too far when he demands the direct participation of his Council and its formal consent to any agreement concluded with the French leaders such as Weygand and Nogues'. General Nogues was commander of all French forces in North Africa, and very hostile to de Gaulle.[7]

Halifax shared Churchill's enthusiasm for an accord with Vichy, and at an internal Foreign Office meeting agreed on 20 November:

> Our aim should be to bring General Weygand, Catroux and de Gaulle together. Rapprochement between de Gaulle and Weygand will be slow. The best we can do is to encourage Weygand, i.e. no waving of a red flag and *no* further operations. [author's italics]
>
> We should multiply contacts with Vichy, e.g. Rougier, Dupuy [Canadian representative in Vichy] . . . we will hold back de Gaulle if Vichy does not attack him on any other French territories that may spontaneously come over in the future . . . the more they show the spirit of resistance the less likely it is that de Gaulle's movement will spread . . . they [Vichy] are quite happy with present position whereby ships are passing through [Gibraltar] and they are getting pretty well what they want.

On the next day Halifax cabled to Hoare, the British Ambassador in Madrid, that the conditions agreed 'constitute merely a provisional arrangement whereby the situation might be held while means are sought of reaching a *modus vivendi*', and on this understanding Britain was prepared to begin economic discussions with a Vichy representative in Madrid. After Rougier's visit Churchill had ordered the Royal Navy not to stop French food ships from their colonies proceeding to French ports in Vichy France.[8]

Rougier went from Vichy to Algiers. Weygand had told him originally in July: 'If the British come with four divisions I will fire on them; if they come with twenty divisions I will welcome them.' Now, after talking to Weygand, Rougier informed the British there would be a 'vast amount of preparatory ground before General Weygand would make a decision one way or the other', and on 30 November he sent a message: 'We could hope for nothing from Weygand.'[9]

Rougier went on from Algiers to Washington. De Gaulle wanted the Americans to be warned against him but Churchill would not agree; the Foreign Office told Lothian he was 'the unofficial intermediary between HMG and Pétain' and he was told: 'Please help him.' At that moment Churchill was fed up with de Gaulle and his entourage in Carlton Gardens, and on this telegram he wrote: 'Good'. This was a low point in Churchill's relations with de Gaulle and the high of his hopes of Vichy.[10]

Rougier arrived in Washington during the first week of December. In London he had been strictly forbidden to tell the Gaullists anything of his negotiations; now, in Washington, he found that the Americans had been kept in the dark. Not realizing this, he told a leading journalist, Walter Lippman and Felix Frankfurter, an intimate of Roosevelt, what had transpired. This provoked Neville Butler, Head of Chancery in the Embassy, to write to Rougier in strong terms that he must be more discreet, and that the British Government would only pay him if he kept quiet. Rougier considered this letter was more one that should have been sent to a secret service agent than to 'a French intellectual who had done his best in difficult circumstances to help the British war effort', and refused to accept British cash, which he termed "Pitt's money" (William Pitt the Younger, British Prime Minister 1783–1801 and 1804–06, in 1793 subsidized Louis XVIII's emigré army with forged currency).[11]

Churchill disliked keeping de Gaulle in the dark, and had on 26 October 1940 minuted to him that something should be said to de Gaulle, 'appraising him of the negotiations with Pétain and Weygand . . . in view of our relations with General Weygand and engagements signed he has a right to feel assured we are not throwing him over'. Britain had promised to protect de Gaulle's forces in Libreville from an attack by Vichy forces from Dakar, but on 1 November the War Cabinet agreed with Churchill not to give de Gaulle the same measure of support at Libreville as they had done at Duala, near Dakar; on the same day Colville noted that, after he had told Churchill how certain circles were condemning de Gaulle's headquarters, Churchill had said that 'de Gaulle is definitely an embarrassment to us in our dealings with Vichy and the French people'. Cadogan noted in his diary: 'de Gaulle is a loser and should be played down.' On 10 November Churchill telegraphed to de Gaulle in Libreville: 'Situation between France and Britain has changed remarkably since you left . . . We have hopes of Weygand in Africa and no-one must underrate advantage that would follow if he were rallied. We are trying to arrive at some *modus vivendi* with Vichy which will minimise the risk of incidents and will enable favourable forces in France to develop.'[12]

On 13 November de Gaulle's troops entered Libreville; two days later the whole of Gabon was in French hands, and by the end of 1940 the French possessions in India, New Caledonia and the New Hebrides had joined the West African colonies in acknowledging the authority of de Gaulle. This did not help to sweeten relations between London and Vichy.

Although Weygand's response to Rougier had been disappointing Churchill decided in December to try again, this time using Dupuy, the Canadian representative in Vichy. Accordingly he drafted a message to Weygand, which was concealed from the de Gaulle camp in London:

If at any time in the near future the French Government decide to cross to North Africa or resume the war there against Italy and Germany we would be willing to send a strong and well equipped Expeditionary Force of up to six divisions to aid the defence of Morocco, Algiers and Tunis. These divisions could sail as fast as shipping and landing facilities were available. We now have . . . considerable spare forces already well trained . . . We are willing to enter into staff talks of the most secret character with any military representatives nominated by you . . . It is most important that the French Government should realize that we are willing to give powerful and growing aid.[13]

Before despatching it Churchill showed the message to Halifax, who on 27 December minuted: 'I agree that the message should go. Dupuy should give it to Weygand, and at the same time transmit it to Pétain.'

Unfortunately at a house party given by Ronald Tree MP, Churchill's Parliamentary Private Secretary (PPS), at which Churchill's friend Brendan Bracken was present, news of Dupuy's mission was leaked to Helen Kirkpatrick, an American journalist. She sent a message to the *Chicago Daily News*, which was passed by the censor because he had not been warned, and published under the headline: 'Pétain tells Britain Vichy will not aid Nazi attack'. The article gave details of both Rougier's and Dupuy's negotiations. Churchill was furious, and wanted Kirkpatrick 'shipped out of the country at the earliest moment'. However Brendan Bracken, a friend of Kirkpatrick's, calmed him down.

At the War Cabinet on 30 December Churchill wondered whether it would be advisable to send a further message to Pétain and Weygand to the effect that the British would give every facility for the mobilization of Admiral Godfroy's French Fleet at Alexandria and for its deployment against the Italians and Germans 'if the situation demanded it'.[14]

Laval was now sacked by Pétain, because he was too pro-German, which encouraged Churchill's hopes of Pétain. Dupuy turned out to be an unsatisfactory emissary. Anti-de Gaulle and unreliable, he became ludicrously pro-Pétain. On 18 January 1941, back in London from Vichy, he sent Churchill a thirty-nine-page report on his experiences in Vichy in November and December 1940, which tried to make Pétain seem more co-operative and more pro-British than he was.

Dupuy told Churchill that Pétain, Darlan and Huntziger (Vichy Minister of War) had spoken to him

> about the possibility of co-operation in North Africa and France under this vital condition – that the present atmosphere of tension between Great Britain and France be maintained as a smoke screen behind which contacts could be made and information exchanged. They also said that if the Germans heard of such collaboration they would immediately crush the French and overrun the unoccupied part of French territory.

On this item Churchill replied that he was ready to enter into a procedure along the lines suggested – that he would like Mr Dupuy to inform the French Government of Britain's readiness to send divisions to North Africa in the event that the French Government decided to abandon the metropolitan territory or considered it opportune to receive British support in North Africa. Churchill said 'it was important to avoid experiences similar to those of Norway, the Netherlands and Belgium'. He entrusted Mr Dupuy with the mission of presenting his point of view to the interested Department of the French Government as well as to the French military authorities in North Africa.

Dupuy continued that Pétain was deeply touched at the possibility of 'somewhat relaxing the blockade', which Churchill had personally authorized Dupuy to state, 'and desired to express his appreciation to Halifax'. (As Halifax was no longer Foreign Secretary, this, according to the Foreign Office, showed how little in touch Pétain was with reality.)[15]

Dupuy also claimed that Pétain had told him that at Mers-el-Kebir Vichy thought there were only two alternatives – to fight or surrender. They would, he said, have sent different instructions to Admiral Gensoul if they had known the French ships would be allowed by the British to go to French ports in the West Indies or to US ports.

Dupuy reported that Vichy would like to collaborate with Britain in the war, but at this stage could only do so by protecting the French Fleet and colonies against German and Italian enterprises. Dupuy added that Pétain had said that the military authorities were organizing the French Army and creating underground forces in the hope that they would be successful in the case of an Allied landing. This *canard* was later frequently retailed to SOE officers, but has no foundation.[16]

According to Eden, who became Foreign Secretary on 1 January 1941, Dupuy did not handle the delivery of Churchill's second message to Pétain 'very skilfully'. He organized Jacques Chevalier, Minister of Public Education, to hand the message to Pétain in the presence of Pierre Etienne Flandin, Vichy Foreign Minister, which Eden thought 'incredibly inept'. Chevalier failed to make Pétain understand that the message was from Churchill himself; instead the Marshal believed it to be from Halifax. Pétain was embarrassed and the message was burnt; he said: 'we have not received it'.

On 6 January Eden suggested that Dupuy should take another copy to Pétain personally and discuss it with him as soon as possible, stressing that it came from Churchill. He told Dupuy that 'the next step is to get the message to Weygand'.

However, a more satisfactory emissary to Weygand in the shape of Colonel Mittelman appeared, and on 17 January he was sent to Algiers with a note from Churchill:

> I take advantage of M. Mittelman's return to send you the text of a personal and secret message which I have been able to convey to Marshal Pétain . . . You may be confident we have a full understanding of the difficulties which surround you but as the days pass and as the prospect of victory broadens out before our eyes we look forward with the greater assurance to the resumption of active collaboration between French and British arms in what is still the common cause.

Weygand made no reply to Churchill's message nor to the offer of six divisions made in December, and the Prime Minister minuted on 12 February:

> we have made Weygand great efforts to which we have had no reply . . . Until he has answered by some channel or other the telegram I have sent him he ought not to be given supplies. Not one scrap of nobility or courage has been shown by these people so far and they had better go on short commons till they come to their senses. The policy of occasional blockade should be enforced as Naval means are available.

All optimism over Vichy disappeared when on 19 April Pétain violated his 'gentleman's agreement' with Churchill that no bases would be ceded to the Germans. He allowed the Luftwaffe to take over Syrian aerodromes to help the revolt by Rashid Ali in Iraq and to bomb the Suez Canal. These planes were serviced by the French, who also sent military supplies to Rashid Ali from their Syrian depots. The Vichy Governor General Dentz also provided trains to convoy arms to Rashid Ali, leader of the Iraqi rebels against British rule. Churchill had tried his best with Vichy, and now with the 'gentleman's agreement' torn up by Pétain he turned anew to de Gaulle.

Dupuy saw Pétain in Vichy in March, but his lengthy report to the Prime Minister about it was described by Churchill's private secretary, Morton, as 'useless', and his views were 'so wrong as to be dangerous'. Churchill agreed. After the fighting with Vichy troops in Syria in June 1941 (described below) Dupuy was firmly told by the Foreign Office that 'we had no special business for him to transact for us in Vichy nor any messages to send', and that it was perhaps a good thing that some of his visits to Vichy should be confined to purely Canadian business. Churchill's flirtation with Pétain was over for good.[17]

There is a strange postscript to the Rougier and Dupuy negotiations. In 1945 Churchill tried to deny they had taken place. Then de Gaulle was head of the provisional French Government and would have been annoyed to hear how far Churchill had gone with Vichy in the autumn of 1940 behind his back, but this was no justification for Churchill trying to hide what he had done in 1940.

Churchill was abundantly justified in his 1940 overtures to Vichy. Since after Mers-el-Kebir and Dakar de Gaulle was making little headway either with recruitment for his Free French forces or with the French Colonial Governors, it was sensible to try for an agreement with Weygand to bring French forces back into the field on the British side. To do this it was necessary to approach Pétain and offer him a *quid pro quo* over the food ships. In addition, there was reason to expect that Weygand would co-operate with de Gaulle.

In France in the summer of 1945 Pétain was being put on trial as a traitor, even though many Frenchmen were rallying to his support; these included Rougier, then in America. Rougier wrote a book giving a full account of the negotiations, expecting that it would be used as evidence in favour of Pétain in his trial. He obtained considerable pre-publication publicity in the USA and this perturbed Halifax and the British Embassy in Washington, who reported their misgivings about what they considered an unfavourable account of British conduct during the war. When this was brought to Churchill's attention he minuted on 30 April 1945:

    1) I do not consider that this question deserves attention at the present time. I am not in favour of a P.Q. on the subject. Halifax need not get excited about it. Naturally it was part of our policy to endeavour to get whatever we could out of Vichy and even at that time when we were all alone I had strong hopes of making a landing in Morocco if the French assisted. You should look up the letter written with the authority of the Chiefs of Staff to General Weygand offering him six divisions.

2) As for the Americans, Admiral Leahy was sitting in Marshal Pétain's pocket at Vichy doing everything in his power to support and stiffen them against the Germans. The Americans have no grounds for complaint against us. I have the script of President Roosevelt's proposed broadcast on the eve of Torch (Invasion of North Africa, November 1942). He addressed Pétain as Marshal Pétain and 'My dear friend the great and trusted hero of Verdun' or words to that effect. With some difficulty I persuaded him to withdraw this, as it would have been spat at in France.

3) I am entirely indifferent to any attacks on my conduct during this period. It will be sufficient to tell the Ambassador that I do not think the matter requires attention at the present time but that he should forward any material connected with it.[18]

But Rougier's allegations could not be ignored, because they were causing a furore in France as well as in the USA and were being reported in the Russian newspapers.

During a preliminary hearing in Paris Pétain refused to give details of how the alleged 'Agreement' with Britain had been negotiated, 'since to do so would be contrary to diplomatic usage'; he would only say that negotiations with Churchill had begun on 24 October 1940 when he, Hitler and Laval met at Montoire, and his whole policy had been inspired by it even when Britain departed from it. He conveniently ignored the fact that his Government had violated the Agreement by consenting to the Germans using the French air bases in Syria in May 1941.

In Paris agitation increased after Pétain's statement, so that Duff Cooper, the British Ambassador, recommended strongly that it should be dealt with by an arranged Parliamentary Question and the publication of a fully documented account of British exchanges with Vichy. In a minute to Eden, suggesting a PQ, Oliver Harvey wrote: 'We have nothing to hide or be ashamed of, but I am afraid our continued silence is helping a campaign of slander designed to denigrate our aims in the war.'

Eden replied to Harvey: 'I have a feeling that a Parliamentary answer will only lead to demand for publication of the papers. (Can we do this at present?) However if Department is so enthusiastic I am prepared to sign a minute to the P.M. asking if we can publish documents if asked to do so.'

Speaight minuted that the documents could be published if the detailed correspondence about abortive proposals for exchanging diplomatic agents with Vichy was omitted; 'the actual documents, viz Rougier's notes for his interview with General Weygand, his letter to the P.M. after his return from Vichy, and the telegram which we sent to him about the upshot of Madrid exchanges are not of the sort usually included in White Papers but there is nothing in them that we need withhold'.

On 28 May Eden minuted to Winston: 'Duff Cooper has written again urging strongly an early statement in order to counter the spreading belief in Paris that a Pact actually existed which is doing us harm. Our statement may lead to a demand for the publication of documents. We need not be afraid of this. There might indeed be some advantage in giving the whole story in a White Paper. That can however be considered later.' Churchill minuted his agreement on 29 May, and a Parliamentary Question was put down by Captain MacEwen, Conservative MP for Berwick and Haddington.[19]

On 5 June Rougier's book *Les Accords*, giving full details of his 1940 negotiations, was published in Canada and received worldwide publicity. Four days later the Foreign Office issued a press statement that there had been 'No secret treaty'.

On the 13th Churchill insisted on replying personally in the Commons to the MacEwen question. His reply was unworthy of him. It was not only economical with the truth, it was tendentious and misleading. He said:

A series of messages were exchanged through British and French representatives at a neutral capital. The object was to obtain assurances that Vichy would not allow Germans to obtain fleet or French colonies or attack colonies which had rallied to de Gaulle. If such assurances were forthcoming we should be prepared to negotiate a *modus vivendi* with limited trade between metropolitan France and African colonies. Replies were unsatisfactory. Emissary saw Halifax and P.M. but came without any specific mission, and object of his visit seems primarily to have been to gauge the state of opinion in this country.[20]

It was a prevarication to say that Rougier had come without a specific mission, and to infer that messages were only exchanged through Madrid with unsatisfactory replies. He was trying to conceal the information that Rougier had taken the terms to Vichy and that Pétain's reply had been considered satisfactory, with the result that orders were given to allow French food ships to pass through Gibraltar. By 15 June the British Embassy in Washington was 'bombarded' by enquiries, and Sir Michael Wright, the British Ambassador in Washington, wrote to London that Churchill's parliamentary statement 'threw no light'.

Churchill and Eden then decided to publish a White Paper. This never occurred because the Churchill Government fell, but on 17 July the Foreign Office issued a press statement:

Les Accords Pétain Churchill [the title of Rougier's book] has been found to contain not only a wholly misleading interpretation of the policy of His Majesty's Government in the negotiations but contains serious misstatements of fact which call for correction. Monsieur Rougier's attempt to prove that the Gentleman's Agreement was later confirmed by Vichy and His Majesty's Government is equally without foundation.

As Foreign Office minutes had proved Rougier correct, it is astonishing that Eden and Churchill should have authorized this statement which the British diplomats knew to be mendacious. It is an unsavoury episode in the history of the Churchill wartime Government. On 17 July the *Times* commented that Rougier's book 'had already caused much enquiry into British policy'.

Incensed by the press statement, Rougier issued his own in Canada on 17 July, pointing out the inconsistencies and prevarications in Churchill's Commons statement and the Foreign Office announcement to the press. Rougier's press statement was sent to London by the Washington Embassy on 21 July in their telegram 5116, which was forwarded to Churchill in Potsdam.

Churchill's conscience must have pricked him, because almost his last act as Prime Minister as he flew back from Potsdam for the General Election result was to minute: 'Ref. telegram 5116. What is the truth?' Clearly he had misgivings. His minute was never answered, because his Government fell on the day it was received, but Hoyer Miller, deputy Under-Secretary, minuted: 'Perhaps you should put Tony Rumbold on to it.' Sir Anthony Rumbold, First Secretary, French Department, minuted unconvincingly: 'We have maintained that the assurances of Pétain were not sufficient to enable us to consider the conclusion of an agreement.' Bevin, the new Foreign Secretary, was told about the Rougier saga, and with Churchill fallen from power the controversy fizzled out.[21]

In his memoirs, Churchill omits any reference to the important Rougier and Dupuy negotiations. His official biographer touches on the 1940–41 negotiations but omits completely the storm caused in 1945 by the Rougier revelations. Nor does Woodward, the official diplomatic historian, refer to the Rougier controversy in 1945.

In early 1941, with Weygand still showing no inclination to make a deal, Churchill began to feel that in spite of his abrasiveness and pride de Gaulle would be the key to French co-operation in the Middle East and Africa. Between January and April 1941 Free French troops helped in Wavell's victories at Bardia, Tobruk and Benghazi, together with the taking of Kub Kub and Massawa in Ethiopia, while General Leclerc raided Mouzouk and Koufra.

On 17 February that year Churchill minuted to Eden that 'an end should be put to the cold shouldering of General de Gaulle and the Free French movement who are the only people who have done anything for us and to whom we have very solemn engagements. The emphasis should be somewhat shifted.' Six days later Churchill wrote to Cadogan that 'we should continue to give increasing support to de Gaulle'. A second honeymoon with the General was beginning.[22]

As soon as Churchill had solved the Iraq problem, Vichy-held Syria became a nightmare for him. In 1940, after the fall of France, both General Mittelhauser, the Governor of Syria, and the French admiral in charge of the Eastern Mediterranean Fleet declared their determination to fight on against Germany despite Pétain signing the armistice. When a week later they received news of the sinking of the French Fleet at Mers-el-Kebir they became hostile to Britain and loyal to Pétain, so that Syria was virtually an enemy country.[23]

In Syria in 1941 there had been hopes that in spite of Mers-el-Kebir Free French supporters might organize a coup to overthrow the Vichy Government. General Catroux, the former Governor General of Indo-China, had come to London and joined de Gaulle; in October 1940 he went out to Cairo to try to set up a Syrian coup. But it came to nothing: Catroux reported to Churchill that the fierce resistance by the Vichy army at Dakar in 1940 against de Gaulle's assault had depressed the Free French sympathisers, and nothing could be done before the spring.

Catroux then considered bidding for the support of the Syrian Arab population and suggested a declaration in the name of the Free French, promising Syria and Lebanon independence with safeguards for essential French rights on the lines of the Anglo–Egyptian Treaty. Churchill was in favour in principle, but agreed with the Foreign Office that it would be unwise to start an Arab revolt. De Gaulle, however, refused to relinquish any French rights in Syria, telling Churchill he was confident that if he was given full facilities for propaganda he could bring the French in Syria over to his side without British armed help.

With his latent desire for an understanding with Vichy, Churchill would probably have been content to let the Vichy regime in Syria wither on the vine under General Dentz, the High Commissioner. However, when intelligence came in May 1941 that the French in Syria were co-operating with the Germans, the planners advised him that the German aim was to destroy the British in the Middle East by a drive through Turkey and the Levant. The Chiefs of Staff had not yet guessed that Hitler was about to attack Russia.

False hopes that Dentz might agree to a Free French occupation of Syria were raised in March 1941 when the British Consul General in Damascus received a friendly visit from Conty, Dentz's deputy during his absence. They had a confidential talk and Conty proved to be anti-Vichy. The Canadian Dupuy had written to Cadogan: 'Officially General Dentz will object to our intervention, but having shown a more or less artificial resistance he will be delighted as well as Vichy to see Syria coming under our control.' As usual, Dupuy was inept and misleading. Dentz did sack General Fougère, the commander of the French troops in Syria and Lebanon, who was proving poisonously anti-British and had made a widely reported speech which amounted to naked Nazi propaganda. But on account of Mers-el-Kebir Dentz himself was strongly anti-British, and he made harsh remarks which resulted in Halifax asking the State Department to make representations to Pétain through Admiral Leahy that Dentz should not be made Minister of War.[24]

Wavell wanted to leave Syria as quiet as possible, but Catroux and de Gaulle were agitating for a tightening of the blockade in the hope that this would lead Dentz to agree to a Free French takeover. The Turks too attached importance to transit rights for Allied troops over Syria.

Cadogan minuted to Eden on 22 April: 'Task of occupation of Syria at this moment and of such conditions as "no more German visits or propaganda" or the right of passage across Syrian territory for Allied troops is pure moonshine. Are we really ready at this moment to conquer Syria? Of course we are not. We really must put these ridiculous ideas out of our head and out of those of Catroux and de Gaulle.' Eden agreed. But as so often, Churchill rejected out of hand the over-cautious views of the Foreign Office and Eden. For him the conquest of Syria was not 'pure moonshine': he was determined to take the country so that Allied troops could reach Turkey. Churchill sent instructions to Wavell to assemble a force either to help Dentz to resist German infiltration or to attack Syria if the French refused to cooperate.[25]

In response to overtures from Britain Dentz said he himself would be ready to resist the Germans, but would have to obey the orders from Vichy. Wavell was less than enthusiastic, replying to Churchill on 17 May: 'I feel strongly that Free French without strong British support would be ineffective and likely to aggravate situation and that original action must be British, to be followed by Free French if successful . . . Hope I shall not be landed with Syria commitment unless absolutely essential. Any force I could send now would be painfully reminiscent of Jameson Raid [the Jameson Raid was an abortive attack in 1895 on the Transvaal which was then under Boer rule] and might suffer similar fate.'[26] This signal infuriated Churchill, coupled as it was with Wavell's previous dragging of his feet over sending a force to Iraq; as has been seen, he decided impulsively to sack Wavell, but delayed the dismissal even though he told Dill that Wavell must go.

Wavell was ordered to 'improvise the largest force that you can manage without prejudice to the security Western Desert and be prepared to move into Syria at the earliest possible date'. There was then a dispute between Wavell and London on the role of the Free French troops. On 21 May the exasperated Wavell threatened to resign, signalling: 'You must trust my judgements in this matter or relieve me of my command.' Churchill answered: 'We must not shrink from running small scale military risks' and told Wavell he must undertake a joint Anglo–French operation or 'arrangements will be made to meet any wish you express to be relieved of your command'.[27]

Dill was horrified at Churchill's cavalier treatment of his fellow general, and wrote to Wavell: 'What a time you are having . . . I do not know whether or not you will pack up on receiving the telegram from the Defence Committee or rather the P.M. . . . From your own personal view you will be sorely tempted to hand in your portfolio – you could hardly go on a better wicket – but from the national point of view it would, I feel, be a disaster.' Dill also wrote to Auchinleck, warning him that he would shortly be replacing Wavell.[28]

Wavell decided to comply with Churchill's instructions. He produced a mixed force of British and Dominion troops to operate alongside the Free French, and on 8 June 1941 launched an attack on Syria with General Sir Henry Maitland Wilson in charge. Consisting of only one division and six battalions of de Gaulle's infantry, it was outnumbered by the Vichy forces. Churchill's hope that the presence of de Gaulle and his troops would cause the French in Lebanon and Syria to overthrow the Vichy yoke was soon dashed. Mers-el-Kebir rankled strongly, and instead of offering only a token resistance General Dentz's forces quickly counter-attacked before the Allies reached Damascus. Fierce fighting followed, but the colonial troops under General Dentz were lukewarm and when Dentz accepted the help of German aircraft defections to the Anglo–Gaullists began.

Wavell explained to Churchill that the Vichy French on 'discovering we had no tanks put up very stout and resolute resistance. They had expected to be attacked in overwhelming numbers on ground and in air and were probably prepared to capitulate after token resistance.'[29] The Vichy French Fleet could give little assistance because of lack of ammunition. Mercifully, casualties at sea on both sides were light until the French submarine *Souffleur* was sunk 4000 yards from shore and only four seamen were able to swim to safety (one of them immediately defected to de Gaulle). Vichy sent air reinforcements; they had to stage at Italian aerodromes at Brindisi and Athens. The pilots arrived worn out because they had refused to sit down in an Italian Air Force mess.[30] Soon a much respected Vichy officer, Colonel Collet, a close friend of General Huntziger, the Vichy Minister of War and Commander in Chief, defected. French resistance crumbled, and on 12 July Dentz surrendered. But the Syrian campaign cost the Allies 4600 killed and wounded, with 6500 losses on the Vichy side.

Churchill was abundantly justified in insisting on the attack on Syria. Otherwise the Germans would have occupied Syria and turned the north flank of the British defence of Egypt and the Suez Canal.

The armistice terms made de Gaulle angry because General Wilson, with Churchill's approval, was allowing Dentz to repatriate his troops to France without insisting that the Free French were allowed first to try and persuade them to defect. In addition the occupying British were as friendly towards the Vichy troops as they were to de Gaulle's. De Gaulle was rude and difficult with Oliver Lyttelton, the Minister of State in Cairo, until Churchill agreed to change a few words in the armistice document. However Dentz continued to repatriate the Vichy troops without the Free French being able to conduct their propaganda until it was learnt that, in contradiction of the rules of warfare, Dentz had sent fifty-two captured British officers to Vichy France; Dentz and his staff were then taken into custody as hostages, which resulted in the speedy return of the prisoners. However only 2500 (including 100 officers) rallied to de Gaulle out of the 24,000 troops under Dentz's command.

Syria did not bulk large in Churchill's calculations after its occupation by Anglo–French troops, although he became very irate when he learnt that Dentz had allowed 600 Germans from the Foreign Legion to be sent back to Vichy France where they would be available to be used again against British troops; he wanted disciplinary action taken against Wilson's staff officers who had allowed this to happen. (French historians ignore the incident of the British POWs and the German Legionaires being transferred to metropolitan France.) Instead Churchill concentrated on Wavell's offensive in the Western Desert, codenamed Battleaxe, and the likelihood that Hitler would invade Russia. Consequently he did not reply to de Gaulle's frequent arrogant telegrams of complaint. Wavell and Lyttleton pointed out to him that de Gaulle's failure even to recognize the existence of the problem of Arab desire for independence in Syria and Lebanon might have 'serious consequences'. Relations became so strained that the General threatened to withdraw all Free French troops from Allied command.

On 4 August Eden warned the War Cabinet that 'the situation in Syria was disturbing. General de Gaulle had adopted a very difficult attitude and there had been signs of collusion between him and the Vichy French', so that efforts were being made to induce him to return to England. But the General could not be persuaded to leave Cairo until September.

Churchill and de Gaulle met in London on 12 September. Churchill, furious with Pétain over the German use of French bases in Syria, knew in his heart of hearts that he must rely on de Gaulle as his principal French collaborator, and after a stormy start to the interview harmony was restored. The British and the Free French recognized Syrian independence, but as the French mandate could not be suspended in wartime General de Gaulle was to exercise the powers of French High Commissioner in Syria.[31]

Success in Iraq and Syria, in spite of Wavell's premonitions, was rich compensation to Churchill for his disappointment over the setbacks to British arms in Greece and Crete and over Keyes' ambitious but abortive plans for amphibious operations in the Aegean. Correctly he wrote in his memoirs that 'our strategical position in the Middle East was greatly improved'.[32] The northern defences of Egypt and the Suez Canal had been made secure, and the threat to Turkey from the south removed. All four sets of operations – Iraq, Greece, Syria and Crete – ran concurrently with the battle in the Western Desert. These had imposed a tremendous strain on air, army and naval forces in the Middle East, and in the summer of 1941 there remained a grave threat to Egypt from Rommel's forces in the desert.

CHAPTER ELEVEN

Wavell and Auchinleck under the lash

CHURCHILL WAS unfair in blaming Wavell for the fall of Benghazi and Rommel's advance to the Egyptian frontier in April 1941. Wavell had informed London that he was leaving only one infantry division and half an armoured division to defend Cyrenaica when he split his forces to find the troops required for Greece. Churchill had accepted this without demur, and if Wavell had suggested leaving more troops in Cyrenaica Churchill would almost certainly have said that Wavell was being over-cautious and depriving Greece of much-needed strength.[1]

Once the decision to go into Greece had been taken, Wavell was forced to take risks, and he had been caught on the hop by the sudden arrival of unexpectedly strong German armoured forces under Rommel. Churchill and the Chiefs of Staff were better informed in London about German moves in Tripoli than Wavell was in Cairo, and had accepted the calculated risk of a weakly defended Cyrenaica.

Early in the war, cypher experts at Bletchley Park had broken the main German Army code, Enigma, and could read their most important radio cypher messages. The decrypts were known as Ultra. The flow of intercepted messages brought a massive traffic, and increasing numbers of German scholars were posted to Hut 3 at Bletchley to interpret the decoded messages. The translations were sent immediately to Churchill at the Ministry of Defence, and extracts were forwarded in strict secrecy to GHQ MEF, the headquarters of Middle East forces in Cairo. There was always a fear that the Germans would discover their Enigma code had been broken and would give up using it; hence the secret was confined to as few as possible. By the spring of 1941 there were enough German experts at Bletchley to provide Churchill with a continuous flow of reliable news about the German Army's intentions in the desert, and this made him feel he could dictate strategy in the Mediterranean to Wavell and later to Auchinleck.

On 20 April news came that a new German armoured division of around 400 tanks had disembarked at Tripoli and would soon be in the line. Wavell asked the CIGS to 'please give his personal assistance because of this disquieting intelligence'. Galvanized by the danger, within two days Churchill organized the removal of 300 tanks from the home forces and their despatch direct through the

126

Mediterranean to Wavell. Only one ship was lost, and 240 out of 300 tanks reached Alexandria on 12 May.

But the Chiefs of Staff expressed grave fears over sending this valuable convoy of tanks through the dangerous Mediterranean. According to Ismay, the COS were strongly against the tank proposal because it weakened the strength of the Army at home and the Mediterranean route involved unwarranted risks. However Churchill railroaded his plan through, and was delighted when the convoy arrived at Alexandria almost unscathed.[2]

Churchill now concentrated on his ardent hopes of an early desert victory. These were enhanced by an Ultra report early in May that Rommel's Afrika Corps was thoroughly exhausted and needed reinforcement and reorganization because of the inadequacy of its supply system, and that it would be impossible for it to achieve anything other than quick raids on Tobruk. Alas, Churchill's high hopes during the first week of May 1941 were to be followed by two British defeats in the desert and the dismissal of Wavell.

Churchill was frustrated because Rommel's small army was keeping Wavell bottled up in Egypt. He told Wavell on 4 May that there were close on half a million men under Middle East command, whereas he did not believe Rommel had more than 25,000 in Africa. Wavell replied that his numbers were impressive on paper but he was short of air support and very short of equipment, particularly tanks, anti-aircraft guns and transport.[3]

Wavell told Churchill that even before the convoy of tanks, known as Tiger, had docked he had issued orders for a desert attack on the assumption that the tanks would arrive safely. The convoy arrived on 12 May, and on the 15th Wavell launched Operation Brevity against Rommel. Although Halfaya Pass, Sollum and Capuzzo were quickly captured, they were soon lost again. Churchill did not appear worried, cabling to Wavell: 'Results of action seem to us satisfactory', and adding 'What are your dates for bringing Tiger tanks into action?' Churchill was determined to force Wavell to throw the newly arrived tanks against Rommel, who the Prime Minister was convinced was enfeebled.

Unfortunately Churchill's tanks (which he called Tiger cubs) were found on arrival at Alexandria to be in an unsatisfactory condition; they consisted of Crusaders, Matildas (the slow-moving infantry tank) and light tanks. The vehicles had been rushed on to the ships without even elementary mechanical checking. At Alexandria all had to be camouflaged and modified for the desert, and many needed overhauls. On 19 May Wavell cabled to Churchill: 'Estimate that Tiger cubs will be in action by end of month will prove optimistic because of air cleaners ['air cleaners' were needed to keep the sand out of the carburettors] etc.' These delays made Churchill angry, but he was optimistic when Wavell told him that D-Day for his attack, codenamed Battleaxe, was 15 June. However, Wavell had also sent the disquieting news that his armoured cars were inferior to the Germans', the Matilda tanks were too slow, and there were too many breakdowns amongst the Crusaders. Thus he could not accept battle with 'perfect confidence' as he had against the Italians. Wavell's plan for Battleaxe was first to defeat Rommel's Panzers and then to link up with the fortress at Tobruk and advance to Mechili, halfway between Tobruk and Benghazi.[4]

Battleaxe started well, but after forty-eight hours everything went wrong, and three days after the assault began the British troops had to withdraw to their start line. After a last-minute dangerous flight to consult with his battle front generals Wavell cabled to Churchill: 'I regret to report failure of Battleaxe.'

Churchill had convinced himself that sending the tanks from Britain through the Mediterranean had given Wavell a 'lethal weapon'. Now nothing remained of his high hopes but dust and ashes. He blamed Wavell, as he did for the Crete disaster, recording in his memoirs that he had been 'discontented' with him over Crete where 'a few more tanks had not been sent', and now he was dissatisfied with his arrangements for the reception of the tanks sent at so much risk through the Mediterranean. He thought Battleaxe 'ill-concerted' with its failure to make a sortie from 'the Tobruk sallyport'. So on 17 June Churchill dismissed Wavell, appointing him Commander-in-Chief India in place of Auchinleck, who was sent to Cairo.[5]

Churchill was wrong in ascribing the failure of Battleaxe to poor generalship: it was a failure of British equipment. Not only were German armoured cars and tanks superior, but Rommel also had an overwhelming advantage in anti-tank guns. At this stage of the war the British had only 2-pounder guns both on their tanks and in artillery anti-tank batteries; the 6-pounders and 17-pounders which were so effective later were not available for Battleaxe. British troops engaged in Battleaxe reported that their 2-pounders were ineffective against the more powerful 50 mm and 75 mm guns mounted on German tanks. Instead, the artillery 25-pounders had to be deployed in an anti-tank role because they had solid, armour-piercing shells. But their muzzle velocity was too slow, and using them in an anti-tank role produced a tactical conflict because the gunners were trained for infantry support.

Rommel had an immense advantage from the high-velocity 88 mm A A guns which, when dug into the ground, became a devastating weapon against British tanks, not only during Battleaxe but until the end of the campaign in North Africa. The Germans made them practically invisible by sinking them into the sand with only their barrels protruding horizontally above ground.

The Chiefs of Staff condoned Churchill's decision to sack Wavell, but Dill thought it necessary to warn Auchinleck that he would be subject to great and often undue pressure from Churchill, adding: 'You should make it quite clear what risks are involved if a course of action is forced upon you which from the military point of view is undesirable. You may even find it necessary in the extreme case to dissociate yourself from the consequences.' This makes it clear how strongly Dill disapproved of Churchill's treatment of Wavell.[6] Unfortunately Churchill never liked Dill, and Dill in return, although he welcomed his forceful leadership, deeply resented Churchill's continual meddling in purely military matters.

Churchill recorded in his memoirs how much he had hoped that Battleaxe would destroy Rommel's 'audacious' force, so that Tobruk would be relieved and

Benghazi recaptured. As the news came of Battleaxe's failure he went down to his home at Chartwell, which was shut up, and walked alone around the valley 'disconsolately' for several hours.[7]

But as usual his spirits soon revived. He was eagerly anticipating war between Germany and Russia. On 31 May the COS reported that Hitler was concentrating a large army on the Russian frontier; on 12 June they gave fresh evidence that Hitler was about to attack Russia. On Sunday the 22nd Churchill was given the news in his bedroom at 4.30 a.m. that Germany had invaded Russia. Although Churchill was a bitter opponent of Communism he immediately rejoiced that Britain had an ally again, and broadcast that night that we would give 'whatever help we can to Russia and the Russian people'.

For twelve months since the fall of France the war had been a crusade with no apparent chance of victory. Once Russia was an ally there were rational grounds for hope again. Churchill had tried hard to wipe out the Russian Revolution after the First World War, and he never withdrew his former attacks on Bolshevism. Yet he realized he must now draw a veil over the misdeeds of the Soviet regime and the appalling character of its leader. His resulting propaganda misled the British public into believing that the Soviet Union was emerging as a proper democracy and that Stalin was a statesman with human qualities. The rank-and-file British trade unionists keenly echoed this view, although Attlee, Bevin and Morrison inside Churchill's coalition Cabinet were always sceptical and cautious about Stalin's likely behaviour.

On the morning of 22 June the British nation, unlike Churchill, was uncertain whether to treat the news as good or bad. Typical was the behaviour of the City. The *Spectator* commented that the Stock Exchange spent the morning endeavouring to make up their minds whether the German aggression against Russia was 'bull' or 'bear'. Eventually it was concluded that 'whatever happened we could hardly be worse off as a result of Hitler's latest somersault'.

In 1940 Stafford Cripps had been the leading political figure in Great Britain in favour of a rapprochement with the Soviet Government; he looked on it as practical in spite of the German–Russian non-aggression pact and the generally favourable attitude of the Russians towards the Germans. At the low point of the war, on 31 May 1940, Churchill agreed to Cripps going as Ambassador to Moscow in place of the long-serving Russian expert William Seeds.

As soon as it was clear that France was on the brink of capitulation Russia had invaded the Baltic states of Lithuania, Latvia and Estonia. Bogus elections followed, in which these states appeared to vote for incorporation in the Soviet Union and to accept Communism. The Russians had also compelled the Romanian Government to surrender to them northern Bessarabia and Bukovina. According to Cadogan, Cripps wanted to recognize all the Russian acquisitions of territory *de jure*, hand over to them all the Latvian, Estonian and Lithuanian ships and gold that had been deposited in London 'and trust to the Russians loving us'. He commented: 'This is just silly.'[8]

Churchill felt bitter towards Stalin over both the Balkans and the Baltic states, and intensely disliked Cripps' much more favourable attitude towards them. He would not agree to Cripps' request on the sound ground that such action would cause resentment in the United States where there was much sympathy for the Baltic countries. In April Cripps reiterated that *de jure* recognition would cause a 'deterioration' in Russo–German relations.

Churchill was scornful of Cripps' despatch, writing back to him on one occasion that it was not worth the trouble of sending it and 'you will get much more out of them by letting these forces work than by frantic efforts to assure them of your love. This only looks like weakness and encourages them to believe they are stronger than they are.'9

It is claimed that when Rudolf Hess flew to England on 11 May he came with Hitler's approval to tell Churchill that Germany intended to attack Russia and to ask Britain to make peace and join forces with Germany. The evidence points to it being entirely Hess's own scheme for a negotiated peace, with the British Empire being left alone if Germany was allowed a free hand in Europe. Churchill wanted to make propaganda out of Hess, but when it was found that the German was deranged he decided that no good use could be made of the incident. However Litvinov, the Russian Ambassador in Washington, told Halifax that when he learnt of the German attack he felt sure Britain had done a deal with Hitler through Hess. Hence he was enormously relieved by Churchill's declaration of support for Russia broadcast on 22 June.10

Until the last moment, in spite of mounting evidence about the build-up of German forces on the Russian frontier, the Foreign Office feared that Hitler would merely give Stalin an ultimatum demanding large and harsh economic concessions, and that the German preparations for the attack were a bluff. Churchill, on the other hand, was sure that Hitler would attack, and as so often his instinct was correct. He insisted on warning the Russians in considerable detail of the German intentions, but the Russians could not believe that Hitler would be so treacherous and dishonest. Eden had a long interview with Maisky, the Russian Ambassador, in London; the late Duke of Portland (formerly William Cavendish Bentinck), who was present, told the author it was clear to him that Maisky would not believe Eden, evidently thinking that the troop movements were part of a war of nerves.11

In the first month of the German–Soviet war the Germans penetrated deeply into Russia with 160 divisions. Then there was a pause, and Hitler decided not to thrust for Moscow but to go for Leningrad and the Crimea.

Churchill eagerly agreed to a joint Declaration with the Russians that there should be mutual help and no separate peace, and on 7 July proudly told Stalin in a personal message that 'we were making very heavy attacks both by day and night upon all German occupied territory and all Germany within our reach', with four hundred sorties the previous day; concluding with 'we have only to go on fighting to beat the life out of these villains'.12

On 20 July Stalin implored Churchill to establish a second front either in northern France or in the Arctic in Norway. Churchill's reaction was that the Russians 'never understood to the smallest degree the nature of the amphibious operation necessary to disembark and maintain a great army upon a well defended hostile coast'; and after the war he recorded that 'Niagaras of folly and misstatement still pour out on this question of the second front'. In July 1941 Britain was so weak militarily that the landing of an army in Europe was out of the question, and Churchill firmly told Stalin so.[13]

Still, on 29 August Churchill offered the Russians 445 Hurricane aircraft which could ill be spared from Britain and for which, as will be seen, there was a crying need in Singapore. Stalin sent lukewarm thanks and reiterated a plea for a second front 'somewhere in the Balkans or France to draw away from the Eastern front 30–40 divisions'. Maisky, sent to talk to Eden and Churchill, pleaded for an immediate landing on the coast of France or the Low Countries. Stalin would not take 'No' for an answer. Churchill wrote to Stalin on 4 September that

> although we should shrink from no exertion there is, in fact, no possibility of any British action in the West, except air action, which would draw the German forces from the East before the winter sets in. There is no chance whatever of a second front being formed in the Balkans without the help of Turkey . . . Whether British armies will be strong enough to invade the mainland of Europe during 1942 must depend on unforeseeable events.[14]

In reply Stalin made the ridiculous statement that Britain could 'without risk' land twenty-five to thirty divisions 'at Archangel or transport them across Iran'. Churchill recorded that it was hopeless to argue with a man 'thinking in terms of so much utter unreality' and Stalin's letters are evidence that in the summer of 1941 the Russian leader was in a state of panic lest German armies should take both Leningrad and Moscow. He was feeling desperate because Kiev was about to fall; Soviet troops were retreating in the eastern Ukraine, and a fresh drive on Moscow was probable.

On 11 September Churchill wrote to Stalin: 'If we could act successfully in Norway the attitude of Sweden would be powerfully affected, but at the moment we have neither the forces nor the shipping available for this project. Again in the South the great prize is Turkey; if Turkey can be gained another powerful army will be available. Turkey would like to come with us but is afraid, and not without reason.' By 6 October he was able to inform Stalin that he intended to run 'a continuous cycle of convoys leaving every ten days with 300 fighter aircraft and 315 tanks during October'.

There was then a nasty hiccup in the Stalin–Churchill relationship: an awkward letter was sent by Stalin on 11 November which said, 'In the present situation there will be difficulty to secure mutual confidence', and he would not invite Generals Wavell and Paget to Moscow as Churchill had suggested. Stalin continued that 'an intolerable situation has been created in the question of the declaration of war by Great Britain to Finland, Hungary and Romania' (who were all fighting against Russia).

Despite pressure from Cripps, Churchill had refused to declare war on Finland, for which nation he had much sympathy; he also had a personal friendship with Field Marshal Mannerheim, the Finnish leader. However, in response to Stalin's blunt request he agreed to a message being sent on 26 November to the Finnish Government that unless by 3 December they ceased to fight Russia, Britain would have no choice but to declare war. Churchill also sent a personal message to Field Marshal Mannerheim saying how grieved he would be 'if out of loyalty to Russia' Britain declared war on Finland, and adding 'surely your troops have advanced far enough and could now halt and make a *de facto* exit from the war'. Mannerheim refused, and to please Russia Churchill agreed reluctantly to declarations of war on Finland, Romania and Hungary on 3 December.

Cripps annoyed Churchill by reiterating the advisability not only of these declarations of war, but also of increased help for Russia. He threatened to resign his post and conduct his opposition to Churchill's policy in the Commons. Winston then drafted a strong letter to Cripps, which shows how he was prepared ruthlessly to override any opposition to his conduct of the war:

> All the same I am sure it would be a mistake from your point of view to leave your post and abandon the Russians and the Soviet cause with which you are so closely associated while all hangs in the balance at Leningrad, Moscow and in the south. Your own friends here would not understand it. I hope you will believe that I give you this advice not from any fear of political opposition which you might raise over here by making out we had not done enough, etc. I could face such opposition without any political embarrassment, though with much personal regret. The Soviet Government, as you must see upon reflection, could never support you in an agitation against us because that would mean that we should be forced to vindicate our action in public which would necessarily be detrimental to Soviet interests and to the common cause. Force of circumstances would compel them to make the best of us. After all, we have wrecked our Air and Tank expansion programmes for their sake, and in our effort to hold German Air power in the west we have lost more than double the pilots and machines lost in the Battle of Britain last year. You must not underrate the strength of the case I could deploy in the House of Commons and on the broadcast, though I should be very sorry to do so. The Government itself was never so strong or unchallenged as it is now. Every movement of the United States towards the war adds to that strength. You should weigh all this before engaging in a most unequal struggle which could only injure the interests to which you are attached. I have taken full note of your wish to come home. Indeed you told me about it before you returned last time. You may be sure I will tell you when to come at the right moment for you and for the cause. It may not be for some months yet.[15]

Fortunately, on account of the declaration of war by Britain on 3 December Cripps withdrew his request to be allowed to leave Moscow, and this formidable Churchillian letter was not sent.

Both the Russians and the British became seriously alarmed about German influence in Iran, then known still as Persia, and the size of the German community which had reached five thousand. They were mainly technicians brought in by the Shah for his modernization programme, but this made them even more dangerous. There was a constant fear of a German-inspired coup on the lines of Rashid Ali's revolt in Iraq.

On 10 July the Russians proposed sending a joint note to the Persian

Government demanding the expulsion of the German colony, and if the Persians did not comply to follow it up with military action. At first the British Cabinet would only agree to half-measures involving the capture of the Abadan oil field without any demand for transit rights of troops and war material for Russia. This was far from strong enough for Churchill. Auchinleck had been recalled to London, and on 31 July Churchill presided at a Chiefs of Staff meeting with Eden and Auchinleck and pressed for tougher action. Despite the timidity of the Cabinet Churchill insisted that an Anglo–Russian note should be presented in Teheran on 17 August demanding the expulsion of the German colony, but again without a demand for transit rights. The Persian reply was unacceptable, and joint Anglo–Russian military operations began on 25 August. Churchill insisted, against Auchinleck's plea of being under-strength, that reinforcements must be sent from Cairo. (The main effort was coming from India.) On 28 August the Shah asked for a ceasefire, but afterwards was un-cooperative.[16]

Lord Hankey's Committee for the Co-ordination of Allied Supplies had told the Chiefs of Staff that only the Persian route gave any possibility of large volumes of supplies to Russia in coming months, and that if this was developed it would be a departure from the policy of providing for the defence of India's north-western countries by maintaining a 'vacuum' beyond them. Churchill was adamant that the Persian route must be expanded to the limit of its capacity regardless of this traditional policy; to do so would require physical control of the Persian railway system. On 3 and 4 September, at meetings of the Defence Committee and the War Cabinet, Churchill insisted it was time to take a firm line with the Persians: the British must exercise complete control over the country for the rest of the war, and especially over the road and railway route to Russia.[17]

On 15 September British and Russian troops moved on Teheran. The Shah abdicated and was succeeded by his son, who agreed to co-operate fully. The entire German colony was interned in Basra; British and Russian troops were able to withdraw from Teheran, but continued to guard the key points on the railway. Once again Churchill's firmness had produced the desired result.

Churchill immediately put plans in hand through the Ministry of Supply and War Transport for substantial increases in the number of locomotives and amount of rolling stock on the Persian railways. He telegraphed to Stalin that he had done so, and that now twelve trains a day instead of the current two would be able to make the journey each way. Locomotives and rolling stock (already converted to oil burners) were being shipped from Britain via the Cape, and the first 48 locomotives and 400 steel trucks were about to start, while the water supply along the railway was being developed.

Churchill's fertile mind loved plans like these. He knew that through the occupation of Teheran and the improved efficiency of the railway he had obtained an important strategic objective. On 30 September he telegraphed again to Stalin:

> I am most anxious to settle our alliance with Persia and to make an intimate efficient working arrangement with your forces in Persia. There are in Persia signs of serious disorder among tribesmen and of breakdown of Persian authority. Disorder if it

spreads will mean wasting our divisions holding down these people, which again means burdening the road and railway communications with movements and supplies of aforesaid divisions, whereas we want to keep the lines clear and improved to the utmost in order to get supplies through to you. Our object should be to make the Persians keep each other quiet while we get on with the war. Your Excellency's decisive indications in this direction will spread forward the already favourable trend of our affairs in this minor theatre.[18]

Already German air and submarine attacks were taking a great toll of ships in the sea convoys to Archangel laden with tanks, aircraft and vital military supplies, and there were doubts whether this northern convoy route could be kept in operation. Churchill did not mind that Stalin might use harsh and ruthless methods in Persia to stop disorder, provided the alternative to the Archangel route to Russia could work at full capacity.

In June 1941 when Auchinleck succeeded Wavell in Cairo as Commander-in-Chief he was, not surprisingly, cautious. He emphasized how essential more reinforcements and more tanks were before he attacked Rommel. His first message to London, on 4 July, came as a shock to Churchill because Auchinleck declared he could not contemplate 'a further offensive' in the Western Desert until Syria was 'secure' (four days later Dentz surrendered), and even then he needed three armoured divisions to ensure success over Rommel because infantry divisions 'were not good enough' for attacks in the desert against armour. Cyprus too, Auchinleck pointed out, required a strong garrison.

Churchill replied that a renewed offensive in the desert ought to be possible in the near future because Auchinleck would soon have five hundred tanks available, and he wanted the attack to be made not later than mid-September while the Tobruk garrison was still 'capable of offensive action'. Auchinleck responded that the tank crews required more training with their new tanks, particularly on the American ones which had just arrived.[19]

Churchill felt it was intolerable for the Eighth Army to stand idle while fierce battles raged between Russia and Germany in the East; he also feared an autumn attack on the Middle East by the Germans from the north, through Anatolia or the Caucasus, which would oblige Auchinleck to divide his forces. He therefore urged his new Commander-in-Chief first 'to snatch a quick victory in the desert'. Auchinleck insisted he could not attack before mid-November, and only then if he received considerable numbers of extra tanks. This produced a deadlock. Auchinleck was summoned to London on 29 July, where he uncompromisingly continued to refuse to attempt an offensive operation until November. Churchill was left with no option but to accept Auchinleck's view or to find another commander. Having sacked Wavell on the grounds of his unsatisfactory performance, he could hardly do the same with Auchinleck before any battle had taken place.[20]

With growing impatience, Churchill had to wait until 18 November for Auchinleck to launch his desert attack, codenamed Crusader. The ensuing long drawn-out operations lasted until the following January and produced a resounding victory, although the quick kill envisaged at first by Auchinleck and Churchill did not materialize. After long, involved, heavy fighting Tobruk was relieved on 29 November, having been besieged since 11 April; Benghazi was recaptured on 24 December. During the fighting, on 26 November Auchinleck dismissed General Cunningham, commander of the Eighth Army, because he thought he had become too defence-minded after losing a large number of tanks; General Ritchie was substituted for him. Churchill endorsed this decision without demur.[21]

Rommel withdrew to a defence line at El Agheila. Auchinleck attempted to penetrate it so as to capture Tripoli and throw the Germans out of North Africa altogether. But a counter-attack by Rommel made this impossible, and to Churchill's chagrin the Germans recaptured Benghazi early in February 1942, when the front became temporarily static, with both sides exhausted.

Churchill attributed the victory to Auchinleck conducting the battle better than Wavell had in the spring. It was a false appreciation. The truth is that Auchinleck's forces were much stronger relative to the Germans than Wavell's had been.[22]

By New Year's Day 1942 the Eighth Army had reached the identical point where Wavell had forced the Italians back in 1940. But the objective of clearing the Germans out of North Africa was not achieved. However, Crusader was a fillip to Churchill's morale which he badly needed after Wavell's desert failure and the disasters in Greece and Crete. Alas, he would have to wait until October 1942 for another military success in the Middle East, while the war with Japan produced disaster after disaster in the Far East.[23]

In December 1941 many German submarines were transferred from the Atlantic to the Mediterranean; they sank the carrier *Ark Royal* and other British ships while Italian human torpedoes crippled the *Queen Elizabeth* and *Valiant* in Alexandria harbour. Additionally Hitler sent back a corps of the Luftwaffe from the Russian front to Sicily, and command of the sea and air in the Eastern Mediterranean suddenly passed into German hands. The crippling of the British Fleet, together with the re-emergence of German air power in Sicily, put paid to Churchill's dream of capturing Tripoli and linking up with the Vichy French in Tunisia.[24]

In February 1942 the German submarines and the Luftwaffe were posing a threat to Malta. Accordingly, Churchill was desperately anxious for Auchinleck to recapture the air bases in western Cyrenaica which he had occupied fleetingly after his December advance before Rommel counter-attacked in January.[25]

Brooke, who had replaced Dill as CIGS, was sympathetic to the difficulties besetting Auchinleck, who had to send away three divisions to the Far East while the Germans were threatening to attack from Turkey. Not so Churchill! He was determined that Auchinleck should launch an offensive against Rommel in March 1942, signalling to Auchinleck on 26 February: 'According to our figures you have substantial superiority in the air, in armour, and in other forces over the enemy. There seems to be danger that he may gain reinforcements as fast as or even faster than you. The supply of Malta is causing us increasing anxiety, and anyone can see the magnitude of our disasters in the Far East'. This crossed with a message from Auchinleck, saying that he fully realized the critical position of Malta and the need to recover the advanced landing grounds, but 'to launch major offensive before 1 June would be to risk defeat in detail and possibly endanger safety of Egypt'.[26]

In a rage, Churchill drafted a stinging reply to Auchinleck; but after Lyttelton, back in London from Cairo, had described the defects in British armour he agreed to a milder one stating that the recapture of the landing grounds in Western Cyrenaica 'in the near future is vital to your whole situation'. Churchill pressed for a convoy from Alexandria to go to Malta, which was cut off and short of all supplies and food; this was almost impossible without fighter protection from western Cyrenaica. But Auchinleck and his colleagues in Cairo again refused to attack before late June or early July.

Finding that long-range pressure had no effect on Auchinleck, Churchill invited him to come home for consultation. Auchinleck turned this down, telling the Prime Minister that in the present 'fluid' state of affairs his duty was to remain on the spot, and asking instead for the CIGS and the Chief of Air Staff to come to Cairo. Churchill refused to send them, and seriously considered sacking Auchinleck. He asked Brooke for his opinion. Brooke replied that the best solution would be a 'return swap' between Auchinleck and Wavell. Winston, irritated, angrily rejected this idea, and instead sent Cripps, assisted by General Sir Archibald Nye, the Vice CIGS, to Cairo. To Churchill's intense annoyance, his two emissaries took Auchinleck's side. Cripps reported that the present British strength in tanks and airpower was such as not to give 'any reasonable chance of a successful offensive' (Auchinleck had been forced to send large numbers of planes to the Far East). Cripps emphasized that he agreed with Auchinleck that to attack before mid-May would be to take 'unwarrantable risks'. Nye confirmed Cripps' report and stressed that a successful offensive depended on superiority in tanks. This view forced Churchill reluctantly to agree to 15 May as the earliest date for an attack.

However, on 6 May Auchinleck stated that he could not start his offensive until 15 June. Not until then, he said, would he have the necessary superiority in tanks. And should the fresh Italian division Littorio arrive in the battle zone the offensive would have to be postponed until August, while if he had to divert forces to aid Turkey no offensive was possible at all.[27]

This continued obstinacy from Auchinleck gave Churchill an unpleasant shock, and he was greatly angered. On 8 May he held meetings of the Chiefs of Staff and the War Cabinet which were attended by Cripps and Lyttelton, both recently returned from Cairo. Churchill wanted to order Auchinleck to attack, but he was persuaded to tone down the instructions. Auchinleck was accordingly told that the Chiefs of Staff, the Defence Committee and the War Cabinet agreed that he ought to fight a major battle, if possible in May, and the sooner the better; and that 'they' would take full responsibility.[28]

At that time Churchill was much influenced by Ultra signals, which disclosed that Rommel was lamenting to his superiors the inadequacies of his equipment and supplies. This news reinforced Churchill's view that Auchinleck should attack as soon as possible. But post-war research has disclosed that Rommel was adept at misleading his superiors about his weaknesses in order to get a better allocation of available supplies. His real strength in the desert was considerably greater than Churchill believed, because the Prime Minister always took Ultra decrypts at their face value; in Cairo, meanwhile, Auchinleck's intelligence had their own means of discovering Rommel's strengths and weaknesses.[29]

Auchinleck countered Churchill's call for an immediate offensive by calling a meeting in Cairo of the Middle East Defence Committee, which had been set up to allow the politicians to consult formally with the Service Chiefs. On 10 May they met, presided over by Richard Casey, the Australian politician who had been appointed Resident Minister in the Middle East in place of Lyttelton; the Junior Minister, Walter Monckton, was also present. They pointed out that the fall of Malta would not necessarily be fatal for Egypt; the landing grounds west of Benghazi would not be operational for at least two months after the attack began; to attack with inadequate armoured forces might well result in the destruction of those troops and endanger Egypt, while it might be to Britain's advantage if the Germans attacked first.

This was the last straw for Churchill. He insisted on an ultimatum being sent to Auchinleck to the effect that the very latest date for the attack must be mid-June to coincide with the Malta convoy and that the Chiefs of Staff, the Defence Committee and the War Cabinet considered the risks to Egypt as less grave than the disaster of losing Malta.[30] Churchill hoped that this direct order, couched in abrupt terms, would push Auchinleck into resignation. Instead, Auchinleck acquiesced. He had been determined not to risk another Battleaxe-style fiasco, but by May a considerable number of the more powerful Grant and Stuart American tanks had arrived together with some 6-pounder guns.

The preceding three months had produced an unhappy deterioration in the relationship between Churchill and Auchinleck on whom Churchill had originally pinned such high hopes; unfortunately the relationship between them became only too reminiscent of that leading up to the sacking of Wavell. But on 26 May, when relations between Churchill and Auchinleck were at their lowest point, Rommel attacked the Eighth Army.[31]

The German offensive resulted in a triumph for Rommel and a disaster for the Eighth Army. Ritchie was outflanked at Bir Hacheim, and a German pincer movement around the Knightsbridge Box (see map) was closed; by 12 June Ritchie, Commander of the Eighth Army, had to order the troops still on the Gazala Line to withdraw, hoping to make a stand on a line running from Tobruk to the south. Unfortunately El Adem and Sidi Rizegh were taken without difficulty by Rommel on the 18th. Tobruk was isolated as the British had to retreat towards the Egyptian frontier, enabling Rommel to take the so-called fortress on 20 June.

Churchill heard the news of the fall of Tobruk while he was with Roosevelt in Washington the following day; he claims it was 'so surprising that he could hardly believe it', while Brooke, who was also there, wrote in his diary: 'Neither Winston nor I had contemplated such an eventuality.' This is strange, because they had received ample warning from Auchinleck. It is possible that Churchill feigned surprise to Roosevelt to wring more supplies out of him. Alternatively, neither he nor Brooke had read Auchinleck's messages carefully enough.[32]

On 10 January Auchinleck had issued Operation Instruction No. 110 to Ritchie about the contingency of a retreat from El Agheila, and included the following paragraph: 'It is NOT my intention to try to hold permanently Tobruk or any other locality west of the frontier.' When this was received in the War Office Kennedy minuted: 'Tobruk might last year have proved another Kut had it not been for the outbreak of the Russian war . . . In my opinion it would be right to avoid such detachments in future.' Brooke made no comment. Nor did Churchill.

On 11 February Auchinleck issued his Operation Instruction No. 111 to Ritchie. It contained this passage:

> If, for any reason, we should be forced at some future date to withdraw from our present forward positions, every effort will still be made to prevent Tobruk being lost to the enemy, but it is *not my intention to continue to hold it once the enemy is in a position to invest it effectively* [author's italics]. Should this appear inevitable, the place will be evacuated, and the maximum amount of destruction carried out in it, so as to make it useless to the enemy as a supply base. In this eventuality, the enemy's advance will be stopped on the general line Sollum–Maddalena–Giarabub, as laid down in Operation Instruction 110.'[33]

These orders were still in force when Rommel began his offensive in May. Therefore it should have been clear to Churchill and Brooke, if they had studied Auchinleck's signals, that their commander had no intention of making Tobruk a redoubt again as in 1941.

On 14 June Churchill cabled Auchinleck and asked to what position Ritchie wanted to withdraw the Gazala troops, adding that 'he presumed there was no question in any case of giving up Tobruk'. Auchinleck replied the next day, that, although he did not intend the Eighth Army to be besieged in Tobruk, he had no intention whatever of giving it up – meaning he intended to hold it unless it became surrounded. Two days before, on a 'black day' for the Eighth Army, Auchinleck had told Norman Clark of the *News Chronicle* and other war correspondents that he did not expect to be able to hold Tobruk; he would not even be able to defend the Egyptian frontier, he said, and would have to fall back to the prepared defensive positions at Alamein.[34] Thus there is no doubt as to Auchinleck's intentions.

On 15 June the Prime Minister cabled Auchinleck to ask if the War Cabinet should interpret his telegram to mean that, if the need arose, Ritchie would leave as many troops in Tobruk as were necessary 'to hold the place for certain'. The following day Auchinleck replied that this was a 'correct interpretation', adding that Rommel was not strong enough to invest Tobruk and 'mask' British forces on the frontier.

However, in accordance with the plan, on 14 June the Eighth Army had ordered preparations for demolitions at Tobruk to be put in hand so as to be ready for evacuation. These were cancelled on the 15th when Churchill's message about holding the place 'for certain' was received.[35]

Just as Churchill's badgering in 1941 forced Wavell into the wrong decision over Greece, so this hectoring of Auchinleck in June 1942 made him change his mind over Tobruk. If the 14 June demolition order had been proceeded with, most of the garrison would have been evacuated. Instead, after an abortive defence it fell, with over thirty thousand troops being taken prisoner and immensely valuable weapons and stores falling into German hands.

Churchill's insistence on Tobruk being defended pushed his general into a gross tactical mistake against his better judgement at the eleventh hour. During a retreat after a losing battle a commander is under intense strain and pressure; interference from above with no knowledge of the rapidly changing local situation is unpardonable. Tobruk ought to have been abandoned, and the disastrous loss in prisoners and equipment must be laid at Churchill's door. At this critical moment for the Eighth Army Auchinleck should not have had to look over his shoulder to Downing Street.

In a memorandum intended for the official history P. McCallum wrote:

> The fact that Tobruk fell must undoubtedly be attributed to the eleventh hour reversal of policy leading to the decision to hold the fortress regardless of the fact that the 8th Army was in full retreat and in the face of an enemy who had been uniformly successful and whose morale must in consequence have been high. It was impossible in the time available to make adequate preparations for the completely new role imposed upon the garrison which until then had been concerned with prevention of raids by land, sea or air.

He added that not only had German tanks greatly improved since 1941, but the Tobruk defence layout 'was out of date tactically'; also much of the wire had been removed, and there were no up-to-date plans of the minefields through which large tracks had been driven to facilitate movement while the anti-tank ditch had filled in. This piece by McCallum does not appear in the published official history.[36]

The fall of Tobruk was a shock to the British public and a central issue in the vote of censure in the Commons on 2 July. Churchill included in his draft speech:

> The fall of Tobruk with its garrison of about 25,000 was utterly unexpected. Not only was it unexpected by the House and the public at large, but by the War Cabinet, by the Chiefs of Staff and by the General Staff of the Army. On the night before its capture we had received a telegram from Auchinleck that he had allocated what he believed to be an adequate garrison, that the defences were in good order and that 90 days' supplies were available for the troops. The decision to hold Tobruk and the dispositions made were undertaken by Auchinleck with the agreement of the Cabinet, of the War Cabinet and their professional advisors.

When Kennedy saw the Prime Minister's draft he minuted to Brooke that it was 'unfair' to Auchinleck. It certainly was grossly unfair, because it did not make clear that Auchinleck's strategy of abandoning Tobruk had been revealed as early as January and that Churchill had not challenged it until the last moment. Also it was incorrect that Auchinleck had stated that the defences were in good order. Brooke asked Churchill 'in fairness to Auchinleck and to obviate any complaint' to make a change, but the Prime Minister refused on the grounds that 'the Ministers who had seen the telegrams did not feel this was necessary'. The documents in the file in the Public Record Office containing Kennedy's and Brooke's comments are closed until 1992, but Kennedy makes his views clear in his memoirs.[37]

Churchill's speech to the Commons included the full text of the paragraph to which Kennedy and Brooke objected. In the debate Aneurin Bevan said devastatingly that 'the nation cannot stand the holding out of Sebastapol for months and the fall of Tobruk in 26 hours'. However, the main criticism of Churchill was of the inadequacies of British tanks and guns compared with those of the Germans. Bevan stated that the Republican Army was using an 8-pounder anti-tank gun in Spain in 1936, and the Commons well knew the deficiency of the 2-pounder from articles in the *Times*.

Sir James Wardlaw Milne, the mover of the censure vote, made a devastating indictment of the Government over tanks and guns, saying that the first British tank, produced in 1916, carried a 6-pounder; he asked what excuse there was for sending men into battle with the scales weighted against them. Both Wardlaw Milne and Leslie Hore Belisha, who had been dismissed as Secretary of State for War by Chamberlain in 1940, claimed correctly that on 11 December 1941 Churchill had misled the House by saying that 'our men met the Germans on equal terms in the matter of weapons'. Belisha said: 'Every military correspond-ent concurs that we were outgunned and that our armour was not as good as the armour of German tanks, and we had sent Mr Westwood to report on equipment in Libya and he wrote " . . . it was essential to have a six pounder gun if we were to defeat the enemy".' (Joseph Westwood, Labour MP for Stirling and Falkirk, had gone to Cairo earlier in the year to report to the Commons.)

Prominent Liberal MP Clement Davies said that in the view of the terrible disclosures 'we should proceed at once to consider impeachment of those responsible.' There was no support for such drastic measures, but the debate made it clear that the House was conscious of the deficiencies not only of the guns, but also of the tanks, and of Churchill's responsibility as Minister of Defence. Churchill's efforts to bluff it out went down badly.

The Economist accurately reflected public opinion, saying, 'Churchill and the Government spokesmen in the Commons and Lords [Lyttelton and Beaverbrook] overlooked that the Libya army was generally supposed, because of authoritative statements, to be as well equipped as the enemy and they would scarcely admit to any deficiencies.' It went on. '. . . the state of opinion in Parliament mirrors the state of public opinion. Surprise, bewilderment and even alarm are widespread: but the wish to hit out indiscriminately against Mr Churchill and his colleagues has always been confined to a petulant few.' Churchill must have realized how vulnerable he had made himself by combining the offices of Prime Minister and Minister of Defence, and he sought a scapegoat for the tank and gun deficiencies which had been revealed in Parliament. Here he was barking up the wrong tree. Both he and the Ministry of Defence had a blind spot over the superiority of German tanks and guns, and had failed to interpret properly reports from the desert.

Auchinleck had reported the short range and inferior performance of the two-pounder guns compared with the German guns, and the mechanical unreliability of cruiser tanks compared with German tanks 'so that at present equipped we must have at least two to one superiority.' According to Colonel Berry, Chief Mechanical Engineer, 8th Army,

> The two pounder as the standard anti-tank gun in the 8th Army was simply too small to prove effective against German armour at over 600 yards. As an anti-tank gun it was virtually useless in the desert . . . I got the impression that the War Office simply did not want to listen to any criticisms of any kind that were made about any equipment that had been sent to the Middle East. It was much easier to criticize the Generals.

He was right.[38]

Berry added: 'Shortly before "Operation Crusader" was about to begin it was found that the suspension arms of the Crusader tank were breaking off like carrots in large numbers . . . we had pushed [January 1942] Rommel right back to El Agheila and he seemed to be nearly finished. I think he would have been if we had not had 200 Crusader tanks under repair.' According to Berry a signal was sent for four hundred water pumps for Crusaders to be flown out to the Middle East, and the reply came back: 'Regret not available in UK.' Berry believes if those water pumps had been available, Rommel's counter-attack would not have succeeded.

Berry also wrote that the Germans had converted a captured British three-inch AA gun manufactured by Vickers to an anti-tank gun which was 'a very effective and powerful weapon'. He said that there were several hundred three-inch guns available in London because they had been made redundant by the 3.7 inch guns so that 'if these had been fitted to twenty-five-pounder gun carriages and rushed out to the Middle East the whole course of the war would have been changed.'[39] Such are the 'ifs' of military history, but Berry's evidence shows Churchill and the War Office had been blind to the inferiority of British equipment in the desert.

On the day he returned to London from Cairo (March 2 1942), having completed his tour as Minister of State Middle East, Oliver Lyttelton told the Defence Committee, 'General Messervy, a very determined man, had expressed the view that with the present tanks we required a 4 to 1 superiority to be certain of victory,' and that at Agedabia and again at El Agheila 'two British armoured brigades had been defeated by inferior enemy forces who had suffered them-selves little loss'; this was 'mainly due to mechanical defects in their [the British] tanks . . . on top of this mechanical failure must be reckoned the superior gun power of the German tanks'. Churchill cross-examined Lyttelton on why the defects in the tanks had not been noticed at an earlier stage, saying, 'Surely every step should be taken to test out material before battle; particularly as the fate of

the whole campaign depended upon the reliability of tanks.' Here Churchill
ignored that he had continually criticised Wavell and Auchinleck for taking too
long before putting tanks into battle after they had been disembarked in the
Middle East.

Churchill also said that the previous May (1941) it had been noticed the
German tanks were firing 4½lb projectiles, and 'no report to this effect had been
sent home . . . surely something should have been done in the intervening period
to counter this gun. A special enquiry should be held as to why no report was
rendered . . . an enquiry was absolutely necessary.'

The Committee invited Attlee to chair an enquiry. He took almost three
months over it; it came before the War Cabinet on June 24 during Churchill's
absence in America. As usual Attlee was succinct, stating that reports about the
German 5 cm gun were rendered both before and after the battle of June 1941,
and said, 'I am not satisfied adequate steps were taken when the November 1941
offensive in Libya was under discussion. It should have been stressed as a factor
of the utmost importance in our calculations.' The Crusader tank, he claimed,
was a 'sad story pressed into production too soon because the situation called for
haste', and six reports had been received between April 21 and June 24 1941
which 'provided ample evidence that the Germans had a weapon of greater power
and penetration to ours'. Attlee continued, 'As a member of the Defence
Committee I cannot recollect the point having been made in any of our
discussions during the planning of Auchinleck's November offensive; the existence of the German heavier gun was certainly never stressed although it was
obviously a factor of greatest importance. Indeed we were given reassuring
information by Auchinleck on March 1 1941 that the Germans had tanks armed
with guns comparable in power with our Crusader tanks'.

Attlee's report revealed that copies of all important telegrams were sent to the
three service departments, and a selection of the more important telegrams were
made for the Prime Minister. Attlee concluded that the reason for this information not being brought to the notice of 'the War Cabinet generally was
almost certainly that the possession of this gun was not at the time regarded as a
factor of special importance'.

The War Cabinet recorded that Auchinleck on his visit to London in July 1941
had said nothing about the superiority of the German guns, and

> . . . it was unfortunate that the Ministers on the Defence Committee should have
> been in the position in which they were asked to take decisions on Defence matters
> without being given knowledge of this gun which was available in this country . . . it
> was incumbent on the War Office to tell the Cabinet all relevant matters together
> with expressions of their judgement; it was not enough that these matters should be
> studied by the Ministers concerned.[40]

The Attlee report was a reflection of Churchill's conduct as Minister of
Defence, and was to be echoed in Parliament a few days later. Churchill returned
to London only four days before the Censure debate, and had no time to consider
the report in detail before he spoke on 2 July. On July 8 Bridges (Secretary to the

Cabinet), asked the Prime Minister if he wished to give any special reconsideration to it in the light of the debate. On his copy Churchill scrawled, 'Yes. Surely someone is going to be punished or at least blamed for the lapses that occurred.' However, the only possible scapegoat was his own Ministry of Defence. Bridges pointed out that all the telegrams from Wavell had been brought to his attention with the copies 'flagged', and advised that 'no action should be taken'. Churchill acquiesced and from then on strained every nerve to make sure the British army was equipped with as many as possible of the more powerful 6-pounder and the even better 17-pounder anti-tank guns, together with better tanks.[41]

After the fall of Tobruk although he was in Washington and not in direct contact with the War Office, Churchill continued to interfere in the day-to-day running of the desert battle. Immediately on receiving the news of the loss of Tobruk he cabled from Washington: 'CIGS Dill and I earnestly hope stern resistance will be made on the Sollum frontier line. Special intelligence [Ultra] has shown stresses which enemy has undergone. Very important reinforcements are on the way. A week gained may be decisive.' The 'very important reinforcements' were three hundred Sherman tanks which Roosevelt had generously offered to Churchill upon seeing the Prime Minister's distress at the news of Tobruk, together with fresh divisions travelling via the Cape. These and the immensely superior 17-pounder anti-tank guns were *en route* for Egypt, but could not be ready – with troops trained to man them – in time to have any influence on the current battle situation.

Churchill's next telegram instructed Auchinleck to use more of his available manpower as infantry in the battle. Auchinleck, exasperated, replied that his need was for more armoured units, who would need time to learn desert fighting, and he dared not draw reinforcements from the precarious Iraq–Syria area, concluding '. . . infantry cannot win battles in the desert so long as the enemy has superiority in armour. Masses of infantry are no good without guns and armour.'

A riled Churchill replied: 'You have over 700,000 men on your ration strength in the Middle East. Every fit male should be made to fight and die for victory; there is no reason why units defending Mersa Matruh position should not be reinforced by several thousands of officers and the administrative personnel ordered to swell the battalions.' The same message contained totally misleading intelligence that 'the President's information from Rome is that Rommel expects to be delayed three or four weeks before he can mount a heavy attack on the Mersa Matruh position. I should think the delay might be greater.' Fortunately Auchinleck was better informed from his own intelligence sources about Rommel's intentions.[42]

It was malicious of Churchill to bombard Auchinleck in this way at the height of the battle, and on the day the last cable was received Auchinleck was in the unpleasant position of having to sack Ritchie and take over command of the Eighth Army in person. It was the worst possible moment for Churchill to nag.

On receiving the news about Ritchie Churchill made some sort of amends for his irritating messages: 'Very glad you have taken over command. Do not vex yourself with anything but battle. Fight it out wherever it flows. Nothing matters but destroying the enemy's armoured force. A strong stream of reinforcements is approaching [meaning the Sherman tanks about to leave the USA]. We are sure you are going to win.'

Auchinleck had realized that the line from Mersa Matruh to the south on which Ritchie had hoped to stand was too weak, and in accordance with his plan husbanded the remains of the Eighth Army. Instead of making a heroic last ditch stand, which would probably have meant the destruction of the Eighth Army, as Churchill wanted, he withdrew in good order to the strongly fortified position at Alamein. Mersa Matruh fell on 29 June and Auchinleck cabled to Churchill in Washington:

> I deeply regret that you should have received this severe blow at so critical a time as a result of the heavy defeat suffered by the forces under my command. I fear the position is now much what it was a year ago when I took over command except that the enemy now has Tobruk which may be of considerable advantage to him not only from the supply point of view but because he has no need to detach troops to contain it as was the case last year.

It might have been better if he had stressed how strong the Alamein position was. Churchill now bypassed Auchinleck, instructing Casey, the Australian Cabinet minister who was Churchill's Resident Minister in Cairo, to organize a last-minute desperate stand in Egypt in case Rommel broke through the defences: 'Mobilise for battle in rearward area. Everyone must fight exactly as they would if Kent or Sussex was invaded. Tank hunting parties with sticky bombs and bombards. No general evacuation; no playing for safety. Egypt must be held at all costs.' As Auchinleck had already closed the training schools to make more men available to fight in the desert, this was an impertinence.[43]

After the fall of Tobruk Churchill plainly had little confidence in Auchinleck, but it is hard to understand why he thought that prodding and pinpricking would help the battle. After the war Auchinleck commented mildly: 'I was not afraid of Churchill. Some people were. But his interference was a disturbing influence on a chap like myself who was concentrating the whole day and night on one thing. I did not need encouragement to beat the enemy although I was glad to get it if things went well.' That is the nearest Auchinleck ever went to criticizing Churchill.[44]

With the June defeat of the Eighth Army Churchill's disbelief in Auchinleck, and his commander's reluctance to be frank with the Prime Minister, made their relative positions impossible. Still, Auchinleck fought one more successful battle. He retreated from the frontier and consolidated his defences around the El Alamein and along the line of low hills to the Quattara depression. He knew that the German supply lines would be dangerously long when their forward troops reached El Alamein.

At dawn on 1 July Rommel attacked the El Alamein positions. The next day the British counter-attacked. By 3 July the Germans were discomfited and Rommel pulled back his forces, leaving mostly Italians to hold the line. By 27 July the first Battle of Alamein was over, and it was a British victory. Auchinleck had robbed

Rommel of his chance of taking Cairo. Unfortunately a major breakout effort by Auchinleck on 22 July had failed. Churchill was grievously disappointed, although Kennedy assured him that Auchinleck was now so strong that he would make a successful attack before long.[45]

Even as Auchinleck was struggling to defeat Rommel at El Alamein in July, Churchill administered a further snub. On 20 November 1941 Auchinleck had insisted on press statements being issued in Cairo, not in London, because 'they were a weapon which could be used against the enemy'. On 7 July Auchinleck was angered because the BBC in London had announced that he was counter-attacking from El Alamein towards the coast road, giving details. He cabled to the CIGS: 'This is intolerable and I must ask that the PM intervenes, otherwise conducting operations becomes impossible.'

Unfortunately his staff had not found out that the censor in Auchinleck's headquarters had passed this message to London for publication. Within a few hours the mistake was discovered and Auchinleck sent a further cable to London: 'Regret further investigation shows information passed by military censor here.' Ignoring Auchinleck's second cable, Churchill, who still resented Auchinleck's insistence on the press releases being made in Cairo, replied personally: 'Censor who released it should be tried by court martial and correspondent who wrote it sent home by Cape. You cannot possibly blame the BBC; there is no second censorship here on your Cairo releases. Recommend you hand censorship over to Minister of State [Casey].' To send such an unkind telegram when Auchinleck was grappling with the crucial first battle of Alamein showed how little regard Churchill had for his General's feelings and is an unpleasant, if unimportant, incident.[46]

Auchinleck was also furious when Churchill wanted him to 'depute' a senior officer on his staff to conduct an enquiry into the fall of Tobruk. He protested vigorously to Churchill who climbed down, saying in excuse that it was a War Cabinet request, not his personal one.[47]

After the Parliamentary debated about the Eighth Army Brooke wrote in his diary: 'It was quite clear something was radically wrong [with the British Army in the Middle East] but not easy at a distance to judge what this something was, nor how far wrong it was.' He wanted to go to Cairo to investigate. With difficulty Brooke obtained Churchill's consent to go, but on July 30, the day before he was due to leave, Churchill decided to go as well. According to Brooke, Churchill felt only his presence would galvanize the battered Eighth Army into reversing their defeat in June. Churchill had also decided to visit Moscow, and would stay in Cairo en route.[48]

Thus Brooke found that instead of forming 'unhurried judgements' about future policy for the desert army, as he had hoped, he had Churchill at his elbow. Auchinleck had not appointed a new Commander to the Eighth Army after Ritchie's dismissal. Churchill decided, without seeing him, that General Gott, who had performed brilliantly in the recent desert fighting, should take over. Here he over-ruled Brooke, who considered Gott 'too tired' and felt Montgomery, who was always bounding with self-confidence, would be preferable. According to Alan Moorehead, 'Gott stood out like a giant in the bitter thankless fighting . . . a great man for England.'[49]

En route Churchill suggested to Brooke that *he* should take over the Eighth Army. Brooke desperately longed to accept so that he could be his own master and escape from Churchill. But with great public-spiritedness he decided that he was more use in London, and that another change of CIGS within a year would be damaging. Then, as soon as they arrived in Cairo, Churchill wanted Brooke to take over from Auchinleck as Commander in Chief in Cairo, with Montgomery as his Eighth Army commander. Sorely tempted, Brooke again refused – he was sure Auchinleck ought to stay in command.

Churchill, who had now talked to Gott and decided he was not 'over tired', dismissed Brooke's suggestion of Montgomery and cabled to the War Cabinet that Gott had been chosen for the Eighth Army. But on the same day Gott was killed in an air accident and Churchill reluctantly fell back on the idea of Montgomery. The Prime Minister also set aside Brooke's objections and insisted on General Alexander replacing Auchinleck. Alexander was at this time in charge of the British force designed for the North African landings, and if Gott had lived Montgomery would have taken over from Alexander.

Churchill describes his conversation with Auchinleck after the dismissal as 'bleak and impeccable'. Churchill was arbitrary in his choice of generals. At this crisis of the war there was no alternative. Selection by committee would have resulted in choosing compromise candidates, and the Prime Minister, with his intense involvement in the details of the fighting in his additional role as Minister of Defence, felt he was in the best position to choose.[50]

If Churchill had not sacked Auchinleck in July 1942 he would have been the British commander for the 1944 cross-Channel invasion. There has been controversy whether Auchinleck was better than Montgomery. Auchinleck's conduct of his desert campaign was definitely first-class; he was defeated not because of his strategy or tactics, but because Rommel's tanks and guns were superior. Both Montgomery and Auchinleck had spent their working lives studying how to make the British Army efficient; both were experts at moving great numbers of men and huge quantities of stores and vehicles at high speed across large distances; both understood how to co-operate with the RAF and Royal Navy and appreciated the immense value of the Ultra signals and other information about the enemy. In addition, both were good at commanding troops of other nations. Auchinleck was cautious, but not as cautious as Montgomery, and it can be said with certainty that Auchinleck would not have made the disastrous mistake of the airborne landing at Arnhem in September 1944; nor would he have quarrelled with Eisenhower and the other American generals as Montgomery did.

It was typical of Churchill's conduct of the war that the decision to let Auchinleck go, and bring in Montgomery, was his own impetuous, off-the-cuff decision taken in the field. The results, however, were such that Churchill cannot be criticized.

CHAPTER TWELVE

The USA and Japan in the war

IN JULY 1941 the alarm bells rang in the Far East. The Vichy Government signed an agreement with the Japanese which allowed the latter to establish air and sea bases around Saigon in French Indo-China. This put the Malay peninsula and Singapore in deadly danger and rendered obsolete all the British defence plans for this area, because by flying across the Gulf of Siam Japanese aircraft could dominate the skies over Malaya. Churchill failed to react to this Far Eastern threat with his usual expertise and mastery of strategy.

The so-called Manchurian Incident of 1931 had developed into an un-declared war between Japan and China; by the end of 1938 the Japanese had captured most of the great cities and ports of China and were astride the important railways, despite strong Chinese resistance. The Chinese Government was forced to take refuge at Chungking and to fight the war from the fertile plains of Sichuan. Here they were handicapped by shortages due to the occupation of the supply routes by the Japanese, but secure against complete conquest behind the barrier of the Yangtse gorges. By the end of 1937 Japan had become dominated by the war party; the Emperor, who was opposed to war, and the peace party could make little headway as victories aroused national pride and made the military leaders popular.

Meanwhile Japan's relations with Russia, the United States and the United Kingdom deteriorated, and the so-called anti-Comintern Pact of 1936 between Japan and Germany was joined by Italy in 1937. Japan thus became almost a totalitarian military state in virtual alliance with Germany and Italy.

The defeat of the British and French armies in Europe in 1940 weakened the position of Britain in the Far East, and Japan allied herself even more definitely with Germany and Italy by the Tripartite Pact of 27 September 1940. Under this agreement the contracting parties undertook to assist each other under certain conditions of which the most important was a conflict with the United States.

Japan had invaded China in 1931; by 1939 they were deep inside Chinese territory, and had occupied all the Chinese sea ports so that the Chinese army was dependent on overland routes. America was strongly hostile to Japan's invasion, but Britain with her European embarrassments could not play as prominent a role as the USA in supporting China.

The Chinese Government in Chungking under General Chiang Kai-shek had at first received a trickle of supplies through Indo-China, Burma and Hong Kong, but the bulk of its assistance came from the Soviet Union via the Russian–Turkish railway in Central Asia. After 1939, however, the only access for outside supplies was via the Burma road.

After the fall of France the Japanese Government expected Britain to surrender to Hitler. Accordingly, although they wanted to avoid war with the United States, the Japanese demanded that the Burma road should be closed at the end of June 1940. Churchill instructed the British Ambassador in Japan, Sir Robert Craigie, to counter this by pointing out that Germany was trying to force Japan into war with America, that Hitler wanted Japan to be weakened by war, and that she would not be able to claim her spoils of victory. Furthermore, closing the road would drive Chiang Kai-shek into the arms of the Russians to the detriment of Japan.

Craigie replied that any delay in closing the road might bring a declaration of war from Japan, and suggested a temporary closure for three months, during which period a special effort would be made to negotiate a lasting agreement with the Japanese. The Chiefs of Staff thought Britain was too weak militarily to risk war with Japan, and the War Cabinet agreed to the three months' closure even though the Americans were opposed to it. Churchill sent a message to Chiang Kai-shek that he was sure the General would understand, and said: 'We shall never press you to any peace against your interests or your policy.' At first Churchill had demurred, but then he realized Britain had no other option, although with his temperament it must have gone against the grain. In the Commons he made it clear that it was only a time-gaining operation and that there was no intention to agree to permanent closure or 'default' on China. To Churchill's irritation Cordell Hull, the American Secretary of State, described the closure as 'an unwarranted inter-position of an obstacle to world trade', although he had agreed beforehand that the United States had no cause to complain because America was unwilling to take a hand in Far Eastern affairs. Churchill had been privately informed by Chiang Kai-shek that the Chinese had enough small arms ammunition for a year's fighting.

British attempts to reach agreement with Japan got nowhere. On 5 September 1940 the Vichy Government signed an agreement by which Japanese troops were given rights of passage through northern Indo-China. On 22 September the Japanese threatened to invade Hanoi unless the Vichy French allowed them to occupy Haiphong and five airports. With Britain under dire threat of invasion and all available forces needed elsewhere, Churchill could do nothing. In addition, relations with Vichy were at a low ebb because of Mers-el-Kebir and Dakar, and there was again no support from the USA. Although Churchill was ready to offer Weygand several divisions if he would declare war against Germany in North Africa, Britain would not allow French reinforcements to go to Indo-China. When in August Vichy sent a Senegalese battalion in the transport ship *L'Espérance* from Djibouti to the east she was stopped by the British and sent to Aden. Two other transport ships consequently went back to Diego Suarez in Madagascar because they too would have been intercepted.[1]

However, the American attitude changed when on 27 September Germany, Italy and Japan announced the Tripartite Pact. Immediately public opinion was alerted in America because it was clear from the way in which the contracting parties undertook to assist each other that the Pact was directed against the United States. Stiffened by Roosevelt, Churchill decided not to renew the agreement to keep the Burma road closed, and clutched at hopes of American assistance raised by Hull telling Lothian that America was ready to hold staff talks about the situation if reopening the road let to a Japanese attack.

Craigie asked from Tokyo whether, if the United States became involved in war against Japan, it would be 'detrimental' to the British war effort because she would be obliged to stop sending war material to Britain. Craigie had discussed this problem with Joseph Grew, the US Ambassador in Tokyo, because Grew wrote to Roosevelt to ask 'whether our getting into war with Japan would handicap our help to Britain in Europe as to make the difference to Britain between victory and defeat'. Churchill was annoyed at Craigie's question. The two had clashed when Churchill went on a lecture tour of America in 1930, and now the Prime Minister minuted to his Foreign Secretary on 4 October:

> This shows the very serious misconception which has grown up in Sir R. Craigie's mind about the consequences of the United States entering the war. He should surely be told forthwith that the entry of the United States into war either with Germany and Italy or with Japan, is fully conformable with British interests.
>
> 2. That nothing in the munitions sphere can compare with the importance of the British Empire and the United States being co-belligerent. That if Japan attacked the United States without declaring war on us we should at once range ourselves at the side of the United States and declare war upon Japan.
>
> It is astonishing how this misleading stuff put out by Kennedy that we should do better with a neutral United States than with her warring at our side should have travelled so far. A clear directive is required to all our Ambassadors in countries concerned.

Uppermost in Churchill's mind was the hope that Japan would attack the USA and that this would bring America into the war on Britain's side against Germany, which otherwise was doubtful.[2]

There now arose a strange contradiction in foreign policy. The War Cabinet had set up the Far Eastern Foreign Policy Committee under Rab Butler. Their instructions were to formulate policy which would prevent Japan attacking the Dutch or British possessions, and they briefed Ambassador Craigie in Tokyo and the Minister in Bangkok, Sir Josiah Crosby, accordingly. Meanwhile Churchill wanted to force Japan to declare war on America, as his minute to Eden of 4 October 1940 shows, but he had at all costs to hide his plan from the Americans; he probably only mentioned it in private to Eden and Beaverbrook.

Churchill did his best to impress Roosevelt with the awe-inspiring consequences of Britain having to fight Japan without American aid; this was one of the Prime Minister's worst bogies at the time. On 15 February 1941 he wrote to the President:

Drifting straws seem to indicate Japanese intentions to make war on us or do something that would force us to make war on them . . . the weight of the Japanese Navy, if thrown against us, would confront us with situations beyond the scope of our naval resources. I do not myself think that the Japanese would be likely to send the large military expedition necessary to lay siege to Singapore . . . any threat of a major invasion of Australia or New Zealand would of course force us to withdraw our fleet from the Eastern Mediterranean . . . You will therefore see, Mr President, the awful enfeeblement of our war effort that would result from the sending out by Japan of her battle cruisers and her twelve 8 inch gun cruisers into the eastern ocean, and still more from any serious invasion threat against the two Australian democracies . . . Personally I think the odds are definitely against that . . . Everything you can do to inspire the Japanese with the fear of a double war may avert the danger. If however they come in against us and we are alone, the grave character of the consequences cannot easily be overstated.[3]

Churchill was urging Roosevelt to take a hard line in the Far East in the hope of eventually involving the United States in the defence of British possessions. However, even more important in the Prime Minister's mind was the idea that if America went to war with Japan she would be more likely to intervene against Hitler. Critics of Roosevelt have termed this 'the back door to war', but the President never gave Churchill any assurance that America would fight if the Japanese attacked British colonies. Churchill was ready to provoke Japan except on the occasions when he feared Americans might not respond as he wanted to a Japanese declaration of war on Britain.

At this date, although Churchill was envisaging war against Japan in alliance with America, he could not reinforce the Far East. He was on the horns of a dilemma. The military strength available to him was totally inadequate. In addition to the Western Desert, Syria, the Dodecanese and the Balkans were a severe drain; Britain could still be invaded, and on top of this Churchill was planning a landing in Norway known as Jupiter. As 1941 unfolded, the Defence Committee discussions over which Churchill presided must have seemed to the Chiefs of Staff like a mad hatter's tea party.

Despite his hope that Japan would provoke America into war, with the consequence that Roosevelt would delcare war on Germany , Churchill objected to the Chiefs of Staff's plans to send more planes to Malaya, minuting on 5 January 1941:

I like all this except the dispatch of so many invaluable aircraft at a time when the danger of war with Japan has receded. In particular the P.B.Y.s [USA light bombers] are urgently needed for the North Western Approaches where vital war operations are in progress. The Air needs may be met later in the year, but not so early as April. Preparations may however be made for the reception of these aircraft, so that their transference could be rapid should the occasion arise. I do not take an alarmist view about the defense of Singapore, at the present time.[4]

When the Chiefs of Staff sent a memorandum asking for 336 aircraft to be the target for the Far East, and for a small immediate increase, Churchill replied on 13 January: 'The political situation in the Far East does not seem to require, and the strength of our Air Force by no means warrants, the maintenance of such large forces in the Far East at the time.' On 10 April he minuted that 'we must not tie up a lot of troops in these regions which we can so easily reinforce from India . . . I view with great reluctance the continued divergence of troops, aircraft and supplies to a theatre which it is improbable will be lighted up unless we are heavily beaten elsewhere.'[5] Not only did Churchill deny increased numbers of aircraft to the Far East, but the omission was compounded by the quality of what *was* sent – obsolete aircraft and insufficiently trained pilots. Instead of Hurricanes and Beauforts, out-of-date Blenheims and Buffaloes were provided.

Churchill had set his heart on a straight bombing offensive of Germany which, coupled with fighter sweeps, he felt could be decisive in defeating Hitler; and although he was ready to risk war with Japan, he could not find it in his heart to divert aircraft from the main enemy. The pilot reinforcements for Singapore came from flying training schools in Australia and New Zealand; most had never flown anything but trainers. The Air Ministry refused the request by Sir Robert Brooke Popham, Commander in Chief, Far East, for facilities for further training in operational flying, and only eight fully trained pilots left Britain for the Far East during January 1941. The trouble was that meeting any request for war material to the Far East meant diverting important items from the Middle East and Britain. The troops in Singapore felt neglected. Buffaloes were the American F2A – their first monoplane carrier fighter; it was a great disappointment, and was later slaughtered by the more agile Japanese Zero fighters. A disgusted US marine officer wrote that to order F2A fighters against Zeros was to order them to commit suicide. It was soon relegated to training service by the Americans after the outbreak of war with Japan.[6]

A grave omission by Churchill was his failure to send a single tank to Malaya. Hundreds of British and American tanks were being expended in the Western Desert and sent (many sunk on the way) to Russia. It is a mystery why, after Churchill had been so impressed by hearing that even a dozen tanks would have saved Crete, he did not authorize their despatch to Malaya. The High Command in Singapore badgered Whitehall for the urgent despatch of tanks and modern aircraft – in vain. Yet in his post-war memoirs Churchill recalls with pride that 3276 tanks and 2665 aircraft were delivered to north Russian ports in 1941 and 1942.[7]

In July 1940 Prince Konoye became Prime Minister of Japan. Konoye was not in favour of war. His Foreign Secretary, Matsuoka, who had been thrust upon him, was ambitious, dictatorial and an admirer of the Nazi regime. Like Konoye he was no militarist and he believed that Japan, by allying herself with Germany, could by peaceful means undermine Britain's position in the Far East so that Japan could become heir to Britain's former political influence and economic domination. He also hankered after playing the role of mediator, perhaps in conjunction with Roosevelt, in the conflict between Germany and Britain. In March 1941 Matsuoka paid visits to Moscow, Berlin and Rome, and in Moscow negotiated a Neutrality Pact under which each side would remain neutral if the other was involved in war with a third party. His intention was to keep Japan out of war with Russia if Hitler attacked the Soviet Union, and also to ensure Soviet neutrality in the event of Japan declaring war on the United States.

In July 1941, much against Matsuoka's wishes, the majority of the Japanese Cabinet and the Air and Army Chiefs decided to violate the neutrality of Vichy Indo-China. Matsuoka was forced to resign, and according to Craigie was in no doubt that this step would inevitably plunge Japan into war. Admiral Toyoda became Foreign Minister; he was intent on a war of conquest.[8]

The Acting Consul General in Saigon, E. W. Meiklereid, reported that the Syrian campaign had embittered local sentiment against Britain and the local newspapers had day after day carried headlines such as 'Frenchmen fighting Frenchmen', but he hoped that with the cessation of hostilities in Syria matters would improve. He wrote that when the first news had been received of the 1940 French capitulation there had been enthusiasm for Britain, who made General Catroux, then Governor of Indo-China, a generous offer of economic and financial assistance (which Catroux was forced to decline because of Japanese hostility). There had also been hope of Indo-China under Catroux breaking away from Vichy, in spite of the resentment over the sinking of the French Fleet at Oran. To prevent this, Pétain had replaced Catroux with Admiral Decoux, who was violently anti-British because of Oran, and although the majority of the French in Indo-China hoped for a British victory 'any hope or desire' of breaking away from Vichy disappeared. However in December 1940 a Communist rising in Cochin-China was put down with severity, and the colony suffered considerably from a lack of essential imports.

Then, according to Meiklereid, Decoux decided to alter his policy towards Britain, and in January 1941 sent the charming and able Captain Juan to Singapore to try to arrange a *modus vivendi* with Britain. Juan was the only strong man in the Government. Decoux was described by the Acting Consul General as 'small physically, as in mental outlook', and overbearing in private and public; while Admiral Bérenger, Commander of French Naval Forces, was the leader of the anti-British faction – the Navy were still bitter about Oran and there was open and spontaneous veneration for Pétain. Decoux reciprocated in his memoirs by describing Meiklereid as 'untrustworthy, stumbling and unpleasant with an Anglophile French wife'.

Much to the credit of Juan in these inauspicious circumstances, he managed to come to a secret agreement in Singapore whereby seventy French aeroplanes lying at Martinique were allowed through by ship. Crosby, the British Minister in Bangkok, advised strongly 'we should not allow a defenceless Indo-China beside a Thailand armed to the teeth'. Crosby was a Jewish Francophile and Thailand was demanding Indo-Chinese territory from France. De Gaulle agreed, provided Decoux gave a guarantee they would only be used in defence. The Foreign Office urged strongly that Indo-China should be strengthened so that it could resist Japanese demands. Ashley Clark, in the British Embassy in Tokyo, made the sensible suggestion that some of the French battleships lying at Toulon should go to Indo-China. Neither Eden nor Churchill reacted, although it would have been difficult for the Germans to prevent this under the terms of the Armistice.

In return for the planes and resumption of trade Decoux agreed not to attack British ships, while Britain undertook not to make propaganda for the Free French, and trade was resumed.

It is not surprising that Churchill agreed to Decoux's suggestion that the British would ban Gaullist propaganda in French Indo-China in January 1941, because, as has been seen in Chapter 10, he had just concluded his agreement through Rougier with Pétain, and felt de Gaulle's Free French would not be of much value to the war effort. However all this was not enough. Only the news that a powerful fleet of British and American battleships was at anchor in Johore Bay would have given the Vichy French the courage to resist Japanese demands and the Americans had refused Churchill's requests for naval cooperation in the Pacific.[9]

Because of the threat imposed by Japan joining Germany and Italy in the September Tripartite Pact, a naval Defence Conference was convened in Singapore in October 1940. Roosevelt did not take the Japanese threat seriously enough, and America was represented only by the Naval Attaché to Thailand.

In November 1940, after the Japanese occupation of Hanoi, Lothian had been asked by the Chiefs of Staff to discuss with Roosevelt the sending of the United States Fleet from Pearl Harbor to Singapore. Lothian's efforts, and further attempts by Churchill, failed to produce any commitment about American naval help at Singapore if reopening the Burma road led to a Japanese attack. Hull told Lothian firmly the Japanese would not come into the war, and that it was impractical to give help to Indo-China.

In January 1941, when Harry Hopkins had arrived in London to talk to Churchill as Roosevelt's personal representative, he stated: 'The isolationists and indeed a great part of the American people would not be interested in a war in the Far East merely because the Japanese attacked the Dutch.'[10] In face of this the War Cabinet would not give the well-disposed Dutch a guarantee, let alone Vichy Indo-China.

On 14 July the Japanese demanded from Vichy the use of eight airfields and the naval bases of Camranh Bay and Saigon; on the 21st Darlan told the US Ambassador in Vichy that he was compelled to meet the Japanese demands. Admiral Toyoda quickly concluded on 29 July a Franco–Japanese agreement for the cession of the bases and for joint defence of Indo-China; this meant Japanese occupation. Vichy was in no position to refuse Japan's demands; nor could Britain bolster her up to resist. Britain had made no offer of military help in Indo-China, nor would Roosevelt give any indication that America would supply military aid.

Roosevelt had told Halifax on 15 July that he thought even if the Japanese did get into Indo-China it would not be 'a very difficult job for the United States and British Governments acting together, when relieved of their European anxieties, to make it impossible for the Japanese to maintain themselves there'. Such a view was not encouraging for Churchill in the present crisis. He minuted to the Chiefs of Staff Committee the next day:

> I must repeat my conviction that Japan will not declare war upon us at the present juncture, nor if the United States enters the war on our side. I agree with the views of the Chiefs of the Staff that we are in no position to declare war upon Japan without the United States being in on our side. Therefore I do not consider that a war between Britain and Japan is likely at the present time. If contrary to the above views Japan should attack us, I am of opinion that the United States would enter the war as the weight upon us would clearly be too great.
>
> Nevertheless, since the threatened Japanese moves in Indo-China are of serious menace to us, further precautions in the Far East should be taken so far as they are possible without condemning us to misfortune in other theatres.[11]

Unfortunately the Chiefs of Staff had no resources with which to reinforce the Far East, and without help from America Vichy could not resist the Japanese demands. In Vichy on 16 July Pétain talked to Admiral Leahy, the US Ambassador. The American told the Marshal that the USA definitely would not change its attitude, and that there was no possibility of his Government sending arms or munitions to French Indo-China even though its strategic value was very evident. Decoux has recorded that the Japanese proceeded with 'febrile haste to position a vast army with considerable air forces in Cochin China and Cambodia' so that it became clear to him they were bent on a war of aggression.[12]

The ready acquiescence of Vichy accelerated the advance of the Japanese; this was a shock to Britain and America. The British and US Foreign Offices were aggravated because Vichy gave legal status to the Japanese military occupation on the specious grounds that they had to do so to forestall de Gaulle and the British. According to the US Secretary of State, Cordell Hull, 'We would not, of course, have expected the Vichy Government to offer any active resistance to the Japanese. But we would have expected it to refrain from giving the Japanese occupation its legal sanction and from falling in with Tokyo's propaganda that the British and de Gaullists were about to seize Indo-China'. Japan's air and naval presence south of Saigon rendered the British plans for the defence of Singapore obsolete. Japanese airfields on the south-west tip of Vietnam were only 350 miles from north Malaya across the Gulf of Siam. And if war came, Japanese land-based torpedo bombers protected by fighters (also land-based) would put British warships on the east coast of Malaya at risk. Churchill entirely failed to understand the gravity of this deadly threat to Malaya and Singapore.

Immediately the United States, Holland and Britain froze Japanese assets and embargoed the export of oil and raw materials as a sign that Japanese aggression had passed the stage when verbal protests or remonstrances had any value. Churchill eagerly concurred. The Japanese reacted by a large-scale Army mobilization; their Navy had been fully mobilized early in July.

American–Japanese discussions had been proceeding desultorily in Washington since spring 1941. Now they became deadly serious, as peace or war hung precariously in the balance. However, Churchill had agreed that the discussions should be left entirely in the hands of the Americans. The American

Ambassador in Tokyo, Grew, was ordered by Washington not to take part in discussion with the Japanese.

The Prime Minister, Prince Konoye, wanted to avoid war, and at the suggestion of the Emperor he asked to meet Roosevelt. This offer was refused out of hand. This was the last dying flicker from the Japanese peace party, and it aroused such bad publicity that on 16 October Konoye was forced to resign.

Meanwhile the economic blockade, and especially the oil embargo, hit the Japanese war economy hard. The new Prime Minister, General Tojo, was determined that unless the blockade was removed Japan should go to war. His Foreign Minister, Togo, was married to a German and had been Ambassador in Berlin; his sympathies were strongly pro-Nazi. However, according to Craigie during the five weeks between assuming office and the outbreak of war he made a determined effort to find an agreement.[13]

Sir William Hayter told the author that in the Foreign Office they felt Craigie was too keen on appeasing Japan at China's expense, and that he was unduly influenced by his Military Attaché, General Piggot, ignoring the sounder advice he got from his Japanese expert sent to Tokyo by the Foreign Office, Sir George Sansom.[14] In a series of telegrams Craigie reported to London that the Japanese were anxious for agreement and were prepared to make concessions. These messages were ill received. Churchill felt that by leaving the negotiations strictly to the Americans there would be a breakdown, which would result in a declaration of war by Japan on the USA with the welcome emergence of America as Britain's ally. Otherwise the most likely scenario was a Japanese attack on British and Dutch Far East possessions, which might not involve the USA in war.[15]

The Japanese Government sent Saburu Kurusu, former Ambassador in Berlin, with an American wife, to Washington to assist the Ambassador Kinisaro Munura there.

On 20 November Kurusu and Munura presented a proposal to Cordell Hull for a settlement based on a return to the *status quo ante* before the Vichy agreement over Saigon. In return for a complete withdrawal of troops from southern Indo-China, and a partial withdrawal, pending a peaceful settlement with China, from the northern part of the country, freezing of assets was to be cancelled and oil and raw materials sold again to Japan.

On receiving from Washington details of the Japanese proposals the Foreign Office telegraphed them to Craigie in Tokyo; he urged that they should be given favourable consideration. His grounds were that it was a matter of extreme urgency to remove the Japanese troops from Saigon, where they were threatening Malaya; in Tokyo he received private information that the Japanese were ready for further compromise, and he informed the Foreign Office that he was confident the terms could be improved.[16]

Meanwhile in Washington Hull drew up promising counter-proposals (known as the *modus vivendi*) which met the Japanese request to end the freezing of assets and withdraw the embargo on raw materials as far as peace time industries were concerned, although no raw material was to be supplied for war.

Craigie had reported that, based on information he considered reliable, his opinion was that the Japanese Cabinet had extracted a pledge from the Army and Navy that 'all preparations for war would at once cease' if the Japanese proposal of 20 November was accepted.[17] Churchill did not want agreement to be reached over the *modus vivendi*, as this would put paid to his hopes of a Japanese attack on America. He needed to play his cards very carefully, because any hint that he was trying to provoke Japan and America into war with each other would be like a red rag to a bull to the isolationists in America; if they seized on it, it would be more difficult for Roosevelt to get permission from Congress to declare war on Germany.

The evidence of Churchill's intention is strong. On 12 September 1941, on a minute from Eden, he minuted 'Yes' against the words 'our right policy is clearly to keep up the pressure [on Japan]'; and against the passage 'We are now engaged in examining Craigie's telegrams. It is important that we should not be too forthcoming . . . we want to make the Japanese feel that we are now in a position to play our hand from strength', he wrote 'Good'.[18]

On 19 October Halifax had cabled that Hull was considering some form of barter agreement, such as a limited amount of American cotton in return for Japanese silk, and although Halifax had stated that Churchill 'attached the greatest importance to a firm front' Hull wanted to know the Prime Minister's reaction. Winston minuted to Eden: 'This is the thin end of appeasement.'

Churchill was now pressing for a joint Anglo–American warning to Japan which would amount to an ultimatum, but had been told that Roosevelt's military advisers were against it because the Americans were not ready to fight in the Pacific. Accordingly he wrote to the President on 5 November that 'what we need now is a deterrent of the most general and formidable character'. Churchill continued that the Japanese were at this time threatening to cut the Burma road, with disastrous consequences for Chiang Kai-shek; he asked Roosevelt to warn the Japanese against such an attack, saying that Britain would 'of course be ready to make a similar communication. No independent action by ourselves will deter Japan because we are so much tied up elsewhere. But of course we will stand with you and do our utmost to back you in whatever course you choose.' But Roosevelt wanted to back away from any strong warning to Japan while he built up American strength in the Pacific, and from Tokyo Grew had sent a long cable saying that sanctions had failed and advocating a softer approach.[19]

The above shows Churchill's mood, and his reaction to the Kurusu–Munura proposals of 20 November was to suggest that demands on the Japanese should be 'pitched high' and 'the price paid low'; therefore he asked for the total evacuation of all naval, air and military forces from China and Indo-China as the *quid pro quo* for the partial relaxation of the embargo for the welfare of Japanese civilians, but no oil. Churchill knew this would be unacceptable to Japan. In response to a personal message from Roosevelt about the proposed *modus vivendi*, Churchill replied on 26 November that it was for the President to handle this business, and that he certainly did not want an additional war. He continued: 'There is only one point that disquiets us. What about Chiang Kai-shek? Is he not having a thin diet? Our anxiety is about China. We are sure that the regard of the United States for the Chinese cause will govern your action. We feel sure the Japanese are most unsure of themselves.'[20] Nothing could have been better calculated to stiffen the Americans, because for them the cause of an independent China was an emotive issue; they looked on themselves as China's chief benefactor and protector. Not only had they made Lend Lease available, but they had also given the Chinese a large dollar credit and allowed United States citizens to form the American Volunteer Group to help China with pilots.

The Netherlands Government supported the *modus vivendi*, but the Chinese protested it was a return to appeasement and would have 'a most discouraging effect on the Chinese Government and people'. Hull decided on the evening of 26 November in view of 'the sharp Chinese reaction' (which Halifax described to him as 'hysterical') and what he called the 'lukewarm British attitude', to hand to the Japanese representatives in Washington not his *modus vivendi* but what amounted to an ultimatum and a flat rejection of the Kurusu–Munura proposal. Halifax reported that Hull had 'lost his temper' when he cancelled the *modus vivendi*; William Hayter, Counsellor to Halifax, minuted: 'I have no doubt at all that this memorandum was put in a fit of petulance', and 'It was a snap decision if ever there was one.'[21]

Hull's loss of temper triggered off the Japanese attack in the Pacific; on such small things as a change of mood the course of history depends. But why did he lose his temper and abandon his statesmanlike *modus vivendi*? Forty-nine years after the event, Sir William Hayter wrote to the author:

> Hull's loss of temper on 26 November can, I think, only be that he resented having been pushed off his *modus vivendi* by Chinese pressure against it and British lukewarmness about it, and having as a result put in a memorandum to the Japanese which the latter were likely to consider as provocation. Hull, as you know, had a short fuse, and I expect all this made him feel cross and uneasy. This is reflected in Roosevelt's message to Churchill saying that 'we must all be prepared for real trouble, possibly soon'. I don't think it is anything more than this.

In his memoirs Hull wrote that it was Churchill's telegram of 25 November, with its anxiety over 'meagre rations', which decided him to cancel the *modus vivendi*.

> After talking it over with his Japanese experts he decided instead to present to the Japanese solely the ten-point proposal for a general settlement to which originally the *modus vivendi* would have been in the nature of an introduction. He felt the slight prospect of Japan agreeing to the *modus vivendi* would not justify the outburst of American public opinion against supplying Japan even limited quantities of oil, together with the violent opposition of the Chinese, while the other interested Governments, whose co-operation was essential, were either unfavourable or lukewarm.[22]

Hull told Halifax and others on 24 November that the US Government wished to try for a temporary agreement with Japan, primarily because the Army and Navy Chiefs often 'emphasised to him' that they needed more time to prepare effectively for the outbreak of war with Japan. Later Hull complained to Halifax about the manner in which the efforts to postpone the row had been 'blown out of the water' by people who did not understand 'how delicate was the balance'; here he was indicating that he resented Roosevelt's receptivity to advice from those outside the State Department.

According to Henry Stimson, Secretary of War, Roosevelt 'blew up' on the morning of 26 November when he phoned him with the news that five Japanese divisions had been embarked on ships and sighted south of Formosa. Stimson claims that thereupon the President instructed Hull to drop the *modus vivendi*. This is improbable, because similar reports had been received previously and there is no mention of this in Hull's papers or memoirs.

Hull's virtual ultimatum of the 26th contained two clauses which all Japanese experts knew would be unacceptable. These were that in return for lifting the oil and economic embargo Japan would withdraw all her forces from China and Indo-China (clause 3); and that the United States and Japan would recognize no Government in China other than that of Generalissimo Kai-shek. (clause 4).[23] Clause 4 meant the abandonment of Japan's puppet Chinese Government in Nanking, which Tojo immediately said was 'derogatory to Japan'.

Craigie's view was that Hull's decision not to proceed with his original counter-proposal was 'crucial and unfortunate', because the *modus vivendi* bore the 'hallmark of constructive statesmanship'. He believed that, had it been presented, war with Japan could have been postponed or even avoided altogether.

But Hull's harsh line of 26 November was the tactic favoured by Churchill, and on the 30th he sent a further message to Roosevelt which he must have calculated would fuel the flames; 'It seems to me that one important method remains unused in averting war between Japan and our two countries; namely a plain declaration, secret or public, as may be thought best, that any further act of aggression by Japan will lead immediately to the gravest consequences . . . we would of course make a similar declaration or share in a joint declaration.' Readers must judge Churchill's motives for themselves, but nothing would be more likely to provoke a proud country like Japan to war than this type of ultimatum on top of the out-of-hand rejection of the Kurusu–Munura proposal made in Washington on 20 November.[24]

Japan was playing a double game. If the negotiations in Washington failed she planned to launch a surprise attack on Britain and the USA, and on 26 November a task force had sailed for a rendezvous in the east Pacific. The commander had been ordered – on receipt of a secret signal, but not before – to launch an attack on Pearl Harbor.

There is no reason to doubt the sincerity of Konoye's intentions to enter into an agreement in Washington so as to remove Japanese forces from China and Indo-China in return for the lifting of the blockade. Grew, the US Ambassador in Tokyo, emphasizes in his memoirs that peace would have been maintained if Konoye had remained Prime Minister. However, after his resignation in October his successor, Togo, was more inclined for war, and Japan's oil shortage had become very serious.[25]

When Hull's virtual ultimatum of 26 November was received the Japanese Admiralty was against war but Tojo, the Minister of War, and the Army Chiefs wanted to fight. On 30 November the Emperor summoned the Navy Chiefs and asked them if they were 'confident of success'. They told him they were. Then Hirohito, like Victor Emmanuel III of Italy, made the greatest mistake of his reign and decided on war. Surprisingly, despite his grave responsibility for the war, Hirohito's dynasty is still ruling Japan today, a situation which the House of Savoy does not share in Italy.

However on 5 December Roosevelt, alarmed both by a decyphered telegram from Tokyo asking the Japanese Ambassador in Berlin to tell Hitler and Ribbentrop secretly that war was imminent, and by reports of menacing Japanese troop and fleet movements, decided to disregard Churchill's harsh advice. Instead he took up a suggestion made originally by Kurusu of sending a personal message to the Emperor, appealing to him 'to give thought in this definite emergency to dispelling the dark clouds'. By the time the Emperor received the message, hostilities had begun. Togo, by now intent on war, did not allow the communication to get through in time.

In his message to Hirohito, Roosevelt revived many of the compromise terms that he had suggested for the discarded *modus vivendi*; this throws doubt on the Stimson tale that the President had instructed Hull to drop the *modus vivendi*. Roosevelt said that evening, 'Well, this son of man has just sent his final message to the Son of God.' (Many Japanese thought their Emperor was a god.)[26]

When he first learnt that Hull was drawing up his *modus vivendi* Churchill showed ambivalence, minuting to Eden:

My own feeling is that we might give Hull the latitude he asks. Our major interest is: no further encroachments and no war, as we have already enough of this latter. The United States will not throw over the Chinese cause, and we may safely follow them in this part of the subject. We could not of course agree to an arrangement whereby Japan was free to attack Russia in Siberia. I doubt myself whether this is likely at the present time. I remember that President Roosevelt himself wrote in 'There must be no further encroachment in the North' at the Atlantic Conference. I should think this could be agreed. The formal denunciation of the Axis Pact by Japan is not in my opinion necessary. Their stopping out of the war is in itself a great disappointment and injury to the Germans. We ought not to agree to any veto on American or British help to China. But we shall not be asked to by the United States.

Subject to the above, it would be worth while to ease up upon Japan economically sufficiently for them to live from hand to mouth – even if we only got another three months. These however are only first impressions.

I must say I should feel pleased if I read that an American–Japanese agreement had been made by which we were to be no worse off three months hence in the Far East than we are now.[27]

This mood soon left Churchill, and it is hard to reconcile his expression 'our major interest is . . . no war' with the evidence of his anxiety to bring about a Japanese attack on America. Perhaps he had cold feet about the defence of Malaya and a conscience about the way which he had starved it of planes and tanks, and wanted 'another three months' to provide reinforcements. However,

British commitments were such that he could do little. More likely, he was hoping for an American naval and military commitment to defend Malaya if he got his three months. Perhaps he baulked for a moment at the prospect of the terrible bloodshed that a war in the Far East would cause.

No firm undertaking of active United States support for Britain or Holland in the event of a Japanese attack was given; for constitutional reasons, Roosevelt could not give it without the approval of Congress. As soon as the Japanese delegates in Washington informed Tokyo of the contents of the final United States Government communication of 26 November orders were given to the Japanese military machine to launch air attacks on Pearl Harbor, southern Thailand and Manila, and to invade southern Thailand and Malaya on 7 December.

At 9 p.m. on 7 December Churchill was informed by his butler at Chequers that the Japanese had attacked the Americans. Immediately he telephoned the President. Churchill said: 'What's this about Japan?'

Roosevelt replied: 'It is true. They have attacked us at Pearl Harbor. We are all in the same boat now.'

Churchill told him: 'Our declaration of war will follow yours within the hour.'

Significantly, when Dudley Pound had told the Defence Committee that 'it would be very awkward if we had to declare war [on Japan] on behalf of the Dutch without the support of the United States', Churchill replied that 'all he wanted to avoid was being landed in an automatic declaration of war . . . and give the [American] anti-British party cause for saying the US were again being dragged into a British war'.

Churchill has recorded that to have the United States 'at our side' gave him 'the greatest joy'; he felt we had 'won', and went to bed and slept 'the sleep of the saved and thankful'. With great skill he had helped to manoeuvre Japan into attacking America, and now America was at last Britain's ally. However, while playing this dangerous game he had failed to commit enough military resources to the defence of Malaya, and if he could have foreseen the disaster that would result he would not have slept so soundly.[28]

Although on the evening of 7 December Churchill went to bed in the certainty that America would join the war against Hitler, this was only hypothetical. There were grave doubts in the Foreign Office as to whether the USA would declare war on Germany, and it was well on the cards that she would be at war with Japan but not with Germany and Italy. Most American historians believe that, if Roosevelt had immediately asked Congress to declare war on Germany, he would have faced strong opposition because the only enemy that had attacked the United States was Japan.

When Hitler talked to Matsuoka, the Foreign Minister, in Berlin in April 1941 the German dictator promised to declare war on America in the event of war between the USA and Japan following Japanese aggression in the Pacific; this pledge was repeated to the Japanese Ambassador in Berlin, Hiroshi Oshima, on 29 November by Ribbentrop. However, in his evidence before the Nuremberg Tribunal Ribbentrop testified that Pearl Harbor came as a complete surprise to the Germans; when Hitler returned to Berlin from the Russian front Ribbentrop presented him with the alternative of staying out of war with the USA because the Tripartite Pact bound Germany only in the event of an attack on Japan, and the German Embassy in Washington cabled that America would want to avoid a 'two front war'.

Entirely underestimating the US military power and greatly overestimating Japan's strength, however, Hitler committed his crowning folly and declared war on the USA on 10 December. We do not know why he did it. If he had not, all the US military effort would have been put into the Far East. At last Churchill's dream of the USA being Britain's ally in Europe against Germany was realized. But at what a cost!

Any lingering doubts about whether Churchill really wanted Japan to attack America in 1941 are removed by the minute he wrote in September 1943 after he had read the printed report by Craigie on the final pre-war negotiations with Japan; Craigie was not repatriated until late in 1942. By describing Pearl Harbor as a 'blessing' Churchill makes it crystal-clear that all along he wanted Japan to attack the United States.

> This despatch throws the blame for the war between Japan and the United States on the failure of the United States to handle properly the compromise proposals of the 20th November 1941. It is therefore a very strange document and one which should be most scrupulously kept secret. A more one-sided and pro-Japanese account of what occurred I have hardly ever read. The total lack of all sense of proportion as between any British or American slips on the one hand and the deliberate scheme of war eventuating in the outrage of Pearl Harbour on the other shows a detachment from events and from his country's fortunes. He also writes of the breach with Japan as if it were an unmitigated disaster. This may be pardoned in an Ambassador whose duty it is to preserve friendly relations with a particular country, and whose judgment is naturally affected by this fact. It was however a blessing that Japan attacked the United States and thus brought America wholeheartedly and unitedly into the war. Greater good fortune has rarely happened to the British Empire than this event which has revealed our friends and foes in their true light, and may lead, through the merciless crushing of Japan, to a new realtionship of immense benefit to the English-speaking countries and to the whole world.
>
> There should be no question of circulating this despatch to anyone. I will however keep my copy for further study for the present.[29]

In his report Craigie argued cogently that the Japanese decision to go to war on 27 November 1941 would not have been taken, or 'definitely' would have been postponed, if their compromise proposals of 20 November had been made the basis of negotiations. He looked on these Japanese proposals as 'the last throw of the Emperor and the moderates in their desire to prevent war'. He condemned the decision by the Americans not to proceed with Hull's *modus vivendi*, and stated that the final reply of the United States Government was couched in terms which Japan was certain to reject. Craigie added that the United States Government should have known there was no chance whatever of Japan accepting the Hull Memorandum of 26 November.

Craigie had toned down some of his passages, but the report included that the lack of response to Japanese peace efforts had resulted in Prince Konoye resigning on 16 October and being succeeded by the more extreme General Tojo. Craigie was emphatic that a more co-operative attitude by America and Britain could have averted the deadlock, in spite of Tojo and Togo being more bellicose than their precedessors. Craigie also argued that it was a great mistake to leave all the negotiations in the hands of the Americans, and that Togo 'even at the eleventh hour' wanted 'not to sow dissension but to discover some means of averting the threatening catastrophe'.

On receiving the Prime Minister's bad-tempered memorandum Eden replied that he 'entirely agreed'. Yet he had not demurred when Craigie's despatch was received and printed, and he had authorized its circulation to the King, the War Cabinet members, the Washington Embassy and within the Foreign Office after Cadogan had produced a Far Eastern Department comment on it. Now he minuted to his Department that 'this should not have been printed', which was criticizing himself. The King's copy was withdrawn before he had read it. The official historian writes that the Foreign Office did not accept Craigie's view that the acceptance of the Japanese proposals of 20 November would have averted or postponed war, or that 'the United States (or Great Britain) could have agreed the proposals'. Of course, for Churchill the attack on Pearl Harbor was not a 'catastrophe' but the 'blessing' for which he had been longing because it brought America into the war against Hitler which, without her aid in Europe, Britain had no chance of winning.

Churchill refused to allow Craigie to be re-employed and even said he should be sent to the Isle of Man, where enemy aliens were interned, as a traitor. However, under Labour after 1945 he was given important appointments in Geneva.

L. H. Faulds, the Japanese expert in the Foreign Office, minuted on the Craigie report that 'we have nothing with which to reproach ourselves since the final result was that the United States came into the war'. Was he right?[30]

For Churchill Britain's victory over Germany was an over-riding objective, and Pearl Harbor made this infinitely more likely. Was he justified in trying to provoke Japan to attack the United States? Did the end justify the means? The immediate result in the Far East was defeat for the Allies, followed by three and three-quarter years of bloody warfare with great loss of life and tremendous suffering on both sides, culminating in atom bombs being exploded over Hiroshima and Nagasaki.

Against this must be weighed the inescapable fact that in 1941 Britain had no prospect of defeating Germany without the aid of the USA as an active ally. Churchill believed Congress would never authorize Roosevelt to declare war on Germany. Also he considered that 'the merciless crushing of Japan' would be of immense benefit to English-speaking countries, and acted over Japan in 1941 with a full awareness of all the grave issues involved. In war, decisions by national leaders must be made according to their effect on the war effort. There is truth in the old adage: 'All's fair in love and war.'

CHAPTER THIRTEEN

Roosevelt and Churchill hand in hand

AFTER AMERICA'S entry into the war Churchill decided he must go to Washington immediately to consult with Roosevelt. He sailed from the Clyde on 12 December 1941 with a strong team of advisers, including Beaverbrook. Dill had been superseded by Brooke as CIGS but Churchill, in spite of tensions between them, decided to take Dill and leave him in Washington as the Permanent Military Representative. It was a sensible choice, and Dill and Churchill got on better in their new relationship.

Churchill's main worry was that America would concentrate on the war with Japan at the expense of Europe. Fortunately the President and his military advisers agreed at once that the Americans would give the European theatre priority, and Roosevelt wanted American land forces to be involved as soon as possible in the West to counteract the public demand to avenge Pearl Harbor by action against the Japanese. To Churchill's delight the Americans enthusiastically agreed to two important measures of unity: a high-faluting Declaration of War Aims, to be signed by all the associated powers and henceforward to be called the United Nations, and a Combined Chiefs of Staff Committee in Washington to co-ordinate the operations and strategy of the armed might of Britain and the USA.

General Marshall, Roosevelt's main military adviser, wanted the British and Americans to concentrate on a cross-Channel invasion. They should, he felt, accumulate as soon as possible the maximum quantity of men and equipment in the United Kingdom (Bolero), while making a contingency plan for an emergency attack in the autumn of 1942 (Sledgehammer) in the event of real danger of a Russian collapse, and a decisive assault on the French coast in 1943 (Roundup). Churchill was opposed, and wanted instead only sporadic attacks on the Continent to enable the conquered populations to revolt, together with a landing in French North Africa so that Anglo–American forces would link up in Tunisia with the Eighth Army, who he confidently hoped in December 1941 would soon force the Germans out of Tripoli.

Roosevelt was disturbed by Churchill's typically adventurous plans for widely dispersed piecemeal landings in support of local uprisings on the Continent, but he did plump for the North African landing. Marshall did not agree. For him North Africa was peripheral. He feared that a substantial diversion of British and

American armies there would leave the Allies too weak for a landing in France, which alone could be decisive in defeating Germany in the West.

The arguments between Marshall and Churchill were not resolved at the Washington Conference (Arcadia), in spite of Roosevelt's support for Churchill's North African plan. At the Conference the differences in temperament and intellect between Churchill and Roosevelt became apparent. Churchill was hoping for a warm, intimate friendship, and romantically longed for a post-war world guided by British and American partnership in which both countries sacrificed their national self-interest. Roosevelt did not share Churchill's vision; he did not want to link America's future too closely with a Churchill-led Britain.[1]

There are 1161 written messages from Churchill to Roosevelt and 788 from the President; there were also many phone calls (largely unrecorded) and nine meetings. Many of these messages were drafted by their respective advisers and they do not always give a reliable clue to their relationship. Their basic bond was hatred of Hitler and Japan, and the way in which they were both determined to defend Western civilization. There is evidence of camaraderie and friendship in the written exchanges, and one special unselfish gesture of friendship when the President offered to divert three hundred of his most modern tanks (Shermans) and guns (SP 105 mm) to Cairo in June 1942 after Tobruk fell. But the camaraderie masked frequent clashes and continual irritations.

Historians have romanticized the Churchill–Roosevelt relationship mainly because in his post-war memoirs Churchill misleadingly defined that relationship as close personal affection combined with identical interests. But detailed study of the British and American archives and personal reminiscences by those then in high places reveal that Anglo–American discord overhung the Alliance. It is not well known that on two occasions Churchill drafted letters to Roosevelt in which he threatened to resign. The first was on 12 April 1942, when Roosevelt argued that because of American public opinion Britain must make an immediate offer to India of independence (see pages 199–201). This made Churchill furious, because he was adamant that Indian independence should wait until the end of the war. The second occasion was on 30 June 1944, when Roosevelt insisted that US divisions must be withdrawn from Italy for the invasion of southern France (Anvil; see pages 278–80), whereas Churchill had set his heart on victory in Italy and an advance into Austria and Hungary to forestall the Russians. Neither letter was sent. Instead, Churchill toned down his drafts, which lie in the archives as indisputable evidence of his resentment against the President.[2] Through clouds of distrust, dislike and discord Churchill worked for an Anglo–American entente, believing that only thus could Britain remain a major power, while Roosevelt always assumed that as the weaker partner Britain must follow America's lead.

How far were the two friends? Following Pearl Harbor in December 1941, when Churchill flew to Washington to stay at the White House for the Arcadia Conference, there was undoubtedly cordiality, warmth and great relief that at last America could wage all-out war openly against Hitler without Roosevelt having to drag public opinion with him painfully in every step of his programme of aid for Britain. There is evidence that Roosevelt found Churchill irritating – especially his trumped up Americanism based on his American mother – and there was a gradual but remorseless cooling off in their relations; while Churchill, immensely proud of Britain's achievement in standing out alone against Hitler, deeply resented being the underdog and the enforced subordinate of a man whom he judged his inferior as a statesman.

After the first Arcadia military discussions Roosevelt was enthusiastic for Churchill to address Congress; he did so on Boxing Day, and was received enthusiastically. The Prime Minister was as confident as if he was in the Commons. However he struck a wrong note with Roosevelt by declaring that in future Britain and America would walk side by side 'in majesty, in justice and peace'. Roosevelt did not see America's destiny as being intertwined with that of Britain. He had a sentimental regard for the British people and he had helped them unselfishly to hold out against Hitler, but he had a prejudice against both the British Empire and the Conservative ruling establishment which Churchill epitomized for him.

Churchill's second address to Congress, in 1943, also annoyed Roosevelt (according to Hopkins), because Congressmen complained afterwards that they only found out what was going on in the war when the British Prime Minister visited Washington, and Churchill injudiciously agreed with some of them in private about this.[3] Churchill was insensitive over this and wrote to his wife on 28 May 1943 that the speech, showing the 'success which has attended our joint efforts, and his part in it', strengthened his friendship with the President; he added that his words had 'had a most electrifying effect . . . they never had had anything like the kind of accounts I give to Parliament and were delighted'. The trouble was that Churchill had done very well what Roosevelt should have been doing.[4]

It would be false, however, to imply that the initial friendship between Churchill and Roosevelt during the Arcadia Conference of 1941 turned to enmity. There was always a strong element of goodwill and understanding between them. They were both big enough to realize that history required them to get along, and that they must meet each other's views as far as possible over the key problems of the war. Thus it was a successful alliance of convenience.

A hint of discord arose when the Soviet Foreign Minister, Molotov, visited London and Washington in May 1942. Molotov found Britain and America at odds on the question of a second front in 1942. Against Churchill's advice, Roosevelt told Molotov that he favoured a cross-Channel invasion in 1942, and gave vague threats that America might concentrate on the Far East unless France was invaded.

Then in June 1943 Roosevelt tried to arrange a private meeting with Stalin, and lied to Churchill about it. The President claimed that with Churchill absent Stalin would be more frank, especially over Poland, the Balkans and the Far East. Churchill always felt that Britain should be the broker between Russia and America, and he flew into a rage because a private meeting between Roosevelt and Stalin implied second-class status for Britain. That private meeting never took place, but damage was done to the Churchill–Roosevelt relationship.[5]

After Arcadia the US Army Planning Staff were not content. They complained that there was no definite commitment to concentrate all Allied resources on an invasion of Europe. The US Joint Strategic Committee reported that the British Isles must be used as a base area for an 'offensive to defeat the German armed forces'. General Marshall wrote a memorandum for the President, pointing out that England was the only place where British and American armies could undertake an attack in co-operation, and that the United States could use larger forces in western Europe than elsewhere because of sea distances and the existing base facilities in England. He ruled firmly against concentrating on the Pacific because of the problem of moving forces there. Marshall accompanied the memorandum with a plan to invade France in April 1943 with forty-eight divisions between Le Havre and Boulogne, and wanted 'all other operations . . . to be subordinate to this major stroke'.[6]

Churchill was relieved that Marshall had turned down any idea of the major American Army effort being in the Pacific, but he was too impatient to wait until 1943 for combined British and American armies to fight the German armies and take the pressure off Russia. He wanted to invade either French North Africa (Gymnast) or northern Norway (Jupiter).

Jupiter was a wild plan which attracted no American support, and the British Chiefs of Staff were horrified at it. Before the entry of America into the war in the summer of 1941 Churchill had become keen on Jupiter, to help the Russians in the event of a German offensive against Murmansk; this action of the Prime Minister's was an attempt to meet Stalin's desperate requests for another front. When in August that year Churchill toyed with Jupiter only three brigades and one mountain regiment trained for Arctic warfare were available and they would not be ready until March 1942, whereas the Germans had six well-equipped divisions between northern Norway and the Murmansk front. The Chiefs of Staff pointed out that the only feasible operation was an Anglo–Swedish attack on Trondheim. However, the Swedes would not concert plans with Britain until they had actually been attacked by the Germans. The Chief of Staff's report was not to Churchill's liking and he unfairly called it a 'catalogue of difficulties'. But the chances of Sweden ever fighting Germany were low, and the 1941 Norway plan was just one more of Churchill's impractical dreams.

Even with the entry of the USA into the war the British Chiefs of Staff told Churchill that Jupiter was 'unsound' because it would absorb unacceptably large quantities of shipping, contribute little to the defence of northern convoys and run the risk of military disaster. The Americans were equally discouraging, but Churchill would not give up his pet scheme. He asked General McNaughton, commander of the Canadian forces in Britain, whom he wanted to play a leading part in the expedition, to make an independent enquiry. But even when McNaughton firmly advised against the operation, Churchill refused to give up the idea. On 16 September 1942 he minuted that McNaughton's report was 'unduly pessimistic', and told the Chiefs of Staff: 'Jupiter with all its costs and risk may well be found not only necessary, but cheapest in the long run.'

He then wanted McNaughton to go to Moscow to talk to Stalin about it, cabling to the Soviet leader that if the Russian staff could make a good plan the President and he would co-operate to the limit of their ability. Moscow was unencouraging, and Jupiter died a natural death. However, until 1944 Hitler believed the British planned a Norway landing, and diverted troops and ships there needlessly, to the Allies' advantage.[7]

At the beginning of April 1942 Marshall and Hopkins flew to London with Marshall's plan, approved by the President. Much to Churchill's annoyance they refused his invitation to stay at Chequers, and instead insisted on plunging immediately into discussions with the British Chiefs of Staff in London. Churchill was relieved that Marshall still rejected the idea of focusing the main American effort in the Pacific, but he was still impatient for early action and emphatically raised the question: 'What is to be done during 1942?' He was very conscious that Russia had survived only by the narrowest of margins in 1941, and there was no certainty that she would be able to withstand another ferocious German assault in the summer of 1942. So Churchill put to the Americans that the Allies should either clear the Germans out of Africa through a landing in French North Africa (Gymnast) or by his pet plan for an operation closer to Russia – a landing in northern Norway (Jupiter).

Marshall brought to London not only a plan for a major invasion of Europe in 1943 (Roundup) but also a contingency plan for an emergency cross-Channel attack in 1942 (Sledgehammer), which Marshall said would 'only be justified if the situation in Russia became desperate' or the German situation in Western Europe became critically weakened. Although Sledgehammer as first presented by Marshall in London was a back-to-the-wall emergency plan, it assumed considerable importance because in the early discussions there were no rival proposals for a land attack on the German armies during 1942, and the Americans wanted it firmly kept on the agenda as a possibility whatever the Russian situation.

Both Churchill and Brooke were ready to discuss Sledgehammer, and Calais and the Cherbourg peninsula were suggested as possible zones of attack. Churchill would not commit Britain to capturing a bridgehead in France in 1942 and the CIGS was even more adamant that it was not practical because the Germans could easily have reinforced their troops and pushed the Allies back to the beaches. At that time Churchill was depressed by the poor showing of the British troops at Singapore, and feared the morale of the new British generation of fighters was not as good as in the First World War. The fall of Tobruk in June 1942 redoubled his fears.

In the end Churchill vetoed Sledgehammer in 1942 except 'if opportunity occurs'. But it was agreed accommodation would be prepared for considerable numbers of American troops in Britain and plans should go ahead at full speed 'for operations on the Continent' (Bolero or Roundup) in 1943. So as Marshall flew back to Washington plans were in a state of flux.

On 20 May, five weeks after Marshall and Hopkins had left London, Molotov, the Soviet Foreign Minister, arrived. Molotov announced that he had come to discuss both a treaty and a second front, but the second front was much the more important. In personal discussions with the Russian Minister Churchill emphasized that it was impossible for Britain and America to draw off large enemy forces from the East during 1942, and that a landing in France which resulted in fiasco would not benefit either Russia or the Allied cause.[8]

Molotov then proceeded to Washington and repeated his request to Roosevelt for a second front in France in 1942 which would draw off forty German divisions. In defiance of Churchill, Roosevelt and Marshall told Molotov they could authorize him to tell Stalin that 'we expect a Second Front this year', and an official statement was issued in Washington and London that 'In the course of the conversations full understanding was reached with regard to the urgent task of creating a Second Front in Europe in 1942.' Churchill, as has been noted, was very angry. He and his military advisers had not agreed, and in May Churchill had warned Roosevelt of the difficulties of a landing in France in 1942.

Back in London, Molotov again asked the British for a second front in 1942. Churchill told him he quite understood there was a danger point in 1942 and that Germany might be stronger in the West in 1943. Therefore he would be very glad if it was possible to do in 1942 what was planned for 1943, which was to invade the Continent with forty or fifty divisions. But he firmly refused to make any commitment to a bridgehead in France in 1942.[9]

To make his position clear and to undo Roosevelt's commitment, Churchill insisted Molotov was handed a memorandum stating that 'We are making preparations for a landing on the Continent in August or September 1942 . . . it is impossible to say in advance whether the situation will be such as to make this operation feasible . . . we can therefore give no promise.' However, Molotov was told firmly there would be a large-scale invasion of the Continent in 1943 with over a million men. He was also told that Britain would consider an operation in the Petsamo area, the Artic point of Finland on the ice-free Barents sea (Churchill's favourite Jupiter plan), and send fighter bomber squadrons to Murmansk at the end of July; it was not what the Russian wanted to hear.[10]

Churchill reported his discussions with Molotov to the War Cabinet on 11 June. They came to an important decision, recording that the Allies should not attempt any major landing on the Continent in 1942 unless they intended to stay there. Churchill had warned them that Sledgehammer was only practical 'if German morale had started to crack'. This Cabinet meeting marked the end of Sledgehammer for Churchill.[11]

Meanwhile Churchill had sent Mountbatten to Washington to cajole the President. Roosevelt, who liked royalty, fell for the Admiral's charm. Mountbatten had been charged by Churchill with the task of convincing the President that Sledgehammer would be a disaster. Roosevelt rapidly agreed in à deux talks (without Marshall) that Sledgehammer was 'off', but declared he could not send a million soldiers to England to wait for Roundup on some unspecified date in 1943. Therefore the President suggested to Mountbatten that United States divisions should attack North Africa, and said he had been 'very struck' by the Prime Minister's plan for Gymnast – just what Churchill wanted.[12]

Immediately he received this news from Mountbatten, Churchill decided to visit Washington again. He was delighted that Roosevelt favoured the North Africa project and, although still very much in favour of the cross-Channel assault in 1943, he was determined to give more immediate help to Russia by a diversion in the Mediterranean.

Churchill arrived in Washington on 17 June, and spent 19 and 20 June in *tête à tête* conversations with the President at his residence, Hyde Park. This was just as well, because the CIGS, who had accompanied Churchill, was opposed to the North African venture and in talks with the Americans found his opposite numbers in complete agreement. The Joint Chiefs of Staff wanted no operation in 1942 in the Mediterranean and preferred to concentrate all available forces for the 1943 cross-Channel invasion.

While the two heads of state were at Hyde Park on 19 and 20 June the Joint Chiefs of Staff had thrashed out their plans and differences in Washington. They agreed that the proposal to build up strength in Britain should be adhered to, but that a cross-Channel landing in 1942 should only be undertaken 'in case of necessity or of an exceptionally favourable opportunity'. The professional Service leaders of both nations were 100 per cent opposed to an immediate operation in Norway or North Africa. Marshall and Brooke, who did not get on well, were for once in agreement: Gymnast would ruin plans for Roundup. They both felt that Gymnast was an 'alternative', not an 'addition', to a 1943 Roundup. But their discussions and consensus were abortive,[13] and this unanimity was shattered abruptly: when they emerged from Hyde Park their political masters were agreed on Gymnast, and the British and American Service Chiefs had to bow to their will.

Both heads of state refused to believe their generals' claim that the North African operation in 1942 would make an invasion of France impossible in 1943. Nor did abandonment of Sledgehammer cause Roosevelt to favour giving priority to the Pacific, which was much feared by Churchill and Brooke. His Chiefs of Staff had recommended to him that the United States should, if Sledgehammer was abandoned, reorder its priorities and concentrate on the Pacific. Roosevelt would not have this, and he sent Hopkins and Marshall back to London on 18 July with firm orders: 'We cannot wait until 1943 to strike at Germany. If we cannot strike at "Sledgehammer" then we must take the second best – and that is NOT the Pacific.' Hopkins and Marshall were told to explore in London a direct attack in French North Africa or the Middle East, where they could reinforce the British in Egypt or the Russians through Iran. Roosevelt concluded: 'Defeat of Japan does not defeat Germany and American concentration against Japan this year or in 1943 increases the chance of complete domination of Europe and Africa . . . defeat of Germany means defeat of Japan probably without firing a shot or losing a life.'[14]

Churchill, convinced of the merits of Gymnast (now rechristened Torch), was delighted with the President's approval of his strategy. Certainly Churchill had played his cards well with Roosevelt, and Mountbatten had worked wonders for him by convincing the President that Sledgehammer should be abandoned in favour of North Africa.

In London, Marshall and Admiral King made it clear to the British that in their view undertaking Gymnast meant there was no possibility of carrying out a full-scale Roundup in 1943, as originally visualized. Brooke agreed, and told the Cabinet so firmly on 24 July, but Churchill continued to ignore the argument.[15]

The Americans, with their orders from the President, argued unsuccessfully with the British for a Cherbourg landing in 1942 as a Roundup preliminary; but, faced with an adamant refusal, they agreed to Churchill's plan for North Africa. Originally the operation was subject to the situation 'on the Russian front by 15 September indicating such a collapse or weakening of Russian resistance as to make 'Roundup' appear impracticable'. By 25 July the Americans had agreed that planning for Torch could begin, and Eisenhower was appointed commander. Churchill cabled to Roosevelt: 'Second front consists of a main body holding the enemy pinned opposite 'Sledgehammer' and a wide flanking movement called 'Torch'.' He overlooked the proviso about the Russian front.[16]

Both Churchill and Roosevelt remained steadfastly blind to their military advisers' reiterated arguments that Torch in the autumn of 1942 ruled out Roundup in 1943. They were both delighted that agreement had at last been reached on a military operation for which plans were under way. Churchill even minuted to the Chiefs of Staff Committee on 23 July that '"Gymnast" although it impinges temporarily on "Bolero" [build-up of US invasion troops in Britain] is NOT at the expense of "Roundup".' Both Churchill and Roosevelt took it that an explicit decision had been made to invade North Africa, and when the decision was made they conveniently forgot the important reservation that this operation should be undertaken only if a collapse of Russian resistance made Roundup impossible. Churchill asked Roosevelt to fix a date for Torch not later than 30 October.[17]

Roosevelt agreed, and told his Chiefs of Staff on 30 July 'that he as Commander in Chief had made the decision that "Torch" should be carried out at the earliest possible date, and that the operation was now our principal objective and it should have precedence over the assembly of US troops in Britain for a Continental invasion'. The fact that Torch had been agreed only as a stopgap was played down by both Churchill and Roosevelt, and the resources which Marshall had designed for the grand cross-Channel invasion of 1943 quickly began to flow away to the Pacific and the Mediterranean. The decision to go for Torch made Roundup impossible, as the generals had predicted all along, and may even have prolonged the war.

During the negotiations with the Americans Churchill was extremely anxious to make a raid in force on France. He toyed with Imperator, a madcap scheme for a two-day landing and an approach to Paris. This was not taken seriously by the Chiefs of Staff, but a landing at Dieppe became a runner in the spring of 1942. The Dieppe operation was known first as Rutter and then as Jubilee. Churchill and the War Cabinet were under severe pressure from both the Russians and the

Americans, together with a vocal section of British public opinion, for a second front in 1942; Churchill believed that a successful Dieppe raid would assuage these pressures. With the Prime Minister's hearty approval the Dieppe operation was born on 11 May 1942 when Mountbatten, as Commander of Combined Operations, recommended it; two days later the Chiefs of Staff approved his outline plan.

It called for a force of infantry, airborne troops and tanks to land at 'lightly defended Dieppe', which lies only 67 miles south of Newhaven, well within range of fighter aircraft from south coast airfields. In spite of objections from Service Chiefs, Churchill wanted to carry out the Dieppe assault willy-nilly in order to pacify Stalin. The Russian armies were in a bad way, with Leningrad in dire danger, and Stalin was demanding a diversionary assault in western Europe; as will be seen, he took ill the Anglo–American decision to postpone until 1943 the main cross-Channel invasion and instead to land in North Africa.

Despite a shocking muddle in the rehearsal, Dieppe was scheduled for 4 July 1942. The aim was to destroy strong points and installations and then withdraw. Troops were embarked amid iron security. Then the weather turned bad and the raid had to be postponed until the 8th. The wind freshened that night, and the commander of the airborne troops refused to fly. The troops, mostly Canadians, were disembarked; security was badly dented by their talk in Portsmouth pubs. Montgomery was in charge of the operation, and he advised firmly that it should be cancelled for all time.

Churchill insisted that Rutter should be resuscitated. Meanwhile Montgomery had flown off to Cairo and had no more responsibility; it became entirely Mountbatten's operation. Churchill was due in Moscow on 12 August, and he felt he urgently needed to tell Stalin of an important assault on Europe.

Mountbatten made the new D-Day for Dieppe 18 August, and the operation was now rechristened Jubilee. Because of RAF objections he agreed to forego the heavy bombers insisted on by Montgomery, and to substitute commandos for airborne troops. Dudley Pound refused adamantly to risk a battleship or a cruiser in the narrow Channel. Churchill, heavily engaged in negotiations with the Americans in London and preparations for his trip to Cairo and Moscow, was too busy to attend to details of Jubilee. The 18th of August was a black day in Imperial military history; on the Dieppe beaches the flower of the Canadian Army was mown down in daylight by an unprecedented concentration of machine guns, field guns and mortars, mostly firing on predetermined lines. There was no surprise about the main assault, and the rate of casualties in the first few minutes was much higher than at any moment on the first day of the Battle of the Somme in 1916. Out of 5086 soldiers who landed, only 1443 returned to England, while the Germans lost no more than 597 killed and wounded. 906 Canadians were killed.

Yet no one took the blame because on 20 August Mountbatten gave the War Cabinet a totally misleading report, claiming a satisfactory, not a disastrous, outcome:

Our naval losses had been extremely light. Two-thirds of the total military forces
. . . were accounted for and had returned to this country. Although tanks had been
got ashore they had been unable to leave the immediate vicinity of the beaches,
owing to the exits being blocked. As a result, the objectives of the forces which had
landed on the central beaches had not been reached. The personnel of one enemy
coastal battery had been wiped out while another battery had been neutralized by a
small party of determined men who had sniped the gun crew. Planning organization
and co-operation between all the Services had been excellent. The air support had
been faultless.

Mountbatten said that the lessons learnt would be invaluable in planning for
Roundup, and that the raid would be carefully examined to evolve new tech-
niques against the very strong German coastal defences. On the 29th the War
Cabinet was told that the Dieppe raid had achieved complete surprise from the
air point of view. It had been three hours after the attack had started before
German fighters had appeared, and six hours before German bombers arrived on
the scene.[18]

In fact Dieppe achieved nothing. The British handed to the Germans on a
plate twenty-eight of their most modern tanks and much other war booty which
provided complete information about up-to-date radios, infantry weapons and
tactics. Mountbatten claimed that for every soldier who died at Dieppe ten were
saved on D-Day, but this is rubbish. Churchill claimed that Dieppe showed how
a frontal assault on a defended port was doomed to failure, and that because of
this vital lesson the Normandy landings were successful. If anyone thought
before Dieppe that infantry could be landed successfully in small boats in
daylight on beaches covered by machine gun fire they needed their heads seen to,
and the plain truth is that lives and equipment were sacrificed recklessly and in
vain.

It was unfortunate that Churchill was too busy to pay attention to the details of
the Dieppe attack as he did over similar proposed assaults from the sea in the
Aegean. Mountbatten did not even refer to the Prime Minister the repeated
requests by the Canadian commander, General 'Ham' Roberts, for a battleship
or a cruiser, and was content with the supporting fire of four destroyers. Although
Montgomery had insisted on heavy bombers and airborne troops to land behind
the objectives, Mountbatten ordered General Roberts to cut out the airborne
troops because gliders were 'too dependent on the weather'. Mountbatten
claimed over-optimistically that commando units landing from the sea could be
substituted with complete safety. It is unlikely that Churchill would have
approved such changes. Roberts' requests for airborne troops, bombers and a
bombardment from a battleship or cruiser were all turned down by Mountbatten
on his own authority.

Churchill took a keen interest in Jubilee, although it is impossible to trace in
the archives his definite written approval before he left for Cairo. From Egypt he
cabled to the War Cabinet on receiving Mountbatten's report, which included a
statement that all those returning whom he had seen 'were in great form', that the
lessons learnt would be 'invaluable for the cross channel invasion', and that his

general impression was that 'the results fully justified the heavy cost'.[19] But the truth dawned on him before long. Beaverbrook confronted Mountbatten at a social function and said: 'You have murdered thousands of my countrymen . . . their blood is on your hands'; criticism in the Canadian press was intensely hostile.

Shortly after Dieppe, at a dinner party at Chequers in Churchill's presence, Brooke had openly attacked Mountbatten, telling him that the planning for Dieppe had been all wrong. Mountbatten exploded and demanded a full enquiry; in December 1942, when Mountbatten finally produced a report on the lessons learnt from Dieppe, Brooke noted that he was 'very disappointed with the paucity of ideas'.[20]

Churchill had told the Commons: 'I personally regarded the Dieppe assault, to which I gave my sanction, as an indispensable preliminary to full scale operations.' In December 1942 the discrepancies between Mountbatten's report and detailed later reports, together with rumours of inefficiency and angry Canadian press comment, made Churchill alarmed that he had misled the Commons. He minuted to Ismay:

> Although for many reasons everyone was concerned to make this business [Jubilee] look as good as possible the time has come when I must be informed more precisely about the military plans. Who made them? Who approved them? What was General Montgomery's part in it? and General McNaughton's part? What is the opinion about the Canadian generals selected by General McNaughton? Did the General staff check the plans? At what point was V.C.I.G.S. informed in C.I.G.S.'s absence?
>
> At first sight it would appear to a layman very much out of accord with the accepted principles of war to attack the strongly fortified town front without first securing the cliffs on either side, and to use our tanks in frontal assault off the beaches by the Casino, etc. instead of landing them a few miles up the coast and entering the town from the back.[21]

Ismay was instructed to make an investigation – after which, Churchill warned, 'I will then consider whether there should be a more formal inquiry and what form it should take.' Ismay consulted with Mountbatten and worked out mollifying replies to Churchill's pertinent questions without letting the Prime Minister know that he had consulted Mountbatten. The replies are inadequate, but Churchill let the matter drop. It is surprising that he retained his intense faith in Mountbatten after the Dieppe incident.

However, when Churchill was writing his memoirs in 1950 he realized that his 1942 questions about Dieppe had never been properly answered and that Stacey, in the official Canadian war history, had been very critical. He consulted with his advisers, Ismay, Pownall and G. R. Allen, asking them who took the decision to revive the plan and why it was not brought to his attention before he left for Cairo at the end of July 1942. They consulted Mountbatten, who wrote to Churchill: 'You were as ever the moving spirit', and begged him to omit from his memoirs his original draft, which made it clear that the Prime Minister had had no hand in the detailed planning (as he would if he had not been abroad). This was true, but in the end Churchill substituted Mountbatten's suggested draft in full, thus shouldering himself with full responsibility for the decision to relaunch, together with the claim that the raid had been necessary and the results of good value. This episode casts doubts on the validity of Churchill's memoirs.[22]

Churchill's draft for his memoirs states that the Dieppe raid was revived on the initiative of Admiral Mountbatten; this Mountbatten crossed out on Churchill's draft. Churchill had also written:

> Before I left England for Cairo and Moscow on August 2, I knew that the operation was to be remounted. Though I took no part in the planning I was in principle favourable to an operation of this character at this time. I naturally supposed that it would be subjected to the final review of the Chiefs of Staff and Defence Committee [of the Cabinet] before whom I should certainly have the main issues brought prior to action had I not been abroad.

Beside this passage Mountbatten wrote: 'Please omit.' Mountbatten also crossed out Churchill's words: 'There is no written record of the revised plan being further examined, nor of any decision to launch it being taken by the Chiefs of Staff or by the Defence Committee or the War Cabinet. Churchill obligingly accepted Mountbatten's amendments; finally he wrote this about Dieppe in his memoirs:

> It was a costly but not unfruitful reconnaissance in force. Tactically it was a mine of experience. It shed revealing light on many shortcomings in our outlook. It taught us to build in good time various new types of craft and appliances for later use. We learnt again the value of powerful support by heavy naval guns in an opposed landing, and our bombardment technique, both marine and aerial, was thereafter improved. Above all it was shown that individual skill and gallantry without thorough organisation and combined training would not prevail, and that team work was the secret of success. This could only be provided by trained and organised amphibious formations.[23]

As there were no heavy naval guns, it is surprising that Churchill was so inaccurate.

Churchill could ill afford to publicize the fact that the Dieppe raid had been a disaster, because in August and September 1942 his prestige as war leader was at its lowest ebb. Worries about why Singapore and Tobruk had fallen could not be soothed by eloquence, and in his memoirs Churchill wrote: 'The chatter and criticism of the press, where the sharpest pens were busy and many shrill voices raised, found its counterpart in the activities of a few score of M.P.s and a fairly glum attitude on the part of the immense majority. A Party Government might well have been overturned at this juncture.'[24]

Many of Churchill's critics wanted him to stay as Prime Minister but to give up the post of Minister of Defence. But Churchill would not consider surrendering any of his power and would have preferred to resign rather than allow someone else to be Minister of Defence under him. He told the Commons he would not be an 'appendage' as Prime Minister 'to make the necessary explanations, excuses and apologies to Parliament when things go wrong'.

Eden, infuriated by Churchill, was convinced that someone else should be Minister of Defence. Eden was popular in the Commons and with the Services;

there is incontrovertible evidence that he told an 'intimate' in 1942 that he would be willing to serve as Minister of Defence under Cripps, and a well concerted move by these two could have toppled Churchill.[25] But Churchill cleverly muzzled Cripps by bringing him into the War Cabinet. Eden was the one man who could bring Churchill down by organizing a cabal within the Cabinet, but his personality was such that he would never strike. At the end of January 1942, after the fall of Singapore, in the vote of confidence in the Commons Churchill survived by a majority of 464 to 1; in July 1942, after Tobruk (see pages 140–43), the vote was 476 to 25 with around 40 MPs abstaining. This was not a crushing victory, because with no official opposition both Labour and Conservative were able to put pressure on most MPs. That so many defied the Whips is evidence of their anxiety about the efficacy of Churchill's leadership and of his dual role of Prime Minister and Minister of Defence.

Churchill's standing with the public after the fall of France in 1940 had been immensely high; his colourful speeches and courageous defiance of the dangers surrounding Britain had made him the hero of the nation. Yet by 1942 although the top civil servants, Service Chiefs and ministers in Whitehall appreciated his role as a morale booster, they distrusted the way he ran the war.

He knew by 1942 that his credit with the public and Parliament was 'not inexhaustible', and that after Tobruk he must fall unless he produced military victories. This influenced his judgement over Dieppe. Major mistakes such as Mers-el-Kebir and sending the Army to Greece were his personal decisions, and his methods of conducting business were disliked exceedingly by those who had to listen to his monologues long after midnight – knowing that the Prime Minister, unlike them, had been refreshed by soothing sleep during their working hours.

In the Lords debate following the loss of Singapore on 25 March two of Churchill's former ministers fiercely criticized the machinery he had set up to run the war, and in particular the Defence Committee; they also complained of Churchill having too much power and his habit of keeping his subordinates at work during the night. After Hankey (whom Churchill had dismissed from the Cabinet in July 1941) had attacked the Defence Committee and Churchill's late working hours, Chatfield (Minister of Defence until Chamberlain fell) said:

> It is much better to do away with the extraordinary position [the state of Defence Committee] as it has grown up and to merge it into the War Cabinet, so that the brains of several men can be applied to the task of making these very vital decisions, which are going to affect us for all time, instead of the burden resting so largely on a single pair of shoulders, however broad, however able, whatever confidence we may have in these shoulders . . . I can assure Your Lordships that I have had representations made to me by those who work in Whitehall that the hours they have to work are perfectly intolerable. It does not lead to efficiency. Nobody is at his best in the Middle Watch . . . I believe it is the height of inefficiency and bad administration to work such hours, which really cannot be necessary, and it only wants a certain amount of sacrifice on the part of different people in order to get a proper working arrangement, efficient in all respects.[26]

Churchill ignored this criticism, and this was unfortunate because many people in high places, although devoted to him for his courage and singleness of purpose, became deeply resentful. As a result they did not always give him 100 per cent co-operation. Brooke has written of 'long drawn out evenings and a desperate longing for bed . . . at the end of a hard week's work to be kept up till the small hours of the morning was, to put it mildly, a very trying procedure', and he 'was fortunate if he did not see Winston for six hours'.

According to General Kennedy (Director of Military Operations) the criticisms in the Lords had no effect on the Prime Minister except that once he said at 11.30 p.m.: 'We had better break off or Lord Hankey will be after us.'[27]

Leo Amery made a significant diary comment on 26 February 1942:

> He [Churchill] seems quite incapable of listening or taking in even the simplest point but goes off at a tangent on a word and then rambles on inconsecutively . . . For the first time I realised he is not only unbusinesslike but overtired and really losing his grip altogether . . . Certainly a complete outsider coming to the meeting and knowing nothing of his reputation would have thought him a rather amusing but quite gaga old gentleman . . . coming out Cripps told me he had been nearly as bad at a meeting earlier in the day.

Harold Nicolson has recorded Sir Frank Markham MP telling him on 14 January 1942 that in order to win the war 'We must get rid of Churchill', while Kenneth Lindsay MP said: 'Cripps was the only possible alternative.' Nicolson did not agree, writing that 'Winston is the embodiment of the nation's will.' Oliver Harvey's diary reveals that Eden complained how difficult the Prime Minister was, and of the devastating effect he had on planning; he stressed the need for a Minister of Defence independent of the Prime Minister.

In his diary Eden wrote on 21 January that Churchill had told him 'the bulk of Tories hated him, that he had done all he could and would be only too happy to yield to another, that Malaya, Australian Government's intransigence and "nagging in House" was more than any man could be expected to endure'. Hugh Dalton in his diaries also gives firm evidence of Churchill's acute depression at this stage of the war. Mary Soames, his daughter, recorded after lunching alone with her mother and father on 27 February 1942: 'Papa is at a very low ebb and he is worn down by the continuous crushing pressure of events'.[28]

In his memoirs Churchill wrote that at this stage of the war it was remarkable he was not dismissed from power or forced to change his methods 'which it was known I should never accept. I should then have vanished from the scene with a load of calamity on my shoulders and the harvest at last to be reaped would have been ascribed to my belated disappearance.'[29]

In 1942 Churchill was not only in a state of intense depression, but he also faced a major political crisis. Yet his standing with the public stayed high, and this saved him. In the light of Churchill's reputation after the war it is hard to believe that his wartime leadership was ever at risk. However, with the victory over Rommel at El Alamein in October 1942 and the successful occupation of Morocco and Algiers the tide of war turned, and no one knew better than

Churchill how to use victories to strengthen his own position in Parliament and with the nation.

Having disposed of Auchinleck and inserted Montgomery, Churchill flew off to Moscow from Cairo on 11 August 1942. His meetings with Stalin and the journey have been vividly described by both Churchill and Brooke in their memoirs. Churchill was obsessed by fear that Stalin and Hitler would come to a separate peace unless Britain agreed to the repeated Russian call for an early second front in western Europe. When Stalin learnt from Churchill in Moscow that instead of an assault on France in 1942 there was to be only an Anglo–American landing in French North Africa, he was furious. Roosevelt, recognizing how difficult it would be for Churchill to placate Stalin, sent his special representative Averil Harriman to Moscow with the rank of Ambassador to give him American moral support.

The conference with Stalin was held in an atmosphere of gloom. The Germans were advancing fast both on Stalingrad and in the Caucasus, and the important oil field of Maikop had just been captured by them. But by sheer force of personality Churchill managed to convince Stalin that Torch would remove pressure on the Russian front by drawing off a great number of German divisions. At first the Soviet leader would not share this view. There were stormy passages, but Churchill magnificently convinced Stalin he had a resolute ally – describing the advantages of freeing the Mediterranean and drawing a crocodile to explain how he would attack 'the soft belly of the crocodile as well as his hard snout'. Harriman emphasized that in spite of the American worries over the Pacific the President's eyes were turned on Europe 'as the primary concern'.

Stalin and his advisers argued fiercely with the British delegation that Torch in 1942, instead of a cross-Channel invasion, breached the commitment given to Molotov by the President and the Prime Minister for a second front that year. Churchill replied that he had been careful not to make any promise to Molotov. This was correct, but of course Roosevelt had made a firm commitment without Churchill's consent. Finally Stalin, on hearing from Churchill an inspired defence of Anglo–American strategy, accepted the decision after Churchill had rashly promised a full-scale cross-Channel invasion in 1943. Then the meeting ended with a banquet in an atmosphere of cordiality.[30]

This marked the high point in Churchill–Stalin relations during the war, but the Russian leader never forgave Churchill for not honouring his pledge for 1943. Despite the arguments of the Chiefs of Staff to the contrary, in Moscow in August 1942 Churchill had persuaded himself that Sledgehammer in 1943 was still possible despite carrying out Torch in the latter part of 1942. Later he admitted that he was too optimistic, but that his conscience was clear because 'he did not deceive or mislead Stalin'. But the consequences were that Stalin never again trusted Churchill fully. Probably the Soviet policy of acquiring Poland and eastern Europe sprang from Stalin's disillusionment over the breach of promise over a second front in 1943.

CHAPTER FOURTEEN

Singapore falls

AS A deterrent to Japanese aggression, from April 1940 Pearl Harbor in the Hawaii Islands was made into the main base for the US Pacific Fleet. At 6 a.m. on Sunday, 7 December 1941 363 planes from Japanese aircraft carriers attacked Pearl Harbor, putting out of action nearly all the battleships there and a large proportion of the Army planes on the airfields, which were lined up wingtip to wingtip as a precaution against sabotage. Fortunately the three American aircraft carriers were at sea; even so, more than 2400 Americans were killed, while Japanese losses were trivial.

The Japanese achieved complete surprise. The Emperor had insisted that a declaration of war must precede the attack. The Prime Minister, Tojo, admitted in evidence at the Tokyo war trials that he told the Emperor he agreed, but then made sure no message was sent to Washington in advance of the attack as the military chiefs were adamant that its success depended on surprise.

As a result Pearl Harbor was enjoying a normal, relaxed, peacetime weekend; the AA guns were not manned, and the pilots were not at alert. A private watching the island's radar screens saw the incoming planes and reported them, only to be told: 'Nothing to worry about.'[1] After rejecting the Japanese proposals on 26 November Hull had sent Admiral Kimmel, who was commanding Pearl Harbor, a warning: 'An aggressive move by Japan is expected within the next few days . . . Execute appropriate defensive deployment.' But Admiral Kimmel ignored this advice, and by an extraordinary muddle a further urgent warning on 6 December, initiated by General Marshall, did not reach the island until after the attack.

Some historians, mostly American, allege that Churchill knew from British Intelligence that the Japanese were planning their attack on Pearl Harbor but deliberately failed to alert Roosevelt. Other American historians argue that Roosevelt used the whole crisis as 'a back door to war in Europe'. Such arguments are based on flimsy evidence and can be ignored. A Foreign Office minute by Ashley Clarke states: '. . . the mystery is how the Americans were caught unawares at Pearl Harbour'.[2]

The Japanese made successful surprise attacks on Hong Kong, Burma and the Philippines, but failed to attain the same degree of surprise as at Pearl Harbor when they attacked the south-east tip of Siam, and the north-east coast of

Malaya, at dawn on 7 December; they did, however, manage to land strong invasion forces from sea transports at Singora and Patani in Thailand, and at Kota Bharu in Malaya. The invasion fleet had been sighted twenty-four hours before by a Hudson aircraft on reconnaissance, and information was received from Saigon that Japanese convoys loaded with troops had put out to sea; it was also reported that Thai frontier guards had been erecting roadblocks on the main road from the Malayan frontier to Singora.

The plan for the defence of the Malayan frontier was not to hold the narrowest strip of the Kra Isthmus but to push British troops into Thai territory and defend Singora and Patani, some forty miles over the frontier. This plan was codenamed Matador. General Percival had been appointed to command the land forces in Malaya in the summer of 1941. He had been briefed about Matador before he left London, and after the war he stated that it had great military advantages because it would prevent the Japanese landing tanks on the beaches, and would provide the RAF with additional aerodromes in Thai territory.[3]

Detailed plans for Matador were worked out; Thai currency was printed and thirty officers, some very senior, were sent in to reconnoitre in plain clothes. They frequently encountered Japanese officers on a similar mission; the Japanese had the advantage of a secret agreement with the Thais to co-operate if they landed at Singora and Patani. The British troops defending the northern Malay frontier were so heavily committed to preparations for Matador that defence works inside Malaya were neglected.

On 4 December the War Cabinet authorized the initiation of Matador and a move into Thailand, but Churchill insisted that the Commander in Chief Far East, Air Marshal Brook-Popham, should 'only' put Matador into operation 'if necessary'. As a result Brook-Popham was uncertain how far he was free to act, and Matador was delayed for three fatal days from 5 to 8 December. In his diary Cadogan noted on Monday, 1 December: 'P.M. against taking any forestalling action in Thailand. Think he is right. Japs are evidently in a fix.'[4]

The clue to Churchill's uncharacteristic indecision over Matador comes in a minute to Eden dated 2 December: 'An attack on the Kra Isthmus would not be helpful to Japan for several months. In any case we should not take forestalling action without a definite guarantee of United States support. Having regard to the supreme importance of the United States being foremost we must be the sole judge of timing the actual moment.'[5] This shows Churchill's worry that the Japanese might attack British or Dutch possessions and not American ones, so that Britain and Holland would be at war without America. Roosevelt could give no firm guarantee of support in such an eventuality without the approval of Congress, which he knew he might well not succeed in getting. In addition Matador, as a British violation of Thai territory, would be badly received in America, especially by the isolationists. Churchill's caution over Matador was purely political; he fully realized how helpful it would be militarily in defending Malaya.

On 4 December Crosby, the British Minister in Bangkok, reported that Japan was offering Thailand territory in French Indo-China and Malaya at British and

French expense, and that the Thai Cabinet was deeply divided. Previously Crosby had argued strongly for a senior British general to go to Bangkok to concert defence plans with the Thai Government and to offer them British arms, because the Thai Prime Minister had asked him for aircraft and military material to resist a Japanese invasion. Eden minuted to the War Cabinet that the British should not give a 'complete negative' and should tell them that we were interested in the Kra peninsula, but wanted an assurance that they would not oppose 'us' if we took action there. The War Cabinet approved sending 'a responsible officer' to Bangkok. However Churchill later vetoed this, saying that Britain could not discuss plans with a non-ally.[6]

Crosby, who had first gone to Thailand thirty-seven years before, was devoted to the Thais and wanted to do everything he could to prevent them yielding to the Japanese. Accordingly he sent a telegram to Brook-Popham on 6 December: 'For God's sake do not allow British forces to occupy one inch of Thai territory unless and until Japan has struck the first blow at Thailand.' Crosby was sincere in his efforts to keep Thailand on the British side, but it was improper for him to interfere with military operations at this stage. Brook-Popham thought Crosby knew the attitude of the Thai Government, and this added to his indecision over Matador. In fact Thailand had already cast the die in favour of Japan, and unknown to Crosby, Luang Pibul, the Prime Minister, had agreed to a military alliance with the Japanese. According to Crosby, this was due to resentment at Britain's unwillingness to give direct military aid, and to last-minute exasperation caused by a personal message to Luang Pibul from Churchill 'There is a possibility of imminent Japanese invasion of your country. If you are attacked, defend yourself. The preservation of the full independence and sovereignty of Siam [Thailand] is a British interest and we shall regard an attack on you as an attack on ourselves.'[7]

It is impossible to agree with Crosby that Churchill's eleventh-hour telegram had any effect on the Thai Prime Minister, but Crosby insisted that Luang Pibul looked on it as a trap to induce Thailand to engage Japan single-handed 'in order that Britain might survive'. This is an improbable interpretation. Luang Pibul had already committed his country and never thought of turning back.

At the Defence Committee on 17 October it was revealed that the Australian Government, backed by the British commanders in the Far East, has asked for the immediate despatch of British battleships to the region as a deterrent to the Japanese; Churchill suggested sending the most modern battleship, the *Prince of Wales*, to join the elderly *Repulse* which was already at Durban in South Africa. Attlee supported him; so did the Foreign Office. Pound, however, was against this plan, stating that Britain needed to keep all the King George V class battleships in the Atlantic because of the danger of the *Tirpitz* breaking out from Tronso in Norway, and the return of the *Scharnhorst* and *Gneisenau* from Brest. Three days later, on Churchill's initiative, the Defence Committee over-ruled Pound, and the *Prince of Wales* and the *Repulse* were ordered to the Far East with Admiral Phillips to command the force.[8]

Originally it was intended that the newly commissioned aircraft carrier

Indomitable should accompany Phillips. Unfortunately on her trials she was damaged in Jamaica and was unable to go. No other aircraft carrier could be spared – a desperate failing. On 2 December the *Prince of Wales* and *Repulse* berthed at Singapore.

Churchill had no responsibility for the tragic fate of these two battleships. He called an emergency meeting on the night of 10 December to consider the future movements of the *Prince of Wales* and *Repulse*, but they had already left Singapore. Churchill suggested they should either go across the Pacific 'to join the remnants of the American Fleet' or they 'should vanish into the ocean wastes' to act as rogue elephants. Churchill did not suggest that the ships should operate on the offensive in the war zone on the Malayan coast.[9]

At a conference on the *Prince of Wales* on 8 December, thirty-six hours before, Phillips stated it was impossible for 'the navy to do nothing' while the Army and the RAF were being driven back. All his staff agreed. Accordingly he sailed from Singapore with his two battleships and four destroyers, known as Force Z, at 5.30 that evening; his intention was to make a lightning raid to smash the Japanese transports at the landing beaches at Singora and Patani at dawn on the 10th. He knew he was at risk from Japanese aircraft operating out of Saigon; unfortunately the Navy and RAF Intelligence had completely underestimated the efficiency and capabilities of Japanese Zero fighters and torpedo bombers. Phillips hoped for fighter protection not only from the Singapore aerodromes, but from the RAF airfields in northern Malaya. But as a result of the abandonment of Matador, within forty-eight hours the Japanese Army had over-run the important RAF aerodromes at Kota Bharu and Alor Star, while Kuantan aerodrome, far away from the fighting, was, according to Admiral Layton, 'abandoned in panic'.[10]

The British would have lost command of the air anyway because of the superior performance of the Japanese aircraft, but the premature loss of Kota Bharu, Alota Star and Kuantan was due to totally inadequate AA defences. The RAF and the Army had quarrels about aerodrome defence measures, and there was what the RAF described as 'inadequate defence'. Thus without Matador not only had the British failed to acquire fresh landing grounds in southern Thailand, but had lost their most northerly ones in Malaya. The RAF lost 50 per cent of their planes during the first forty-eight hours, mainly from Japanese attacks on the aerodromes from the air.[11]

The signals exchanged between Phillips and the War Room in Singapore, setting out his requirements for fighter protection, are dramatic and tragic.

He signalled:

Copy of Naval requirements for Air co-operation
9th 10th December, 1941. Original returned by
W/Cdr. Chignell to C.O.S. E.Fleet

1. A. 2°37' North 106°28' East at 0500/9
   B. 3°25' North 106°40' East at 0800/9
   C. 6°15' North 103°17' East at 0001/10
2. Thence to destination at 0600/10
3. Speed of advance. 17 knots
4. Return route unknown
5. What is desired
   A. Reconnaissance to about 120 miles to North of force during daylight 9th.
   B. Reconnaissance of 100 miles, mid point SINGORA 10 miles from coast, starting northwesterly point first light 10th.
   C. Fighter protection near SINGORA at daylight 10th.

Note by A.O.C. on original request on paper in pencil. Shown by W/Cdr. Chignell F.A.V.O. to A.O.C. on 8/12. A.O.C. wrote in pencil on top left hand corner:- I can provide A. I hope to be able to provide B. I cannot provide C. Wing Cdr Chignell took this back to C of S Eastern Fleet.

Secret Naval Message

C.Z.M. (R) A.O.C.F.E., G.O.C. Malaya from C-in-C E.F. C-in-C F.E.
    Intend sailing at 1100Z/8/12/41 with *Prince of Wales*, *Repulse* and four destroyers with the object of attacking enemy transports reported between Singora and Pattanni.
2. This force will be known as Force Z.
3. Speed of advance will be 17 knots and course will be shaped through:-
   Point A 02 degs. 37'N. 106 degs. 28'E
   Point B 03 degs. 25'N. 106 degs. 40'E
   Point C 06 degs. 15'N. 103 degs. 17'E
4. Anticipate arrival off objective dawn 10th December.
5. Request all Dutch forces concerned may be informed accordingly. Acknowledge.

                                        T.O.O. 0452Z/8/12/41

The replies to Phillips from the RAF were:

FIRST REQUEST 'I can manage.'
SECOND REQUEST 'I hope to be able to manage.'
THIRD REQUEST 'I cannot manage.'

A note on the bottom of the record reads:

> The reason for the A.O.C.'s refusal of fighter cover was that the distance from the aerodromes in Singapore to the position of the Fleet when defence was required was not within fighter range.

When Phillips set out he believed the aerodromes in northern Malaya were still operational in British hands; instead the fighters were now all at Singapore. On receipt of the refusal of air cover at Singora he turned back to Singapore during the night of 9–10 December, knowing also that his force had been sighted by the Japanese.[12]

So on the morning of 10 December, instead of being in action off Singora, Phillips' Force Z was well on its way back to safety in Singapore. However, a message had been received in Singapore from Kuantan during the night that a Japanese invasion fleet was approaching the shore. This was imagination. The Indian troops gazing out to sea on the alert during the night reported they had seen 'many lights' out at sea. The Indians were panicky because they had heard of the surprise Japanese landings at Kota Bharu, where the defending troops had been annihilated. Their British officers were sceptical, but the report was passed on to Singapore – for what it was worth – as 'unconfirmed'. Naval Intelligence then made the culpable mistake of passing it on to Phillips on the *Prince of Wales* as a confirmed report of a Japanese landing at Kuantan. Immediately Phillips changed course and steered for Kuantan. Reconnaissance by a plane from the *Prince of Wales* and a destroyer reported 'All clear' at Kuantan, and Phillips turned again for Singapore at 08.00.[13]

At 11.18 Force Z, sixty miles east of Kuantan, was attacked by 34 high-level bombers and 51 torpedo bombers (twin-engined monoplanes) from land bases near Saigon. For security reasons Phillips had not reported his change of course, and no fighter protection was in the area. Not until 11.30 did the war room at Singapore learn that Phillips had gone to Kuantan, and then only from the pilot of the plane from the *Prince of Wales*, which had landed at Penang.

By 13.20 both the *Repulse* and the *Prince of Wales* had been sunk by torpedoes. A squadron of eleven Buffaloes from Singapore arrived over the scene at 13.15, ten minutes after the *Prince of Wales* had capsized. They saw the Zeroes departing in the distance, and destroyers picking up the survivors from the two battle-ships.[14]

Japanese planes and submarines made no effort to interfere with the rescue operations, which was chivalrous and a welcome contrast to their behaviour during the rest of the war. 42 out of 69 officers, including the captain, and 754 out of 1240 ratings were saved from the *Repulse*; and 90 officers out of 110, and 1195 out of 1502 ratings, from the *Prince of Wales*. Phillips was drowned.

It is fascinating, if not altogether useful, to speculate whether, if the false report of a Japanese landing at Kuantan had not been sent to Singapore and then carelessly repeated by Naval Intelligence to Phillips, the battleships would have sailed safely out of range of the land-based torpedo bomber aircraft from Japanese-occupied Saigon and into the safety of the waters around Singapore. However, the greatest criticism of the overall strategy is that the only fighters available at Singapore to give cover to Admiral Phillips' Force Z were a few out-of-date and difficult-to-manoeuvre Buffaloes which, even if they had arrived in time, could have done little to save the battleships from the Japanese torpedo bombers and the faster and more agile Zero fighters.

When on 10 December the tragic news reached London, Churchill was working on his boxes in bed. Dudley Pound telephoned him; Churchill thought his voice sounded odd. After a cough and a gulp Pound said: 'Prime Minister, the *Prince of Wales* and *Repulse* have both been sunk by the Japanese – we think by aircraft. Tom Phillips is drowned.'

Churchill replied: 'Are you sure it's true?'

Pound said: 'There is no doubt at all.'

Churchill has recorded that he had never received a more direct shock. He said to his secretary, who was working with him in his bedroom, 'Poor Tom Phillips.' Forty-eight hours later Churchill was able to telegraph to Roosevelt: 'I am enormously relieved at the turn world events have taken', and to Eden, who was *en route* to Moscow, 'The accession of the United States makes amends for all.'[15]

Churchill insisted on the Admiralty making detailed enquiries into the reason for the sinking of the battleships. His only written comment on the Admiralty papers was to ask why did they not use 'smoke' (camouflage smoke) when attacked. Pound replied that smoke was unlikely to hide ships from attacking aircraft. Pound advised the Prime Minister that 'no useful purpose would be served' by a Board of Enquiry, and Churchill agreed. The USA now had two battleships based in the Pacific; the British none; and the Japanese ten. Japan had complete command of the sea and air.[16]

According to the reports of the captain of the *Repulse*, W. B. Tennant, and Captain L. H. Bell, the senior surviving staff officer of the *Prince of Wales*, the situation at Kota Bharu was obscure when Phillips sailed on the evening of 8 December. He had reason to expect that fighters could cover him from both Kota Bharu and Alor Star aerodromes, but in fact the Japanese had over-run them in the initial assault. The two officers also reported that neither Phillips nor the commanders on the spot in Singapore had 'reasonably accurate information about the strength, types and efficiency of the Japanese Air Forces in Indo China', and consistently adverse reports of the capabilities of the Japanese Air Force 'may have caused Phillips to underestimate the air threat'. War experience up to this time was that attacks by torpedo aircraft were not carried out at long range, that attacks by dive bombers were confined to a distance of 200 miles from aerodromes, and that high-level bombing against modern capital ships was not expected to cause vital damage. Phillips was 400 miles from the Saigon aerodromes when he was sunk. Both Churchill and Phillips belonged to the school of thought which believed that battleships could hold their own against enemy aircraft. Suddenly they had been proved tragically wrong.[17]

Once the Japanese had secured firm footholds at Singora and Kota Bharu, the British Army was not strong enough to halt them. The greatest British shortage was in tanks. They had none, while on the first day the Japanese landed considerable numbers of light and medium tanks which were able to manoeuvre in the rice fields on the coastal belt; in addition, Japanese aircraft could fly at will over the battlefield.

Churchill was almost culpably ignorant of the weakness of the British Army. In his defence it must be pointed out that he had sent Duff Cooper, Chancellor of the Duchy of Lancaster and a member of the Cabinet, to give him a personal report on the situation. Cooper arrived in Singapore on 9 September 1941. He had been a failure as wartime Minister of Information and was always an inept minister; but Churchill clung to him loyally because he had resigned from the Chamberlain Cabinet at the time of the Munich crisis and was the only Conservative minister to support Churchill publicly in his all-out opposition to Chamberlain's Munich settlement. During his three months in Singapore before war started Duff Cooper gave Churchill no indication of the tragic weakness of the British Army, although he recounts in his memoirs that he had been convinced by George Sansom, the Foreign Office Japanese expert, that a Japanese attack was inevitable.[18]

His long report on the defences of Malaya, dated 29 October, is a classic piece of ineptitude. After explaining that the system by which two Commanders in Chief, one for the Far East and one for China, lived side by side in the naval base at Singapore was 'unsound' and had led in practice to 'considerable inconvenience', and pointing out that 'there was one G O C Malaya and an A O C Far East at the other end of the Island', all he told Churchill about the defence situation was this:

> The impression that I personally formed from such enquiries as I made into the state of the defences of Malaya and Burma led me to the conclusion that the former was somewhat over insured at the expense of the latter. When I expressed this opinion to C in C India he told me that he shared it. He also strongly held the view that the defence of Burma should be under C in C India [Wavell].[19]

Coming from a Cabinet Minister who had held the posts of First Lord of the Admiralty and Secretary of State for War, this was supine. The Service Chiefs in Singapore told him of their lack of tanks, anti-tank guns and modern fighter aircraft. It is a mystery why he did not consider it his business, as Churchill's representative and adviser, to produce a technical list of their requirements in terms of planes and military material. If he had reported these deficiencies to Churchill, surely the Prime Minister would have taken some urgent action to remedy them. Duff Cooper made a deplorable impression in Singapore on the Malayan Civil Service, the military commanders and on the Governor, Sir Shenton Thomas, whose authority he undermined.

Brigadier Smyth VC, a divisional commander in Malaya in 1941 and later a Conservative Minister, has written: 'If Duff Cooper with the ear of the Prime Minister had only whispered into it "Tanks and aeroplanes for Malaya" surely this great man would have issued one of his famous "action this day" directives and something would have materialised. Surplus tanks were available in the Middle East and were in fact sent to Burma a few months after Singapore fell.' General Percival has recorded:

> During the whole of the four months he was in Singapore Duff Cooper hardly ever visited Malaya Command Headquarters. He dined with me once at Flagstaff House but I was never asked either to his house or his office, either in peace or war. He had no grasp whatever of the Army machine and allowed himself to be influenced by people who for years had been critical of the Government of Malaya. The result was confusion.[20]

As soon as war was declared, Churchill appointed Duff Cooper Resident Cabinet Minister at Singapore for Far Easten Affairs.

The Malaya campaign was one of the blackest chapters in British military history. The Japanese were able to bomb the infantry from low heights almost at will, and to use their command of the sea to land behind the defended localities. Tanks were used by the Japanese with skill, and the British were, as already noted, woefully short of anti-tank guns. Fighting in France in 1940 had shown up the weakness of British anti-tank guns, and a much better 17-pounder was now in service in the Middle East. But none of these were sent to Malaya, and instead the Army had to rely on a few 6-pounders or the 25-pounder field gun used in an anti-tank role. The infantry commanders preferred to use the 25-pounders to call down defensive fire when the Japanese attacked, and did not look upon them as anti-tank guns. In addition, although the Chief Engineer, General Simson, had pressed for the establishment of anti-tank positions, and to that end had made dumps of materials together with concrete cylinders and steel ropes and chains to hold them together, so that the enemy tanks could be brought to a halt and destroyed, few of these defences were erected. As a result the Japanese tanks caused havoc and disorganization against unprotected infantry. Not until 11 December was Percival authorized to spend more than £500 on a defence work without War Office approval, which took weeks to obtain; after that date he was given a free hand. Perhaps this was too small a departmental detail for Churchill as Minister of Defence to be aware of, but it demonstrated the general malaise.[21]

The war in the Far East opened with disaster for the British at sea and in the air. Worse quickly followed on land. Within forty-eight hours the Japanese used their tanks to maul the British troops advancing into Thailand, so that they had to retreat. After that the Japanese never lost the initiative; their general staff had planned the campaign efficiently and with the same meticulous attention to detail that Montgomery was later to put into his attack at El Alamein and into the cross-Channel invasion. The result was that all went according to their plan. Kuala Lumpur fell on 11 December, and Penang on the 19th; many undamaged landing boats fell into Japanese hands, and they made good use of them. The attack on the island of Singapore began on 8 February. Evacuation of Penang was followed by a careless broadcast by Duff Cooper, who said that 'the majority of the population of Penang had been evacuated'. He was referring to the Europeans only, and this gaffe shattered Asian morale. Shenton Thomas had to deny it in another broadcast. A fortnight later, with the water supply cut and his fellow generals unwilling to launch the counter-attack he wanted against the numerically inferior Japanese, General Percival surrendered and 130,000 British went into captivity. It was the largest surrender in British history.

On his return to London, Admiral Layton, the former Singapore Naval Commander, wrote that the Japanese produced

> a practically continuous daily air effort of 100 to 150 combat aircraft over Malaya, of which about 60 per cent were high performance fighters. In the air our aircraft were outnumbered customarily by odds of 4 or 5 to one. Since our machines were on the whole inferior in quality it is not surprising that they were overwhelmed . . . the torpedo bomber squadrons on which we had mainly relied to attack the enemy expeditionary force at sea were a broken reed.

Layton added that 'the result was an unparalleled disaster, because we lost the whole of Malaya in fifty-six days, and on the seventieth day Singapore surrendered. There was only one real reason why we lost Singapore, and that is we were unable to provide forces strong enough to defend it.'

Layton continued:

> The land forces, though sounding sufficient on paper and in ration strength, were ill supplied with weapons and backwards in training. The air force had estimated 167 against the target of 336, and most of these were of inadequate performance or obsolescent. The Buffalo fighter with which three squadrons were equipped, proved definitely inferior to the Japanese navy 'o' Zero fighter, and the Singapore flying boats and Vildebeeste torpedo bombers were so far behind modern types as to be almost useless, while frontier aerodromes defended only by naval 3 inch guns without predictors were almost helpless . . . with the collapse of our air effort the army's task was made ten times more difficult.

When Churchill received Layton's devastating report he minuted: 'There is no advantage in circulating this report or entering into correspondence with the Admiral at so busy a time. It should be put by until the end of the war.'[22] General Percival was unable to report until after the end of the war because he became a POW. No official enquiry has ever been conducted into the débâcle of the Malaya campaign.

As the news of the fighting became worse and worse, Churchill's minutes and telegrams became frantic. He had gone to Washington to meet Roosevelt and was away from London for one month. From Washington he watched the situation in Malaya deteriorate disastrously. On 15 December he sent a telegram to Duff Cooper, asking him 'to state in what way you think the military campaign is not being well conducted'. This put Duff Cooper in a quandary, because in October he had not reported the deficiencies of the Army and now he was well aware that the lack of tanks, anti-tank guns and AA guns was making the position of the troops impossible. In a letter taken to London by Captain Tennant of HMS *Repulse* he fell back on criticism of Brook-Popham and Percival:

Sir Robert Brooke-Popham is a very much older man than his years warrant and sometimes seems on the verge of nervous collapse. I fear also that knowledge of his own failing powers renders him jealous of any encroachment on his sphere of influence . . . The Governor, Sir Shenton Thomas, is one of those people who find it impossible to adjust their minds to war conditions. He is also the mouthpiece of the last person he speaks to . . . much influenced by his Colonial Secretary, a sinister figure called Stanley Jones who is universally detested in the Colony, where he is accused of having been defeatist since the beginning of the war . . . General Percival is a nice, good man who began life as a schoolmaster [incorrect]. I am sometimes tempted to wish he had remained one. He is a good soldier, too – calm, clear-headed and even clever. But he is not a leader, he cannot take a large view; it is all a field day at Aldershot to him. He knows the rules so well and follows them so closely and is always waiting for the umpire's whistle to cease fire and hopes that when that moment comes his military dispositions will be such as to receive approval.[22]

As a result of this letter Stanley Jones was dismissed, on orders from London—much against the wishes of Sir Shenton Thomas and to his extreme annoyance. Jones' colleagues in the Malayan Civil Service were outraged—in fact he was a popular man and not defeatist at all.

Finally Churchill realized how Duff Cooper was letting him down. He minuted the letter: 'This is a shocking tale,' and that Duff Cooper's pre-war reports had given no indication of his poor opinion of Percival. Cooper's appointment in the Far East was terminated by Churchill on 7 January, and he was recalled to London.

On 16 December Churchill, concerned about bad news of the fighting in northern Malaya, wrote from Washington to Ismay: 'Beware lest troops required for defence of Singapore island and fortress are used up or cut off in Malay peninsula. Nothing compares in importance with fortress. Are you sure we shall have enough troops for prolonged defence? Consider with Auchinleck and C W [Commonwealth] Government moving one Australian division from Palestine to Singapore.'[23] But the military problem was not, of course, the number of troops – rather it was lack of equipment. Churchill was also under a misconception in describing Singapore as a 'fortress'; it was a naval base, never a fortress.

A remarkably prescient appreciation of the defence of Malaya was written in July 1940 by C. A. Vlieland, then Secretary of Defence, Malaya. He was known as Starchy Archy because of his habit of putting on a dinner jacket every night, but this was really an affectionate nickname. He stated that 'the real threat came from the north', and that Singapore would be 'completely useless' if the other side held the peninsula; 'it is abundantly clear' to the Japanese that a sweep from the Thai–Malay frontier down to the back door of Singapore would be so easy that they would be 'mad to plan their adventure otherwise'. He went on that Japanese air power would be decisive, and that once the enemy had 'driven us out of the north-western plains complete disaster would follow inevitably'. Vlieland favoured Operation Matador, but thought that if it was carried out only at the 'eleventh hour (HMG would never agree . . . until the last moment)' it would be a mistake. An 'eleventh-hour' Matador of course, is what occurred.[24]

Vlieland's report was badly received both by the commanders in the Far East and in Whitehall, because it contradicted all the standing beliefs. Churchill probably never saw it. This was a pity, as it would have cleared up his delusions. When his cogent appreciation was ignored by the authorities, Vlieland resigned.

The problem of providing reinforcements for Malaya haunted both Churchill and the Chiefs of Staff. There was a serious quarrel between Churchill and Curtin, the new Australian Labour Prime Minister. In 1940, when Churchill became Prime Minister, Menzies had been Prime Minister of Australia. He was inspired by Churchill's defiant leadership and one of his most enthusiastic supporters. Menzies came to London and attended War Cabinets, but was dismayed by the lack of interest in Far East defence both in Whitehall and by Churchill. When Menzies resigned in August 1941 Fadden of his own party succeeded him, but led them to defeat in the election of October 1941.

Fadden had insisted on the relief of the two Australian brigades at Tobruk. This was done with great difficulty by the Royal Navy, using the few moonless nights, and resulted in the loss of a minelayer and damage to a cruiser, two destroyers and two supply ships. As a result of disputes over the use of their forces the Australian Government had sent a Cabinet Minister, Sir Earle Page, to London. After attending a Defence Committee, chaired in Churchill's absence on Christmas Eve 1941 by Attlee, Earle Page was gravely dissatisfied; Attlee rang up Brooke to 'find out if we were ready for Defence Committee to keep Australians quiet as they were fretting about reinforcements for Singapore'. On Christmas Day the Australian representative in Singapore cabled to his Government that the deterioration in the Malay peninsula was becoming a landslide and that 'the only thing that might save Singapore would be immediate despatch from Middle East of powerful reinforcements, large numbers of fighter aircraft and ample operational personnel'.

Immediately Curtin, who had succeeded Menzies as Prime Minister, cabled to both Churchill and Roosevelt in Washington that the reinforcements earmarked for Singapore were utterly inadequate and that he would 'gladly accept United States command in Pacific'. This was pressuring Churchill by threatening that Australia would secede from London's orbit. Churchill replied:

> We do not share your view . . . that there is the danger of early reduction of Singapore fortress . . . you have been told of the air support which is already on the way . . . we have instructed C in C Middle East to concert a plan for sending fighters and tanks to Singapore immediately the situation in Libya permits . . . you may count on my doing everything possible to strengthen the whole front from Rangoon to Port Darwin.

That was not good enough for Curtin, who the next day wrote in a signed article in the *Melbourne Herald*:

We refuse to accept the dictum that the Pacific struggle must be treated as a subordinate aspect of the general conflict ... The Australian Government, therefore, regards the Pacific struggle as primarily one in which the United States and Australia must have the fullest say in the direction of the democracies' fighting plan. Without any inhibitions of any kind, I make it quite clear that Australia looks to America, free of any pangs as to our traditional links or kinship with the United Kingdom. We know the problems that the United Kingdom faces ... But we know, too, that Australia can go and Britain can still hold on. We are, therefore, determined that Australia shall not go.

This unexpected bombshell from the Australian Prime Minister arrived in Washington while Churchill was in the midst of delicate negotiations with his ally over the future conduct of the war, and coincided with the Prime Minister's first heart attack.

The Australian Prime Minister had embarrassed Churchill in front of Roosevelt, and Churchill was angry. He knew that his own weakness had been to treat troops from the Commonwealth as if they were British vassals. He cabled to Attlee: 'I hope there will be no pandering to this ... If the Malayan peninsula has been starved for the sake of Libya and Russia no-one is more responsible than I, and I would do exactly the same again.' Sir Ian Jacob, who was with Churchill, recorded in his diary:

The Australian Government have throughout the war taken a narrow, selfish, and at times a craven view of events in contrast to New Zealand ... I fear the Prime Minister's treatment of Mr Menzies is somewhat to blame. He has never really understood the Far East problems and has deliberately starved Singapore in favour of the Middle East without paying enough attention to the feelings of Australia ... I am afraid we will have a lot of bother with Australia.[25]

Churchill cabled to Auchinleck, asking him to spare four Hurricane fighter squadrons and an armoured brigade equipped with American tanks. Auchinleck complied generously, but it was too late. Before these reinforcements could arrive, Singapore was lost.

In Washington Marshall called for a unified command in the Far East and, much to Churchill's and the Chiefs of Staff's surprise, suggested Wavell as Supreme Commander. Churchill felt this was an empty compliment because Wavell's new command would in all probability soon be obliterated by the Japanese. Dill wrote to Brooke: 'It would be fatal to have a British Commander responsible for the disasters that are coming to the Americans and ourselves.' Still, the unified command gave the Australians the feeling that their demands were being satisfied, and their co-operation improved.

Roosevelt and Churchill agreed on creating the American, British, Dutch, Australian Command (ABDA), and Wavell was put in charge. Wavell, who knew little of the Far East, had written to Brooke Popham six weeks before: 'I should be most doubtful if the Japs ever tried to make an attack on Malaya and I am sure they will get it in the neck if they do so.' He must have been horrified when a telegram from Churchill appointing him reached him in Delhi on

30 December. Manfully he accepted the appointment, but he wrote to Dill that he had been handed 'not just a baby, but quadruplets'.[26]

On 1 January 1941 the Chiefs of Staff had tabulated the reinforcements which would eventually reach the Far East: Malaya would receive a British division, an Indian division and an armoured brigade. Burma would get two divisions, as would Java and Sumatra in the Netherlands East Indies; Churchill and Curtin agreed that two Australian divisions and a Corps headquarters should be pulled out of the Middle East without a precise destination.[27]

All this was pie in the sky. The only reinforcements which could reach Malaya in time were 18th British Division, already at Cape Town, and 17th Indian Division from India. However, Churchill still cherished hopes that extra troops could arrive in time to save Singapore, although his military advisers were by now sure that final disaster could not be averted. Curtin sent Churchill another blast on 8 January:

> It is naturally disturbing to learn that the Japanese have been able to overrun so easily the whole of Malaya except Johore . . . It is observed that the Eighth Australian Division is to be given the task of fighting the decisive battle . . . I urge on you that nothing be left undone to reinforce Malaya . . . I am particularly concerned in regard to air strength, as a repetition of the Greece and Crete campaigns would evoke a violent public reaction.

Two weak and inadequately trained infantry brigades from 17th Indian Division had arrived in Singapore, but it looks as if Churchill was becoming aware of the bleak prospects for Singapore because he replied mildly and almost plaintively:

> I do not see how anyone could expect Malaya to be defended once the Japanese obtained command of the sea and while we are fighting for our lives against Germany and Italy. The only vital point is Singapore Fortress and its essential hinterland . . . I do not accept any censure about Crete and Greece. We are doing our utmost in the Mother Country to meet living perils and onslaughts. We have sunk all party differences and have imposed universal compulsory service, not only upon men, but women. We have suffered the agonising loss of two of our finest ships which we sent to sustain the Far Eastern war . . . I hope therefore you will be considerate in the judgment which you pass upon those to whom Australian lives and fortunes are so dear.

When Churchill returned to London on 17 January after a month's absence in Washington he was still confident that the island of Singapore could be held for at least two months, so that there would be time for reinforcements to arrive. He was soon disillusioned, however, and took it ill. In a telegram from Washington dated 14 January he had asked Wavell: 'Are you sure you can dominate with Fortress cannon any attempt to plant siege batteries?', and pointed out that 'the vital need is to prolong defence of the island to last possible minute, but I hope it will not come to that'.

Wavell's reply, received in London on the 21st, was a warning that he doubted whether the island could be held for long once Johore was lost, and

Until quite recently all plans based on repulsing seaborne attack on island and holding land attack in Johore or further north, and little or nothing was done to construct defences on north side of island to prevent crossing Johore Strait . . . Fortress cannon of heaviest nature have all-round traverse but their flat trajectory makes them unsuitable for counterbattery work. Could certainly not guarantee to dominate enemy siege batteries with them. Supply situation unsatisfactory.

Wavell continued that many of the remaining troops were of 'doubtful value', and he was sorry to give 'a depressing picture, but I do not want you to have false picture of island fortress'.[28] In fact most of the coast defence guns could be swivelled round to fire to the north, but there were almost no supplies of high-explosive shells to deal with attacking troops – only armour-piercing ones, which were useless against attacking ground forces and field guns.

The lack of HE shells for the big guns represented shocking negligence on the part of the War Office and the Ministry of Defence. Further supplies could only be drawn from Portsmouth. One may well ask why during his three months in Singapore Duff Cooper, considering his experience at the Admiralty and War Office, failed to notice the situation. Surely if he had put everything into his job, as Churchill expected him to do, he could have brought this glaring deficiency to light in time.

Petulantly Churchill minuted to the Chiefs of Staff that he was 'staggered', because it had never occurred to either him or Dill in Washington that Singapore 'was not entirely fortified against attack from the north'. He continued angrily:

> What is the use of having an island for a fortress if it is not to be made into a citadel? To construct a line of detached works with searchlights and crossfire combined with immense wiring and obstruction of the swamp areas and to provide the proper ammunition to enable the fortress guns to dominate enemy batteries planted in Johore, was an elementary peace-time provision which it is incredible did not exist in a fortress which has been twenty years building. If this was so, how much more should the necessary field works have been constructed during the two and a half years of the present war? How is it that not one of you pointed this out to me at any time when these matters have been under discussion? More especially should this have been done because in my various minutes extending over the last two years I have repeatedly shown that I relied upon this defence of Singapore Island against a formal siege, and have never relied upon the Kra Isthmus plan.
>
> I was repeatedly informed at the time of the Japanese landing that . . . there could be no question of an advance southward until the Spring. Pray look this up and find out who and what was the foundation of this opinion so violently falsified by events . . . most disquieting to me that such frightful ignorance of the conditions should have prevailed.

Churchill warned that if the Japanese broke across the Johore Straits in small boats it would be 'one of the greatest scandals that could possibly be exposed'.[29]

Well might Churchill rail against the Service Chiefs who had so neglected the defence of the Malayan peninsula; warning after warning had been ignored. However, as Vlieland has explained, Singapore was defenceless once the Japanese occupied Johore to the north. It was a naval base without planned land defences, as well as a city with an enormous civilian population and an inadequate water supply. A prolonged defence against an enemy equipped with tanks and possessing overwhelming air superiority was impossible.

Nevertheless Churchill now ordered that the defence of Singapore Island must be 'maintained by every means'; the city of Singapore was to be converted into a citadel and 'defended to the death. No surrender must be contemplated and the Commanders, staffs and principal officers are expected to perish at their posts.'[30] The Chiefs of Staff conveyed Churchill's message to Wavell – omitting, not surprisingly, the instruction 'to perish at their posts'. In theory Churchill could no longer send orders to Wavell who, as Supreme Commander of ABDA, was subject to the joint control of America, Britain, Holland and Australia; but on 20 January he sent a personal message: 'I expect every inch of ground to be defended, every scrap of material or defences to be blown to pieces to prevent capture by the enemy, and no question of surrender to be entertained until after protracted fighting amid the ruins of Singapore City.'

Wavell sent back a telegram stating that prolonged defence of Singapore Island was 'improbable'; as a consequence, on 21 January Churchill suddenly changed his mind and suggested to the Chiefs of Staff that the naval and military installations at Singapore should be made useless to the Japanese, and the reinforcing troops and aircraft on their way there diverted to Burma. 'We may, by muddling things and hesitating to take an ugly decision, lose both Singapore and the Burma road. It is certainly not worth losing all our reinforcements and aircraft to prolong the defence for only a few weeks.' The Prime Minister asked his advisers if it was not 'throwing good money after bad' to send more reinforcements to Singapore instead of to Burma, and he told the Defence Committee that 'we could not now consider Singapore a fortress'.[31]

This change of mind was realistic and typical of Churchill's quick reaction to a changing military situation. Unfortunately it was not acted upon. The Chiefs of Staff were indecisive. By an oversight the Australian Sir Earle Page was shown copies of Churchill's secret minutes advocating abandoning the policy of re-inforcement of Singapore. Page immediately informed his own Prime Minister, and on 23 January Curtin telegraphed to Churchill that evacuation of Singapore 'would be regarded here and elsewhere as an inexcusable betrayal'.[32]

A three-day debate on Malaya took place in the Commons from 26 to 29 January; Churchill argued brilliantly that it was the right strategy to 'accept' weakness in the Far East, which had been a peaceful theatre, and to deliver an offensive in Libya and to aid Russia; this was 'in no way invalidated by the unexpected naval misfortunes and the heavy forfeits we have paid and will have to pay in the Far East'. Many MPs had strong misgivings but Churchill's oratory, although it glossed over the mistakes, won the day; only one vote, that of James Maxton, the extreme left-wing Independent Labour MP, was recorded against him. Churchill was overjoyed, but as he left the Commons the London evening papers bore ominous headlines that the Japanese were within eighteen miles of Singapore, and that the Germans had entered Benghazi.

There is no doubt that Curtin's message of 23 January containing the words 'inexcusable betrayal' caused Churchill to change his mind and to allow the whole of 18th Division to go to Singapore, although he denied this after the war. Australia was proving a difficult ally, but her continued wholehearted co-operation was vital. At the meeting of the Defence Committee on 26 January Churchill and Page had a row: the Prime Minister told the Australian that he had 'unintentionally misled his Government'. Page replied that he was well within his rights, and had only sent a factual account of the decision disclosed to the Defence Committee 'together with his own observations'. In face of Australian opposition no more was heard of diverting the reinforcements to Burma and 18th Division sailed on to Singapore, although Wavell cabled on the same day that the Japanese move into Burma could be held and that all should be well 'provided reinforcements arrived'. As early as 29 December Wavell had asked for 18th Division to be sent to Burma instead of Singapore. His request was turned down, and this was a disastrous mistake.[33] There is some mystery as to why Wavell did not argue more strongly that the reinforcements must be diverted to Burma, because he made no secret of his view that Singapore was a lost cause. But probably he realized from his previous clashes with Churchill that once the Prime Minister had made up his mind it was like banging your head against a brick wall to argue with him, and from London too the Chiefs of Staff made it clear that they supported Churchill.

Elements of 18th Division arrived on 29 January in Singapore; 44th Indian Infantry Brigade, seven thousand Indian and two thousand Australian reinforcements, together with an Australian machine gun battalion, had arrived a week before. Although unready for battle, they were thrown into the line immediately. All were captured except those who died when Singapore fell fourteen days later. Fifty-one Hurricanes arrived in crates, but their air speed was drastically reduced because they were equipped with desert air filters; this meant that at heights below 20,000 feet they were outperformed by Japanese Zeros.

By now the Singapore aerodromes were under too heavy air attack for the Hurricanes, and they were operating from Dutch aerodromes in Sumatra. Churchill was furious that the valuable Hurricanes sent from the Middle East were not more effective in action, minuting on 27 January:

> The latest telegrams from Singapore show only one Hurricane in action and 14 in 24 hours. We know 51 arrived on the 13th but had to be uncrated, etc. It is necessary for me to know how many of these are ready. Have they all been uncrated or are they still only coming into action? I must have a clear account of each of the 51 Hurricanes. Is it alive; is it wounded; is it dead?
>
> It is most important to get this before the 48 now being flown off the *Indomitable* come into action. It is a fortnight since I asked for a daily return of Singapore Hurricanes, and I have not had a single word since then. Pray see that I am properly informed; the whole battle turns on the arrival of these Hurricanes and on the rest of the 18th Division.[34]

He was wrong; the battle had already been lost. Fortunately the forty-eight Hurricanes from the *Indomitable* never arrived; nor did Auchinleck's Tank Brigade. If they had, they would also have been lost under the policy of throwing good money after bad. Air Marshal Maltby, who had replaced Air Marshal Fulford after his nervous breakdown, reported the RAFs performance with the Hurricanes suffered from not being 'homogenous squadrons and having too large a proportion of freshly trained pilots without experience of shooting'.

The Prime Minister's minutes reveal his anguish as the inexorable Japanese advance continued, and reports came in that 'the enemy is able to attack and land on our coasts almost at will'. He minuted to the Admiralty on 22 January:

> This is really not good enough. Here we have been absolutely out-manoeuvred and apparently out-fought on the west coast of Malaya by an enemy who has no warship in the neighbourhood. Consequently our forces are made to retire from successive positions, precious time is gained by the enemy and a general state of insecurity engendered in our fighting troops. The shortcomings are only too evident. Why were the enemy allowed to obtain all these craft? We apparently have none or very few, although these were waters we until recently controlled. Secondly, when mention is made of heavy machine-gun fire from the banks . . . how is it the enemy hold these banks? They cannot be manning with machine-guns points commanding every part of the sea down which these barges must come.
>
> You should surely call for much more precise reports. This command of the western shores of Malaya by the Japanese without the possession of a single ship of war must be reckoned as one of the most astonishing British lapses recorded in naval history. I am sorry to be disagreeable, but I look for a further report of a far more searching inquiry.[35]

But exhortation could not avert the inevitable, and Singapore was surrendered on 15 February. It was a black moment for Churchill, and he was subjected to fierce criticism. Eden describes his mood as one of 'troubled discomfort'. Cripps had been difficult and insisted on being in the War Cabinet; the Australians were furious with Churchill, and there is evidence that he had a terrible fear that British soldiers were not as good fighting men as their fathers had been. Wavell had telegraphed about 'a lack of real fighting spirit' both in Malaya and in Burma; neither British, Australians or Indians 'have shown any real toughness of mind and body'. Fighting conditions, Wavell admitted, were difficult but should not have been 'insuperable'.[36]

By losing Singapore and surrendering 150,000 local, Indian, Australian and British troops Britain had suffered the most ignominious defeat in her military history. The water supply had been damaged, and the local commanders would not obey Churchill's dictum to fight to the last man even though the numerically inferior attackers were almost out of ammunition.

The last fortnight of February 1942 found Churchill at his most depressed point during the whole war. However, with characteristic resilience he soon put the disasters behind him and used his talents to the full to deal with the new problems assailing the Allies.

Hong Kong and Borneo had already fallen before Singapore, and now Burma was threatened. The French in Indo-China had submitted to the Japanese without fighting. The United States army of 140,000 in the Philippines was beaten by a smaller Japanese army than had triumphed in Malaya. In Java on

18 March 1941 the Dutch General Ter Poorten surrendered with 98,000 Dutch and 8000 British, American and Australian troops. The same day, Rangoon fell.

Churchill refused to admit that defeat in the Far East was final. Instead, he dreamt of winning everything back with the help of American arms, so that the *status quo ante* could be restored. However, the Americans were to dictate strategy in the Far East, and recovering French, British and Dutch colonial possessions was far from being amongst their war aims.

The day after Singapore capitulated Churchill minuted to Ismay that one brigade of the Australian Corps returning home from Libya should be diverted to defend Burma.[37] The Australian Government refused point-blank and insisted they came home instead. This was the writing on the wall. Britain's prestige had been heavily dented by the collapse of her Far Eastern possessions, and the bonds linking the British Empire together had irrevocably loosened.

The Western Powers were devastatingly humiliated by the Japanese in the Far East. When in 1945 the American victory over Japan allowed them to return to their former colonies France, Holland and Britain's standing with the native races had disappeared. Eventual departure was painful for the British; swift and distasteful for the Dutch; and long and bloody for the French. Above all it was the disastrous seventy-day war in Malaya which made the restoration of European power in the East impossible.

CHAPTER FIFTEEN

Churchill and India 1942–45

THE OUTBREAK of war in the Far East put India at risk and it was of enormous importance for British and American strategy to keep the Indian people enthusiastic for an Allied victory over Japan. In September 1939 the Viceroy Lord Linlithgow, a bluff, straightforward and likeable Tory aristocrat, had obtained from Mahatma Gandhi, leader of the majority Indian Congress Party, the promise of 'full and unconditional support' for Britain on the understanding that after the war the India Act of 1935 would be implemented to give India independence. Unfortunately Gandhi did not abide by this promise.

When Churchill became Prime Minister in May 1940 the then Secretary of State for India, the Marquis of Zetland, resigned because he knew his and Churchill's views on Indian independence were too far apart. Churchill was emotionally opposed to giving India independence, and he appointed his old friend, Leo Amery, who was a passionate supporter of the Empire, to succeed Zetland. Soon after Amery took on the India Office, Churchill told him that he refused to fix an agreed date for Indian independence. Amery then wrote to the Viceroy that Churchill 'reacts instinctively and passionately against the whole idea of any Government of India other than that which he knew forty years ago' although he added that in the end Churchill realized there was no feasible alternative to eventual independence.[1]

Under the 1935 India Act, which Churchill had strenuously opposed, there was to be a central Federal Government, although defence and foreign affairs were reserved for Britain. However, it was laid down that clauses in the Act precluding complete self-government were 'transitional' and that India would in due course become a Dominion. If the Baldwin and Chamberlain Governments had implemented the Act a united India might have been well on its way to *de facto* Dominion status by the outbreak of war in 1939.

Instead progress was slow, and when India declared war on Germany in 1939 it was an arbitrary act by the Viceroy without democratic or constitutional assent. This was resented by the Indian politicians, although Indian troops fought gallantly against the Germans and Italians. To encourage full Indian co-operation in the war effort a pledge of Dominion status immediately after the war was made in August 1940, but defence and foreign affairs were to remain in the

Viceroy's hands. As a result the 'August' offer was rejected by the Indian National Congress.

Before Singapore Churchill had contemplated going to India to consult with Indian leaders about the formation of an Assembly to work out a constitution after the war, and also to meet Chiang Kai-shek. Given Churchill's intransigence about Indian independence, it was as well that this plan was abandoned.[2]

After the announcement of the Atlantic Charter in September 1941, Indian Congress leaders had turned to Roosevelt and asked for American help in obtaining independence. There was much sympathy for India in America, but Churchill firmly told the Commons in September 1941 that the Atlantic Charter did not apply to the British Empire. In 1942, as the Japanese brushed aside the weak defences in Burma, adjacent India was in deadly danger. The dilemma for Churchill was how to keep India committed to the war without the offer of immediate full independence. Fortunately, on 30 December 1941 the Indian Congress had voted in favour of supporting the war with Japan.

During Churchill and Roosevelt's talks over Christmas 1941, the main point of friction had arisen when Roosevelt urged Winston to identify himself with the President's idealistic post-war aims, which included the end of colonialism and independence for India. On 10 March, in a private letter, Roosevelt suggested to Churchill the creation of a temporary Dominion Government in India for five or six years, because this might 'cause the Indians to become more loyal to the British Empire', although he softened his argument by writing 'it is strictly none of my business'. Churchill did not reply.

On 12 March Roosevelt told the Indian High Commissioner to the United States, Bajpai, that 'British policy in India had moved in a groove for the last twenty to thirty years'. Dominion status was, he thought, the right policy, adding that the United States had accelerated Philippine solidarity by fixing the date for those islands' independence.[3] Churchill even told Harriman that the great bulk of India's fighting forces were Moslems antagonistic to independence, saying 'there is ample manpower in India willing to fight'.

Chiang Kai-shek, too, pressurized Churchill to change his policy over India. But Churchill replied: 'The Allies should not interfere in each other's internal affairs,' and pointed out that Britain had abstained from involvement in internal Chinese disputes with the Communists.[4]

In Cabinet Bevin and Attlee questioned Churchill's rigidity over Indian independence, and the Indian moderates under Tej Bahadur Sapru appealed to the Prime Minister for a 'bold stroke', with the elevation of India to Dominion status. Attlee prepared a memorandum for the Cabinet, writing, 'Now was the time for statesmanship . . . a representative with power to negotiate within wide limits should be sent to India now.'

There were threats of Cabinet resignations, and in March 1942 Cripps, who had come back to London after being Ambassador to Moscow and was now in the War Cabinet as Lord Privy Seal, offered to go to India as negotiator. Churchill had little choice but to agree in face of the strong pressure from Roosevelt and his dependence on Labour support after defeats in battle had shaken public confidence in his leadership.

Cripps went out to India in March 1942, authorized to give precise definition to the August 1940 offer which was to come into operation immediately after the war. Moderate Indian leaders would have been agreeable to the proposed new constitution, which *inter alia* gave India the right to secede from the Commonwealth. Jinnah, the Moslem leader, and Nehru, President of the Indian National Congress, were also ready to negotiate, but not Gandhi, who declared it was 'a blank cheque on a crashing bank'. As a result of Gandhi's obstinacy the offer of a new constitution was rejected out of hand by the Congress Working Committee, and on 10 April negotiations were broken off, to Churchill's relief.[5]

Cripps handled the negotiations admirably, making it clear that he would stay only a little time, and that there would be no chance of making India another offer in wartime. Churchill showed statesmanship in putting his authority behind a plan which was in accordance with neither his previous views nor his inclinations.

Roosevelt had sent out to India his personal representative, Louis Johnston, who was sympathetic to the Indians. American public opinion had been unanimous that the British proposals were fair and ought to be accepted. He had little time for Indian demands for control of their own defence. However, Cripps was unable to convince Indian opinion that the plan represented a real change of heart. Many Indian politicians accepted Cripps' sincerity but were obsessed by the fear that, when he departed, they would have to treat again with the India Office, which they looked upon, in common with the Viceregal Lodge, as the symbol of their 'servitude'.

Roosevelt's response to the collapse of the negotiations was unusually critical. On 12 April he wrote to Churchill asking him to postpone Cripps' departure from India until 'one more final effort' had been made, adding that he could not agree with Churchill's message to him that public opinion in the United States believed the negotiations had failed on broad general issues. 'The general impression here is quite the contrary. The feeling is almost universally held that the deadlock has been caused by the unwillingness of the British Government to concede to the Indians the right of self-government, notwithstanding the willingness of the Indians to entrust technical, military and naval defense control to the competent British authorities.'

Roosevelt went on to say that, if Japan successfully invaded India after the negotiations were allowed to collapse, 'the prejudicial reaction on American public opinion can hardly be overestimated'. The President told Harry Hopkins, who was in London, to give the letter 'immediately' to the Prime Minister because 'we must make every effort to prevent a breakdown'.

This letter made Churchill furious. According to Hopkins, 'the string of cuss words lasted for two hours in the middle of the night', and the Prime Minister told him he was ready to resign 'if that became the best way to quiet American concern about India and maintain the wartime alliance'. Well might Churchill curse, because he had sacrificed his own personal feelings over India, and in a statesmanlike move sent Cripps, whose views were anathema to him, with authority to negotiate a settlement – yet the President showed no understanding. Churchill drafted a reply:

1. I am greatly concerned to receive your message because I am sure that I could not be responsible for a policy which would throw the whole sub-continent of India into utter confusion while the Japanese invader is at its gates. A Nationalist Government such as you indicate would almost certainly demand, first, the recall of all Indian troops from the Middle East, and secondly, they might in my opinion make an armistice with Japan on the basis of free transit through India to Karachi of Japanese forces and supplies. From their point of view this would be the easiest course, and one entirely in accord with Gandhi's non-violence doctrines. The Japanese would in return no doubt give the Hindus the military support necessary to impose their will upon the Moslems, the Native States and the Depressed Classes.

2. I cannot feel that the common cause would benefit by emphasizing the serious differences which would emerge between our two countries if it were known that against our own convictions we were conforming to United States public opinion in a matter which concerns the British Empire and is vital to our successful conduct of the war in the East.

3. I should personally make no objection at all to retiring into private life, and I have explained this to Harry just now, but I have no doubt whatever that Cabinet and Parliament would be strongly averse from reopening the Indian constitutional issue in this way at this juncture. Far from helping the defence of India, it would make our task impossible.

4. Nevertheless I will of course if you desire it bring your message before the Cabinet at its earliest meeting on Monday. You may be sure I will do everything in my power to preserve our most sympathetic co-operation. Any serious public divergence between the British and United States Governments at this time might involve both of our countries in ruin.

It represented a crisis in the relationship between the President and the Prime Minister, but it is inconceivable that Churchill really had any intention of resigning. He wanted to bring home to Roosevelt how exasperated he was by this interference in British affairs. Emotionally he was opposed to Indian independence, and he knew he had been much criticized for this attitude; on top of that he was certain that to grant independence at this moment of extreme danger from Japanese attack would be military suicide. This view was shared by most British experts on India.

Churchill's draft was not sent. Instead he wrote:

I could not decide such a matter without convening the Cabinet which was not physically possible till Monday. Meanwhile Cripps had already left . . . You know the weight which I attach to everything you say to me but I did not feel I could take responsibility for the defence of India if everything has to be thrown into the melting pot . . . Anything like a serious difference between you and me would break my heart and surely deeply injure both countries.

It was fortunate that Cripps had left India before Roosevelt's letter arrived.

Hopkins reported by telephone to Roosevelt Churchill's resignation threat, and the President wisely softened his attitude over India, realizing that Churchill's full co-operation was more important than immediate Indian independence. Later Churchill wrote that Roosevelt 'was keeping off the grass', and expressed his true feelings in his memoirs, where he wrote: 'I was thankful that events had already made such an act of madness impossible.'[6]

At the end of March Churchill and the Chiefs of Staff agreed there was a grave fear that Japan might invade Bengal or Ceylon and put the whole Indian Empire in dire danger. On 5 April a large enemy fleet approached Ceylon and sank two British cruisers, and the island was heavily bombed from aircraft carriers. Churchill asked Roosevelt to make a diversion with the US Pacific Fleet to relieve the pressure on the Indian Ocean, saying that the Japanese had control of the Bay of Bengal and the waters around Ceylon. Wavell's view was that 'we shall never regain control of the Indian Ocean and Bay of Bengal, and run risk of losing India' unless he was sent reinforcements. But Roosevelt would not accede to Churchill's request, and Britain could find no resources to reinforce Wavell. Thus it was fortunate that the raid on Ceylon marked the limit of Japan's westward expansion. Instead, Japan concentrated on the south-west Pacific and threatened Australia.[7]

When the Australians, alarmed at the Japanese threat to their homeland, pressed for the return home of their two infantry brigades in Ceylon which were vital for the defence of the island, Wavell sent a message: 'The War Cabinet must really make up their mind whether or not they propose to defend India and Ceylon seriously.' Churchill replied that the Australians would stay in Ceylon until British reinforcements arrived; this was typical of his treatment of the Dominion powers, because Australia had only agreed to 'a temporary loan of their units'.[8]

However, the Ceylon situation was relieved when on 24 April the War Cabinet agreed to launch an attack on Vichy-held Madagascar on the Cape – Middle East route. There were grave fears that Vichy might allow the base at Diego Suarez at the northern end to be used as a submarine base by the Japanese, as had happened in Indo-China. The operation known as Ironclad employed three infantry brigades, which after the capture of Madagascar were intended to be available for Ceylon.

Plans to seize Madagascar had been discussed with de Gaulle, but there had been fears of provoking the Vichy Government, to which Laval had recently returned. Relations between Churchill and de Gaulle were at a very low ebb because of the dispute over Syria, and Churchill had ordered the General not to leave Britain. The previous Anglo–French adventures at Dakar and Syria had failed, and the British military chiefs advised Churchill that Free French participation would be likely to produce stubborn resistance; Churchill expected little resistance from General Anet, the Vichy Governor of Madagascar, perhaps because Clemmie Churchill had once met him on a train and found him 'a most charming man'. The *Economist* commented shrewdly in March that Decoux's behaviour in Indo-China had been 'shameless and may well be repeated by Anet' in Madagascar, and it was 'an odd fact about minor Vichy officials that they are prepared to defend French territory to the last but only against the democracies'. The *Economist* was correct, and Anet organized strong resistance; nevertheless Diego Suarez was taken two days after the landing on 5 May, although no attempt was made to occupy the rest of the island.[9]

General Anet was told he could remain in office if he collaborated with the British, and he signed a treaty of capitulation. This agreement with the pro-Vichy Anet infuriated de Gaulle. Churchill and Eden were adamant that Madagascar could not be handed over to de Gaulle while the dispute over Syria continued, but by 3 October, after Anet had shown signs of treachery, the capital, Tananarive, was taken and an armistice concluded. De Gaulle's nominee, General Gentilhomme, was allowed to take over Madagascar. It was an unpleasant episode in the Churchill–de Gaulle relations, but with the appointment of Gentilhomme the open quarrel between the two leaders ended.[10]

Once Diego Suarez was occupied Churchill wanted the troops engaged in Madagascar to be sent to India, and he elaborated to the Chiefs of Staff plans for 'a general amphibious air, land and sea operation against Burma for the autumn and winter of 1942 for which he wanted landing craft prepared locally with a proportion sent from home'. However, Wavell found that internal conditions in India made it impossible to prepare for local amphibious operations in Burma.[11]

The working committee of the Indian Congress which had rejected the Cripps offer in April became obsessed with the belief that Britain was on the verge of defeat, and demanded the immediate withdrawal of British rule in India. Lord Linlithgow, the Viceroy, had no alternative but to declare the Indian National Congress an illegal association, and to intern Gandhi and other political leaders.

Gandhi then made a call for the British 'to quit India' and launched a campaign of civil disobedience. He seriously believed the Japanese would leave India alone if the British left, and advocated only passive resistance if Japan did invade. Linlithgow called it 'the most serious rebellion since 1857 [the Indian Mutiny]', and the total numbers of rioters killed by troops and police amounted to 850 – not quite up to Mutiny standards, but grave enough with the Japanese at the gate. Serious rioting occurred over large areas and there were prolonged strikes in the heavy industries. Hundreds of railway stations, post offices and police stations were destroyed or damaged, although Moslem opinion was entirely opposed to the revolt. It was certainly not a propitious moment to plan a campaign to recapture Burma.

Still, Wavell was determined to launch some type of offensive against the Japanese. After a lull in the fighting, with the terminus of the Burma road, Lashio, and all central Burma in Japanese hands, he decided to try and seize the port of Akyab on the Arakan coast. In spite of the civil disturbances he made two brigades of Indian and British troops ready for a direct seaborne attack. But the Japanese were well dug in and Wavell had grossly underestimated their efficiency in a jungle terrain. The two brigades were virtually destroyed, and suffered 2500 casualties before they were withdrawn.

Churchill, who had been enthusiastic for the operation, was intensely disappointed, but he distracted attention from this wretched failure by spotlighting the achievements of Brigadier Orde Wingate's Chindits in northern Burma. In February and March 1943 these three thousand men, supplied by air, carried out operations in the rear of the Japanese lines; on 24 March they made a more or less successful overland return to India, but they had lost half their number. Psychologically it was a success and gave British and Indian morale a much-needed boost. The Japanese were forced to alter their plans, and for the rest of 1943 Burma remained relatively quiet.

During 1944 Churchill became disturbed at the lack of British progress in the Far East, despite the great numbers of soldiers in India and the size of the Fleet in the Far East now that the Mediterranean was under Allied control. It had become clear to him that Roosevelt would not allow American forces to be used to pave the way for the re-establishment of British, French and Dutch rule in their former Far Eastern possessions. Significantly, Roosevelt had promised the Philippines independence as soon as the war with Japan ended, and he wanted Indo-China not to return to French Government but to be placed under a trusteeship to prepare it for self-government. Cadogan declared that American policy towards Indo-China was 'sinister'. Later Roosevelt even gave orders that American forces were not to give aid to French units fighting the Japanese in Indo-China.[12]

With reason Churchill argued that if Burma, Borneo and Malaya were to return without difficulty to British rule after hostilities, it was imperative that the prestige of British arms became high in the Far East.

During 1943 Churchill had shown enthusiasm for an attack on the Andaman Islands, formerly used to house convicts, in the eastern part of the Bay of Bengal. Operation Buccaneer, as it was known, required considerably more landing craft than were available because, as will be seen, he was now even keener on operations in the eastern Aegean. This imposed prior claims on landing craft, which in any case were in short supply because so many were required for the planned cross-Channel invasion. In June 1944 Churchill had approved a proposal agreed with the Australian and New Zealand Prime Ministers for a British sea and land offensive based on Australia to take Amboina, between Australia and the Philippines, and from there to launch an attack to recapture Borneo. With difficulty the Americans had been persuaded to approve this plan.

Then Churchill, preoccupied with the need to recapture Singapore and Malaya before the Japanese were defeated by the Americans, abruptly changed his mind. Instead he developed great enthusiasm for Culverin, an operation to capture the northern tip of Sumatra which could be used as a base for an attack on Malaya.

He told a Chiefs of Staff meeting on 24 June 1944 that he was 'distressed that in the American strategic plan the British in the Far East were either cut out altogether or subordinated to MacArthur [Supreme Commander South West Pacific Area]', and went on:

> The political importance of our making some effort to recover British territory must not be underrated. Rangoon and Singapore are great names in the British eastern world, and it will be an ill day for Britain if the war ends without our having made a

stroke to regain those places and having left the whole Malayan peninsula alone until it is evacuated as the result of an American-dictated peace at Tokyo, even though there is a very small British force in the American armies.

On 6 July he told another Chiefs of Staff meeting that the British would be 'in a most humiliating position in the Far East if the Americans could turn round and claim they alone had defeated Japan . . . there were enormous forces in the Indian Army on our payroll and it would be a scandal not to make use of these forces.' He revealed his gnawing worry about the necessity of British troops recapturing former British possessions by adding:

The British contribution to the recapture of our Empire in the Far East is minute. The shame of our disaster at Singapore could, in his opinion, be wiped out by our recapture of that fortress. He still favoured an operation in November of this year for the capture of the island of Simalur, to be followed by the capture of the tip of Sumatra. We would then obtain air domination of Singapore and Malaya.[13]

This view did not find favour with the Chiefs of Staff present. Brooke, Cunningham and Portal insisted there would not be sufficient land forces available until after the defeat of Germany. Eden wrote in his diary that the Prime Minister became very irritated at the reaction of his advisers.

The next week, on 14 July, Churchill returned to the attack. When the Chiefs of Staff reiterated their advice to use bases in Australia for an attack on Amboina, Churchill said he would not have it because it meant condemning 'the vast forces in India to inaction save for those that would be engaged in the swamps of Burma'. He was convinced the right course was 'to mount an operation from Ceylon at the earliest possible date' to capture the north of Sumatra, and thereafter to advance against Malaya and recapture Singapore. Eden supported Churchill over Culverin, but pointed out that the necessary troops and landing craft could not be found in time, while Attlee said: 'Despite Culverin's obvious attractions there was no chance of it taking place within a measurable time.'[14]

On 9 August, when the campaign in France was going so well that it looked as if the end of the war with Germany was near and large forces could be released for the Far East, Churchill told the Chiefs of Staff that the capture of Rangoon (Vanguard) must be given priority, and plans for the recapture of Singapore put in readiness as soon as forces were available. At Quebec on 12 September he told the Chiefs of Staff: 'Britain's ultimate object must be the recapture of Singapore.'[15]

Wavell had now been made Viceroy in succession to Linlithgow and Earl Mountbatten had replaced him as Commander in Chief Far East. Mountbatten and the Chiefs of Staff argued with Churchill that a campaign to retake Rangoon and open up land communications with Chiang Kai-shek would use up all available land and air forces in the Far East until the war with Germany allowed extra divisions to be sent, and an attack on Singapore must be left until much later. They also wanted Britain to offer America the British Fleet in the Far East for operations against the Japanese homeland, or in the south-western Pacific under MacArthur from Australian bases. Churchill disliked this idea, and on 12

September, with the triumph of the Allied Armies in France and Belgium, when it looked as if Germany was on the brink of defeat, wrote a minute that the capture of Sumatra was a stepping stone to Singapore, adding: 'Here is the supreme British objective in the whole of the Indian and Far Eastern theatres. It is the only prize that will restore British prestige in this region.'[16]

At this stage, with every nerve strained to defeat Germany, the Chiefs of Staff were reluctant to prepare plans for Singapore, and their minds boggled at what they called 'the fundamental problem . . . the movement of 370,000 men and 24,000 vehicles from the European theatre to India in the shortest time'. Had Germany collapsed in September 1944, Churchill would have insisted on such an operation, but the failure of the Arnhem operation between 17 and 24 September enabled Hitler to halt the Allied advance, restabilize the crumbling Western Front and prolong the European war until the end of April 1945. At Quebec in September, Churchill and Roosevelt had approved a plan to send six British divisions from Europe to Mountbatten in India; but by October it was clear that nothing could be spared from Europe.

It was a bitter pill for Churchill that the invasion of Sumatra had to be called off. With the prospect of an early end to the war in Europe Churchill had had great hopes of a brilliant victory in the Far East too if he transferred divisions from Europe to India to reconquer Burma. He bitterly rued that Arnhem and the German success in defence in Italy made these plans inoperable, although Eisenhower had agreed to let 1st Airborne Division, refitting in England, and other divisions go direct to the Far East without returning to the Continent. On 5 October Churchill told Mountbatten sadly, 'I am very sorry indeed that we have not been able to carry out this operation [the recapture of Burma] on which I had set my heart, but the German resistance both in France and Italy has turned out to be far more formidable than we had hoped. We must clean them out first.'

The result was that in 1945 the Far East war was more than ever in the hands of the Americans, and when Germany was finally defeated in May 1945 Britain's part in the Japanese war had been minor. Chiang Kai-shek's efforts had not come up to Churchill's expectations, with the result that the British campaign in Burma became purely a private war to restore British rule, and made no contribution to final victory over Japan.

Mountbatten's forces liberated Rangoon five days before the German surrender, and a British contingent of two battleships, four aircraft carriers and three cruisers had arrived in Australian waters and were helping in American operations in the Ryuku Islands preparatory to the invasion of Okinawa. Churchill now insisted on throwing the largest possible British striking force against Japan with priority for the recapture of Singapore (Operation Zipper), and an assault was planned for the autumn of 1945. Churchill approved the final plans for Singapore enthusiastically at a Chiefs of Staff meeting on 5 July 1945, the day before the General Election.

This was a statesmanlike move by Churchill, abundantly justified by results – because when Japan surrendered, Operation Zipper was accomplished without opposition and thus British government in Singapore and Malaya was resumed with the backing of a powerful army. This was a sharp contrast to Indonesia, where the Japanese had permitted a degree of self-government under Sokarno and other nationalist leaders; the Dutch were unable to regain control after a small British force had landed to disarm the Japanese. The re-entry of the Dutch troops coincided with mass support for an independence movement, and widespread disorder occurred as soon as British forces withdrew.

In Indo-China the Japanese surrender to the Allies left a confused situation in which a resurgent France found herself faced with revolutionary nationalism. In March 1945 the Japanese had ended French administration after Decoux had continued to govern during the uneasy period after the Vichy Government fell. Neither the Dutch nor the French received any support from US forces. In Malaya, so hated were the Japanese that there was general delight at the return of the British, and thanks to Churchill the Army was powerful enough to deal with an outbreak of banditry by a few thousand Chinese Communists.

CHAPTER SIXTEEN

North Africa and Casablanca

WHEN AUCHINLECK's troops were defeated in the desert in July 1942 Hitler's world power was terrifying despite the US entry into the war. German armies were advancing into the foothills of the Caucasus and might simultaneously reach Cairo and the Nile. Northern Australia and India were threatened by the Japanese, who dominated the Bay of Bengal. It was not certain that the military potential of the USA would be in action before Japan and Germany controlled both Europe and Asia, while the mounting toll of Atlantic sinkings of merchant ships by German submarines threatened Britain with starvation.

Churchill was overawed neither by his precarious political position at home nor by the daunting task ahead. He threw all his energies into organizing a confrontation with German armies as soon as possible so as to draw German strength off Russia. The alternative lay between waiting for Roundup across the English Channel in 1943, or an attack in the autumn of 1942 on the French North African colonies. Churchill's temperament was such that he could not bear the prospect of US and British armies staying idle until the spring of 1943, but he failed to realize that diverting resources to the Mediterranean must inevitably mean postponing Roundup until 1944 except for small-scale operations. He was deeply conscious of the promise he had made to Stalin, first for an attack in Europe in 1942, and then for a major cross-Channel assault in 1943. As the Russian military position became more and more precarious Churchill became more and more enthusiastic for the immediate combined British–American North African operation, Torch. As has been seen, both he and Roosevelt deluded themselves that Torch did not make a 1943 Roundup impossible.

French North Africa was controlled by Vichy. They had no intention of declaring for the Allies because they still felt that Hitler was winning the war and they did not want to provoke the Germans to breach the armistice terms. The rulers in Vichy lived in Hitler's shadow, and even those who were anti-German had little sympathy for Britain after Mers-el-Kebir, Dakar and the Syrian war. Pétain was popular with the 300,000-strong French Army and the naval units in North Africa, and there was little support for de Gaulle, so that there was no chance the Allies would be allowed to land unopposed in French North Africa.

Roosevelt, unlike Churchill, believed there would be little French resistance provided the British role could be concealed and de Gaulle's Free French excluded. The Americans were fully conscious of the French hatred of the British inspired by Mers-el-Kebir, but from their intelligence reports they received misleading news of the Vichy French attitude towards themselves and assumed on false evidence that most of the local French commanders in North Africa would welcome an American expeditionary force. Accordingly an American commander, General Eisenhower, was appointed, and at one time Churchill even considered sending British troops ashore in American uniforms.

The British and the Americans were divided over strategy for Torch. The Americans were cautious and wanted to land at first only on the Atlantic coast in Morocco, and not to go into the Mediterranean until they had a firm base in the west. They were frightened that Franco would allow the Germans into Spain, so that Hitler could seize Gibraltar and close the Straits behind the Allied invading fleet. Churchill argued that the correct plan was to capture the whole of North Africa in one fell swoop, and before the Germans could intervene to land at Oran, Algiers, and as far east as Bone. Churchill was right, and if Bone had been included in the first assault there was every chance that Tunis would have fallen before the Germans could send troops there.

This conflict of views between Roosevelt and Churchill and their respective Chiefs of Staff is well documented in a lengthy exchange of written messages between the two heads of state. Eventually a compromise was reached and the two Allies agreed that additional landings inside the Mediterranean should be made at Oran and Algiers though not at Bone. The decision not to go for Bone meant that the North African campaign lasted for seven months instead of a few weeks because Bone (400 miles east of Algiers) lay only 200 miles from Tunis, and as a result the lengthy and costly fighting in Tunisia might have been avoided.[1]

Churchill feared above all else that the Axis powers would establish themselves in Tunis, and it was worthwhile running considerable risks to forestall the Germans there. In London Eisenhower, with enthusiastic support from Churchill, planned landings at Bone and Philippeville on D-Day plus three, but in Washington the American Chiefs of Staff were still reluctant to risk their invasion fleet passing through the Straits of Gibraltar and were downcast at the heavy losses still being inflicted on the latest Malta convoys.

At this stage of the war Churchill was on bad terms with de Gaulle because of shilly-shallying by the Free French over the independence of Syria and Lebanon, and de Gaulle's petulant demand for control of Madagascar. The two met on 30 September and there was a flaming row which resulted in relations being almost severed. Roosevelt was even more prejudiced against de Gaulle than Churchill, because the Free French had seized the islands of St Pierre and Miquelon, off Newfoundland, at Christmas 1941, shortly after the USA had given Vichy an assurance that the United States would respect the *status quo* in that area. This action was taken by Roosevelt and Hull as an insult to the United States. Eden was always trying to improve relations between Churchill and de Gaulle, but in a sharp note in June 1942 the Prime Minister snubbed the Foreign Secretary:

It is very easy to make the kind of case you have set down out of all the shameful things the Vichy Government have said. This does not alter my wish or extinguish my hope to have the French Fleet sail to Africa and to get an invitation for British or American troops to enter French North Africa. Nor does it alter the fact that at any rate for some time to come Vichy is the only party that can offer these good gifts . . . President Roosevelt has the same feelings as I have about all this and so I believe have the Chiefs of Staff . . . There is much more in British policy towards France than abusing Pétain and backing de Gaulle.[2]

As has been noted, in late 1940 and early 1941 Churchill had high hopes of co-operation from Pétain, but these sank to nothing when the Anglophobe Darlan became Vice President of the Council in 1941, and when in April 1942 the even worse Laval assumed control of the Vichy Government. Churchill was in no doubt that 'the establishment in French North Africa would remain loyal to Vichy'. Roosevelt did not agree, and was dangerously overoptimistic. America had continued diplomatic relations with Vichy although as a protest the US Ambassador, Admiral Leahy, had remained on extended leave when Laval came to power. Thus America was able to take soundings in North Africa through Robert Murphy, a career diplomat who was appointed Consul General in Algiers in December 1940. Murphy had had considerable experience in France before the war, and played a key role in American–French relations, acting as a roving Ambassador for Roosevelt. Under Murphy in French North Africa were a number of American vice consuls whose main role was the gathering of intelligence. When the Americans proposed that Murphy should contact a number of Vichy adherents in North Africa who would co-operate with American invading forces Churchill raised no objection; he agreed that the de Gaulle organization in London should be told nothing of the plans for Torch, although they could be revealed to co-operative Vichy plotters in North Africa and France.

Because of the firmness with which the French had resisted the 1940 British effort to capture Dakar, Hitler considered the Vichy regime in North Africa reliable, and he allowed it to be responsible for its own defence. Weygand took advantage of this to reorganize the Army, but his frank anti-German sentiments led him to be recalled in 1941. By then he had an Army of 120,000 men and 400 aircraft. Weygand declared he would fight *contre quiconque*, and his fierce defence of France's neutrality was shared by his successor, General Juin, and the residents general in Morocco, Tunis and French West Africa (Dakar) – General Nogues, Admiral Esteva and Pierre Boisson.

Murphy established relations with senior officers in the Vichy Army both in unoccupied France and in North Africa; they reported that to outward appearances Torch must be an American operation and must not contain any of de Gaulle's forces. Churchill concurred, although he warned Roosevelt on 1 September that 'if the political bloodless victory, for which I agree there is a good chance, should go amiss a military disaster of very great consequence will supervene. We could have stormed Dakar in September 1940 if we had not been cluttered up with preliminary conciliatory processes. It is that hard experience that makes our military experts rely so much on the simplicity of force.'[3]

Churchill was alive to the danger of a determined French defence of North Africa, but Roosevelt still had a blind spot. The American President replied to Churchill on 3 September: 'An American expedition led in all three phases by American officers will meet little resistance from the French Army in Africa. On the other hand a British-commanded attack in any phase or with de Gaullist cooperation would meet with determined resistance.' Churchill warned Roosevelt: 'Free French have got inkling and are leaky.'[4]

Unknown to Churchill, Murphy was taking soundings from Darlan, who stressed how important it was to avoid doing anything to precipitate drastic German retaliation against Vichy. However, Darlan told Murphy through Leahy that he would consider coming to North Africa himself, bringing with him all the valuable elements of the French Fleet, if he was assured of American military and economic help.

The situation was complicated because the Americans, to whom Churchill had delegated responsibility for all preliminary political contacts with the French, had discovered General Giraud, who had escaped dramatically from a German fortress, and looked upon him as the knight in shining armour who would be able to persuade the French in North Africa not to resist an American invasion. Mistakenly the Americans put their faith in Giraud, not Darlan; Giraud proved a broken reed because the key French commanders in North Africa were pro-Darlan and has scarcely more use for Giraud than for de Gaulle. However the Americans believed General Mast, number two to Juin in Algiers, and Giraud's devoted supporter, when he told Murphy optimistically that Giraud could neutralize all French Army and Air Force resistance in North Africa. Mast was told by Murphy in strict secrecy that 7 November was D-Day for the invasion, and he did his best – but to little avail – to stop any resistance, as did General Bethouard, number two to Nogues.

On the night of 5 November the Torch convoys sailed through the Straits of Gibraltar bound for Oran and Algiers, while other American convoys, bound for the Atlantic coast, were on their way direct from American ports. The Germans and Italians were certain that the Allies in the Mediterranean were heading for Benghazi and Tripoli, and made no attempt to interfere by sea or air. If the convoys had gone to Bone or even Tunis or Bizerta only the French, not the Germans or Italians, would have opposed them.

The landings met heavy French resistance. Mast and Bethouard had been unable to persuade General Nogues at Casablanca or General Juin in Algiers to allow the American Army to land peacefully. At Oran and Casablanca the French fought back determinedly for two days, and at Casablanca nearly drove the attacking Americans back into the sea. At Algiers, although anti-Vichy forces took the main aerodrome at Blida, there was initial resistance. The situation was confused by Darlan being in the town. He had gone to Algiers to visit his son, who was sick in hospital, although he may well also have been influenced by Leahy's hints that an American occupation was in the offing. Darlan was angry when he saw Murphy on the morning of 8 November. He told the American that with a little more time he might have been able to bring over not only unoccupied

France, but all North Africa, to the Allied cause. Fortunately Juin, after consulting with Darlan, agreed not to fight, but not before substantial casualties had been suffered on both sides.

In April 1941 the Germans had forced Pétain to replace Darlan with Laval as Vice President of the Council, but Pétain remained Commander in Chief of all the French forces. Because of the contacts established by Murphy with Darlan the Americans expected Eisenhower to do a deal with him. Darlan told Eisenhower he would take over full authority, civil and military, in French North Africa in the name of Pétain, and, after cabling to Pétain, ordered a ceasefire while fighting at Oran and Casablanca was still in full swing. Hitler summoned Laval to meet him in Munich and insisted that Pétain should disown Darlan. Pétain did so formally, although he sent Darlan by secret code a message of good wishes and encouragement. Eisenhower was delighted; he had satisfactorily solved an appalling political situation.

Without Darlan Giraud was impotent, but in return for Giraud recognizing him as the supreme civil authority Darlan appointed the General to the position of Commander in Chief French Forces in North Africa as promised to him by the Allies. Eisenhower, dismayed by the fierce French resistance at Oran and in West Africa, immediately confirmed this arrangement; it meant that North Africa was firmly on the Allied side although under Darlan, who was contaminated by Vichy. Nogues and Boisson announced their loyalty to the Darlan regime: all resistance ceased, and the French co-operated with the invading forces. Eisenhower reported from Algiers that Giraud had been powerless to stop French resistance and was suspected of 'treachery', but 'all concerned now profess themselves ready to support the Allies provided Admiral Darlan tells them to do so . . . they are absolutely not willing to follow anyone else'; he was convinced that the Allies needed a strong military Government of some kind in North Africa.[5]

At first Churchill was gravely disconcerted. In 1940 he had deeply distrusted Darlan's honesty and frequently declared in public that he could not trust Darlan's promise never to allow the French Fleet to fall into German hands. Churchill's anger with him had been heightened when, in return for trifling concessions by Hitler, the Frenchman agreed in May 1941 to allow the transit of German war material across Syria to aid the anti-British rebels in Iraq. Churchill described him as 'a bad man with a narrow outlook and a shifty eye. A naval crook is usually a bad kind of crook.' The British press echoed Churchill's view of Darlan.[6]

On 11 November Churchill reminded Roosevelt that the British were under 'quite definite and solemn obligations to de Gaulle and his movement' and warned against 'the creation of rival French emigré Governments each favoured by one of us'. The next day he argued that Darlan should only be recognized if he could bring over the French Fleet from Toulon; Darlan was trying, unsuccessfully, to do precisely this. Nevertheless on 13 November Churchill yielded, albeit reluctantly, and told the President he agreed Darlan should be recognized as the legal authority; however the arrangements were 'neither permanent nor healthy', but must be accepted 'for maintaining local and interim equilibrium and for securing the vital position in Tunisia'.[7]

Churchill showed real statesmanship in agreeing to the *ad hoc* arrangement made by Eisenhower with Darlan in Algiers in spite of his pent up personal hostility and prejudice against Darlan. However British public opinion, incited by Churchill to believe that Darlan was the villain who had made Mers-el-Kebir inevitable, was outraged. Hostile questions were asked in the Commons, and a motion was tabled in the Commons 'That this House is of the opinion that our relations with Admiral Darlan and his kind are inconsistent with the ideals for which we entered and are fighting this war'. In secret session on 10 December, in a speech regarded by many as his most brilliant, Churchill allayed these criticisms. He himself felt that this speech changed opinion more decisively than any other he made during the war.[8]

It was nearly 600 miles from Algiers to Tunis, with only one road and one very slow railway. Fortunately, with the Eisenhower–Darlan agreement the co-operation of French railway officials and the French Army was secured; other-wise it would have been impossible to mount an immediate attack on Tunisia. Had American ships arrived at Bone or Bizerta on 8 November they would probably have been received with 'mooring lines, not gunfire'. It is known from post-war evidence that Admirals Derrien and Esteva, who were in charge, were ready to co-operate with the Americans, even though they were both tried and wrongly condemned to imprisonment in March 1945 for their part in what had happened in Tunisia two-and-a-half years earlier. When Derrien was given a message from Roosevelt by the US Consul in Bizerta in the middle of the night of 8 November, to the effect that the landings were about to begin, he declared himself sympathetic, but added: 'You had better hurry up; the Germans will be here within forty-eight hours.'

On the 9th German aircraft began to land troops on the main Tunisian military aerodrome. As no resistance had been ordered by Vichy, the French allowed them to land. At midday on 10 November Derrien received Darlan's order for a ceasefire, but he thought it irrelevant because no fighting against the Americans had taken place. He ordered the French troops to avoid all contact with Germans and to withdraw from the ports to the hills behind the littoral. On 11 November, as soon as the news came through that the Germans had invaded the Vichy-controlled zone of France, Darlan and Juin telephoned orders to resist the Germans. General Barre, in charge of the Army, was ready to fight when Juin told him it was 'time to bash the Boche [*On va taper sur le boche*]'. Derrien issued a proclamation to the troops that 'the enemy is Germany and Italy. Go to it,' But when Esteva realized no Americans would turn up in Tunisia he became fainthearted, and ordered 'strict neutrality against all belligerents'. The next day the Germans and Italians took over in strength. A great opportunity had been lost.

The British 78th Division soon landed at the ports of Bougie and Bone and were received with enthusiasm by the French. They linked up with Barre's French troops on 19 November, but the Germans and Italians held them twenty

1. Churchill becomes Prime Minister in 1940. The Tories had wanted Halifax as
Prime Minister instead.

2. The War Cabinet in the dark days of 1940. Standing, left to right: Sir Archibald Sinclair, A.V. Alexander, Viscount Cranborne, W.S. Morrison, Lord Moyne, Captain Margesson, Brendan Bracken. Seated, left to right: Ernest Bevin, Lord Beaverbrook, Anthony Eden, Clement Attlee, Winston Churchill, Sir John Anderson, Arthur Greenwood, Sir Kingsley Wood.

3. East Enders warm to Churchill during the 1941 Blitz.

4. Churchill, having sacked Auchinleck, relaxes in the garden of the British Embassy, Cairo, with South African Prime Minister Smuts in August 1942.

5. Churchill overcomes obstacles on a battle course in England in November 1942.

6. The summit, Tehran, November 1943. Stalin, Churchill and his hard-worked interpreter Major Birse.

7. Churchill patches up his quarrel with de Gaulle as they review Free French troops at Marrakesh, March 1944.

8. Churchill comes to Ramsgate to console victims of German bombardment.

9. Churchill visits Eisenhower during the tense days of preparation for the cross-channel invasion.

10. Churchill enthusiastically greeted by troops in Normandy bridgehead, June 1944.

11. Montgomery charms Churchill with promises of an early break out from Normandy, August 1944.

12. Montgomery, Churchill and Brooke triumphant on the banks of the Rhine on March 26 1945. But the Americans had stolen their thunder with a surprise river crossing 19 days previously.

13. After VE Day. The Prime Minister with his victorious Chiefs of Staff (left to right: Portal, Brooke and Cunningham) in the garden of 10 Downing Street.

14. Stalin, Roosevelt and Churchill at the Yalta Summit, February 1945. The Russians had already overrun Poland.

15. Buckingham Palace balcony, VE Day. Churchill with the King and Queen.

16. Walthamstow, July 1945. Churchill appeals in vain for a parliamentary majority in the General Election.

17. Potsdam, July 1945. Stalin greets Churchill at the conference table.

miles away from Tunis. Heavy rains set in, and an Allied attack on Tunis could not be renewed until after the Eighth Army entered Tripoli on 23 January 1943.

Thus Torch was only a limited success, but it had enabled the British and American armies to get to grips with the Germans, and consequently an important part of the German Army and Luftwaffe was diverted from the Russian front. However, Churchill's plan of clearing North Africa in time for a cross-Channel invasion in 1943 was to be frustrated.

Darlan's promises to Churchill that the French Fleet would never fall into German hands were resoundingly fulfilled. After the landings, on 11 November the Germans denounced the armistice and occupied the whole of France; they allowed a 'neutrality' zone around Toulon, where eighty ships of the French Fleet were in harbour. Darlan had sent an 'invitation', but not a definite order, to Admiral de Laborde, the naval commander in Toulon, to sail these ships to West Africa on 12 November. But de Laborde rudely refused, and the ships stayed in Toulon. French sailors dreaded another Mers-el-Kebir, but Pétain kept his promise that the French Fleet would be scuttled to save it from falling into German hands.

On the night of 26–27 November 1942 Hitler ordered two columns of SS into Toulon naval dockyard in a surprise attack, followed by 4500 German sailors to take over the French Fleet. It was a close-run drama. The first the French knew was when German tanks loomed up outside the gates of the arsenal and the naval port. Admiral de Laborde immediately ordered boilers to be lit and preparations made for scuttling. As German tanks broke down the gates and drove along the quays the black darkness was lit up by the glare of explosions in ships, docks and workshops. At all points the Germans were too late, and by dawn seventy-five warships had been destroyed or had escaped. The Germans had possession of the greatest French naval port, but with empty hands. The shooting war between France and Britain had ended. French honour was redeemed, and Darlan's pledge to Churchill of 18 June 1940 was fulfilled.[9]

However, it would have been more glorious for France if the French ships at Toulon had sailed to join Darlan as soon as the Germans violated the armistice. After the liberation Admiral de Laborde was tried and condemned to death, but the sentence was commuted to life imprisonment. The officers and men were willing to sail; they only awaited the order from de Laborde – and it was not given.

From Cairo in August Churchill had told the War Cabinet that 'we were heading for disaster under the old regime. A complete change of atmosphere has taken place.' Montgomery fulfilled Churchill's high hopes. At the end of August Rommel launched a tank attack to outflank the Alamein line from the south. The Eighth Army defence was excellent, and on 2 September Rommel had to withdraw from all the ground he had gained. According to some military experts, if Montgomery had reacted quickly with a strong counter-attack he might have 'ended Rommel's army for good', without the celebrated costly attack which followed in October.[10]

Montgomery's enormously strengthened Army could hardly fail to win a setpiece battle. The Eighth Army numbered 230,000 against Rommel's 80,000, of whom only 30,000 were Germans, the remainder being Italians. Montgomery had at least a thousand front line tanks, including 347 of the new, heavily gunned American Shermans, which were far superior to the tanks available to Wavell and Auchinleck and as good as those of the Germans. Rommel had fewer tanks. In the air the British had 1500 aircraft against Rommel's 350. In addition, Rommel's were a long distance from his supply ports, whereas the Eighth Army was within a few hours' drive of their well-stocked bases around Cairo. Finally, the Axis armies were short of petrol and rations because of Allied sinkings of their supply convoys.

Churchill had wanted to stay in Cairo to see the fighting, and was as impatient as he had been with Wavell and Auchinleck for Montgomery to launch a major offensive. He asked for a start date in mid-September but Montgomery would not be hustled, and Churchill had to be content with D-Day in the third week of October – fourteen days before Torch was due.

On 20 October Churchill signalled to Alexander: 'All our hopes are centred upon the battle you and Montgomery are to fight.' On 23 October the Battle of El Alamein opened. At first it did not go well. British tank losses exceeded Rommel's by four to one, and after a week's fighting Rommel's army was unbroken.

Nasty rumours began to circulate in Downing Street and Whitehall, as they had over Wavell's and Auchinleck's failed offensives, because the attack seemed little nearer to its objectives than when it had started. On 28 October Churchill told the CIGS, after Eden had been unnecessarily pessimistic about the battle, that the signals from the Middle East were 'particularly disquieting, and the attack must be resumed before Torch; a standstill would be proclaimed as a defeat'. On 29 October Brooke was woken up with the draft of an 'unpleasant' telegram to Alexander which Churchill wanted to send. As soon as the two met, the Prime Minister gave Brooke a 'storm of reproach'. Churchill said: 'What was your Montgomery doing now allowing the battle to peter out? He had done nothing now for the last three days and now he was withdrawing troops from the line. Why had he told us he would be through in seven days if all he intended to do was to fight a half-hearted battle?'[11]

When Brooke flared up, Churchill said he was dissatisfied with the conduct of the battle and would immediately hold a Chiefs of Staff meeting under his chairmanship where it would be discussed with other members of the War Cabinet. At the meeting Brooke was faced with fierce complaints from Churchill that Montgomery was not showing a 'true offensive spirit' and had 'lost grip'. Brooke hotly denied these 'unfair' charges against his colleague; Smuts agreed with Brooke, while Attlee and Lyttleton said that any hint that the commanders on the spot had lost the confidence of the British Government would be 'disastrous' at this critical moment.

Churchill was dissuaded from sending the offensive telegram, which ran: 'We . . . were somewhat concerned to see that on the 27th the attack on Kidney Ridge by two battalions was the only substantial thrust. And now by your sitrep most units appear to be coming back into reserve . . . we should be grateful if you could tell us if you have any substantial large scale attacks impending.' The message actually sent was milder, but still contained an implied criticism: 'The Defence Committee feel that the general situation justifies all the risks and sacrifices in the relentless prosecution of this battle.'[12]

Casey, Resident Minister of State in Cairo, was ordered by Eden to go to Eighth Army Headquarters and report back to London; he was told by Montgomery's Chief of Staff, after he suggested sending a message to Churchill that things were not going well, 'Tell Whitehall not to bellyache.' The Prime Minister was on the brink of a showdown with Montgomery. However, on the afternoon of 28 October the battle turned in the British favour, and late in the evening Churchill was shown an Ultra decrypt of Rommel's signal to Hitler describing the situation as 'grave in the extreme with petrol short . . . signs that very strong British forces are preparing to break through from the north.' The Prime Minister then apologised to Brooke, and was especially nice as he showed the CIGS the message.[13]

The final push, codenamed Supercharge, went in on 1 November. The Germans were worn down by the enemy's greater number of tanks: on 2 November there were only 35 German and 20 Italian battleworthy tanks, as against over 500 British, and by the afternoon Rommel was in full retreat. In London, Ultra decrypts by lunchtime on 3 November revealed that Rommel had told Hitler that his army faced 'a desperate defeat' from which he could only 'extract remnants'. After twelve days' fighting the Battle of El Alamein had been won, and it was the turning point of the war. Churchill had the victory he longed for, and his political position was once more impregnable, while the allied High Command had the boost to morale which they had sorely needed before the hazardous Torch operation.[14]

On 5 November the *Daily Mirror* carried the headline: 'Rommel Routed. Huns Fleeing in Disorder', and there were similar stories in all the leading British and American nationals. With the desert victory and the end of the fighting in North Africa, Churchill declared that 'we had won one of the greatest victories ever won by the British Empire in the field'. He ordered church bells, silent since Dunkirk, to be rung on Sunday, 15 November.

Unfortunately Montgomery did not follow up as skilfully as he had conducted the setpiece battle. General G. P. Roberts, commander of the 22nd Armoured Brigade, told the author: 'The mistake was that we *all* went and all needed supplies at once, which caused problems. Soon there were shortages, especially of petrol.' General Harding, commander of 7th Armoured Division, wrote that the pursuit produced 'terrible confusion' because too many troops were engaged; he felt his own division could have gone through on its own if other divisions had not been competing for the available petrol and supplies, Monty was being 'over cautious carrying out the pursuit on too broad a front'.[15]

So Montgomery won an historic victory at Alamein, but bungled the aftermath and missed the opportunity of surrounding Rommel's remaining forces with a ring of armour. Instead Rommel's army escaped to fight again. First he stood at

El Agheila. Here again was a heaven-sent chance to destroy the Germany army. But Montgomery gave him a fortnight to reorganize and the moment was lost. Thus Rommel withdrew into Tunisia, where his army helped to prolong the North African campaign until May.

However, after the dramatic victory of Alamein Montgomery had become Churchill's blue-eyed boy, and the Prime Minister did not send the kind of prodding and goading messages about the slow advance which had upset Wavell and Auchinleck. They would have been better justified with Montgomery and Alexander than with their predecessors, and might have been effective.

At the end of 1942 Churchill could congratulate himself upon having secured all North Africa (apart from Tunisia) from the Atlantic to the Nile. His pecker was up, and the victories were magnified out of proportion in the press. In fact, Eisenhower's failure to link up with Eighth Army tanks in Tunisia was a severe setback to the overall Allied plans. By Christmas the Germans had assembled sixty thousand men and two hundred tanks in Tunisia and the Allied attack had ground to a halt. After Pearl Harbor, Churchill had predicted in Washington that by the beginning of 1943 the whole of North Africa would be in Allied hands, with footholds in Sicily and Italy, so that Roundup could go ahead that year. But this was far from the case. A cross-Channel invasion was now out of the question, with great numbers of ground forces and landing craft tied up in the Mediterranean.

Anxious to make sure that Roundup would take place in August or September 1943 and to implement his pledge to Stalin, Churchill planned for a three-power conference in January 1943, hoping that it would initiate preparations for a cross-Channel operation. On 3 December he wrote to Roosevelt that such a conference was 'the only way of making a good plan for 1943'. Roosevelt agreed to come to North Africa. On the same day Churchill asked Stalin to join him and Roosevelt in North Africa, writing: 'We must decide at the earliest moment the best way of attacking Germany in Europe with all possible force in 1943 . . . such a decision can only be settled between the Heads of Government . . . with their high expert authorities at their side.'[16]

Churchill realized that his high hopes for a cross-Channel invasion in 1943 depended on the Germans being pushed out of Tunisia in the early months of that year. But Hitler's decision to reinforce his North African armies under General von Armin was to destroy Roundup's chances in 1943 – both Churchill and Roosevelt were ludicrously overoptimistic about the operations in North Africa. In his letter suggesting the Casablanca Conference Churchill had written to Roosevelt: 'We may reasonably expect Tunisia will be settled by the end of December and Tripolitania by the end of January. All prospect of attack in Europe depends on early decision.' Roosevelt replied that he expected Tunis and Bizerta settled by 15 January and Rommel's army liquidated by the time of the Conference. This was wishful thinking, and it is the key to why the Allies drifted into abandoning Roundup in 1943.

Stalin refused to leave Moscow, but he took Churchill's message as a reiteration of the promises to invade France in 1943. He was to be grievously disappointed. Ominously, in his reply the Russian dictator wrote: 'I am awaiting your reply to the paragraph of my preceding letter dealing with the re-establishment of the Second Front in Europe in 1943' – thus reminding Churchill of the ever-present fear of a separate German–Russian peace and a return to the Molotov–Ribbentrop accord.

Luxurious hotels and villas in Casablanca were chosen for the Conference, and it was scheduled for mid-January 1943. As usual Churchill wanted the best of two worlds, and his plans were centred on more Mediterranean operations in 1943 combined with an attack in great force on the French coast. His professional advisers warned him that this was impossible, and that a choice must be made between the two. He refused to accept this situation; but was not single minded over a Mediterranean strategy, although this has been implied by some historians.

On the day when Churchill proposed the Casablanca meeting to Stalin and Roosevelt he harangued the Cabinet at length about 'swinging back towards a Western Front' in 1943, and said repeatedly that North Africa must act as a 'springboard' and not a 'sofa' for future action. Previously he had urged attacks on Sardinia and Sicily. Brooke was concerned, knowing it was impossible to attack in the Mediterranean and the Channel at the same time.[17] He argued that the best plan was to eliminate Italy, bring in Turkey and finally to liberate France. He emphasized that all this depended on Russia 'holding out', but by the end of 1943 this seemed 'a safe bet' because she had beaten off the attacks on Moscow, Leningrad and Stalingrad. At that time Churchill was being heavily pressurized by Stalin, Marshall, Stimson and Beaverbrook for a second front. There was popular agitation from the Beaverbrook press for an invasion of France, and large propaganda meetings took place in the Albert Hall and Trafalgar Square.

Roundup in 1943 would mean transferring all the landing craft from North Africa to Britain; Marshall wanted this to be done, and advised Roosevelt that there were immense logistical difficulties about further Mediterranean operations, which he described as 'dabbling wastefully'. But Hitler was staking a lot on defending the Tunisian peninsula, and refused even to consider abandoning the German foothold in North Africa. During December 1942 and January 1943 he continued to fly men and supplies across the narrow sea channel from Sicily to Tunis, even though the Allies were sinking more and more German convoys. On 1 December von Arnim attacked the Americans at Kasserine Gap in Tunisia. The inexperienced US troops fled, and from American dumps the Germans captured enough supplies for two divisions. An end to the Tunisian campaign was no longer in sight.

On 11 December Dill cabled from Washington that Marshall wanted to close down all operations in the Mediterranean once Tunis was taken, and to concentrate on Roundup and a move through Turkey. Brooke disagreed completely, and on 15 December presented the Prime Minister with a Chiefs of Staff paper rejecting all the arguments for a Western Front in 1943 in favour of a Mediterranean policy aimed at pushing Italy out of the war and bringing in Turkey.

Reluctantly, Churchill gave way to the arguments of his professional military advisers. After listening to their strong views, Churchill stated that he 'saw no alternative to the strategy recommended by the Chiefs of Staff'. But he soon changed his mind. He knew that Marshall and the Joint Chiefs of Staff in Washington would back a 1943 cross-Channel invasion, and he persevered in his efforts to make his own point of view prevail. One factor that weighed strongly with him was that Stalin had become much more friendly, and abandoning the second front in France in 1943 would surely create grave problems with Russia.

On 29 December Churchill, reinforced by news that Marshall and the Joint Chiefs of Staff in Washington were determined to concentrate on France in 1943, sent a note to the War Cabinet:

> Once we have cleared the North African shore several important enterprises open up in the Central Mediterranean, and the success of the Russian armies presents us with favourable opportunities in the near east. The question arises therefore whether combined and concurrent operations can be organized from the west and the south, and if the answer is in the affirmative which theatre should be considered the major or the minor.

The Chiefs of Staff replied: 'Our policy should be to exploit Torch as vigorously as possible and at the same time to build up Bolero [the cross-Channel project] to the greatest scale. This does not accord with the view of the US COS which is that we should go full ahead on Roundup and holding in North Africa.' They went on to say that knocking Italy out of the war and bringing in Turkey would afford earlier and greater relief to Russia than if the Allies were to concentrate on Bolero to the exclusion of all other operations, observing that at best a force of no more than three divisions could be put on the Continent in the late summer of 1943, while the Germans had twenty-four effective divisions in France.[18]

To his consternation, Brooke found that the Prime Minister was ignoring the decision agreed at the Defence Committee on 16 December, and at the Defence Committee on 29 December he had to argue with Churchill all over again the merits of the Mediterranean against France. Churchill was as obstinate as ever, but once again he was forced to give way to the professional expertise of his advisers and he finally agreed to priority for the Mediterranean. However, he insisted on the Americans being told that there would be 'the greatest possible concentration of forces in the United Kingdom with a view to re-entry on the Continent in August or September 1943, should conditions hold out a good prospect of success'.

Fortified by Churchill's agreement, on 31 December the Chiefs of Staff finalized their report on Anglo–American strategy, giving strong arguments why a cross-Channel invasion would not be advisable in 1943. This was the British brief for Casablanca, but Churchill, as ever, deviated from it several times in favour of Roundup – to the consternation of his advisers. The report reads:

> If we go in for the maximum Bolero with the intention of assaulting the Continent in 1943 we must be ready to strike by September. Thereafter weather conditions will

progressively deteriorate. The strongest Anglo–American force which we could assemble in the UK by that date for an attack upon Northern Europe would be some 13 British and 9 American Divisions with perhaps a further 3 American Divisions collecting in the UK. 6 Divisions are probably the maximum which could be organised for assault forces. Assembling the above forces would have the following effect. We should have to accept only a small increase in the scale of bomber offensives against Germany and Italy from now onwards. This would be due to giving a higher priority to passage of US soldiers across the Atlantic and to the need for bringing over a larger proportion of army support types of US aircraft. Too we should have to abandon all amphibious operations in the Mediterranean thereby giving Germany the opportunity she so desperately needs for rest and recuperation and Italy a chance to steady her morale.

Even if we accepted the above curtailment of our activities in other theatres we should probably find that the expedition we had prepared was inadequate to overcome the scale of German resistance existing when the time came for assault. The scale of the old Roundup was a total of 48 British and American divisions; since then the defences of the French coast and the German garrison in France have been increased to some 40 divisions. [This shows how North Africa had made a 1943 Roundup impossible.]

In short the adoption of this strategy would mean a relaxation of pressure on the Axis for 8 or 9 months with incalculable consequences to the Russian front and at the end of the period no certainty that the assault on France could be carried out; or even if it were carried out that it would draw any land forces from the Russian front. [Strong arguments.] While we follow the policy of bombing and amphibious operations in the Mediterranean our surplus resources can be devoted to the build up in UK . . . any decision to re-enter the Continent would have to allow three months for collection of landing craft.[19]

Armed with this brief, the CIGS and the other British Chiefs of Staff arrived in Casablanca on 12 January 1943 and immediately plunged into discussions with their US counterparts. They soon found that Roosevelt did not share Marshall's preference for Roundup. On 11 November 1942 he had asked Churchill for a survey of the possibilities of attacking Sardinia, Sicily, Italy, Greece and the rest of the Balkans, including obtaining Turkey's support for an attack through the Black Sea on Germany's flank. This inspired Churchill to plan attacking the 'soft underbelly' of the Axis.

However, the main worry of the British was that the Americans would decide to send the lion's share of their available forces to the Pacific, and make Mediterranean France a subsidiary theatre. The Americans for their part were suspicious that, once Germany was defeated, Britain would leave the Americans to continue the war against the Japanese with little help. Fortunately, by the time Churchill and Roosevelt arrived on 13 January these mutual suspicions had been removed, and the British were very glad to learn that America was going to give the defeat of Germany priority over that of Japan.

The state of play at the beginning of the Casablanca talks was that the British Chiefs of Staff were wholeheartedly in favour of more operations in the Mediterranean. Churchill, while giving lip service to this preference, could at any moment be blown off course in favour of the cross-Channel operation; he hoped against hope that both operations would be possible in 1943, although he was frequently warned by Brooke that it could not be. In Ian Jacob's words, Churchill 'was in agreement on a programme of operations which the military people thought beyond our powers, e.g. Sicily, Italy and Roundup all in 1943'.

The American Chiefs of Staff were almost unanimous in support of a cross-Channel invasion in 1943, but they could not carry the President with them. In addition, when the British Chiefs of Staff actually talked to Marshall they found his views were not quite as strong as they had feared, although he was to 'fight a strong rearguard action in defence' of Roundup in 1943 and was opposed to 'interminable operations' in the Mediterranean.[20]

At the first meeting of the Combined Chiefs of Staff, on 14 January, to Churchill's great relief Admiral King stated that the general division of resources should permit only 30 per cent to go to the Pacific. At the same meeting Brooke was able to convince the Americans that the British would not run out on them in the Pacific when Germany was defeated, and later Churchill offered even more binding assurances which completely removed American fears on that score. However, a note of contention remained because the Americans refused to give priority – especially in terms of naval resources – to the defeat of Germany before that of Japan, as Britain had hoped.

Churchill had to use all his powers of statesmanship to bring the Conference to a satisfactory conclusion from the British point of view. When he arrived he cabled to Attlee: 'Conditions most agreeable. I wish I could say the same of problems.'

Fortunately he triumphantly overcame these problems, and the Combined Chiefs of Staff agreed in a paper entitled *Memorandum on the Conduct of the War in 1943* that 'operations in Europe would be conducted with maximum forces which can be brought to bear', and in order to ensure that these operations 'are not prejudiced by the necessity to divert forces to retrieve an adverse situation elsewhere adequate forces shall be allocated to the Pacific; these operations must be kept within such limits as will not jeopardise the capacity to take advantage of any favourable opportunity that may present itself for the decisive defeat of Germany in 1943.' As the official historian has written: 'Important concessions were made to the British fear that the Americans in the Pacific were biting off more than they could chew.'[21]

This memorandum endorsed the British Chiefs of Staff's memorandum of 31 December, and when the Combined Chiefs of Staff met Roosevelt and Churchill on 18 January there was accord and harmony. They agreed to undertake the invasion of Sicily, codenamed Husky, as soon as the Germans were cleared out of North Africa, and recorded that this would make Roundup in 1943 impossible as the landing craft required for Husky could not be sent back to the United Kingdom in time. So the troops and equipment assembling in Britain were to be only an emergency force waiting for 'an opportunity target'.

At Casablanca Mountbatten, Chief of Combined Operations, argued for an invasion of Sardinia, codenamed Brimstone, in place of Sicily, on the grounds that it would be less costly, would leave resources over for operations in the eastern Aegean to encourage Turkey to enter the war, and might free resources for a landing from the sea in Burma (Operation Anakim). Churchill strongly opposed Mountbatten, feeling he could tell Stalin that Sicily was a substitute for the second front as it was part of Europe (ie. ½ mile from the mainland across the Straits of Messina), whereas the capture of an island, like Sardinia, far from the Italian coast, would be peripheral. Brimstone became his *bête noire.* On 17 January Churchill cabled to Attlee that 'the President is strongly in favour of the Mediterranean being in prime place. He also seems increasingly inclined to operation Husky instead of Brimstone. This is what I should like. Admiral King even went so far as to say that if it was decided to do Husky he would find the necessary escort.' [22]

Churchill's cable to Attlee for the War Cabinet on 20 January reveals that he was still hankering after operations both across the Channel and in the Mediterranean during 1943, and that Roosevelt felt similarly, regardless of the view of the professionals: 'Full preparation for Husky to go ahead . . . At home Bolero is to go ahead as fast as our commitments allow with a view to Sledgehammer of some sort this year or a return to the Continent with all available forces if Germans show definite signs of collapse. FDR and I were in complete agreement.'[23]

He reiterated this to Attlee on the 23rd: 'We have secured the priority of Mediterranean over Roundup without prejudice to the maximum development of Bolero'. And to Smuts, Prime Minister of South Africa, on 27 January he cabled: 'We have found it possible to plan a heavy attack across the Channel for the Autumn in order to engage as heavily as possible the German forces and wear down his air power.'

This was an exaggeration. The Joint Chiefs of Staff were prepared to consider limited operations such as an assault on the Channel Islands or other raids, or even 'seizing and holding' a footing in the Cherbourg peninsula, but the realistic assumption had been made that a large-scale invasion of France against the German opposition available there was out of the question. However, the Joint Chiefs of Staff emphasized that the strongest possible force should be assembled in Britain ready to re-enter the Continent in the event of a German collapse, and to Churchill's satisfaction the planning of a cross-Channel operation was entrusted to a British general, F. E. Morgan. Under him began the detailed planning for an attack either in 1943 or in 1944, which eventually resulted in the invasion of 6 June 1944 – Overlord.[24]

On the conclusion of the Casablanca Conference Roosevelt and Churchill sent a long joint statement to Stalin that 'Our immediate intention is to clear the Axis out of North Africa, and open an effective passage through the Mediterranean for military traffic', and to 'launch amphibious operations in the Mediterranean at the earliest possible moment'. With Roosevelt's permission, Churchill amplified this with 'we intend in July or earlier if possible to seize Sicily'. Stalin replied that 'the establishment of a second front in the West is envisaged only in August–September . . . it is extremely important to deliver the blow from the west in the spring or early summer [of 1943] and not to postpone it until the second half of the year'.[25]

Churchill made a second effort to propitiate Stalin, but it only brought the riposte: 'Fully realising the importance of Sicily I must however point out that it cannot replace the second front in France . . . I deem it my duty to warn you in the strongest possible manner how dangerous would be from the view point of our common cause further delay in the opening of the Second Front in France.'[26]

Churchill was apprehensive about the effect of the first message at the receiving end, cabling Attlee: 'Nothing in the world will be accepted by Stalin as an alternative to our placing 50 or 60 divisions in France by the Spring of this year. I think he will be disappointed and furious with this joint message. I thought it wise that the President and I should both stand together. After all our backs are broad.' Roosevelt, who had not met Stalin, did not share this anxiety, but, as will be seen, the consequences were catastrophic.[27] Stalin never again trusted America or Britain, and the fact that the Anglo–American assault came a year later than originally planned meant that all of eastern Europe passed under the Soviet yoke.

When the Conference ended Churchill invited Roosevelt to Marrakesh for a night's relaxation in a luxurious American-owned villa; he hoped there would be time then for a far-ranging, intimate discussion *à deux*. Roosevelt enjoyed the trip to Marrakesh, but evaded any long talk with Churchill.

The President did not want to talk politics to Churchill; they were too far apart over British colonialism, and he told his son Elliot that he looked on Churchill as an old-fashioned imperialist intent on regaining and holding all the pre-war British possessions and on reinstating the French in their colonies. Roosevelt made clear his outspoken hostility to the British and French Empires, saying to Elliot:

> Why does Morocco inhabited by Moroccans belong to France? Or take Indo-China . . . Why was it a cinch for the Japanese to control that land? The native Indo-Chinese have been so flagrantly downtrodden that they thought to themselves: Anything would be better than to live under French colonial rule . . . Don't think for a moment that Americans would be dying in the Pacific tonight if it hadn't been for the shortsighted greed of the French and the British and the Dutch . . . When we've won the war I will work with all my might and main to see to it that the United States is not wheedled into the position of accepting any plan that will further France's imperialistic ambitions or that will aid or abet the British Empire in its imperial ambitions.

Roosevelt's resentment against British colonialism was triggered when, *en route* for Casablanca, he had stopped off at Bathurst in the British colony of Gambia. There he had been appalled at the conditions of the natives; he thought they had a life expectancy of only twenty-six years and were treated worse than cattle, which lived longer. With such ideas seething in his mind it was just as well that Roosevelt did not have a heart-to-heart political talk with Churchill at Marrakesh. Yet on 26 January the President wrote a letter to the King of England which he showed to Churchill. It was a masterpiece of diplomacy, but not strictly accurate: 'As for Mr Churchill and myself I need not tell you that we make a perfect matched team in harness and out – and incidentally we had lots of fun together as we always do. Our studies and unanimous agreement must and will bear fruit.'[28]

At Casablanca Churchill was still pursuing his long-standing will-o'-the-wisp of bringing Turkey into the war on the Allied side. On 27 January he wrote to Smuts: 'I am off to Turkey where I have been most cordially invited by the Turkish President and his Government. My object will be to kit them up as well as possible with arms and to trust to the march of events to bring them in at the climax of the Mediterranean campaign.' On the same day he wrote to Attlee:

> I agreed with the President that while he took the lead in China and North Africa the British Government should play the hand with Turkey . . . I have no wish to press them into the war immediately. They must first be kitted up. But the time will come in the summer when they may feel able to take an even more forthright view than it is evident they are now adopting. You will see how vital it is to the whole of the Mediterranean combination that this additional weight should be thrown in when the climax is reached, and also how important that we should be able to plaster Ploesti [Romanian oilfields] with our bombs.

In London, Eden and Attlee did not share Churchill's optimism over Turkey. They had told Churchill that this Turkish proposal was open to 'several serious objections', and that the Turkish Ambassador in London had reported 'no change' in the Turkish attitude – 'we feel extremely doubtful if you would get anything substantial out of them. Our experience in 1941 was that a promise extracted in Cyprus was promptly gone back on in Angora [Ankara] . . . surely we should at least clear North Africa first.'

Attlee and Eden were right, and Churchill's mission was fruitless. He met the Turkish Prime Minister and his colleagues with a train near the Turkish frontier in Syria. The Turks, as frightened of the Russians as they were of the Germans, wanted arms from the Allies more to strengthen themselves against the former than to make attacks on the latter. In any case, with the Germans and Italians occupying Rhodes and the Dodecanese Islands, Smyrna could easily be blockaded by the Axis.[29]

Churchill made it clear to the Turks that if they wanted a place at the peace conference, and to have the full benefit of the system of security which 'we hoped to construct, they must not hesitate too long to enter the ranks of the victorious powers'. The Prime Minister was sure they saw the point of this. However, he realized their main preoccupation was Russia and he argued with them that this was the time to make a real effort to improve their relations with the Russians. Churchill even sent a message to Stalin: 'The Turks are apprehensive of their position after the war in view of the great strength of the Soviet. I told them that in my experience the USSR had never broken an engagement or treaty; that the time for them to make a good arrangement was now, and that the safest place for Turkey was to have a seat with the victors as a belligerent at the peace conference.'[30] To the Cabinet Churchill cabled: 'They would, I am sure, be very responsive to any gesture on part of the USSR . . . I have established very close personal relationship with Inonu [the Turkish Prime Minister].' Stalin made no purposeful response; nor did Inonu. As the War Cabinet had predicted, Churchill met a humiliating rebuff.

The year 1943 was to be one of conferences for Churchill. Casablanca was followed by a Washington conference, Trident, from 11 to 25 May. This Conference failed to solve the controversy raging between the American and British Chiefs of Staff as to whether or not the Italian mainland should be invaded after Sicily was taken. After Turkey Churchill had been out of action with pneumonia, while the commanders responsible for planning the invasion of Sicily were fully occupied with the capture of Tunis, which did not fall until 7 May, the day after Churchill sailed for America from the Clyde.

Trident is best described as a 'muddle'. The British Chiefs of Staff favoured invading Italy. The COS report of 10 May said: 'There will be a period of 9–10 months before we can launch offensive into Northern France . . . the first essential will be to make certain there will be no diminution of the threat to Germany's southern front . . . we must eliminate Italy which would give us great opportunities for exploitation.' They wanted a bridgehead in southern Italy, and preparations for exploitation across the Adriatic. They concluded that the Mediterranean offered opportunities for action in the coming autumn and winter at the same time as

> we prepare for a cross channel operation in 1944, and in fact the collapse of Italy if it were followed by an Allied landing in the Balkans and a [German] withdrawal to a line covering the Danube basin might have such repercussions in Hungary, Bulgaria and Roumania as to make it very difficult for Germany if still heavily committed in Russia to continue much longer.'[31]

Churchill became a reluctant convert to a Mediterranean strategy and no Roundup in 1943. John Grigg writes that Churchill was only converted by a process 'not far removed from a sleight of hand', because Brooke cunningly told him that after the landing craft required for a cross-Channel invasion had been used for Husky they would be required again for the Mediterranean after the initial landings to exploit the success, and could not be sent back to Britain.

Once converted, Churchill argued aggressively at Trident for Husky. When Eisenhower reported from Algiers that there would be little chance of success in Sicily 'if there were substantial well armed and fully organized German ground forces' of more than two divisions, Churchill demolished this argument with:

> If the presence of two German divisions is held to be decisive against any operation of an offensive or amphibious character open to the million men now in North Africa, it is difficult to see how the war can be carried on. I trust the Chiefs of Staff will not accept these pusillanimous and defeatist doctrines . . . What Stalin would think of this, when he has 185 German divisions on his front, I cannot imagine.[32]

Finally at Trident on 19 May the Combined Chiefs of Staff agreed that there should be further operations in the Mediterranean after Husky, although it was left vague what they should be. The target date for invading France was fixed as 1

May 1944, and in preparation by November 1943 seven divisions should be withdrawn from the Mediterranean for Overlord.

Churchill argued strenuously in Washington for ambitious operations in the Mediterranean against the 'soft underbelly' of the Axis, and wanted plans drawn up for attacks in the Balkans and a seaborne assault on Rhodes and the Axis-held islands in the eastern Aegean. But these did not appeal to the Americans, and it was decided that to solve the impasse Marshall should go with Churchill to Algiers to decide on the Mediterranean plans.

Marshall was anxious to curtail operations in the Mediterranean and to concentrate on Overlord which he believed must be the vital theatre. However, he decided not to argue incessantly with Churchill. As a result of the Marshall–Churchill visit to Algiers it was decided that the question of whether or not the conquest of Sicily was to be followed by an invasion of the mainland should be left to the *ad hoc* judgement of Eisenhower. When Churchill found that Eisenhower had scheduled his assault on Sicily for the end of July, he persuaded him to bring it forward to the 10th.

Eisenhower promised the Prime Minister that if Husky went well he would invade mainland Italy. Churchill told the American that 'my heart lies in the invasion of southern Italy but the fortune of battle might necessitate another course. The alternative between Sardinia and southern Italy involved the differences between a glorious battle and a mere convenience.'[33]

On 9 July a great armada sailed from Malta and North Africa to attack Sicily. There were more troops and ships in the Sicilian assault than in the initial Normandy landing in 1944. 115,000 British Empire and 66,000 American troops took part in the largest amphibious operation in history. The Italian Army had no heart for the battle, but fierce German opposition was encountered from fifty thousand German troops on the island, and it was thirty-eight days before Axis resistance ceased.

As the fighting in Sicily developed in the Allies' favour the seventy-six-year-old American Secretary of War, Henry Stimson, came to London. His talks with Churchill did not go well. Afterwards Stimson wrote that they went at it 'hammer and tongs'. Stimson charged Churchill with being opposed to Roundup. Churchill countered that, having pledged himself to it, he would go through with it loyally; but, perhaps unwisely, the Prime Minister talked of 'the channel being full of corpses of defeated allies'. Stimson formed the impression that Churchill was so keen on finding an easy way of ending the war without a trans-Channel assault that the USA must constantly be on the lookout against Mediterranean diversions which would make Roundup in early 1944 impossible. Stimson reported his views emphatically to both Marshall and Roosevelt.

Stimson flew on to Algiers, where he told Eisenhower that Churchill was 'obsessed with the idea of proving to history that invasion of the Continent by way of the Balkans was wise strategy and would repair whatever damage the misfortune at the Dardenelles had done to Churchill's reputation'; in addition he was apprehensive that the Prime Minister would try to avoid the commitment of the British and American Governments to invade France the following spring.

This put Eisenhower on the horns of a dilemma. He felt that if he did not exploit the victory in Sicily he would be accused of missing the boat, and he did not like the idea of his own Government slamming on the brakes just when the going was good. He had also already drafted a note for the Combined Chiefs of Staff saying, that as soon as Messina fell 'We proceed across the strait to the toe of Italy.' This acute division had to be resolved, and a top-level conference known as Quadrant, was called for mid-August in Quebec to produce an agreed plan of action.[34]

Suddenly everything changed. On 25 July King Victor Emmanuel III arrested Mussolini and replaced the Fascist Government by one led by Field Marshall Badoglio. Immediately it became clear that the new Italian Government wanted to break loose from Germany and make peace with the Allies. As Roosevelt and Churchill gathered on 7 August with their advisers in Quebec, the glittering prize of an unopposed landing in Italy lay before their eyes. It was a dramatic moment; instead of Churchill's Mediterranean strategy being abandoned, it seemed as if its fruits would soon be gathered.

CHAPTER SEVENTEEN

The Italians surrender, 1943

AFTER WAVELL had demolished Graziani's army in Libya in January 1941, Churchill was in favour of offering soft terms to Italian dissidents if they would topple Mussolini. Yet in the summer of 1943, when Italy was down and out, nothing but unconditional surrender was offered to anti-Fascists. Thus the heaven-sent opportunity for the Allies to land unopposed in Italy after the fall of Mussolini was lost.

At the final press conference at Casablanca on 24 January 1943 Roosevelt had announced that no terms would be offered to Germany, Japan or Italy, and nothing but 'unconditional surrender' accepted. Originally both Roosevelt and Churchill had wanted to exclude Italy, feeling wisely that the time had come to appeal to the Italian anti-Fascists, and that applying unconditional surrender to Italy would defeat their purpose. Accordingly Churchill cabled to London with the proposal that unconditional surrender should be demanded from Germany and Japan, but not from Italy: 'Omission of Italy would encourage break up [of tottering Fascist rule]. FDR likes idea.' But the War Cabinet cabled back the tough reply: 'Cabinet unanimous that Italy must be threatened with unconditional surrender. Knowledge of rough stuff coming to them should have desired effect on Italian morale.'[1]

Unconditional surrender in 1943 was in stark contrast with Churchill's attitude in 1940 and 1941 after he had received reports from the Foreign Office of sinking Italian morale, the desire of the people to get out of the war, and powerful anti-Fascist opposition. Then he initiated plans for raising a Free Italian Force to fight on the British side (the Garibaldi Legion); for the establishment of Cyrenaica as a 'free' Italian colony 'to be petted and made prosperous'; for cash bribes to Italian naval officers to induce them to sail their ships to Alexandria and surrender them; and for a search to be made for an Italian de Gaulle to lead an anti-Fascist Italian army outside Italy.

Churchill embarked on all this with deadly seriousness, yet he made no reference to it in his memoirs, neither have his official biographer nor the official historians. The plans became abortive and reflect little credit on either Churchill or his Foreign Secretary, Eden.

Shortly after Wavell's desert victory Lord Davies, the Conservative newspaper magnate and a close friend of Churchill's, wrote to Churchill suggesting that a

Free Italian Army called the Garibaldi Legion should be raised from Italian prisoners of war in Egypt, 'to fight fascism'. A copy was sent to Eden, who had recently become Foreign Secretary. Nicholls and Sargent in the Foreign Office approved the idea, and, fortified by their support, Eden sent a memorandum to the Prime Minister on 6 February 1941:

> Dalton's organisation [SOE, the underground organisation set up to sabotage and subvert the enemy] are with concurrence of the Service Departments preparing leaflets to be dropped on Italian Forces if there should be any sign later on that as a result of their dislike of the Germans numbers of the Italian forces are prepared to come over to us.
>
> In the leaflet addressed to *Italian sailors* it is proposed to say:
>
> His Britannic Majesty's Government solemnly pledges itself to give hospitality and protection to you and to your ships in the naval base of Alexandria. HBMG pledges itself further not to exert the slightest pressure to make you and your ships fight against Germany and Fascist tyranny. Complete freedom of choice will be left to you between taking up the fight against Germany and total abstention from conflict while putting your ships well out of reach of the rapacious German claws.
>
> The leaflet also states that in both cases Italian sailors (officers, petty officers and men) will receive the same treatment and the same pay as the Royal Navy.
>
> The proposed leaflet to *Italian airmen* urges them to join in the fight for the liberation of Europe from German tyranny and advises them if their machines run the risk of being captured by the Germans to fly them to a British air base.
>
> The leaflet further pledges HMG to give Italian airmen who do this the same treatment as that of the R.A.F.
>
> I have no doubt that the line suggested both to the Italian Fleet and Italian airmen is the right line. Do you approve? If you do, Dalton's organisation will get ahead with the preparation of the leaflets.[2]

Churchill enthusiastically minuted to the Chiefs of Staff on 11 February that not only did he agree to the raising of an anti-Mussolini army in Egypt, but that he wanted to establish Cyrenaica as a Free non-Fascist Italian colony, to be treated even better than the French colonies who had declared for de Gaulle:

> I see no reason why you should not consider raising an anti-Mussolini or Free Italian force in Cyrenaica. Volunteers might be called for from the 100,000 prisoners we have taken. There must be a great many who hate Fascism. We might even rule Cyrenaica under the Free Italian flag and treat it in the same way as de Gaulle's colonies are being treated subject to our military control. Anyhow, I wish Cyrenaica to be petted and made extremely comfortable and prosperous, more money being spent upon them than they are intrinsically worth. Can we not make this base a place for starting a real split in Italy and the source of anti-Mussolini propaganda? We might make it a model of British rule, hold it in trust for the Italian people and have 4,000 or 5,000 Italian troops sworn to the liberation of Italy from the Germans and Mussolini yoke. This could be run as world propaganda. The matter raises wide political considerations and I am sending a copy of this minute to the Foreign Secretary.

In response to this minute a committee of representatives from the Foreign Office, Admiralty, War Office, Air Ministry and SOE met two days later to 'consider the possibility of a Free Italian movement in Cyrenaica or other Italian colony'. Eden signified that he favoured a Free Italian Army, but he thought 'nailing the Italian flag to Cyrenaica required considerable thought'.

Sir Leonard Woolley, the archaeologist and leading expert on Egypt and the Arab world, was then working in the War Office. He produced devastating objections to Churchill's scheme, pointing out that an Italian Cyrenaica 'would lose us all sympathy from Arabs everywhere who would regard it as a betrayal of the local Arabs', and that Cyrenaica ought to be attached to Egypt which would satisfy both the Senussi [tribe] and the King of Egypt and his Government. But Woolley's opinion was ignored by the Committee, who endorsed the Prime Minister's initiative by concluding that a Free Italian Cyrenaica would make a voluntary surrender of the Italian Fleet easier, and that from the propaganda point of view the existence of a Free Italian colony would be excellent. However, they noted that such a development would be looked upon as a betrayal by the Arab population of Cyrenaica, who were extremely anti-Italian. It might therefore be better to set up the Free Italian colony in Eritrea, and in any case it would be difficult to provide the necessary imports to sustain Cyrenaica in view of the present supply position in the Mediterranean. The RAF and the Admiralty were lukewarm, and the War Office were not keen on the idea of the Free Italian Army. The War Cabinet approved the Report, which was printed and circulated, and on 7 March a cable was sent to Cairo to discover the response of Wavell and the British Ambassador to Egypt, Sir Miles Lampson (later Lord Killearn), who had an Italian wife:

1. His Majesty's Government have had under consideration the reaction of (a) a Free Italian colony in Cyrenaica: this colony to be run under the Free Italian flag and treated, *ceteris paribus*, as are Free French colonies, and (b) the raising of a Free Italian force from among Italian prisoners to be stationed in Cyrenaica.

2. Main advantage of this scheme would be that from point of view of propaganda the existence of a Free Italian colony would enable us to encourage Italians to hope that the future of their country is not necessarily tied up with Germany and Fascism. Secondly it might, if and when the time comes, facilitate the voluntary surrender of whole or part of Italian fleet, since Italians might find it easier to take their ships to what was still an Italian colony than to an enemy port. Italian fleet might in that case provide an Admiral as leader of the movement.

3. (a) Do you consider that a Free Italy movement could be created in Cyrenaica among the existing civil population? (to His Majesty's Ambassador only) Could the large Italian colony in Egypt supply any useful recruits including potential leaders? (to all) No leaders are available in this country.

(b) What are the chances of raising a Free Italian force amongst Italian prisoners of war? What numbers could safely be recruited? Could questioning of Italian prisoners be directed to this end?

(c) What are your views on the above from the purely military/naval/air points of view and from the standpoint of administration, supply and particularly security? In any event His Majesty's Government attach importance to both Italian and Arab population of Cyrenaica being made as comfortable and prosperous as possible under war conditions.

(d) What would be the reactions to these proposals among the Arabs of Cyrenaica, in Egypt, and in the Arab world in the Middle East generally?

4. Would you see any advantages in setting up a Free Italian movement in Eritrea?[3]

Shortly afterwards Eden arrived in Cairo. On 14 March, after discussing the Prime Minister's suggestions with Lampson, Wavell and Longmore, the Air Chief in the Middle East, he replied that the existing civilian population in Cyrenaica was not promising material because they had been selected as 'promising Fascist colonists'. Wavell felt strongly that as long as there was a danger of a counter-attack from Tripoli it would be dangerous to experiment with a Free Italian organization in Cyrenaica, and all were agreed that reactions amongst the Arabs of Cyrenaica, of Egypt and the Arab world generally would be 'unfavourable'.[4]

Churchill's enthusiasm for a prosperous Free Italian Cyrenaica soon became stillborn, and for the rest of 1941 the argument centred on whether the Egyptians or the Senussi should rule in Cyrenaica. In January 1942 Churchill agreed to a Commons statement that because of the help rendered by the Senussi against Britain's enemies, Cyrenaica would under no circumstances be placed under Italian rule, thus begging the question of rewarding Egypt with a slice of former Italian territory.

Wavell took Churchill's suggestion of a Free Italian Army seriously, and a search was made for an Italian de Gaulle. General Bergonzoli (called Electric Whiskers because of his enormous side-whiskers) was considered, until it was discovered he was a 'mountebank'. Freya Stark, the well known Arabist, in Cairo wrote a memorandum forecasting with strange optimism that 'two thirds of Italian prisoners were anti-fascist' and should be put under sympathetic Maltese guards. Eventually it was decided that no progress would be made with the Italian prisoners in Egypt, but that there might be a more favourable reception amongst those sent to India. Nothing materialized from the Indian efforts, and the plan for a Free Italian Army withered on the vine.[5]

In November 1940 the British Legation in Sweden was informed that anti-Fascist senior naval officers wanted to surrender the Italian Fleet to Britain to prevent it being turned over to the Germans, and would consider negotiating. Churchill was enthusiastic to begin discussions, and minuted that he wanted to take a personal interest; on 25 November the War Cabinet approved further contacts. In March 1941 the Legation reported that the Italian naval officers to whom they had spoken had indicated that surrender was impractical at the moment because it would be impossible to safeguard the families of the personnel involved, but the anti-Fascists nevertheless hoped that Britain would not exploit her victory 'vindictively when final Italian defeat comes, but rather concentrate upon saving Italy from German domination'.

After consultation between Churchill, Eden and the First Lord of the Admiralty, on 9 March a signal was sent to Stockholm:

Following message may be given to Swedish intermediary to pass on to his anti-fascist contacts: 'We re-affirm our previous offer that we shall gladly receive any units of the Italian Fleet that may come to us, and we will do our best to escort merchant ships with families.

'If a real effort is made by the Italian Fleet to avoid falling under German control and evidenced by the sending of important units to British overseas ports, this fact would undoubtedly weigh with us when considering terms of peace with Italy, and we should do our best to save Italy from German domination both before and after the final peace conference.'[6]

On 14 March a strange message came from the Stockholm Legation about the Italian Battle Fleet. A list was produced, showing prices varying from 15,000 dollars for a torpedo boat to 300,000 dollars for a battleship; there was also to be compensation for the families of the officers from the surrendering ships. Half these amounts were to be paid if the ships were sabotaged, and a deposit of 600,000 dollars was to be deposited in a United States bank. Victor Mallet, the British Minister in Stockholm, described the 'go-between', Walters, as having 'real guts and love of adventure', although he had told the Foreign Office in December that Walters was 'a man with the shadiest of reputations'.

Churchill wanted to accept, and minuted accordingly to the Admiralty. The reply was that the chances of success were small, but the necessary payments were so small compared to the prizes to be gained that the gamble appeared worthwhile. Mallet was told: 'While chances of the scheme succeeding appear slight, we accept it in principle'. On the signal Churchill scrawled: 'Admiralty. Foreign Office – This all seems fantastic. WSC. 20.3.' A further communication was received on 19 July, and the Foreign Office replied: 'Our side of the bargain still holds.'[7] Nothing more was heard, and how genuine the approach was remains an unsolved mystery. Sir Peter Tennant and Captain Harold Denham RN, who handled the matter in the Legation at Stockholm, both told the author that they are convinced the approach was genuine.

This incident is further evidence of how much more inclined Churchill was to a soft peace with a non-Fascist Italy in 1940 and 1941 than in 1943 when the King and Marshal Badoglio wanted to surrender. On Christmas Day 1940 Churchill had broadcast to the Italian nation that Mussolini alone was responsible for the war between two friendly countries, and he invited the people of Italy to overthrow the Duce. At that time overtures for peace from anti-Fascists would have been well received in London. In 1943 they met hostility.

Mussolini's overthrow took Churchill completely by surprise. It should not have done. The Italian Royal Family had made soundings in both Lisbon and Geneva, but were told that if the King deposed Mussolini Italy would only be offered unconditional surrender. Badoglio and Caviglia, two famous Italian generals of the First World War, sent messages through SOE in Berne that they had 'a powerful and influential following'; they wanted to seize power, set up a Military Government and form an anti-Fascist army from Italian prisoners of war in North Africa. On 18 January the Cabinet decided to make no response.

However, Cordell Hull had suggested that the American and British Foreign

Offices should define an agreed policy about the acceptability of Italian anti-Fascist personalities. Eden replied to Hull that there was no one in Italy who could overthrow Mussolini, and that the King was 'a docile servant of fascism', while the Fascist Party was still united and the moderate Fascists were impotent. Eden continued that it was useless to offer tempting peace terms to the Italian people because the minimum that would attract them would be a guarantee of their pre-war frontiers, and this was not possible because of the claims of Yugoslavia and (surprisingly) Austria. Roosevelt and Hull disagreed, but failed to soften the British line. Churchill, who did not favour Eden's hard line, did nothing to moderate his Foreign Secretary.[8]

However the War Office put pressure on Eden, and on 17 February 1943 Eden circulated to the War Cabinet a Memorandum about the Badoglio/Caviglia approach. The Italians had suggested that a well-known anti-Fascist, General Pesenti, should fly out as an emissary and be the focus for the anti-Fascist Italian Army. Eden would not give his consent and wrote:

> Our present line is to make no promises whatsoever but merely to offer Italians (through our propaganda) the alternatives of sinking or surviving. We do not promise them a suit of clothes or food. We hope that this tough line supplemented by heavy raids and the threat of invasion will suffice to frighten the Italians out of the war . . . The United States Government, however, are clearly anxious that some ray of hope should be held out to the Italians about their future, and I have just received from Hull a formula which I think should meet the case.
>
> We should hold out to the Italian people without making any specific or territorial commitments the hope that Italy as a nation will survive the defeat of the Fascist Government and that neither we nor our Allies have territorial ambitions with respect to such territory as is and always has been Italian.

Churchill was anxious for the Pesenti plan to be considered by the Cabinet as soon as possible, and squiggled on the memorandum: 'A Cabinet before you go.' But it was not considered for another twenty-eight days, when the War Cabinet approved the idea of General Pesenti being brought out of Italy. By now it was too late: the Fascists had blocked his escape route by arresting the pilot of the plane he was going to use.[9]

The remnants of the old democratic parties in Italy had formed an organization known as the Partito d'Azione. In May 1943 they contacted the Allies through SOE in Berne, and La Malfa, who became a leading Italian politician after the war, offered to go to London via Switzerland to learn what terms would be offered to an anti-Fascist democratic Government. When he was told that only unconditional surrender would be acceptable, he refused to go. Other peace moves came from right-wing anti-Fascists such as Alberto Pirelli and Adriano Olivetti of the famous industrial families. Again, they were told that nothing but unconditional surrender would do. Eden, more than Churchill, was responsible for nipping these promising peace overtures in the bud. Finally, a few days before his fall from power Mussolini made an eleventh-hour effort to rat on Hitler and sent Bastianini, his Under Secretary at the Foreign Office, to Lisbon with instructions to try and get to London to negotiate. While this was being considered in London Mussolini fell, and Bastianini no longer had any standing.[10]

Eden relied too much on reports from D'Arcy Osborne, the British Minister inside the Vatican. On 24 July 1943, the day before Mussolini was arrested, Osborne wrote: 'I do not expect any serious or successful movement from any quarter against the Fascist Government.' He was too closely cloistered in the Vatican. On 25 July Mussolini was deposed and Italian fascism was dead.

It was sad that there had been no previous contact with King Victor Emmanuel and Marshal Badoglio, because on 25 July there was only one German division in central Italy, and the British and Americans could have arrived fast by air and sea in Italy if a plan had been agreed in advance. But Hitler immediately poured troops into the country and made plans to occupy Rome and depose the new Government. However, on 27 July Churchill told the Commons: 'The only consequence of the Italian Government staying under the German yoke will be that in the next few months Italy will be seared and scarred and blackened from one end to the other . . . we should let the Italians, to use the homely phrase, "stew in their own juice" for a bit and hot up the fire to the utmost.'

This proved to Hitler that no immediate deal between the Badoglio government and the Allies was likely; it also spotlighted for the King and Badoglio the difficulties they would have in changing sides. Dino Grandi, former Ambassador in London, and a leading Fascist, who had engineered the overthrow of Mussolini, wanted an immediate switch so that the Italians could fight alongside the Allies, but Badoglio dilly-dallied in the vain hope that Italy might stay neutral for the remainder of the war.

In a Foreign Office memorandum, Gladwyn Jebb, now Lord Gladwyn, then an assistant Under Secretary, wrote that if the Government persisted in demanding unconditional surrender it would be difficult to obtain the 'purely military armistice' which was urgently required. He added: 'It is pretty evident that fascism is being liquidated and that the army plus the House of Savoy is making a desperate effort to put itself in a position in which it can obtain what it considers to be "reasonable terms of surrender" for Italy. But it is equally plain that neither the King nor the Army would consider "our own terms reasonable".' Cadogan commented: 'It is an awful prospect if it means that when the Italians ask for an armistice there is to be a telegraphic blitz between the Prime Minister, President and Ike, and Ike's Chiefs of Staff and Combined Chiefs of Staff, before we can send an answer.'[11]

Unfortunately this is what occurred, and the Allies threw away the prize which was theirs for the taking during the first fourteen of Badoglio's forty-five days of rule – the secession of the Italian Army, Fleet and Air Force intact, with the minimum interference from the Germans. Instead, the British and American Governments began a long haggle over the armistice terms – to the horror of Eisenhower, who had fixed 9 September for the invasion of Italy with a large seaborne landing at Salerno (Husky).

Approaches were soon made in Lisbon. On 4 August the Marchese d'Ajeta went there on behalf of Badoglio and saw Campbell, the British Ambassador.

Churchill received his report on board ship while *en route* to Quebec; it stated that the King's and Badoglio's first thought was to make peace, but they had 'no alternative but to make a show of going on with the fight'. Churchill sent the report to Roosevelt with the message: 'I send it to you for what it is worth, which is substantial. It certainly seems to give inside information.' But Eden minuted: 'My own strong feeling is that there is nothing in this approach.'

Simultaneously an Italian diplomat, Berio, arrived in Tangier with a message – not altogether true – that Italy was in the hands of the Germans and the Allies should land in the south of France or the Balkans to take the pressure off the Italians. Churchill's reaction was to tell Roosevelt:

> Badoglio must understand that we cannot negotiate but require unconditional surrender, which means the Italians should place themselves in the hands of the Allied Governments who will then state their terms. These will provide for an honourable capitulation. Badoglio's emissary should be reminded at the same time that the Prime Minister and the President have already stated that we desire in due course Italy should occupy a respected place in the new Europe.

Impishly Churchill added to the draft of their message to Roosevelt: 'It will at any rate make it easier for them to decide whom to double cross next.' But Churchill insisted that bombing of Italy must continue, although Roosevelt's emissary at the Vatican, Tittman, implored that it should be stopped or at least confined to purely military objectives.[12]

Roosevelt's reaction was not to Churchill's liking. Irrelevantly he suggested that Italy should concede territory to the Slovenes: 'Trieste, Fiume and Pola should constitute free outlets for all countries.' His idea was that these towns should have a territory 'say ten miles long and 15 miles deep, and that they should have an international administration under an Italian, a Yugoslav and perhaps an American or British'. The Prime Minister would not discuss this, saying it was a matter for a post-war peace conference.

Churchill, Eden and the Americans argued inconclusively over the terms of the surrender document which the Italians must sign, but were adamant that it must include 'unconditional surrender'. Eden wrote from London to Churchill in Quebec: 'I am sure we should insist expressly on unconditional surrender before we name our terms . . . any other course would inevitably involve us in long and tortuous negotiations.' Churchill replied: 'Do not miss the bus, and merely harping on unconditional surrender may mean no surrender at all.' This wise statement had no effect on the anti-Italian Eden, who wrote back: 'I quite understand your wish to sugar the pill for the Badoglio Government . . . I feel having stated so categorically in public that we insist on unconditional surrender we are bound to tell Badoglio's emissary this.'[13]

The Badoglio Government in Rome, terrified of the German military presence in Italy, now had no thought except to concert plans with the Allies to throw the Germans out; unfortunately discussion of a complicated surrender document prolonged the negotiations needlessly. Alexander, Eisenhower and Macmillan at Allied Force Headquarters in Algiers were driven frantic by the leisurely progress made by their Governments. Macmillan cabled to London that Eisenhower should be allowed to sign a document in an emergency which would take Italy out of the war overnight. But the Allies remained bogged down, haggling over the terms of the armistice.[14]

Desperate at the time being lost while the Germans strengthened their grip on Italy, Badoglio sent a third emissary to Lisbon – General Castellano. At last negotiations began in earnest, but it was not until 4 September, five days before the Salerno landings were due, that a short armistice imposing unconditional surrender was signed at Casabile in Sicily. Badoglio and Eisenhower agreed to announce the armistice simultaneously on 8 September, and an American airborne division was to land on the Rome airfields that night. The Italians had sufficient armour and troops around Rome to defend these aerodromes but the commander, General Carboni, panicked at the last moment and persuaded Badoglio to call off the air landings.

In the nick of time, after attempts to get out of it, Badoglio announced the Cassibile armistice on 8 September a few hours before the landings began at Salerno. This was fortunate, as otherwise Italian submarines might have played havoc with the Allied invasion fleet. It was a tragedy for Italy that the proposed airborne invasion did not take place, because if the Italian Army had emerged from being an enemy fighting side by side with the Americans successfully against the Germans, her post-armistice treatment would have been much more favourable. In a draft for the official history Miss J. Hamilton of the Cabinet Office historical section, with access to all the official documents, wrote: 'The two German divisions near Rome were tied up by seven Italian divisions including two armoured, and reinforcements could never have reached them either from the north or the south. Rome would have fallen into Allied hands and the German troops would soon have had to give up their positions in the Alban Hills which controlled the two roads to Naples.'[15] She is correct. Strangely the official histories ignored Miss Hamilton's percipient comment and give the impression that the planned airborne operation, known as Giant Two, was ill conceived. At the time Churchill gave a misleading account in the Commons, saying the airfields around Rome were already occupied by the Germans so that the air landing was impossible.

Giant Two was a perfectly good military operation, but it depended on the Italian generals being enthusiastic about changing sides. Instead the Italian War Office ignored the detailed plans made by the Americans to facilitate the landings and no firm orders came from the Government. The King and Badoglio threw away the splendid chance generously given to Italy by Eisenhower to make a glorious exit from the Axis and throw away her Fascist past. Instead the Italian Army, without orders, melted away: the soldiers making their way home on foot, or by bicycle, train or tram, while the Germans behaved with extreme brutality to those who were trapped by them.

Yet the Italian Fleet sailed in perfect order to Malta. After the war General Bedell Smith, Chief of Staff to Eisenhower, and his German opposite number, General Westphal, wrote that in their view the Germans would have been forced to evacuate southern and central Italy in a hurry if the air landing had taken place. The Italian General Castellano, who was closely involved in the planning, is even more emphatic that it would have been a resounding success. The US official history comes to the same conclusion.[16]

The Italian armour around Rome held the Germans, but the cowardly Badoglio persuaded the King to flee from Rome in the early hours of 9 September and the Italian divisions around the capital, left leaderless, stopped fighting. The Germans at Salerno, instead of being cut off, were able to hold the invaders, so that the Allied Fifth US Army and the British Eighth Army could only crawl up the Italian peninsula and Rome was not taken until June 1944. The opportunity for a quick victory had been frittered away. Churchill's plan had been to knock Italy quickly out of the war and then clear the decks for the Balkans and the 1944 cross-Channel invasion of France. Instead, up to thirty divisions were pinned down in Italy until the end of the war, so that they were not available for the second front; in addition immense demands were made on Allied shipping. Churchill had prevailed over an Italian campaign, but he could not win the war there.

CHAPTER EIGHTEEN

Eastern Aegean frustrations

CHURCHILL WAS agog to exploit the Italian surrender by pushing the Germans out of Rhodes and the Dodecanese Islands so that the sea route through the Dardanelles to Russia could be opened. He was longing to erase from history the memory of his failure at Gallipoli in the First World War. His hopes might have been realized if the Italian army in the Aegean had shown more guts and loyalty to their King. Alas, they did not. In addition, the Americans did not share Churchill's enthusiasm for the eastern Aegean.

One glance at the map shows that Rhodes is the key to the Dardanelles. Churchill also had great hopes that if Rhodes became an Allied base Turkey might declare war on Germany. Months before the Italian surrender GHQ Middle East under General Wilson had worked out a plan to assault Rhodes, codenamed Accolade. D-Day was fixed for 1 September; 8th Indian Division and other picked troops had been trained for it. Unfortunately Eisenhower at Allied Forces Headquarters (AFHQ) was in command in the Mediterranean, and all the resources were in his hands. Churchill could not give him orders, and before the unexpected Italian collapse Eisenhower ordered most of the specialized assault shipping away from the Mediterranean and either to the Far East or back to Europe for the far off invasion of France. For this reason Churchill's longed for assault on Rhodes was aborted, and after the surprise Italian surrender it could not be reinstated at short notice.

On the day after the overthrow of Mussolini, at Churchill's instigation the British Chiefs of Staff urged the Americans to put a 'standstill' order on all landing craft and assault shipping in the Mediterranean which were scheduled to leave for other theatres of war; not to do so, they said, 'would be a profound mistake since Italy was in measurable distance of collapse'. Washington objected strongly on the grounds that this was a breach of the Trident agreement and said the USA would not propose operations in the Mediterranean requiring 'additional resources'. This controversy produced what the official historian calls an Anglo–American 'storm'; it evaporated when it was reported to the Quadrant Conference at Quebec that a reassessment showed Eisenhower had more landing craft than he could use for Husky, and the 'standstill' order was revoked on 19 August. But Churchill soon regretted his agreement to abandon the 'standstill' order.[1]

When Wilson asked Eisenhower to spare him for Accolade four squadrons of fighter aircraft together with transport aircraft for one parachute battalion group, Eisenhower said this could not be provided without damaging the prospects for the invasion of Italy. He cabled to London on 12 August that 'he viewed with considerable alarm the prospect that Accolade would draw upon reserves urgently required for the main business of knocking Italy out of the war; instead he wanted to concentrate on one thing at a time and abandon Accolade for the time being'. Churchill was very conscious that in the Middle East Command Wilson had over half a million men, half of whom were fighting troops, but unfortunately when the surrender of Italy came on 8 September shipping and landing craft were in such short supply in Middle East Command that Wilson was only capable of mounting small-scale landings if opposition was going to be encountered.[2] A co-belligerent Turkey could have provided the air landing grounds and ships needed, but despite all Churchill's hopes she was far from coming into the war – although she was prepared to give the Allies help towards taking the Dodecanese Islands.

Two days after Mussolini's fall Churchill minuted: 'I hope that the planners are all keyed up with plans for taking Rhodes on the assumption that the Italians ask for an armistice.' And on 2 August he minuted again:

Here is a business of great consequence to be thrust forward by every means. Should the Italians in Crete and Rhodes resist the Germans and a deadlock ensue we must help the Italians at the earliest moment engaging thereby also the support of the population.

The Middle East should be informed today that all supplies to Turkey may be stopped for the emergency and that they should prepare expeditionary forces not necessarily in divisional formations to profit by the chances that may offer.

There is no time for conventional establishments but rather for using whatever fighting elements there are. Can anything be done to find at least a modicum of assault shipping without compromising the main operation against Italy? It does not follow that troops can be landed from armoured landing craft. Surely provided they are to be helped by friends on shore a different situation arises. Surely caiques, ships and boats can be used between ship and shore.

I hope the staffs will be able to stimulate action which may gain immense prizes at little cost though not at little risk.

Churchill was delighted when Wilson proposed a fresh Accolade with one infantry division, two armoured regiments and a parachute battalion. Eisenhower did not help, because on top of his refusal to allow more sea and air transport he insisted he must have 8th Indian Division for Italy, although Wilson had been counting on them for Rhodes. As a result the new Accolade needed six weeks of preparation before it could be mounted.

Churchill was disappointed when he was told that after an Italian armistice any enterprise other than a 'walk in' against Crete or Rhodes, or small-scale opposed raids, was impossible unless Eisenhower would provide more resources.[3] As a result, when the Italians surrendered on 8 September no force could be landed on Rhodes. All that could be done was to parachute in at dawn on 9 September a

Major Doleby with a message from Wilson to the Italian Governor, Admiral Inigo Campioni, that if the Italians could round up the Germans he would be able to send an infantry brigade and tanks on the 15th.

Campioni immediately agreed to fight the Germans, who numbered only 6000 against 37,000 Italians, but he reported to the British that he could not continue a prolonged battle unless the British attacked the island from the south immediately. By a trick General Scaroina, commander of the 13,000-strong Regina Division, and his headquarters were captured on 9 September, and although the remaining Italian units under General Forgiero, the overall local army commander, fought on they were for some reason 'without orders'. During the afternoon of 10 September the Germans parleyed with Campioni, threatening to kill Scaroina and 3000 Italian soldiers whom they had captured. In addition they threatened indiscriminate air bombardment of the towns, and as they had captured the main airfield of Maritza on the first day this would have been an inhuman slaughter. So Scaroina sent a note to Campioni advising an armistice. By 17.00 on 10 September, knowing no British help would come until 15 September, Campioni had agreed that the Italian soldiers would lay down their arms and leave the Germans in military control of the island under their General Kleeman while he, Campioni, remained the civil Governor. It was desperately unlucky that on Rhodes Campioni, Forgiero and Scaroina should have proved to be men of straw. Surprisingly, both Campioni and Scaroina were given gold medals by the Royal Italian Government, and Campioni was executed after being tried by a Fascist tribunal a year later for his part in organizing the resistance. Many Italian soldiers disapproved of the armistice and escaped to Cos and Leros.[4]

Wilson's message after the Rhodes capitulation was galling for Winston:

> We got a mission there . . . and the Italian Commander Campioni seemed ready to co-operate 48 hours later. However he threw in his hand and made a pact with the German commander in the island although there are 35,000 Italians to 7,000 Germans. It was a great pity that we were ordered to send to India the ships which we had asked to be allowed to hold for an assault loaded brigade. If we could have pushed this brigade into Rhodes on the day after the armistice was signed I think we could have seized and held the island.[5]

This shows the folly of the Allies not trying to concert military plans with the Italians during the six weeks between the fall of Mussolini and the armistice; then Rhodes could have been saved.

Meanwhile Churchill issued a war cry to Wilson: 'Kick spur and practice.' Fortunately on Cos, Leros, Samnos and some smaller islands the Italians had obeyed the armistice terms, and Wilson immediately reinforced them with British troops. Cos was the most important because it had a major aerodrome and was close to Rhodes. On 21 September Wilson reported that his plans to assault Rhodes before the end of October with 10th Indian Division and 9th Armoured Brigade were ready. D-Day was fixed for 23 October. On 4 October strong German forces attacked Cos. Without the possession of the Cos airfield, Accolade would be doubly difficult. Churchill sent a frenzied signal to the defenders of Cos as soon as he learnt of the attack; this shows his intense concern about Rhodes – it is unusual for a Prime Minister to write to a battalion commander.

Following for Lieutenant-Colonel Kirby or O.C. Cos. Personal from the Prime Minister:
We rely on you to defend this island to the utmost limit. Every measure is being taken to help you. Tell your men the eyes of the world are upon them. Tell the Italians that a terrible fate will befall them if they fall into the hands of the Hun. They will be shot in large numbers, including especially the officers, and the rest taken not as prisoners of war, but as labour slaves to Germany. If they strike hard for freedom and for the United Nations, they will be sent home to Italy at the first opportunity.

To Tedder, who commanded the RAF in Cairo, he signalled: 'The Prime Minister to Air Chief Marshal Tedder. Cos is highly important and a reverse there would be most vexatious. I am sure I can rely upon you to turn on all your heat from every quarter, especially during this lull in Italy.' And more mildly to Eisenhower: 'We are much concerned about Cos, and are sure you will do all in your power to prevent a vexatious injury to future plans occurring through the loss of Cos.'[6]

After twenty-four hours' fighting the British and Italians on Cos surrendered with the loss of three fine British infantry battalions. Churchill's plans to open the Dardanelles were thwarted. On 7 October, ignoring his previous snub, he tried again to persuade the American President to divert forces from Italy for the capture of Rhodes, and even to divert landing craft and assault ships from Overlord. After receiving a plea from Wilson for more shipping for his tanks, 'plus an extra brigade from central Mediterranean to arrive night of D-Day plus 1 would greatly accelerate completion of operation [assault on Rhodes]', Churchill wrote to Roosevelt:

1. I am much concerned about the situation developing in the Eastern Mediterranean.
2. It may, indeed, not be possible to conduct a successful Italian campaign, ignoring what happens in the Aegean. The Germans evidently attach the utmost importance to this Eastern sphere and have not hesitated to divert a large part of their straitened air force to maintain themselves there. They have to apprehend desertion by Hungary and Roumania and a violent schism in Bulgaria. At any moment Turkey may lean her weight against them. We can all see how adverse to the enemy are the conditions in Greece and Yugoslavia. When we remember what brilliant results have followed from the political reactions in Italy induced by our military efforts, should we not be short sighted to ignore the possibility of a similar and even greater landslide in some or all of the countries I have mentioned? If we were able to provoke such reactions and profit by them our joint task in Italy would be greatly lightened.
3. What I ask for is the capture of Rhodes and the other islands of the Dodecanese. The movement northward of our Middle Eastern Air Forces and their establishment in these islands, and possibly on the Turkish shore, which last might well be obtained, would force a diversion on the enemy far greater than that

required of us. It would also offer the opportunity of engaging the enemy's waning air power and wearing it down in a new region. This air power is all one, and the more continually it can be fought the better.

4. Rhodes is the key to all this. I do not feel the present plan of taking it is good enough. It will require and is worth at least up to a first-class division, which can, of course, be replaced by static troops once the place is ours. Leros, which for the moment we hold so precariously, is an important naval fortress, and once we are ensconced in this area air and light naval forces would have a most fruitful part to play. The policy should certainly not be pursued unless done with vigour and celerity requiring the best troops and adequate means. In this way the diversion from the main theatre would only be temporary, while the results may well be of profound and lasting importance.

He concluded that withdrawing landing craft and assault ships for one division from the build-up of Overlord without altering the zero date 'would be well worth while'. This produced an almighty snub for Churchill from Roosevelt, who replied on the same day:

I do not want to force on Eisenhower diversions which limit the prospects for the early successful development of the Italian operations to a secure line north of Rome. I am opposed to any diversion which will in Eisenhower's opinion jeopardize the security of his current situation in Italy, the build-up of which is exceedingly slow, considering the well-known characteristic of his opponent, who enjoys a marked superiority in ground troops and Panzer divisions.

It is my opinion that no diversion of forces or equipment should prejudice 'Overlord' as planned. The American Chiefs of Staff agree. I am transmitting a copy of this message to Eisenhower.[7]

Churchill was now in a state of acute tension over Rhodes. Brooke wrote in his diary:

I can control him no more. He has worked himself into a frenzy of excitement over the Rhodes attack, has magnified its importance so that he can no longer see anything else and has set his heart on capturing this one island even at the expense of endangering his relations with the President and the Americans and the future of the Italian campaign . . . He is placing himself quite unnecessarily in a false position. The Americans are already desperately suspicious of him and this will make matters worse.[8]

Churchill was angry, and the next day he fired back two more pleas to the President. The first stated that failure to take Rhodes would constitute a cardinal mistake in strategy and that there was plenty of time to 'produce a diversion for the conquest of Rhodes and restore it to the battle front for Italy before we reach the German fortified line'. The second informed Roosevelt that 'the Middle East was stripped bare at the moment when great prizes could be cheaply secured'. Churchill also proposed that he should go to Tunis and meet Marshall there on 10 October, with the aim of seeing if round the table together they could fit in the Rhodes operation without detriment 'to the advance in Italy'.

This produced another immediate resounding snub, showing how America was now the senior partner, providing much greater forces and resources for the war against both Japan and Germany. Roosevelt reiterated that there should be no diversion of force from Italy that would jeopardize the security of the Allied armies there, and that no action towards a minor objective should be allowed to prejudice the success of Overlord.

As for Churchill's proposed attendance at a conference with the commanders in Tunis, he dismissed this out of hand with 'I cannot participate. Frankly I am not in sympathy with this procedure under the circumstances.' Churchill now could not go to Tunis, but immediately on receiving Roosevelt's message he fired off a signal to Wilson:

> You should press most strongly at the Conference for further support for 'Accolade'. I do not believe the forces at present assigned to it are sufficient, and if you are left to take a setback it would be bad. It is clear that the key to the strategic situation in the next month in the Mediterranean is expressed in the two words 'Storm Rhodes'. Do not therefore undertake this on the cheap. Demand what is necessary and consult with Alexander. I am doing all I can.[9]

According to General Ismay, 'the very word Balkan' was anathema to the Americans, and they were determined not to allow Churchill's enthusiasm for the Aegean to 'lead to our getting seriously involved in that part of the world and to a further postponement of Overlord.' During the Conference Eisenhower brushed aside the British commander's arguments, but the British were lukewarm in their support of the Prime Minister.[10]

The conference of commanders agreed that resources in the Mediterranean were not large enough to undertake Accolade: 'we must choose between Rhodes and Rome. To us it is clear we must concentrate on Italian campaign. We recommend Accolade be postponed until weather and air conditions make the operation a reasonable undertaking. Suggest examine the situation after capture of Rome.' Alexander told Churchill: 'We left no stone unturned to meet your wishes and I am only sorry and disappointed we could not find the way.'

Bitterly disappointed, Churchill accepted the decision. In his memoirs he wrote that 'it was one of the sharpest pangs I suffered in the war . . . When so many grave issues were pending I could not risk any jar in my personal relations with the President.' The episode represented a head-on collision between Churchill and Roosevelt, who backed Eisenhower and Marshall to the hilt.[11]

Churchill's reply on 9 October to Roosevelt's second snub shows his intense displeasure; also that he did not accept the decision with as good grace as he implies in his memoirs:

> At your wish I have cancelled my journey [to the Tunis Conference] . . . I am afraid however [that your message to Eisenhower] will be taken as an order from you and as closing the subject finally. This I would find very hard to accept. I hope therefore that you will make it clear that the Conference is free to examine the whole question in all its bearings. I ask that the Conference shall give full free patient and unprejudiced consideration to the whole question after they have heard the Middle East point of view . . . Cancellation [of Accolade] will involve loss of Leros . . . and the complete abandonment by us of any foothold in the Aegean which will become a

frozen area with most unfortunate political and psychological reactions in that part of the world instead of great advantages.[12]

Churchill had found himself impotent to influence Eisenhower's decision, but Wilson and his commanders in Cairo operated a purely British headquarters; thus they were subject 100 per cent to Churchill in his role as Minister of Defence. Shocked by the unwelcome news of the fall of Cos, he sent to Cairo a peremptory questionnaire which amounted to castigation, as he had done with Wavell and Auchinleck after their desert reverses:

1. I do not understand why you have not reported the measures you are taking to rescue and support the garrison of Cos which is fighting in the hills. No explanation has been furnished us why a seaborne attack by seven transports escorted by only three destroyers encountered no opposition and was not effectively attacked when unloading or when returning either from the air or from the sea. Did you foresee the possibility of a seaborne attack? If so, it was surely the Naval Conmander-in-Chief's responsibility to point out that all his naval forces were dispersed in which case other arrangements could have been made.

2. What are you going to do now to resist the attack on Leros and Samnos to which you refer as likely? Strong reinforcements in cruisers and destroyers have now been sent you. With such forces at your disposal do you consider another seaborne attack on these islands possible observing the enemy have only three destroyers? How is it that none of our submarines was able to attack the seven transports all the hours they were lying off Cos? Why did the Hunts [destroyers] not attack?

3. You report that the troops on Cos have no artillery and no mortars. They have been in occupation for nearly ten days and you should explain the condition of their equipment. Is it possible that the Durham Light Infantry Battalion did not even have its unit equipment in mortars?

4. On all the above you should report immediately after consulting with your naval and air colleagues, realising that you three are the responsible authorities conducting these operations and that you are answerable for their success and for the early reporting of deficiencies. It is quite right to run risks in the conditions prevailing but foresight and energy are all the more required in such circumstances. The loss of these islands and the garrisons you have put into them will constitute a most vexatious miscarriage for which the fullest explanations will be required.

Churchill minuted to the Chiefs of Staff:

3. The question, however, arises, was this possibility foreseen in any way by the Middle East Commanders-in-Chief or by Admiral John Cunningham. We certainly were not aware that the enemy possessed any effective naval forces in these waters. We have a right to expect a reasonable measure of care in the execution of plans by the authorities on the spot. They are responsible for the proper conduct of the operation. If they needed help they should have asked for it and not allowed a situation to arise where absolutely nothing was available except the two submarines on patrol.

4. There seems also to be an inhibition on the part of the Admiral to allow the four Hunts he has to attack the transports for fear of the enemy's air power. The question arises whether these vessels are capable of defending themselves to a very large extent if working as a flotilla, and whether in the circumstances they should

not have attacked on the night of 3rd/4th October. There seems to be a certain air of feebleness and helplessness . . .

5. More precise questions arise in regard to the military force. Why are we told, for instance, that it had no mortars? Surely mortars are an integral part of every *company's* equipment. Ten days were available for the build-up, during which time ordinary ships could enter the harbour. There was plenty of time to land a few anti-tank guns, and it is not seen why the island could not have been reinforced and preparations made to defend it effectively.

6. All the above should be considered by the Chiefs of Staff. These minor operations must not be neglected by those in charge of them. Everything must now be done to retrieve the position. The possession of Cos is essential to the attack on Rhodes. It is to be considered whether the force assembling for Rhodes should not be used to retake Cos and capture the Germans who have landed there, other forces being gathered for Rhodes later on . . . The comparative pause in the operations in Italy and the need for the build-up of General Montgomery's tail give a certain breathing space in which a great effort should be made to tidy things up in the Dodecanese.[13]

This criticism prompted Wilson, against his better judgement, to defend Leros, Samnos and Castelrizo, although Churchill's suggestion that Cos should be recaptured was not taken seriously either by the Chiefs of Staff in London or in Cairo. Churchill was delighted at the decision to keep a toehold in the Aegean, and he cabled to Wilson: 'Cling on if you possibly can. It will be a splendid achievement.' However, Wilson had stated that although the holding of Leros and Samnos was not impossible, their maintenance was going to be difficult and would depend on Turkish co-operation. Churchill was to be disappointed again.[14]

The Turks were giving valuable help, allowing British warships to sail through their territorial waters and carrying supplies in Turkish ships to Leros and Samnos. But British naval shipping losses were heavy because of the German air superiority. Between 9 September and the end of October five destroyers and two submarines were sunk, in addition to four cruisers and two destroyers damaged. Such losses were unacceptable, and the prolonged defence of the islands in the northern Dodecanese depended on more help from the Turks, who met Eden and Allied representatives in Cairo on 5 November. The British asked for six squadrons of fighters to be allowed to operate from south-west Anatolia immediately. Eden argued that with Turkish help the Dardanelles could be open for convoys to Russia, and stressed the advantages for Turkey of being on the winning side. But the Turks feared German reprisals: they said the Luftwaffe would attack Istanbul, 'which would burn like matchwood', and that the German divisions held in reserve in Bulgaria would attack them. The Turks demanded forty RAF squadrons and thirty AA batteries in Turkey before they would consider declaring war. This was impossible. If Rhodes had fallen there was an outside chance of Turkey joining in the war; without Rhodes there was none.[15]

Without Turkish air bases Leros proved, as Wilson had forecast, 'indefensible'. The British had sent in three infantry battalions and had strong artillery support from the Italian garrison. After four thousand German troops landed on

11 November German control of the air enabled them to bomb the island continuously, and to drop parachute troops. Leros surrendered on 17 November, and the other islands were evacuated. The three infantry battalions on Leros became POWs.

Although the Italians on Leros were loyal to the armistice terms, they did not give the military help needed to save the island. Wilson informed Churchill on 30 October that the Italians were co-operating only halfheartedly, and statements by Badoglio were not enough. The Italian commander on Leros, Mascherpa, never left his dugout and had no grip on the situation; while most of his naval and military staff were unreliable, so that it was essential he was relieved by someone with 'more spunk', and 'he must place himself and his staff under our command.' The Italian Government in Brindisi ordered Mascherpa to place himself completely under British command and sent in picked Italian officers, but to no avail.

Churchill did not criticize Wilson over the fall of Leros, cabling instead: 'I approve your conduct of operations there. Like you, I feel this is a serious loss, and like you I have been feeling fighting with my hands tied behind my back. I hope to have better arrangements made.' Churchill's 'better arrangements' were that combined British and Russian pressure might bring Turkey into the war. Once again this was a will-o'-the-wisp.[16]

Churchill, Roosevelt and Stalin arranged to meet at Teheran on 28 November after a preliminary Roosevelt–Churchill conference in Cairo on 21 November. This was the fourth top-level conference of 1943.

In Cairo the Prime Minister pleaded with Roosevelt that 68 landing craft, intended to depart on 15 December for Overlord, should remain in the Mediterranean, and that Wilson should be given the modest help he needed to capture Rhodes. The Americans were up in arms at once. Ismay recorded that they were 'haunted by the ghost of Gallipoli' and feared that Churchill, instead of backing Overlord to the hilt, wanted to get a footing in what they regarded as 'his favourite hunting grounds, the Balkans. The Americans firmly ruled operations in the Aegean must be fitted in without any detriment to other operations.' Ismay commented: 'that ruled them out altogether'. The Americans had valid reasons for their suspicions. Brooke wrote in his diary *en route* from Cairo to Teheran: 'He [Churchill] is inclined to say to the Americans, "Alright, if you won't play with us in the Mediterranean we won't play with you in the English Channel."'[17]

When the Big Three met at Teheran, unfortunately Churchill had a nasty, feverish cold and lost his voice. But this did not prevent him taking a full share in the discussions. Churchill told the Conference that the very large Anglo–American forces in the Mediterranean must not stay idle during the six months before Overlord began. He wanted them to advance to the Pisa–Rimini line in Italy, and to hold it with minimum forces while using their surplus troops to land either in the south of France or Istria in the northern Adriatic and advance to Vienna through the Ljubljana Gap. Churchill insisted that the immediate subsidiary objective should be to persuade Turkey to enter the war, to seize the Aegean islands and to open the Dardanelles for convoys to Russia.

Stalin did not agree. He was sure Turkey would not come into the war and did not much mind if they did not; he attached minor importance to opening the Dardanelles, pointing out that the last Arctic convoy had got through unscathed, while the capture of Rome and northern Italy was desirable but not of great importance. Instead Stalin wanted Overlord to go ahead at the earliest possible moment, supported by as large an operation as possible in the south of France, compared to which taking Rome was 'a mere diversion'. The Russian leader was keen to keep the Allies out of the Balkans and would not give any post-war promise to Turkey about the future of the Dardanelles.

At Teheran agreement was reached that Overlord should take place in May 1944 and be accompanied by a new Russian offensive. Roosevelt agreed with Churchill that there were merits in landings both in the south of France and in Istria. These proposed operations were to become the subject of acute division between the Americans and Churchill later.

At Teheran the Big Three discussed the future of Poland. Churchill started it up by saying that 'personally he thought Poland might move westwards . . . If Poland trod on some toes, that could not be helped, and he hoped the three of them could form some sort of policy which they could press upon the Poles after discussing it without the Poles present.' Eden said what Poland lost in the east she might gain in the west.[18]

At the second meeting about Poland Stalin declared that the Polish Government in exile was in contact with the Germans and killing partisans (Communists). This was untrue. Eden undiplomatically referred to the Curzon Line as the Molotov–Ribbentrop Line after Stalin had said that after the war he wanted to return to the 1939 frontiers. A strange discussion followed, in which Churchill said the Poles would be 'fools' if they did not accept the Curzon Line, with Lwow also going to the Russians and parts of Germany ceded to Poland. Churchill's words were: 'I am not going to make a great squawk about Lwow.' At a further meeting Churchill said 'nothing would satisfy the Poles', but he might be able to get a formula for Stalin which gave him Polish territory up to the Curzon Line with Poland receiving East Prussia, Oppeln and German territory up to the Oder–Neisse Line. Stalin said he would agree to the Prime Minister's formula provided the Russians got the warm water port of Königsberg, which 'would put Russia on the neck of Germany'.[19]

The Curzon Line was the armistice line suggested in July 1920 by the then British Foreign Secretary, Lord Curzon, when the Soviet Union was fighting the newly created Polish Republic. In August 1920 the Poles unexpectedly threw back the Bolsheviks in a series of brilliant attacks and occupied large tracts of former Tsarist territory. By the Treaty of Riga in 1922 much of the Russian territory occupied by the victorious Polish Army was ceded to Poland. However in 1939, when the Russians invaded Poland after her crushing defeat by Hitler's armies, under a secret clause of the Molotov–Ribbentrop Agreement the Curzon Line, with minor alterations, became the Russian western frontier.

Thus at Teheran Churchill sacrificed the hard-won Polish victory of 1920 and betrayed the ally for whom Britain had gone to war. War is the art of the possible, but in negotiations with a thug like Stalin only iron firmness produces results.

The text of the Yalta Conference of 1945, fifteen months later, reads: 'The big three considered the Curzon Line to be the eastern frontier of Poland.' All Polish protests were in vain.

Roosevelt proposed the permanent dismemberment of Germany and emphasized his wish for the separation of Prussia, and for three separate zones of occupation after the war. The three leaders quickly agreed to the dismemberment of Germany, and to incorporate parts of East Prussia into the Soviet Union. This decision had important consequences, and was to be used by the Nazi propaganda machine to good effect to bolster up German morale to fight when all seemed lost.

Overall, the Teheran Conference marked a change in the Churchill–Roosevelt relationship: Roosevelt tended to side with Stalin at Churchill's expense. Stalin agreed that Churchill and Roosevelt should meet President Inonu of Turkey and pressurize him to bring Turkey into the war. The discussions should be held without Russian participation, although the Russian diplomat Vishinsky would be available if required. Inonu agreed to come to Cairo, and between 4 and 7 December Inonu, Roosevelt and Churchill had conversations there.

At Teheran, when Stalin had raised the question of warm water ports (meaning in this instance a port in the Mediterranean for Russia), Churchill replied that 'there were no obstacles'. Stalin immediately said: 'The question of the regime of the Dardanelles would have to be considered. Russia had no outlet and perhaps a new regime would help them.' Knowing that giving Russia new rights in the Dardanelles would alienate Turkey, Churchill said he wanted to get Turkey into the war and this was an awkward moment for raising this question; while Roosevelt stated that if Turkey went to war the Dardanelles ought to be free to the commerce of the world, including Russia, 'subject to policing by the policing nations'. Churchill also injudiciously told Stalin that if Turkey did not enter the war her 'rights' to the Dardanelles and Bosphorus could not remain unaffected.[20]

The Treaty of Sèvres of 1920 proposed that rights of passage through the Bosphorous and the straits of the Dardanelles between the Black Sea and the Mediterranean should be controlled by an International Commission and should be opened to all vessels, including warships. The subsequent Straits Convention of 1923 modified this arrangement by permitting free passage for merchant shipping and for warships up to 10,000 tons in time of peace. It additionally set up an International Straits Commission at Istanbul. This was then rescinded by the Montreux Convention of 1936, which gave back control of the straits to Turkey. These changes were hotly opposed by the Soviet Union, who considered them as a threat to her Black Sea coast.

Thus at Teheran Roosevelt was taking the Russian side in the long-standing controversy over policing the Dardanelles, and Churchill's last remark was that he certainly thought 'the regime of the Straits deserved review'. Inonu had no idea that the Big Three had discussed the future of the straits: Roosevelt and Churchill were far from frank in hiding from him what they had said to Stalin.

Turkey wanted an Allied victory but was terrified of both Russia and Germany. The rout of the British in the Dodecanese Islands had reduced their will to enter the war and von Papen, the German Ambassador in Ankara, had suggested that in the event of a German victory Turkey might be given the Dodecanese. Hitler rejected this because it would antagonize the Greeks.[21]

Inonu made it clear to Churchill and Roosevelt that he was ready to make preparations for co-belligerency, but he baulked at any infiltration of personnel who could not be camouflaged and who would produce an immediate declaration of war by Germany – for which he was not prepared. Churchill offered Turkey twenty squadrons of fighters to be based at Smyrna and Bodrum, where the British had already constructed aerodromes. Roosevelt imprecisely offered some American bombers; he also emphasized the great benefits to Turkey from joining the war, 'particularly from the point of view of Turkish relations with Russia which would be put on the best possible footing, and said Russia desired Turkish friendship and was not likely to betray Turkey'. He gave lukewarm support to Churchill, but stressed that air protection would be available 'at once', and made the impractical suggestion that British military personnel could come in 'plain clothes'.

Churchill was conscious of the way in which Hitler had eliminated other nations by lightning attacks without a declaration of war, and proposed to turn the tables on him by placing British and American combat squadrons on Turkish airfields in a surprise move. He proposed to Inonu that, while Germany was making protests and Turkey giving diplomatic replies, 'there would be a steady continuation of reinforcement and preparation' during which Turkey should continue to send supplies to Germany, 'including chrome (but only a little)'. On the morning of 5 December Roosevelt talked to the Turkish representatives without Churchill, and undid any good Churchill had done by suggesting a delay of four or five months in which there could be political conversations with the Americans, British and Russians and full disclosure of 'Allied military plans, e.g. Crete, Rhodes, etc.'[22]

Unlike Roosevelt, Churchill was intent on a declaration of war by Turkey within six weeks and had suggested a date between 15 and 20 January. The American President ignored this, and the Conference ended with everything in the air and the Turks stalling hard. Afterwards Churchill proposed that on 15 February the Allies would request permission from the Turks to send in air squadrons, but if the Turks refused the Allies would send them to another theatre of war and give up hope of wartime co-operation with Turkey. If the Turks agreed, the sea route to Turkey would be opened. Churchill's timetable for Turkish entry had been put back, but how strong his hopes were for bringing Turkey in and opening the Dardanelles is shown by his minutes of 22 and 23 December to the Chiefs of Staff:

> I am not prepared at this stage to the abandonment of the operation [the capture of Rhodes and the subsequent return of landing craft to Anvil – the invasion of the south of France]. To abandon Hercules [new codename for Rhodes] is to abandon the prize for which all our efforts are directed upon Turkey, and also by leaving the

sea routes to the Dardanelles unopened to prevent our reinforcement of Turkey
. . . subsequent to her entry into the war. Till we are masters of the Aegean we have
only the trickling railway. To have Turkey enter too late to sandwich Hercules
before Anvil is certainly not the policy we have been pursuing and the facts must be
reviewed. For the present we must persevere.

On 23 December he was rather more resigned, minuting: 'I recognize that if
the Turks will not play we may have to sacrifice the Aegean policy especially if
it is marked up so high and slow. I hope however that this decision will not be
taken till after full exploration of the whole scene . . . I wish to keep it open for
the next three or four days.'[23] Churchill at the time was in Carthage, recuperat-
ing from pneumonia which had laid him low *en route* for London from Cairo.

In January 1944 Air Marshal Sir John Linnel went to Ankara with a mission to
set up military talks. The Turks were warm but non-committal. Churchill's
patience gave out. He realized the Turks had decided they had more to gain than
lose by remaining neutral. On 29 January Churchill instructed that Linnel should
be withdrawn and that no more military materials should be sent to Turkey.
Churchill's vision of a belligerent Turkey and the opening of the Dardanelles, for
which he alone had striven so hard, had proved a mirage, and neither the
Russians nor the Americans had given him the support he wanted.[24]

CHAPTER NINETEEN

Tito and Mihailovic blunder

AS HIS hopes of opening the Dardanelles faded, Churchill turned to a plan for a front in Yugoslavia. He did not want to send an expeditionary force there; instead he hoped to use the Yugoslav resistance to prepare the ground for the Eighth Army to make an amphibious landing in Istria and then to drive through the Ljubljana Gap into Austria and on to Vienna. This did not appeal to the Americans, but Churchill persisted. Plans were drawn up by Alexander at Caserta in Italy and approved by the Chiefs of Staff in London and the War Cabinet. The Istria plan was only abandoned during the Malta Conference as late as January 1945.

By the middle of 1943 resistance to the Germans by the Serbs and Croats in Yugoslavia offered a promising field. Loyalists to the King under General Mihailovic (who had been made Minister of War in the exiled Yugoslav Government of King Peter) and the Communists under Tito unfortunately not only detested each other, but fought each other in bloody internecine strife with the Communists, the persistent aggressors. After Teheran Churchill decided that Tito's Communists would render more valuable help than Mihailovic, and against Foreign Office advice he decided to back the former and disown the latter. This decision he soon regretted, but in his initial enthusiasm for Tito he involved himself personally in the intricacies of Yugoslav resistance, without sufficient or proper understanding of its complexities.

Hitler behaved like a savage towards the Yugoslavs after their army capitulated in April 1941. He at once broke up the country. Slovene territory was annexed by Germany, Italy and Hungary. The bulk of Macedonia was given to Bulgaria, but some was incorporated in Italian-occupied Albania. An independent Croat State was set up, nominally under the Duke of Spoleto (a close relation of King Victor Emmanuel III of Italy) but actually controlled by a Croatian terrorist, Ante Pavelic, and his Ustase party supported by Axis troops. The new Croatian state consisted of the former Croatia-Slavonia, Bosnia-Hercegovina, and part of Dalmatia. Most of the Dalmatian coast was annexed by Italy, while Montenegro became an Italian protectorate. Serbia, where the capital, Belgrade, lies, was held under German military occupation with a German-controlled government under General Nedic; he was not a quisling, but had decided that further active resistance could only cause useless loss of life after the Germans had announced that a hundred Serbs would be killed in reprisal for each German soldier killed.

After the lightning German campaign in 1941, the Yugoslav King and Government had fled to London, the Army had surrendered, and 350,000 Serbs became POWs – Croats were set free. Some Serbs, especially in the mountainous south, had gone home. A few dozen, led by Colonel Mihailovic, gathered in the hills of central Serbia and began to organize resistance. Mihailovic was a veteran of the Turkish war of 1912 and of the First World War and knew the terrible cost of premature guerrilla action. Moreover, along with his fellow Serbs, he was soon anguished by the outbreak of barbarous massacres in Croatia as the Ustase tried to rid the new state of ethnic Serbs, Jews and gipsies. Half a million Serbs were reported killed; hundreds of thousands fled into Serbia. All Mihailovic could do at that stage was to send a few of his officers into Bosnia to help Serb communities defend themselves.

After the German attack on Russia in June 1941 the Communist Party of Yugoslavia, which had been banned before the war and had opposed their country's taking part in an 'imperialist war' which did not concern the workers, was ordered by Moscow to start resistance. Their leader was Josip Broz, known as Tito, who had been the party's underground organizer in Russian pay. The party's guerrilla forces were known as Partisans. They went into action in order to take pressure off the Soviet Union. This put Mihailovic in a dilemma, because though he thought any large-scale action premature he could not risk losing the support of patriotic Serbs: if he did not lead them into action they might join the Partisans. The Communists were trying to take control of all resistance groups.

News filtered back to Cairo and London about resistance by guerrillas in Yugoslavia. The preliminary British Government view was that premature insurrection should be discouraged because it would have little military effect while producing savage reprisals. Mihailovic hoped to organize forces from the mountains which could be launched to attack the enemy at an opportune moment.

As early as September 1941 a British liaison officer, Major Hudson, had landed in Montenegro and joined Mihailovic's headquarters. He found there was no co-operation between Tito's Partisans and the Mihailovic Royalist force, known as Cetniks. Soon a message came through from Hudson that the Communist Partisans were attacking Mihailovic; Allied efforts at forming a common front came to nothing. In the spring of 1942 Hudson reported that the Cetniks were being molested by the Partisans, who were receiving support from the Axis powers; German local commanders wanted to stifle the resistance by making the Yugoslav groups fight each other. This was correct: the Germans had given some of Tito's officers safe conduct passes so that they could discuss with the German command a local truce which would make it easier for Tito's forces to attack Mihailovic's. However, Hitler refused out of hand to allow his generals to have anything to do with 'Communists'.

Major Archibald Jack has recorded:

On the 13th of March 1943, a meeting took place at Tito's request, between three Partisan leaders, Djilas, Velebit and Popović, who were very important figures, and the German General Dippold. The Partisan delegation stressed that they saw no reason for fighting the German Army, but wished solely to fight the Četniks – that means Mihailovic's troops, the Loyalists – and that they would fight the British should the latter land in Yugoslavia. That was a pledge to the Germans on behalf of Tito. Furthermore, they proposed a cessation of hostilities between Germans and Partisans: Velebit and Djilas were flown in German planes from Sarajevo to Zagreb for further discussions. But Ribbentrop, for some reason, forbade all further contact with the Partisans.[1]

Meanwhile the British sent messages to Mihailovic urging him to carry out the maximum amount of sabotage against the enemy's bridges and railways. Inadequate drops of food, dynamite and arms were made to him through SOE Cairo. He did useful work, but was severely hampered by Tito's Partisans attacking his troops. A more senior officer, Colonel Bailey, a mining engineer who had lived in Yugoslavia since 1928, was now sent to Mihailovic. Early in 1943 he suggested extra support for Mihailovic and no dealing with Tito, whose Partisans he claimed were antagonizing the civilian population.

However, contradictory information was received from SOE in Cairo, which, having been infiltrated by Communists, alleged that Tito's movement was more active and a better horse to back; SOE also sent claims emanating from Tito that Mihailovic was co-operating with the Italians and the Nedic Government. These had some substance: the Italians were supplying the Cetniks with food and arms to help them fight off attacks by the Partisans, who also threatened Italian safety.[2]

Peter Boughey of the Yugoslav section of the SOE London headquarters said after the war that 'we certainly told Mihailovic to be in touch with the Italians and wanted him to be able to get Italian weapons when the Italians withdrew, collapsed or surrendered'. Jack has also recorded that 'In Serbia the Home Guard was the Nedicefsi under General Nedic whom Mihailovic treated as a traitor but the Nedicefsi were an enormous help to the Resistance'; on one occasion a Nedic sergeant arranged for him to go in a horse and cart to reconnoitre the railway bridge at Sabac.[3]

In February 1943, when Churchill was in Cairo after the Casablanca Conference, SOE Cairo gave him a paper based on the latest reports from the British liaison officers with Mihailovic and on Cairo decrypts of certain German cyphers. This made it clear that Mihailovic was not collaborating with the Germans but had concluded local pacts with the Italians in order to repel Partisan attacks on his units. It also explained that Mihailovic's policy was to conserve his manpower so as to be able to launch a strong attack on the Germans when the Italians changed sides. At that time, as has been seen in Chapter 17, Field Marshals Caviglia and Badoglio and General Pesenti were in touch with the Allies through the British Legation in Berne, with a view to a separate peace. The Italian generals in Yugoslavia, aware of these negotiations, were making plans accordingly and must have communicated to Mihailovic their expectation of changing sides or becoming neutral.[4]

During March Enigma decrypts showed increasing German alarm at the collaboration between Mihailovic and the Italians, and ordered that 'no Cetnik formations whose leaders are in touch with Mihailovic are to be spared'. The decrypts also showed that the Germans had become aware that Mihailovic was hoping to turn the Italians into an ally if they made a separate armistice, and gave details of German plans for the contingency of an Italian collapse. On 4 March the Chiefs of Staff concluded: 'On balance taking the long view, the better military alternative was to continue to back Mihailovic because he would provide some organization and control whereas under the Partisans chaos would probably ensue when the Axis forces were defeated.'[5]

Thus Churchill faced a dilemma. He was immensely eager to support armed insurrection in Yugoslavia and to intensify all guerrilla activity. He agreed that British officers should go into Croatia and Slovenia to make contact with Tito and report whether air supplies should be sent to him as well as to Mihailovic.

Meanwhile Mihailovic incautiously stated in Bailey's presence on 28 February 1943 that he would accept Italian assistance, and that he was receiving little help from the English who with their 'traditional perfidy' were trying to use the Serbs for their own strategic ends while King Peter and his Government were 'virtually prisoners in English hands', so that it was his duty to exterminate the Partisans. This caused Churchill (in Eden's absence) to send a note to the Yugoslav Prime Minister in exile in London, stating that he could not justify to the British public support for a movement whose leaders maintained his enemies were not the German and Italian invaders of his country, but fellow Yugoslavs. At the same time the Prime Minister told Mihailovic he hoped to increase 'our supplies' to him, but only if he was assured that the supplies would not be used for attacking his fellow countrymen; he also minuted to Cadogan that Mihailovic was 'certainly maltreating us, but he was also double crossing the Italians. His position was terrible and it was not much use preaching to the "toad beneath the harrow" and we should not forget how very little help we could give.'[6]

Unfortunately Churchill and the Foreign Office now became misled by false information supplied by SOE in Cairo. Their headquarters, known as MO4, had been infiltrated by Communists who consistently maligned Mihailovic and played down his operations while lauding Tito to the skies and grossly exaggerating the scale of his attacks on the enemy. Until March 1943 British policy had comprised full support for Mihailovic, who was hailed as the first great leader of covert resistance in Axis-occupied Europe. Then SOE cast doubts on his role. Bailey's mission was supplemented by several British Liaison Officers, who went out to local detachments together with considerable supplies from the air.

The SOE office in Cairo became dominated by Captain (later Major) James Klugman, who had become a dedicated Communist at Cambridge at the same time as Anthony Blunt, Guy Burgess, Donald Maclean and John Cairncross. His activities are disclosed in Andrew Boyle's book *The Climate of Treason* and Simon Freeman's *Conspiracy of Silence*. Boyle writes: 'Klugman was a most effective Soviet apparatchik who was principally responsible for the massive sabotage of the Mihailovic supply operation and keeping from London impressive information about the activities of the Mihailovic forces.' During his undergraduate days the Labour Cabinet Minister Denis Healey was a friend of Klugman's. In his autobiography Healey records that, while at SOE in Cairo during the war, Klugman was 'simultaneously an agent of the Comintern for which he had started recruiting spies in Cambridge in 1934'.[7]

Within the Cairo office Klugman handled the W/T (radio) reports of all the British liaison officers in Yugoslavia, including editing them and writing policy memoranda for GHQ MEF and the Foreign Office. Because of doubts instilled by Klugman about Mihailovic, the British Government sent a note to the Cetnik leader on 9 May to the effect that 'we' were prepared to continue to support him provided he ceased collaboration with the Italians and General Nedic, and co-operated with the Communist guerrillas. The Yugoslav Government in London denied to the Foreign Office that Mihailovic had co-operated with either Nedic or the Italians, but agreed to pass the note to the General. Again at Klugman's instigation, the High Command in the Middle East instructed Mihailovic to withdraw his forces across the River Ibar into Serbia, and said that Yugoslavia should be divided into districts, with Mihailovic recognized in east Serbia and Tito in Croatia. Mihailovic objected and refused to obey.

This led to a conflict of views in London. The Foreign Office claimed that the Middle East instruction to Mihailovic to withdraw had been sent on the false premise from SOE in Cairo that the Cetniks had been defeated in battle by the Partisans, who were now the most formidable anti-Axis element in Yugoslavia. Neither SOE HQ in London nor the Foreign Office believed this, and recommended that the withdrawal order to Mihailovic should be rescinded; from Yugoslavia Bailey telegraphed that he agreed.

The Foreign Office had become suspicious of the authenticity of the reports from SOE in Cairo. It was known that Klugman was a Communist, and at the end of 1942 a junior officer of the Balkan Section of SOE was sentenced to seven years' imprisonment for passing secrets to the Communist Party of Great Britain. It is impossible to discover whether these suspicions were passed on to the Prime Minister.[8]

With Churchill's consent the order to Mihailovic was cancelled and both guerrilla leaders were told firmly that support was dependent on no operations being carried out against the other. At this stage King Peter and his Government left London for Cairo to be in closer touch with the Yugoslav resistance.

On 23 June Churchill minuted to Ismay, with reference to a Middle East report on the situation in Yugoslavia, 'All this is of highest importance . . . I understood when I was last in Cairo that an additional number of aircraft were to be made available. I consider . . . that this demand should have priority even on the bombing of Germany.' At the Chiefs of Staff Conference the same day he stressed the importance of giving 'all possible support to the Yugoslav anti-Nazi movement with the small number of additional aircraft which must be provided if necessary at the expense of the bombing of Germany and of the anti-U Boat war . . . this would be a small price to pay for the diversion of Axis forces,' and said every effort should be made to increase supplies to 500 tons per month.[9]

When the Italians surrendered on 8 September 1943 Peter Solly-Flood, a British commando major with Mihailovic who had formerly been in the Foreign Office, went to see General Oxilia commanding the Italian Venezia Division at Berane; this division controlled an area of Montenegro leading south into Albania and east to Sandzak on the road to the Serbian heartland. Both Flood and Oxilia were fluent in French; Oxilia told the former diplomant that he would put his division at the disposal of the Allies immediately, but he was under the impression that Britain was backing Tito's forces. Flood convinced him that was not so and that the Italian should co-operate with Mihailovic. Oxilia agreed, and the Loyalists took over the civil government in Berane and the surrounding territory.

Tito immediately moved against Mihailovic's troops in the area with the full weight of his army. General Oxilia attempted to persuade the Loyalists and Partisans not to fight each other, pointing out that they had a great opportunity if they combined to thrust to the sea. The Titoites refused, telling Oxilia to keep out of Yugoslav internal politics. The Partisans, with the help of their British Liaison Officer, Major Hunter, swore to the Italians that they alone had the support of the Allies, and the BBC joined in by describing the Loyalists as 'enemies', which impressed the Italians.

This, and the number of Tito's troops who rushed into the Mihailovic territory, convinced Oxilia he must throw in his lot with Tito. SOE in Cairo doctored the news to give the Italians the impression they should back Tito, and ordered the British Liaison Officers (BLOs) to stop Mihailovic sending in more troops to join the Venezia Division. The result was that General Oxilia turned over all his reasources to the Titoites who took over from the Loyalists, and this was a watershed in determining the result of the conflict between Mihailovic and the Communists.

However Churchill, misled by SOE in Cairo, began to place exaggerated hopes on Tito's value and mistrusted Mihailovic. He decided to send Fitzroy Maclean, Conservative MP for Lancaster and a former diplomat, as his personal emissary to Tito. Brushing aside opposition from Lord Selborne, who had succeeded Dalton as the Minister responsible for SOE, Churchill insisted Maclean was promoted to the rank of Brigadier. F. W. Deakin, a Fellow of Wadham College and a friend of Churchill, who had assisted him with his book *Marlborough, his Life and Times*, had been parachuted to Tito in May 1943 as leader of the first mission to Tito.

Maclean, who arrived at Tito's headquarters at the end of September 1943, found that the surrender of Italy had much increased the strength of the partisans. In collaboration with Italian divisions based on Split, they had occupied Istria and the mountainous country between Trieste and the Austrian frontier for a short period. In addition, they had taken great quantities of arms from the Italian depots (including those of the Venezia Division which had so nearly gone to the Loyalists). However the Germans soon re-occupied this territory and the port of Split.

After one long interview with Tito and without verifying the truth on the ground, Maclean sent a report which reached the Foreign Office on 12 November. It was misleading. Maclean accepted at face value a preposterous claim by Tito that his forces amounted to two hundred thousand, and that he had control over large areas completely liberated from the enemy. Maclean stated that the Partisans were organized on Communist lines with political commissars, but claimed that 'their effective political organisation afforded equal treatment to members of all races and religion'. He added that 'the other political parties were still allowed some latitude'. He did not explain how this could be reconciled with 'equal treatment'. Maclean also noted that the Partisans would not allow anti-monarchical propaganda. He recommended strongly that the British Government should 'discontinue our support for Mihailovic and increase aid to Partisans in view of the fact that he was encouraging or at best failing to prevent collaboration between his forces and the enemy'. He believed that Tito must take power when the Germans withdrew, whereas Mihailovic, who was pan-Serb and anti-Croat, was discredited and could never unite the country.

This report had a great influence on Churchill, although the Foreign Office thought that Maclean had considerably exaggerated Tito's strength. They were correct. Tito had no more than sixty thousand all told and his force was inferior in numbers to Mihailovic's. The Foreign Office also insisted there was no proof that Mihailovic had ordered collaboration with Germany or was even conniving in the activities of his subordinates. In fact only one decrypt (according to the official history) offered evidence of Cetnik collaboration with the Germans. This, on 19 November, instructed the German forces not to interfere with a drop to Mihailovic because 'it was a good means of diverting Bolshevik hopes'. In August American liaison officers with Mihailovic reported that Partisans at Pristina had put the Germans 'on to Mihailovic's tail'.[10] The Foreign Office pointed out that if Britain abandoned Mihailovic and supported Tito 'we would land ourselves with a communist state closely linked to the USSR after the war who would employ the usual terrorist methods to overcome opposition'. They advised that support should not be withdrawn from Mihailovic while the possibility of an arrangement between King Peter and Tito was studied.

During November further reports of alleged co-operation between Mihailovic and Nedic and the Germans were sent to London by Klugman at Cairo, accompanied by statements that Mihailovic was no longer carrying out sabotage in spite of the presence of British liaison officers (BLOs) and supplies from the air. Both statements were false.[11]

The BLOs with Tito were kept out of the way by 'minders' so that they could not observe at first hand the sabotage expeditions, and were always kept at arms length from the units by political commissars. With Mihailovic, on the other hand, BLOs commanded raiding parties in person like Lawrence of Arabia.

Enigma decrypts contradicted the reports being sent by Klugman to London. They gave no evidence of Cetnik–German collaboration – rather that the Germans were set on Mihailovic's destruction. In July 1943 Hitler suggested a high reward should be put on the heads of both Mihailovic and Tito. In August it was learnt that the Abwehr in Dubrovnik had warned Berlin that the Cetniks were thirsting for revenge on German troops and the German general there had complained he did not have enough forces to engage the Cetnik bands.

That summer Enigma decrypts left no doubt that at the highest level the Germans remained set upon Mihailovic's destruction, and in July Hitler suggested a higher price should be put on the head of Mihailovic than on that of Tito. Only two Enigma decrypts referred to collaboration before November 1943 which made the Foreign Office suspicious of Klugman's and Deakin's allegations.[12]

Reports of the successful disruption of railways and the blowing of bridges were sent back by W/T to Cairo from the BLOs with Mihailovic. A recent book by one of them, Michael Lees, entitled *The Rape of Serbia*, lays bare the deception practised by Klugman. Lees has found a cache of recently released SOE files in the Public Record Office containing the operational logs of the Mihailovic missions between June 1943, and compared his own signals and those of his colleagues from the field in Yugoslavia with the reports submitted by Klugman to London and GHQ MEF. He found that the BLO reports were falsified in order to denigrate Mihailovic. For example, in late July 1943 Lees was ordered to sabotage the Belgrade–Salonika railway – a vital link for the Germans. With 150 of Mihailovic's Cetniks he crossed the Bulgarian border and was about to carry out his planned attack when a signal came from Klugman ordering him to abandon the operation. Lees is convinced this was Tito-inspired. At that time the Germans were rushing troops back from Greece for their sorely pressed Italian front. Lees soon afterwards derailed two trains on lines vital to the Germans.[13]

Brigadier Armstrong, a regular soldier, was parachuted to Mihailovic in late September 1943. He organized raids led by British officers which resulted in five important railway bridges being blown on the Belgrade–Salonika line. Yet these important demolitions only secured 'passing reference' in the SOE Cairo reports to higher authority. In November Major Jack, with the help of the Cetniks, brought down the Midjedge bridge, one of the largest and most important over the River Drina, in an action involving 2500 Cetniks who had previously captured Visegrad and in the accompanying fighting killed 200 Germans. This was reported to SOE in Cairo, but Klugman failed to send the news to London or GHQ MEF. Klugman and the BBC attributed it quite falsely to Tito's Partisans. The PRO archives reveal that between Armstrong's arrival in September and December 1943 Robert Purvis, Michael Lees and George More made many successful sabotage raids. In spite of this Klugman made sure the lion's share of air drops went to Tito.[14]

After the Italian surrender Klugman sent reports alleging that the Cetniks were collaborating with the Serbian State Guard, the police force allowed by the Germans to the Nedic Government. It was quite different from the Ustase, a Fascist Croat force recruited by the Germans, who consistently attacked both the Cetniks and the Partisans and carried out atrocities. The Nedic State Guards were anti-German and ready to co-operate with the Cetniks. The Foreign Office commented that 'this may indicate that Nedic was half hearted in his support for the Nazis'.[15] In November the Foreign Office asked Armstrong for a report on Mihailovic's activities, and on the 7th he sent a 5000-word document. Had Churchill read it he would have been in no doubt that the Cetniks were dominant in Serbia, as active against the Germans as the Partisans were, and worth backing on military grounds – quite apart from political considerations. However, Klugman managed to delay Armstrong's report in the Egyptian office of SOE in Cairo, and it was not received in London until 12 December. This date is important, because on 9 December in Cairo Churchill had come to the irrevocable decision to sack Mihailovic and to devote all resources to Tito.

The Armstrong report stated that Mihailovic desired to carry out 'extensive operations, and had been upset by a 'falling off in air sorties and by the current BBC propaganda in favour of Tito; the anti-German activities of Mihailovic's forces had been nullified by their anxiety to deal with the Partisans, who attacked them all the time. It continued:

Greatest mistrust and apprehension, however, derive from the conviction of all Jugoslavs here that the present one hundred per cent support of Partisans by BBC, including gross misrepresentation of known facts, plus minimum mention of Mihailovic's activities, plus greater material support he believes we give the Partisans, plus fact that it is clear to him that a BLO with Partisans is always believed in preference to a BLO with his forces, all add up to mean that British have completely sold Jugoslavia down the river to the Russians . . .

He is convinced that we have agreed that Jugoslavia shall fall within the Russian sphere of influence after the war but will not say so now so that we may callously extract maximum advantage from his forces now. Consequently, he will have to fight his own battle with the Partisans after the war without material, moral or political support from us.

These apprehensions are enhanced by the rapidity of the Russian advance in the Ukraine, the slowness of the Allied advance in Italy and the lack of any indication of an Allied invasion of the Balkans, and the consequent fear that the Russians may reach the Danube or Bulgar–Serb frontier before Allied troops set foot in Jugoslavia. Apprehensions are particularly marked at the moment as it is feared Moscow conference may have resulted in increasing favouring of Partisans at Mihailovic's expense.

Brigadier Armstrong is encountering great difficulties because Mihailovic hoped he would bring reassurances on some of the above points. The fact that we took no advantage of the arrival of a senior officer to do so, plus clear indication that Armstrong has no control whatever over BBC broadcasts, volume of sorties and supplies or via you over Partisan activities in disputed areas, has caused sharp reaction in direction of doing nothing operationally and restricting contact with this mission to a minimum.

There must be no further favouring the Partisans by the Russians and should they later take an active interest in operations in Yugoslavia they must send representatives and supplies and provide propaganda to both sides equally imposing the same safeguards as we do. We believe a suggestion to send a Russian representative to this HQ would not be rejected out of hand. For our part we must face squarely the fact that there is a moral responsibility on us to offer immediate rewards to all resistance groups.[16]

Armstrong asked for three hundred air 'sorties per month per side to demonstrate to the Yugoslavs beyond doubt our good faith and dispel misgivings about perfide Albion'.

Churchill had been inspired by Maclean's misleading report about Tito and was bursting with enthusiasm to help the Partisan leader, seeing in Yugoslavia the opportunity to make the Balkans a theatre of war. On 9 December he summoned Deakin to dinner in Cairo. Deakin, who had returned to Cairo by air via Brindisi from Tito's headquarters two days before, was cross-questioned about the situation in the area where Tito operated. The next day Maclean and Deakin were called to Churchill's bedroom. Maclean had already reported to Churchill his personal view that Mihailovic should be abandoned in favour of Tito; he had also made it clear that after the war Tito would endeavour to transform Yugoslavia into a Communist country, with all its evils. This had produced from Churchill the retort: 'Do you intend to live there?'

Churchill had been impressed with the evidence (emanating from SOE Cairo) that Mihailovic was co-operating with the enemy, and Deakin was subjected to a two-hour interrogation over how to interpret various captured German and Cetnik documents, which he had been given at Tito's headquarters, concerning 'the links between Mihailovic and his commander with the Italians and Germany'. Deakin wrote: 'It was a miserable task. The questions were pointed and searched out every detail within the range of my knowledge, and as I talked I knew that I was compiling the elements of a hostile brief which would play a decisive part in any future break between the British Government and Mihailovic.' Deakin was entrusted by the Prime Minister with informing King Peter, who was in Cairo, that the British Government had concluded that Tito was strong, while Mihailovic was collaborating with the enemy.[17]

These documents are damaging to Mihailovic, but are contradicted by the operations log of his BLOs. Deakin had passed the period between 25 May and 2 December with Tito's forces while they had been attacked by the Germans. He had helped in negotiations with the Italians at Split after the 8 September armistice, and shared dangers with Tito from German air raids which had caused numerous casualties. Before Deakin's arrival the Partisan leader had been distrustful and cold with British liaison officers, and Deakin was justifiably pleased because he had broken down Tito's reserve and established a friendly relationship. However, Deakin had no first-hand knowledge of the successful sabotage operations carried out by the liaison officers with Mihailovic, nor of his strength in Serbia nor of the truth of the alleged co-operation of the Loyalists with the Germans. Nor did he know of Tito's attempted co-operation with the enemy. However, since he was Churchill's friend and pre-war colleague his attitude towards the Yugoslav rivalry was a strong factor in making up Churchill's mind. This is clear from the Prime Minister's later minutes.

There is no doubt that Churchill was made fully aware that, if Tito triumphed over Mihailovic, Yugoslavia would be a Communist state after the war.

Unfortunately there is no written record of Churchill's discussions with Deakin and Maclean in Cairo in December 1943. Deakin had no political axe to grind; he was an unbiased witness, but he knew only one side of the story and had been fed tales of Mihailovic's bad faith by experienced Communist propagandists at Tito's headquarters.

The Foreign Office had asked Armstrong to fly out to Cairo with his Serbo-Croat-speaking political adviser, Colonel Bailey, to give the Prime Minister his version of the Yugoslav situation. The invitation was not passed on by Klugman, and Mihailovic's case went by default. In addition to this Fitzroy Maclean had recruited Randolph, Churchill's son, for his mission to Tito. Randolph was then in Cairo without a job; although resourceful and courageous, his temperament and drinking habits made him unsuitable for the commandos to whom he had attached himself, and none of their commanders wanted him. Randolph threw himself enthusiastically into the Tito cause; Churchill was devoted to his son; as a result the Prime Minister became emotionally involved in the British mission to Tito. Had Randolph and Maclean been sent to Mihailovic instead of Tito, the outcome would have been different. It is hard to believe that Maclean recruited Randolph for his abilities, it was his influence with his father that made him attractive to Maclean.

On 10 December the die was cast. Churchill decided irrevocably to abandon Mihailovic and to support Tito to the hilt. He had difficulties in implementing this policy, but he railroaded it through against the opposition and doubts of Lord Selborne, of the Foreign Office, GHQ MEF, the British Ambassador to the Royal Yugoslavian Government, and the SOE in London. Soon he rued it bitterly.

On 8 December Armstrong had been ordered to hand a personal message to Mihailovic from Wilson to blow two bridges over the Rivers Moravo and Ibar. It had been decided that, if Mihailovic failed to carry out this order, that would be the excuse to withdraw all help from him. But Mihailovic agreed to do so and issued orders to this effect, though he said he could not undertake the operation until the middle of January and needed more supplies by air. However, as Churchill had decided on 9 December to have no more to do with Mihailovic, the last thing the Prime Minister wanted was for the Cetniks to have a dramatic success over these bridges. No supplies were sent, and no pressure was put on Armstrong from Cairo for the operation to be carried out.[18]

On 26 December Armstrong reported that Mihailovic wanted to stop the civil war against the Partisans, to fight the Germans, and to meet Tito with a view to an alliance. Armstrong added he thought this was entirely due to Mihailovic's fear that otherwise he might lose British support. Eden thought 'it was too much of a death bed repentance'. Stevenson, the British Ambassador to the Yugoslav Government in Cairo, suggested the fact that Mihailovic had not complied immediately with the order to blow the bridges might serve as an excuse to break with him. Eden did not agree, replying:

It might be awkward if Mihailovic [succeeds]. [He] did not after all refuse to carry out test operation but has merely asked for a fortnight's grace to make his plans to complete the operation successfully at a moment when we may be telling King Peter he must get rid of him. I think therefore that there would be advantage in telling him at once that we do not want him to carry out operation. Please discuss this was GHQ MEF with a view to instructions being sent accordingly to Brig. Armstrong if they agree.

However, before this message reached him Brigadier Armstrong had himself 'reconnoitred the area, selected a target and urgently requested small quantities of stores for this purpose'. The SOE in Cairo reported that the 'operation would certainly be difficult'.[19]

En route from Cairo to London Churchill fell ill with pneumonia in Algiers on 17 December, and after he recovered he went to Marrakesh to convalesce. Here, feeling well again, he set about running the war free of the trammels of the Chiefs of Staff and the War Cabinet. Brooke put in his diary: 'Most of the difficulties are caused by the P.M. in Marrakesh and trying to run the war from there.'[20]

In two letters to his father at the end of December, Randolph pointed out that the Foreign Office were insisting that Maclean return to Tito's headquarters to implement their policy of trying to bring the Partisans and the King together, which was contrary to Churchill's intentions. Wilson had cabled to Churchill:

> There is grave danger that Foreign Office efforts to bring together Tito and Mihailovic will result in considerable diminution of partisan movement. From military aspect it would be better for His Majesty's Government to face the embarrassing position of having two Governments than for Germans to be relieved of having to retain many active divisions in Yugoslavia.

Eden wrote to Churchill in Marrakesh:

> . . . it would be a mistake to promise Tito to break with Mihailovic. If we have a public and spectacular breach with Mihailovic our case against him for treachery must be unanswerable . . . I am still without evidence of this. Breach with Mihailovic whenever it comes will certainly attract a great deal of attention both here and in America and I should have liked to have moved in step with Russians and Americans if we could.

The Prime Minister would have none of this, and replied that he was convinced of Mihailovic's guilt.

> This was confirmed not only by people like Deakin who have come back from Tito's forces, but by many of the officers serving in the MIH[ailovic] area. I have been convinced by the arguments of men I know and trust [Maclean, Deakin and his son] that Mihailovic is a millstone tied round the neck of the little King and he has no chance till he gets rid of him. Once Mihailovic has been dismissed Maclean and Randolph will have a chance to work on Tito for the return of the King, perhaps in a military capacity.

On 6 January Churchill was even firmer, cabling to Eden: 'My unchanging object is to get Tito to let the King come out and share his luck with them. I believe dismissal of Mihailovic is essential policy. Please note Mihailovic never did anything about test operation.' It looks as if SOE misinformed the Prime Minister about the test.[21]

Spurred on by Maclean and Randolph, Churchill decided on his own to abandon Mihailovic. On 8 January 1944, in a letter taken by hand by Maclean, he wrote to Tito: 'I am resolved that that British Government will give NO FURTHER MILITARY SUPPORT TO MIHAILOVIC [author's capitals] and will give all help to you, and we should be glad if Royal Yugoslav Government would dismiss Mihailovic. It would not be chivalrous or honourable for GB [Great Britain] to cast him [the King] aside.' Here he was jumping the gun. There had been no consultation with the Chiefs of Staff nor the War Cabinet; while Eden had objected, as has been seen. On 9 January Eden circulated Churchill's letter to Tito with a long report on Yugoslavia in a printed memorandum to the Cabinet, giving as his view: 'It would be unwise to back Tito and abandon Mihailovic.'

On 16 January Churchill arrived back in London, where once more he had to govern in a more conventional way, consulting with his Cabinet colleagues and the Chiefs of Staff. A wrangle between him and Eden over Tito ensued. This is contrary to the impression given in Churchill's memoirs.

Stevenson reported from Cairo that 'the whole situation fundamentally changed from the moment the Partisans declared themselves to be in open revolution against the King and Government'. He advised against sacking Mihailovic, but said that judging by the US and Soviet representatives in Cairo it would be difficult to persuade them to agree. Internal Foreign Office minutes on Stevenson's missive suggested that an immediate break would be a mistake unless a *quid pro quo* about recognizing the King could be secured from Tito, and Eden summed up: 'There is force in all this. Had we not better wait the P.M.'s decision?' Churchill merely minuted to Eden: 'What progress has been made towards procuring the dismissal of Mihailovic by King Peter?'[22] However, at the end of November 1943 Tito had summoned a bogus political congress of his supporters at his headquarters at Jajce. He formed an *ad hoc* Provisional Government which formally deprived the Royal Government of all its right, and forbade the King to return.

From Tito's headquarters Maclean reported that Tito was 'frankly delighted' by Churchill's message on 8 January, and neither he nor his advisers attempted to disguise the importance they attached to it. Tito's reply arrived on the 13th, and two days later Churchill wrote to Tito:

I can understand the position of reserve which you adopt towards King Peter. I have for several months past been in favour of advising him to dismiss Mihailovic and to face the consequent resignation of all his present advisers. I have been deterred from doing this by the argument that I should thus be advising him to cast away his only adherents. You will understand I feel a personal responsibility towards him. I should be obliged if you would let me know whether his dismissal of Mihailovic would pave the way for friendly relations with you and your Movement and, later on, for his joining you in the field, it being understood that the future questions of the Monarchy is reserved until Yugoslavia has been entirely liberated . . . I much hope that you will feel able to give me the answer you can see I want.

A week later, Maclean reported that Tito had told him that he would be willing to send out a representative to the King to discuss future co-operation between them as soon as Mihailovic and the present Government had been dismissed, and the Provisional Government accepted as legal, on the understanding that the question of the monarchy was reserved until after the liberation. 'On my then raising the question of the King's return to Yugoslavia Tito said this could only be arranged if the State repealed their resolution of 29th November [at the Jajce Conference] on the subject. He pointed out that the King was discredited in the eyes of the people by long association with Mihailovic and the Government.

Stevenson, forwarding Maclean's reply from Cairo, commented '. . . He [King Peter] is being asked to throw away all his cards . . . we would in my view be incurring a very great weight of responsibility if we were to advise him to buy at such a price [disowning Mihailovic] the right merely to discuss co-operation with a representative of Tito . . . ought not the discussion to precede dismissal of Mihailovic and the Government?'

Churchill dismissed this with: 'Stevenson vacillates feebly on the subject of Mihailovic and the King,' and said King Peter's one hope of getting back to Yugoslavia lay in ridding himself of Mihailovic and contacting Tito.[23]

Eden did his best to delay Churchill's impetuous move to break with Mihailovic, writing on 19 January:

> Reports from our liaison officers show that Mihailovic undoubtedly still commands wide support in Serbia . . . If Mihailovic is dropped what will happen to the Serbs who now support him? Some might go over to Tito but the majority would probably either continue inactive or follow Mihailovic or some of his henchmen into the enemy camp. Unsatisfactory though Mihailovic is, there are still two Bulgarian divisions looking after him [the Bulgarians were allies of the Germans]. But if the King and Tito were to come together then no doubt virtually all Mihailovic's followers would go to them. That is why I should prefer to know that we can bring King Peter and Tito together before urging King Peter to break with Mihailovic . . . Naturally to Maclean Tito is all white and Mihailovic all black. I have a suspicion that grey is a more common Balkan colour.

Eden asked Churchill to spend half an hour with Selborne (the Minister responsible for SOE) to hear the evidence and pronounce judgement because 'Selborne has through SOE a good deal of information about Mihailovic's conduct over a long period'. Churchill might have been told by Selborne of the London suspicions that SOE in Cairo had become Communist dominated, but he refused to talk to him. Instead, as so often, he disregarded Eden's advice and went ahead with sacking Mihailovic.[24]

Maclean telegraphed his own view that Britain should advise King Peter to accept the conditions about the Jajce conference repealing their resolution because they represented the King's sole chance of continuing to reign. Neither Stevenson nor the Foreign Office agreed.

Tito's continued reference to the bogus Jajce conference was galling to

Churchill but he stuck to his guns encouraged by Randolph's letters, and on 17 February he ordered the withdrawal of all the BLOs and Brigadier Armstrong from Mihailovic. Eden weakly agreed, although he wrote to Maclean that Britain could not recognize the Jajce Provisional Government.

On 25 February Churchill wrote to Tito informing him of the decision and asking him to invite King Peter to join the Partisans: 'you can understand that I cannot press him to dismiss Mihailovic, throw over his Government, and cut off all contact with Serbia before knowing whether he can count on your support and co-operation'. Churchill had made an enormous miscalculation, and his belief that Tito would play ball with the King was pathetic. Tito hated the monarchy and the former Belgrade Government as much as he hated the Germans, and would never allow the King any place in his Communist state.

Churchill's decisions brought trouble from the Americans, who not only refused to withdraw their Mihailovic missions but wanted to send more OSS officers, the US equivalent of SOE, under the auspices of Donovan. Eden warned Churchill that the Americans were 'far from accepting a final break with Mihailovic'. Accordingly Churchill wrote to Roosevelt: 'I have great admiration for Donovan, but I do not see any centre in the Balkans from which he could grip the situation.'

Yet the Americans persisted, and Churchill wrote again to Roosevelt: 'If American mission arrives at Mihailovic's headquarters it will show throughout the Balkans a complete contrariety of action between Britain and the United States. The Russians will certainly throw all their weight on Tito's side which we are backing to the hilt. I hope and trust this may be avoided.' Roosevelt protested that the mission was purely for intelligence, but in view of Churchill's objections he agreed to cancel it. Friction between America and Britain over the Balkans came to a head when the Americans after all sent a mission with Macdowell to Mihailovic at the end of August 1944. Churchill told Roosevelt: 'Colonel Donovan is running a strong Mihailovic lobby just when we have persuaded King Peter to break decisively with him and when many of the Cetniks are being rallied under Tito.' This produced the astounding reply from Roosevelt: 'The mission of OSS is my mistake. I did not check with my previous action of last April. I am directing Donovan to withdraw his mission.'

It is unlikely Roosevelt actually made a mistake because on the same day as he wrote to Churchill he instructed Donovan: 'In view of British objection it seems best to withdraw mission to General Mihailovic.'

Tito complained bitterly about the Allies maintaining relations with Mihailovic. Wilson replied they were only for air crew rescue and evacuation of Allied personnel and to collect intelligence. Donovan's representative at Mihailovic's headquarters, Colonel Macdowell, was outspokenly anti-Communist and at first refused to leave; finally he was evacuated on 2 November 1944. His report is an indictment of British policy towards Mihailovic.[25]

All the BLOs with Mihailovic were brought to Bari by air at the end of May 1944. Armstrong and his officers were furious at being recalled, and against the orders of SOE Cairo some BLOs went on carrying out sabotage although this was concealed by Klugman in Cairo. Armstrong wrote a full and accurate report. Not surprisingly Churchill was unhappy when he read Brigadier Armstrong's final report on his mission, commenting to the Foreign Office: 'I find this report most disquieting. Brigadier Armstrong does not bear out the often repeated tale of Mihailovic's co-operation with the enemy. Yet he was with him all the time, wasn't he? I have never understood on what the evidence rests although I have asked a score of times.' Churchill now suspected Maclean and Randolph had led him up the garden path, and Deakin had been fed false information at Tito's headquarters.[26]

Some BLOs travelled 150 miles from their operational areas in southern Serbia to Pranjani for evacuation. The party after picking up rescued air crews totalled 110, and they encountered no Partisans on the march which was all through Cetnik-held territory. Mihailovic's troops defended the aerodrome against the Germans for their departure. On arrival in Bari they were shown a map with pins showing the whole of their escape route held by Tito's forces. An identical map had been prepared for the Prime Minister by SOE in Cairo. The BLOs were so angry that they pulled out the pins. This shows how Klugman in Cairo was duping his superiors.[27]

Despite receiving mounting quantities of military aid now totally denied to Mihailovic, Tito became non-cooperative and refused to see King Peter. Churchill's high hopes that abandoning Mihailovic would result in a united Yugoslavian Government disappeared. On top, as the official historian points out, Churchill had the 'uneasy feeling that they [Tito's Partisans] might still be eliminating the remaining Cetniks with arms supplied by us rather than undertaking widespread operations against German communications in Serbia'. In fact Tito was hardly operating against the Germans, and concentrating on fighting the Cetniks.[28]

Macdowell in his final October 1944 report wrote:

> . . . members of this mission personally observed sufficient instances of Partisan avoidance of German troops and installations in Serbia during August and September to require the conclusion which the undersigned (Colonel Macdowell) unhesitatingly accepts – that during this period at least the Partisan army made no serious effort to fight Germans or hinder their retreat, but concentrated on attacking Nationalist troops who in some instances were attacking Germans.
>
> . . . all the evidence including much collected earlier by British and American liaison officers cries out against the hypocrisy and dishonesty of the Partisan effort to destroy the Nationalist movement by labelling it quisling or collaborationist. By this attack they have only succeeded in depriving the Allies at this moment of the services of well seasoned troops eager to attack the Germans if only relieved of the pressure of Partisan attacks.

By the time the Macdowell Report reached Churchill his final disillusionment with Tito was complete. Churchill asked Tito to meet him early in August in Naples, after the Yugoslav had rudely refused to come to Caserta to talk to Wilson. Tito accepted Churchill's invitation. The Prime Minister recorded that the Naples meeting 'further weakened his faith in Tito'. After unsatisfactory discussion a memorandum was prepared for Tito stating that His Majesty's

Government would continue to supply war material in increasing quantities, but expected Tito to contribute to the unification of Yugoslavia and to agree to meet King Peter on Yugoslavian soil. Renewal of the civil war would stop Allied supplies, and the Royal Yugoslavian Navy and Air Force could not be brought under Partisan control. Complications were arising over the Yugoslav Navy and Air Force, which were loyal to the King; they were never resolved. Churchill now feared the truth was that Tito had used the massive Allied support to destroy the loyalist Cetniks and carry out his communist revolution.

During a later discussion in Naples Tito said untruthfully that any fighting by his Partisans against the Cetniks was only in self-defence, and he asked for Istria to be ceded to Yugoslavia after the war. Churchill was eager for an amphibious landing in Istria by the Eighth Army; he told Tito that the question of an Allied move into Istria in collaboration with the Partisan forces would have to be discussed with Roosevelt, so that the 'status' of Istria must not be prejudged, and although it might be a good thing to remove Istria from Italian sovereignty, the matter must be left to a post-war peace conference. Meanwhile the territory, as soon as occupied, must be administered by an Allied Military Government. Tito annoyed Churchill by stating sulkily that he could not agree to any Italian civil administration there, and demanded that Yugoslavs should be associated with any administration of the territory.

After the Naples meeting Churchill wrote a minute to Eden which shows how short-lived was his honeymoon with Tito: 'It would be well to remember how great a responsibility would rest with us after the war' when all the arms in Yugoslavia would be in Tito's hands, so that he could subjugate the whole country with weapons supplied by the Allies. Eden, resentful that the decision to abandon Mihailovic had been railroaded through the War Cabinet against his advice, replied that Churchill has persistently 'pushed Tito' in spite of Foreign Office warnings, and that British policy in Yugoslavia had been determined by short-term 'military expediency' rather than 'a long-term political interest'; the Foreign Office had disliked the plan of forcing King Peter to break with Mihailovic before the position of the anti-Communists in post-war Yugoslavia had been studied. Eden was right. Churchill was the prisoner of his own impetuosity, and had been misled by the Communist-infiltrated SOE Cairo office. Now it was impossible for him to remedy the position.[29]

In September Tito further aggravated Churchill by complaining strongly that the Allies were still supplying arms to Mihailovic and maintaining relations with him. The first charge was untrue: no arms were being sent. However, the American missions had refused to withdraw. Churchill prepared a stiff reply, stating his increasing concern that a large proportion of the arms sent to Tito were being used against his countrymen and not against the Germans; also that he was much disappointed that Tito had failed to implement his promise to try to form a united Yugoslav Government with King Peter. The Prime Minister hoped that in place of making minor complaints Tito would not forget 'the much larger matters in which we who had done so much to help him had not received sufficient satisfaction'.

Tito had established himself on the British occupied island of Vis because he had been chased out of his mainland headquarters by the Germans. But Churchill's letter could not be delivered because Tito had flown out of Vis to Moscow in a Russian plane, even though the RAF and Royal Navy were protecting him. Churchill was furious. He thought Tito's behaviour in vanishing was 'unpardonable', and Harold Macmillan, British Resident Minister in the Mediterranean, was told to threaten the Partisan leader's representatives in Vis that unless Tito formed a united Yugoslav Government Britain would be unable to deal with him at a peace conference.

On 29 August 1944 Churchill had written to Roosevelt:

> I have never forgotten your talks to me at Teheran about Istria and I am sure that the arrival of a powerful army in Trieste and Istria in four or five weeks would have an effect far outside purely military values. Tito's people will be awaiting us in Istria. What the condition of Hungary will be then I cannot imagine but we shall at any rate be in a position to take full advantage of any great new situation.[30]

Churchill's ambition was for an Allied army fighting side by side with Tito's Partisans in Istria, to force a passage through the Ljubljana Gap and on to Vienna. This was to take place after September, when the Eighth Army were to storm the Gothic Line, north of Florence, which defended Venice and the Lombardy plain.

While Churchill was in Naples meeting Tito he was enthusiastic for the Eighth Army to make an amphibious landing in Istria. On 8 October 1944 he held a top-level conference there with the Foreign Secretary, the CIGS and Generals Wilson and Alexander. Alexander asked for three American divisions to be sent direct from their homeland to Italy, and the Prime Minister suggested that the current Eighth Army offensive in the Apennines should be stopped, and 'the effort switched to Istria', claiming that it would not be like the failure of Anzio, where the Americans near Rome had been driven back to the beach head after a successful landing, because the British would have the support of Tito's Partisans. He had no inkling that Tito would refuse to co-operate in land operations with the British forces. Alexander was delighted, proposing to hand over the whole of the Italian front to the US Fifth Army, and to prepare the Eighth Army to go in either at Split or into Istria to give him a 'two handed punch'. General Wilson said that late November was the earliest possible date for the operation.

Churchill then suggested 'the amphibious operation might be launched against the north-east coast of Italy behind Kesselring', but was told there were no suitable beaches between Ancona and Trieste. Brooke was lukewarm, and pointed out that the Americans would be most unlikely to release any divisions for Istria; Churchill promised to send telegrams to Roosevelt taking the 'general line' that the winter would bring present Italian operations to a standstill and that the President should be asked to spare two to three divisions for an amphibious operation against the Istria peninsula.

The Eighth Army plan for Istria, on which Churchill was so keen, is unimpressive. The first objectives would be the ports of Pola, Fiume, Trieste and Ruvigno, and the troops would 'concentrate' on the north exit through the Ljubljana Gap. The Army planners were not confident about the help which Tito might give, pointing out that the scattered Italian Resistance was violently 'anti' the Yugoslav Partisans, who were themselves weak, and that it would be unwise 'to count on any considerable help from Partisans'. The planners were even doubtful about being able to take Trieste. Two divisions would be required for the assault, and with a total of five divisions Pola and Ruvigno could be taken, although they had doubts about Trieste. The Germans had a big group of airfields in the Udine–Monfalcone area, but few planes. The Eighth Army report concluded ominously that 'if we got bottled up in Istria we should have achieved nothing after a considerable expenditure of effort by naval, air and military. If Germans could make three reserve divisions available he could hold the line against anything but superior forces.'

However, as has been seen, Roosevelt, backed strongly by Marshall, would not consider diverting any divisions to the Mediterranean for the Istria plan. It therefore withered on the vine, although it was not finally abandoned until the Malta Conference at the end of January 1945. It is difficult to understand why Churchill badgered away for this impractical operation. But the Eighth Army attack on the Gothic line was a costly failure. Alexander held a conference of officers and told them they were going to 'open the road to Vienna'. Instead, after seventy-two hours the attackers were nearly back to their start line. First Armoured Division ran into a concentration of 88 mm guns dug in within prepared defence positions, and suffered such heavy losses that they could not be reformed. Since many US and French divisions had left Italy for southern France the attack could not be remounted, and the Italian campaign became a stalemate.

Unfortunately the British had no faith in the Italian Partisans operating behind the German lines. If as many resources had been sent to them as to Tito, an amphibious landing at the mouth of the Po could have been planned which would have made it impossible for the Germans to hold the Gothic Line. The War Office were misled by reports that Mussolini had raised Fascist divisions, and they underestimated the fighting potential of the Italian Resistance. There was no co-operation between the SOE sent to them and the Plans Section of Alexander's headquarters at Caserta. The late Field Marshal Harding, Alexander's Chief of Staff, told the author that the British Government insisted that the great bulk of supplies and airpower in the Balkans were used in support of Tito and not for the Italian Resistance, while at Caserta they had no information to make them believe the Italian Resistance could be a potent force in disrupting the German defences.

Churchill had been disappointed when Montgomery refused to make amphibious landings on the Adriatic behind the German lines in the autumn of 1943 (apart from one brilliantly successful action at Termoli), and this made him feel that Yugoslavia offered better opportunities. The military dividend from the massive effort in support of Tito was negligible; almost all went into the civil war between the Partisans and the Royalists. Churchill's policy of attacking the 'soft underbelly' of the Reich would have had every chance of success if he had left Mihailovic and Tito to their own devices, written off the Aegean and put everything into Italy. Then the Eighth Army could have advanced through the Veneto and on to Vienna in October 1944, before the Russians arrived in Austria. This is a neglected 'might have been' of history. Churchill was anxious for Tito's forces to attack the Germans in preparation for his pet Istria operation which was now to be an amphibious assault. When Tito asked for field guns, which he would not be able to operate technically, a small British force strong in artillery, led by Brigadier Floyd, was landed near Dubrovnik in December 1944. It was known as Floyd Force. One can imagine Churchill's anger when the Free Yugoslav Radio, operated by Tito, put out this statement: 'No agreement had been signed concerning the entrance of English and American troops into our territory such as has been signed with the Soviet Government.' On 12 January 1945 Tito sent a message he wanted Floyd Force withdrawn, and ordered it back to the sea at Dubrovnik.[31]

At the same time there were reports of atrocities against non-Communist civilians in Dubrovnik, and of rudeness and restrictions on the movement of British soldiers in Yugoslavia. Partisan commanders had refused to allow into Yugoslav ports British warships (including minesweepers which were trying to clear a route for supply ships), and on one occasion Partisan shore batteries had been given orders to fire on any ship which could not produce authority for passage from Tito. Churchill had already told Wilson on 20 November:

> My confidence in Tito which was weakened when I met him in Naples has been destroyed by his levanting from Vis in all the circumstances which attended his departure. We have agreed with the Russians to pursue a joint policy towards him and Yugo 50–50. There is nothing in this to prevent the landing of the British light forces . . . There is no question of recognising Tito at the present time as anything more than the leader of the guerrillas who should be aided in every possible way . . . Maclean should return as soon as possible.

Churchill spent a considerable time composing a stiff message to Tito. He consulted with Wilson, who was back in London for a short visit, and with Brooke and the Foreign Office. After numerous alterations Churchill told Tito he was astonished at the treatment of Floyd Force; he insisted that British forces must have 'every facility' for co-operation with the Partisans. He continued that British public opinion would require any group or political party in Yugoslavia to be genuinely free to put forward candidates in the forthcoming elections, and to express their views about the monarchy by a free plebiscite.

The Prime Minister pointed out emphatically that Tito's ambitions 'to occupy Italian territories on the north of the Adriatic might be leading him to suspect and dislike every military operation carried out by us on the Yugoslav coast against the Germans', but that all territorial questions must be reserved for the peace conference. By now Churchill's disillusion with Tito was complete, and he became determined to stop Tito from seizing Italian territory and imposing Communism on Yugoslavia against the will of the people.

Maclean was ordered to deliver the message personally to Tito. He reported on 6 December that the Partisan leader was considerably taken aback and apologized for his subordinates, saying he wanted an agreement to cover the operations of Allied forces on Yugoslav territory on exactly the same terms as he had given the Russians.

Maclean was told that verbal assurances and promises were 'insufficient', and that definite information was required on the points in the Prime Minister's note. A written reply was received from Tito on 21 December, stating that he did not suspect British motives in landing troops on Yugoslav territory or on territory on which Yugoslavia had claims; and he did not want to prejudice the decisions of the peace conference. In addition, Tito gave the strongest assurances that elections in Yugoslavia would be free, and that there would be a plebiscite over the monarchy. This was tendentious. Naively Stevenson and Eden minuted that 'the terms were on the whole even better than we had hoped'. Churchill was not impressed, but in his reply wrote: 'Let me assure you that we are friends and that we intend to remain so.'[32] At that moment Churchill felt he must do everything possible to keep on good terms with Tito as his co-operation was vital for the Istria landing, which Churchill still saw as a short cut to ending the war.

The Russian Army had taken Belgrade on 21 October 1944, and were advancing on Austria through Romania and Hungary. This made the forcing of the Ljubljana Gap an easier task. In addition, there were strong diplomatic arguments in favour of forestalling a Russian occupation of Austria. Churchill had been shocked by Stalin's refusal to help the Polish uprising in Warsaw in September. Now in December the growing hostility of the Russians and their forces' behaviour in the territories now occupied by them gave him grounds for grave fears about Soviet post-war intentions. Churchill had pressed both the diplomatic and the military arguments for Istria on Roosevelt at the Quadrant Conference in Quebec in September 1944. By January 1945 the diplomatic argument had become stronger.

However, as the defeat of Germany appeared imminent both the British and American Chiefs of Staff pressed for a withdrawal of divisions and landing craft from the Mediterranean to the Pacific. Churchill himself was enthusiastic to mount Skipper – the campaign to retake Malaya, which would require some of the resources needed for Istria. In spite of pleas by Brooke, the Americans adamantly refused to make extra divisions or landing craft available for Istria. Finally on 29 January at the Malta Conference Churchill agreed that some divisions in Italy could go to reinforce Montgomery's army in western Europe, and Italy could become a minor front. Istria was off, and Churchill ceased to take the same detailed interest in Tito.

Mihailovic's position became desperate after the Russian occupation of north-east Yugoslavia in late September 1944. His troops were pushed into a pocket with the Russians and the Partisans on one side, and the Germans on the other. Any Cetniks who fell into Tito's hands were massacred. Mihailovic himself

would not co-operate with the Germans, but some of his subordinate commanders organized the formations still loyal to the King to co-operate with the
Germans in resisting Communist attacks. After the Russian occupation of
Belgrade on 21 October Tito set up a nominally non-Communist Government,
but in fact exercised all power personally as a dictator. Stalin and Churchill had
agreed to a 50–50 division of influence in Yugoslavia. It was in fact 100 per cent
Russian.

Meanwhile Tito increased his demands for military supplies. Churchill
refused, minuting to Eden in March 1945:

> My feeling is that henceforward we should back Italy against Tito . . . the fact that
> we are generally favourable to Italian claims at the head of the Adriatic will give us
> an influence over Italian interests as against communists and wild men which may
> assist the integration of the Italian state. I have lost my relish for Yugoslavia . . . On
> the other hand I hope we may still save Italy from the Bolshevik pestilence.

On 20 April he stated: 'We ought not to throw away our substance in a losing
game with Soviet Russia in Titoland.' When at the end of April 1945 Eden wrote
that 'he did not despair entirely of Yugoslavia, and in order to maintain our stake
in the country we should equip the Yugoslav air force', the Prime Minister
ordered: 'Our supplies to Tito should dwindle and die without another moment's
delay, and no further deliveries are to be made. The above must be taken as a
decision.' The Americans agreed. Churchill noted that Tito was trying to rush
territorial claims against both Italy and Austria, and to face Great Britain and the
United States with a *fait accompli* by sending troops into Italian and Austrian
territories before the British Eighth Army arrived.[33]

In February Alexander had gone to Belgrade and firmly told Tito that when
British troops occupied Austria he would need to control Trieste and the whole
of the territory west of the 1939 frontier between Italy and Yugoslavia – in other
words, all of Istria. Alexander explained that this would be without prejudice to
the frontier 'set' in the final peace settlement. Tito said he would agree to the
establishment of Allied Military Government provided he was allowed to retain
the 'civil administration', which he claimed to have already in part of this
territory. Nothing was agreed. The United States would not consent to a
demarcation line and insisted on Military Government over the whole of Istria
(now referred to as Venezia Giulia). Alexander brought back the mistaken
impression that he had obtained Tito's verbal agreement to the Allied occupation
of Trieste. Meanwhile the Yugoslavian press, controlled by Tito, conducted an
intense propaganda campaign for Venezia Giulia to be incorporated in
Yugoslavia.

A sudden collapse by the Germans in front of both the Eighth Army and the
Russians brought Tito's and Alexander's troops racing towards Trieste at the
end of April 1945. Alexander was ordered to set up an Allied Military Government over the whole of Venezia Giulia, and if the Yugoslavs refused to 'withdraw'
to consult the Combined Chiefs of Staff about 'further action'; this meant war

against Tito – the only medicine he understood. However, the Americans did not stand firm.

On 2 May, as New Zealanders of the Eighth Army accepted the surrender of Trieste from the Germans, they found (to Churchill's disgust) Yugoslav troops moving into the town, extending their occupation to the Isonzo river and entering the Austrian provinces of Carinthia and Styria. At once Tito carried out in Venezia Giulia, and particularly in Trieste, executions and widespread deport-ations of Italians, especially those influential enough to oppose annexation of the territory. Many of those deported were also summarily executed on arrival in Yugoslavia, as were Royalist Yugoslav troops who fell into the hands of the Partisans.

Churchill thought there was 'not much use in arguing with Tito', and that force was the only solution. The Yugoslavs had neither tanks nor planes and could not have put up a sustained resistance to an Allied attack. Churchill signalled to Alexander that 'our line' with Tito should be that all would be settled at the peace conference, and meanwhile 'peace and goodwill should reign on all contacted fronts'. But there was no goodwill on Tito's side.

American support was essential. Unfortunately President Truman, who had now succeeded Roosevelt, sent a message to Churchill that he wished to avoid the use of American forces in combat in the Balkan political area. If Roosevelt had lived, the outcome would have been different. Truman, new to the game, understood nothing of the issues involved in Venezia Giuila. Roosevelt had always believed Tito to be a ruthless Communist; and he had never shared Churchill's short-lived enthusiasm for the man in late 1943 and early 1944, and had to be dragged reluctantly into abandoning Mihailovic.

Still, for a moment Truman considered war. On 12 May he sent a robust telegram of encouragement to Churchill, stating that the USA could not allow 'uncontrolled land grabbing or tactics all too reminiscent of Hitler and Japan'; therefore they must insist on complete and exclusive control of Trieste and Pola. He added: 'I do not believe that Tito or Russia wants to provoke a major clash while American armies are in Europe.' Churchill told the War Cabinet on 13 May that he understood Truman had sent his message after consulting his Chiefs of Staff, and intended that British and American troops should move into the area by force if Tito did not withdraw. However, Truman suddenly weakened and told the Prime Minister on the 14th that unless Tito actually attacked he could not involve the United States 'in another war'; he also refused to make a standstill order to stop United States troops moving out of Italy.

Churchill was bitterly disappointed. In response to another entreaty from Churchill, Truman replied that Alexander, with help from Eisenhower, should reinforce his front line troops to such an extent that the Yugoslavs would realize the firmness of our intentions and 'our preponderance of force'. But he added ominously that he was 'most anxious to avoid interference with the despatch of US troops to the Pacific'.

Stalin now suggested a compromise, with a 'demarcation' line agreed between Alexander and Tito. Churchill was strongly opposed. He told Truman we ought to refuse to negotiate; on 2 June he added that a military operation would be 'sharp and short' and that he hoped Truman would act in the spirit of his message of 12 May. However, Truman was still determined to avoid any fighting. Thus Churchill was forced to eat humble pie and rescind his order to Alexander to occupy all Venezia Giulia up to Pola. Reluctantly Churchill accepted an agreement made on 9 June, under which Tito's army withdrew from Austria and Trieste but remained behind an agreed demarcation line which left the bulk of Venezia Giulia in Yugoslav hands.[34] Churchill dared not risk war with Tito without the USA, as it would open a rift which Stalin would exploit to the hilt.

The new Yugoslav state was totalitarian, with only the pretence of elections; it was run by a series of committees nominated by the Central Government. No political criticism was permitted, and secret police had unlimited powers of arrest and execution without trial. In 1947 the Treaty of Paris assigned the occupied parts of Venezia Giulia to Yugoslavia permanently, and today no Italian families live in this territory. The Italian communities are only commemorated by residents' associations in Rome, Milan and other large Italian towns and cities. Churchill's decision to back Tito against Mihailovic produced little if any military benefits, and was a disaster for the people of Yugoslavia. This he never denied after the war.

A ghastly postscript was the British decision to send back to Tito around thirty thousand anti-Communist Yugoslav troops and civilians who had surrendered with the Germans. This occurred ten days after Tito's troops had withdrawn behind the Alexander demarcation line, which removed all possibility of combat between the British and the Yugoslavs. On arrival in Tito's hands they were massacred and thrown into mass graves, an incident which received enormous publicity in the 1990 Aldington/Tolstoi libel case. The decision to return the Royalist Yugoslavs was made during the General Election of 1945, in breach of a British Government order, while Churchill was over-engaged and Eden was ill and devastated by the loss of his favourite son in action. The decision was effectively taken at a lower level, but responsibility must rest upon the Prime Minister and the Foreign Secretary. Controversy still rages over who was to blame.

Mihailovic was captured by Tito's troops in 1946, and Churchill asked Bevin, the Foreign Secretary, to intervene on his behalf. The Attlee Government took no action. Brigadier Armstrong and other BLOs who had fought with him submitted a memorandum to the court, giving particulars of ten important military operations carried out against the Germans up to February 1944, and of the aid given to Allied prisoners of war and shot-down airmen. The court refused to consider this evidence, and after a summary trial Mihailovic was executed.[35]

At a dinner in Brussels in December 1945 Churchill was reported as saying: 'During the war I thought I could trust Tito . . . but now I am aware I committed one of the biggest mistakes of the war.' Eden said after the war, at the Carlton Club, 'My biggest regret of the war was abandoning Mihailovic.'[36]

If the Greek left-wing parties could have produced a leader as effective as Tito while the country was under German occupation Greece might have ended the war with an unwilling acceptance of a Communist regime imposed by Soviet methods. It can equally be argued that if Belgrade had been as accessible as Athens a relatively small British occupation force could have entirely altered the course of events in Yugoslavia. Fortunately, Churchill's policy was as successful in Greece as it was unsuccessful in Yugoslavia.

King George II of Greece and his Government moved to Crete after the German occupation in April 1941, but were soon driven out of there to London. The Greek Government had been carried on under the virtual dictatorship of General Metaxas until his death in January 1941, when the King and his ministers tried to continue with the same type of government, leaving the constitution suspended indefinitely.

As in Yugoslavia, Greek guerrillas in the mountain valleys organized resistance to the Germans. The Government's move into exile triggered off outspoken opposition to the King, who had condoned the harsh dictatorship of Metaxas. As in Yugoslavia, there was bitter hostility between the Communist and non-Communist guerrillas. The Communist fighters were known as the National Liberation Front (EAM) and the People's Liberation Army (ELAS). The anti-Communists under Zervas (known as EDES) were republican and hotly opposed to the restoration of the monarchy. British officers were dropped to the guerrillas, who blew some important bridges.

Churchill sent the Greek King to Cairo in April 1943. In August he secured with difficulty a paper-thin agreement between ELAS and EAM on one side and EDES on the other to agree to fight the Germans and set up an administration in Cairo under Papendreou, a Social Democrat; but it was accompanied by a declaration that the Greek parties would only agree to the return of the King after a plebiscite. Meanwhile Britain kept the Royal Government in existence as the only properly constituted political administration.

In April 1944 a Greek infantry brigade which Churchill hoped would fight in the Italian campaign mutinied against the King, as did the crews of five ships of the Royal Hellenic Navy. In November EAM–ELAS attacked the non-Communist guerrillas, with a view to seizing control when the Germans withdrew.

On 12 October the Germans evacuated Athens, and British troops who could ill be spared from Italy were sent by plane to the Megara airfield. However, Papendreou did not have enough troops to keep order, and on 1 December the Communists plunged Athens into civil war, attacking the police and the British garrison. Churchill did not hesitate, ordering General Scobie, who was in charge in Athens: 'We have to hold and dominate Athens. It would be a great thing for you to succeed in this without bloodshed if possible but also with bloodshed if necessary.' Churchill had in mind Balfour's celebrated telegram[37] in the 1880s to the British authorities in Ireland, 'Don't hesitate to shoot', which was sent through the open telegraph line in the Post Office. This action was heavily criticized, but prevented loss of life.

Macmillan, the minister responsible in the Mediterranean, flew to Athens. Together with General Scobie and Leeper, the Ambassador to Greece, he agreed that the situation was out of control and that the only solution was to make Archbishop Damaskinos, Primate of Athens, Regent immediately. In London Churchill asked the King of Greece to agree, but he refused. Churchill was reluctant to appoint Damaskinos against the wishes of the monarch, since he was still hoping for a restoration. The Prime Minister's original view was that Macmillan and Leeper were asking 'that a lawful King should be compelled against the advice of his Ministers to install a dictator or quasi dictator in the person of the Archbishop of whose character and intentions he [the King] was in doubt'. Instead Churchill suggested a Regency of Three approved by the King.[38]

At this stage public opinion in America and Britain held that ELAS and EAM were 'friends of democracy' who were being attacked by reactionary forces. There was little realization of the true complexion of the Communist guerrillas, nor of their atrocities. In addition there were widespread demands that the King of Greece should abdicate and not return to his country unless summoned by a plebiscite.

Roosevelt suspected that Churchill's love of monarchies made him eager for a restoration which was no longer practical, and telegraphed on 13 December 1944 explaining that 'it had not been possible to take a stand along with you on the present course of events in Greece; even an attempt to do so would bring only temporary value to you and would in the long run do injury to our basic relationship'. Roosevelt demanded the appointment of a Regent and the King's abdication.[39]

Churchill bowed to the inevitable and concurred. Once Churchill gave way over the monarchy Roosevelt promised full co-operation in putting down the rebels in the capital. Churchill then flew on Christmas Day to Athens, which he found under shell and machine-gun fire. By sheer force of character Churchill forced Damaskinos to become Regent and form a Goverment without Communist members; in return Churchill promised more British troops to clear the Communists out of Athens. Once back in London Churchill persuaded the King to agree, and to issue a public statement that he would not return to Greece unless summoned by a free and fair expression of the national will. By 11 January the Communist guerrillas had been defeated. They signed a truce, and peace was restored. By his statesmanlike withdrawal of his objections to a Regency, and his prompt and decisive action in Athens, Churchill had saved Greece from the fate of Yugoslavia.

CHAPTER TWENTY

D-Day to long-delayed
German surrender

Prior to the Quebec Conference in September 1943 it had been assumed that the overall commander of the Normandy invasion would be British. With US approval, Churchill had promised the CIGS the post. Brooke was delighted, recording in his diary that when in August 1942 Churchill had asked him to take over command of the Eighth Army it had given rise to 'most desperate longings . . . and for sheer thrill and freedom of action it stood in a category by itself and not to be compared with a staff appointment'. When on 9 July 1943 Churchill told Brooke he wanted him to be Supreme Commander of operations across the Channel, Brooke put in his diary: 'It would be the perfect climax to all my struggles to guide the strategy of the war', and he was 'too excited to go to sleep'.

On 12 August, a few days before the Quebec Conference, Roosevelt told Churchill that because the American forces would be so much larger numerically than those of the British in the later stages of the European invasion he had decided that Marshall, not Brooke, must command. Callously Churchill ignored his offer to Brooke of the previous month and complied with alacrity. The CIGS recorded: 'It was a crushing blow to hear from him that he was now handing over the appointment to the Americans . . . Not for one moment did he realise what this meant to me. He offered no sympathy, no regrets at having had to change his mind, and dealt with the matter as if it were one of minor importance.' Brooke called it a black day.[1]

Roosevelt soon regretted his choice of Marshall. He had become overdependent on him and felt 'he could not sleep at night in Washington without having him at his side'. Instead of Marshall, Eisenhower was then selected. But Churchill had to nominate the British commander under Eisenhower (21 Army Group).

Montgomery had fallen from grace because of the poor performance of the Eighth Army in the Italian campaign. They had been successful in the invasion of Sicily, but General Patton's Army had snatched the headlines from them by reaching Messina first, and much of the German Army had been allowed to escape to the mainland. A nasty quarrel between Montgomery and Alexander on the one side, and Patton and Eisenhower on the other, over whether the Americans or the British or both should use the main road north from Catania to Messina, produced tension in Anglo–US relations.

The campaign in Italy had turned sour on Montgomery. The Eighth Army landed without opposition at Reggio on the toe of Italy on 4 September 1943. The main assault came at Salerno on the 9th, with US Fifth Army and British X Corps under General Mark Clark. Montgomery was slow in closing the gap between the two armies, so that the Germans nearly pushed the Salerno invasion forces back into the sea. For this he was much criticized. Unarmed war correspondents linked up with the US Fifth Army forty-eight hours before the Eighth Army troops did, which showed his shortcomings.

Montgomery was again so slow advancing up the Adriatic coast that Churchill became frustrated. The Prime Minister coined the meaningless phrase, 'Whoever holds Rome holds the title deeds to Italy', disregarding the fact that Rome had only been the Italian capital for seventy-three years and that her main industrial base was several hundred miles further north. On 4 October Montgomery, conscious of Churchill's irritation at his lack of speed, cabled direct to the Prime Minister: 'We have advanced a long way and very quickly . . . When I have got control of Termoli Campobasso I will advance with my whole strength on Pescara and Ancona and I look forward to meeting you in Rome.' Montgomery was staking his claim for the command of the British troops in north-west Europe.

Churchill wanted Montgomery to undertake amphibious assaults behind the German line, and was delighted when on 20 October Eighth Army commandos made a spectacularly successful landing in the German rear at Termoli. This advance made the important airfields at Foggia safe from a German counter-attack, so that they could be utilized for raids deep into eastern Europe upon which Churchill set much store.

On 28 November Montgomery launched his attack over the Sangro. This would, if successful, lead to the capture of Rome. Bombastically he announced, 'We will hit the Germans a colossal crack', and after a successful first day said, 'My troops have won the battle as they always do. The road to Rome is open.' He was mistaken. His attack ground to a halt and the Pescara–Rome lateral road was not taken until June 1944. If Montgomery had stayed in Italy he would have finished the war with a sadly dented reputation. Brooke noted in his diary on 14 December after visiting the Eighth Army: 'I am rather depressed about what I have seen . . . Monty is tired out, and Alex fails to grasp the show . . . Monty saw little hope of capturing Rome before March . . . no longer any talk of turning left by his forces to capture Rome.'

But Churchill still had faith in the victor of Alamein, and on Christmas Eve 1944 Churchill told Montgomery he was to command the cross-Channel invasion. It had been decided that American troops should come under British command in the initial assault stage within 21 Army Group, and that Eisenhower would only establish his Supreme Headquarters Allied Expeditionary Force (SHAEF) on the continent after the breakout from the bridgehead. The Americans would have preferred Alexander, whom they found easier and more co-operative than Montgomery. Montgomery had been abrasive towards Patton in Sicily and to General Mark Clark in Italy. However, the American generals admired Montgomery's expertize and confidence, and as Churchill had been co-operative over an American Supreme Commander Roosevelt readily agreed to Montgomery's appointment.

At the end of 1943 Churchill was convalescing in Morocco from the pneu-monia which had struck him after the Teheran Conference. Montgomery arrived on 1 January 1944 in Marrakesh, where Eisenhower was a fellow guest, and immediately saw Churchill, who was in bed surrounded by official papers. The Prime Minister greeted him warmly, handed him a bulky document entitled 'Operation Overlord', and told him to read it. Montgomery, who disliked Churchill's habit of talking into the dead of night, took it away, and by next morning had briefed himself. He, like Eisenhower, was unhappy about it; he gave Churchill a typed report which condemned the plan on the grounds that the front for the initial landings was too narrow.

The Montgomery memorandum weakened Churchill's faith in General F. E. Morgan, Chief of Staff to the Allied Commander, who had drafted the original Overlord plan. Churchill agreed enthusiastically with Montgomery's view, stat-ing it was an advantage to invade a long continental coastline from an island because 'our forces are concentrated at the start, while the army are forced to spread themselves out over a wider range'. Churchill and Clemmie took Montgomery for a picnic, on which the General delighted the Prime Minister by describing the technical essentials for an opposed seaborne landing. Churchill insisted that the Allies must not use the word 'invasion' until they crossed the German frontier. He objected to Roosevelt's recent phrase 'Assault upon Fortress of Europe'; instead he insisted upon 'Liberation of Europe from Germans . . . we must not make a present to Hitler of the idea that he is the defender of Europe which we are trying to invade'. Churchill cabled the Chiefs of Staff, endorsing all Montgomery's points; Eisenhower fully agreed.

Although Montgomery was to make many mistakes, he was the right choice. Aged fifty-six, he was an expert in modern war technology, and perhaps best of all supremely confident in his own ability to lead a combined US–British Army to victory. No other British general was so well equipped for the job.

In London Morgan was replaced as Chief of Staff by the American General Bedell Smith. When US generals objected to Montgomery talking about giving orders to them, Montgomery tactfully said he would command the British and Canadian troops but that he would 'suggest' to General Bradley 'the scheme of manoeuvre for the Americans'. Enthusiastically Eisenhower and his staff agreed to Montgomery's plan to upgrade the assault force from three divisions to five on the first tide, with two more, plus an airborne division, to follow on the second tide. Marshall readily agreed to provide more landing craft, but to Churchill's disappointment this meant postponing D-Day from early May to early June.

The only point of conflict between Montgomery and the Americans was whether Overlord should be accompanied by an assault on the Mediterranean coast of France (Anvil), which would take American divisions away from the Italian campaign. Montgomery, backed by Churchill, opposed Anvil. But

Eisenhower, supported by Marshall, would not give it up. At Marrakesh on 1 January Montgomery had told Churchill it would be ninety days before Anvil had any beneficial effect on Overlord.[2] Churchill now went over the heads of the military, and appealed to Roosevelt. To the Prime Minister's consternation, at the end of June the President insisted that Anvil must go ahead, writing: 'We can, and Wilson confirms this, immediately withdraw 5 divisions (3 US and 2 French) from Italy for Anvil. The remaining 21 will provide Alexander with adequate ground superiority.' Over Churchill's *cri de coeur* not to diminish the Italian forces because they would all be necessary for a landing in Istria, Roosevelt wrote:

> The difficulties in this advance would seem far to exceed those pictured by you in the Rhone valley ignoring the effect of organised resistance groups in France . . . it is doubtful if within a decisive period it would be possible to put into the fighting beyond the Ljubljana Gap more than six divisions . . . I cannot agree to the employment of US troops against Istria and into the Balkans, nor can I see the French agreeing to the use of French troops . . . For purely political considerations over here I would never survive even a slight setback to Overlord if it were known that fairly large forces had been diverted to the Balkans.

The Presidential election was due early in 1945.[3]

Churchill's heart was, of course, set on an Allied advance from Italy into Istria and on over the Ljubljana Gap to Vienna. Alas for his plans! As Brooke put it: '. . . the Americans now begin to own the major strength on land, in the air and on the sea'. By July 1944 the Americans had over 11 million men under arms, the British only 5 million. America was the senior partner, and Roosevelt's message shattered Churchill's hopes. He took it ill and threatened resignation, drafting a reply to the President:

> The whole campaign in Italy is being ruined . . . If my departure from the scene would ease matters by tendering my resignation to the King I would gladly make this contribution, but I fear that the demand of the public to know the reasons would do great injury to the fighting troops . . . I am supported by the War Cabinet and by the British Chiefs of Staff. Therefore I think I have a right to some consideration from you, my friend.[4]

The Prime Minister was wrong in claiming he had the support of the British Chiefs of Staff. Churchill, Brooke, Portal and Cunningham discussed the President's message on 30 June; Brooke summed it up: 'I thought at first we might have trouble with him; he looked like wanting to fight the President. However in the end we got him to agree with our outlook which is "Alright if you want to be damned fools sooner than fall out with you which would be fatal, we shall be damned fools with you and we shall see that we perform the role of damned fools damned well."' The meeting concluded that American insistence on Anvil was motivated by domestic politics, not military factors, and 'further discussion was useless'.[5]

Churchill abandoned his draft and wrote that Eisenhower disliked Anvil (this was incorrect), and that Montgomery had stated it would take ninety days for Anvil to influence Overlord.

There is no doubt that an advance up the Rhone valley begun at the end of August could easily be blocked and stemmed by a smaller number of German troops who could come either through the tunnels from Italy or from southern Germany. I doubt whether you will find that three American divisions supported by seven French, 80 per cent native, divisions from Morocco, Algiers and Tunis, will have any important strategic effect on Eisenhower's and Montgomery's battle 500 miles to the north. His Majesty's Government must on the advice of their Chiefs of Staff enter a solemn protest.

The late Field Marshal Lord Harding, then Chief of Staff to Alexander, told the author that the removal of the American and French divisions for Anvil put paid to his and Alexander's plans for victory in Italy.[6]

It was an ungracious acceptance. By the time Anvil was launched on 16 August the German armies in Normandy had been defeated and Hitler had decided not to defend the Rhône valley. Even so, it was four weeks before the Anvil landing forces could take part in the main battle. As soon as the Germans began to crumble in Normandy Churchill pleaded with Roosevelt, again in vain, for Anvil to be cancelled or diverted to the west coast of France in Brittany. This relentless and persistent demand by the Americans for Anvil was a running sore for the Prime Minister, who had become obsessed by what he saw as glittering opportunities in Istria.

The dread of the coming battle in Europe lay like a black cloud over Britain. Over four years of war – for part of the time without any real hope of victory – had sapped the energy of the nation. The older generation was worried by memories of the bloodbath of the Somme and Passchendale in 1916, and the inevitable fearsome casualties of trench warfare. The home army was frustrated: after four years of hard training they had known no battles. A small proportion were survivors from the fiasco of Dunkirk. Veterans of the First World War were unable to understand why they had won in 1918 but had been defeated in 1940 and why, until Montgomery took over, the British Army had lost all its battles except for Wavell's victory over the Italians. Senior officers bored and frightened their juniors with reminiscences of trench warfare which appeared out of date to young men expert in W/T communications, mechanized mobile warfare and RAF support.

Montgomery found that the average young soldier expected to die in Overlord, and he decided he must go on a morale-boosting tour of the troops. He was right. After four years of exhortation the Churchill magic was wearing thin, and a fresh input was required. Montgomery enjoyed the limelight and had a flair for personal appeals. He had spent all his adult life with soldiers, and he loved and understood them. In early 1944 he mesmerized the servicemen and the armaments factories with his speeches, and revelled in his sudden personal popularity.

In him young men and women saw a survivor of the First World War who had mastered the art of modern warfare and, unlike the other generals, had won all his battles against the Germans. He made them believe he could make good use of the modern technology in which they had been trained, and could lead them to victory over Hitler's armies which had seemed invincible until Alamein. And instead of going to France as in 1939 with bayonets against sub-machine guns and with useless 'Boyes' anti-tank rifles, now they were a properly equipped, well-trained army which would sweep all before it. This message Montgomery put across successfully, and he did a fine job in raising morale at the precise moment when it was essential.

Churchill appreciated how Montgomery was helping the troops' morale, but he feared his General was becoming so popular and receiving such publicity that he was edging in on Churchill's own position as national leader. In addition Montgomery began to show an interest in politics, which the Prime Minister found unwelcome, so he initiated messages asking him to stop his tours, while the BBC were told to cut down on his invitations to broadcast. Montgomery paid no attention. He knew the good he was doing and that he could leave the details of planning to his excellent staff, but he also knew very well how the D-Day landing would test the morale of his troops.

Montgomery was famous for his black beret, to which were affixed several divisional crests. Churchill objected to this, and asked the King to query with Montgomery if this was in the best of taste. Montgomery told the King when he was at Buckingham Palace that, as all the soldiers knew his beret, it was worth 'at least an army corps' and it was vital he should go on wearing it. The King, succumbing to Montgomery's charm, raised no objection.

On 7 April 1944 Churchill was present at an historic occasion – the presentation of the D-Day plans at Montgomery's old school, St Paul's. Churchill learnt, as did the other 111 people present (all sworn to strict secrecy) that Montgomery's aim was for the British on the east flank to draw off the German armour, and that when this was done the Americans would drive through on the west down the Cherbourg peninsula and then turn east to rout the German Army from the south.

Montgomery told the conference that the Prime Minister would arrive with a large cigar in his mouth and that his smoking ban would be lifted then; he did so in such a puckish way that there was a roar of laughter. Churchill told the conference that the operation would not have been feasible in 1942 or 1943, but now he had the greatest confidence in the plans and 'we were going to write a glorious page in the history not of one country or of two, but of the world'. At Anzio the British had lost a great opportunity; we must learn the lesson and this time push our spearheads forward quickly. Churchill spoke without vigour, and when he finished looked as if he was going to burst into tears. However, the audience was 'tremendously impressed and inspired'.

That day the Prime Minister seemed tired and old. He was worried, for that week he had endured difficult Cabinets over the proposed pre-invasion bombing of French roads and railways. Eden and Churchill were violently opposed because of the likelihood of high civilian casualties, but Eisenhower insisted it must go ahead. However, after his pep talk the conference dispersed with a friendly atmosphere amongst British, Canadians and Americans, and a confidence that all would go well.

In his diary Brooke commented: 'Monty started with a good speech. Churchill was in a weakly condition looking old and lacking vitality.'[7] A week before he had described Churchill as 'in a desperately tired mood. I am afraid he is losing ground rapidly. He seems quite incapable of concentrating for a few minutes on end and keeps wandering continuously . . . said he was feeling desperately tired.' Cadogan commented the same week: 'I really am fussed about the P.M. He is not the man he was twelve months ago, and I really don't know whether he can carry on.' General Kennedy commented that at St Paul's 'He looked puffy and dejected and his eyes were red.' But as usual Churchill was resilient, and quickly recovered his ebullience.[8]

The final top-level pre-invasion conference was again held at St Paul's, with the same service top brass, on 15 May, and this time with the King as well as Churchill. Once again Montgomery was supremely confident and lucid. He concluded: 'We shall have to send the soldiers into this party seeing red. We must get them completely on their toes having absolute faith in the plan and imbued with infectious optimism and offensive eagerness.' Air Chief Marshal Sir Arthur Harris told the conference that even at this late hour strategic bombing of Germany could be an adequate substitute for invasion. For a long time Churchill had hoped this was true, but now it was an irrelevance for him. The King embarrassingly stammered out a few words. Churchill this time did not speak; he arrived for lunch, and was cheerful and genial. The conference broke up with a smell of victory in the air, and Churchill seemed far more confident than in April. The die was cast. D-Day was 6 June. He had complete faith in Montgomery, and after having had to galvanize his generals for four years at last he had a man after his own heart.[9]

As D-Day approached, Churchill agitated to witness at first hand the Normandy landings. On 30 May he informed the King of his intention at their weekly Buckingham Palace lunch; the King immediately replied that he would come too, and suddenly Churchill saw the folly of his suggestion.[10]

. The controversy over the bombing of French bridges and railways continued to haunt Churchill, but Eisenhower would not curtail his demands. However, one of Churchill's quirks was that he liked to have a pet aversion on which he could let off his tensions. With the strain of waiting for D-Day, the Prime Minister worried more and more about the large numbers of administrative vehicles and personnel which showed up on the charts of loading priorities. He now began to query the loading programme. The War Office could give him no satisfactory answer; all they were able to say was that Montgomery's planning staff had certified that these scales were essential.

A week before D-Day Churchill went down to 21 Army Group HQ, which had now moved to Portsmouth, and there suggested to Montgomery that he (Churchill) should address the latter's staff on the subject of unnecessary vehicles and unnecessary clerical personnel. Characteristically Montgomery would have none of it, and said to Churchill:

It would be unwise for you to speak to my staff. Even if I have made mistakes it is now too late to put them right. The loaded trains are on the way to the ports and many of the boats are already loaded. To alter things now would dislocate

'Overlord'. I myself am sure that every single man and vehicle is necessary. If you do not believe me and insist on last-minute alterations you must have lost confidence in me.

It was a tense moment. Suddenly Churchill saw that he had left things too late, and that Overlord was beyond his control. He could not afford a quarrel with Montgomery at this eleventh hour. He was almost certainly right about the loading priorities and the unnecessary personnel, and undoubtedly he still thought so, but now he bowed to the inevitable. Montgomery led him out of his office and introduced him to his waiting staff, all of whom knew what the two men had been discussing. Churchill rose to the occasion and acknowledged defeat, saying with an impish grin: 'Gentlemen, today I must not talk to you.' A clash between the two dedicated leaders had been averted, but it had shown that Montgomery knew how enormously powerful was his own position *vis-à-vis* the Prime Minister. The incident did nothing to make the General more modest. Hamilton, Montgomery's official biographer, says Churchill almost burst into tears. In 1946 Churchill threatened to sue Alan Moorehead if he published an account of this incident. It became the Field Marshal's favourite story in his old age.[11]

The Overlord landings went according to Montgomery's plan on 6 June, except for the US Omaha beach where the issue was in doubt for many hours; but the Allied troops were contained in the bridgehead by determined German infantry and armour under General Rommel. For Montgomery the result was disappointing. He needed a large-scale map to point out the territory he had gained. He had never promised that the British Second Army would break out; only that they would draw off German armour and so weaken the Germans in front of General Bradley's Army that the Americans would have no great difficulty in breaking out down the Cherbourg peninsula.

Montgomery confidently went on telling everybody that the battle was going well according to his plan, since around Caen he had drawn off the bulk of the German armour from the US front. But at St Paul's he had promised the air marshals he would capture the airfields around Caen and advance far enough to make them safe for use. This he could not deliver, but he personally did not care whether the RAF and USAAF operated from French or British airfields.

On 3 July Montgomery wrote a long letter to Eisenhower boasting how he had drawn off Rommel's Panzers to the British front, thus enabling the Americans to take Cherbourg and regroup without the threat of Panzer attacks. Montgomery was justified; Ultra decrypts had revealed that only one battered Panzer division was opposite the Americans. But Eisenhower and the American generals, backed by Air Marshal Tedder (second in command at SHAEF), disliked the 'always right' tone of the letter and were very critical of Montgomery. Inadvisedly, on 10 July Montgomery had claimed to Eisenhower that Caen had been captured. This was untrue – the British had taken only part of the town.

In London Eisenhower complained to Churchill that 'Monty was bogged down and over cautious'. According to Brooke, Churchill listened sympathetically to the American. This produced a furious four-hour quarrel between the

Prime Minister and the CIGS on the evening of 6 July, with Churchill abusing Montgomery because he was not advancing fast enough, at which Brooke flared up and demanded why the Prime Minister 'could not trust his General for five minutes'. Brooke put in his diary: 'He said he never did such a thing. I then reminded him that in front of a large gathering of Ministers, he had torn Alexander to pieces for lack of imagination and leadership in continually attacking Cassino. He was furious with me but I hope it has done some good for the future.' Eden noted in his diary: 'a deplorable evening'; Admiral Cunningham's comment was: 'There is no doubt the PM was in no state to discuss anything . . . very tired and too much alcohol'.[12]

Montgomery and Bradley scheduled their main breakout attack to start on 20 July. The British assault south of Caen was codenamed Goodwood, the American push Cobra. Goodwood was a partial success, drawing almost all Rommel's armour to the British front and inflicting heavy damage on them, but no breakthrough was achieved. Unfortunately for Montgomery, Cobra had to be postponed until 24 July because of bad weather, which had also brought the Goodwood attack to an end. The delay was nearly fatal for Montgomery, and the American generals pressed Eisenhower for their British colleague to be sacked. At this moment Montgomery had upset the temperamental Churchill, who was at his edgiest because flying bombs were causing intense damage to London (see page 307), and desperately anxious for the Allied armies to advance more quickly from Normandy to capture the flying bomb sites on the Calais coast.

On 18 July Churchill sent a message to Montgomery that he would visit him. Up to his eyes over the breakout, the last thing Montgomery wanted was to have his time wasted, and with Goodwood faltering he could not bear the Prime Minister breathing down his neck. Rashly he signalled to Eisenhower that he did not want to receive the Prime Minister. Eisenhower told Churchill this, suggesting that instead he went to see Cherbourg and then sailed along the British beaches without visiting his General. Churchill was livid, and Montgomery was in grave danger of losing his command.

The Prime Minister informed Eisenhower that he would fly over on the 21st to drive around the Cherbourg peninsula and visit several of 'the alleged rocket strips'; he added ominously, 'I have no intention of visiting General Montgomery's HQ and he should not concern himself about me in any way.' And he told Brooke, with venom:

> With hundreds of war correspondents moving about freely this cannot be considered an unreasonable request from the Minister of Defence. If however General Montgomery disputes about it in any way the matter will be taken up officially, because I have both a right and a duty to acquaint myself with the facts on the spot.

Montgomery's fat was in the fire.

On the 19th, according to Brooke's diary, Churchill, still in bed at 09.30, was raging against Montgomery for stopping his visit to him in France: 'Haig had always allowed him in the last war as Minister of Munitions. He would not stand it. He would make it a matter of confidence, etc. etc.' At this stage Brooke was annoyed with Churchill, noting in his diary on 20 July: 'Winston goes off skylarking instead of giving decisions months overdue'.

Brooke, who had scheduled a visit to Montgomery for that day, realized the moment of crisis had come for his friend. As soon as he landed at the airstrip, Brooke informed Montgomery that Eisenhower 'has been expressing displeasure and accusing Monty of being sticky and of not pushing sufficiently on the Caen front with the British while he made the Americans do the attacking on the right', and that Churchill had taken these complaints very seriously. He firmly told Montgomery to go into his caravan and write to the Prime Minister, inviting him to his forward Tactical Headquarters. Montgomery wrote in his own handwriting:

> My Dear Prime Minister
>
> I have just heard from the C.I.G.S. that you are proposing to come over this way shortly; this is the first I have heard of your visit. I hope that you will come over here whenever you like; I have recently been trying to keep visitors away as we have much on hand.
>
> But you are quite different, and in your capacity as Minister of Defence you naturally are above all these rules. So as far as I personally am concerned I hope you will visit Normandy whenever you like; and if I myself am too busy to be with you I will always send a staff officer. And if you ever feel you would like to stop the night and stay in one of my caravans – which will be held ready for you at any time.
>
> Yrs sincerely
> B.L. Montgomery

Montgomery did not show the letter to the CIGS – he dared not, since it contained the untruth that he had not 'heard' of the proposed visit.

The letter worked 'like magic'; certainly it saved Montgomery. Churchill telephoned Brooke that he was delighted with it, and felt ashamed about all he had said in the morning. Late on the 19th he signalled Montgomery: 'Thank you very much for your letter.' On the first draft he had dictated: 'You may be sure that I shall never be a burden but only a prop if ever needed.' He put his fountain pen through this phrase, thinking perhaps that there might arise an occasion when he would have to be a 'burden', and also, that he must not make his General any more conceited than he already was.

The Prime Minister visited Montgomery on 25 July. All went well. Montgomery, having seen the red light, exerted his charm to convince the Prime Minister, that the campaign was going according to plan. Montgomery himself was optimistic, mainly because Ultra signals showed the Germans in the US sector to be in poor shape. Ultra also confirmed that Goodwood had drawn almost all the German armour to the eastern front, so that the prospects for a swift American triumph with Cobra were excellent. All this Churchill lapped up greedily; when he returned to London he said that 'all was going well in Normandy', telling the War Cabinet that he had never seen 'a happier army'. Montgomery wrote to his friend General Frank Simpson at the War Office: 'The PM has just been here very friendly. I gave him a bottle of brandy as a peace offering.' He could not have found a better present – at that stage of the war there was hardly a bottle of French brandy left in London.[13]

Eisenhower lacked the British General's supreme confidence and, exasperated by his lofty attitude, was on the brink of asking Churchill to sack him. At I a.m. on 25 July Churchill telephoned Eisenhower, who thought this would be a good moment to ask the Prime Minister to get rid of Montgomery, knowing from his previous conversations how angry Churchill was with his General. During a half-hour conversation the American probed to find out what Churchill's reaction would be, only to discover that the Prime Minister was solidly on Montgomery's side. Eisenhower told his aide de camp, Captain Henry Butcher, that Montgomery had sold the Prime Minister a 'Bill of Goods' at his Normandy headquarters and 'the P.M. is supremely happy with the situation'; the American realized that, no matter how maddening Montgomery might be, he must live with him.[14]

Montgomery was right. The Cobra offensive under General Patton went through the weakened enemy lines like butter, and the Germans could not counter-attack because their six Panzer divisions were held in front of the British near Caen. The key road junction of Avranches fell on I August, and Bradley's divisions streamed into Brittany while Patton's army turned east to cut off the Germans from the rear. Soon the Allies were on the Seine, and on 25 August Paris fell.

Churchill's visit to Montgomery in Normandy on 25 July coincided with the news of the Stauffenberg bomb plot which nearly killed Hitler on 20 July. Brigadier Sir Edgar Williams told the author that he was present when Montgomery asked the Prime Minister: 'What is going on with this revolution in Germany?' According to Williams,

> Churchill was completely nonplussed. He sat on the only stool in the map caravan in silence. Then I remember very clearly he produced a long chain with keys and unlocked two despatch boxes. They were full of papers, all mixed up. He said 'There is something about it in here.' As Monty and I scrabbled through the papers with Cabinet documents and Ultra decrypts all muddled up Churchill began to mumble to himself rhetorical phrases for a speech about the overthrow of the Nazis.
>
> I suddenly realised that Winston had come from London with all this stuff in his despatch case unread, and that he was 'naked' in face of the possible sudden end of the war. I was amazed that he was unbriefed of what was going on in Germany. I felt sure that von Kluge [commanding the German armies in Normandy in succession to Rommel, who had been wounded] was contemplating a battlefield surrender.[15]

Williams was correct: Churchill had no prior inkling of the plot. The conspirators, led by Stauffenberg and Adam von Trott had made repeated efforts to talk to the Allies through diplomats in the neutral capitals of Stockholm, Berne, Lisbon and Madrid. But neither the Americans nor the British would communicate with them. They were told 'nothing but unconditional surrender' even if they formed an anti-Nazi Government.

Ever since he had become Prime Minister Churchill had insisted on 'absolute silence' in response to any peace overtures from Germans, instructing Eden early in January 1941: 'Our attitude to all such enquiries should be absolute silence.' Foreign Office officials disliked this ruling because they thought that by talking to

German dissidents they could obtain a lot of information about conditions in Germany. They pressurized Eden to ask Churchill to relax his ruling, and on 10 September 1941 the Foreign Secretary wrote to Churchill: 'such messages occasionally throw interesting light on internal difficulties and tendencies in Germany'. The Prime Minister replied categorically: 'I am sure we should not depart from our policy of absolute silence. Nothing would be more disturbing to our friends in the United States or more dangerous with our new ally, Russia, than the suggestion that we were entertaining such ideas. I am absolutely opposed to the slightest contact.' On the minute Eden noted: 'I do agree and am in fact relieved at your decision. The case in favour was, I thought, worth a mention. A.E.'

Churchill penned on Eden's minute: 'Please keep.' Clearly he wanted to make sure that the Foreign Office did not back-pedal on his decision that there should be 'absolute silence', and he bears a heavy responsibility for refusing to encourage the anti-Nazi German patriots who might have been able to bring the war to an end. But Eden was weak in not pressing his Department's view.[16]

Adam von Trott, a Rhodes scholar and a close personal friend of Stafford Cripps and his son, was one of the most active conspirators. He constantly sought contact with the British Government so that he could report what peace terms would be given to an anti-Nazi Government, because this would be an inducement to the dissident generals to abandon Hitler. His efforts went unrewarded. Through Dr Visser't Hooft, the Secretary of the World Council of Churches in Geneva, who made a trip to London, he sent a memorandum to Cripps in May 1942 asking that the 'complete uncertainty of the British and American attitude towards a change of Government in Germany' should be ended; he stated that there was a powerful resistance movement, whose members included politicians, generals and civil servants, who wanted to kill Hitler and make peace. Wheeler-Bennett, the German expert, had considerable influence on both Churchill and Eden. Surprisingly, he recommended that the Visser't Hooft memorandum should be ignored and said that Trott, a former friend of his, was dishonest. Eden and Churchill concurred. This brought an outspoken protest from Cripps, then a member of the War Cabinet, who told Eden that he 'completely failed to understand Trott – who or what he stood for'. Churchill and Eden ignored Cripps' protest.[17]

Bishop Bell of Chichester went to Sweden in May 1942 and saw Hans Schoenfeld and Dietrich Bonhoeffer of the German Protestant Church. In Stockholm Schoenfeld informed Bell of the existence of a strong opposition to Hitler which had existed before the war. He said that the course of the war had given it a chance which it was waiting to seize. The opposition, according to Schoenfeld, was made up of members or former members of the state administration; large numbers of former trade unionists who had built up a network of key men in the main industrial posts; high officers in the Army and State police; and leaders of the Protestant and Catholic Churches, 'exemplified' by the protests against Nazi tyranny by the Protestant Bishop Wurm of Württemberg and Bishop von Preysing of Berlin.

This opposition intended to destroy Hitler, Himmler, Goering, Goebbels and the leaders of the Gestapo, S S and S A and in their place establish a Government composed of strong groups of those mentioned above. Their programme, of which Schoenfeld supplied a written memorandum, was principally to include considerable decentralization of German Government; a free Polish and Czech nation and reparations for damages caused by Germany to other nations; national and social life orientated towards Christianity; and repeal of the Nuremberg laws and restoration of property to the Jews. (The Nuremberg laws had deprived Jews of their civil rights.)

Schoenfeld was later joined by Bonhoeffer, who said the opposition hoped to mobilize the Army and the nation against the Nazis. They stressed that they were embarking on a highly dangerous project, and that it was therefore 'extremely important to know the Allies' attitude to a Germany purged of Hitler'.

Bell asked Bonhoeffer to give him the names of the chief conspirators. Bonhoeffer replied that they were generals Beck and Hammerstein, the politician Goerdeler, the former trade union leaders Leuschner and Kaiser, and that Beck and Goerdeler were joint leaders, while Schacht, Prince Louis Ferdinand (son of the Kaiser) and leading Protestant and Catholic bishops were involved. He also said that there was an organization representing the opposition in every Ministry and in all the big towns and cities, and mentioned Kluge and Witzleben amongst the Army generals. Finally Bonhoeffer summed up their discussion by asking Bell to get replies from London to the following questions. Would the Allied Governments, once the whole Hitler regime had been overthrown, be willing to treat with a *bona fide* German Government for a peace settlement as described above, including the withdrawal of all German forces from occupied countries and reparation for damages, and to say so privately to an authorized representative of the opposition; or could the Allies make a public pronouncement in clear terms to the same effect?

Bonhoeffer told the Bishop that Trott would be 'ideal' as an intermediary. Bell discussed all this with Mallet [Head of the British Legation in Stockholm], who reported to the Foreign Office that 'this was something more than one of the usual peace feelers'. Bell wanted Dr Ahrenstorm of the World Council of Churches in Geneva or Dr Visser't Hooft to go to Stockholm to help as an intermediary.

As soon as the Bishop got back to London he asked to see the Foreign Secretary. Patrick Hancock of the Foreign Office German Department noted that the Secretary of State might explain to the Bishop the Government's attitude to peace feelers, in other words 'absolute silence'. Christopher Warner minuted: 'The claims sound very exaggerated.' He commented, correctly, that 'this might chime in with the move from Adam Trott via Visser't Hooft who had come from Geneva to London. It will be interesting to hear what the Bishop has to say.' Strang agreed that Eden should see the Bishop, and Cadogan wrote:

What would be interesting would be to see what any group of this kind can *do*. We are not going to negotiate with any Government in Germany that has not thoroughly purged its soul and we must have some convincing of *that* and we have got to be convinced first. Total defeat and disarmament is probably the only possible answer.

The Bishop's message fell on stony ground. The Foreign Office already knew from other sources of the existence of the plot, but refused to take it seriously or consider how to encourage the anti-Nazis. Eden saw the Bishop at the end of June 1942, listened courteously to what he had to say, read Schoenfeld's memorandum, and confirmed that some of the names given by Bonhoeffer were known by the Foreign Office. Because other feelers had reached him from other countries he said he had to be scrupulously careful not to enter into even an appearance of negotiations independently of the Russians and Americans. He wrote to Bell on 17 July that no action could be taken. So these overtures from impeccable sources were greeted with Churchill's strictly imposed 'absolute silence'.[18]

On 10 March 1943 Bishop Bell initiated a debate on the Hitlerite state in the House of Lords. He referred to the pastoral letter by Bishop von Preysing condemning the Nazis and their 'terrible ways', saying that steadfast and conspicuous opposition was expressed by the Catholic and Protestant Churches; the volume of Church protest was astonishingly great; and that Britain must distinguish between the Hitlerite state and the German people. Lord Simon, the Lord Chancellor, replied: 'We desire to encourage in every way we can the opposition inside Germany which has been described by the reverend prelate.'[19]

This was untrue, as Adam von Trott was to find when plans to assassinate Hitler came near to completion. In Stockholm in March 1944 he found that the British had no intention of talking to the Resistance, which Simon said the Government wanted to encourage. Churchill would not allow British diplomats to meet him. In Geneva Trott contacted both the British and the Americans, with the same result. This made him, according to journalist Elizabeth Wiskemann, an old English friend, 'a broken man'. In June Dulles, Head of OSS in Berne received a confidential message from Gisevius, a German whom he trusted, giving advance news of a plan to murder Hitler. He reported to the British and US Governments: 'Dramatic events may be pending', and said that the news confirmed his previous report about the plot's organization and that the Resistance would overthrow Hitler and set up a responsible Government. According to Dulles in July, the plotters wanted to prevent as much as possible of Germany falling into Russian hands; the new Government would order a planned retreat from the West and the transfer of the best divisions to the East.

In June 1944 Trott tried again with the British in Stockholm, and gave a memorandum to a secret service agent. He confirmed that plans to overthrow Hitler were at an advanced stage, but the plotters could not accept unconditional surrender because they would be unable to counteract the mass slogan of 'having stabbed the fighting forces in the back' – a slogan which would be bound to recur even more violently than it did after 1918. Churchill and Eden ignored this memorandum.

On 18 July, in a Supply Committee debate in the House of Commons, the rights and wrongs of unconditional surrender and the terrifying consequences of the Teheran Conference on the German people were raised, together with the Goebbels propaganda about it. Eden decided to make an off-the-cuff reply and complained petulantly that he could not give a 'redefinition of unconditional surrender' when he had only a few minutes' warning. He read out to the House part of an uncompromising statement by Churchill of 22 February 1944, and ignored a more generous statement by Attlee on 6 July. He emphasized that the Government were not going to allow themselves to be put into a similar position vis-à-vis Germany as they had been because of Wilson's fourteen points (which were ignored during the Treaty of Versailles discussions) at the end of the First World War; and he claimed, with no evidence to support him, that British propaganda to Germany 'has not been unsuccessful'.

Thus as the gallant Resistance inside Germany prepared their coup to end the war by killing Hitler and forming an anti-Nazi Government on 20 July they were given no help. Rommel was in on the plot, and on 12 July he convinced Kluge, who had replaced Rundstedt as Commander in Chief in the West, that the Allies were bound to defeat the Germans and that continuation of the war would punish Germany for nothing. They decided that, if Hitler would not negotiate a peace, he must be liquidated. If the Resistance could kill Hitler, both Kluge and Rommel would support a new Beck–Goerdeler Government, and call on Montgomery to negotiate surrender terms under which the Germans would leave their heavy equipment in France, and withdraw their troops behind the Rhine to help their Eastern armies to keep the Russians out of Germany.

Rommel had already opened a radio link with the Americans, and on 2 and 9 July medical personnel and severely wounded had been passed through the lines. Hitler was furious when he heard of this. On 16 July, after discussions with Kluge, Rommel prepared what he called a 'Blitz' message to Hitler, stating that his troops 'were fighting heroically', but that the German front would crumble inevitably 'within fourteen days to three weeks', and: 'It is my duty to state this clearly.'

The conspirators in Berlin, through their accomplice General Karl Stülpnagel, Military Governor of Paris, sent a message to Rommel that Stauffenberg would try to kill Hitler at his war conference on 20 July, and a Beck–Goerdeler Government would be proclaimed to replace the Nazis. Kluge agreed to co-operate if Hitler was killed; on 17 July Rommel told Stülpnagel he would act 'openly and unconditionally' as soon as Hitler was liquidated, whether Kluge went along with him or not. But that evening Rommel's car was attacked by Spitfires and he was taken to hospital severely wounded. Now the conspirators' hopes in the West rested on Kluge. But he was spineless and vacillating.

On 20 July Stauffenberg's bomb exploded during Hitler's conference at Rastenburg. Unfortunately the Führer was only wounded and not killed, and the revolt in Berlin was quickly snuffed out, with the immediate execution of Beck and Stauffenberg.

In Paris Stülpnagel and his fellow conspirators received a telephone call that the coup was 'on' and Hitler dead. Later they received a message that 'all was lost'. As planned, Stülpnagel had ordered the arrest of over a thousand Gestapo in Paris; they were put in prison without violence. When the news came that the plot had failed in Berlin, Stülpnagel drove to Kluge's headquarters in a last desperate attempt to persuade him to surrender the Western Front and continue the uprising from France. According to General Blumentritt, one of Kluge's senior staff officers, when Kluge first heard the news that Hitler was dead he said: 'If the Führer is dead we ought to get in touch with the other side at once.' Unfortunately soon afterwards a message came from Keitel at Rastenburg that Hitler was only wounded. Kluge's nerve failed, and by the time Stülpnagel arrived at his headquarters, La Roche Guyon, he had decided irrevocably to turn his back on the conspirators.

Stülpnagel argued desperately, but Kluge remained adamant that he had only agreed to co-operate once Hitler was dead. It is conceivable that his personal oath of loyalty to Hitler weighed with him. Kluge even threatened Stülpnagel with arrest. In return Stülpnagel considered blackmailing Kluge by threatening to expose his promise to join the plot, but eventually decided to return to Paris and release the Gestapo officers. Stülpnagel's role had become clear to the Gestapo, and the next day he was summoned back to Berlin and arrested after a failed attempt at suicide.

The Normandy campaign went atrociously for Kluge. A counter-offensive against the advancing Americans was ordered by Hitler, against his General's advice. Faithfully Kluge, who had suggested a retreat to behind the Seine, executed the Führer's orders, but his remaining Panzer divisions were sacrificed uselessly. Thereupon Kluge changed his mind again and tried to surrender.

On 15 August Kluge was out of contact with his staff all day. At Hitler's headquarters an Allied radio signal was monitored, asking where Kluge was. Immediately Hitler suspected that Kluge was trying to negotiate an armistice, and said it was 'the worst day' of his life. Kluge's son-in-law, Dr Udo Esche, who later gave Kluge cyanide with which to commit suicide, told Allied interrogators after the war that Kluge had discussed with him the idea of surrendering and 'went to the front lines but was unable to get in touch with the Allied com-manders'. George Pfann, secretary to General Patton's Third US Army, stated that Patton vanished for an entire day in mid-August and, when he returned, said he had tried to make contact with a German emissary who had not turned up at the appointed place. Brigadier Sir Edgar Williams, Montgomery's Chief of Intelligence, told the author he could recall the day when Kluge was reported missing and he had warned Montgomery they might get something from him at any moment.

Late that night Kluge reappeared at his headquarters and said his radio van had been damaged by enemy aircraft in the morning, so he could not stay in touch as he visited his forward units. This did not satisfy Hitler, who immediately sacked Kluge and replaced him with a fanatical Nazi, Field Marshal Model. Kluge wrote to Hitler: 'My Führer, make up your mind to end the war. The German people have undergone such untold suffering that it is time to put an end to this frightfulness.'

Too late Kluge, who had such difficulty in making up his mind, had tried to end the war and failed. He committed suicide on his way back to Germany, knowing that his part in the plot had been revealed to Hitler.[20]

The above is evidence that by his intransigence and refusal to countenance talks with dissident Germans, Churchill threw away an opportunity to end the war in July 1944. He was always frightened that unilateral negotiations, without the Russians, might edge Stalin into a separate peace with Hitler. Post-war evidence proves this improbable. In addition, with memories of the Cabinets at the time of Dunkirk Churchill feared that peace talks might destroy the will of the nation to fight.

After the war Churchill stated he had been

> misled by his assistants about the considerable strength and size of the anti-Hitler Resistance, . . . in Germany there lived an opposition which was weakened by their losses and an enervating international policy, but which belongs to the noblest and greatest that the political history of any nation has ever produced. These men fought without help from within or from abroad – driven forward only by the restlessness of their conscience. As long as they lived they were invisible and unrecognisable to us, because they had to camouflage themselves. But their death made the resistance visible.

Wheeler-Bennett gave callous advice to Churchill:

> It may now be said with some definiteness that we are better off with things as they stand today than if the plot of 20 July had succeeded and Hitler had been assassinated. In this event the 'Old Army' Generals would have taken over . . . and put into operation a peace move already prepared in which Germany would admit herself defeated and sue for terms other than Unconditional Surrender. In the failure of the plot we have been spared the embarrassment both at home and in the United States which might have resulted from such a move, and moreover the present purge is presumably removing from the scene numerous individuals who might have caused us difficulty not only had the plot succeeded, but also after the defeat of Nazi Germany . . . the Gestapo and the S.S. have done us an appreciable service in removing a selection of those who would undoubtedly have posed as 'good' Germans after the war while preparing for a third World War. It is to our advantage therefore that the purge should continue since the killing of Germans by Germans will save us from future embarrassment.[21]

From Germany came the news that dissident generals and politicians had been tried and executed. Churchill accepted Wheeler-Bennett's briefing for the debate in the Commons on 12 August and killed the remaining hopes of the Resistance, saying 'The highest personalities in the Reich are murdering one another or trying to, while the avenging armies of the Allies close upon the doomed and ever-narrowing circle of their power.' He was supported by Greenwood, who said: 'It would be a fatal mistake if . . . we were to present any better terms to the militarists of Germany than we have done to the discredited Nazis.'

Only Richard Stokes and George Strauss dissented from the Government line. Strauss said that now we knew there is a strong element in the German army which thinks that continuance of the war is foolish and suicidal, we should change our whole policy. How can one expect a movement of that sort to be widespread and broad-based if the Germans have nothing to go on except the repeated cry of 'unconditional surrender' and statements daily by Dr Goebbels over the wireless telling the people that if Germany is conquered we are going to cut Germany up and do awful things to its men and women?'

Stokes intervened to add: 'By the Prime Minister too.'

Strauss was heavily barracked when he went on to say that Goebbels' propaganda claimed that after the Allies' victory 9 million German people in Upper Silesia, East Prussia and the Sudetenland would be transported. He finished by saying that the Allies should immediately declare their terms 'and help the next crack in Germany to develop into a fissure that will rend the army and nation in twain'. He wrote to the author that he was proud he had made the speech, but the mood of the House was that they would not countenance a separate peace with the German opposition.

Stokes argued for a revocation of the Teheran Conference decisions on dismembering Germany and a return to the Atlantic Charter, with a declaration that it was sincerely meant that the German people should have the kind of Government they wanted after the war. He forecast that the German people would give in 'if they were told . . . not only that they are not going to be shot, but that they have something to hope for'. Like Strauss, Stokes was jeered by both Labour and Conservative MPs, including the present Lord Hailsham.

From the Seine Montgomery's armour raced to Brussels and Antwerp. At Antwerp Montgomery made the mistake of not informing his commanders that the Albert Canal was one of the principal waterways of Europe, and a strong defence line. General Roberts, commanding the leading armoured division, told the author: 'I did not appreciate the significance of the Albert Canal and the Germans did not blow the crucial bridge for twelve hours after we got there.' Montgomery also made the mistake of using airborne troops to link up with them; this action produced grave losses among the best fighting men. The decision to go for Arnhem was taken while Churchill was in Quebec for a conference with Roosevelt. He was not involved in the plan.

As the Allied armies surged across France and liberated Belgium reaching the German and Dutch frontiers in early September, Hitler was able to rally the Germans behind him because the alternatives seemed so appalling. The Teheran Conference was made out by Goebbels to mean that Germany would be robbed of her eastern provinces and half of her territory, and that several million people would be deported. Under Albert Speer and Karl Saur arms production soared, and a new peak was reached as late as August 1944. Churchill's hard line in the 2 August Commons debate helped Hitler to resist to the end, while Goebbels cleverly coined the phrase 'total slavery'. According to the diary of von Hassell, the anti-Nazi diplomat, the Stauffenberg plotters were convinced that the 'unconditional surrender' formula 'jeopardised and possibly destroyed the six years of work by the anti-Nazi conspirators'.

Several months earlier, as soon as Eisenhower had taken command of the invasion forces in January 1944, he demanded that he should be allowed to present a much more attractive scenario to the German forces. On 15 January Churchill firmly ruled against this, pointing out that the Allies had agreed at Teheran that the Russians could take over vast quantities of German machinery, and that other powers might have similar claims, while Stalin was asking for 4 million Germans to work for many years in 'building up the ruin they had caused in Russia'; therefore 'a frank statement of what is going to happen to Germany would not necessarily have a reassuring effect upon the German people, and that they might prefer the vaguer terrors of unconditional surrender'. Cadogan minuted on the Prime Minister's paper that it 'rather shook him', and Eden agreed. Bedell Smith, Eisenhower's Chief of Staff, insisted that the psychological moment for an attractive announcement to the Germans would be after the bridgehead was well established, and that it would be impossible in default of such a declaration to exploit 'the crisis which would undoubtedly arise in the German army after a successful landing'.[22]

The British Cabinet inconclusively debated 'unconditional surrender' with Eisenhower's staff, but no agreement about a declaration was reached before the invasion began on 6 June. Eden produced a draft declaration, but Churchill opposed it in the War Cabinet on 13 March and it was turned down. Cripps wanted to include 'no mass reprisals against the German people and we do not desire to see the peoples of Germany engulfed in economic collapse which would infect the whole of Europe'. This was not to Churchill's liking; he ignored the fact that the only way to undo the damage being done by Goebbels was to abandon 'unconditional surrender' and state what was proposed for a liberated Germany.

Eisenhower refused to accept the War Cabinet's decision, and on 19 April told the Foreign Office that he would raise the matter strongly with the Prime Minister at lunch at Downing Street that day. Eden noted that Eisenhower had not managed to raise it 'while I was there, but I had to leave at 3 p.m.'

In April Eisenhower's staff asked again for a definition of 'unconditional surrender' in advance of D-Day, together with a summary of Anglo–American principles upon which Military Government in Germany would be conducted. They also requested an effort to create a mood in the German General Staff as a result of which 'necessary political steps might be undertaken by a German Badoglio for unconditional surrender'.[23]

When he went abroad in March Eden instructed the Foreign Office to try and persuade Churchill to agree. Churchill's minute in reply on 19 April was that he did not like 'Generals shivering before the battle' and he wanted it left to the Americans, reiterating:

> The actual terms contemplated for Germany are not of a character to reassure them at all if stated in detail. President Roosevelt and Marshal Stalin at Teheran wished to cut Germany into smaller pieces than I had in mind. Stalin spoke of very large mass executions of over 50,000 of the staff and military experts . . . There are a lot of other terms implying the German ruin and indefinite prevention of them arising

again as an Armed Power . . . Unconditional Surrender was interpreted in a very favourable manner in the case of the Italians . . . I must say I think it is all wrong for the Generals to start shivering before the battle.[24]

Roosevelt then proposed that he should make a unilateral declaration to the German people. He cabled his draft to the Prime Minister on 20 May. It contained the words: 'Only Germany and Japan stand out against all the rest of humanity . . . the Allies do not seek the total destruction of the German people. They do seek the total destruction of the philosophy of those Germans who have announced that they could subjugate the world.' Whether Roosevelt's statement could have been used by Allied propaganda to defeat Goebbels' claims is debatable: it was far from what Eisenhower and Bedell Smith wanted to soften up the German fighting forces. Cadogan minuted: 'The statement itself is not bad and generally on the right lines.' Churchill disagreed. Brendan Bracken, Minister of Information, minuted: 'R's draft was sloppy and silly, and no substitute for tripartite declaration we have proposed.' Eden's comment was 'Better be silent before battle.'

On 24 May, with the invasion of Normandy only a few days off, the War Cabinet considered Roosevelt's proposed statement and rejected it. Smuts, a member of the War Cabinet, said:

> It ought to be postponed until Germany has been thoroughly beaten on all three fronts. We have said nothing to Germany yet since 'Unconditional Surrender' – a declaration which has been very bad propaganda from our point of view. Our next word to Germany should be first class propaganda, a document to which Germany would listen, issued at a time when they would pay most attention. This is an inopportune moment.

Eden said the message should be the basis of conclusion of hostilities and be made by the three leaders, because if Roosevelt made a statement alone the Germans would be in doubt about the views of the Russians and the British.

The Prime Minister said the Government should postpone any action until it sensed victory, and the text of the suggested communication might conceivably be taken as a peace offer which must be agreed by the three Allies. The War Cabinet agreed with the Prime Minister and concluded that it was far too late as an alternative to get a tripartite statement agreed now with Stalin before D-Day. Churchill cabled Roosevelt:

> I think myself your message might be taken as a peace feeler. Cabinet showed considerable concern at the tone of friendship shown to the Germans at this moment when the troops are about to engage.
>
> At Teheran my suggestion of dismemberment and isolation of East Prussia was considered far too modest for you and UJ. [Uncle Joe, i.e. Stalin]. How are the Poles to be compensated if they do not get East Prussia and certain territories up to the lines of the Oder in return for the Curzon line which the Russians will certainly demand?
>
> We here earnestly hope you will not make it in its present form and above all at the present time. There was also feeling that a document so grave addressed to the

enemy should emanate from the three principal Allies. I may add that nothing of this document would get down to the German pill boxes and front line in time to affect fighting troops.

Stalin agreed with Churchill and on 26 May cabled Roosevelt 'The proposed appeal cannot bring a positive effect. Return to question when favourable circumstances arise.' Roosevelt then threw in the sponge, so when the invasion started on 6 June Eisenhower was forbidden to make any announcement about a soft peace and the attraction of surrender to German soldiers.[25]

A gratuitous boost to Goebbels' propaganda was given at the September 1944 Quebec Conference when Roosevelt and Churchill endorsed the Morgenthau Plan, which stated that after the war metallurgical, chemical and electrical industries on the Ruhr and Saar must be closed down and dismantled, and that Germany should be converted into a country 'primarily agricultural and pastoral in its character'. Once again Churchill acted without his colleagues' approval, but Eden, who was opposed, did not have the support of the other members of the Cabinet. In a cable sent to Eden from Quebec Churchill wrote that he and Lord Cherwell favoured the plan because it meant that Britain would be able to export to Germany goods to the value of £3–10 billion annually which would otherwise have been produced by Germany herself. The Foreign Office view was that Morgenthau was misguided and 'we' must destroy the Nazi system, but 'always remember a starving and bankrupt Germany would not be in our interest'. However, while Eden himself was *en route* to Quebec Churchill cabled the text to Attlee, and the next day, 16 September, the War Cabinet cabled their warmest congratulations to the Prime Minister without apparently considering the consequences of converting Germany into a 'primarily agricultural and pastoral country', and oblivious of the Foreign Secretary's disagreement.[26]

In his memoirs Churchill wrote that he made a mistake in agreeing to the Morgenthau Plan. In excuse he claims that at first he was violently opposed. This may be true, but the anti-German bigot Lord Cherwell soon convinced him that it would be of great economic help to Britain after the war. In fact Churchill quickly became enthusiastic, strengthening the draft joint memorandum by inserting the word 'pastoral' after 'turning Germany into a country primarily agricultural'! In the memoirs Churchill gives the impression that the policy of 'pastoralising' Germany was soon abandoned. This is incorrect.[27] After Churchill initialled the Plan it was never cancelled; it was even put into effect to a limited extent by the Allied Military Government after hostilities ceased. Colville told the author that Churchill realized he had accepted the Plan without considering his colleagues' contrary views, but that did not worry him. Colville suspected that Churchill never gave it serious thought, merely initialling it because he was keen on getting Roosevelt, as a *quid pro quo*, to initial his (Churchill's) plan for a 50–50 division of all atomic products between the United Kingdom and the United States.

Halifax reported from the Washington Embassy on 25 September 1944:

The attribution of the plan to Mr. Morgenthau loads the scales against it.

(a) He is one of the least popular American officials while Mr Hull, who has fairly clearly admitted the divergence, is one of the most popular (and thereby dramatised it).

(b) Mr Morgenthau is not regarded as an expert on foreign affairs, while Mr Hull is so regarded.

(c) Many Americans are patently anti-semitic and therefore particularly inclined to suspect the objectivity of a Jew on Germany . . .

An Associated Press article had stated: 'Morgenthau's thesis is opposed by Hull and violently opposed by Stimson; Hopkins is thought to support him (Morgenthau) and Harry White has drawn up plans; the alleged trend of the Treasury argument is that elimination of Ruhr industry will boost that of Britain and so make the Beveridge Plan realisable.' (Churchill and a large section of the Conservative Party thought the Beveridge Plan [which proposed children's allowances, a free Health Service and better provisions for those in poverty] would throw too much of a strain on the taxpayer because of the cost of extra social services.) Halifax also commented that, although Morgenthau was heavily criticized, there was 'no mistaking the increasing sentiment in favour of the tough treatment which the administration were known to favour'.

Immediately Goebbels' propaganda ministry put out the tale that 'Clemenceau had said there were 23 million Germans too many, but that now Morgenthau wanted to exterminate 43 million Germans'. Soon the Political Warfare files of the Foreign Office were full of reports from neutral countries of the propaganda value to Goebbels of Morgenthau. The German people, by and large, believed that they were going to be treated brutally and forced into starvation. A further Goebbels embellishment was that anyone trying to leave the country after the war would be shot on the frontier. The routine reports from the Political Warfare Executive on German propaganda leave no doubt about the damage being done. On 2 October 1944 the Political Warfare report ran:

Greatest prominence given to Morgenthau alleged proposals for the economic subjugation of Germany. Newspapers report, under many headings, Morgenthau surpasses Clemenceau who claimed there were 40 million Germans too many . . . Morgenthau was described as the leader of the agitation 'who sings the same tune as the Jews in the Kremlin and demands complete annihilation of the German industry, dismemberment of the country and extermination of half the population' . . . Roosevelt was reported to have amplified the plans of his bosom friend the finance Jew Morgenthau and developed a programme of pitiless extermination . . . Eisenhower's orders to the allied troops on crossing the German frontier were interpreted as no food for the German population plus compulsory registration for deportation . . . as a result Goebbels said every house in Aachen [then being attacked by the Americans] should resemble a fortress.

Unfortunately, in Washington Morgenthau irresponsibly made statements which could be construed that Germans leaving would be shot by armed guards; he also gave a long list of categories of officials to be executed. Goebbels spotlighted again and again that the author of the Plan was a Jew. The appalling damage and casualties from British and American bombing were interpreted to the German people by Goebbels as an integral part of the Morgenthau Plan.

In Normandy, by September 1944 Hitler's armies had suffered a defeat far more severe than the Kaiser's in 1918. Instead of considering surrender, Hitler found extra manpower for new divisions and for the manufacture of arms through an intense combing out of all able-bodied Germans and by an un-scrupulous use of slave labour from occupied countries. Even twelve-year-olds were taken out of school to dig fortifications, and the new battalions contained a chillingly high proportion of schoolboys. By mid-October, when six weeks earlier defeat had seemed inevitable, Hitler had raised twelve new divisions for the Western Front. They included factory workers, shopkeepers and petty officials. Schoolboys transformed overnight into fighting soldiers had known no Govern-ment nor faith other than Nazi; fighting for Hitler had a romantic appeal for them and they resisted like demons. All this had become possible because of the gigantic boost given to German fighting morale by the Morgenthau Plan, coupled with the sinister threat to the future of all Germans inherent in 'unconditional surrender'.

Eden and other Cabinet ministers urged Churchill to rescind the Morgenthau Plan, but Churchill replied that he had been much struck by the depth of feeling which would be stirred by a policy of 'putting Germany on her feet again' – because of the hatred which Germany had aroused – and 'it would be a mistake to try to write out on little bits of paper what the vast emotions of an outraged and quivering world would be either immediately after the struggle is over or when the inevitable cold fit follows the hot . . . there is therefore wisdom in reserving one's decision as long as possible'.

In the autumn of 1944 Eisenhower's staff at SHAEF were alarmed by the high morale of the German fighting forces. Eisenhower returned to the attack over the question of a soft peace and demanded the offer of terms which would induce the Germans to stop fighting. Dismayed by the fighting qualities of Hitler's new armies, on 21 November he sent a long telegram to London and Washington stating that German resistance was 'very tough' and that unless the phrase 'unconditional surrender' could be modified he saw no end to the war except after a long and bitter process of fighting. He went on: 'If unconditional surrender must be adhered to, then everything possible should be done by propaganda and subversive means to soften German morale.' He asked London to go into these matters which 'could not be dealt with by SHAEF'.

On 25 November the Prime Minister telegraphed to Eisenhower: 'It would be a mistake to show the Germans that we are anxious for them to ease off their desperate opposition.' At least this showed that Churchill was aware of the high morale of Hitler's fighters, but he vetoed any proclamation to the German people.

Churchill and Roosevelt never understood the use the Nazis could make of the link between the Morgenthau Plan and unconditional surrender. Eisenhower's message, based on field reports of German morale and the abundant evidence from Political Warfare about German propaganda, should have made it crystal-clear that to expedite an early end to the war unconditional surrender and the Morgenthau Plan must be repudiated. The day after Roosevelt received Eisenhower's *cri de coeur* he cabled Churchill that the Combined Chiefs of Staff in Washington would like a declaration to break down German morale. Churchill replied that he had consulted all his Cabinet and his Chiefs of Staff and

> we all gravely doubt whether any such statement should be made. I do not think that the Germans are very much afraid of the treatment they will get from the British and American armies or governments. What they are afraid of is a Russian occupation, and a large proportion of their people being taken off to toil to death in Russia, or as they say, Siberia. Nothing that we can say will eradicate this deep seated fear.
>
> 2. Moreover, U. J. [Uncle Joe (Stalin)] certainly contemplates demanding two or three million Nazi youth, Gestapo men, etc., doing prolonged reparation work, and it is hard to say that he is wrong. We could not therefore give the Germans any assurances on this subject without consultations with U.J.
>
> 3. It seems to me that if I were a German soldier or general, I should regard any such statement at this juncture, when the battle for Cologne is at its height, as a confession of weakness on our part and as proof positive of the advantages of further desperate resistance. The Chiefs of the Staff and Ministry of Information both independently agree with me that this might well be the consequence of any such announcement now. I do not see any alternative to the General Grant attitude 'To fight it out on this line, if it takes all summer'.

Roosevelt disagreed, and wanted to issue a statement including the words: 'We do not seek to devastate or eliminate the German people . . . we seek the elimination of Nazi control and the return of the German people to the civilization of the rest of the world'. But Churchill would not have it, and Roosevelt did not persist. Thus S H A E F never got the antidote they wanted to Goebbels' propaganda, which they were sure was boosting the morale of the enemy soldiers. Meanwhile the defeated remnants of the German Army fought as stoutly as ever against both the Russians and the Anglo–US forces, and Hitler's Ardennes offensive at Christmas 1944 nearly recovered Brussels, Antwerp and most of the rest of Belgium.[28]

By December 1944 the euphoria which followed the defeat of Hitler's armies in Normandy had disappeared with the failure of the airborne landing at Arnhem in September, which should have opened the way into Germany. Hitler had raised new armies with high morale, the product of Goebbels' astute propaganda that unconditional surrender and the Morgenthau Plan meant a dreadful future for the German people after defeat.

Efforts by the British and American armies to reach the Rhine before winter set in were blocked; the attack by the Americans east of Aachen, on which high hopes were pinned, failed, and instead of being on the Rhine the Americans were held on the River Roer. The British had cleared all the Netherlands west and south of the Meuse, but were making slow progress towards the banks of the Rhine. Churchill and Roosevelt agreed that Germany had in effect lost the war, but it would need another hard slog before the Allies could link up with the Russians and occupy Berlin.

With the winter stalemate, bickering broke out between Montgomery and Eisenhower. Montgomery wanted to concentrate the assault in the north and to command substantial US forces, but unfortunately the American generals objected to serving under Montgomery. Churchill and the CIGS thought Eisenhower was frittering away the opportunities by attacking on two fronts instead of concentrating on the north as Montgomery wanted. On 10 December Churchill and Eisenhower discussed the problem inconclusively in London, and afterwards Brooke prepared a paper which Churchill confidently expected would bulldoze Eisenhower into agreeing to the Montgomery plan. But in London Eisenhower dismayed Churchill by saying he did not expect to cross the Rhine before May 1945.

Suddenly the stalemate ended. On 16 December Hitler hurled two strong Panzer armies in a surprise attack on the Americans' weakest point in the Ardennes. The German tanks immediately drove deep behind the American lines, creating panic and shooting up convoys of 'soft' vehicles. By the 18th the situation was grave. Brussels and Antwerp were threatened, and it seemed that the Germans might drive through to the coast. Montgomery signalled: 'The general situation is ugly as the American forces have been cut clean in half and the Germans can reach the Meuse at Namur without opposition. The command set-up here has always been faulty, and now it is quite futile; Ike [Eisenhower] should place me in operational charge of all troops on the northern half of the front.'

As soon as Churchill read Montgomery's signal he became excited and, according to General Sir Frank Simpson, Director of Military Operations at the War Office, drafted a signal to Montgomery ordering him to take action at once 'with XXX Corps on some thrust line or other'. Simpson and Brooke were appalled because Churchill would be ordering about Montgomery's formations (as he had done with Wavell's and Auchinleck's), forgetting that such orders could now only come from the Supreme Commander, Eisenhower. They pointed out to the Prime Minister that Eisenhower must give the orders, and it was quite impossible for anyone in London to decide how Montgomery should act because they did not know the circumstances on the ground. Reluctantly Churchill agreed not to contact Montgomery direct and asked Brooke what he could do instead. The CIGS advised the Prime Minister to telephone Eisenhower and suggest that the whole of the northern half of the front should be under one commander, preferably Montgomery.

So Churchill telephoned the Supreme Commander, with the delicate task of persuading the American to put his divisions under an Englishman. He began tactlessly, saying that Eisenhower should work 'on a pincer nip from the north and south upon the German offensive bulge', and went on to make his request that Montgomery should be placed in overall command of the northern effort. Testily Eisenhower replied that he had already asked Montgomery to take over. Brooke and Simpson were always worried when Churchill, an enthusiastic amateur strategist, involved himself in details of the fighting, and they were immensely relieved at the news. Churchill now revived the phrase he had used to Wavell after the fall of Benghazi in 1941: 'The tortoise has stuck his head out too far.' This time it had.[29]

Fortunately, thanks to Montgomery's well-organized counter-attack and the complete air supremacy of the Allies, the German Ardennes offensive was halted. It was finally pinched out when US troops under Montgomery joined up with the other Americans on 6 January 1945 at Houffalize; the Battle of the Bulge, as it was known, was over. But relations between Montgomery and Eisenhower had gone from bad to worse. Churchill incautiously advised Montgomery to hold a press conference; it was a disaster. Cocksure Montgomery described his own part in over-glowing terms; this was rewritten by the Germans for their radio stations in a skilful piece of black propaganda to give the impression that Montgomery had said he 'personally had saved' the Americans from disaster.

Eisenhower wrote to Marshall that both the Prime Minister and he had tried every device at hand to counteract the feeling, but 'no single incident that I have ever encountered throughout my experience as Allied Commander has been so difficult to combat as this outburst in the papers'. Churchill did his best to calm the situation, but the notorious press conference was a key factor in Eisenhower's later disastrous decision to withdraw American troops from Montgomery's command and to allow the Russians to take Berlin.[30]

Montgomery had fixed 23 March for a setpiece battle in which the British 21 Army Group and the Ninth US Army (also under Montgomery's command) would cross the Rhine at Wesel and then march triumphantly on to Berlin. The operation was called Plunder, and to Montgomery's horror Churchill insisted on being present. On 2 March the Prime Minister had told General de Guingand (Montgomery's Chief of Staff) on a visit to Montgomery that he intended to watch the Rhine crossing, saying belligerently that he had discussed it with Eisenhower, who had said: 'You will be all right if you go forward in a tank.' Montgomery annoyed Churchill by not taking the suggestion seriously, telling Simpson that 'it was just not on to have the Prime Minister meandering around in the middle of the battle disturbing the Commanders who were running it'.

Churchill expressed his irritation to Brooke, who accordingly wrote to Montgomery on 7 March: 'If the Prime Minister is not allowed to come you will have the seeds of serious trouble ahead. When the P.M. gets such ideas into his head nothing will stop him.' In his diary Brooke wrote: 'I am not happy with this trip. He will be difficult to manage and has no business to be going. All he will do is to endanger his own life unnecessarily and get in everyone's way and be a damned nuisance to everybody. But nothing can stop him.' Making the best of it, Montgomery wrote to Brooke: 'If the P.M. is determined to come there is only one course of action and that is to ask him to stay at my camp. Then I can keep an eye on him and see he goes only where he will bother no-one. I have written him a letter which should please the old boy.' Montgomery must have remembered the tricky situation when he tried to keep Churchill away from Normandy the previous July.

As then, Churchill was delighted with Montgomery's letter, replying on 11 March:

> My dear Field Marshal,
>   I was delighted to receive your letter . . . I am resolved to be no hindrance to you, and you must consider yourself absolutely free from any obligation during this important battle. I would not come if I thought there was the slightest chance of my getting in your way. I will come on D minus 1 with (only) the CIGS.
>   . . . it would be necessary for me to have somewhere 20 or 30 miles back, a train or perhaps a railway coach where I can keep a private secretary and Mr Rinna who deals . . . with facilities for scrambling messages.
>   I may add that General Eisenhower suggested to me when I talked my wishes over that a tank would be the best way of seeing things.
>   Yours very sincerely,
>   Winston S. Churchill

Montgomery told Grigg, the Secretary of State for War: 'I did not want him so I invited him to keep the peace', and 'I am expecting the P.M. here on 23. He seems to be getting restless and querulous. Why he wants to go about in dangerous places I cannot imagine. He may quite likely get shot up. However it is his own affair. I shall make it quite clear to him that he goes to these dangerous places against my definite advice, and then leave it to him. I shall be far too busy to attend to him.'[31]

Montgomery's meticulous planning secured a bridgehead over the Rhine on the first day of Plunder. However, his glamour was dented because the Americans had unexpectedly captured a bridge at Remagen on 7 March to establish an earlier bridgehead.

Churchill arrived at Montgomery's headquarters with Brooke to witness Plunder. From the west bank of the Rhine Churchill saw through his field glasses numbers of British gliders and towing planes being shot down over the German positions as airborne troops carried out a spectacular and successful attack which made a substantial contribution to that day's victory. Churchill minuted to Eden: 'We had a jolly day.' This shows little feeling about the British airborne casualties he had witnessed.

On the following day Churchill, Brooke and Eisenhower met in a small house overlooking the Rhine which was an American Corps headquarters. The Prime Minister went on at length about the enormity of a cable from the Soviet Foreign Minister, Molotov, in which the Russian complained bitterly and unreasonably about Alexander's handling of surrender negotiations with the German Army in Italy. Molotov complained that these were carried on behind the backs of the Russians. At this battlefield conference Churchill formed the impression that Eisenhower was as keen as himself to enter Berlin before the Russians, and Montgomery demonstrated with the help of maps how he would advance from his Rhine bridgehead and on to Berlin.

But Eisenhower was far from frank. He had already made up his mind to shift his main attack away from Montgomery in the north to the Americans in the centre, and he wanted to leave Berlin to the Russians. Eisenhower overlooked the fact that he had a duty to Churchill to discuss his plans with him before he changed his strategy; it is amazing that he failed to let Churchill know he no longer wanted to capture Berlin. The Supreme Commander's staff had become obsessed with misleading reports that Hitler was preparing a last-stand redoubt in the mountains on the Italian–Austrian frontier in an effort to create the legend of a fight by unconquered immortal Nazism – a legend which would plant the seeds for a Third Reich reincarnation at some future date. The most favourable interpretation which can be put on Eisenhower's behaviour at his 25 March conference with Churchill is that he had not firmly made up his mind not to go for Berlin, and he baulked at incurring the spontaneous rage of the Prime Minister and an unpleasant discussion while his plans were still fluid.

Both Churchill and Roosevelt were seeking as glamorous as possible a role for their respective nation's armies in the final triumph, because this would be of considerable importance in post-war elections. Churchill was anxious to hold a General Election as soon as possible after the armistice; the Conservatives were doing badly in by-elections, and he hoped to capitalize on his reputation as 'the architect of victory' in a snap election. He felt he could emulate Lloyd George's steamroller majority in the 'Khaki Election' of December 1918 in the afterglow of the defeat of the Kaiser. Thus Berlin was very important to him.

Marshall, on the other hand, was encouraging Eisenhower to give the major part of the final victory to the Americans. In addition, there was American jealousy of Montgomery. One of Eisenhower's staff stated at the time that 'Monty wants to ride into Berlin on a white charger wearing two hats', and according to Eisenhower's biographer the feeling at SHAEF in March 1945 was that the principal British concern was not to finish the war, but to make a hero out of Montgomery. On 24 March Eisenhower wrote to Marshall that 'there is some influence at work that insists on giving Montgomery credit that belongs to other Commanders'.

By 27 March Montgomery's advance over the Rhine was rolling away, meeting little resistance. After his conference with Churchill and Eisenhower on the 24th Montgomery believed the agreed Allied plan was that, once he was well into the plains of Germany, he should send his armour at top speed towards both the Baltic and Berlin. He knew that Churchill looked on Berlin as 'a priority objective', and the Prime Minister had explained to him on the 24th that the occupation of the city before the Russians arrived would be an important factor in the subsequent peace.

Relaxed, confident and unsuspecting, on 27 March Montgomery signalled to Eisenhower:

Today I issued order to Army Commanders for the operations about to begin . . . My intention is to drive hard for the line of the Elbe using the [US] ninth and [British] second armies. The right of the ninth army will be directed on Magdeburg and the left of the second army on Hamburg . . . I have ordered ninth and second armies to move their armoured and mobile division forward at once to get through to the Elbe with all the possible speed and drive . . . My Tac HQ moves to the northwest of Bonninghardt on Thursday, 29 March. Thereafter my HQ will move to Wesel Münster Widenbruck Herford Hanover – thence by autobahn to Berlin I hope.

Eisenhower saw red, and in his anger he behaved strangely. He had little patience with Montgomery, who had infuriated him on many occasions during the campaign. What now sent him round the bend was that Montgomery had assumed (innocently enough, because nothing had been said at the Churchill conference on 24 March) that US Ninth Army would stay under his command for the final victorious drive to Berlin. Worse, in Eisenhower's mind, was that he thought Montgomery was once more usurping the prerogative of deciding how the Allied troops would march through Germany, even though American troops vastly outnumbered British. On top of this, Eisenhower had been made aware that Marshall, Patton and the other American generals, as well as US public opinion, would be enraged if many American troops stayed much longer under Montgomery's command.

Eisenhower considered Montgomery's signal 'imperious', and whatever qualms he had previously had about antagonizing Churchill went out of the window. For once the Supreme Commander was curt and clear in his reply to Montgomery; he quashed out of hand the Berlin proposal and withdrew US Ninth Army from British command. He told Montgomery that command of US Ninth Army must revert to the American General Bradley, and that the future role of Montgomery's XXI Army Group would be to protect Bradley's northern flank. On the same day, without consulting either Washington or London, Eisenhower cabled direct to Stalin in Moscow that his plan was for the armies under his command to link up with the Russians at Dresden, thus making it clear that he intended Berlin to be left to the Russians. In another signal copied to London he told Marshall he did not intend to capture Berlin.

A further shock for Churchill and Montgomery was Eisenhower's: 'You will see that in none of this do I mention Berlin. So far as I am concerned that place has become nothing but a geographical location. I have never been interested in this. My purpose is to destroy the enemy.' Even more bitter for Churchill and Montgomery was the signal's last paragraph, which indicated that the final role for Montgomery in the victory would be modest. Eisenhower ordered XXI Army Group to 'cross the Elbe without delay, drive to the Baltic coast of Lübeck and seal off the Danish peninsula'.

On 1 April Montgomery wrote to Simpson, in a letter intended for the Prime Minister's eyes:

> Ike may be saying that I set my forces in motion for the Elbe without consulting him. The true facts are that on 25 March when I took the Prime Minister and the CIGS to meet Ike and Bradley at 15 US Corps HQ I got hold of Ike and Bradley and had a talk with them round the map.
>
> I explained my plan of moving up to the Elbe line and drew on the map the right boundary that I suggested for 21 Army Group: i.e. between me and Bradley. The only comment made by Ike was that he thought Magdeburg, which is on the Elbe, should be inclusive to Bradley. I had drawn it inclusive to me. I at once agreed and Bradley agreed also. No other comment was made, though on that day Ike must

have known that he was going to take the 9th Army away from me, and that he intended the main thrust to be south-east towards Dresden so as to join up with the Russians in that area . . . On March 28 I issued my written directive to my armies. On the same day I received the blow from Ike in his directive in which he agrees with my plan and removes the 9th Army from me. A very good counter-attack.

All very dirty work. It is useless to try and deny the events of March 25.

Increasingly worried by Russian intentions, Churchill desperately wanted Allied troops to take Berlin. So he went into action to try to reverse Eisenhower's decision, telephoning him on 29 March to emphasize the political importance of Berlin as a counter-balance to the imminent Russian occupation of Vienna. He followed this up next day with:

> Withdrawal of US 9th Army from 21 Army Group may stretch Montgomery's front so widely that his offensive role may peter out . . . I do not consider myself Berlin has lost its military and certainly not its political significance . . . While Berlin remains under German flag it is the most decisive point in Germany . . . I prefer the plan on which we crossed the Rhine, namely that the 9th US Army should march with 21 Army Group to the Elbe and beyond to Berlin.'[32]

The Prime Minister wrote in similar terms to Roosevelt on 1 April. But neither Roosevelt nor Eisenhower would budge, and Roosevelt's reply amounted to a snub. Nevertheless Churchill tried again with Eisenhower, writing on 2 April: 'I deem it important that we should shake hands with the Russians as far east as possible.' Eisenhower, supported by Marshall and the President, again refused to yield, though he cabled to Marshall: 'If the COS consider that the Allied effort to take Berlin should outweigh purely military considerations I would cheerfully adjust my plans.'

With the American forces in Europe outnumbering the British by two to one, Churchill had no option but to give up the longed for prize of Berlin. With good grace he wrote to Roosevelt:

> I still think it was a pity that Eisenhower's telegram was sent to Stalin without anything being said to our Chiefs of Staff . . . The changes in the main plan have turned out to be less than we first supposed. My personal relations with General Eisenhower are of the most friendly character. I regard the matter as closed, and to prove my sincerity I will use one of my very few Latin quotations, 'Amantium irae amoris interatio est.' [Roosevelt's staff translated the Latin as 'Lovers' quarrels always go with true love.'][33]

Roosevelt died suddenly on 11 April and was succeeded by Harry Truman, who had been Vice President for three months but kept well out of foreign affairs. Edward Stettinius, who Roosevelt had made Secretary of State when Hull became ill in December 1944, immediately gave Truman a briefing on international problems, which included the information that 'Churchill is inclined to press his position with the Russians with what we consider unnecessary rigidity. The British are anxious to buttress their position *vis-à-vis* United States and Russia both through exerting leadership over the countries of western Europe and through knitting the Commonwealth more closely together.' This was an omen that the precarious solidarity between Churchill and Roosevelt would not continue under the new regime.[34]

On 4 May the Germans in front of Montgomery surrendered, and on the 7th Eisenhower accepted the unconditional surrender of all German forces. However, the Russians were in both Berlin and Vienna. Churchill had written to Eisenhower in his unproductive letter of 1 April: 'If the Russians take Berlin as well as Vienna their impressions will be that they have been the overwhelming contributor to our common victory . . . which will raise grave and formidable difficulties.' Churchill was right, and the iron grip of Communism descended on a far greater part of Europe than if his policy had prevailed.

CHAPTER TWENTY-ONE

Invasion worries: gas, anthrax and de Gaulle

SIX DAYS after the Normandy landings, on 12 June, the first of Hitler's secret weapons, the V1 – codenamed Crossbow – landed on Britain. During the next two weeks two thousand more arrived. On 27 June Herbert Morrison, the Home Secretary, reported to the War Cabinet that the V1s had killed 1600 people, seriously injured 4500 and damaged 200,000 homes; there was a 'serious deterioration' in civilian morale. Between 30 and 40 tons of bombs were being dropped on London every day, and almost 50 per cent of the RAF fighters were diverted to shooting down the flying bombs. The V1 was followed on 8 September by the even more devastating V2, which flew too high for fighter aircraft to destroy. But the main danger from the new weapons was that they would disrupt central Government in London, and seriously damage weapons production.

Churchill became more rattled by the flying bombs than by any other setback in the war, and snapped at his colleagues. When Morrison circulated a note comparing the weight of high explosive delivered by aircraft and flying bombs the Prime Minister fired off an angry minute at the Secretary of State for Air (Sir Archibald Sinclair): 'Why were the 30–40 tons of bombs dropped "by the Robot" doing so much damage when two or three thousand tons were dropped on Berlin or Munich and the German people seemed to get away with it alright?' Churchill followed this up with 'Sinclair [Secretary of State for Air] must feel rather uncomfortable' and it was 'a great reflection on our inventive science that we did not develop the idea . . . you certainly should not feel good and the Air Ministry go away wagging your tails about this. If we had started four years ago on a plan of this kind we might now be able to make great economies in our bomber force and save a great many lives in good crews and pilots.' However, having written this he got his irritation under control and deleted the final sentence.

Up to 16 July Crossbow had demolished 13,000 houses in London compared to 214,000 destroyed by Allied bombing in Hamburg in July 1943. Churchill asked: 'Why have the enemy been able to carry on when one considers the effect of the comparatively light scale of flying bombs on this country?' The answer, which his civil servants did not give, was that the Germans had to carry on because they were impotent to organize public opposition to Nazidom, and on top of this Goebbels' propaganda had now instilled in them the hope of victory from Hitler's secret weapons.[1]

The Secret Service controlled a number of double agents in London; after capture they had been offered the choice between death and transmitting to the Germans misleading messages made up by the British. The War Cabinet conceived the plan that these double agents might be used to give false news of where the bombs landed, so that the Germans would change their direction. Some double agents had been ordered by their German controls to obtain large-scale maps so that they could radio precise details of the landings; this showed how crucial the enemy considered the operation.

The War Cabinet's first plan was to lead the Germans to believe that flying bombs aimed at Portsmouth and Southampton had been particularly successful, so that they would be tempted to increase the number of bombs launched on these cities and decrease those directed at central London. Statistics showed that fatal casualties in London were five times more per bomb than in Southampton. But this plan was rejected because it would have meant moving barrage balloons and AA batteries away from London, and civil defence services in the two cities were mostly part-time.

On 6 July Churchill made two propositions. The first was that a hundred German towns with populations of between two and five thousand should be selected for total destruction by aerial bombardment. Ten were to be destroyed on the first night; the rest would be obliterated at the rate of one for every day that the flying bomb attacks continued.

The second proposal was sensational: the Prime Minister was ready to authorize the use of poison gas if it could be shown that it was a matter of life or death for Britain or would shorten the war by a year. (He ignored the fact that a few weeks earlier he had said there was no question of using gas in the Normandy invasion, and Montgomery had ordered the soldiers to leave their gasmasks behind.) He continued:

> It is absurd to consider morality on this topic when everybody used it [gas] in the last war without a word of complaint from the moralists or the Church. On the other hand, in the last war the bombing of open cities was regarded as forbidden. Now everybody does it as a matter of course. It is simply a question of fashion changing as she does between long and short skirts for women. I want a cold-blooded calculation made as to how it would pay us to use poison gas, by which I principally mean mustard.
>
> We would probably deliver twenty tons to their one . . . If the bombardment of London really becomes a serious nuisance and great rockets with far reaching and devastating effect fall on many centres of Government and labour I should be prepared to do ANYTHING [Churchill's capitals] that would hit the enemy in a murderous place. I may certainly have to ask you to support me in using poison gas. WE COULD DRENCH THE CITIES OF THE RUHR AND MANY OTHER CITIES IN GERMANY IN SUCH A WAY THAT MOST OF THE POPULATION WOULD BE REQUIRING CON-STANT MEDICAL ATTENTION. [author's capitals.] I do not see why we should have all the disadvantages of being the gentlemen while they have all the

advantages of being the cad . . . It may be several weeks or even months before I shall ask you to drench Germany with poison gas and if we do it, let us do it 100 per cent. In the meantime, I want the matter studied in cold blood by sensible people and not by that particular set of psalm-singing uniformed defeatists which one runs across now here now there . . . I shall of course have to square Uncle Joe [Stalin] and the President, but you need not bring this into your calculations at the present time. Just try to find out what it is like on its merits.[2]

On 25 July Churchill, irritated by the delay, sent the Chiefs of Staff a sharp reminder, insisting on having the report within three days. Forty-eight hours later the Joint Planning Staff Report ordered by the Chiefs, was ready for Churchill and the War Cabinet; it stated that 'gas would help only if it proved impossible to force the German lines in Normandy by conventional methods. It would give a major though fleeting advantage, but would not help at all in the drive across France. The effects of gas on the flying bomb sites would be negligible.' The Joint Planning Staff (JPS) were also against Churchill's suggested reprisal bombings, ostensibly because of the diversion of effort from more important targets. They thought that the best counter-measure would be to use the double agents – who in any case *had* to be used – to induce the Germans to land the bombs where they would do the least damage.[3]

Churchill liked this plan to mislead the enemy, and Sir Findlater Stewart, Chairman of the Home Defence Committee, was asked how best this could be done. He assessed the effect on the casualty rate and on war production of moving the point of impact to different places. Analysis of 1076 bombs that fell on London between 22 June and 12 July showed that if the average range of the V1 general pattern could be shortened by six miles there would be great relief to central London and overall casualties would be satisfactorily reduced. The density of bombs per square mile in Whitehall and the City would fall from 2.8 to 0.7, a reduction of 75 per cent. Against this more would land in the southern suburbs. In Bromley the density would increase from 1.7 to 3.6 per square mile; in Orpington from 0.6 to 2.6. The Chiefs of Staff concluded that there was an 'overwhelming case' for trying to move the bombs to the south.

However, Herbert Morrison and Oliver Lyttelton, the Minister of Production, disagreed. Morrison was sceptical about the success of the manoeuvre (probably because he was not in on the secret of the existence of the double agents and their use by the Deceptionists); while Lyttelton thought that overall damage to factories and absenteeism (although as much as 50 per cent in some places) would not be affected. This disagreement had to be settled by Churchill, and thanks to him the War Cabinet concluded that it would be a serious matter to assume any degree of responsibility for action that would affect the areas against which the flying bombs were aimed, although it was agreed that the Deception authorities 'should arrange that the information conveyed to the enemy as regards the point of impact and timing of the arrival of the bombs was such as would create confusion in his mind and present him with an inaccurate picture'. The Deceptionists were usually given a very free hand, but in this instance

Churchill insisted on their instructions being submitted to him for his personal approval.[4]

Duncan Sandys, Churchill's son-in-law, who had been given responsibility for combatting the V weapons, was not invited to the ministerial meetings which took this decision. He asked for it to be reconsidered, pointing out that the Germans' aiming point was Charing Cross but that their bombs were falling short, so that the effective central landing point was Dulwich in South London. He felt that the War Cabinet feeding 'confusing information' would result in the enemy discovering the true concentrations, so that the focus of the bombing pattern would be moved to central London – with disastrous results. He was in no doubt that it would be much safer to mislead the Germans positively by informing them that the bombs were overshooting the target (although they were actually falling short), and estimated that this ruse could reduce monthly casualties by 12,000. He also estimated that, if the focus of the bombing pattern was shifted fairly and squarely to central London, monthly casualties would increase by 3000. But Edward Bridges, Secretary to the Cabinet, told Sandys that the War Cabinet felt if the information came out that they had authorized action which meant south-east London got a heavier discharge of flying bombs and sustained 'heavier casualties than at the present time the Government's position would be indefensible'.

To the consternation of Morrison, who sat for a south London constituency, on 9 August Sandys succeeded in getting the War Cabinet to reconsider their decision. The issue was clouded because, due to the paramount need for secrecy, several ministers were not aware how potent a means of misinformation the double agents were. One argument deployed against changing the decision was that property in the south-east, to which a greater weight of bombs would be diverted, was of lighter construction than that in central London, and although the houses were more widely spaced the total damage would be greater. On 15 August the War Cabinet ruled that 'the Deceptionists' object should be to ensure there was no deterioration in the position and that the enemy did not shift his pattern of bombs to the north west'.[5]

Churchill was desperately keen to halt the flying bombs, even if it meant razing one hundred German towns to the ground or drenching the Reich with mustard gas. Yet he would not argue in favour of the Chiefs of Staff's moderate recommendation, which he could have persuaded his colleagues to accept, about protecting central London and the machinery of Government.

Charles Cruickshank, one of the official historians, wrote in an article published in May 1980: 'He [Morrison] was not interested in the Chiefs of Staff claim that it would benefit the war effort to encourage the Germans to drop their bombs short, or the fact that it would save many lives . . . but he said quite unequivocally that he was afraid of the politically damaging consequences if it ever came out that the War Cabinet had attempted to intervene'. Churchill, too, must have feared the political consequences of doing anything positive to shift the target area of the flying bombs. Thousands of people are alive in the south-east suburbs of London today, and in central London a great many more are dead, because the Chiefs of Staff's advice was not accepted.[6]

The 27 July report of the JPS to the War Cabinet was against mustard gas but contemplated biological warfare, by which they meant anthrax germs, and Churchill did not rule out using anthrax. The JPS did not produce any political or military argument against dropping anthrax germs on German cities. They ruled it out purely because not enough anthrax bombs could be accumulated in time.

On 28 February 1943 a paper on anthrax by Lord Cherwell was read out to a secret session of the Chiefs of Staff. The typist was instructed to leave blanks which Cherwell filled in by hand – it was the closest Allied secret of the war apart from the atom bomb. 'N' was substituted for 'anthrax':

> There is no known cure . . . no prophylactic. N [anthrax] spores . . . may lie dormant on the ground for months or perhaps years but be raised like very fine dust by explosions, vehicles or even people walking about . . . Half a dozen Lancasters could apparently carry enough, if spread evenly, to kill anyone found within a square mile and to render it uninhabitable thereafter . . . This appears to be a weapon of appalling potentiality, almost more formidable, because infinitely easier to make, than tube alloy [the code name for the atom bomb]. It seems most urgent to explore and even prepare the counter measures, if any there be, but in the meantime it seems to me we cannot afford not to have N [anthrax bombs] in our armoury.

After what he described as a 'most secret consultation with my military advisors' Churchill gave instructions that an order for half a million anthrax bombs should be placed with the Americans, adding: 'Pray let me know when they will be available. We should regard it as a first instalment.'[7]

In September 1941 Churchill had authorized experimentation with anthrax bombs. Gruinard island, off the north-west coast of Scotland was chosen as an experimental site, and in the summer of 1943 the RAF dropped anthrax bombs on it. All the sheep died of anthrax, and the island has been sealed off ever since. The JPS paper on 27 July had this to say about anthrax: 'N [anthrax] is the only biological agent which could probably make a material change in the war situation before the end of 1945.' Fortunately the US production of anthrax bombs was behind schedule and the JPS stated that 'there was no likelihood of a sustained attack being possible before the middle of 1945'. Churchill, who had received objections to both gas and anthrax warfare from Eisenhower and Roosevelt, abandoned the plans only reluctantly with 'I am not at all convinced by this negative report [the JPS report of 27 July, advising against both gas and anthrax]. But clearly I cannot make headway against the parsons and warriors at the same time. The matter should be kept under review and brought up again when things get worse.'[8]

Fortunately for mankind things got better, not worse, and most of the flying bomb sites were over-run by British troops. The Chiefs of Staff thought victory so near that they asked permission to discontinue work on both anthrax and mustard gas bombs. On 1 March 1945 Churchill issued the necessary order.

It is a shock to find that Churchill contemplated initiating mustard gas and anthrax attacks on Germany, and shows to what straits a national leader can be driven when his plans go wrong. Churchill felt terrible because, as victory seemed near with the collapse of Hitler's army in Normandy, the sudden appearance of the flying bombs made it possible for the Germans to turn the tables on Britain by paralysing the Government and devastating Whitehall. But before passing an ethical judgement it should be remembered that he never issued a definite order for chemical or germ warfare, and it may well be that when it came to the crunch he would have baulked at violating the Geneva Convention. The USA was not a subscriber to the Geneva Convention, but Roosevelt and his advisers were dead against gas and germ warfare.

In 1944, as D-Day grew near, Churchill's patience with de Gaulle had worn thin. At the Casablanca Conference in January 1943 the Free French leader at first refused to attend to meet General Giraud because he looked on all those who had been loyal to Vichy as traitors to France; on top of this the Anglo–American co-operation with Darlan in Algiers had been anathema to him. He failed entirely to appreciate how great an asset Darlan had been to the Allies by ordering an armistice when American troops were in difficulty, and acting as head of a French Government who did all they could to help the North African battles. After Darlan's murder on Christmas Eve 1942 authority had passed smoothly to General Giraud, and Churchill was anxious to unite the French in Algiers with de Gaulle's Free French. When de Gaulle refused to go to Casablanca, Churchill drafted a note 'that if he did not come the British Government would review their attitude towards his movement while he remained at its head', and if he rejected the invitation 'We shall endeavour to get on well without you.' Churchill told Eden: 'If in his phantasy [sic] of emotion he rejects the chance now offered I shall feel his removal from the headship of this movement is essential to the further support of the Free French movement by HMG . . . Kick him pretty hard.' Eden was more sympathetic to de Gaulle than the Prime Minister was, and with great tact he eventually persuaded de Gaulle to go to Algiers. There he met Roosevelt and Giraud, and agreed that his Free French would join the provisional committee in Algiers.[9]

In Algiers de Gaulle jockeyed Giraud into a minor position on the French National Committee, an action which in Churchill's and Roosevelt's eyes weakened the military potential of the French forces outside France. In May 1943 in Washington, after hearing strong American denunciation of the Frenchman, Churchill telegraphed that the War Cabinet ought to consider urgently whether de Gaulle 'should not now be eliminated as a political force'. Fortunately the War Cabinet, under Eden and Attlee in Churchill's absence, would not have this. Eden cabled back about the danger, if de Gaulle was driven out, that he would become a national hero and 'we would find ourselves accused by both Gaullists and Giraudists of interfering improperly in French internal affairs with a view to treating France as an Anglo–American protectorate'.[10] By 8 November 1943 de Gaulle was virtually in sole command of the French Committee in

Algiers, although he had started off on an equal footing with Giraud who had now been relegated to commander of the armed forces.

After strong British pressure, in July 1943 elections had been held in both Syria and Lebanon. Despite intense propaganda by the French, these resulted in an overwhelming victory for the anti-French national parties. In Lebanon the new Government under Riadh es Solh announced that they would unilaterally abrogate the French mandate from the League of Nations. De Gaulle, with an order not approved by his Committee, told the French Delegate General, Helleu, to dissolve the Lebanese Parliament, suspend the constitution and appoint a pro-French head of Government. The new President and ministers were put in prison. Outraged, the British demanded the release of the Lebanese ministers, failing which they said they would be set free by the British Army and martial law proclaimed.

A furious de Gaulle denounced this action as a British attempt to oust the French from the Levant; Catroux called it another Fashoda (the 1898 Imperial confrontation between France and Britain when the French established a military post on the Nile in a challenge to Britain's colonial claims in the region) and said that 'Perfide Albion' was humiliating France. He thundered against Churchill, who he considered was behind it all. However, all the British Cabinet including the pro-de Gaulle Eden were shocked, and the French were forced to free all the imprisoned ministers. This resulted in both the Syrian and Lebanese Governments categorically refusing to recognize the French mandate or to negotiate a treaty with France. Churchill wrote to Roosevelt: 'These lamentable outrages are a foretaste of what de Gaulle's leadership of France means . . . I assure you there is nothing that this man will not do if he has armed forces at his disposal.' Roosevelt's opinion of de Gaulle was even lower than Churchill's.[11]

In December de Gaulle further prejudiced his position with Churchill by arresting Pierre-Etienne Flandin, former Foreign Minister, together with Peyrouton, former Vichy Minister of the Interior, and Boisson. The last-named had given the order to fire on the British fleet at Dakar in 1940, but had redeemed himself by delivering Dakar to the Americans in 1942. Churchill minuted to Eden that 'this was proof the French Committee was unfit to be considered in any way the Trustees of France but rather small and ambitious intriguers'.[12]

Roosevelt gave Eisenhower what amounted to an ultimatum, backed by Churchill, that 'in view of the assistance given by the Allied armies during the campaign in Africa by Boisson, Peyrouton and Flandin, de Gaulle should be ordered to take no action against them'. Churchill would have agreed, but Eden pointed out that this might mean the wholesale resignation of de Gaulle and his colleagues; on hearing that no trials would take place until France was liberated, Roosevelt agreed to rescind the order. Both Roosevelt and Churchill feared the effect of de Gaulle's resignation on public opinion in their countries.

In January 1944, while convalescing at Marrakesh, Churchill, invited de Gaulle to stay. At first the Frenchman refused, to Churchill's intense annoyance, but later he sensibly changed his mind. The Prime Minister wrote to Hopkins: 'I shall do my utmost to make him realise the disservice he does to France by his known hostility to our two countries.' After a sticky start the meeting was a partial success, and for once the two parted upon almost cordial terms.[13]

Churchill was more favourably disposed to de Gaulle than Roosevelt, who adamantly refused to consider the French Committee of National Liberation (FNCL) under de Gaulle being the provisional authority in a liberated France. The Americans insisted there should be Military Government (AMGOT), and printed its own military francs for the use of the troops. On 15 March 1944, without consulting Churchill, Roosevelt issued an order to Eisenhower telling him that 'he might consult the FNCL' and could also deal with any other French authority if he deemed it desirable, but not the Vichy Government. Eden's reaction was that this was dangerous because 'the Resistance movement and the majority of French opinion was overwhelmingly behind de Gaulle and that if we were to treat the National Committee of Liberation with apparent mistrust we should damage Anglo–French relations'.[14]

The British press and many MPs were clamouring for full co-operation with de Gaulle, and Churchill asked Roosevelt to be forthcoming and invite the Frenchman to Washington. Roosevelt replied, 'I will extend no formal or informal invitation.' However, the President raised no objection to Churchill inviting de Gaulle to Britain before D-Day, though he refused to send Stettinius to meet him.

De Gaulle arrived in Britain on D-Day minus one, 4 June. Churchill, to everyone's annoyance, was now living in a train close to the invasion military headquarters near Portsmouth where, according to Eden, there was only one bath and one telephone: 'Churchill was always in the bath, and General Ismay always on the telephone, so that physically we were nearer the battle but it was almost impossible to conduct any business.' Churchill had written to de Gaulle 'welcoming him to these shores'; walking down the metals he stretched his arms out to greet the General, who responded coldly.

The conference which followed on the train was a failure. De Gaulle resented Churchill's suggestion that he should ask Roosevelt to receive him in Washington, saying: 'Why should I submit my candidacy for authority in France to Roosevelt? The French Government exists'; he also complained bitterly about the decision to issue AMGOT francs, finishing with: 'OK make war with your counterfeit money' [fausse monnaie]. Churchill replied: 'If you want us to ask the President to agree to give you the title deeds of France the answer is NO.' The conversation became a shouting match, in which Bevin and Eden intervened in de Gaulle's favour; this made Churchill even angrier and the General even more difficult.

De Gaulle then had an interview with Eisenhower, who was nearby. This again was unsatisfactory. De Gaulle flared up when Eisenhower said he had prepared a proclamation to the French people. 'By what right?' shouted de Gaulle, and he refused to broadcast after Eisenhower; he also refused to allow his carefully picked French liaison officers to accompany the landings if the AMGOT money was introduced. (Similar Italian liaison officers had been invaluable at the time of the landings in Italy, giving information about the Germans and the

Resistance.) Churchill, in a towering rage, wanted to send de Gaulle back to Algiers because he was 'an enemy' and must not be allowed to re-enter France.[15]

The landing in France was carried out without any agreement over French civil administration or AMGOT currency and no French liaison officers, but at the eleventh hour, as the paratroopers were dropping from the sky, de Gaulle broadcast to the French people; he did it magnificently.

Meanwhile Duff Cooper worked on de Gaulle, and Eden on the Prime Minister. Harvey noted in his diary 'The Prime Minister is almost insane at times in his hatred of de Gaulle.' Eventually Churchill relented and allowed de Gaulle to visit the bridgehead in France, minuting to Eden:

Although I could adduce many reasons against any compliments being paid to a man who has shown himself so entirely free from any sympathy with us or the Americans or the efforts we are making to liberate his own country, yet I feel like you somewhat compromised by the references I made to him visiting France before his new misbehaviour began. I do not know the situation in Bayeux. It may easily be under long range shell fire. It would not be possible for de Gaulle to hold a public meeting or gather a crowd in the streets. He would no doubt like to have a demonstration to show he is the future President of the French Republic. I suggest he should drive slowly through the town, shake hands with a few people and then return.

Remember there is not a scrap of generosity about this man who only wishes to pose as the saviour of France . . . without a single French soldier at his back.

He wrote similarly to Roosevelt, adding de Gaulle would give no address in France 'but a statement which we still have power to censor on his return . . . The responsibility is mine.' Roosevelt replied that the visit might stimulate the French underground, over which 'he' (de Gaulle) had authority.[16]

The night before he went to France, 13 June, de Gaulle dined with Eden and Attlee. During dinner a messenger brought a handwritten note from Churchill to Eden suggesting that, if de Gaulle had forbidden the twenty liaison officers (who he had given permission to go to France) to take AMGOT currency with them, the visit should be cancelled. Sensibly, Eden and Attlee decided to ignore this rather petty note.[17]

In the early afternoon of 14 June de Gaulle arrived off the coast of France in a French destroyer and landed from a 'duck' on Courseulles beach. Montgomery's staff were disconcerted because his party numbered nineteen, not three as expected. De Gaulle had brought three French chauffeurs because he insisted on being driven in France only by French people. Fortunately the chauffeurs' landing craft was delayed, and they were left on board the destroyer so de Gaulle could not ask Montgomery's officers to hand over their jeeps to his French soldiers.

The military traffic congestion was intense, and at first few noticed de Gaulle. However, at one stop he heard the noise of horses' hooves. It was the local parish priest on a rough pony. The priest said: 'You are my hero, and the hero of all France. May I shake your hand?' The General replied: 'As you are the first

Frenchman to greet me on French soil not only will I shake your hand, but I will hug and kiss you.'

De Gaulle's jeep proceeded slowly through the traffic towards Montgomery's headquarters at the Château of Creuilly, between Courseulles and Bayeux. De Gaulle, who disliked Montgomery, was paying only a courtesy call and had refused a lunch invitation. At the next traffic jam de Gaulle noticed two gendarmes with bicycles standing on the verge. He asked the British officer driving his jeep to stop and let him out to talk to them. He said, 'Will you do me a favour?' They replied they would do 'anything for you'. The General said, 'Good. Bicycle to Bayeux. Go round all the streets and tell the people of Bayeux General de Gaulle will be speaking in the main square at 4 p.m.' Montgomery's officer driving the jeep did not understand French.

De Gaulle's plan was not, as Churchill wanted, to shake a few hands and go away. Nor was it impossible, as Churchill believed, to hold a public demonstration in undamaged Bayeux despite its closeness to the front. The two gendarmes did their job well. When de Gaulle appeared in the main square, every inhabitant of Bayeux who could leave his or her house was there. It was a moving occasion. The townspeople all burst into cheers or tears, 'amid an extraordinary display of emotion'. Everyone who heard de Gaulle's speech was moved beyond words; he seemed the reincarnation of a fighting France which was throwing aside the ignominious defeat of 1940. Even Montgomery's officers had tears in their eyes. Having removed the Vichy-appointed prefect who, to de Gaulle's fury, still had a photograph of Pétain on his wall, and inserted his own man – thus aborting AMGOT – de Gaulle agreed to return to Courseulles. But instead, in the words of the Foreign Office, he 'did a bunk', to the horror of the British officers, and asked his staff to book rooms for the night in Bayeux. Downing Street was informed at once and Churchill ordered that de Gaulle was to be put under 'very polite restraint' if he did not turn up at 5 p.m. to re-embark.

De Gaulle then went to Isigny, the only other sizeable place in the bridgehead. To his distress this town – unlike Bayeux, which the British had been careful not to bomb or shell – had been practically destroyed by the Americans. There he gave another address which was received as rapturously as at Bayeux. However, Montgomery gave strict orders forbidding de Gaulle to spend the night in France, and very late that evening he re-embarked at Courseulles, to everyone's relief.[18]

De Gaulle's antics in France maddened Churchill, who told Duff Cooper he 'would describe the whole of de Gaulle's past career, and denounce him as the mortal enemy of Britain'. Fortunately a wiser mood returned. The Prime Minister read a Foreign Office report that a British intelligence officer who had been in the bridgehead from 9 to 12 June had spoken to scores of French men and women of all ages, and 'there is one name, and one name only, on every lip – de Gaulle'.

About this there is no doubt and no two opinions. The testimony was overwhelming and indeed seemingly unanimous. There was no question of any emotional reaction, but rather the quietly accepted fact that he was their leader . . . the

Normans are the coldest and unemotional of all the French types and the testimony is perhaps all the more striking that at a town meeting in Bayeux soon after the city's liberation de Gaulle's name was greeted with prolonged and almost rapturous applause . ... Exactly the same view was taken of de Gaulle in the country as in the town.[19]

This *prima facie* evidence, coupled with further reports of de Gaulle's rapturous reception by the crowds in Bayeux and Isigny, convinced Churchill that to get the best military performance out of the Resistance and the Free French fighting units he must accept de Gaulle. On 20 June Churchill wrote to Roosevelt asking him to invite the Frenchman to Washington. Roosevelt agreed. De Gaulle went. American public opinion was enthusiastic for him, and he charmed the President, who wrote to Churchill on 11 July that he was prepared to accept temporarily *de facto* the FNCL as the authority for civil administration in France. The idea of AMGOT was dead.[20]

An armoured French division with American tanks under General Leclerc played an important part in the breakout from Normandy and the fall of Paris on August 25, 1944. De Gaulle went to Paris the day after its liberation and was received with exultation. On 10 November Churchill flew to Paris with his wife and his daughter Mary. On the following day, Armistice Day, Churchill and de Gaulle walked down the Champs Elysées, which was lined with troops and crowds of civilians. Ismay recorded that 'the pent up emotion of perhaps half a million Parisians broke loose like a flood. Some were cheering; some were laughing; some were sobbing. All were delirious.' Churchill recalled: 'De Gaulle was the perfect host that day.' His long-standing hostility to the French leader had ended.[21]

The Prime Minister intervened to help de Gaulle during the Battle of the Bulge in January 1945, when the Frenchman had fallen out with Eisenhower. The Supreme Commander had decided to abandon French territory in Alsace, announcing on 28 December that Strasbourg would be evacuated. This was a political blunder. De Gaulle refused to agree to the evacuation, writing to Eisenhower that 'whatever happened, the French will defend Strasbourg'. He ordered his General, de Lattre Tassigny, 'to take matters into your own hands and guarantee the defence of Strasbourg'. On 31 December the Germans launched an offensive against the city. Eisenhower ordered the French and American troops in the area to withdraw to the Vosges and abandon Strasbourg. The French believed, with reason, that the Germans would take reprisals against the citizens, and that to lose the city without a fight would be disastrous for the prestige of de Gaulle's provisional Government.

On 2 January 1945 General Leclerc rushed to S H A E F headquarters at Versailles and told Eisenhower's Chief of Staff, Bedell Smith, that the French would not obey the order to withdraw, and that de Gaulle had ordered de Lattre Tassigny to defend the city. Bedell Smith replied that this was 'insubordination'. 'All right,' replied Leclerc, 'in that case we will forbid the American troops the use of the French railways.' DeGaulle cabled Roosevelt that the French Government could not accept 'a deplorable and strategically unjustifiable withdrawal,' and sent a copy to Churchill, adding only: 'I ask you to support me.' Roosevelt replied that it was a purely military question and must be settled by Eisenhower alone.

But Churchill was more generous to the French head of state who had caused him so much trouble. He immediately went to Versailles where he, de Gaulle, Leclerc and Brooke argued fiercely with Eisenhower, who finally caved in and agreed that Strasbourg should be held. With his previous experience of de Gaulle, Churchill wisely saw that the Allies were close to a most damaging break with the French.

Undoubtedly Churchill's statesmanlike intervention saved Strasbourg. In his memoirs he says de Gaulle expressed his gratitude. But according to Leclerc's detailed account in his own memoirs, when he and de Gaulle got into the car to leave Versailles Leclerc suggested Churchill had some right 'to expect at least a word of thanks'. 'Bah,' de Gaulle replied, and relapsed once more into 'apparently gloomy contemplation'.[22]

CHAPTER TWENTY-TWO

===

Potsdam and atom bombs

IN 1942 the Japanese conquered the Far East up to a line from Mandalay in Burma through Sumatra, Java and Timor to the middle of Papua New Guinea. A drive by them to capture Port Moresby in Papua, close to Australia, was foiled by the Australians when the Japanese were only twenty miles away. The Solomon and Marshall Islands also fell.

However, as long as the sea route from Hawaii to Australia stayed in Allied hands American, Far Eastern and Australian forces could be easily reinforced. The Japanese had wrongly forecast the American reaction; the angry nation immediately set about building a military machine capable of waging a war on two fronts, and in spite of priority for Europe and the Mediterranean the Japanese defensive perimeter was soon threatened from several different directions. In May 1942 a Japanese task force intended for Port Moresby, in an effort to isolate Australia, was turned back at the Battle of the Coral Sea.

The final act in the drama of the Japanese effort to dominate the Pacific and to establish what they called the 'South East Asia co-prosperity sphere' was played out at Midway Island on 3 and 4 June 1942. Midway, the westernmost of the Hawaiian chain of islands, lies one thousand miles west of Pearl Harbor, which was now the only American base west of San Francisco. If the Japanese had seized Midway they could have swept on to Hawaii and Pearl Harbor. This time the Japanese did not surprise the Americans. Admiral Nimitz had the advantage of having broken the Japanese naval code, and thus was forewarned of the presence of the powerful Japanese naval striking force and transport ships. When the Japanese approached Midway the American carrier force was at sea awaiting them. In the fighting the Japanese lost all four of their aircraft carriers, with disastrous casualties amongst their trained pilots. Ignominiously the Japanese Admiral Yamamoto turned back as soon as he learned of the loss of his carriers. This was another real Allied victory in the Far East to consolidate that won at the Battle of the Coral Sea. The Japanese had only two first-line carriers left, and from now on the American Fleet with their new Essex class carriers outclassed the Japanese.

During 1943 the Joint Chiefs of Staff argued continuously about the comparative merits of Admiral Nimitz's plan for a drive through the central Pacific and General MacArthur's design for the main drive to be made through New Guinea

and into the Philippines. The British were left out of the arguments and
Churchill's plea for operations in the Bay of Bengal was disregarded. By 1944 the
American build-up in the Pacific made it possible to begin both drives. In June
1944, in trying to repel American landings, the Japanese Navy received a
crushing defeat at the Battle of the Philippine Sea off the Mariana Islands. Even
worse disaster struck the Japanese Fleet on 20 October 1944 at Leyte, the largest
naval battle in history. Determined to prevent the Americans recapturing their
former air bases, the Japanese risked a decisive battle – only to lose four aircraft
carriers, three battleships and ten cruisers. From then on the Americans had
undisputed command of the sea and MacArthur's troops were able to make
spectacular advances on land.

Then, in April 1945, the Americans assaulted Okinawa, between Formosa and
Japan. The Japanese High Command knew that possession of this island would
put the mainland at the mercy of US bombers and ships, and they resisted
desperately – but in vain. Japanese suicide pilots (kamikaze) sank 25 ships and
damaged another 165. By 21 June all Okinawa was in US hands, at a cost of over
12,500 American lives; but in an amazing display of fatalism and foolhardy
courage over 100,000 Japanese had died in a fanatical display of devotion to the
Emperor. Even civilians were told (and many believed) that in dying for their
country they would be rewarded in the afterlife as if they had been soldiers dying
in battle.

In June 1945 the possession of air bases in Okinawa put American fighters and
bombers within easy range of the Japanese mainland; and the American Fleet,
now reinforced by British ships from forward anchorages in the Ryukus, was able
to engage in almost continuous action against Japan. Tokyo and other large towns
and cities were devastated by bombing from both carriers and land-based
aircraft. At the same time Japan's sea and air power had been so reduced, and her
capacity to produce and transport war supplies so crippled, that she was almost
helpless in face of the threat of invasion. The end of the Pacific war was in sight.

The question for the Japanese Government when Germany capitulated in
May 1945 was whether to continue the war to the bitter end or to seek a
surrender. Tojo had been succeeded as Prime Minister by General Koiso in
September 1944, which meant that the military element in the Government
became less influential. Immediately peace overtures to the British and Americans began through the neutral countries of Portugal, Switzerland and Sweden.
General Koiso was replaced in April 1945 by Admiral Suzuki, who was known to
be in favour of a negotiated peace and declared that 'national existence is in
danger'. The peace overtures redoubled. Yet to all of them the British and
Americans returned the reply: 'No negotiations, only Unconditional Surrender.'
By July 1945 the physical damage to Japan from aerial bombing was so great that
it was madness to continue the war.

Unfortunately the alternative American strategy of the atom bomb now
erupted on the scene. Originally British scientists were far ahead of their US
counterparts in research on nuclear fission. French physicists, too, were working
on exploring the possibilities of a controlled chain reaction using uranium with

heavy water slowing down the neutrons; early in 1940 the French Secret Service bought up the world stock of heavy water which on the fall of France was transferred to Britain together with the French research team. In July 1941 it was reported to Churchill that 'a Uranium bomb is practicable and likely to lead to decisive results in the war'. Research in Britain then moved much faster than in America, so that in August US scientists suggested joint research to the British, and in October 1941 Roosevelt wrote to Churchill proposing that 'extended efforts may be coordinated or even jointly conducted'. The British response was negative, mainly because of fear of breach of security by American scientists.

However, with America's entry into the war in December 1941 everything changed. US scientists were given access to all British secrets, and in a few months the Americans had not only caught up but moved well ahead. Sir John Anderson, the Cabinet minister in charge, told Churchill in July 1942 that the necessary production plant would be so huge that 'its erection in this country will be out of the question during the war'. The flow of information back to Britain dried up, and nuclear research became almost 100 per cent American. Anderson wrote: 'We cannot afford after the war to face the future without this weapon and rely entirely on America, should Russia or some other power develop it.'

Churchill was perturbed, and thanks to his personal intervention a document was signed by him and Roosevelt at the first Quebec Conference in August 1943, agreeing that neither country would use nuclear weapons nor pass on information about their manufacture to any third country without the other's consent. Churchill disclaimed 'any interest' in 'industrial and commercial aspects beyond what may be considered by the President of the United States to be fair and just in harmony with the economic welfare of the world'. Thus atomic research was formally handed over to America. R. V. Jones, the Government's scientific adviser, has written of this: 'It seemed to me we had signed away our birthright on the scientific development post war of nuclear energy.' Many of the author's generation of Oxford undergraduates, who passed the motion at the Union that they would never fight for King or Country, felt it was a birthright they could gladly shed.[1]

By the time of the second Quebec Conference, in September 1944, an atomic warhead was approaching completion; Churchill and Roosevelt agreed that the bomb 'might perhaps after mature consideration be used against the Japanese'. At that moment there were false hopes of an imminent German military collapse. Churchill, made conscious of the security risks by Lindemann, later Lord Cherwell, his scientific advisor, insisted strongly that no one else should be told. Roosevelt agreed. Stalin's un-cooperative attitude over Poland was making the President and the Prime Minister cautious towards their ally. Roosevelt promised full co-operation with Britain after the war 'for military and commercial purposes'. But Truman did not honour his predecessor's pledge.

When Roosevelt died, on 12 April 1945, Truman had no idea that America was almost ready to launch an atom bomb attack. Suddenly he had to take on direct responsibilities towards mankind. As soon as he was briefed, Truman set up a committee to study all aspects of atomic energy, including whether to use it to bring about a Japanese surrender. The committee was told that an atomic bomb would be ready for operational use in early August if a test in July was satisfactory. Responsibility lay primarily with the Americans, although under the Churchill–Roosevelt agreement British consent was still needed for the use of the atom bomb against Japan. As will be seen Eden, and to a lesser extent Churchill, were now to become partly responsible and assume some of the guilt, if it was guilt, for the atom bomb attacks on Japan. On 2 July the British gave their formal consent to the atom bomb being used against their Far Eastern enemy.

Joseph Grew, US Ambassador in Tokyo until the outbreak of war, had been made Assistant Under Secretary for Foreign Affairs in Washington. He was the leading Japanese expert in America and felt strongly that to avoid prolonging the war the USA should tell Japan formally that unconditional surrender would not lead to the ruin of the country and that the Emperor could remain on the throne after capitulation. However, Truman would not go further than saying on 8 May after the German surrender that 'Unconditional Surrender does not mean the extermination of the Japanese people.' The American press and some members of the influential International Pacific Relations Conference demanded that the Emperor should be treated as a war criminal, and Faulds in the Far Eastern Department of the Foreign Office minuted: 'The spate of foolish talk in the US about the Emperor has unquestionably stiffened Japanese determination to fight to the last gasp.'

The chief British Foreign Office expert on Japan was Sir George Sansom. He had spent many years at the Embassy in Tokyo, and after the Pacific war began had been transferred to the Embassy in Washington as Minister. He was an outstanding Japanese scholar and had a high reputation owing to his authoritative history of Japan. Sansom agreed 100 per cent with Grew that it was essential to assure the Japanese that the Emperor's powers would not be removed after surrender if there was to be a speedy end to the war.[2]

The Sansom–Grew view was not challenged by Japanese experts either then or now. The late Professor Richard Storry wrote authoritatively and definitively: 'The monarchy must be preserved at all costs. This was their one irreducible demand. A Japan without an Emperor was inconceivable . . . they were ready to sue for peace if only the formula of 'unconditional surrender' could be modified by an allied pledge not to tamper with the institutions of the Japanese monarchy.'[3]

On 27 May Grew told Sansom he proposed to speak to the President and ask him to make an announcement that unconditional surrender would not mean any interference with the position of the Emperor. Grew impressed on Sansom that it was 'a very nicely balanced question' whether, in view of American public opinion and hostility to the Emperor, the Government could afford to sponsor such a statement. Sansom had reported to the Foreign Office from Washington that Grew's position with regard to the Emperor was 'rather delicate', because influential senior civil servants and politicians wanted to defer to American public opinion and overthrow the Emperor, who was much hated on account of Pearl Harbor and the atrocious treatment of American POWs by the Japanese. In his messages to London Sansom stressed the discord between the US and British

POTSDAM AND ATOM BOMBS

views on the future of the Emperor. On 30 May, at Grew's insistence, the State Department showed Sansom (for his own information and not as an official communication) a draft document setting forth the policy of the US Government. To Sansom's concern it included the words 'suspension of constitutional powers of the Emperor and all organs for consideration and formulation of policy [e.g. Parliament] their functions to be assumed by military Government'.

The Foreign Office told Grew through Sansom that they agreed that unqualified insistence on unconditional surrender was prolonging Japanese resistance. Grew had considerable support within the State Department and from Stimson and other members of the administration, but when Grew and Truman spoke the President told him he accepted the contrary view which was held by Byrnes, who Truman had made Secretary of State in place of Stettinius.[4]

However Grew was able to convince Stimson, Secretary of State for War, who was Chairman of the Committee controlling the atom project, that to obtain an early surrender it was essential to make a formal offer of the retention of the monarchy. On 2 July Stimson submitted a memorandum of the utmost importance to Truman. It proposed an ultimatum which contained this key passage:

> Withdrawal [of Allied Forces] as soon as there has been established a peacefully inclined Government of a character representative of the masses of the Japanese people. I personally think that *if in saying this we should add that we do not exclude a constitutional monarchy under her present dynasty it would substantially add to the chances of success*. (author's italics.)

If this advice had been accepted, there would have been no need to drop the atom bombs. However, many American officials feared Congress would question the enormous expenditure on atom research if the bomb was not used; a significant comment comes from Admiral Leahy: 'the scientists and others wanted to make this test [operational use of the atom bomb] because of the vast sums that had been spent on the project. Truman knew that, and so did the other people involved.'[5]

On 16 July the Americans successfully completed the atom bomb experiment, and immediately went forward with plans to launch bombs on Japan. On the same day Stimson again drew the President's attention to his 2 July memorandum about the Emperor remaining, but without success.

Eden had taken little interest in the problem of the Japanese surrender, but he was concerned when he learned that the USA had four thousand Military Government officers being trained at the University of Michigan for duties in the post-war military administration of Japan. On 20 May 1945 he wrote to Churchill:

> We have reason to believe that the Americans have been doing a great deal of planning on this subject and that it is reaching an advanced stage. My views are that we should take part in the military occupation of Japan after her defeat if there is an Allied occupation . . . we should share in the political control of Japan and in the planning of that control as we have done in Europe.
>
> If you agree . . . I suggest that the study of the problems involved should be set in

motion without delay, and left to the COS and to the FO to arrange in agreement how the work should be done.[6]

Churchill minuted his agreement.

Eden appears unconscious of the arguments about the need to retain the Emperor in order to obtain a Japanese surrender. At the end of May he became seriously ill with a gastric ulcer and was ordered a complete rest. His condition was aggravated by the tragic news that his favourite son, Simon, had been killed while flying with the RAF in Burma, and he was too ill to take part in the General Election apart from recording one broadcast. Instead he stayed at his country house at Binderton in Kent.

Churchill too ignored the problem of the Japanese monarchy, although he was enthusiastic for the return of the European monarchies. The General Election campaign absorbed all his energies from between 15 June and 5 July. When it was over he was exhausted and went to France for a holiday where, according to Colville, he hardly looked at his boxes. Cadogan wrote that when he got to Potsdam the Prime Minister had done no work since he left London. Significantly, neither Eden nor Cadogan mentions the Emperor in their diaries; nor does Churchill mention him in his post-war memoirs.

Eden came to London for a Cabinet on 10 July but was below par, and only just well enough to fly to Potsdam for the final wartime summit with Churchill on the 15th. According to Cadogan, once at Potsdam Churchill 'refused to do any work or read anything', and when in conversation with the Americans, at every mention of a topic he 'set off on a wild rampage'.[7]

Meanwhile the Far Eastern Department of the Foreign Ofice had recalled Sansom to London for consultation, and conscientiously formulated arguments likely to exploit the American division of opinion and reinforce Grew and Stimson against Byrnes in influencing Truman. In this they were following the Prime Minister's instructions to proceed in accordance with the views of the Chiefs of Staff, because Churchill and Eden were not available.

On 20 June Sansom produced a long memorandum in which he wrote: 'Instead of surrendering the constitutional powers of the Emperor it would seem preferable to work through these powers or through whatever state administration they find in being in Japan.' He suggested these views should be communicated to the State Department in Washington. As the memorandum represented the agreed views of the COS and the Foreign Office Cadogan did not think there was anything which needed Cabinet approval at the time, but he was anxious for British views to be taken into consideration by the Americans in view of the likelihood that the question would be discussed at Potsdam. Sterndale Bennett, Head of the Far Eastern Department, minuted: 'Question of Emperor is likely to be crucial and cannot be avoided in any discussion with the Americans.'[8]

How right he was became even clearer when Michael Wright, Counsellor at the Washington Embassy, was told by General Donovan on 20 June that he wanted Hirohito placed on the 'hit list' of war criminals. The Foreign Office minuted that this was definitely not Grew's view, and that it would be better not to discuss it further with Donovan. Donovan was influential in the White House as Head of the Office of Strategic Services (OSS).

Sterndale Bennett minuted that the Sansom memorandum represented the agreed view of the chief Japanese experts in Britain and that the Chiefs of Staff concurred. Owing to the non-availability of Churchill and Eden the Chiefs of Staff and the Foreign Office pushed ahead. On 17 July they sent a telegram to Washington based on Sansom's memorandum and asked Halifax to make an oral communication based on it. The telegram stated in paragraph 7:

> It seems worth pointing out also that the best chance of getting the Japanese in the southern areas to lay down their arms will be to require the Emperor to send them his commands in that sense by Imperial Messenger. Unless the troops in those areas receive an Imperial Command to cease fighting there is a considerable risk that they will ignore any capitulation which is made in Japan proper and will continue a hopeless struggle until they are all mopped up.

This was sensible. Only the Emperor could stop the Japanese war machine (although it did not follow automatically that the Emperor must be retained as ruler after surrender).

Eden read this telegram in Potsdam on 19 July and threw a heavy spanner into the works; he scrawled on it in pencil: 'I do not want to recommend to the Americans that Emperor should be preserved. They would no doubt like to get such advice and then say they had reluctantly concurred with us . . .'

The telegram of 17 July based on Sansom's views had been despatched; it was now cancelled and altered, and a new paragraph 7 substituted: 'Might it not be preferable for the Allies instead of suspending the constitutional powers of the Emperor to work through these powers or whatever state administration they may find in Japan using economic sanctions to secure compliance.'

Cadogan comments in his diary that both Churchill and Eden 'had been out of the picture for some time lately'. Eden was in no way an expert on Japan. Yet he became petulant and obstructive evidently feeling the Department were not treating him with sufficient respect. He did not realize that the grim problem of securing the Japanese surrender without the horrific use of atom bombs hinged on the Emperor being allowed to remain. On reading the telegram Eden wrote: 'I do not like this telegram; it should not have been sent without my seeing it. It deals with important issues of policy which are essentially for me. Please telegraph at once to Washington that no action is to be taken upon it and if it has been taken, it is to be cancelled. Dept. must be rebuked for having done this. Matter could well have been referred to us here.'

The Far Eastern Department were amazed by their master's comment. Sterndale Bennett minuted that the 17 July telegram 'was in accordance with approved policy'; he later deleted 'policy' and wrote 'course of action', meaning that in line with Churchill and Eden's instructions the Foreign Office had obtained 'the Chiefs of Staff approval and therefore there was no need to refer it to Eden before despatch'. On a minute that the 17 July telegram might be 'allowed to stand as a planning study' Eden shows further signs of petulance; he did not suggest any alternative policy but wrote: 'This is too subtle for me. F.O. does commit me until July 26 [Election day] A.E.'9

The Foreign Office obeyed the Foreign Secretary and cabled Halifax asking him to cancel their advice. Thus British opposition to Byrnes' view that the Emperor must go was not expressed, and the State Department drafted an ultimatum to Japan without reference to the Emperor remaining. Meanwhile the experimental atom bomb had been successfully exploded, and Churchill told Truman that he agreed atom bombs should be dropped on Japan after the issue of an ultimatum.

On 12 July the Prime Minister, Suzuki, after conferring with the Emperor, had instructed the Japanese Ambassador in Moscow to ask Stalin personally whether Prince Konoye the former Prime Minister would be received in Moscow as an envoy in an attempt to negotiate a surrender on behalf of the Emperor. The Russians turned a deaf ear, claiming that by the time the message had been delivered Molotov and Stalin had departed for the Potsdam Conference with the British and American leaders.

Stalin told Churchill at a private dinner on 18 July that he had replied to the Mikado's approach 'that as the message had been in general terms and contained no concrete proposals the Soviet Government could take no action'. From Stalin's further statements Churchill noted it was evident that Russia intended to attack Japan soon after 8 August. After this news of Japanese peace efforts Churchill did nothing to try to dissuade Truman from unleashing his atom bombs.10

On 22 July Churchill and Eden met Truman and Byrnes, and the decision was taken to drop an atom bomb on Japan if she refused to accept unconditional surrender. Churchill revealed this to the British COS at lunchtime next day, and Brooke described the Prime Minister as 'completely carried away. [Churchill said] it was no longer necessary for the Russians to come into the Japanese war; the new explosive alone was sufficient to settle the matter. Furthermore, we now had something in our hands which would redress the balance with the Russians.' Brooke said Churchill declared: 'Now we could say, "If you insist on doing this or that, well . . ." And then where are the Russians?' The CIGS tried to calm Churchill's optimism based on the results of one experiment, and 'was asked with contempt what reason I had for minimizing the results of these discoveries. I was trying to dispel his dreams and as usual he did not like it.' Truman told Stalin of the atomic bomb next day, the 24th; the Soviet leader merely nodded his head and muttered: 'Thank you.'11

On 24 July at Potsdam the American delegation showed their draft ultimatum to Japan to the British. Conflicting advice had been received from Hull and the American joint Chiefs of Staff, but Byrnes had ruled firmly that there was to be no mention of the Emperor remaining. Eden had been briefed by the Foreign Office:

There is no organised group in Japan who could overthrow the Government; the mass of the people are loyal to the Emperor and therefore obedient to the lawfully constituted administration. The proclamation would have a better chance of success if it is framed in recognition of these facts. It may indeed fail unless these facts are recognised.

Eden did not show this brief to Churchill, and on the top of Eden's copy Cadogan wrote in his own hand: 'This was not shown to the P.M.' (Perhaps Cadogan was sending a coded message for future generations of historians that Eden had failed in his duty but that there was nothing that he, as a civil servant, could do about it.) Instead Eden, ignoring the Foreign Office advice, minuted to Churchill: 'I think we must accept the American draft.' Churchill concurred, and on 26 July an ultimatum known as the Potsdam Declaration, in the names of the USA, Britain and China, was issued to the world. It called for unconditional surrender to prevent 'the utter devastation of the Japanese homeland', and said 'there must be eliminated for all time the authority and influence of those who have deceived and misled the people of Japan into embarking on world conquest'. There was no mention of the new and terrible instrument of destruction which the Allies were poised to deliver, and the Japanese were given the impression that their beloved Emperor must abdicate.[12]

The American Chiefs of Staff agreed with the Stimson view that the Japanese must be allowed to retain the Emperor in order to bring about a quick surrender. They gave Churchill one more chance to intervene in favour of the Emperor. He would not take it.

On 17 July Ismay had sent a minute to Churchill that the combined Chiefs of Staff had discussed unconditional surrender at Potsdam and it was generally agreed:

> . . . if this involved the dissolution of the Imperial dynasty there would be no-one to order the cease fire in outlying areas and fighting might continue in various British and Dutch territories and also in China for many months or even years. Thus from the civilian point of view there was a good deal to be said for retention in Japan of some central authority who would command attention . . . they asked whether you yourself would be prepared to raise the point with the President.
>
> We replied that as the Americans were so very much the predominant partner in the war against Japan you might feel reluctant to take the lead in the matter; but we agreed to inform you at once . . .'

Churchill took no action. He clearly felt he had done all he could when lunching with Truman the day before, and he was not going to interfere now.

By this time Japan was in a dreadful state. Aircraft from American and British carriers, as well as from the Marianas, Iwojima and Okinawa, ranged over the length and breadth of the country. Forty per cent of the built-up area, comprising more than sixty towns and cities, had been destroyed. Professor Storry wrote:

> For mile after mile the huge urban area from Tokyo through Kawasaki to Yokohama presented the spectacle of charred wood and ashes with scarcely a building standing. It was much the same at Osaka, Nagoya and Kobe . . . Little

more than one million tons of merchant shipping out of some ten million remained afloat . . . the navy had been reduced from some two and a quarter million tons to less than two hundred thousand.

Yet very large and efficient land forces remained in Malaya, Indo-China, Borneo and Burma, as well as in Japan itself.[13]

Immediately the British General Election result was announced, the Churchill Government resigned. Attlee and Bevin, respectively the new Prime Minister and Foreign Secretary, arrived in Potsdam late on 28 July, and after rushed and exhausting meetings eventually saw Stalin at 10.30 p.m. for a private talk. The Russian leader repeated what he had told Churchill about the Japanese proposal that Russia should act as mediator. This time Stalin explained that he had not answered the first letter from the Japanese Ambassador in Moscow because it had not contained a 'sufficiently definite proposal'. The Japanese Ambassador, he said, had now stated that the proposed mission of Konoye to Moscow was to end the present war and negotiate questions of Soviet–Japanese relations, and that the mission would have the special authority of the Emperor, who wanted to avoid further bloodshed on both sides. Stalin told the British the communication contained nothing not already known, and was simply a further attempt to obtain the collaboration of Russia in Japanese policy. Therefore the Soviet Government had 'returned an unhesitating negative'.[14]

Churchill wrote in his memoirs: 'There was never a moment's hesitation at the Conference [Potsdam] whether the bomb should be used or not.' He did not know of the Attlee–Bevin–Stalin late-night meeting of 28 July after he had left. However, Bevin and Attlee failed to appreciate the importance of Stalin's remarks about the Emperor. They had no discussion with Stalin and merely thanked him. According to the archives they ignored the information, and regarded Churchill's agreement to drop the atom bomb as a *fait accompli*.[15]

Even though the ultimatum meant his own abdication the Emperor was in favour of accepting it. However Suzuki, now eighty years old, did not respond.

Eden had minuted in Potsdam that the ultimatum could be released to the world press. For some unexplained reason the Americans issued it as a press statement and did not make any communication to Japan through the Japanese ambassadors in the neutral countries of Sweden, Portugal and Switzerland, even though they knew the Japanese were expecting to hear from them through these channels. If it had been an official declaration to the Japanese Government, Suzuki would almost certainly have responded and perhaps staved off the atom bombs. Instead he concerted his plans with the Emperor and instructed Sato the Japanese ambassador in Moscow on 2 August:

> The battle situation has become acute. There are only a few days left in which to make arrangements to end the war . . . a request was made to the Soviet Union, in accordance with the Imperial will, for her mediation in terminating the war . . . the despatch of a special envoy was . . . decided upon . . . it is our intention to make the Potsdam Three-Power Declaration the basis of the study regarding the terms. It is requested that further efforts be exerted somehow to make the Soviet Union enthusiastic over the special envoy . . . Since the loss of one day relative to this

present matter may result in a thousand years of regret, it is requested that you immediately have a talk with Molotov.[16]

The Russians, as could be expected, ignored Sato's intervention; Stalin and Molotov did not return to Moscow until 6 August, and Molotov refused to see Sato until the 8th when, ignoring the request for mediation, he told him that Russia had declared war on Japan. However, the Americans were reading all Japanese coded signals to Sato from Tokyo, and it is inconceivable they did not decode this momentous telegram which revealed that the Japanese were desperate to capitulate. The Potsdam Conference had broken up on 2 August and Truman, Byrnes and Stimson were all travelling. The British were not informed by the Americans of the content of the telegrams.

When the State Department learnt of Japan's intention to make the Potsdam Declaration 'the basis of the study regarding terms' it would have been awkward, but not impossible, to convene a fresh emergency summit. They took no action. If Churchill had been informed of the contents of the 2 August message from Suzuki to Sato and he had been still Prime Minister he might have taken urgent action and altered the course of history. It is much less likely that Attlee would have done anything. Responsibility for ignoring the Moscow development which made it clear that Japan was about to capitulate lies on the State Department in Washington.

On 6 August the Americans dropped an atom bomb on the industrial city of Hiroshima, causing horrendous damage, even though, as we have already seen in Storry's words: 'Washington knew, in fact, that the Japanese were desperately trying to seek peace.'[17] A second atom bomb was dropped on Nagasaki on the 9th, causing similar devastation.

Prior to resigning as Prime Minister Churchill, with the help of Lord Cherwell and Sir John Anderson, drafted a press statement for the occasion of the delivery of the atom bomb on Japan. On 29 July Churchill sent it to Attlee, writing that it required 'immediate consideration in view of what is in prospect'. He added that he had drafted it 'in the first person as I should have made it myself, but it would be quite easy to put into the third person as an announcement by you'.[18]

Attlee came to the conclusion that the statement should be released as Churchill's own, and told Truman this. The President replied: 'I think you are very generous to release Mr Churchill's statement in toto.' However, perhaps the right explanation is that Attlee now had qualms about his inaction after Stalin had told him of the Japanese intention to surrender on 28 July, and did not want to be associated with atom bombs. The statement was released by the Ministry of Information to coincide with the news of the first atom bomb, and although he was now Leader of the Opposition, responsibility (and credit, if any) devolved on Churchill. Churchill was statesmanlike: 'it is now for Japan to realise in the glare of the first atomic bomb which had smitten her what the consequences will be of an indefinite continuance of these terrible means of maintaining the rule of law in the world. We must indeed pray that these awful agencies will be made to conduce to peace amongst nations'. Truman, on the other hand, was materialist and banal; 'We spent 20 billion on the greatest scientific gamble in history and won,' the *Times* leader said two days later; 'everyone will now hope . . . there will be no need to drop another'. On the same day the paper printed a letter from a Carlton Club member; 'Posterity will condemn those who have first used it . . . by creating the most awful precedent in the history of mankind', and the *Times* correspondence column was soon filled with letters expressing approval or strong condemnation.[19]

Ehrman, the official historian, in his unpublished chapter for Part VI of Grand Strategy, argues that the Americans were influenced by Russia's entry into war against Japan to drop the atom bombs as soon as possible. They wanted to shorten the war in order to limit Soviet participation and influence at the subsequent peace conference. Ehrman's arguments languish unread in the Public Record Office because this chapter was expurgated by the Cabinet Office after the book had been printed and circulated in Whitehall – presumably because it might give offence to the Russians.[20] In this context, surprisingly, Professor Dilks has suggested that it was partly because 'it would remove the need to pay a high price for Russia assistance in the Far East' that Churchill consented to the use of the atom bombs. Ehrman's suppressed chapter does not support this view.

The Americans had no more atom bombs ready for use, but the Japanese did not know this. The Russians were advancing at whirlwind speed, and on 13 August Tokyo was raided by 1500 planes from Allied carriers cruising at will off the coast. The next day Suzuki and the Emperor, despite fanatical opposition from the 'war-to-the-end' faction, insisted that the Potsdam Declaration be accepted subject to the retention of the Emperor. The Pacific war was over. When Japan's acceptance was reported in Washington the British Embassy cabled London to say that there was a 'clamour' in the USA for the removal of the Emperor, who was regarded as the symbol of Japanese militarism. However Truman and Attlee conceded that from the moment of surrender 'the authority of the Emperor and the Japanese Government to run the State should be subject to the Supreme Commander of the Allied Powers'. If this concession had been made in the Potsdam Declaration three weeks earlier, Japan would have surrendered without atom bombs.[21]

A last-minute plan by the British, codenamed Mimsy, might also have saved the world from the horrors of the atom bombs. It crops up first in a memorandum from the London Controlling Section (LCS – the codename of the War Cabinet 'Deceptionists') to the Chiefs of Staff on 12 July 1945, and was concocted in Mountbatten's Far East Headquarters. In London the Deceptionists pointed out it was not a deception plan but rather 'a plan based on the use of deception machinery', under which one of the Japanese double agents would send a direct message from Mountbatten to Emperor Hirohito. Once direct contact was established between the two, it was hoped that surrender terms could be negotiated without further bloodshed.

Unfortunately 12 July was during the period after the General Election, when both Churchill and Eden were out of action. According to Harvey, Churchill and

Eden were both 'quite exhausted' . . . they could no longer look at the problems properly or read the papers about them. 'It had become mere improvisation', and, as has been noted, Churchill hardly looked at his boxes at this time. As a result neither the Prime Minister nor the Foreign Secretary took any interest in Mimsy, and it perished on the vine during those vital weeks between 12 July and 6 August when mankind was given notice of its possible fate at Hiroshima.[22] If Mountbatten and the High Command in the Far East had had the courage of their convictions and moved fast the war might have ended less devastatingly.

In London the plan was put forward by Peter Fleming (brother of the novelist Ian Fleming) and was favoured by Colonel John Bevan, head of LCS in the Cabinet office; after long discussion over detail it was approved by Sir George Sansom, the Foreign Office Japanese expert, and William Cavendish Bentinck, later the Duke of Portland, then an Assistant Under-Secretary. On 26 July Fleming minuted that, as Bevan and Sansom had approved it, the plan for Mimsy should go to the Chiefs of Staff Committee. Fleming feared Washington's reaction would be unfavourable and asked the Chiefs of Staff to mention Mimsy 'on a high plain verbally', as this 'would be invaluable to a project which the experts agree is promising'. But with Churchill and Eden unavailable there was nothing which Brooke and his colleagues could do.

On 3 August two copies of the Mimsy plan were forwarded to the Chiefs of Staff with a note that it would not be an easy project to clear with Washington, and that it should be put into force 'as soon as possible' as its chances of success would be greatly reduced after D-Day of Olympic (the atom bomb attack on Japan).

As the American official line was that Hirohito should not be allowed to remain as ruler after hostilities ceased, Washington might have rejected it, but it was of such supreme importance that it should have been put to Truman. If Mountbatten, who was enthusiastic for the plan, had got through to Hirohito we know he would have found the Emperor co-operative. Hirohito had met and liked Mountbatten when he visited London in the 1920s.

Instead, Mimsy was overtaken by events. On 6 August the first atom bomb was dropped on Hiroshima, and it was followed three days later by the second, which devastated Nagasaki. Four days after Hiroshima Mountbatten gave the COS an outline of Mimsy and 'drew attention to the advantage which we should gain if it were to succeed.' The COS asked the Deceptionists for a further report.

Mimsy is a might-have-been of history, but again the papers languish unread in the Public Record Office and it is hardly known. However, the only close surviving British friend of the then Empress, Alice Morland, whose husband and father were both British Ambassadors in Tokyo, has written to the author that in her view Hirohito would not have responded to an approach through the 'lowly Lord Mountbatten' but only to one from another sovereign.[23]

When Churchill arrived, tired, at the Potsdam Conference his other three main unsolved problems were the future of the Baltic states, Poland and eastern Europe. At the time Britain and America were immensely strong in Europe, and with the American possession of the atom bomb Stalin was not in a position to reject out of hand British and American demands.

Unfortunately Truman had never visited Europe and had little knowledge of European history. In addition he was obstinate and dependent on the anti-British Byrnes, who was now Secretary of State in place of the fine statesman Cordell Hull. Worn out by the strain of the war, Hull had resigned on 31 December 1944 and was succeeded by Edward Stettinius, who was 'a pain' to British diplomats. Truman had great admiration for Byrnes, who had been Roosevelt's principal economic adviser, and on assuming office appointed him his adviser on foreign affairs, and then in July to replace Stettinius. Thus Byrnes' first task on taking over was to accompany Truman to Potsdam.

Unlike Roosevelt and Hull, Truman and Byrnes would not give Churchill wholehearted support in his efforts to prevent Russia dominating countries which had been free and independent before the war. As a result, at Potsdam Britain lost the day over the Baltic states, Poland and eastern Europe. Churchill was intensely worried by the likelihood of losing the General Election. He faltered, and after he had fallen from power in the final days of the Potsdam Conference Attlee and Bevin were abject. However, Truman and Byrnes bear major responsibility for the Iron Curtain which descended for forty-five years on Europe.

Churchill recorded for the Foreign Office his impressions of Truman when they met for the first time for lunch at Potsdam. He did not repeat these favourable remarks in this memoirs:

> He was good enough to say that this has been the most enjoyable lunch he had had for many years and how he earnestly hoped the relations I had with President Roosevelt would be continued between him and me. He invited personal friendship and comradeship and used many expressions at intervals in our discussion which I could not easily hear unmoved. He seems a man of exceptional character and ability.[24]

The two were antipathetic, and Churchill's claim that they got on well is incorrect.

The Baltic states – Latvia, Lithuania and Estonia – which had previously been free and independent countries, had been compelled to give up their independence and become republics of the Soviet Union when the Hitler–Stalin agreement came into operation in September 1939. In June 1941 Germany overran these states, absorbing them and instituting a regime of terror, oppression and deportations, together with a plan of mass colonization to make them a part of greater Germany.

The Baltic states were always on the side of the Allies. They never succumbed to the blandishments of Ribbentrop, and would not join the bloc of the Axis states. During the Nazi occupation the German war machine was sabotaged by organized Partisans, and although the German occupation authorities ordered mobilization four times, they did not succeed in raising a single division.

With the German withdrawal Russia re-established her sovereignty. Churchill had wanted to insist that Stalin restored these states' independence after the war, and had this in mind when he drafted the Atlantic Charter. However in March 1942, when Stalin demanded they were allotted to Russia in the Treaty which was eventually signed in May 1942, Churchill had cold feet. He feared that, with the Germans at the gates of Moscow, a flat negative might tempt Russia into a separate peace with Hitler. On 7 March he telegraphed to Roosevelt: 'The increasing gravity of war has led me to feel that the principles of the Atlantic Charter ought not to be construed so as to deny Russia the frontiers she occupied when Germany attacked her . . . I hope that you will be able to give us a free hand to sign the Treaty which Stalin desires as soon as possible.'[25]

In April 1945 the Foreign Office set out the British position. This had been agreed by Churchill and Eden, but was never put to the War Cabinet:

> It was understood between us and the Russians that we would not oppose their claim that the Baltic States have now become constituent States of the Soviet Union. This clause disappeared from the final text of the Treaty, but the Russians no doubt consider we are at least under a moral obligation to adhere to the understanding . . . we have not recognized, and do not recognize, the absorption of the Baltic States into the Soviet Union and have hitherto been able to avoid any public pronouncement on the question of sovereignty . . . de facto Governmental powers . . . have since July 1940 been exercised by the Soviet Government (except for the period when the territories were in German occupation) . . . we have recognized no change in the international status of the Baltic States, but that status will have to be settled at the Peace Conference.

In a note prepared for Churchill and signed by Eden on 10 July, just before the Potsdam Conference, the Foreign Office stated:

> *Baltic States*
> If the Russians requested our recognition of their annexation of these small states we had numerous demands to make in return, and especially with regard to our interests in the countries.[26]

In July 1945 there were many press rumours that the status of the Baltic states would be discussed at Potsdam. This resulted in a spate of letters to the Foreign Office and Churchill from the representatives of free Lithuania, Estonia and Latvia, and from the President of the Committee of Liberation of Baltic States in Berne. The Churchill Government had by now refused to recognize the former Baltic ministers in London as having any official capacity, and no reply was sent to any communication by them, not even to those addressed personally to Churchill.

On unanswered letters to Churchill (forwarded to him in Potsdam) from Vaclovas Sudxhaskas, the Lithuanian Minister in London who had been resident since 1939, on the subject of Britain recognizing the independence of the Baltic states, Allen minuted: 'We shall, of course stall on this occasion if it comes up here.'[27] This epitomizes Eden's and Churchill's stance at Potsdam. Successive Labour and Conservative Governments after the war treated the states as *de facto* but not *de jure* part of the Soviet Union and were still doing so at the time of the dramatic declaration of Lithuania's independence in 1990. In the event the status

of the Baltic states never appeared on an agenda at Potsdam, and neither Eden
nor Churchill raised it.

It is a sad story, and Churchill's ready agreement at a bad moment in the war
that the Atlantic Charter should not apply to the Baltic states (on top of his
refusing to agree that it should apply to the British Empire, as has been seen)
casts doubts on his sincerity over the Atlantic Charter. It is easy to excuse
Churchill for not pressing the independence of the Baltic states during the
critical times of the war when Stalin might have done a deal with Hitler. It is
harder to excuse his inaction at Postsdam.

As Stalin's armies advanced into eastern Poland the Soviet authorities acted as
though the eastern provinces were part of the Soviet Union and denounced
protests from the Polish Government in Exile in London as 'Polish Imperialism'.
In April 1943 they had suddenly broken off all relations with the London Poles,
and instead recognized a League of Communist Poles in the Soviet Union; the
Russians set them up as a 'provisional administration' at Lublin in Poland in July
1944 as the Soviet armies crossed the River Bug, the former Russian/Polish
frontier. Thus there were two rival Governments claiming to rule Poland, and
the Soviet-sponsored Lublin administration had the advantage of being in
possession.

At Teheran, as has been seen, in 1942 Roosevelt and Churchill had conceded
to Stalin the Soviet claims to eastern Poland, and Churchill had announced to the
Commons Poland's right to compensation by the annexation of parts of East
Prussia. Churchill was gravely alarmed when hostilities with Germany ceased
because Russia was treating not only Poland, but also Hungary, Romania and
Bulgaria, as satellite states. Churchill considered 'the Soviet menace' had
replaced 'the Nazi foe'.

Meanwhile, with the help of the Russian armies the Lublin administration
under Bierut had taken over complete control of Poland, carrying out the
liquidation and deportation of political opponents, instituting press censorship,
and making free elections impossible because opposition parties were not
allowed to operate. On top of this British and American journalists and observers
were denied access to Poland, in direct contravention of the Yalta agreement.
Only with the wholehearted support of Truman could Churchill stop Stalin
imposing his will not only on Poland, but also on eastern Europe where
conditions were similar to those in Poland. These former free countries in the
Balkans were being reduced to satellite states under Communist rule.

Churchill felt strongly that illegal and unconstitutional Russian domination of
so much of Europe violated the Yalta Agreement, and that the American and
British armies should therefore not withdraw to the occupation zones agreed at
Yalta. Anglo–American forces, chiefly American, occupied 'the centre and heart
of Germany', an area some 400 miles long and 120 miles deep at its greatest
depth. Churchill defined this occupation by British and American Armies and
Air Forces as a 'mighty armed power'; he wanted to use this allied strength to
thwart Russia, and to hold a summit conference as soon as possible after the
German surrender to tie Stalin down with a written and enforceable agreement.

Unfortunately President Truman was, unlike Roosevelt, a difficult ally, and according to Churchill the new President and his advisers thought naïvely that Europe would 'settle down into a quiet and happy peace'.[28] On 11 May Churchill wrote to Truman, suggesting that he should invite Stalin to a Summit and saying that he doubted very much whether any enticements would get a proposal for such a meeting from Stalin, although he was likely to respond to an invitation. Churchill added the ominous words: 'Meanwhile I earnestly hope that the American front will not recede from the now agreed tactical line.' The Soviet–Allied demarcation line was a considerable distance behind the 'tactical line', which was the point at which American and British troops had met the Soviet Army before the ceasefire, and Churchill stressed: 'I feel every minute counts.' Churchill also gave Truman a warm invitation to visit London *en route* to the Summit, wherever it was to be. Truman replied coldly the next day:

> I would much prefer to have Stalin propose the meeting and believe it is worthwhile to endeavour, through our Ambassadors, to induce him to propose the meeting. If such an effort fails, we can then consider our issuing an invitation jointly or severally.
>
> When and if such a meeting is arranged, it appears to me that in order to avoid any suspicion of our 'ganging up' it would be advantageous for us to proceed to the meeting place separately.

Churchill was furious at this off-hand refusal of his cordial invitation, and also at the suggestion of 'ganging up'. He recorded in his memoirs that this telegram conveyed 'the difference of views', and on the day he received it he composed and sent his 'Iron Curtain' telegram, the importance of which he spotlights in his memoirs. Churchill emphasized his concern about the American Armies and Air Force moving out of Europe, and said the Canadian Army would also leave, while the French

> are weak and difficult to deal with so that anyone can see that in a very short space of time our armed power on the continent will have vanished except for moderate forces to hold down Germany . . . I feel deep anxiety because of their [Russian] overwhelming influence in the Balkans except Greece, the difficulties they make about Vienna, the combination of Russian power and the territories under their control or occupied, coupled with the Communist technique in so many other countries, and above all their power to maintain very large armies in the field for a long time.
>
> What will be the position in a year or two when the British and American armies have melted . . . and when Russia may choose to keep two or three hundred Divisions in the field?'
>
> An iron curtain has been drawn down upon their front. We do not know what is going on behind. There seems little doubt that the whole of the regions east of the line Lübeck–Trieste–Corfu will soon be completely in their hands. To this must be added the further enormous area conquered by the American armies between Eisenbach and the Elbe which will, I suppose, in a few weeks be occupied, when the Americans retreat, by the Russian power . . . and then the curtain will descend again . . . Thus a broad band of many hundreds of miles of Russian occupied territory will isolate us from Poland.

The next day Churchill aimed a shorter missive at Truman, asking him to hold a Summit with Stalin 'as soon as possible and wherever possible' some time in June. Churchill this time stated that he doubted very much if Stalin would agree, because 'time is on his side if he digs in while we melt away'.[29]

Truman and Byrnes did not share Churchill's fears of the Soviet Union establishing a permanent Communist domination of the countries it occupied militarily; nor did they realize the urgency of re-establishing freedom and independence in these countries while American military might in Europe still put Russia in a weak negotiating position. To Churchill's frustration the President did not even reply to the important and cogent arguments in his 'iron curtain' telegram, nor to a second urgent telegram of the next day. Fourteen days later, to Churchill's horror and dismay, Joseph E. Davis, the former US Ambassador in Russia (who was sympathetic to the Communist regime), arrived in London with a message that Truman proposed to meet Stalin alone in Europe before any Summit was held. Churchill was devastated. Angry already about Truman's 'ganging up' suggestion, he has recorded that this American attempt to reach a singlehanded understanding with Russia on the main issues was an 'affront'. He rejected the proposal out of hand, and Truman climbed down. It was not an auspicious start for the vital Summit, at which Anglo–American solidarity was essential to prevent Russia becoming master of all eastern Europe.

Stalin agreed with Truman on a Summit at Potsdam near Berlin around 15 July. On 1 June Truman informed Churchill, who cabled back: 'Why not July 1st, 2nd or 3rd?' Truman replied that he could not manage any date earlier than the 15th, ignoring Churchill's plea about urgency, and also the imminence of the withdrawal of the American Army from the large area ahead of the Yalta demarcation line which they were occupying. Having failed to bring forward the meeting of the Big Three, Churchill now importuned Truman not to withdraw the American Army from 'the whole centre and heart of Germany'.

The President replied that the tripartite agreement about zones had been agreed by Roosevelt at Yalta after 'long consideration and detailed discussion' with Churchill, and he was advised it would prejudice relations with Stalin if he did not implement the decision; therefore all American troops would start to withdraw on 21 June. Churchill could not oppose the decision, but he recorded that it 'struck a knell in his breast' and that Britain and America were going to the conference table with 'nothing to bargain with and all the prospects of the future peace of Europe might well go by default'. In Europe the American Army numbered three million to the British one. Churchill cabled to Truman on 4 June:

> I view with profound misgivings the retreat of the American army to our line of occupation in the central sector, thus bringing Soviet power into the heart of Western Europe and the descent of an iron curtain between us and everything to the east . . . you and I will have to bear great responsibility for the future. I still hope that the date [of the Summit Conference] will be advanced.

But his plea fell on deaf ears.[30]

At Potsdam Churchill argued strongly that there must be guaranteed free elections in Poland, and that the German territory between the east and western Neisse should not be ceded to Poland because the enormous agricultural production there was essential for feeding Germany. Stalin would not yield, and Winston allowed the differences to remain unsettled until he and Eden returned to England for the Election result. Churchill recorded later that he intended to have a 'showdown' at the end of the Potsdam Conference, and if necessary a public break with Stalin, and that no Government of which he was the head would have agreed to the over-running by Russian armies of territory up to and beyond the western Neisse. Truman had thrown away the best card in the Allied hand by withdrawing American troops from the large part of Germany which they occupied east of the Yalta demarcation line, and at Potsdam seemed unconscious that vast territories would fall under Russian control and become satellites.

In 1953 Churchill told John Colville that he lamented having to cut out from Vol. VI of his war history (because Eisenhower was President) the story of how the 'United States gave away, to please Russia, vast tracts of Europe – the British General Election had occupied too much of his attention which should have been directed to stemming this fatal tide. If FDR had lived and had been in good health he would have seen the red light in time to check the American policy'; Truman was a novice 'bewildered by responsibilities which he had never expected.'[31]

The General Election result brought Churchill's efforts at Potsdam to an untimely conclusion. Neither the new Prime Minister nor his Foreign Secretary, Bevin, would take a firm stand over Poland. They quickly reached agreement with Stalin to recognize the Lublin Government, leaving Poland firmly in Russian hands as a Soviet Communist satellite. On 30 July Attlee and Bevin announced they accepted that Polish administration could be extended to the western Neisse.

Instead of Churchill's 'show down' there were naïvely accepted Russian assurances that free elections would take place in Poland early in 1946. Bevin told the Commons on 20 August 1945 that he expected the opposition parties would have 'full liberty' to make their own programmes and put up their own candidates. This was wishful thinking. Britain had gone to war to save Poland's independence, and had spurned Stalin's aid in 1939 for fear of communism advancing into Poland. Churchill later wrote at Potsdam Truman and Byrnes 'great object was not to get drawn into siding too closely with Britain against Russia'.[32]

At Potsdam Eden, with support from Byrnes, had argued with Molotov that there was no freedom of the press in the ex-satellite countries of Hungary, Romania and Bulgaria, and no possibility of free democratic elections being held. Both Byrnes and he emphasized that if the elections were held with press censorship neither America nor Britain would recognize the regimes. They both also complained vigorously because Russia had removed from Romania oil-producing equipment which had belonged to other European countries and not to Germany. Molotov refused to agree to the setting up of a committee to consider the question of ownership, and rejected the idea that the property of Allied nationals in satellite countries must not be treated as war booty. The Russians would yield nothing on questions relating to Czechoslovakia or the Balkans. Yet after the Conference was over Attlee said: 'We found greater willingness than hitherto to admit the Press to South East Europe though whether we shall see free elections is more open to doubt.' With great weakness the Labour Government had given in to Stalin on all the points where Churchill claims he would have stood firm.

Bevin was less optimistic in the Commons on 20 August, saying with frankness that in the Balkans 'The impression we get from recent developments is that one kind of totalitarianism is being replaced by another.' He was right, and the Iron Curtain descended on the Balkans for forty-five years.

Conclusion

WHAT OUGHT we to make of this fine patriot? Without him Britain would have succumbed in 1940. No other British statesman could have created the same faith in victory and inspired the nation to fight on wholeheartedly when all seemed lost. Alone Winston Churchill saved Western civilization from destruction at the hands of the Nazis.

It was touch and go whether he or Halifax became Prime Minister when Neville Chamberlain resigned. Both wanted the job. Churchill clinched it in his favour on 9 May 1940 when he stayed silent after Halifax had asked him and Chamberlain whether a wartime Prime Minister could be in the House of Lords. This silence made Halifax realize that, even if he was Prime Minister, Churchill would have to be Minister of Defence, and in this capacity would dominate policy and steal nearly all the limelight in the Commons.

The majority of Conservative MPs wanted Halifax, not Churchill. Churchill's irresponsibility over Indian independence and the Abdication Crisis, and his exaggeration of the strength of the Luftwaffe, had been seized on (until he joined the Cabinet in 1939) by the Conservative Whips in order to denigrate him. On top of this it was known that as First Lord of the Admiralty he had been irresponsible during the Norwegian campaign.

The over-riding factor was that Churchill alone had clean hands over the appeasement of Hitler; all the other candidates were contaminated. Only Winston could enlist enthusiastic Labour and Liberal support for the Government in the Commons and unite the nation in the moment of defeat. Churchill could not purge his Cabinet of all former appeasers, but his choice of Ernest Bevin was brilliant and showed his acute political awareness and finesse.

Those close to him have made abundantly clear in post-war memoirs that the whole atmosphere at 10 Downing Street changed overnight. Instead of the customary shilly-shallying the desks were cleared for action, and he himself made at speed the crucial decisions – often without proper consultation. But this was inevitable if the day was to be saved. The expression 'Britain's finest hour' was coined as his magnificent speeches in the Commons and his broadcasts galvanized the nation to fight in an all-out effort and, although there were only flimsy grounds for confidence, his obvious faith in final victory inspired the nation.

No sooner had he taken office than he had to make an unpalatable decision about withdrawing the BEF to the Channel ports. Since he had been in the War Cabinet at the time he knew only too well that this was exactly what Lloyd George had so rightly refused to allow Haig to do in March 1918. However, Churchill appreciated correctly how poor the French Army was in 1940 compared to its predecessor in 1918, and without hesitation he made the decision in the nick of time to evacuate from Dunkirk the tiny but vital British regular Army and first-line territorial divisions. Then, despite much soul searching, he refused to waste the few precious RAF fighter squadrons on a despairing defence of France. Thus Britain became impregnable.

Churchill was wrong to state in his memoirs that while France was being over-run the War Cabinet never discussed peace terms. The minutes show that Halifax and Chamberlain wanted to make overtures to Hitler through Mussolini, involving the sacrifice of Gibraltar, Tunis and Djibouti to the Italians. Churchill would have none of this and was ready to let Halifax resign. But such was his concern that his colleagues' lack of robustness might endanger the nation's will to resist that no word of the War Cabinet's discussions was leaked, and Churchill gave strict orders there was to be 'absolute silence' in future in response to any overtures from the enemy through neutral capitals. This edict had unfortunate consequences when the German Resistance sought British aid in their gallant efforts to topple Hitler.

In his memoirs Churchill has falsified history not only over the pusillanimity of Halifax and Chamberlain in 1940, but over other important episodes. Relentlessly he concealed important parts of the history of the Second World War. Why? He had nothing of which to be ashamed. He was Victor Ludorum of his own generation, and no wartime Prime Minister can escape blunders. However, not only are his memoirs tendentious in places, but in the 1950s when he returned to Downing Street he put pressure on the official historians in the Cabinet Offices to conceal chunks from the archives. As the first official war histories were being prepared for publication it became clear that the Attlee Government was likely to fall and that Churchill would soon be Prime Minister again. Newly released archives show how Acheson, Secretary to the Cabinet Offices Historical Section, and his colleagues (but not Admiral Cunningham) funked publishing anything which might incur Churchill's disapproval. This in no way detracts from Churchill's war leadership, but many facets of the history of the war have been distorted and only now, by detailed analysis of the archives, can the truth be revealed.

Martin Gilbert's detailed official biographies suffer because the source notes mostly refer to Churchill's private archive, which will not be made available to researchers for another ten years. However, I have found in the PRO, with considerably more detail and background, duplicates of all the important papers cited. It appears that Churchill did not retain in his archive papers which he did not want to be made public.

Churchill made a major mistake – possibly his gravest wartime blunder – by ordering the sinking of the French Fleet at Mers-el-Kebir on 3 July 1940.

Instantly France became an enemy. This resulted in ten thousand casualties in the fighting in Syria in 1941, while in Indo-China Vichy France tamely handed over to the Japanese her naval and air bases on the Gulf of Siam, thus making Singapore and Malaya indefensible. The War Cabinet and the Chiefs of Staff disagreed with Churchill over the Mers-el-Kebir decision. Admirals North, Cunningham and Somerville were strongly opposed. Yet in his memoirs Churchill implied there was complete agreement. Another consequence was that when the Allies landed in North and West Africa in 1942 they met fierce French resistance which, but for the provident presence of Admiral Darlan in Algiers, would have resulted in the US assault force being pushed back into the sea in West Africa. Then, once it was clear to Churchill that Darlan, whom he detested, would be an asset, Churchill agreed to co-operate with him. This was statesmanship.

It is not widely known that in late 1940 Churchill concluded an agreement with Pétain. Realistically Churchill accepted that the Free French under de Gaulle were making no headway, and that if the French armed forces were to be of value again against Germany Vichy co-operation was necessary. The Churchill–Pétain Gentleman's Agreement was torn up by Pétain unilaterally when he allowed the Axis the use of French air bases in Syria in 1941, but Churchill's effort was well worth making. In the summer of 1945 details of the 1940 Churchill–Pétain deal were leaked, and with the approaching trial of Pétain in Paris it attracted enormous publicity.

The way in which Churchill then tried to deny its existence is both shaming and inexplicable. De Gaulle was the ruler of France, and the details were offensive to him; still, it had made sense in December 1940 to court Pétain. Neither Churchill nor his official biographer mentions the furore over this agreement at the time of the Pétain trial in 1945; nor do they discuss Churchill's efforts to cover it up.

It was a disaster to send a high proportion of Wavell's Middle East fighting forces to Greece in 1941. This was not a unilateral decision by Churchill, although as usual he wanted adventurous action. Eden tipped the scales in favour of the expedition, and the War Cabinet were fully consulted and agreed – as did Wavell, GOC Middle East. Wavell's agreement may have been conditioned by fear that otherwise Churchill would dub him cowardly. The messages sent by Churchill to Wavell over Crete, Syria and Iraq are so peremptory and over-riding that it is hard to believe they were being addressed to one of the nation's most distinguished soldiers. Later, Auchinleck and Wilson had to endure similar treatment. Churchill remembered, perhaps too well, that during the First World War Generals Haig, Robertson and Henry Wilson concealed important information from Lloyd George. Churchill was determined that his generals should not do the same. Only Alexander and Montgomery were immune from this harsh treatment, and Churchill momentarily lost faith in Montgomery twice – first when Alamein hung in the balance, and again when the breakout from the D-Day Normandy bridgehead was delayed.

As the fear of invasion of Britain receded Churchill itched for offensive action to raise the nation's morale. The Chiefs of Staff advised him there were no spare forces, but he would not accept this. Roger Keyes was an old friend from Dardanelles days who echoed Churchill's longings; his passion for dramatic amphibious landings was manna for Churchill. Impulsively Churchill made Keyes Head of Combined Operations, and had to be dissuaded from giving him even higher command. Churchill found Keyes' inventiveness and ardour an antidote to what he considered the over-cautiousness of the Chiefs of Staff.

Unfortunately Keyes was impractical and ill-informed about the capabilities of the Army; he was also jealous and quarrelsome. His incompetence was transparent to the Chiefs of Staff but not to the Prime Minister, who became obsessed with the idea of capturing the island of Pantellaria, between Malta and Sicily. The attraction of Pantellaria was its aerodrome with underground shelters for aircraft; the island had neither water nor harbour and Admiral Cunningham, commanding in the Mediterranean, considered the problem of maintaining it after its capture a 'nightmare'. The Germans and Italians had complete air superiority in that area, and occupying the island would have entailed unacceptable casualties for the RAF and the Navy.

In fact the capture of Malta by the Axis was more feasible, and it would have been attempted if Mussolini had been able to prepare a sensible plan. Instead, the Italian General Staff produced such a ridiculous plan, including using the water buses from Venice as landing craft, that the German General Staff would not even consider it.

Eventually, after Keyes had mucked up a large-scale amphibious exercise in the Highlands, Churchill became exasperated by the continual flow of well-justified complaints from the Chiefs of Staff and reluctantly sacked him. The official historians could have lightened their tomes if they had disclosed more details of the comic correspondence between Keyes and Churchill during Keyes' period as Head of Combined Operations.

Churchill's reaction when Hitler invaded Russia in June 1941 was statesman-like and admirable. Disregarding his long antagonism to Communism, he gasped with relief because he at least had an ally. With generosity and courage he diverted aircraft, tanks and other vital military equipment to Stalin, using the dangerous north Russia convoy route. He brushed aside all doubts at home about aid for Russia, and was most helpful to Roosevelt who encountered serious opposition from Catholics and other anti-Russian groups in the USA to the idea of sending supplies to Russia.

Indeed, Churchill seriously weakened British strength in Malaya by sending tanks and planes to Russia when the forces chiefs in Singapore were clamouring for them. Here Churchill had a blind spot. He failed to realize that, once Vichy France had given Japan the naval and air bases near Saigon, the short distance over the Gulf of Siam made Malaya vulnerable. All plans for defending Singapore should have been immediately revised. They were not, and a dangerous situation arose.

Instead Churchill played with fire. The abortive Atlantic Conference with Roosevelt in the summer of 1941 convinced him that the President would be unable to carry American opinion with him and declare war on Germany unless Japan attacked America in the Far East. He then pressurized America to provoke Japan into attacking. The despatches of the British Ambassador in Tokyo, Craigie, and those of the United States Ambassador, Grew, leave no doubt that in 1941 Japan could have been kept out of the war if the oil blockade had been eased. Churchill opposed this, and persuaded the Americans to take a hard line. Churchill's gamble succeeded. In December 1941 the Japanese attacked the Americans at Pearl Harbor as well as British and Dutch possessions. If the Japanese had attacked only the British and the Dutch and left the Americans alone it is doubtful whether Roosevelt could have persuaded Congress to declare war on Japan. Nor was there a certainty that, once America was at war with Japan, she would declare war on Germany. Fortunately Hitler – against Ribbentrop's advice – made the monumental mistake of declaring war on the USA. The Foreign Office were very worried immediately after Pearl Harbor that America might not go to war with Germany, but Churchill, with his remarkable political intuition, slept well that night without doubts.

Churchill was furious when, after a belated return to London, Craigie wrote a long despatch pointing out that war with Japan could have been averted if Britain and America had encouraged the Japanese peace party by softening the blockade, as he and Grew had advised. Churchill's rage with Craigie for stating a clear truth was unjustified. His petulant minute to Eden that Craigie's despatch was not to be circulated indicates that he had an uneasy conscience about his behaviour over Japan. It is a mystery why he was so concerned. After all, his plan had worked and resulted in the otherwise unattainable objective of making America an ally against Germany, and all's fair in war.

Churchill would not allow Craigie to be re-employed. But the top echelons of the Foreign Office disagreed with Churchill, and as soon as the Churchill Government fell he was given an important post. The Craigie incident is hardly known about and finds no place either in Churchill's memoirs or in his official biography.

The months after America's entry into the war were bitterly disappointing for Churchill. The Far East became a disaster area, and he knew in his heart of hearts that he bore a heavy responsibility for not sending tanks and modern planes to defend Singapore when he was risking war with Japan.

Having dismissed Wavell, Churchill had high hopes that under Auchinleck the Eighth Army would drive the Axis out of North Africa. These hopes were dashed when Rommel attacked; then Churchill lambasted Auchinleck mercilessly. This was another of his blind spots – believing that the defeats in the desert in 1942 were due to poor generalship, not to the lower quality of British tanks and guns – although once he realized the truth he made ample amends. Tobruk was lost because of Churchill's interference with Auchinleck, who had decided it was indefensible; Churchill's signals made him reverse his decision, and thirty thousand Allied troops were made prisoner.

When he and Roosevelt met as Allies for the first time in January 1942 Churchill had grave fears that the Americans would concentrate on the Far East to avenge Pearl Harbor and make Europe a secondary theatre. Much to his relief, Roosevelt and Marshall spontaneously declared that Europe must be the first priority. However, he was frustrated because Marshall insisted that America should put all her available forces into a build-up in Britain for a cross-Channel invasion in 1943. With his temperament Churchill fretted for earlier action against Hitler's armies, and he was desperately worried since he had promised an early second front in Europe, that Stalin would seek a separate peace with Hitler. Post-war evidence shows that his fears had little foundation. So Churchill pressed the Americans for an attack on French North Africa in the autumn of 1942, and they agreed. Was he right?

In his book *1943 The Victory That Never Was* John Grigg produces cogent arguments why a 1943 cross-Channel invasion would have been successful and shortened the war. In 1943 beach defences in Normandy were non-existent and the German troops on the Russian front, which would have been needed as reinforcements, were much further away from France. It is difficult to contradict Grigg's arguments, and the controversy over whether a Mediterranean strategy in 1942 was correct will never be resolved.

Churchill was more courageous than the Americans over North Africa. The Americans' first plan envisaged only landings in West Africa, and Churchill had to cajole them into crossing the Straits of Gibraltar and landing at Algiers. Once this had been conceded, Churchill was 100 per cent correct in urging that the most easterly landings should be made at Bone. The Americans funked this, but had they landed at Bone, Tunis would have been taken in a first assault; as a result the Axis would have been cleared out of North Africa within weeks, not months.

Both Roosevelt and Churchill grossly underestimated the will of the French in North Africa to resist invasion; they were sure that if American troops landed they would be received with open arms, and it was even suggested that the British should wear American uniforms. Neither leader appreciated how the iron had entered the French soul after the massacre of Mers-el-Kebir and the Syrian battles.

Such is Churchill's reputation that it is hard to believe his premiership was ever at risk. But in 1942, with the disaster of Singapore and the defeats in the desert, his popularity sank and he was insecure. In Whitehall those in the know attributed the defeats to Churchill's personal decisions, although they never underrated his value as a morale-booster. There was a move favoured by Eden for him to remain as Prime Minister but to give up being Minister of Defence. Churchill's predictable reaction was that he would rather resign altogether than remain as Prime Minister with someone else as Minister of Defence. Certainly with his method of conducting the war it would be impossible, and there was no one with his initiative, energy and resolution to fill the post. However, Montgomery's resounding defeat of Rommel at Alamein and the partial success of the North African campaign swiftly restored Churchill's position and he became unassailable.

In January 1943 Roosevelt and Churchill came together at Casablanca to decide Allied policy. It was a crucial meeting, but the decisions were fudged. As usual Churchill wanted the maximum of action everywhere, with attacks on Sicily, Italy and the eastern Aegean islands as well as a cross-Channel invasion during 1943. The two leaders eventually agreed that the North African campaign, which was in the doldrums with both Montgomery and Eisenhower bogged down, made a full-scale landing in France in 1943 almost impossible. The crucial decision made at Casablanca was to attack Sicily after North Africa was cleared. This meant postponing the cross-Channel invasion, and Churchill feared that Stalin would receive the news very badly. No decision was made at Casablanca to invade the Italian mainland.

Casablanca was overtaken by the Italian surrender in September 1943. Although in 1940 and 1941 Churchill had wanted to offer anti-Fascist Italians a tempting soft peace, now in 1943, with Italy down and out, all such thoughts had left him. Overtures came from the leaders of the former political parties and from Royalist generals. Churchill, much to the approval of the Italophobe Eden, ignored them. Thus, when the King of Italy toppled Mussolini on 25 July 1943, Churchill was taken by surprise. If plans had been concerted beforehand with the anti-Fascists, Anglo–American forces could have taken over Italy without opposition, as Hitler too was caught unawares. There was an appalling delay over the armistice However, Mussolini's overthrow made the Allies decide to invade Italy. This meant that any lingering hopes of cross-Channel action in 1943 were dead.

The Italian campaign was only partially successful, and the Allies were held by fierce German resistance in the south. Churchill had hoped that when Italy surrendered the eastern Aegean islands held by the Italians would fall into Allied hands, and thus open the Dardanelles route to Russia.

The Dardanelles was an emotive issue with him. In 1915 he had been made the scapegoat for the costly failure of the Gallipoli expedition, and had been dismissed from the Asquith War Cabinet. He had overstated the argument for capturing the Dardanelles straits and linking up with Russia to end the stalemate on the western front and finish the war quickly. This was widely looked on as a ghastly blunder, and he felt the shadow of the Dardanelles always hanging over him. In 1943 he had great hopes that opening the Dardanelles would enable British and American forces to link up with the Russians and strike at Germany from the east. Then his despised First World War strategy would be vindicated. By sheer bad luck his hopes were dashed. Italian Generals in Corsica loyally obeyed the Armistice and kept strong German forces at bay until a French army landed. In the Aegean the Italians did not do the same.

Rhodes was the key to the eastern Aegean; here Italian troops outnumbered Germans by four to one. Alas, the Italian generals were lily-livered. A British liaison officer parachuted successfully to them on the day of the Italian armistice, but when he told the Italians that a British force could not arrive for four days they feebly surrendered to the Germans. Churchill's plan to open the Dardanelles was accordingly torpedoed.

Churchill refused to accept defeat over the Aegean. Cos, Leros and smaller islands were held by the Italians, and in spite of strong opposition they were reinforced, ignoring the deadly domination of the skies by the Luftwaffe from airfields in Greece and Rhodes. The result was disaster. *Inter alia* three good battalions were forced to surrender on Leros; other losses in men, ships and planes were heavy, without benefit to the Allies.

At the Tehran Conference in November 1943 Churchill was frustrated by the Aegean defeat. He fell back on the plan for which he had hankered since 1941 – to bring Turkey into the war as an ally. He was chasing a will-o'-the-wisp. Turkey was as frightened of Russia as she was of Germany; while both Roosevelt and Stalin were lukewarm about making an ally of Turkey. However, Churchill persisted, pressing his arguments vigorously and even contemplating offering Turkey Greek islands as bait.

When in Cairo in December 1943 Turkey firmly refused Churchill's blandishments, Churchill refused to give up hope of a link-up with the Russians in eastern Europe. His hopes turned to Yugoslavia, from where there were reports of resistance to the Germans from both Royalist and Communist guerrillas and the remnants of the Italian army of occupation. Unfortunately S O E in Cairo had been infiltrated by active Communist agents. They misled Churchill and his advisers into believing that the Royalist guerrilla leader, Mihailovic, was collaborating with the Germans and fighting only against the Partisan Communists under Tito. The reverse was true. Tito's Communists were not fighting the Germans, and his sole aim was to make Yugoslavia a Communist state after the war. Against the advice of Eden and the Foreign Office, Churchill insisted on all-out support for Tito and none for Mihailovic. This was a disastrous error.

His honeymoon with Tito was short. Churchill's ambition was to land a powerful amphibious force in Istria on the Italian border with Yugoslavia. It would link up with Eighth Army as soon as they were victorious in Italy, and then cross the Ljubljana Gap to join the Russians in Austria. He felt a link-up with the Russians in eastern Europe might avoid the bloodbath likely to result from a cross-Channel invasion. Tito had no intention of allowing British troops to fight in Yugoslavian territory, and when a small force actually landed he ordered them out. Churchill's faith in Tito was entirely misplaced, but once his eyes were open to Tito's real intentions he admitted he had made a mistake. However, so bent was Churchill on the Istrian landings that when Roosevelt placed obstacles in its way he offered to resign.

Criticism has been levelled at Churchill over Dieppe and his handling of India and the Jews. This should not be taken seriously. A recent well-researched book (Villa, *Unauthorised Action*) proves that Churchill had no responsibility for the decision to attack Dieppe in 1942; but in his memoirs, in response to pressure from Mountbatten, he rewrote paragraphs which misleadingly exempt Mountbatten from blame.

Over India Churchill had a gut feeling that independence should not be promised, and in conversation with colleagues created difficulties. Yet with statesmanship he sent Stafford Cripps, a devotee of independence, to India with instructions to negotiate a settlement by which India would have independence once the war was over. These overtures were rejected by Gandhi and the Indian leaders, for which Churchill was in no way to blame. Yet to Churchill's intense annoyance Roosevelt demanded that India should be given independence while the war continued. This would have had disastrous repercussions on the Indian Army, which was vital to the allies, and Roosevelt's letters caused Churchill to threaten resignation.

Professor Michael Cohen, author of *Churchill and the Jews*, alleges that Churchill's support of Zionism before the war was insincere, and castigates him for not following up a minute he wrote to Sinclair, Secretary of State for Air, advocating the bombing of the Auschwitz concentration camp. The RAF did not do so, and no documents exist to show that Churchill ever repeated this request. It is likely that he discussed the matter with Sinclair verbally, as he saw him frequently and they were old and close friends. Anyway, would the bombing of concentration camps have saved many inmates' lives? Why would bombs kill guards rather than prisoners? It is wrong to denigrate a great Englishman on such flimsy grounds.

Montgomery was an inspired choice to command the cross-Channel invasion in 1944. No other British or American general was so well up to the task, and the original plan, which Montgomery immediately rejected, would have been a disaster. Not so wise was Churchill's refusal to grant Eisenhower's request to broadcast to the German troops messages offering them a soft peace if they surrendered; this might have undermined their morale. Instead they were told to expect nothing but unconditional surrender, to be followed by the horrors of the Morgenthau Plan; this prolonged the war. The concept of unconditional surrender was produced at Casablanca by Roosevelt, but Churchill concurred, even though he tried unsuccessfully to exclude Italy, which would have been a bonus during the long drawn-out negotiations for an Italian armistice. The Morgenthau Plan to pastoralize Germany was again Roosevelt's – with which Churchill, unduly influenced by Cherwell, acquiesced too readily without consulting Eden. This Plan was one of the grave errors of the war, as Goebbels was able to use it to bolster Nazi morale by claiming that it promised ghastly conditions for all Germans if the war was lost. Churchill never expressed repentance for either unconditional surrender or the Morgenthau Plan.

In July 1944, when Germany seemed defeated because of the Normandy victory, the flying bombs and especially the V2s rattled Churchill more than anything else in the war. At this time his usual judgement deserted him. He wanted to retaliate with poison gas, and only with difficulty was he restrained – by evidence from the Chiefs of Staff that it would be counter-productive.

Inadvisedly Churchill suggested that Montgomery should hold a press conference after the triumphant end of the Battle of the Bulge in January 1945. Little did he realize what damage to Anglo–American relations his cocksure General could do. By taking credit for saving the American Army Montgomery reduced his relations with Eisenhower to a new low. As a result, Eisenhower decided he would leave Berlin and Vienna to the Russians and consigned the British troops to a minor role in the final battle. Churchill was up in arms but met a brick wall with Roosevelt. Wisely he realized that America was now the senior partner;

although he knew that Eisenhower's plan would alter the map of Europe for the worse after the war, sensibly he withdrew his objections.

It was a tragedy that before the German surrender Roosevelt died and Cordell Hull had to retire from the State Department due to ill health. Churchill then had to deal with Truman and Byrnes, neither of whom had either a proper understanding of the European problems or faith in Churchill's judgement. As the Americans began to withdraw their troops from Europe after the armistice Churchill realized it was imperative to hold a peace conference with Stalin as soon as possible, while Britain and America were still militarily strong on the ground. Truman could not see this, and Stalin was able to delay the conference until the end of July, by which time much of the American Army of occupation had been withdrawn to the Far East. Militarily Stalin was dominant in Europe, and well aware of it.

The most important item at the Potsdam Conference was whether or not to finish off Japan with atom bombs. The Americans were anxious to use the bombs although their chief Japanese expert, Grew, advised that Japan would surrender without them if the Emperor was allowed to remain. Exactly the same advice came from the Japanese experts in the British Foreign Office. Churchill (although Eden was more to blame) ignored this advice and agreed with Truman that atom bombs should be dropped on Japanese cities. For this it is hard to forgive him.

By the end of the war Churchill was tired and not the man he had been in 1940. On top of this, the General Election campaign wore him out. Before Potsdam he hardly looked at his boxes, and, faced with an appalling crisis by Stalin's obvious intention to impose the iron grip of Communism on all eastern Europe, he faltered; he agreed to a Communist Government in Poland, and then went home to find his Government defeated at the polls. He claimed that if he had returned to Potsdam after winning the election he would have had a 'showdown' with Stalin over the Balkan states – Hungary, Romania and Bulgaria. He could have achieved little, for Britain's bargaining position was poor.

Controversy over Churchill will continue, and more secrets will be revealed. Nevertheless by searching in the key archives I have dispelled some of the fog thrown over his role by official historians, his own memoirs and his official biography. Despite many blunders and hasty, impetuous decisions, only one verdict is possible. He was a great wartime leader.

Source notes

Initials and numbers refer to classification in the Public Record Office. DBFP are *Documents on British Foreign Policy*. DDI are *Documenti Diplomatici Italiani*. DDF are *Documents Diplomatiques Françaises*. DGFP are *Documents on German Foreign Policy*. IMT is *Internationl Military Tribunal*. FRUS are *Foreign Relations United States*. EP are Eisenhower's papers at Abilene, Kansas, USA.

The official war and diplomatic histories were published before the fifty years rule was reduced to thirty years, and their source notes cannot easily be reconciled with the PRO catalogues. However in the later published official history by Professor F. H. Hinsley, *British Intelligence in the Second World War; Its Influence on Strategy and Operations*, the PRO references are quoted and it is invaluable.

Martin Gilbert's two volumes of the official biography of Churchill during the Second World War contain a mass of detail – rather unconnected – about Churchill's wartime activities. Their value to researchers is sadly diminished because most of the sources quoted are to Churchill's private papers, which will not be available to the public for many years, although nearly all the documents cited are also available in the PRO.

Professor Kimball's recently published three volumes *Churchill and Roosevelt* contain all the written wartime messages between the two.

The late Professor Parkinson's two volumes, *Blood, Toil, Tears and Sweat* and *A Day's March Nearer Home*, are an excellent guide to the War Cabinet and Chiefs of Staff documents.

François Kersaudy's book *Churchill and de Gaulle* covers in detail Churchill's wartime relations with de Gaulle, but does not include French Indo-China. For this it is necessary to consult the much maligned Admiral Decoux's autobiography, *A la Barre de l'Indochine*. The true story of the controversy over the sinking of the French Fleet at Mers-el-Kebir cannot be found in the official histories nor in Churchill's own memoirs or in his official biography. In 1950 Commander Stitt RN was given access to all the official documents, and after consultation with the French he wrote a definitive account for the official history. This was rejected by the official historian because it contradicted Churchill's memoirs, and it has never been published. It is Cab 103/541 in the PRO.

There is no authoritative book on the Potsdam Conference; the late Professor Richard Storry's *History of Modern Japan* describes the Japanese surrender.

The most authoritative book on Churchill's behaviour during the Malay campaign is Raymond Callahan's scholarly *Worst Disaster; Fall of Singapore*. (Published only in America.)

Michael Lees has discovered a cache of documents about Tito and Mihailovic, in the Public Record Office, and his recently published *Rape of Serbia* confounds the accepted view of Yugoslav resistance and exposes the Communist infiltration of SOE in Cairo, which led to Churchill's hideous mistake in abandoning Mihailovic and backing Tito. (Published only in America.) As I was writing the book the Churchill memoirs were published in a single abridged edition, which I have quoted where possible.

CHAPTER 1

1 *Spectator*, 4 June 1937; 5 August 1938.
2 Middlemass, *Baldwin*, page 1009. Rose, 'Baffy', *Diaries of Rose Dugdale*, page 34.
3 Author's conversations with T. D. Martin, Godfrey Nicholson and Quentin Hailsham.
4 DGFP Series, C, Vol. 5, page 134. Prem 1/194.
5 Chamberlain Papers. Macmillan, *Winds of Change*, page 469.
6 Harvey, *Diplomatic Diaries*, page 91.
7 Eden, *Facing the Dictators*, page 598. Dilks, *Cadogan Diaries*, page 70.
8 Barnes, *The Empire at Bay*, page 499.
9 Churchill, *Second World War*, Vol. I, page 201.
10 Cohen, *Churchill and the Jews*, pages 101, 147.
11 Cmnd 6019. HMSO.
12 Rose, op cit, page 115.
13 Lamb, *The Drift to War*, pages 270–4.
14 Lamb, op cit, page 262.
15 Cockett, *Twilight of Truth*, pages 114 et seq.
16 Lamb, op cit, page 331.
17 Churchill, *The Second World War*, Vol. I, page 318.

CHAPTER 2

1 IMT, Vol. X, pages 422, 465. DGFP, Series D, Vol. VII, pages 564–6.
2 DBFP, Series 3, Vol. VII, pages 518–19. Prem 1/331. FO 371/22981. DGFP, Series D, Vol. VII, pages 509–13, 527–8.
3 Cab 66/1. FO 371/23131.
4 Prem 1/395.
5 FO 800/328. Deutsch, *Conspiring Against Hitler in Twilight War*, pages 166–7.
6 Prem 1/380.
7 Chamberlain Papers, Prem 1/443. Halifax Letters, FO 800/328. Prem 1/379.
8 Prem 1/330. FO 800/326.
9 Prem 4/100/6.
10 FO 371/24363. Taylor, *Beaverbrook*, pages 404–6. Lamb, *The Ghosts of Peace*, pages 136–7.
11 Gilbert, *Churchill*, Vol. VI, page 149.
12 FO 371/23097. FO 371/23131. Adm 205/2.
13 Adm 295/2.

CHAPTER 3

1 Adm 205/4. Except where otherwise stated, the account of Catherine is based on Adm 205/1–6 and Adm 1928–9.
2 Hough, *First Sea Lord*, page 330.

3 Churchill, *Second World War*, Vol. I, page 325.
4 Letter to author from Sir Peter Tennant. He spent the whole of the war at the British Legation in Stockholm.
5 Cab 66/5.
6 Adm 199/1945.
7 Churchill, op cit, Vol. I, page 432.
8 Letters to author from Admiral Sir Hector Maclean, Rear Admiral John Grant and the Earl of Selkirk (former First Lord), September and October 1990.
9 Marder, *From the Dardanelles to Oran*, page 146.
10 Cab 65/2.
11 Cab 65/4; Cab 80/6; Adm 199/1929.
12 Cab 65/11.
13 Ibid. Gilbert, *Churchill*, Vol. VI, page 190, quoting from Butler's diaries.
14 Colville, conversation with author.
15 Woodward, *British Foreign Policy in the Second World War*, Vol. I, pages 75–80. Lamb, *The Ghosts of Peace*, page 134.
16 Cab 65/5.
17 Cab 65/12.
18 Adm 215/2.
19 Woodward, op cit, pages 78, 101–2.
20 Adm 116/4240. Magnetic mines on Rhine in Adm 215/2.
21 Denham, *Inside the Nazi Ring*, pages 1–5. After the war Captain Denham RN, with the help of Stephen Roskill, tried without success to find his signals in the Public Record Office. His view is that they were the subject of 'official weeding'.
22 Cab 65/6.
23 FO 371/24834. Cab 83/5.
24 Macleod and Kelly (ed.), *Ironside Diaries*, 1937–40, pages 257–8.
25 Cab 65/12. Adm 205/4. Churchill, op cit, Vol. I, page 493.
26 Cab 65/12.
27 Kersaudy, *Norway 1940*, page 154. Cab 65/12.
28 Cab 99/3. Kersaudy, op cit, pages 166–8.
29 Ironside, op cit, page 278.
30 Prem 1/404.
31 Kersaudy, op cit, pages 113–14. WO 106/1859. adm 199/485. Cab 80/105. Cab 79/80.
32 Cab 80/105. Cab 79/85. Adm 199/485. WO 106/1898.
33 FO 371/24834.
34 Cab 103/313.
35 *RUSI Journal*, December 1972. Marder, op cit, page 173.

CHAPTER 4

1 Birkenhead, *Halifax*, page 455. Colville, conversation with author.
2 Wheeler-Bennett, *Action This Day*, pages 49–50.
3 Wheeler-Bennett, op cit, page 220.
4 Wheeler-Bennett, op cit, page 22.
5 Gilbert, *Churchill*, Vol. VI, page 600.
6 Soames, *Clementine Churchill*, page 290.
7 Cab 65/7. Cab 65/13. Prem 2/188/1.

8 Cab 65/13.
9 Horne, *To Lose a Battle*, page 444. Lamb 'Kluge' in *Hitler's Generals*, ed. Barnett, pages 399–400.
10 Cab 69/1.
11 Cab 65/13.
12 Ibid.
13 Dilks, *Cadogan Diaries*, page 291.
14 Cab 65/13.
15 Birkenhead, op cit, page 458.
16 Cab 65/13.
17 Dalton, *The Fatal Years*, page 336. Harvey, *Diplomatic Diaries of Oliver Harvey*, pages 376–7.
18 Colville, conversation with author.

CHAPTER 5

1 Spears, *Assignment to Catastrophe*, Vol. I, page 318.
2 Cab 65/13.
3 Cab 69/1.
4 Marshall Cornwall, *Wars and Rumours of War*, pages 139, 143.
5 Churchill's decision to agree to Marshall Cornwall's request for two more divisions was communicated to the Chiefs of Staff at their meeting on 5 June in Churchill's absence. Cab 69/1. Cab 79/4. WO 106/1697. Gilbert, *Churchill*, Vol. VI, page 471.
6 WO 106/1619.
7 Churchill, *Second World War*, Vol. II, page 134.
8 WO 106/1619. WO 106/1620. Colville, *Fringes of Power*, page 154.
9 Fraser, *Alanbrooke*, page 168. WO 106/1774. Bryant, *Turn of the Tide*, page 169.
10 WO 106/1774.
11 Marshall Cornwall, op cit, page 170.
12 Kimball, *Churchill and Roosevelt, The Complete Correspondence*, Vol. I, pages 45–51. FRUS 1940, Vol. III, pages 53–5. Cab 21/952. Cab 65/7. Colville, op cit, page 155.
13 Colville, op cit, page 160. Cab 65/7.
14 Parkinson, *Blood, Toil, Tears and Sweat*, pages 41–43. Cab 65/7.
15 Amouroux, *Le 18 Juin 1940*, pages 20–58.
16 Trevelyan, *Defence of the Roman Republic*, page 231.

CHAPTER 6

1 Amouroux, *Le 18 Juin 1940*, page 216.
2 Amouroux, op cit, pages 220–31. Marder, *From the Dardanelles to Oran*, pages 190–3.
3 Amouroux, op cit, pages 219, 220, 226. Marder, op cit, page 192. Adm 200/4. Prem 3/174/1.
4 Amouroux, op cit, pages 224–6.
5 Amouroux, op cit, page 220.
6 Churchill, *Second World War*, Vol. II, page 202.
7 Amouroux, op cit, page 223.
8 Cab 65/13. Parkinson, *Blood, Toil, Tears and Sweat*, pages 55–6.
9 Cab 65–17. Churchill, op cit, Vol. II, page 206.
10 Amouroux, op cit, pages 231, 253. Cab 101/95. Marder, op cit, page 211. Adm 205/4.

11 Adm 205/4. Adm 186/800. Cab 65/7. Marder, op cit, pages 205–11.
12 Marder, op cit, page 193. Amouroux, op cit, pages 235–57.
13 Prem 3/179/1. Prem 3/179/4.
14 Cab 101/95.
15 Adm 186/800.
16 Marder, op cit, page 267.
17 Marder, *Operation Menace*, pages 120–41. Keyes Papers, Churchill College, Cambridge. Varilon, *Mers el Kebir*, pages 92–3.
18 Cab 65/17. Cab 69/1.
19 Cab 65/15.
20 Prem 3/416.
21 Cab 103/186. Churchill, op cit, Vol. II, page 208 et seq.
22 Cab 103/541.
23 Woodward, *British Foreign Policy in the Second World War*, Vol. I, page 403. Playfair, *Mediterranean and Middle East*, Vol. I, page 137.

CHAPTER 7

1 Eden, *The Reckoning*, page 182. Gilbert, *Churchill*, Vol. V, page 951.
2 Cab 120/237.
3 Woodward, *British Foreign Policy in the Second World War*, Vol. I, page 335.
4 Lamb, *The Ghosts of Peace*, pages 143–6. FO 800/322. Woodward, op cit, Vol. I, page 385.
5 Kimball, op cit, pages 68–69. Prem 3/462/2.
6 Kimball, *Churchill and Roosevelt*, pages 89–119. Prem 3/462/3.
7 Kimball, op cit, page 223.
8 Freidel, *Franklin D. Roosevelt. A Rendezvous with Destiny*, page 384.
9 Butler, *Grand Strategy*, Vol. III, pages 118–24. Churchill, *Second World War*, Vol. III, page 387.
10 Harvey, *War Diaries of Oliver Harvey*, page 31.
11 Butler, op cit, Vol. III, page 130.
12 Cab 65/19.
13 Cab 79/13.
14 Freidel, op cit, page 394.
15 Freidel, op cit, pages 392–4.

CHAPTER 8

1 Lewin, *The Chief: Field Marshal Lord Wavell C in C and Viceroy 1939–1947*, pages 36–40.
2 Churchill, *Second World War*, Vol. II, pages 376–83, 397.
3 Ismay, *The Memoirs of Lord Ismay*, page 195. Cab 69/1. Eden, *The Reckoning*, page 178.
4 Prem 3/288/1. Lewin, op cit, pages 60–1.
5 Prem 3/288/1. Lewin, op cit, page 68.
6 Lewin, op cit, page 91. Prem 3/309/2.
7 Kennedy, *The Business of War*, pages 73–5.
8 Prem 3/309/2.
9 Von Creveld, *Hitler's Strategy 1940–41: The Balkans Clue*, pages 63–5.
10 Prem 3/309/2. Lewin, op cit, page 82. Kennedy, op cit, pages 75, 106. Cab 65/7.

11 Prem 3/309/3.
12 Parkinson, op cit, pages 195–7. Cab 65/21.
13 Cab 65/22.
14 Ibid. Parkinson, *Blood, Toil, Tears and Sweat*, page 206. Churchill, op cit, Vol. III, page 90.
15 Kennedy, op cit, page 85. Cab 65/22. Parkinson, op cit, page 207.
16 Cab 65/22. Churchill, op cit, Vol. III, page 93.
17 Kennedy, op cit, page 92.
18 Prem 3/309/3. Lewin, op cit, pages 103–4.
19 Churchill, op cit, Vol. III, page 151.
20 Prem 3/309/2.
21 Ibid.
22 Ibid.
23 Prem 3/290/1. Prem 3/290/3.
24 Cab 69/2. Prem 3/309/3.
25 Prem 3/309/3.
26 Kennedy, op cit, page 61. Prem 3/288/1.
27 Churchill, op cit, Vol. III, page 243.
28 Wheeler-Bennett, *Action This Day*, page 86. Colville, *Fringes of Power*, pages 390–1.
29 Prem 3/309/4. Butler, *Grand Strategy*, Vol. II, page 513.
30 Prem 3/290/4. Kennedy, op cit, page 115.
31 Cab 65/18. Parkinson, op cit, pages 249–50. Cab 65/95.

CHAPTER 9

1 Colville, *Fringes of Power*, page 753. Wheeler-Bennett, *Action This Day*, page 62.
2 Leasor, *War at the Top*, page 119.
3 Prem 1/418. Leasor, op cit, pages 120–1.
4 Churchill, *Second World War*, Vol. III, page 51 et seq. Kennedy, *The Business of War*, page 63.
5 Playfair, *Mediterranean and Middle East*, Vol. I, page 308.
6 Eden, *The Reckoning*, page 180. Cab 69/1.
7 Prem 3/330/7.
8 Cab 69/2.
9 Churchill, op cit., Vol. III, pages 700–1.
10 Prem 3/124/1. Seymour, *British Special Forces*, page 67.
11 Prem 3/124/1. Prem 3/124/3. Seymour, op cit, pages 68–9.
12 Cab 100/3. Prem 3/330/7.
13 Prem 3/330/7.
14 Cab 106/3. Prem 7/321/7.
15 Leasor, op cit, pages 122–35.
16 Prem 3/330/7. Leasor, op cit, pages 122–5.
17 Prem 288/1.
18 FO 371/30124. Marshall Cornwall, *Wars and Rumours of War*, pages 178–9.
19 Marshall Cornwall, op cit, page 181.
20 Prem 3/309/4. Churchill, op cit, Vol. III, pages 224–9.
21 Ismay, *The Memoirs of Lord Ismay*, page 207. Lewin, *The Chief*, page 138.
22 Prem 3/309/4.

CHAPTER 10

1 FO 371/24361. Rougier, *Mission secrète à Londres*, page 67 et seq.
2 FO 371/49142.
3 FO 371/49141. Rougier, op cit, page 197.
4 FO 371/24361.
5 Cab 127/14.
6 FO 371/24361.
7 FO 371/24363.
8 FO 371/24363. FO 371/24361. Rougier, op cit, page 255.
9 Rougier, op cit, page 63. FO 371/24363. FO 371/49141.
10 FO 371/24363.
11 Rougier, op cit, page 125.
12 Gilbert, *Churchill*, Vol. V, pages 864–8. Colville, *Fringes of Power*, page 283. Dilks, *Cadogan Diaries*, page 334. Prem 3/186/A/5.
13 FO 371/28234.
14 Prem 3/126/1. FO 371/28234. Bracken pointed out that Kirkpatrick was a good friend of Britain's, and the *Chicago Daily News* was 'a great paper and . . . a staunch friend of England'.
15 FO 371/28234.
16 Ibid. Conversation with Professor M. R. Foot, author of *SOE in France*.
17 FO 371/28234. FO 371/28235.
18 FO 371/49141.
19 Ibid.
20 Ibid.
21 *Times*, 17 July 1945. FO 371/49143.
22 Kersaudy, *Churchill and de Gaulle*, page 130.
23 FO 371/24327.
24 FO 371/27290.
25 FO 371/27284.
26 Prem 3/390/3, Lewin, *The Chief*, page 139.
27 Cab 69/2. Prem 3/290/3.
28 Connell, *Wavell Supreme Commander*, page 462.
29 Prem 3/309/3.
30 Tute, *The Reluctant Enemies*, pages 177–81.
31 FO 371/24302. FO 371/28545. FO 371/28561.
32 Churchill, *Second World War*, Vol. III, page 296. FO 371/24302. FO 371/28545. FO 371/28361. Tute, op cit, pages 169–81.

CHAPTER 11

1 Playfair, *Mediterranean and Middle East*, Vol. II, page 24.
2 Cab 79/10. Ismay, *The Memoirs of Lord Ismay*, page 202. Parkinson, *Blood, Toil, Tears and Sweat*, page 228.
3 Prem 3/309/4. Butler, *Grand Strategy*, Vol. II, page 524.
4 Prem 3/309/4.
5 Ibid.
6 Playfair, op cit, Vol. II, pages 172–6. Butler, op cit, Vol. II, pages 530–52.
7 Churchill, *Second World War* (abridged), page 444.
8 Dilks, *Cadogan Diaries*, page 321.

9 Prem 3/170/1.

10 Dilks, op cit, page 389.

11 Interview by author with Duke of Portland. An account of this talk between Eden and Maisky is in FO 371/29465.

12 Prem 3/170/1.

13 Churchill, *Second World War*, Vol. III, page 339.

14 Prem 3/170/1.

15 Ibid.

16 Butler, op cit, Vol. III, pages 646–50.

17 Butler, op cit, Vol. III, page 189.

18 Prem 3/170/1.

19 Prem 3/290/1.

20 Ibid. Prem 3/286.

21 Churchill, *Second World War*, Vol. III, page 501. Warner, *Auchinleck, the Lonely Soldier*, page 117.

22 Prem 3/284/12 ('The Tank Parliament').

23 Warner, op cit, pages 89–90. Playfair, op cit, Vol. III, Appendix VIII.

24 Warner, op cit, page 117.

25 Prem 3/284/12.

26 Prem 3/290/5.

27 Ibid. Butler, op cit, Vol. III, page 452. Churchill, *Second World War*, Vol. IV, page 262.

28 Cab 65/30.

29 Warner, op cit, page 247.

30 Prem 3/290/3. Cab 65/30. Parkinson, op cit, page 408.

31 Butler, op cit, Vol. III, pages 458–61. Prem 3/290/2. Prem 3/290/3. Prem 3/290/4.

32 Churchill, *Second World War* (abridged), page 584. Bryant, *Turn of the Tide*, page 408.

33 Kennedy, *The Business of War*, page 243. WO 216/2238A. Cab 44/97.

34 Prem 3/290/4. Warner, op cit, pages 271–3.

35 Prem 3/290/4.

36 Cab 101/40.

37 Kennedy, op cit, page 245.

38 Prem 3/284/12.

39 Ibid.

40 Prem 3/290/4. Warner, op cit, page 89. Playfair, op cit, Vol. III, Appendix VIII.

41 Warner, op cit, page 117.

42 Prem 3/290/4. Playfair, op cit, Vol. III, Appendix VI.

43 Prem 3/290/4.

44 Warner, op cit, page 245.

45 Kennedy, op cit, page 255.

46 Prem 3/290/4.

47 Prem 3/290/3.

48 Bryant, op cit, page 431.

49 Moorehead, *Year of Battle*, pages 247–53.

50 Churchill, *Second World War* (abridged), page 596. Bryant, op cit, pages 441–52.

CHAPTER 12

1 Woodward, *British Foreign Policy in the Second World War*, Vol. II, pages 92–101. Letter to author from Capitaine de Vaisseau Huan, the French naval historian.

2 Cab 120/517. Grew, *Turbulent Era*, page 1256.

3 Kimball, *Churchill and Roosevelt*, Vol. I, page 156.

4 Cab 126/6/5.

5 Prem 3/156/3.

6 Air 23/1865. Parrish, *Encyclopaedia of World War Two*, page 183.

7 Churchill, *Second World War*, Vol. IV, page 245.

8 FO 371/35957.

9 FO 371/27767. FO 371/27758. FO 371/27759. Decoux, *A la Barre de l'Indochine*, page 261. The text of the little-known Jouan-Layton Agreement and relevant papers are on FO 371/27761–3.

10 Woodward, op cit, Vol. II, page 112.

11 Prem 3/252/6A.

12 Decoux, op cit, page 155.

13 FO 371/35957. (Craigie, final report on his mission to Japan.) Hull, *Memoirs*, page 1039.

14 Sir William Hayter, letter to author 16 May 1990.

15 FO 371/35957.

16 Ibid.

17 Ibid.

18 Cab 120/517.

19 Prem 3/367/A. Kimball, op cit, Vol. I, page 265. Butler, *Grand Strategy*, Vol. III, page 257.

20 FO 371/35957. Kimball, op cit, Vol. I, page 278.

21 Kimball, op cit, Vol. I, page 277.

22 Sir William Hayter, letter to author, 25 May 1990. Hull, op cit, page 1081. Hull refers to 'meagre rations', although Churchill wrote 'thin diet'.

23 Dilks, *Cadogan Diaries*, page 415. Friedel, *Franklin D. Roosevelt*, page 400. FRUS 1941, Japan II, pages 706–20.

24 FO 371/35957. Kimball, op cit, Vol. I, pages 1278–9. Prem 3/156/3.

25 Grew, op cit., page 1373.

26 Butler, *Grand Strategy*, Vol. III, page 380. Friedel, op cit, page 402. Dilks, op cit, page 415.

27 Cab 120/517.

28 Gilbert, *Churchill*, Vol. IV, page 1258. Prem 3/158/1. Churchill, op cit, Vol. III, pages 537–9.

29 Friedel, op cit, pages 408–9. *IMT*, Vol. 5, pages 6–9; Conversation between Robert Craigie Junior and author. FO 371/35957.

30 FO 371/35957. Woodward, op cit, Vol. II, page 178. Faulds, minute on 12 October 1942 in FO 371/35957.

CHAPTER 13

1 Grigg, *1943, The Victory That Never Was*, page 18.

2 Kimball, *Churchill and Roosevelt*, Vol. III, pages 225–9, Vol. I, page 447.

3 Grigg, op cit, page 90. Sherwood, *Roosevelt and Hopkins*, page 729.

4 Soames, *Clementine Churchill*, page 337.

5 Kimball, op cit, Vol. I, pages 488–500. Kimball, op cit, Vol. II, pages 244, 259.

6 Butler, *Grand Strategy*, Vol. III, pages 315–400.

7 Butler, op cit, pages 646–50 Howard, *Grand Strategy*, Vol. IV, page 34.

8 Kimball, op cit, Vol. I, pages 495–500. Butler, op cit, Vol. III, page 79.
9 Butler, op cit, Vol. III, page 595.
10 Butler, op cit, Vol. III, page 682.
11 Cab 65/30.
12 Butler, op cit, Vol. III, page 622.
13 Bryant, *Turn of the Tide*, page 405.
14 Sherwood, *Roosevelt and Hopkins*, page 605.
15 Sherwood, op cit, pages 607–10. Cab 65/28.
16 Kimball, op cit, Vol. I, page 542.
17 Howard, *Grand Strategy*, Vol. IV, page XXV.
18 Cab 65/31. Parkinson, *Blood, Toil, Tears and Sweat*, page 948.
19 Villa, *Unauthorised Action*, pages 19–50.
20 Taylor, *Beaverbrook*, page 538. Villa, op cit, page 18. Driberg, *Beaverbrook*, page 291. Cab 127/24. WO 100/4115.
21 Prem 3/256. Villa, op cit, page 27. Prem 3/256.
22 Villa, op cit, pages 21, 39. Churchill, *Second World War*, Vol. IV, page 510.
23 Ismay Papers, Kings College, London. Quoted by Villa, op cit, page 40. Churchill, op cit, Vol. IV, page 510.
24 Churchill, op cit, Vol. IV, page 304.
25 Grigg, op cit, page 35.
26 Hansard, House of Lords, 25 March 1942. Grigg, op cit, page 36.
27 Bryant, op cit, page 302. Kennedy, *The Business of War*, page 229.
28 Barnes, *Empire at Bay*, page 779; Nicolson, *Diary and Letters*, page 205. Harvey, *War Diaries*, page 15. Rhodes James, *Eden*, page 262. Pimlott, *Second World War Diaries of Hugh Dalton*, pages 370, 390, 433. Soames, op cit, page 28.
29 Churchill, *Second World War* (abridged), pages 621–2.
30 Woodward, *British Foreign Policy in the Second World War*, Vol. II, pages 255–76.

CHAPTER 14

1 *Encyclopaedia of World War Two*, page 487. Duff Cooper, *Old Men Forget*, page 291. Cooper claims he told the Americans when he visited Pearl Harbor that it was risky to allow 'several hundred aeroplanes to lie wing tip to wing tip'. Prem 3/158/1.
2 All the sources making allegations against Roosevelt are listed in *Troy International Journal of Intelligence and Counter Intelligence*, Vol. 3, No. 3. Kimball lists some American critics of Roosevelt in *Churchill and Roosevelt*, Vol. II, page 275. FO 371/35957.
3 Cab 106/45.
4 FO 371/31860. Dilks, *Cadogan Diaries*, page 415. Parkinson, *Blood, Toil, Tears and Sweat*, pages 320–1.
5 Prem 3/395/3.
6 FO 371/28135. FO 371/28126.
7 Kirby, *War Against Japan*, Vol. I, page 180. FO 371/31860. Prem 3/156/5. Leasor, *War at the Top*, page 164.
8 Cab 69/2. Air 23/1865.
9 Gilbert, *Churchill*, Vol. VI, page 1271.
10 Air 23/4745. Prem 2a/3/42.
11 Air 23/1865. Letter to author from A. P. H. Humphrey.
12 Air 23/4745.

13 Letters to author from A. P. H. Humphrey.
14 Air 23/4745.
15 Gilbert, op cit, Vol. VI, pages 1273–4.
16 Prem 3/163/3.
17 Prem 3/163/2.
18 Duff Cooper, op cit, page 293.
19 FO 371/27856.
20 Smyth, *Percival and the Tragedy of Singapore*, pages 99–100. Letter to author from A. P. H. Humphrey.
21 Cab 106/45.
22 Cab 106/45. Prem 3/161/2. Letter to author from A. P. H. Humphrey.
23 Prem 29/3/42.
24 Vlieland Papers, Liddell Hart Centre, Kings College, London.
25 Callahan, *Worst Disaster: Fall of Singapore*, pages 163, 229–3. Cab 120/517. Ian Jacob, *Diary*, quoted by Callahan, op cit, page 234.
26 Kirby, op cit, pages 257–8. Brook-Popham Papers, Liddell Hart Centre, King's College, London. Connell, *Wavell, Supreme Commander*, page 690. Fraser, *Alanbrooke*, page 284.
27 Butler, *Grand Strategy*, Vol. III, page 407.
28 Cab 120/615. Prem 3/169/2.
29 Gilbert, op cit, Vol. VII, page 46.
30 Cab 65/9.
31 Cab 69/4. Prem 3/169/2. Ismay, *The Memoirs of Lord Ismay*, page 247.
32 Cab 69/4. Callahan, op cit, pages 238–59. Gilbert, op cit, Vol. VII, page 50.
33 Cab 65/19. Churchill, *Second World War* (abridged), page 524. Kirby, Vol I, op cit, page 259.
34 Cab 120/615.
35 Ibid.
36 Eden, *The Reckoning*, page 272. Prem 3/169/2.
37 Cab 120/517.

CHAPTER 15

1 Glendevon, *Viceroy at Bay. Linlithgow*, page 182.
2 Gilbert, *Churchill*, Vol. VII, page 33.
3 Glendevon, op cit, page 227.
4 Dallek, *Franklin D. Roosevelt and American Foreign Policy 1932–1945*, page 324. Barnes, op cit, page 809.
5 Barnes, op cit, pages 730–8.
6 Kimball, *Churchill and Roosevelt*, Vol. I, pages 445, 448. Prem 4/48/9. Churchill, *Second World War*, Vol. IV, page 219. Conversation between author and Philip Mason.
7 Butler, *Grand Strategy*, Vol. III, page 487. Cab 79/10.
8 Cab 65/25.
9 Kersaudy, *Churchill and de Gaulle*, page 185. *Economist*, 21 March 1942.
10 Kersaudy, op cit, pages 200–13.
11 Gilbert, op cit, Vol. VII, page 105.
12 Friedel, *Franklin D. Roosevelt*, page 596.
13 Cab 79/77.
14 Ibid.

15 Cab 79/79. Cab 128/144.
16 Bryant, *Blind Victory*, page 267.

CHAPTER 16

1 Kimball, *Churchill and Roosevelt*, Vol. I, pages 557–642.
2 Kersaudy, *Churchill and de Gaulle*, pages 207–9. Butler, *Grand Strategy*, Vol. IV, page 145.
3 Butler, *Grand Strategy*, Vol. IV, page 133.
4 Kimball, op cit, Vol. I, pages 589–90.
5 Howard, op cit, pages 173–4.
6 Howard, op cit, pages 152.
7 Kimball, op cit, Vol. II, pages 3–10. Howard, op cit, page 175.
8 Churchill, *Second World War*, Vol. IV, page 573.
9 Tute, *The Reluctant Enemies*, pages 271– 90.
10 Cab 65/28.
11 Bryant, *Turn of the Tide*, page 512.
12 Cab 79/23. Bryant, op cit, pages 512–13.
13 Howard, op cit, pages 68–9. Bryant, op cit, pages 512–14. Hinsley, *British Intelligence in the Second World War*, Vol. II, page 441.
14 Hamilton, *Monty, the Making of a General*, pages 838–40.
15 General Roberts, conversation with author. Hamilton, *Monty, Master of the Battlefield*, page 19.
16 Prem 3/420/1.
17 Bryant, op cit, pages 529–30.
18 Prem 3/499/7.
19 Ibid.
20 Matloff, *Strategic Planning for Coalition Warfare*, pages 24–5. Cab 65/28. Howard, op cit, page 240.
21 Howard, op cit, page 240–245, Cab 65/28.
22 Cab 120/76. Cab 120/77. Prem 4/72/1. Prem 3/420/3, which covers the Casablanca Conference.
23 Prem 3/420/3. Cab 120/76.
24 Prem 4/72/1. Cab 120/76.
25 Ibid.
26 Churchill, op cit, pages 575–8.
27 Prem 3/420/3.
28 Prem 4/72/1. Elliot, Roosevelt, *As He Saw It*, pages 75, 114–15.
29 Prem 3/420/3.
30 Cab 120/77.
31 Cab 99/22.
32 Grigg, *1943, The Victory That Never Was*, pages 86–7. Cab 99/22. Howard, op cit, page 368.
33 Cab 120/83.
34 Stimson, *On Active Service in Peace and War*, pages 225–6. Butcher, *Three Years with Eisenhower*, page 317.

CHAPTER 17

1 Howard, *Grand Strategy*, page 283.
2 FO 371/29927. Lamb, *The Ghosts of Peace*, pages 147–56.
3 Ibid. FO 371/29924. FO 371/29927.
4 FO 371/29924.
5 FO 371/29936.
6 FO 371/29940. Denham, *Inside the Nazi Ring*, pages 132–49.
7 FO 371/29940. Denham, op cit, pages 113–40. Lamb, op cit, pages 160–66.
8 FO 371/37262. Prem 3/249/9.
9 Prem 3/249/9.
10 De Luna, *Storia del Partito d'Azione*, pages 17–61. Pirelli, *Taccuini 1922–1943*, pages 450–5.
11 FO 371/32623.
12 Prem 3/249/3.
13 Ibid. FO 371/37333.
14 FO 371/37264.
15 Cab 101/124.
16 Castellano, *La Guerra Continua*, pages 135–65, 222. After the war General Bedell Smith wrote to General Castellano, who negotiated the armistice and the plan for the airborne landing near Rome: 'I shall always regret bitterly we were not able because of the attitude of the Italian military command in the Rome district to undertake our projected airborne operation for securing the city of Rome and its environs. You yourself are aware with what determination and goodwill this operation was planned. I believe personally it could have been successful.' General Westphal, Chief of Staff to Field Marshal Kesselring, wrote in similar terms to Castellano.

CHAPTER 18

1 Butler, *Grand Strategy*, Vol. IV, pages 505–7.
2 Butler, op cit, Vol. IV, pages 489–90.
3 Prem 3/3/3.
4 Letter from Professor A. Santoni, Professor of Naval History at Pisa University, to the author. A. Levi, *Official Italian Naval History of World War Two*, Vol. XVI. *Avvenimenti in Egeo*, pages 6–7, 23–4, 41, 69–70, 80. Zangrandi, *1943, 25 Luglio 8 Settembre*, pages 99–100.
5 Prem 3/3/3.
6 Ibid.
7 Kimball, *Churchill and Roosevelt*, Vol. II, pages 497–9, 501. Prem 3/3/3.
8 Bryant, *Triumph in the West*, page 51.
9 Kimball, op cit, Vol. II, page 502. Prem 3/3/3. Butler, *Grand Strategy*, Vol. V, pages 96–7.
10 Ismay, op cit, page 323.
11 Prem 3/3/3. Churchill, *Second World War* (abridged), page 711.
12 Kimball, op cit, Vol. II, pages 508–13.
13 Prem 3/3/3.
14 Churchill, *Second World War*, Vol. V, page 193.
15 Ismay, *The Memoirs of Lord Ismay*, pages 330–1. Prem 3/3/3.
16 Prem 3/3/3.
17 Ismay, op cit, page 336. Bryant, op cit, page 71.

18 Cab 120/113.
19 Ibid.
20 Ibid.
21 Cab 101/113.
22 Cab 120/113.
23 Prem 3/3/1.
24 Woodward, *British Foreign Policy in the Second World War*, Vol. IV, pages 172-3.

CHAPTER 19

1 Jack, interview of 18 March 1989, recorded in Imperial War Museum.
2 Cab 101/126. This is a 190-page draft for the official historians, written by Miss J. Hamilton of the Cabinet Offices Historical Section, with handwritten corrections by Sir William Deakin.
3 Beloff, *Tito's Flawed Legacy*, page 78. Jack, op cit.
4 Hinsley, *British Intelligence in the Second World War*, Vol. III, Part I, page 141. Cab 121/676. WO 106/5689A.
5 Hinsley, op cit, page 147. WO 208/2019. Cab 121/670. Deakin, *Embattled Mountain*, page 153.
6 Woodward, *British Foreign Policy in the Second World War*, Vol. III, pages 290-1.
7 Boyle, *Climate of Treason*, page 345. Healey, *The Time of My Life*, page 38.
8 Woodward, op cit, Vol. III, pages 292-3. FO 371/37612.
9 Churchill, *Second World War*, Vol. V, pages 410-11. Letter to author from Peter Solly Flood. Lees, *Rape of Serbia*, pages 100-3.
10 Hinsley, op cit, pages 149, 153. Cab 121/531. Woodward, op cit, Vol. III, pages 296-7. FO 371/37612.
11 FO 371/37620.
12 Jack, op cit. Hinsley, op cit, Vol. III, page 151. Defe 3/573. Col MacDowell's report of U.S. mission with Mihailovic (October 1944) is in Martin, *Web of Disinformation*, pages 379 etc.
13 Lees, *Rape of Serbia*, pages 156-9.
14 Lees, op cit, page 32. WO 202/162. FO 371/59469.
15 Hinsley, op cit, Vol. III, page 139. Cab 101/126.
16 FO 371/39167.
17 Deakin, op cit, pages 261-3. Prem 3/511/2.
18 Cab 101/126. Lees, op cit, page 260. Prem 3/511/2.
19 FO 371/37260. Prem 3/511/2.
20 Bryant, *Triumph in the West*, page 130.
21 Prem 3/511/2. FO 371/37260.
22 Ibid (both files).
23 Cab 101/126.
24 Prem 3/511/2.
25 Cab 101/126. Kimball, op cit, Vol. III, page 308. MacDowell report, op cit.
26 FO 371/44273.
27 Lees, op cit, pages 75, 284-5.
28 Woodward, op cit, page 348.
29 Cab 101/126. Martin, op cit, pages 393-400.
30 Cab 101/126. Woodward, op cit, Vol. III, pages 348-52. Kimball, op cit, Vol. III, page 500. Butler, *Grand Strategy*, Vol. V, page 392.

31 Cab 101/126. Cab 120/591. WO 204/8035.
32 Prem 3/513/6. Woodward, op cit, Vol. III, pages 354–7.
33 Cab 101/126.
34 Woodward, op cit, Vol. III, pages 368–74.
35 FO 371/59408.
36 *Sunday Telegraph*, 29 July 1990. Jack, op cit.
37 Churchill, *Second World War* (abridged), page 869.
38 Woodward, op cit, Vol. III, page 417.
39 Woodward, op cit, Vol. III, pages 420–1. See FO 371/48812 for Churchill minute.

CHAPTER 20

1 Bryant, *Turn of the Tide*, pages 659–62, 702–7.
2 Lamb, *Montgomery in Europe*, pages 56–8. Prem 3/336/3.
3 Kimball, *Churchill and Roosevelt*, Vol. III, page 222.
4 Kimball, op cit, Vol. III, pages 225–54. Bryant, *Triumph in the West*, page 225. Butler, *Grand Strategy*, Vol. VI, page 19. Prem 3/271/8.
5 Bryant, op cit, page 168.
6 Kimball, op cit, Vol. III, pages 227–9.
7 WO 215/12. WO 219/255. Lamb, op cit, pages 75–84. Kennedy, *The Business of War*, pages 327–8. Parkinson, *A Day's March Nearer Home*, pages 279–81. Bryant, op cit, page 180.
8 Bryant, op cit, page 175. Dilks, *Cadogan Diaries*, page 621. Kennedy, op cit, page 327.
9 WO 219/255.
10 Churchill, *Second World War*, Vol. V, page 536.
11 Lamb, *Montgomery in Europe*, page 85. Hamilton, *Monty, the Making of a General*, page 592.
12 Bryant, op cit, page 229. Gilbert, *Churchill*, Vol. VII, page 844.
13 Lamb, op cit, pages 141–4. Prem 3/339/1.
14 Butcher, *Three Years with Eisenhower*, page 536.
15 Brigadier Sir Edgar Williams, conversation with author.
16 Prem 4/100/8.
17 Lamb, *The Ghosts of Peace*, pages 255–60. FO 371/30912.
18 Lamb, *The Ghosts of Peace*, pages 252–4. FO 371/33055. FO 371/30912.
19 Hansard, House of Lords, 10 March 1943.
20 FO 371/39087. Lamb, *The Ghosts of Peace*, pages 290–6.
21 Churchill's remarks about the Resistance have been quoted by several German historians including Pechel in *Deutscher Widerstand*. Doubts on whether Churchill really said these words have been cast, but Churchill wrote on November 19 to Walter Hammer of Hamburg:

> Since the receipt of your letter I have had a search made through my speeches for the passage to which you and Count Hardenburg refer; but so far no record can be found of any such pronouncement by me. But I might quite well have used the words you quote as they represent my feelings on this aspect of German affairs.

The author is indebted to Professor Helmut Krausnick of Stuttgart for this information. Wheeler-Bennett's minute is on FO 371/39062.
22 FO 371/39024.

23 Ibid.
24 Prem 3/197/2.
25 Lamb, *The Ghosts of Peace*, page 234. Cab 65/46. Prem 3/197/2. FO 945/10.
26 Woodward, *British Foreign Policy in the Second World War*, Vol. V, page 222. Prem 3/197/2. FO 954/10.
27 Kimball, op cit, Vol. III, page 317.
28 Lamb, *The Ghosts of Peace*, pages 239–45. FO 371/38548. FO 371/38560. FO 371/39083. Prem 3/195/2. Prem 3/197/3. Kimball, op cit, Vol. III, pages 408–9, 403–5.
29 Lamb, *Montgomery in Europe*, pages 309–10. Simpson Archives, Imperial War Museum.
30 Prem 3/334/6. Lamb, *Montgomery in Europe*, pages 324–32.
31 Grigg Archives, Churchill College, Cambridge. Prem 3/339/11.
32 Lamb, *Montgomery in Europe*, pages 364–85. Dawnay Archives, Imperial War Museum. Simpson Archives, op cit. Prem 3/398/5.
33 Kimball, op cit, Vol. III, page 612.
34 Kimball, op cit, Vol. III, page 633.

CHAPTER 21

1 Cruickshank (the official historian) 'Flying Bombs' in *War Monthly*, No. 76, May 1980. *Times*, 6 May 1980, London Diary.
2 Prem 3/89. Def 2/1252.
3 Prem 3/89. Cab 79/77.
4 Cruickshank, op cit.
5 Ibid.
6 *Times*, 6 May 1980, op cit.
7 Prem 3/65.
8 Cab 120/782. Harris and Paxman, *A Higher Form of Killing*, pages 68–105.
9 Eden, *The Reckoning*, page 362. Cab 120/76.
10 Cab 65/38. FO 371/36047.
11 Kersaudy, *Churchill and de Gaulle*, pages 299–301.
12 Prem 3/182/3.
13 Ibid.
14 FO 954/9 Part 1.
15 Kersaudy, op cit, pages 338–45. Cab 66/50. Lacouture, *De Gaulle Le Rebelle*, pages 767–77.
16 Harvey, *War Diaries of Oliver Harvey*, page 343. FO 371/41994. Kimball, op cit, Vol. III, pages 185–7.
17 Eden, op cit, page 456. FO 954/9 Part I contains Churchill's handwritten note to Eden.
18 FO 371/49144. Lacouture, op cit, pages 778–81.
19 FO 954/9 Part I.
20 Kimball, op cit, Vol. III, pages 195, 205, 240.
21 Kersaudy, op cit, pages 374–5.
22 Nobecourt, *Hitler's Last Gamble*, page 260. Lamb 'Ardennes Offensive' in *World War II Investigator*, June 1988. Pogue, *Supreme Commander*, page 401 suggests Churchill went to Versailles at de Gaulle's invitation. Certainly Churchill was enthusiastic for de Gaulle at this stage of the war.

CHAPTER 22

1 Parker, *Struggle for Survival: History of the Second World War*, pages 235–7. Jones, *Most Secret War*, page 595.
2 FO 371/46453.
3 Storry, *A History of Modern Japan*, page 229.
4 Grew, *Turbulent Era*, pages 1421–44. FO 371/46447.
5 Butler, *Grand Strategy*, Vol. VI, page 288. Leahy, *I was There*, page 514.
6 FO 371/46477. Stimson and Bundy, *On Active Service in Peace and War*, pages 361–70.
7 Dilks, *Cadogan Diaries*, page 765. Colville, *Action this Day*, page 51.
8 FO 371/46447. Woodward, *British Foreign Policy in the Second World War*, Vol. V, pages 522–33.
9 FO 954/3 and 954/4 cover the Potsdam Conference. FO 371/46433, Dilks, op cit, page 764.
10 Prem 3/430/6.
11 Parkinson, *A Day's March Nearer Home*, page 504. Bryant, *Triumph in the West*, pages 477–8. Cab 101/45.
12 FO 934/3. Woodward, op cit, page 511.
13 Storry, op cit, pages 227–8. Ehrman, 'Atom bombs', unpublished in Cab 101/45, pages 247–8.
14 FO 934/3.
15 Butler, *Grand Strategy*, Vol. VI, page 639.
16 Ibid, page 308. Grew, op cit, page 1275.
17 Storry, op cit, page 229.
18 Prem 8/109.
19 *Times*, 7 August 1945. *Times*, 10 August 1945.
20 Cab 101/45.
21 Dilks, op cit, page 771. FO 371/46453.
22 Harvey, *Diplomatic Diaries of Oliver Harvey*, page 385. Dilks, op cit, page 765.
23 WO 203/5769A. Cruickshank, *Deception in World War Two*, pages 210–20. Cruickshank, in *War Monthly*, No. 88. 'Mimsy' Lady Morland, letter to author. Letter to author from Philip Ziegler.
24 Prem 8/34.
25 Kimball, op cit, Vol. I, page 399.
26 FO 371/47043. Woodward, op cit, Vol. V, page 354.
27 FO 934/4.
28 Churchill (abridged), op cit, pages 931.
29 Cab 120/186.
30 Churchill (abridged), op cit, pages 933–5.
31 Colville, *Fringes of Power* page 658. Churchill (abridged), op cit, pages 935–93.
32 Churchill (abridged), op cit, page 954.

Bibliography

Amouroux, Henri, *Le 18 Juin 1940* (Paris, 1990)
Amery, Julian, *Approach March* (London, 1973)

Barnes, John and Nicholson, David, *The Empire at Bay: the Leo Amery Diaries 1929–45*
    (London, 1988)
Bennett, Ralph, *Ultra and Mediterranean Strategy 1941–45* (London, 1989)
Beloff, Nora, *Tito's Flawed Legacy* (London, 1985)
Birkenhead, Earl of, *Halifax* (London, 1965)
Boyle, Andrew, *Climate of Treason* (London, 1979)
Bryant, Arthur, *Triumph in the West 1943–46* (London, 1959)
—*Turn of the Tide* (London, 1957)
Butcher, Harry C., *Three Years with Eisenhower* (London, 1946)
Butler, J. R. M., series editor *Grand Strategy*
    Gibbs, Norman, Vol. I (London, 1956)
    Butler, J. R. M., Vol. II (London, 1957)
    Gwyer, J. M. A., Vol. III, Part 1 (London, 1964)
    Butler, J. R. M., Vol. III, Part 2 (London, 1964)
    Howard, Michael, Vol. IV (London, 1972)
    Ehrman, John, Vol. V (London, 1956)
    —Vol. VI (London, 1956)

Callahan, Raymond, *The Worst Disaster: Fall of Singapore* (USA, 1977)
Castellano, Giuseppe, *Come firmai l'armistizio di Cassibile* (Milan, 1945)
—*La Guerra Continua* (Milan, 1963)
—*Roma kaputt* (Rome, 1967)
Chamberlain, Neville, papers, Birmingham University
Churchill, Winston S., *The Second World War*
—I *The Gathering Storm* (London, 1948)
—II *Their Finest Hour* (London, 1949)
—III *The Grand Alliance* (London, 1951)
—IV *The Hinge of Fate* (London, 1951)
—V *Closing the Ring* (London, 1952)
—VI *Triumph and Tragedy* (London, 1954)
—*The Second World War* (abridged) (London, 1989)
Cohen, Michael J., *Churchill and the Jews* (London, 1985)
Collier, Basil, *Defence of Great Britain* (London, 1957)

Colville, John, *The Fringes of Power* (London, 1985)
Connell, John, *Wavell, Supreme Commander 1941–43* (London, 1969)
Creveld, Martin L. van, *Hitler's Strategy 1940–41, the Balkan Clue* (London, 1973)
Cockett, Richard, *Twilight of Truth*, London 1989
Cruickshank, Charles, *Deception in World War Two* (Oxford, 1981)
—'Flying Bombs', *War Monthly* No. 76, May 1980
—'Mimsy', *War Monthly* No. 88, May 1981

Dallek, Robert, *Franklin D. Roosevelt and American Foreign Policy* (New York, 1979)
Dalton, Hugh, *The Fatal Years: Memoirs 1931–45* (London, 1957)
Dawnay, Christopher, wartime papers, Imperial War Museum
Decoux, Jean, *A la barre de l'Indochine* (Paris, 1949)
De Luna, Giovanni, *Storia Del Partito D'Azione* (Milan, 1982)
Deakin, F. W. D. *The Embattled Mountain* (London, 1971)
Denham, Henry, *Inside the Nazi Ring* (London, 1984)
Deutsch, Harold *Conspiracy Against Hitler in Twilight War* (London, 1968)
Dilks, David (ed.), *The Diaries of Sir Alexander Cadogan 1938–1945* (London, 1971)
Driberg, Tom, *Beaverbrook* (London, 1956)
Documents on British Foreign Policy, Series 3, Vol. VII, HMSO (London, 1959)
Documents on German Foreign Policy (Washington, 1949)
Duff Cooper, Alfred, (Viscount Norwich), *Old Men Forget: the autobiography of Duff Cooper* (London, 1953)
Duroselle, J. B., *L'Abime 1935–45* (Paris, 1982)

Eden, A., *Facing the Dictators* (London, 1962)
—*Memoirs: The Reckoning* (London, 1965)
Edmonds, Robin, *The Big Three: Churchill, Roosevelt and Stalin* (London, 1991)

Freidel, Frank, *Franklin D. Roosevelt: A Rendezvous with Destiny* (USA, 1990)
Fuchser, Larry William, *Neville Chamberlain and Appeasement* (Toronto, 1982)

Gates, Eleanor M., *End of the Affair* (London, 1981)
Gilbert, Martin, *Winston S. Churchill – Finest Hour 1939–41* Vol VI, (London, 1983)
—*Winston S. Churchill – Road to Victory 1941–45*, Vol. VII, (London, 1986)
Glendevon, John H., *Viceroy at Bay* (London, 1971)
Grew, Joseph C., *Turbulent Era*, Vol. II., *A Diplomatic Record of 40 years 1904–1945* (London, 1953)
Grigg, John, *1943: The Victory That Never Was* (London, 1980)
Grigg, P. J., personal papers, Churchill College, Cambridge

Hamilton, Nigel, *Monty, the Making of a General* (London, 1981)
—*Monty, Master of the Battlefield* (London, 1983)
Harris, Robert and Paxman, Jeremy, *A Higher Form of Killing* (London, 1982)
Harvey, John, (ed.), *The War Diaries of Oliver Harvey* (London, 1978)
—*The Diplomatic Diaries of Oliver Harvey* (London, 1978)
Healey, Denis, *The Time of my Life* (London, 1987)
Hinsley, F. H., *British Intelligence in the Second World War*, Vol. III, Part I (London, 1984)
Hoffman, Peter, *The History of the German Resistance 1933–45* (London, 1977)
Horne, Alastair, *To Lose a Battle, France 1940* (London, 1969)
Hough, Richard, *First Sea Lord* (London, 1969)
Hull, Cordell, *The Memoirs of Cordell Hull* (London, 1948)

Ismay, Lord, *The Memoirs of Lord Ismay* (London, 1960)
IMT, *Proceedings of International Military Tribunal, Nuremberg* (Nuremberg 1947–49)

Jack, Major William, Memorandum, Imperial War Museum, 1984
Jones, R. V., *Most Secret War* (London, 1978)

Kennedy, John, *The Business of War* (London, 1957)
Kersaudy, François, *Churchill and De Gaulle* (New York, 1982)
—*Norway 1940* (London, 1990)
Kimball, Warren F., *Churchill and Roosevelt, the Complete Correspondence*, Vols I–III
    (Princeton, 1984)
Kirby S. W., *The War Against Japan*, Vol. I, *The Fall of Singapore* (London, 1957)

Lacouture, Jean, *De Gaulle de ribelle* (London, 1943)
Lamb, Richard, *Montgomery in Europe 1943–46* (London, 1983)
—*The Ghosts of Peace 1935–45* (Salisbury, 1987)
—*The Drift to War 1922–39* (London, 1989)
—'Kluge', *Hitler's Generals*, ed. Correlli Barnett (London, 1983)
—'Ardennes Offensive World War II', *Investigator*, June 1988
Leahy, W. D., *I Was There* (London, 1950)

Leasor, James and Hollis, Gen. Sir Leslie, *War at the Top* (London, 1959)
Lees, Michael, *The Rape of Serbia* (USA, 1990)
Lees-Milne, James, *Harold Nicolson, Vol. II, 1930–68* (London, 1981)
Levi, A., *Avvenimenti in Egeo dopo l'Armistizio: Official Italian Naval History of World War
    Two*, Vol. XVI (Rome, 1957)
Lewin, Ronald, *The Chief, F. M. Lord Wavell Commander in Chief and Viceroy 1939–47*
    (London, 1980)

Macleod, R. and Kelly, D. (eds.), *Ironside Diaries 1937–40* (London, 1962)
Macmillan, H., *Winds of Change* (London, 1966)
Marder, Arthur J., *From the Dardanelles to Oran*, (London, 1974)
—*Operation Menace* (London, 1976)
Marshall-Cornwall, James, *Wars and Rumours of War* (London, 1984)
Martin, David, *The Web of Disinformation: Churchill's Yugoslav Blunder* (New York, 1988)
Matloff, Maurice and Snell, Edwin, *Strategic Planning for Coalition Warfare 1943–44*
    (Washington, 1953)
Middlemass, Keith and Barnes, John, *Baldwin* (London, 1969)
Moorehead, Alan, *A Year of Battle* (London, 1973)

Nicolson, Nigel, *Harold Nicolson: Diaries and Letters 1939–45* (London, 1967)
Nobecourt, Jacques, *Hitler's Last Gamble: Battle of the Ardennes* (London, 1967)

Ollard, Richard, *Fisher and Cunningham* (London, 1991)

Parker, R. A. C., *Struggle for Survival* (Oxford, 1989)
Parkinson, Roger, *Blood, Toil, Tears and Sweat* (London, 1973)
—*A Day's March Nearer Home* (London, 1974)
Parrish, Thomas, *Encyclopaedia of World War Two* (London, 1978)
Pechel, Rudolf, *Deutscher Widerstand* (Germany, 1947)

Pimlott, Ben, *The Second World War Diaries of Hugh Dalton* 1940–45 (London, 1986)
—*Dalton's Diaries* (London, 1989)
Pirelli, Alberto, *Taccuini 1922/43* (Italy, 1984)
Playfair, Maj. Gen. I. S. O., *The Mediterranean and Middle East*, Vol. I (London, 1954)
—Vol. II (London, 1956)
—Vol. III (London, 1960)
—(volume editor) Jackson, Gen. Sir William and Gleave, Group Captain T. P. Vol. VI. Parts 1 & 2 (London, 1984), Part 3 (London, 1987)
Pogue, Forrest C., *Supreme Commander* (Washington, 1954)

Rhodes James, Robert, *Anthony Eden* (London, 1986)
Rose, N. A., *Baffy: Diaries of Rose Dugdale* (London, 1973)
Roosevelt, Elliott, *As He Saw It* (New York, 1946)
Roskill, Stephen, 'Marder, Churchill, and Admiralty 1939–43', *Royal United Services Institute Journal*, December 1972
Rougier, Louis, *Mission Secrète à Londres* (Paris, 1947)
Ryan, Cornelius, *The Last Battle* (London, 1966)

Seymour, William, *British Special Forces* (London, 1985)
Sherwood, Robert E., *Roosevelt and Hopkins* (New York, 1948)
Shirer, William, *The Rise and Fall of the Third Reich* (London, 1959)
Simpson, Sir Frank, personal papers, Imperial War Museum
Simson, Ivan, *Singapore: Too Little, Too Late* (London, 1970)
Smyth, John, *Percival and the Tragedy of Singapore* (London, 1971)
Soames, Mary, *Clementine Churchill: the biography of a marriage* (London, 1979)
Spears, Edward, *Assignment to Catastrophy*, Vol. I (London, 1954)
Stimson, Henry L. and Bundy, McGeorge, *On Active Service in Peace and War* (London, 1949)
Storry, Richard, *A History of Modern Japan* (London, 1960)

Taylor, A. J. P. *Beaverbrook* (London, 1972)
Trevelyan, George, *Defence of the Roman Republic* (London, 1907)
Trionfera, Renzo, *Valzer Di Marescialli 8 Settembre '43* (Milan, 1979)
Tute, Warren, *The Reluctant Enemies* (London, 1989)

Varilon, Pierre, *Mers el Kebir (avec documents inédits)* (Paris, 1949)
Varsori, Antonio, 'Italy, Britain and the Problem of a Separate Peace During the Second World War 1940–43', *Journal of Italian History*, Vol. I, No. 3, 1978
Villa, Brian Loring, *Unauthorized Action* (Oxford, 1989)
Vlieland Papers (King's College Archives, London)

Warner, Philip, *Auchinleck, The Lonely Soldier* (London, 1981)
Wheeler-Bennett, J., *Action This Day* (London, 1968)
Woodward, Sir Llewellyn, *British Foreign Policy in the Second World War*, Vol. I (London, 1970), Vol. II (London, 1971), Vol. III (London, 1972), Vol. IV (London, 1975), Vol. V (London, 1976)

Zangrandi, Ruggero, *1943 25 Luglio–8 Settembre* (Milan, 1965)

Selective chronology of the
Second World War

1939
1 September   Germany invades Poland
3 September   Great Britain and France declare war on Germany
17 September   Red Army invades Poland
27 September   Germans take Warsaw
28 September   German–Soviet Friendship Treaty; partition of Poland agreed
30 November   Red Army invades Finland

1940
12 March   Finnish–Soviet Treaty; major territorial concessions made to Soviet Union
28 March   French and British agree not to conclude peace or armistice without mutual
consent
9 April   German forces occupy Denmark and invade Norway
9 April–June   Anglo–French forces capture Narvik but obliged to evacuate. Trondheim
landing force evacuated
10 May   German forces invade Low Countries and France
10 May   Churchill appointed Prime Minister and Minister of Defence; forms all-party
Coalition Government
15 May   Holland surrenders
26 May   War Cabinet consider and reject negotiations with Hitler through Mussolini
27 May–4 June   Dunkirk evacuation
28 May   Belgium surrenders
10 June   Italy declares war on Great Britain and France
22 June   German–French Armistice signed
3 July   British bombard French fleet at Mers-el-Kebir; nearly 1500 French sailors killed
10 July–15 September   Battle of Britain
2 September   Anglo-American 'Destroyers-Bases' agreement signed
17 September   Hitler postpones invasion of Britain (Operation Sealion)
23 September   British and Free French attack Dakar unsuccessfully
27 September   Tripartite Pact between Germany, Italy and Japan
23 October   Louis Rougier, Pétain's secret emissary, sees Churchill without de Gaulle's
knowledge
28 October   Italy invades Greece
5 November   Roosevelt elected US President for third term
12–14 November   Molotov's visit to Berlin
21 November   Churchill telegraphs Rougier with Heads of Agreement with Pétain via
Lisbon Embassy

1940

9 December   British forces under Wavell launch Western Desert offensive and destroy 14 Italian divisions

18 December   Hitler issues directive for invasion of Soviet Union (Operation Barbarossa)

1941

22 January   British take Tobruk

12–14 February   General Rommel and Deutsches Afrika Korps arrive in Tripoli

7 March   British forces land in Greece

8 March   US Senate approves Lend-Lease Bill

March–June   British capture Eritrea and Abyssinia

30 March   Axis launch offensive in North Africa; take Benghazi, surround Tobruk and advance to Egyptian border

7 April   Germans invade Yugoslavia (capitulates 17 April) and Greece

1 May   Germans drive British out of Greece

2 May   British invade Iraq; Iraqi rebellion collapses (30 May)

20 May–1 June   Battle of Crete; British forced to evacuate

8 June   British and Vichy French fight in Syria

21 June   Churchill dismisses Wavell and replaces him with Auchinleck

22 June   Germany invades Soviet Union (Operation Barbarossa)

7 July   US forces arrive in Iceland

12 July   Anglo–Soviet Mutual Assistance Agreement

25 July   Japanese forces occupy French air and naval bases near Saigon in Indo–China; US Government freezes assets and stops oil supplies

August–September   Konoye proposes summit meeting with Roosevelt; USA and Japanese negotiate in Washington

12 August   Roosevelt and Churchill meet at Placentia Bay, Newfoundland; Atlantic Charter signed but results negligible

25 August   Anglo–Soviet forces occupy Iran

8 September   Germans beseige Leningrad

10 September   Germans take Kiev

18 October   Tojo replaces Konoye as Japanese Prime Minister

24 October   Lend-Lease extended to Soviet Union

18 November   British launch Western Desert offensive; Tobruk relieved, 6th December

2 December   German offensive against Moscow (Operation Typhoon) halted in outskirts of capital

6 December   Red Army launches counter-offensive outside Moscow

7 December   Japanese attack Pearl Harbor, Philippines, Hong Kong and North East Malaya

10 December   Japanese sink *Prince of Wales* and *Repulse* off east coast of Malaya; Japanese take Guam

11 December   Germany and Italy declare war on United States, to Foreign Office's relief

25 December   Japanese take Hong Kong

22 December 1941–14 January 1942   Churchill and Roosevelt meet at Arcadia Conference in Washington, and agree to give Europe priority

1942

21–28 January   Axis launch counter-offensive in Western Desert; retake Benghazi and drive British back to Gazala

1942
15 February   Singapore surrenders
19 February   Japanese bomb Port Darwin, Australia
27–29 February   Battle of Java Sea; Japanese take Dutch East Indies
4–9 April   Japanese force British fleet to withdraw to East Africa
9 April   Japanese take Bataan
20 May–10 June   Molotov visits London and Washington; Anglo–Soviet Treaty of
   Alliance
27 May   German battleship *Bismarck* sunk
May–June   Gazala Battle; German victory; Egypt invaded
4–7 June   Battle of Midway Island; first major Japanese setback
18 June   Churchill and Roosevelt meet at Second Washington Conference
21 June   Tobruk surrenders; Churchill informed while with Roosevelt in Washington
1 July   Axis launch unsuccessful offensive on El Alamein
8 August   Churchill replaces Auchinleck with Montgomery
12 August   Churchill and Stalin meet in Moscow for first time
16 September   Battle for Stalingrad begins
23 October–3 November   Battle of El Alamein; first major British victory over Germans
8 November   Anglo–American invasion of North Africa (Operation Torch); Germans
   occupy southern France, Corsica and Tunisia; French sink battle fleet in Toulon
   harbour
December   German forces halt Anglo–American advance on Tunis
24 December   Darlan, Governor of French North Africa, assassinated in Algiers

1943
January   Churchill and Roosevelt meet at Casablanca and decide to invade Sicily;
   Giraud and de Gaulle make agreement
23 January   British forces take Tripoli
2 February   German forces surrender at Stalingrad
May   Churchill and Roosevelt meet at Third Washington Conference (Trident)
12 May   Axis surrenders in Tunisia; all North Africa freed
10 July   Anglo–American forces invade Sicily
25 July   Dismissal of Mussolini; Badoglio Government puts out peace feelers
August–September   Churchill and Roosevelt meet at First Quebec Conference
   (Quadrant) and Washington
8 September   Italian Armistice announced
9 September   Anglo–American landings at Salerno; Germans made fierce resistance;
   Naples taken (30 September)
October–November   Moscow Conference of Allied Foreign Ministers
November   Churchill, Roosevelt and Chiang Kai-shek meet at First Cairo Conference
   (Sextant)
6 November   Red Army retakes Kiev
November–December   Churchill, Roosevelt and Stalin meet at Teheran Conference
   (Eureka)
December   Churchill and Roosevelt meet at Second Cairo Conference; Churchill decides
   to abandon Mihailovic and back Tito exclusively

1944
22 January   Anglo–American forces land at Anzio but forced back to bridgehead

1944
27 January   Red Army raises siege of Leningrad
4 June   American forces enter Rome
6 June   Allied forces land in Normandy (Operation Overlord); de Gaulle visits Normandy beach head
12 June   First German V-1 hits London
13 June   Goodwood attack fails; Churchill doubts Montgomery
20 July   German officers attempt to assassinate Hitler in Stauffenberg bomb plot
25 July   Churchill visits Montgomery
25 July   Polish Committee of Liberation established in Lublin
1 August   Warsaw Rising begins; Poles surrender 2 October
16 August   Invasion of southern France (Operation Dragoon)
25 August   Paris liberated
September   Churchill and Roosevelt meet at Second Quebec Conference (Octagon)
3 September   British take Brussels
11–8 September   First German V-2 hits London
17–30 September   Anglo-American air landings at Arnhem fail
October   Churchill and Stalin meet in Moscow (Tolstoy)
18 October   British land in Greece
20 October   Red Army enters Belgrade; US forces land in Philippines
23 October   British, Soviet and US governments recognize de Gaulle's Committee as Provisional Government of France
23–26 October   Battle of Leyte Gulf; destruction of Japanese fleet
7 November   Roosevelt elected US President for fourth term
16 November   German forces launch Ardennes counter-offensive (the Battle of the Bulge); Montgomery takes over command of half US front
December–January   British forces suppress left-wing insurrection in Greece
25–28 December   Churchill visits Athens; Greek Regency established (31 December)

1945
January–February   Churchill and Roosevelt meet at Malta
4–12 February   Churchill, Roosevelt and Stalin meet at Crimean Conference, Yalta (Argonaut)
4 February   US takes Manila
7 March   US crosses Rhine near Remagen
20 March   Churchill watches Montgomery's troops cross Rhine
1 April   US lands on Okinawa
12 April   Death of Roosevelt; Truman becomes US President
13 April   Red Army takes Vienna
19 April   US forces take Leipzig
25 April   Soviet and American troops meet on Elbe
29 April   Germans in Italy surrender
30 April   Death of Hitler
2 May   Red Army takes Berlin
8 May   German surrender signed in Berlin
9 May   Red Army takes Prague
5 July   General Election in Great Britain – Labour Party victory announced (26 July)
17 July   Berlin Conference, Potsdam (Terminal) Churchill, Stalin and Truman; Attlee replaces Churchill on 29 July

1945
16 July　First atomic experiment at Alamogordo, New Mexico
26 July　Anglo–American ultimatum to Japanese
6 August　US launches atomic attack on Hiroshima
8 August　Soviet Union declares war on Japan; Red Army invades Manchuria
9 August　US launches second atomic attack on Nagasaki
14 August　Japan capitulates

WAR CABINET, MAY 1940

Prime Minister and Minister of Defence	Winston Churchill
Lord President	Neville Chamberlain (resigned, October 1940)
Lord Privy Seal	Clement Attlee
Foreign Secretary	Lord Halifax
Minister without portfolio	Arthur Greenwood

NOTE:

August 1940　Lord Beaverbrook, Minister of Aircraft Production, joined the War Cabinet.

October 1940　Ernest Bevin, Minister of Labour, Sir Kingsley Wood, Chancellor of the Exchequer, and Sir John Anderson (first as Lord President, and then from September 1943 as Chancellor of the Exchequer, after the death of Kingsley Wood) all joined the War Cabinet.

December 1940　Halifax was appointed Ambassador in Washington; Eden succeeded him as Foreign Secretary and became a member of the War Cabinet.

June 1941　Oliver Lyttelton was appointed Minister of State in the Middle East, and entered the War Cabinet.

February 1942　Beaverbrook resigned (as Minister of War Production); Sir Stafford Cripps succeeded Attlee as Lord Privy Seal and became a member of the War Cabinet; Attlee, who became Deputy Prime Minister, remained in the War Cabinet; Greenwood and Wood left.

March 1942　Richard Casey (a member of the Australian Parliament) was appointed Minister Resident in the Middle East and became a member of the War Cabinet. Lyttleton became Minister of War Production.

October 1942　Cripps resigned as Lord Privy Seal and left the War Cabinet, while Herbert Morrison (Home Secretary) entered it.

November 1943　Lord Woolton, Minister for Reconstruction, entered the War Cabinet.

Some members of the Roosevelt Administration, 1940–45

President	Franklin Delano Roosevelt
Vice-President	Henry A. Wallace (succeeded by Harry S. Truman, January 1945; Wallace became Secretary of Agriculture)
Secretary of Commerce	Harry Hopkins (resigned from the Cabinet, August 1940)
Secretary of Interior	Harold L. Ickes
Secretary of Labour	Frances Perkins

Secretary of the Navy	Frank Knox
Secretary of State	Cordell Hull (succeeded by Edward R. Stettinius, Jr., previously Lend-Lease Administrator in November 1944)
Secretary of the Treasury	Henry Morgenthau, Jr.
Secretary of War	Henry L. Stimson

NOTE:

In July 1945 Truman appointed James Byrnes Secretary of State in succession to Stettinius and he accompanied Truman to Potsdam.

Major figures in the Second World War

ALEXANDER, Albert, V. (later Lord of Hillsborough), First Lord of the Admiralty, 12 May 1940 to May 1945.

ALEXANDER, General (later Field Marshal) Sir Harold R. G., C in C Burma, February 1942 to 15 August 1942; GOC in C Middle East.

ALI, Rashid, Prime Minister of Iraq, 1940 to 31 January 1941; Iraqi leader after coup 3 March 1941, fled 30 May 1941.

AMERY, Leopold, Secretary of State for India and Burma May 1940 to 1945.

ATTLEE, Clement R., Lord Privy Seal until 19 February 1942, then Deputy Prime Minister and Dominions Secretary.

AUCHINLECK, General Sir Claude, C in C India 27 January 1941 to 5 July 1941. GOC in C until 15 August 1942; C in C India from 20 June 1943.

BAUDOUIN, Paul, French Under-Secretary for Foreign Affairs until 17 June 1940; Foreign Minister until October 1940.

BEAVERBROOK, Lord, Minister of Aircraft Production from 14 May 1940 to 1 May 1941; then Minister of State until 29 June 1941, when became Minister of Supply until 4 February 1942, then first Minister of Production until 19 February.

BEVAN, Aneurin, Editor, *Tribune*. Labour MP.

BEVIN, Ernest, Minister of Labour and National Service from 13 May 1940.

BRACKEN, Brendan, (later Lord), Churchill's Parliamentary Private Secretary until 20 July 1941, then Minister of Information.

BOISSON, Pierre, Governor General of French West Africa.

BRIDGES, Sir Edward, Permanent Secretary of the Cabinet Office and Secretary of the War Cabinet.

BROOKE, General (later Field-Marshal) Sir Alan F., Commander, British forces in France, June 1940; C in C Home Forces 20 July 1940 until 25 December 1941 when appointed Chief of the Imperial General Staff.

BROOK-POPHAM, Air Chief Marshal Sir Robert, C in C of three services in Far East, October 1941 (first to take this unified appointment) until December 1941.

BUTLER, Richard Austen, Parliamentary Under-Secretary for Foreign Affairs until 21 July 1941; became President of the Board of Education until 1944.

BYRNES, James, Advisor to Roosevelt; Secretary of State July 1945.

CADOGAN, Sir Alexander, Permanent Under-Secretary at the Foreign Office from 1 January 1938.

CAMBON, Roger, Minister at French Embassy, London, until 5 July 1940.

CAMPBELL, Sir Ronald Hugh, British Ambassador at Paris until mission withdrawn 24 June 1940.

CASEY, Richard G., First Australian Minister to America, 1940 to February 1942, then British Minister of State, Cairo, until 1944.

CATROUX, General Georges, Free French High Commissioner and de Gaulle's representative in Near East, 1940; C in C Free French, Levant 1941 to 1943.

CHAMBERLAIN, Neville, Lord President of Council until 3 October 1940.

CHURCHILL, Winston, British Prime Minister from 10 May 1940.

CHIANG KAI-SHEK, Marshal, President Chinese Republic.

CIANO, Count Galeazzo, (Mussolini's son-in-law), Italian deputy Foreign Minister until February 1943.

COLVILLE, Sir John, Private Secretary to Neville Chamberlain and Winston Churchill.

COOPER, Alfred Duff (later Lord Norwich) Minister of Information from 12 May 1940; Chancellor of Duchy of Lancaster from 20 July 1941 including period as Minister of State, Singapore until January 1942.

CRAIGIE, Sir Robert, British Ambassador at Tokyo until declaration of war, December 1941, and then not re-employed.

CRANBORNE, Lord (later Lord Salisbury), Secretary of State for Dominions from 3 October 1940 to 19 February 1942.

CRIPPS, Sir Stafford R., British Ambassador at Moscow 12 June 1940 to 4 February 1941; leader of House of Commons and Lord Privy Seal until became Minister of Aircraft Production 22 November 1942.

CROSBY, Sir Joseph, British Minister in Thailand until December 1941.

CUNNINGHAM, General Sir Alan, Commander of British forces in Kenya and Somaliland, 1940; Commander, 8th Army until 25 November 1941. (Brother of Admiral Sir Andrew)

CUNNINGHAM, Vice-Admiral (later Admiral of the Fleet, Viscount of Hyndhope) Sir Andrew B., C in C Mediterranean Fleet 1 June 1939 until 1 April 1942; member of British mission to Washington and the CCS from November 1942 to 20 February 1943. (Brother of General Sir Alan).

CURTIN, John, Australian Prime Minister, October 1941 until death in June 1945.

DALTON, Hugh, Minister of Economic Warfare from 15 May 1940 to 22 February 1942, then President of the Board of Trade.

DARLAN, Admiral, J. F., C in C French Fleet; Minister of Marine under Pétain from 16 June 1940: Vice-Premier and Foreign Minister from 9 February 1941 (Flandin) to April 1942, when became head of Vichy French armed forces.

DECOUX, Admiral, French Governor General, Indo China 1940 to 1945.

DENTZ, General Henri, French High Commissioner in Syria and the Lebanon 1940 to 1941.

DILL, Lieutenant-General (later Field Marshal) Sir John G., Chief of the Imperial General Staff from 10 June 1940 (Ironside) to 25 December 1941, then Head of British Military Mission to Washington.

EDEN, Anthony (later Lord Avon), Secretary of State for War, 12 May 1940 until 22 December 1940, then Foreign Secretary.

EISENHOWER, General Dwight David, Assistant Chief of Staff in charge of Operations Division, Officer of US Chief of Staff until June 1942; Commanding General, European Theatre, until November 1942; C in C Allied Forces, North Africa.

FADDEN, A. W., Australian Prime Minister, 25 August 1941 until October 1941.

FREYBERG, Sir Bernard Cyril, VC, GOC New Zealand Forces, November 1939 to 1945; Commander of Imperial and Greek Troops in Crete, 1941.

GAULLE, Charles de, Under-Secretary of State for National Defence under Reynaud, June 1940; President of the (Free) French National Committee.

GEORGES, General Alphonse Joseph, French Army Commander North-East, May to June 1940. Friend of Churchill's.

GIRAUD, General Henri, Commander of French Forces in North Africa.

GOERING, Hermann Wilhelm, Reich Commissioner for Air.

GORT, General Lord, VC, Governor of Gibraltar until April 1942; Governor and C in C Malta.

GREENWOOD, Arthur, Minister without Portfolio, 11 May 1940 until 22 February 1942.

GRIGG, Sir James P., Permanent Under-Secretary of State for War, 26 October 1939 until 5 March 1942; became Secretary of State for War on 22 February 1942 until 1945.

HALDER, General Franz, Chief of Staff, German Army, until 24 September 1942.

HALIFAX, Lord Edward, Foreign Secretary until 22 December 1940, then Ambassador at Washington.

HANKEY, Lord, Minister without Portfolio until 11 May 1940, then Chancellor of Duchy of Lancaster until 20 July 1941; Paymaster General.

HARRIMAN, William Averell, special representative of President Roosevelt in Britain with rank of Minister from March 1941; representative in London of Combined Production and Resources Board from July 1942.

HESS, Rudolf, Nazi Party Deputy Leader. Flew to England, Spring 1941.

HITLER, Adolf, German Chancellor from 1933.

HOARE, Sir Samuel, Secretary of State for Air until 11 May 1940; British Ambassador at Madrid until end of war.

HOLLIS, General L. C., Senior Assistant Military Secretary to War Cabinet.

HOPKINS, Harry, Presidential special adviser and representative from January 1941.

HORE-BELISHA, Leslie, MP, Secretary of State for War in Chamberlain's Government from 1937 to 5 January 1940.

HULL, Cordell, American Secretary of State until 1944 when he resigned from ill health.

INONU, General Ismet, President of Turkish Republic, 1938 to 1950.

IRONSIDE, General Sir W. Edmund, CIGS until 10 June 1940, then C in C Home Forces, until 19 July 1940.

ISMAY, Major-General Sir Hastings L., Deputy Secretary (Military) to War Cabinet and Churchill's representative on COS Committee from 2 May 1940.

JACOB, Sir Ian, Assistant Military Secretary to War Cabinet.

JOUAN, Captain, Liaison officer between French Indo-China and Singapore.

KEITEL, Field Marshal Wilhelm, Chief of Supreme Command of German armed forces.

KENNEDY, Major-General Sir John Noble, Director of Military Operations, War Office 1940 to 1943.

KERR, Sir Archibald J. K. C., British Ambassador at Moscow from 4 February 1942.

KEYES, Admiral of the Fleet, Sir Roger, MP, Director, Combined Operations HQ, August 1940 to October 1941.

KING, Fleet Admiral Ernest J., Chief of US Naval Operations C in C US Fleet.

KING, Mackenzie, Canadian Prime Minister.

KURUSU, Saburo, Special Japanese envoy to Washington, 15 November to December 1941.

LAVAL, Pierre, Vichy Foreign Minister October 1940 (Baudouin) until 13 December 1940; returned as Foreign Minister and Prime Minister in April 1942.

LAYTON, Vice-Admiral Sir Geoffrey, C in C Eastern Fleet 11 December 1941 until 5 March 1942.

LEAHY, Fleet Admiral William D., American Ambassador to Vichy 1940 until May 1942, then Chief of Staff to President until 1949.

LINDEMANN, Professor F. A. (Lord Cherwell from 1942), scientific adviser to Prime Minister.

LINLITHGOW, Victor Marquis of, Viceroy of India 1936 to 1943.

LITVINOV, Maxim, Soviet Foreign Minister 1930 to 3 May 1939; Soviet Ambassador to Washington from November 1941.

LORAINE, Sir Percy, British Ambassador to Rome 1939 until withdrawal of mission, 11 June 1940.

LOTHIAN, Philip Kerr, Lord, British Ambassador at Washington 1939 until his death on 12 December 1940.

LYTTELTON, Oliver, President of Board of Trade from 3 October 1940 to 29 June 1941 (Duncan); Minister of State, Middle East, until 12 March 1942, when became Minister of Production (Beaverbrook had left the Ministry on 18 February).

MACARTHUR, General Douglas, Commanding General of the American Far East Command from July 1941; Supreme Commander, Far East.

MARSHALL-CORNWALL, General Sir James, Commander of British Forces in France in June 1940 after Dunkirk; Churchill's emissary to Turkish Government 1941; built El Alamein line 1942.

MAISKY, Ivan, Soviet Ambassador at London, 1932 to 1943.

MARSHALL, General George C., Chief of Staff, US Army, from 1931.

MATSUOKA, Yosuke, Japanese Foreign Minister, 1940 to 18 July 1941.

MENZIES, Robert Gordon, Australian Prime Minister and Minister for Defence Co-ordination, 1939 until 25 August 1941; opposition member of Advisory War Council 1941 to 1944.

MOLOTOV, Vyacheslav Mikhailovich, Soviet Foreign Minister, May 1939 to 1949.

MONNET, Jean, Chairman, Franco–British Economic Co-ordination Committee, 1939 to 1940; member, British Supply Council in Washington, 1940 to 1943.

MONTGOMERY, General (later Field Marshal) Bernard L., Commander, Southern Command from December 1941; Commander 8th Army from August 1942 to December 1943, then Commander 21 Army Group.

MOUNTBATTEN, Lord Louis (of Burma); Chief, Combined Operations, until October 1943.

MUSSOLINI, Benito, Italian Dictator from 1925 until 25 July 1943.

NICOLSON, Harold G., Parliamentary Secretary at Ministry of Information 17 May 1940 to 20 July 1941. Diarist.

NOMURA, Admiral Kichisaburo, Japanese Ambassador to Washington, February 1941 to December 1941.

ODEND'HAL, Admiral, Head of French Naval Mission to Britain, 1940.

PAGE, Sir Earle, Special Australian representative in London.

PAGET, General (later Sir) Bernard C. T., C in C designate to Far East 1941; instead C in C Home Forces 25 December 1941 until July 1943.

PAPAGOS, General (later Field Marshal) Alexander, commander of Greek armies, 1940 to 1941.

PERCIVAL, General A. E., GOC, Singapore, 1941.

PÉTAIN, Marshal Henri Phillippe, Vice-President of the French Council under Reynaud from 18 May 1940 to 16 June; French Premier in Vichy Government.

PHILLIPS, Rear-Admiral Tom, Vice-Chief of Naval Staff 1 June 1939 to 21 October 1941; then C in C Eastern Fleet until he was drowned in December 1941.

PLEVEN, René, member Anglo–French Co-ordination Committee, 1940; then Secretary-General of French Equatorial Africa.

PORTAL, Air Chief Marshal Sir Charles F. A., Chief of the Air Staff from 25 October 1940.

POUND, Admiral of the Fleet Sir Dudley, First Sea Lord and Chief of Naval Staff from 12 June 1939 to 15 October 1943.

POWNALL, Lieutenant-General Sir Henry R., Vice-CIGS from 19 May 1941 to 5 December 1941, then C in C Far East.

RAEDER, Admiral Erich, Chief of the German Naval Staff.

REYNAUD, Paul, French Premier from 21 March 1940 until 16 June 1940.

RIBBENTROP, Joachim von, ex-wine merchant; German Ambassador to London 1936 to 1938; Foreign Minister 1938 to 1945.

RITCHIE, General Neil, Deputy Chief of General Staff, Cairo, June to November 1941; Commander, 8th Army, until 25 June 1942.

ROMMEL, General (later Field Marshal) Irwin, Commander German forces in North Africa from February 1941, and later in Normany until July 1944.

ROOSEVELT, Franklin D., President of the United States.

SARAJOGLU, Sukru, Turkish Foreign Minister, 1938 to 1942.

SIGEMITSU, Namoru, Japanese Ambassador to London until December 1941.

SIMON, Sir John (later Lord), Chancellor of the Exchequer to 12 May 1940 when became Lord Chancellor.

SIMPSON, General Sir Frank, Director Military Operations War Office 1943 to 1945.

SINCLAIR, Sir Archibald, Secretary of State for Air from 11 May 1940.

SMUTS, Field Marshal Jan, Prime Minister of South Africa.

SOMERVILLE, Admiral Sir James F., Commander, Western Mediterranean 1940 to 1941; C in C Eastern Fleet from 5 March 1942.

SPEARS, General Edward, Military Liaison officer with de Gaulle.

STALIN, Generalissimo Joseph, Soviet leader and C in C.

STARK, Admiral Harold R., American Chief of Naval Operations.

STAUFFENBERG, Berthold von, senior German staff officer who headed the bomb plot to kill Hitler on 20 July 1944.

STIMSON, Henry L., American Secretary of State for War.

TEDDER, Air Marshal Sir Arthur W., AOC in C Middle East 1 June 1941 until 11 January 1943; then Deputy to Eisenhower at SHAEF.

THOMAS, Sir Shenton, Governor General Straits Settlement until February 1942.

TOJO, General Hideki, Japanese Prime Minister from 16 October 1941.

VANSITTART, Sir Robert G., Chief Diplomatic Adviser to Foreign Secretary until 25 June 1941.

WARDLAW-MILNE, Sir John, Conservative MP and Chairman of the all-party Finance Committee.

WAVELL, General Sir Archibald P., GOC in C Middle East until 5 July 1941; C in C India and Far East 21 June 1941 until 20 June 1943, ABDA commander December 1941 to February 1942. Later Viceroy of India.

WELLES, Summer, American Under-Secretary of State, 1937 to 1943.

WEYGAND, General Maxime, Minister of Defence under Pétain from 16 June to October 1940, then Delegate General, Algiers and C in C French Africa.

WILSON, General Sir Henry Maitland, Commander, British Army of the Nile, 1939 to 1940; GOC in C Cyrenaica, March 1941; and Commander of forces in Greece in the same month; Commander of Allied forces in Syria and Transjordan, summer 1941; GOC Persia-Iraq from December 1941; 16 February 1943 became GOC in C Middle East.

Index

Aachen, 299
Aaland Islands, 23
Aalesund, 40
Aandalsnes, 36–40
Abadan oil field, 133
Abbeville, 47
Abdication Crisis (1936), 4, 12, 339
Abdullah, Amir, Regent of Iraq, 108, 110
Abyssinia (Ethiopia), 4, 6, 85, 121
Accolade, Operation, 237, 238, 239, 242
Acheson, A. B., 42, 71, 72, 340
Adam, General Wilhelm, 12
El Adem, 137
Aden, 148
Admiralty: Churchill returns to, 14; phoney
    war, 20–1; Norwegian disaster, 22–7,
    34–6; and the French Fleet, 66, 68; loss
    of *Prince of Wales* and *Repulse*, 184; and
    the proposed Free Italian movement,
    228–9; and the Italian surrender, 230–1
Adriatic Sea, 224, 245, 269, 277
Aegean, 125, 172, 203, 221, 225, 237–45,
    248–9, 269, 345–6
Afrika Corps, 127
Agedabia, 141
Agheila *see* El Agheila
Ahrenstorm, Dr, 288
Air Ministry, 151, 228–9, 307
Ajeta, Marchese d', 233–4
Akyab, 202
Alamein *see* El Alamein
Albania, 87, 88, 250
Albert Canal, 293
Aldington libel case, 273
Alexander, A. V., 63–4, 67, 70
Alexander, General Sir Harold, 146, 214, 216,
    341; and Pantellaria project, 100–1;
    Churchill dominates, 101; Operation
    Pilgrim, 104; and the Italian surrender,
    234–5; and the Aegean, 242; and
    Yugoslavia, 250, 267, 271, 272–3; attack
    on Gothic Line, 268; Italian campaign,
    276, 284, 302; Normandy landings, 279

Alexandria, 39, 66, 67, 84, 97, 116, 127,
    135, 227, 228
Algeria, 67
Algiers, 67, 114, 176, 208, 210, 225, 312
Ali, Rashid, 108, 109–10, 118, 132
Aliakhmon line, 88, 89, 90
Allen, G. R., 173, 333
Alor Star, 181, 184–5
Alsace, 317
Altmark, 31
Altmayer, General, 54
Amboina, 203, 204
American, British, Dutch, Austrian Command
    (ABDA), 190–1, 193
Amery, Leo, 7, 10, 20, 43, 176, 197
AMGOT, 314, 315, 316, 317
Amiens, 47, 48
Anakim, Operation, 221
Anatolia, 134, 244
Andaman Islands, 203
Anderson, Sir John, 321, 329
Anet, General, 201–2
Anglo-German Naval Agreement (1935), 58
Ankara, 106, 107, 223
anthrax, 311–12
anti-Comintern Pact (1936), 147
Antigua, 76
Antwerp, 293, 299, 300
Anvil, Operation, 164, 248–9, 278–80
Anzio, 267, 281
Apennines, 267
Arabs, 229–30
Arakan coast, 202
Arcadia Conference (1941), 163–5
Archangel, 24, 131, 134
Arctic, 130, 168
Ardennes, 299, 300–1
Argentina, 79
Ark Royal, 25, 65, 69, 135
Armstrong, Brigadier, 257, 258–9, 260, 261,
    264–5, 273
Arnhem, 146, 205, 293, 299
Arnim, General von, 216, 217

Arras, 47, 48, 58
Arta, Gulf of, 87
Ashley Clarke, 152–3, 178
Asquith, H. H., 14, 345
Asquith, Violet, 9
Associated Press, 297
Athens, 87, 88, 94, 124, 274, 275
Atlantic, Battle of (1940), 81, 82, 100
Atlantic Charter (1941), 79–81, 198, 293, 333, 334
Atlantic Conference (1941), 342–3
atom bombs, 162, 311, 320–3, 326, 328, 329–31, 348
Attlee, Clement, 4, 61, 71, 180, 312; Munich Crisis, 9; and Churchill's political exile, 11; and the Norwegian disaster, 31; refuses to support Chamberlain, 44; in Churchill's War Cabinet, 48; Pantellaria project, 100; attitude to Stalin, 129; enquiry into tank deficiencies, 142; and the fall of Singapore, 189–90; and Indian independence, 198; Far Eastern campaign, 204; and El Alamein, 214; Casablanca Conference, 220–3; and Churchill's Turkish proposal, 223; and Yugoslavia, 273; and German dissidents, 290; Potsdam Conference, 328, 332, 337–8; Japanese surrender terms, 329; and the atom bomb, 329
Auchinleck, General Sir Claude, 108, 109, 133, 177, 214, 243; takes over from Wavell, 83, 123; 128; Western Desert campaign, 92, 134–46, 207; Churchill's peremptory treatment of, 136–46, 341, 343; fall of Tobruk, 137–44; success at Alamein, 144–5; dismissal, 146; Malayan campaign, 190
Augusta, USS, 79
Auphan, Admiral, 64
Auschwitz concentration camp, 347
Australia, 151, 180; and outbreak of war, 17; Greek campaign, 96, 97; and the Malayan campaign, 189–91; and the fall of Singapore, 193–4, 195; refuses to send troops to Burma, 196; Japanese threat, 201, 207, 319; attack on Amboina, 203, 204
Austria, 6–7, 164, 232, 250, 269, 270, 271–3
Avranches, 286
Azores, 103

Badoglio, Field Marshal, 226, 231–2, 233–6, 245, 252
Badouin, Paul, 60, 63, 68
Baghdad, 108, 109–10
Bahamas, 76
Bailey, Colonel, 252, 253, 254, 260
Bajpai, Sir Girja Shankar, 198
Baku, 30, 32, 33
Baldwin, Stanley, 3–4, 5, 11, 48, 58–9, 79, 197

Balfour, Arthur, 274
Balfour Declaration (1917), 8
Balkan Pact, 107
Balkans, 89–91, 106, 129, 150, 219, 225, 245–6, 334, 338
Ball, Sir Joseph, 12, 18
Baltic Sea, 22–4, 25–8, 35
Baltic states, 20, 129–30, 332–4
Bardia, 86, 121
Bardufoss aerodrome, 36
Barents Sea, 168
Barham, 70
Bari, 264, 265
Barre, General, 212
Bartlett, Vernon, 10
Baruch, Bernard, 9
Basra, 108, 133
Bastianini, Guiseppe, 49, 232–3
Bathurst, 222
Battle of Britain (1940), 11, 74, 82, 100
Battleaxe, Operation, 124, 127–9, 137
Bayeux, 316–17
BBC, 111, 114, 145, 255, 257, 258, 281
Beaverbrook, Lord, 9, 149, 163, 217; Abdication crisis, 4; peace proposals, 19–20; Dunkirk evacuation, 48; Pantellaria project, 100; fall of Tobruk, 140; Dieppe raid, 173
Beck, General, 288, 290
Bedell Smith, General, 235–6, 278, 294, 295, 317
BEF see British Expeditionary Force
Belgium, 15, 17; peace moves, 18; Germany invades, 44, 46; capitulates, 47, 49; liberation, 293; Ardennes offensive, 299
Belgrade, 91, 93, 250, 274
Bell, George, Bishop of Chichester, 287–9
Bell, Captain L. H., 184
Bengal, 201
Bengal, Bay of, 201, 203, 207, 320
Benghazi, 86, 87, 91–3, 107, 121, 126, 129, 135, 137, 193, 210, 301
Berane, 255
Bérenger, Admiral, 152
Bergen, 28, 31, 33, 34–5, 36, 41
Bergonzoli, General, 230
Berio, Alberto, 234
Berlin, 10, 290–1, 301, 302–6, 307, 347
Bermuda, 76
Berne, 252, 286
Berry, Colonel, 141
Besançon, 58
Bessarabia, 129
Bethouard, General, 210
Bevan, Aneurin, 140
Bevan, Colonel John, 331
Beveridge Report, 46, 297
Bevin, Ernest, 8, 121, 129, 273, 314; in Churchill's Cabinet, 46, 339; and the

Atlantic Charter, 80; Potsdam
  Conference, 328, 332, 337–8
Biddle, Eric, 64
Bierut, Boleslav, 334
biological warfare, 311–12
Bir Hacheim, 137
Bismarck, 65, 96
Bizerta, 67, 210, 212, 216
Black Sea, 219, 247
Blackshirt Movement, 4
Blake, Admiral Sir Geoffrey, 42, 72
Bletchley Park, 126
Blida, 210
Blumentritt, General, 291
Bodrum, 248
Boisson, Pierre, 70, 209, 211, 313
Bolero, Operation, 163, 167, 170, 218, 221
Bone, 208, 210, 212, 344
Bonham Carter, Violet, 8
Bonhoeffer, Dietrich, 287, 288, 289
Boothby, Robert, 7
Bordeaux, 60, 63, 64, 67
Borneo, 195, 203
Bornholm Channel, 23
Bosnia-Hercegovina, 250, 251
Bosphorus, 247
Bothnia, Gulf of, 22, 25, 28, 37
Boughey, Peter, 252
Bougie, 212
Boulogne, 166
Bourne, General Alan, 98
Boyle, Andrew, 253–4
Bracken, Brendan, 7, 9, 116, 295
Bradley, General, 278, 283, 284, 286, 304
Brest, 180
Brevity, Operation, 127
Briare, 58
Bridges, Edward, 45, 142–3, 310
Bridgwater by-election (1938), 10
Brighton, 74
Brimstone, Operation, 220–1
Brindisi, 124
Brisk, Operation, 103
British Empire, 165
British Expeditonary Force (BEF), 46–8, 49,
  51, 52, 55, 56–7, 58, 340
British Guiana, 76
Brittany, 54–5, 56, 60, 280, 286
Brockett, Lord, 18
Bromley, 309
Brooke, General Sir Alan, 163, 167, 169–70,
  245, 267, 279, 300, 318; and the fall of
  France, 54, 55–6, 57; Western Desert
  campaign, 135–40, 145–6; and the
  Dieppe raid, 173; criticism of Churchill,
  176, 261; meetings with Stalin, 177; and
  the fall of Singapore, 189; Far Eastern
  campaign, 204; and El Alamein, 214–15;
  Mediterranean strategy, 217, 224;
  Casablanca Conference, 220; and the

attack on Rhodes, 241; and Yugoslavia,
  269; Normandy landings, 276, 281–2,
  283–5; on the Italian campaign, 277;
  Ardennes offensive, 300–1; Operation
  Plunder, 301–2; and the atomic bombing
  of Japan, 326
Brook-Popham, Air Chief Marshal Sir Robert,
  151, 179, 180, 188, 190
Bruce, Stanley, 50
Brussels, 293, 299, 300
Buccaneer, Operation, 203
Buccleuch, Duke of, 18
Buffalo aircraft, 151
Bug, River, 334
Bukovina, 129
Bulgaria, 89, 107, 240, 244, 250, 334, 337
Bulge, Battle of the (1945), 301, 317–18, 347
Burma, 178, 185, 191, 193, 195, 196, 202–3,
  205, 221, 319
Burma road, 148, 149, 153, 156, 193, 202
Butcher, Captain Henry, 286
Butler, J. R. M., 28, 41
Butler, Neville, 115
Butler, R. A., 13, 17, 29, 45, 75–6, 149
Byrnes, James, 323, 324, 326, 329, 332, 336,
  337, 348

Cabinet Office, 330, 340
Cadogan, Sir Alexander, 6–7, 17, 19, 49,
  50–1, 107, 112, 113, 115, 121, 122, 129,
  162, 179, 203, 233, 253, 282, 288–9,
  294, 295, 324, 327
Caen, 283, 284–5, 286
Cairo, 84, 106, 126, 137, 145, 207, 214, 243,
  245
Calais, 55, 167, 284
Cambodia, 154
Campbell, Sir Ronald Hugh, 34, 59, 60, 63,
  233–4
Campioni, Admiral Inigo, 239
Camranh Bay, 153
Canada, 17, 171, 173
Canary Islands, 103, 104
Cape Town, 101
Capuzzo, 127
Carboni, General, 235
Carinthia, 272
Carlton Club, 330
Carthage, 249
Casablanca, 67, 71, 103, 210, 211
Casablanca Conference (1943), 216–17,
  218–23, 227, 312, 344–5, 347
Caserta, 265, 268
Casey, Richard, 137, 144, 145, 215
Caspian Sea, 30
Cassibile, 235
Cassino, 284
Castellano, General, 235, 236
Castelrizo, 102–3, 244
Catalina flying boats, 80

Catania, 276
Catapult, Operations, 67, 71
Catherine, Operation, 22–8, 31
Catholic Church, 78, 289
Catroux, General, 114, 121–2, 152, 313
Caucasus, 134, 177, 207
Cavendish Bentinck, William (Duke of
    Portland), 130, 331
Caviglia, Field Marshal, 231–2, 252
Cavour, Count Camillo di, 61
Cetniks, 251–4, 256–8, 260, 264, 265, 266,
    270
Ceylon, 201, 204
Chamberlain, Sir Austen, 4, 5–6
Chamberlain, Neville: recalls Churchill to
    Cabinet, 3; and occupation of Rhineland,
    5; and the Anschluss, 6; Cabinet, 6;
    Munich Agreement, 7, 9–10, 11, 12;
    Sudetenland crisis, 9–11; Polish
    guarantee, 11, 20; tries to discredit
    Churchill, 12–13; outbreak of war,
    13–14, 15–17; peace moves, 18–19, 30,
    48, 50; Norwegian disaster, 25, 28–31,
    34–6, 37–9, 43–4; resignation, 44, 339;
    in Churchill's War Cabinet, 48; and the
    Dunkirk evacuation, 48; and the fall of
    France, 58; proposed Anglo-French
    union, 59; defeatism, 75; and India, 197
Channel Islands, 103, 221
Charing Cross, 310
Chartwell, Kent, 8, 9, 129
Chasseurs Alpins, 37, 71
Chatfield, Lord, 16–17, 35, 175
Chautemps, Camille, 60
chemical warfare, 308–9, 311–12
Chequers, 167
Cherbourg, 56–7, 67, 167, 170, 221, 281, 283,
    284
Cherwell, Lord (Professor Lindemann), 20,
    296, 311, 321, 329, 347
Chevalier, Jacques, 117
Chiang Kai-shek, 147–8, 156–7, 158, 198,
    204, 205
Chicago Daily News, 116
Chiefs of Staff Committee, 45–6, 98
China, 147–8, 156–8, 327
Chindits, 203
Chungking, 147–8
Churchill, Clementine, 8–9, 46, 201, 278, 317
Churchill, Randolph, 4, 8–9, 76, 260, 261–2,
    264, 265
Churchill, Winston: political exile, 3–14;
    relations with Eden, 7, 12; financial
    problems, 8, 9; marriage, 8–9; outbreak
    of war, 13–14; phoney war, 14, 15–21,
    345; Norwegian disaster, 22–42, 43–4;
    becomes Prime Minister, 44–5; direct
    control of conduct of war, 45–6;
    Germany attacks France, 46–7; Dunkirk
    evacuation, 47–8, 53, 55; maintains

British morale, 48; War Cabinet, 48; and
    proposed approach to Mussolini, 49–51;
    and the fall of France, 53–62; proposed
    Anglo-French union, 59–61; and the
    French Fleet, 63–9, 71–3, 340–1; Dakar
    operation, 69–70; vets official histories,
    72, 340; Battle of Britain, 74; popularity,
    74, 176–7; relationship with Roosevelt,
    75, 164–6, 247; American warships,
    76–7; Lend-Lease, 77–8; meeting with
    Roosevelt, 78–81; North African
    campaign, 82–7, 91–3; Greek campaign,
    87–97, 274–5; Keyes' influence on,
    98–106; wants to bring Turkey into war,
    106–8, 131, 223–4, 237, 238, 245–6,
    247–9; and Iraq, 108–10; negotiations
    with Vichy France, 111–21, 341; relations
    with de Gaulle, 121, 201–2, 208–9,
    312–15, 317–18; and Syria, 121–5;
    Western Desert campaign, 126–9,
    134–46; and the German invasion of
    Russia, 129–32; and Persia, 132–4; fall of
    Tobruk, 137–44; and weaknesses of
    British Army, 139–43, 185, 187–8, 343;
    threat from Japan, 147–60; and
    Indo-China, 152–3; America enters war,
    160–2, 163; Arcadia Conference, 163–5;
    Jupiter plan, 166–7; plans European
    invasion, 167–8; plans North African
    landings, 169–70; Dieppe raid, 171–4;
    criticism of his handling of war, 174–6;
    meetings with Stalin, 177; and Pearl
    Harbor, 178; Far Eastern campaign, 180,
    203–6; loss of Prince of Wales and Repulse,
    184–5; Malayan campaign, 185–96; fall
    of Singapore, 187–95; first heart attack,
    190; and India, 197–202; Operation
    Torch, 207–13; and El Alamein, 213–16;
    Casablanca Conference, 216–17, 218–33,
    227; Mediterranean strategy, 217–19,
    224–5, 226; Trident Conference, 224–5;
    Quebec Conference, 226; proposed Free
    Italian movement, 227–30; Italian
    surrender, 230–6, 237; and the Aegean,
    237–45, 248–9; Teheran Conference,
    245–8, 334; and Yugoslavia, 250,
    253–73; pneumonia, 261, 278; Italian
    campaign, 276–7; Normandy landings,
    276, 277–86; tiredness, 281–2; and the
    flying bombs, 284, 307–12; and German
    dissidents, 286–93; terms for German
    surrender, 294–9; Ardennes offensive,
    300–1; Operation Plunder, 301–2; and
    capture of Berlin, 303–6; 1945 General
    Election, 303, 324, 328, 332, 337;
    considers use of chemical and biological
    weapons, 308–9, 311–12; and de
    Gaulle's return to France, 316–17; and
    the atom bomb, 321–2, 326, 328, 329;
    Japanese surrender terms, 323–7,

329–31; Potsdam Conference, 324, 331–4, 335–8; and the Baltic States, 332–4; achievements, 339–48

Ciano, Count, 84

Cicero (spy), 106

Citrine, Walter, 8

Civil Service, 45

Clark, General Mark, 277, 278

Clark, Norman, 138

Clemenceau, Georges, 297

Clyde, River, 104, 163, 224

Coastal Command, 80

Cobra, Operation, 284, 285, 286

Cochin-China, 152, 154

Cohen, Michael, 347

Collet, Colonel, 124

Colville, Sir John, 18, 20, 30, 44, 45, 55, 59, 95, 98, 115, 296, 324, 337

Combined Operations, 98–9

Commandos, 102, 104

Committee for the Co-ordination of Allied Supplies, 133

Commonwealth, 79, 199

Communism, 129; in post-war Europe, 306, 336, 348; in Yugoslavia, 250–4, 256, 259–60; in Greece, 274–5

Compass, Operation, 84–6, 106

Concarneau, 60

Confederation of Free French Equatorial African States, 71

Conservative Parliamentary Foreign Affairs Committee, 5–6

Conservative Party: Churchill's political exile, 3–4; peace moves, 18; and the Norwegian disaster, 43–4

Conty (Vichy official in Syria), 122

Cooper, Duff, 10, 119, 185–6, 187–8, 192, 315, 316

Coral Sea, Battle of (1942), 319

Corbin, Charles, 33, 34, 35

Cork, Admiral the Earl of, 23, 24, 25, 26, 30–1, 39–40

Cornwall, General Marshall, 53–5, 56–8, 106–8

Cornwallis, Sir K., 108

Corsica, 345

Cos, 94, 239–40, 243–4, 345–6

Cotentin peninsula, 57

Courseulles, 315–16

Craigie, Sir Robert, 148, 149, 152, 155, 156, 158, 161–2, 343

Crete, 27, 87, 93–7, 101, 103, 108, 109, 128, 151, 238, 274

Creuilly, 316

Crimea, 130

Cripps, Sir Stafford: negotiations with Russians, 32, 129–30, 131, 132; and Western Desert campaign, 136; criticism of Churchill, 175, 176; and the fall of Singapore, 195; and Indian

independence, 198–200, 202, 346; and German dissidents, 287; and terms for German surrender, 294

Croatia, 250, 253, 254

Croats, 250, 251

Cromwell, Oliver, 43

Crosby, Sir Josiah, 149, 152, 179–80

Crossbow, 307–12

Cruickshank, Charles, 310

Crusader, Operation, 92, 134–5, 141

Crusader tanks, 141–2

Culverin, Operation, 203–4

Cunningham, General Sir Alan, 90, 95–6, 99, 102–3, 106, 135, 204, 279, 342

Cunningham, Admiral Andrew, 68, 69, 83, 284, 340, 341

Cunningham, Admiral John, 69, 70, 72, 243

Curtin, John, 189–90, 191, 193–4

Curzon, Lord, 246

Curzon Line, 246–7, 295

Cyprus, 134, 223

Cyrenaica, 91, 92, 93, 94, 97, 126, 135–6, 227, 228–30

Czechoslovakia, 6–7, 9–12, 338

D-Day (Normandy landings), 276, 277–86

Dahlerus, Berger, 13

Daily Express, 9, 19, 48

Daily Mirror, 215

Dakar, 68, 69–70, 72, 111, 115, 118, 121–2, 148, 201, 207, 209, 313

Daladier, Edouard, 16, 30, 31, 32, 33, 37–8, 61

Dalmatia, 250

Dalton, Hugh, 5, 11, 51, 176, 228

Damaskinos, Archbishop, 275

Danzig, 13

Dardanelles, 24, 27, 38–9, 225, 237, 240, 244, 246, 247–9, 345

Darlan, Admiral J. F., 53, 63–8, 69, 86, 113, 153, 209, 210–12, 213, 312, 341

Darnley, Earl of, 18

Davies, Clement, 140

Davies, Lord, 227–8

Davis, Joseph E., 336

De Gaulle, General Charles: proposed Anglo-French union, 59–60; and the Mers-el-Kebir attack, 68; Dakar operation, 69–71; Churchill's negotiations with Vichy, 111–15, 118; relations with Churchill, 121, 201–2, 208–9, 312–15, 317–18; and Syria, 122, 124–5; and Indo-China, 152, 154; and Madagascar, 201–2; and North Africa, 207–11; return to France, 315–17; Battle of the Bulge, 317–18

Deakin, Sir William, 255, 257, 259–60, 261, 265

Deceptionists, 309–10, 330–1

Decoux, Admiral, 152–3, 154, 201, 206

Defence Committee, 85, 150, 175; and the fall of France, 53, 54; Greek campaign, 97; opposition to Pantellaria project, 99–101; and Persia, 133; and El Alamein, 215; and Mediterranean strategy, 218

de Lattre Tassigny, General, 217

Denham, Captain Harold, 35, 231

Denmark, 17, 24, 35

Dentz, General Henri, 118, 122–4, 134

Derrien, Admiral, 212

Derry, T. K., 28, 41, 42

Diego Suarez, 148, 201–2

Dieppe, 54, 170–4, 175, 346

Dijon, 60

Dilks, Professor, 330

Dill, General Sir John, 86, 91, 135, 163, 190–1; Dunkirk evacuation, 47; fall of France, 56; Churchill's Massawa plan, 57–8; and Churchill's treatment of Wavell, 82, 85, 128; and the Greek campaign, 87–90, 93–4; opposition to Pantellaria project, 99–100; and Turkey, 106; and Syria, 123; Mediterranean strategy, 217

Dippold, General, 252

Djibouti, 49, 148

Djilas, Milovan, 252

Dodecanese islands, 91, 99, 106, 108, 150, 223, 237, 238, 240, 244, 248

Doleby, Major, 239

Dombás, 37

Donovan, General, 264, 324–5

Dormer, Sir C., 32, 35–6

Dowding, Air Chief Marshal Hugh, 46

Dresden, 304

Drina, River, 257

Duala, 115

Dubrovnik, 257, 269

Dugdale, Baffy, 4

Dulles, 289

Dulwich, 310

Dunkerque, 68, 73

Dunkirk, 16, 47–8, 49, 52, 53, 55, 64, 68, 215, 280, 292, 340

Dunkirk, 65

Dupuy, Pierre, 114–18, 121, 122

Durban, 180

Durent, River, 55

E-boats, 99

EAM (National Liberation Front), 274, 275

East Africa, 85, 86–7, 91

East Prussia, 246, 247, 293, 295, 334

Eastern Europe, 332, 334–5, 337–8

The Economist, 140, 201–2

EDAS, 274

Eden, Sir Anthony, 58–9, 82–3; and occupation of Rhineland, 5; resignation from Chamberlain's Cabinet, 6–7; relations with Churchill, 7, 12; Munich Crisis, 9; and Churchill's political exile, 11; and outbreak of war, 16; fall of France, 55–6; becomes Foreign Secretary, 78; and the Atlantic Charter, 80; Operation Compass, 84–5; Greek campaign, 88–90, 341; Pantellaria project, 99–100; Churchill dominates, 101; visits to Turkey, 107; and Churchill's negotiations with Vichy, 117, 119–20; and Syria, 122, 124–5; and the German invasion of Russia, 130; Far Eastern policy, 149; and American entry into war, 162; wants to be Minister of Defence, 174–5; criticism of Churchill, 176; fall of Singapore, 195; Far Eastern campaign, 204; and Churchill's relations with de Gaulle, 208–9; and El Alamein, 214–15; and Churchill's Turkish proposal, 223; proposed Free Italian movement, 227–30; and the Italian surrender, 232–3, 234; Aegean campaign, 244; Teheran Conference, 246; and Yugoslavia, 260–4, 266, 270, 271, 273; Normandy landings, 281, 284; and German dissidents, 286–7, 289–90; terms for German surrender, 294–6, 298; and de Gaulle, 312–15; and the atom bomb, 322; Japanese surrender terms, 323–8, 330–1; and the Baltic States, 333–4; Potsdam Conference, 337; Suez Crisis, 44, 76

Eden, Simon, 324

Edward VIII, King, 4

Egypt, 82, 83, 84, 91–2, 124, 137, 229–30

Ehrman, John, 330

Eighth Army, 137–9, 141, 143–4, 145–6, 163, 213–15, 236, 250, 266, 267–8, 271–2, 276, 277

Eisenhower, General Dwight David, 146, 205; Operation Torch, 170, 208, 211, 212, 216; Sicilian campaign, 224, 225–6; and the Italian surrender, 233–5; and Accolade, 237, 238; and the Aegean, 240–3; and Yugoslavia, 272; Normandy landings, 276, 277–8, 281–6; supports Operation Anvil, 279; terms for German surrender, 294, 295–6, 298–9; Ardennes offensive, 300–1; quarrel with Montgomery, 300, 301; Operation Plunder, 301–2; and capture of Berlin, 302–6; German surrender, 306; objections to chemical and biological weapons, 311; meeting with de Gaulle, 314; Battle of the Bulge, 317–18, 347

ELAS (People's Liberation Army), 274, 275

El Alamein, 138, 144–5, 176, 186, 213–16, 280, 341

Elbe River, 304

El Agheila, 91, 135, 138, 141, 216

Enigma, 126, 253, 256–7

Epirus, 87

Epping, 10
Equatorial Africa, 69–71
Eritrea, 57, 86, 87, 229
Esche, Dr Udo, 291
L'Espérance, 148
Esteva, Admiral, 209, 212
Estonia, 20, 129, 332–4
Ethiopia see Abyssinia

Fadden, A. W., 189
Far Eastern Foreign Policy Committee, 149
Farouk, King of Egypt, 229
Fashoda Incident (1898), 313
Faulds, L. H., 162, 322
Fehmarn, 23
Fernet, Admiral, 112
Finland, 25, 27, 30–2, 131–2, 168
Finnish Expeditionary Force, 31
First World War, 22, 23–4, 48, 237, 280, 290
Fisher, Lord, 23–4, 27
Fiume, 234, 268
Flandin, Pierre-Etienne, 117, 313
Fleming, Peter, 331
Fletcher, Commander Reginald, 18
Florina, 92
Floyd, Brigadier, 269
Floyd Force, 269
flying bombs, 307–12, 347
Focus, 7–8, 9
Foggia, 277
Forbes, Admiral Sir Charles, 35
Force Z, 181–4
Foreign Legion, 71, 124
Foreign Office: and Poland, 20; confidence in
    final victory, 74; dislikes Churchill's
    friendship with Roosevelt, 75; and de
    Gaulle, 112, 114; and Churchill's
    negotiations with Vichy, 120; and Syria,
    122; German invasion of Russia, 130; and
    Indo-China, 152, 154, 155; and Pearl
    Harbor, 178; and Italy, 228–9, 231–2,
    233; and Yugoslavia, 253, 254, 256,
    257–8, 260–2, 266, 269; German
    dissidents, 286–7, 288–9; terms for
    German surrender, 284, 296, 297; de
    Gaulle's return to France, 316–17;
    Japanese surrender terms, 322–3, 324–7;
    and the Baltic States, 333
Forgiero, General, 239
Formosa, 158
Fortune, General, 54, 55
Fougère, General, 122
France: and occupation of Rhineland, 5;
    Churchill's admiration for French Army,
    12; and invasion of Poland, 15–16; and
    the Norwegian disaster, 30, 32, 37–8;
    Germany attacks, 46–9; Dunkirk
    evacuation, 47–8, 53; fall of, 53–62;
    proposed Anglo-French union, 59–61;
    armistice, 61, 63, 65, 67, 69; Fleet, 63–9,

71–3, 112, 113, 117, 121, 152–3, 211,
    213, 340–1; planned landings in, 166,
    167–8; Dieppe raid, 171–4; and
    Indo-China, 206; Normandy landings,
    221–2, 276, 277–86; Operation Anvil,
    278–80; de Gaulle's return to, 315–17;
    Battle of the Bulge, 317–18; liberation of
    Paris, 317; atom bomb research, 320–1;
    see also Free French; Vichy France
Franco, General, 61, 208
Franco-Soviet Pact (1936), 5
Frankfurter, Felix, 115
Free French: capture Massawa, 58; Dakar
    operation, 69–71; and Churchill's
    negotiations with Vichy, 111–15, 118;
    Churchill improves relations with, 121;
    and Syria, 122–5; and Madagascar,
    201–2; and North Africa, 208–11;
    Churchill's relations with de Gaulle,
    312–15
Free Yugoslav Radio, 269
Freeman, Simon, 253
French Committee of National Liberation
    (FNCL), 314, 317
French Equatorial Africa, 113
French National Committee, 312–13
French War Committee, 33, 48–9
Freyberg, General B. C., 94, 96
Fulford, Air Marshal, 195

Gabon, 113, 115
Gallipoli, 14, 39, 237, 245, 345
Gallivare, 28–9, 30
Gallup Polls, 74
Gambia, 222
Gamelin, General, 15, 16–17, 38, 58
Gandhi, Mahatma, 197, 199, 202, 346–7
Garibaldi, Giuseppe, 61–2
Garibaldi Legion, 227, 228
gas, poison, 308–9, 311–12, 347
Gascoigne, A. D. F., 111
Gävle, 23, 25
Gazala Line, 137, 138
General Elections: December 1918, 303;
    November 1935, 4; July 1945, 273, 324,
    325, 328, 330, 332, 337, 348
General Strike (1926), 11
Geneva, 289
Gensoul, Admiral, 66, 67–8, 72, 73, 117
Gentilhomme, General, 202
George II, King of Greece, 88, 274, 275
George VI, King of England, 18, 44, 162,
    222–3, 281, 282
Georges, General, 56
German Protestant Church, 287, 289
Germany: rearmament, 4, 6, 11–12;
    occupation of Rhineland, 5; Anschluss,
    6–7; Munich Agreement, 7, 9–10;
    Sudetenland crisis, 9–11; occupies
    Czechoslovakia, 11; invades Poland, 13,

German Protestant Church – *cont'd*.
15–17; non-aggression pact with Russia, 13;
and peace moves, 18–19; and the
Norwegian disaster, 22–42, 43–4;
invades Low Countries, 44, 46; fall of
France, 46–9, 54–62; French armistice,
63, 65, 67, 69; and the French Fleet,
63–5, 67; calls off invasion of Britain, 74;
invades Russia, 78, 122, 124, 129–32,
177, 342; sinks American ships, 81; North
African campaign, 86, 91–3, 126–8,
134–46; attacks Greece, 87–97, 101–2;
and Iraq, 108–10; and Syria, 122–3;
Enigma code decyphered, 126;
community in Persia, 132–3; control of
Eastern Mediterranean, 135; declares war
on America, 160–1; Allied landings in
Europe planned, 167; Dieppe raid,
171–2; defeat in Europe, 205; Operation
Torch, 207–13, 216; attacks Toulon, 213;
defeat at El Alamein, 213–16; Sicilian
campaign, 225; strengthens Italy, 233;
and the Italian surrender, 235–6; defence
of Rhodes, 239; and the Aegean, 240–5;
Teheran Conference proposals, 247; and
Yugoslavia, 250–8, 265, 268, 270–1;
driven out of Italy, 276–7; Normandy
landings, 280–6, 291, 298; dissidents,
286–93; terms for surrender, 293–9;
Ardennes offensive, 300–1; surrenders,
306; flying bombs, 307–12; and the Baltic
states, 332; Anglo-American occupation, 334
Germersheim, 33
Gestapo, 288, 291
Giant Two, Operation, 235
Gibraltar, 49, 66, 100, 208, 210
Gilbert, Martin, 28, 340
Giraud, General, 210, 211, 312–13
Gisevius, Hans-Bernd, 289
Glen Line, 27, 101, 102, 103
Gneisenau, 180
Godesberg ultimatum (1938), 11
Godfroy, Admiral, 116
Goebbels, Joseph, 70, 288, 290, 293–9, 308,
347
Goerdeler, Carl, 288, 290
Goering, Hermann, 13, 17, 18, 29–30, 288
'Golden Square', 108
Goodwood, Operation, 284, 285
Goree Island, 70
Gort, General Lord, 17, 46, 47, 53, 58
Gothic Line, 267, 268
Gott, General, 145–6
Grandi, Dino, 233
Grant, Admiral John, 26
Grant tanks, 137
Graziani, Marshal, 82, 84, 227
Great Bitter Lake, 102
Greece, 86, 125, 126; Italy attacks, 84;
Germany attacks, 87–97, 101–2; assault

on Kasos, 101–3; Communists removed
from, 273–5
Greenwood, Arthur, 31, 48, 292
Greer, USS, 81
Grew, Joseph, 149, 155, 156, 158, 322–3,
324–5, 343, 348
Grigg, John, 224, 302, 344
Gruinard Island, 311
Gubbins, Colin, 15
Guderian, 47
Guingand, General de, 301
Gustavus V, King of Sweden, 31
Gymnast, Operation, 166, 167, 169–70

Haakon VII, King of Norway, 35
Habbaniya, 108–9, 110
Haig, Field Marshal, 340, 341
Halfaya Pass, 127
Halifax, Lord Edward, 17; Sudetenland crisis,
10; Polish guarantee, 11; outbreak of war,
13; peace moves, 18–19, 29–30, 48–52;
and the Norwegian disaster, 23, 25,
28–30; and Chamberlain's resignation,
44, 339; in Churchill's War Cabinet, 48;
and the fall of France, 59; proposed
Anglo-French union, 59, 60; and the
French armistice, 63; defeatism, 75–6;
dislikes Churchill's friendship with
Roosevelt, 75; becomes Ambassador to
America, 78; and the Atlantic Charter,
80–1; Pantellaria project, 99–100;
negotiations with Vichy France, 111,
113–18; and Churchill's Far Eastern
strategy, 156; terms for German
surrender, 296–7; Japanese surrender
terms, 325–6
Hamburg, 307
Hamilton, Duchess of, 27
Hamilton, Miss J., 235
Hamilton, Nigel, 283
Hammer, Operation, 36, 37, 38
Hammerstein, Colonel General von, 288
Hancock, Patrick, 288
Hankey, Lord, 133, 175–6
Hanoi, 148, 153
Harare, 91
Hardanger Fjord, 41
Harding, Field Marshal Lord, 215, 268, 280
Harriman, Averil, 177, 198
Harris, Air Chief Marshal Sir Arthur, 282
Harvey, Oliver, 6, 51, 80, 119, 176, 315,
330–1
Hassell, Ulrich von, 293
Hawaii, 178, 319
Hayter, Sir William, 155, 157
Healey, Denis, 254
Heligoland, 35
Helleu, Jean, 313
Hercules, Operation, 248–9
Hereward, 102

Hess, Rudolf, 130
Himmler, Heinrich, 288
Hirohito, Emperor of Japan, 147, 155, 159, 161, 178, 320, 322–8, 330, 331
Hiroshima, 162, 329, 331
Hitler, Adolf: occupies Rhineland, 5; Anschluss, 6–7; rearmament, 6; appeasement, 7–8; Munich Agreement, 9–10, 12, 30; Sudetenland crisis, 10; Godesberg ultimatum, 11; occupies Czechoslovakia, 11; invades Poland, 13, 15–17; non-aggression pact with Russia, 13; and peace moves, 18–19; Norwegian disaster, 35, 38, 43–4; ruthlessness, 38; invades Low Countries, 44; proposed peace offers, 49–51; and the French Fleet, 67, 69; calls off invasion of Britain, 74; sinks American ships, 81; North African campaign, 86, 209, 211, 216, 217; attacks Greece, 87, 96; attacks Yugoslavia, 91; invades Russia, 122, 124, 129–30; and Japanese entry into war, 159; declares war on America, 160–1, 343; Arnhem operation, 205; attacks Toulon, 213; defeat at El Alamein, 215; strengthens Italy, 233; and Yugoslavia, 250–1, 256–7; German opposition to, 286–93; Stauffenberg bomb plot, 286, 290–2; Churchill fears Stalin will make separate peace with, 292, 333; Normandy landings, 298
Hoare, Sir Samuel, 7, 29, 114
Hoesch, Leopold von, 5
Hogg, Quintin (Lord Hailsham), 10, 293
Holland see Netherlands
Holland, Captain, 67–8, 72, 73
Hollis, General, 98, 105
Home, Lord, 5–6
Home Defence Committee, 309
Hong Kong, 148, 178, 195
Hopkins, Harry, 78, 79, 153, 165, 167, 169, 199–201, 297, 313–14
Hore Belisha, Leslie, 140
Houffalize, 301
House of Commons: Norway debate, 43–4; and the Mers-el-Kebir attack, 69; Crete debate, 97; and Churchill's negotiations with Vichy, 119–20; fall of Tobruk, 139, 140–1; Dieppe raid, 173; debate on Malaya, 193; hostility to Darlan, 212; and German dissidents, 290, 293
House of Lords, 175–6
Hoyer Millar, Sir Frederick, 121
Hudson, Major, 251
Hull, Cordell, 79, 208; on closure of Burma road, 148, 149; hopes to keep Japan out of war, 153–9, 161; ultimatum to Japanese, 157, 159; and Pearl Harbor, 178; and the Italian surrender, 231–2; terms for German surrender, 297; illness,

305; Japanese surrender terms, 326; retirement, 332, 348
Hungary, 20, 91, 131–2, 164, 240, 270, 334, 337
Hunter, Major, 255
Huntziger, General, 116, 124
Hurricane aircraft, 131, 194–5
Husky, Operation, 220–1, 224, 225, 237

Ibar, River, 260
Iceland, 78, 80, 81
Imperator, Operation, 170
Independent Labour Party (ILP), 19, 193
India, 79, 133; moves towards independence, 3–4, 164, 197–201, 339, 346–7; Free French in, 115; Japanese threat to, 201, 202, 207; 'quit India' campaign, 202
India Act (1935), 197
India Office, 197, 199
Indian Army, 108
Indian Congress Party, 197
Indian National Congress, 202
Indian Ocean, 201
Indo-China, 147, 148, 152–5, 158, 179–80, 195, 201, 203, 206
Indomitable, 181, 194
Indonesia, 206
Inonu, Ismet, 107–8, 224, 247–8
Inskip, Sir Thomas, 6
International Pacific Relations Committee, 322
Iran (Persia), 108, 132–4
Iraq, 87, 108–10, 118, 125, 132
Iron Curtain, 332, 335, 336, 338
Ironclad, Operation, 201
Ironside, General Sir W. Edmund, 36–7, 38, 46, 57
Irving, David, 28
Irwin, General, 69, 70
Isigny, 316–17
Isle of Man, 162
Ismay, General Pug, 39, 45–6, 57, 82, 98, 104, 109, 127, 173, 188, 196, 242, 245, 254, 314, 317, 327
Istanbul, 107, 244, 247
Istria, 245, 246, 250, 255, 266, 267–9, 270, 271, 279, 280, 346
Italian Navy, 230–1
Italy: Churchill's enthusiasm for Mussolini, 4–5; invasion of Abyssinia, 4, 6; peace moves, 49–51; enters war, 61–2; Libyan campaign, 82, 84, 86; attacks Greece, 84, 87; East African campaign, 87, 91; Pantellaria base, 99; Operation Torch, 212–13; Trident Conference, 224; Sicilian campaign, 225–6; proposed Free Italian movement, 227–30; surrender, 79, 230–6, 237, 238; and the Aegean campaign, 245; and Yugoslavia, 252–3, 255; Allies recapture, 267, 276–7, 345; Resistance, 268; and Trieste, 271–3
Iwojima, 327

Jack, Major Archibald, 251–2, 257
Jacob, Sir Ian, 41, 190, 220
Jajce Conference (1943), 262, 263–4
Jamaica, 76, 181
Jameson Raid, 123
Japan, 58, 135, 206; growing threat from, 147–60; attacks Pearl Harbor, 158, 160–2, 163, 178; America declares war on, 160–1; Malayan campaign, 179, 185–96; and Thailand, 179–80, 186; sinks *Prince of Wales* and *Repulse*, 181–5; fall of Singapore, 187–95; threat to India, 201, 202; war with America, 319–20; atom bomb attacks, 322, 323, 326, 329–31; surrender terms, 322–31; bomb damage, 327–8; Mimsy plan, 330–1
Java, 191, 195–6, 319
Jean Bart, 65, 66, 67
Jebb, Gladwyn, 233
Jerusalem, Mufti of, 108
Jews, 7–8, 288, 346, 347
Jinnah, Mohammed Ali, 199
Jodl, General, 12, 15, 16
Johnston, Louis, 199
Johore, 153, 191–3
Joint Planning Staff (JPS), 39, 309, 311
Jones, R. V., 321
Jones, Stanley, 188
Juan, Captain, 152
Jubilee, Operation, 170, 171–3
Juin, General, 209, 210, 211, 212
Jupiter, Operation, 150, 166–7, 168
Jutland Bank, 35

Kaiser, Jakob, 288
Karlsruhe, 33
Kasos, 101–3
Kasprzycki, General, 15
Kasserine Gap, 217
Kattegat, 23
Kearney, USS, 81
Keitel, General, 12, 15, 16, 291
Kelly, HMS, 106
Kennedy, Major-General Sir John, 86, 88, 89, 96, 99, 138, 139–40, 145, 176, 282
Kennedy, Joseph, 19, 75
Kenny, Rowland, 40–1
Kenya, 82, 83, 84, 86
Keren, 87, 91
Kersaudy, François, 42
Keyes, Admiral Sir Roger, 18, 38, 43, 69, 98–106, 125, 342
Kiev, 131
Kimmel, Admiral, 178
King, Admiral, 170, 220, 221
King, Mackenzie, 17
Kirby, Lieutenant-Colonel, 240
Kirkpatrick, Helen, 116
Kirkwall, 41
Kirkwood, David, 18

Kleeman, General, 239
Kluge, General von, 47, 54, 286, 288, 290–2
Klugman, Captain James, 253–4, 256, 257–8, 260, 264
Knatchbull-Huggesen, Sir Hugh, 106, 107–8
Knightsbridge Box, 137
Koiso, General, 320
Königsberg, 246
Konoye, Prince, 151, 155, 158, 162, 326, 328
Kota Bharu, 179, 181, 183, 184–5
Koufra, 121
Kra isthmus, 179, 180, 192
Kristallnacht, 10
Kuala Lumpur, 186
Kuantan, 181, 183–4
Kub Kub, 121
Kurusu, Saburu, 155–9

Laake, General, 36
Laborde, Admiral de, 213
Labour Party, 11, 198–9
La Malfa, Ugo, 232
Lampson, Sir Miles (Lord Killearn), 229–30
Lansbury, George, 18
Lashio, 202
Latvia, 20, 129, 332–4
Laval, Pierre, 7, 60, 111, 113, 116, 119, 201, 209, 211
Laycock, General Robert, 95
Layton, Admiral, 181, 187
Leads, The, 27, 32, 33, 35
League of Nations, 4, 8, 19, 27, 313
League of Nations Union, 9
Leahy, Admiral, 119, 122, 154, 209, 210, 323
Leapfrog, Operation, 104–5
Lebanon, 108, 122, 123, 124, 313
Lebrun, Albert, 60, 61
Leclerc, General, 121, 317–18
Leeper, Sir Reginald (Rex), 274–5
Lees, Michael, 257
Le Havre, 54, 55, 166
Leicesters, 40
Le Mans, 55
Lend-Lease, 77–8, 157
Leningrad, 130, 131, 171, 217
Leopold III, King of Belgium, 18
Leros, 94, 239, 244–5, 345–6
Les Portes, Hélène, 61
Le Tréport, 54
Leuschner, Wilhelm, 288
Leyte, 320
Libreville, 71, 113, 115
Libya, 82, 86, 87, 94, 106, 107, 140, 227
Lindemann, Professor *see* Cherwell, Lord
Lindsay, Alexander, 10
Lindsay, Kenneth, 176
Linlithgow, Lord, 197, 202, 204
Linnel, Air Marshal Sir John, 249
Lippman, Walter, 115

Lisbon, 233–4, 286
Lithuania, 20, 129, 332–4
Littorio, 136
Litvinov, Maxim, 130
Ljubljana Gap, 245, 250, 267, 268, 270, 279, 346
Lloyd, Lord, 64, 67
Lloyd George, David, 43, 51–2, 78, 303, 340, 341
Locarno Treaty (1925), 5, 58
Lochmanar, 40
Lofoten, 105
Lolland, 23
Lombardy plain, 267
London, flying bombs, 284, 307–8, 309–11
London Conference of Jews and Arabs, 8
Londonderry, Earl of, 18
Longmore, Air Marshal Sir Arthur Murray, 106, 230
Lorient, 67
Lothian, Lord, 17, 23, 75, 77–8, 114, 149, 153
Louis XVIII, King of France, 115
Louis Ferdinand, Prince, 288
Luang Pibul, 180
Lübeck, 304
Lublin, 334, 337
Luftwaffe, 244, 339; bombs Poland, 15; Norwegian disaster, 38; Greek campaign, 91, 94, 95, 96; in Sicily, 135; Operation Torch, 213
Lulea, 22, 25, 27, 28, 29, 30, 37
Lustre, Operation, 88–90, 93, 95–6
Luxembourg, 22
Lwow, 246
Lyttelton, Oliver, 124, 136, 137, 140, 141–2, 214, 309

MacArthur, General, 203, 204, 319–20
McCallum P., 139
MacDonald, Malcolm, 4
MacDowell, Colonel, 264, 265
Macedonia, 89, 250
MacEwen, Captain, 120
MacGovern, John, 19–20
Mackesy, General, 39–40
Maclean, Fitzroy, 255–6, 259–60, 261–4, 265, 270
Maclean, Admiral Sir Hector, 26
Macmillan, Harold, 6, 7, 10, 44, 76, 234–5, 267, 274–5
McNaughton, General, 166–7, 173
Madagascar, 148, 201–2, 208
Madrid, 286
Maginot Line, 58
Maikop oil field, 177
Mainz, 33
Maisky, Ivan, 32, 130, 131
Malaya, 147, 150, 151, 154, 159–60, 179, 181–3, 185–96, 203–4, 205–6, 270

Maleme airport, 94–5
Mallet, Victor, 231, 288
Malta, 27, 49, 91, 93, 97, 99, 101, 135–6, 137, 208, 225, 235, 342
Malta Conference (1945), 250, 268, 270
Maltby, Air Marshal, 195
Manchurian Incident (1931), 147
Mandalay, 319
Mandible, Operation, 101
Manila, 160
Mannerheim, Field Marshal, 131
Marder, Arthur, 27, 42
Mariana Islands, 320, 327
Marieham, 23
Maritza airfield, 239
Markham, Sir Frank, 176
Marrakesh, 222, 261, 278
Marseilles, 16
Marshall, General George, 169, 170, 241, 301; and the North African campaign, 163–4, 217; plan to invade France, 166, 167, 218, 344; and Pearl Harbor, 178; and the Malayan campaign, 190; and the Mediterranean strategy, 220, 225; Normandy landings, 276, 278; and capture of Berlin, 303–5
Marshall Islands, 318
Martinique, 152
Mary, Queen, 45
Mascherpa, Admiral Luigi, 245
Massawa, 57–8, 121
Mast, General, 210
Matador, Operation, 179, 180, 181, 189
Matilda tanks, 12, 47, 84
Matsuoka, Yosuke, 151–2, 160
Maxton, James, 19, 20, 193
Mechili, 93, 128
Mediterranean, 49, 83, 86, 97, 217, 224–5; Pantellaria project, 99–100; Germany takes control, 135; North African landings, 169–70; Operation Torch, 208–13; Churchill wants standstill order, 237; Russian access to, 247
Megara airfield, 274
Meiklereid, E. W., 152
Melbourne Herald, 189–90
Menace, 69
Menzies, Sir Robert, 17, 88, 90, 96, 189, 190
Mers-el-Kebir, 67–9, 70, 71–3, 117, 118, 121, 122, 123, 148, 175, 207, 208, 212, 340–1
Mersa Matruh, 84, 143, 144
Messer, Fred, 18
Messervy, General, 141
Messina, 226, 276
Messina, Straits of, 221
Metaxas, General, 274
Meuse, River, 299, 300
Middle East Defence Committee, 137
Midjedge bridge, 257

Midway Island, 319

Mihailovic, General, 250–66, 269, 270–1, 272, 273, 346

Military Co-ordination Committee, 35, 37, 39, 45

Milne, Sir James Wardlaw, 140

Mimsy (Plan), 330–1

Ministry of Defence, 141, 142–3, 174–5, 192

Ministry of Economic Warfare (MEW), 22

Ministry of Information, 329

Ministry of Supply and War Transport, 133

Miquelon, 208

Mittelhauser, General, 121

Mittelman, Colonel, 117

Model, Field Marshal, 291

Mohammed Riza Pahlevi, Shah of Persia, 133

Molotov, Vyacheslav, 32, 165, 168, 177, 302, 326, 329, 337–8

Molotov-Ribbentrop Agreement (1939), 13, 20, 217, 246

Monckton, Walter, 137

Monnet, Jean, 59

Montenegro, 250, 251, 255

Montgomery, General Bernard, 74, 244, 270, 290, 291; appointed to Eighth Army, 145–6; Dieppe raid, 171–3; El Alamein, 186, 213–16; Italian campaign, 268, 276–7; Normandy landings, 277–86, 308, 347; Arnhem, 293; Ardennes offensive, 300–1; quarrel with Eisenhower, 300, 301; and Operation Plunder, 301–2; and capture of Berlin, 303–5; German surrender, 306; and de Gaulle's return to France, 315–16; relations with Churchill, 341; Battle of the Bulge, 347

Montoire, 111, 119

Montreux Convention (1936), 247

Moorehead, Alan, 146, 283

Moravo, River, 260

More, George, 257

Morgan, General F. E., 221, 278

Morgenthau Plan, 296–9, 347

Morland, Alice, 331

Morocco, 61, 67, 112, 113, 176, 208, 278

Morrison, Herbert, 11, 43, 44, 129, 307, 309, 310

Morton, Desmond, 118

Moscow, 130, 131, 145, 217, 333

Mosley, Sir Oswald, 4

Mountbatten, Lord Louis, 106, 168–9, 170, 171–4, 204, 205, 220–1, 330–1, 346

Mouzouk, 121

Munich, 307

Munich Agreement (1938), 7, 9–10, 11–12, 30, 185

Munura, Kinisaro, 155–8

Murmansk, 166, 168

Murphy, Robert, 209–11

Mussolini, Benito, 6, 13, 29, 268, 342; Churchill's enthusiasm for, 4–5, 7;
invasion of Abyssinia, 4, 6; peace moves, 49–51; Libyan campaign, 84; Greek campaign, 87; fall of, 226, 227, 231–3, 239, 345

mustard gas, 308–9, 311–12

Nagasaki, 162, 329, 331

Namsos, 36, 37, 38, 39, 40

Namur, 300

Nanking, 158

Naples, 265–6

Narvik, 22, 25, 27–40, 43, 68

National Government, 3–4

Neame, General, 93

Nedic, General, 250–1, 252, 254, 256, 258

Nedicefsi, 252

Nehru, Jawaharlal, 199

Neisse, River, 337

Nelson, 65

Netherlands, 17, 44, 46, 153, 154, 157, 179, 196, 206, 299

Neutrality Pact (1941), 152

New Caledonia, 115

New Guinea, 319–20

New Hebrides, 115

New Zealand, 17, 94, 96, 97, 151, 203

Newall, Air Marshal Cyril, 15, 28, 46

Newfoundland, 76, 79, 208

News Chronicle, 76, 138

Nicholls, Philip, 108, 228

Nicolson, Harold, 7, 176

Nile, River, 207, 313

Nimitz, Admiral, 319

Nogues, General, 114, 209, 210, 211

Nord Fjord, 41

Normanbrook, Lord, 45

Normandy, 57

Normandy landings (1944), 172, 225, 276, 277–86, 291, 298, 299, 308, 341

North, Admiral, 66, 72, 341

North Africa, 58, 61, 82–7, 91–3, 112, 135, 163–4, 166, 167, 169–70, 207–13, 216, 344

Norway, 22–42, 43, 130, 150, 166–7

Norwegian Expeditionary Force, 24

nuclear weapons, 320–3, 326, 328, 329–31, 348

Nuremberg laws, 288

Nuremberg Trials, 25, 160

Nuri, General, 108

Nye, General Sir Archibald, 136

O'Connor, General, 83

Odendhal, Admiral, 64

Oder-Neisse Line, 246

Office of Strategic Studies (OSS), 264, 325

Okinawa, 205, 320, 327

Olivetti, Adriano, 232

Olympic, Operation, 331

Omaha, 283

Oppeln, 246
Oran, 66, 67, 68, 70, 72, 152, 208, 210, 211
Orion, 39
Orpington, 309
Osborne, D'Arcy, 233
Oshima, Hiroshi, 160
Oslo, 35
Ostend, 98
Ottawa Agreement, 79
Overlord, Operation, 221, 225, 240, 241–2, 245–6, 278–86
Oxford by-election (1938), 10
Oxford Union, 321
Oxilia, General, 255

Pacific war, 319–20
Page, Sir Earle, 189, 193, 194
Paget, General, 131
Palestine, 8, 83, 84, 109–10
Pantellaria, 99–101, 104, 342
Panzer Corps, 47, 283, 286, 291, 300
Papagos, General Alexander, 88, 89, 93
Papen, Franz von, 248
Papendreou, George, 274
Papua New Guinea, 319
Paris, 58, 170, 286, 290–1, 317
Paris, Treaty of (1947), 273
Partisans (Yugoslavia), 251–70, 272
Partito d'Azione, 232
Patani, 179, 181
Patton, General, 276, 277–8, 286, 291, 304
Pavelic, Ante, 250
Pearl Harbor, 153, 158, 160–2, 163, 178, 319, 322, 343
Peel Commission, 8
Penang, 183, 186–7
Percival, General, 179, 186, 187, 188
Persia (Iran), 108, 132–4
Pesenti, General, 232, 252
Pétain, Marshal Henri, 60, 125, 316; armistice, 61; and the French Fleet, 63, 213; negotiations with Churchill, 109, 111–21, 209, 341; trial, 118; and Indo-China, 152–4; and North Africa, 207, 211
Peter II, King of Yugoslavia, 250, 251, 253, 254, 256, 259, 261–6, 271
Petsamo, 27, 168
Peyroutin, 313
Pfann, George, 291
Philippeville, 208
Philippine Sea, Battle of (1944), 320
Philippines, 178, 195, 198, 203, 320
Phillips, Admiral Tom, 34, 36, 101, 180–5
Phipps, Brigadier, 40
Piggot, General, 155
Pilgrim, Operation, 103, 104
Pirelli, Alberto, 232
Pisa, 245
Pitt, William the Younger, 115

Pius XII, Pope, 29
Playfair, General, 71–3
Pleven, René, 59
Plunder, Operation, 301–2
Po River, 268
Pola, 234, 268, 272
Poland, 58, 177; Chamberlain's guarantee, 11; Germany invades, 13, 15–17; Russian invasion, 20; Teheran Conference, 246–7; Warsaw uprising, 270; and terms for German surrender, 295; under Russian domination, 334–5, 337
Polish Corridor, 13
Political Warfare Executive, 297, 298
Pomerania, 24, 27
Ponsonby, Lord, 18
Popović, General Koca, 252
Port Moresby, 319
Portal, Air Chief Marshal Sir Charles, 204, 279
Portsmouth, 171, 192, 282, 308, 314
Portugal, 320, 328
Potsdam Conference (1945), 121, 324, 326, 328, 329, 331–4, 336–8, 348
Potsdam Declaration (1945), 327, 329, 330
Pound, Admiral Sir Dudley, 23–9, 42, 63–7, 83, 89, 99–100, 103, 106, 160, 171, 180, 184
Pownall, General, 41–2, 173
Prague, 11
Pranjani, 265
Preysing, Bishop of Berlin, 287, 289
Prince of Wales, 24, 79, 180–1, 183–5
Provence, 112
Prussia, 246, 247
Prytz, Bjorn, 75–6
Public Record Office (PRO), 17, 72, 140, 257, 330, 331, 340
Purvis, Robert, 257

Quadrant Conference, Quebec (1943), 226, 237, 270
Quattara depression, 144
Quebec Conferences, 204, 205, 226, 237, 270, 276, 296, 321
Queen Elizabeth, 135

R4, plan, 35
Raeder, Admiral, 25
Rangoon, 196, 203, 204, 205
Rastenburg, 290–1
Red Army, 20
Red Sea, 57–8
Reggio, 277
Remagen, 302
Renouf, Admiral, 102
Repulse, 24, 25, 35, 180–1, 183–5, 188
Resistance, 64
Resolution, 70
Reuben James, USS, 81

Reynaud, Paul, 32, 33–4, 37–8, 46, 49, 51, 53, 54, 59, 60–1, 75
Rhine, River, 32–3, 299, 300, 301, 302, 303
Rhineland, 5, 15, 59
Rhodes, 94, 99, 101–2, 223, 225, 237–44, 248–9, 345–6
Rhône valley, 280
Rhys Davies, John, 18
Ribbentrop, Joachim von, 76, 159, 160–1, 252, 332, 343
Ribbentrop-Molotov non-aggression pact (1939), 13, 20, 217, 246
Richelieu, 65, 66, 67, 68, 70
Riga, Treaty of (1922), 246
Rimini, 245
Rio, Alphonse, 60
Ritchie, General, 135, 137, 138, 143–4, 145
Riza Pahlevi, Shah of Persia, 132–3
Roberts, General G. P., 215, 293
Roberts, General 'Ham', 172
Robertson, General, 341
Rodney, 35, 65
Roer, River, 299
Roman Catholic Church, 78
Romania, 91, 107, 129, 131–2, 240, 270, 334, 337
Rome, 233, 235, 236, 242, 246, 277
Rommel, General Irwin: and the fall of France, 47, 55, 56; North African campaign, 86, 91–3, 107, 109, 125, 126–9, 134–8, 141, 143, 146; defeat at Alamein, 144–5, 176, 213–16; Normandy landings, 283, 284, 286; and Stauffenberg bomb plot, 290
Roosevelt, Elliot, 222
Roosevelt, Franklin Delano: peace moves, 19, 29; and the Norwegian disaster, 23; and the fall of France, 59, 63; relations with Churchill, 75, 164–6, 247; refuses to join war, 75; gives warships to Britain, 76–7; and the Royal Navy, 76; Lend-Lease, 77–8; re-elected, 77; meeting with Churchill, 78–81; and Pétain, 119; and the fall of Tobruk, 137–8, 143; threat from Japan, 149–50, 153–60; Japan attacks Pearl Harbor, 160, 178; Arcadia Conference, 163–5; plans European invasion, 168; plans North African landings, 169–70; fall of Singapore, 189–90; and Indian independence, 198–201, 347; and Indo-China, 203; Far Eastern campaign, 205; Operation Torch, 207–10, 212; Casablanca Conference, 216–17, 218–23, 227; resentment against British colonialism, 222; Quebec Conference, 226; and the Italian surrender, 232, 234; and the Aegean, 240–3; Teheran Conference, 245–7, 294, 295, 334; and Yugoslavia, 264, 267–8, 272; and Greece, 275; Normandy

landings, 276, 278; supports Operation Anvil, 279; terms for German surrender, 295–6, 299; and capture of Berlin, 305; objections to chemical and biological weapons, 311–12; and de Gaulle, 313, 314, 317; Battle of the Bulge, 317–18; and the atom bomb, 321; Yalta Agreement, 336; death, 305, 348
Roskill, Stephen, 42, 68
Ross and Cromarty by-election (1936), 4
Rosyth, 35
Rougier, Louis, 111–15, 118–21, 153
Roundup, Operation, 163, 167, 169, 170, 172, 207, 216, 217, 218–20, 221, 224, 225
Royal Air Force (RAF), 15, 16, 48, 146; Operation Susan, 71; Battle of Britain, 74; Greek campaign, 90, 91, 95; Dieppe raid, 171; and the fall of Singapore, 181, 195; and the proposed Free Italian movement, 229; Normandy landings, 283; anthrax bombs, 311
Royal Marine, Operation, 32–4
Royal Navy, 65, 146; and the Mers-el-Kebir attack, 69; in event of British defeat, 76; Greek campaign, 87, 93, 95, 96; Pantellaria project, 99
Rufisque, 70
Ruge, General, 36
Ruhr, 46, 296, 297, 308
Rumbold, Sir Anthony, 121
Runciman, Walter, 10
Rundstedt, Field-Marshal von, 290
Rupert, Operation, 35
Rushcliffe, Lord, 18
Russia *see* Soviet Union
Russo-Finnish War, 25, 27, 31, 32
Rutter, Operation, 170–1
Ruvigno, 268
Ryuku Islands, 205, 320

SA, 288
Saar, 296
Saigon, 147, 153, 155, 179, 181, 184
St Lucia, 76
St Nazaire, 67
St Paul's School, 281, 282, 283
St Pierre, 208
St Valéry, 55
Salerno, 233, 235, 236, 277
Salonika, 87, 88
Salter, Alfred, 18
Samnos, 239, 244
Sandys, Duncan, 57, 310
Sangro, 277
Sansom, Sir George, 155, 185, 322–3, 324, 325, 331
Sapru, Tej Bahadur, 198
Sardinia, 104, 217, 219, 220–1, 225
Sargent, Sir Orme, 108, 228
Sato, Naotake, 328–9

Saur, Karl, 293
Scandinavia, Norwegian disaster, 22–42
Scapa Flow, 35, 104
Scaroina, General, 239
Scarpanto, 99, 102
Schacht, Hjalmar, 288
Scharnhorst, 180
Schoenfeld, Hans, 287–8, 289
Scobie, General, 274
Scotland, 104
Seal, Eric, 45
Sealion, Operation, 82
Sebastopol, 140
Secret Service, 34, 35, 308
Sedan, 46
Seeds, William, 129
Seine, River, 286, 291, 293
Selborne, Lord, 255, 260, 263
Selkirk, Earl of, 26–7
Senegal, 69–70
Senussi tribe, 229, 230
Serbia, 250–1, 252, 254, 258, 259
Serbian State Guard, 257–8
Serbs, 250–1
Seton-Watson, Professor, 11
Sèvres, Treaty of (1920), 247
SHAEF (Supreme Headquarters Allied
    Expeditionary Force), 277, 298–9, 303,
    317
Sherman tanks, 143, 144, 164, 214
Sherwood Foresters, 40
Shrapnel, Operation, 103
Siam, Gulf of, 24, 147, 154
Sicily, 91, 99, 135, 216, 217, 219, 220–1,
    225–6, 276
Sidi Barrani, 84, 86
Sidi Rizegh, 137
Siegfried Line, 12, 15–16
Silesia, 293
Silverman, Sydney, 18
Simalur, 204
Simon, Sir John (Lord Simon), 23, 27, 77, 289
Simonovitch, General, 91
Simpson, General Sir Frank, 285, 300, 301,
    304–5
Simson, General, 186
Sinclair, Sir Archibald, 8, 9, 31, 43, 61, 100,
    307, 347
Singapore, 131, 167, 174, 175; Japanese
    threat, 147; weakness of defences, 150–1,
    154; naval Defence Conference, 153; loss
    of *Prince of Wales* and *Repulse*, 181–4, fall
    of, 187–95; recapture, 203–6
Singora, 179, 181, 183
Sirte, 86
Skipper, Operation, 270
Skoda, 11–12
Sledgehammer, Operation, 163, 167, 168,
    169–70, 177, 221
Slovenes, 234

Slovenia, 253
Smuts, Field Marshal Jan, 17, 51, 214, 221,
    223, 295
Smyrna, 223, 248
Smyth, Brigadier, 186
Soames, Mary, 176, 317
SOE, 117, 228–9, 231, 232, 252, 253–4, 255,
    257–8, 259, 261, 263, 265, 266, 268, 346
Sofafi, 86
Sogne Fjord, 41
Sokarno, Achmad, 206
Solh, Riadh es, 313
Sollum, 84, 127, 143
Solly-Flood, Peter, 255
Solomon Islands, 319
Somaliland, 57, 82, 85
Somerville, Admiral, 66, 67–9, 72, 341
Somme, 48, 53, 58
Sorenson, Reginald, 18
Souffleur, 124
South Africa, 17, 77, 83, 180
Southampton, 308
Soviet Union: non-aggression pact with
    Germany, 13; and Poland, 20, 334–5,
    337; and the Norwegian disaster, 24–6,
    30–2; proposed bombing of Baku oil
    fields, 33; German invasion, 78, 122, 124,
    129–32, 177, 342; fear of coup in Persia,
    132–4; Neutrality Pact with Japan, 152;
    Roosevelt wishes to meet Stalin privately,
    165–6; and Jupiter plan, 167; demands
    for second front, 168, 171, 207, 216–17;
    Churchill meets Stalin, 177; and Turkey,
    223–4; Teheran Conference, 245–7;
    advances on Austria, 269, 270; occupation
    of part of Yugoslavia, 270–1; terms for
    German surrender, 294, 299; and capture
    of Berlin, 302–6; Japanese surrender
    terms, 326, 328–9; Potsdam Conference,
    328, 332, 335–8; and the atom bomb,
    330; and the Baltic states, 332–3
Spain, 15, 100, 140, 208
Spanish Civil War, 6
Spears, General, 7, 53, 60
Spectator, 3, 129
Speer, Albert, 293
Speaight, R. L., 119
Split, 255, 259, 267
Spoleto, Duke of, 250
SS, 288
Stacey, Charles P., 173
Stalin, Joseph: non-aggression pact with
    Germany, 13; and the Baltic states, 20;
    Churchill fears he will make separate
    peace with Hitler, 30, 292, 333; invades
    Germany, 129–32; and Persia, 133–4;
    Roosevelt tries to arrange private meeting
    with, 165–6; and Jupiter plan, 167; wants
    second front opened, 168, 171, 207,
    216–17, 218, 221–2; meetings with

Stalin, Joseph – *cont'd*
Churchill, 177; and the Casablanca
   Conference, 221–2; and Turkey,
   223–4; Teheran Conference, 245–6,
   294, 295, 334; Warsaw uprising, 270; and
   Yugoslavia, 271, 272–3; terms for
   German surrender, 294, 295–6,
   299; and capture of Berlin, 304; and
   the atom bomb, 326; Japanese
   surrender terms, 326, 328–9; Potsdam
   Conference, 328, 335–8, 348; and
   Poland, 334–5
Stalingrad, 177, 217
Stamp, Lord, 20
Stampalia, 99
Stark, Admiral, 78
Stark, Freya, 230
Stauffenberg, Claus, 286, 290, 293
Stavanger, 31, 33, 34, 39, 41
Sterndale Bennett, Sir John, 324–5
Stettinius, Edward, 305, 314, 323, 332
Stevens, Campbell, 19
Stevenson, Ralph, 260, 262, 263, 270
Stewart, Sir Findlater, 309
Stimson, Henry, 158, 159, 217, 225–6, 297,
   323, 324, 327, 329
Stitt, Commander, 71–3
Stock Exchange, 8, 9, 129
Stockholm, 286, 289
Stokes, Richard, 18, 19, 292, 293
Storry, Richard, 322, 327–8, 329
Straits Convention (1923), 247
Strakosch, Sir Henry, 9
Strang, Sir William, 112, 113, 288
Strasbourg, 317–18
Strasbourg, 65
Stratford plan, 39
Strauss, George, 292–3
Stuart tanks, 137
Student, 108, 110
Stuka bombers, 47
Stülpnagel, General Karl, 290–1
Styria, 272
Suda Bay, 87, 93, 94, 102
Sudan, 82, 86
Sudetenland, 9–11, 293
Sudxhaskas, Vaclovas, 333
Suez, 49, 101
Suez Canal, 118, 124, 125
Suez Crisis (1956), 44
Sumatra, 191, 194, 203–4, 205, 319
Supercharge, Operation, 215
Supreme War Council, 16–17, 20, 28, 30,
   31, 33, 37, 38, 53, 58
Susan, Operation, 71
Suzuki, Admiral, 320, 326, 328–9, 330
Sweden, 22, 23–31, 75–6, 166, 230–1, 287,
   320, 328
Switzerland, 320, 328
Syria, 33, 87, 106, 108, 118, 121–5, 134, 150,
   152, 201, 313

Taha Pasha, 108
Tananarive, 202
Tangier, 111
Tedder, Air Marshal, 240, 283
Teheran, 133
Teheran Conference (1943), 245–8, 278, 290,
   293, 294, 295, 334, 346
Tennant, Captain W. B., 184, 188
Tennant, Sir Peter, 231
Ter Poorten, General, 196
Termoli, 268, 277
Thailand, 152, 160, 179–80, 186
Thomas, Sir Shenton, 185, 187, 188
Thrace, 107
Thyssen, Baron, 28
Tiger convoy, 127
The Times, 9, 120, 140, 330
Timor, 319
Tirpitz, 180
Tito, Marshal, 250–73, 346
Tittman, Harold H., 234
Tobruk, 86, 87, 92–3, 121, 127, 128, 134–5,
   137–44, 145, 167, 174, 175, 189
Togo, Shigeriori, 155, 158, 159, 162
Tojo, General Hideki, 155, 158, 159, 162,
   178, 320
Tokyo, 320, 327, 330
Tolstoi, Count Nikolai, 273
Torch, Operation, 119, 169–70, 177, 207–13,
   214, 215, 218
Toulon, 67, 68, 152–3, 211, 213
Tours, 58, 63
Toyoda, Admiral, 152, 153
Trades Union Act, 46
Tree, Ronald, 116
Trevelyan, George, 61
Trident Conference (1943), 224–5, 237
Trieste, 234, 255, 267, 268, 271–3
Trinidad, 76
Tripartite Pact (1940), 147, 149, 153, 161
Tripoli, 82, 86–7, 88, 90, 91, 99, 126, 135,
   163, 210
Trondheim, 31–2, 34–40, 43, 98, 166
Tronso, 180
Trott, Adam von, 286–9
Truman, Harry S.: and Yugoslavia, 272–3;
   and capture of Berlin, 305–6; and the
   atom bomb, 321–2, 323, 326, 329–30;
   Japanese surrender terms, 323, 324;
   Potsdam Conference, 332, 335–7,
   348
Truth, 13
Tunis, 49, 208, 210, 213, 224, 242, 344
Tunisia, 86, 99, 135, 148, 163, 208, 212–13,
   216, 217
Turkey, 20, 122, 125, 136, 219; Dardanelles
   landings, 39; Churchill wants to bring
   into war, 106–8, 131, 233–4, 237, 238,
   245–6, 247–9; and Mediterranean
   strategy, 217, 218; and the Aegean

campaign, 244; and the Teheran
Conference, 247–8

U-Boats, 98
Ukraine, 131
Ultra signals, 87, 88, 126, 127, 136–7, 143,
    146, 215, 283, 285
United States of America; restricts Jewish
    immigration, 8; peace moves, 19; and the
    Norwegian disaster, 31; fall of France, 59,
    63; refuses to join war, 74–5; gives
    warships to Britain, 76–7; Lend-Lease,
    77–8; Roosevelt and Churchill meet,
    78–81; Germany sinks ships, 81;
    Churchill's negotiations with Vichy
    France, 114–15, 119, 120; threat from
    Japan, 148–50, 153–60; Japan attacks
    Pearl Harbor, 158, 160–2, 163, 178;
    enters war, 160–2, 163; Arcadia
    Conference, 163–5; plans European
    invasion, 167–8; plans North African
    landings, 169–70; and Indian
    independence, 198–201; Far Eastern
    campaign, 205; Operation Torch, 207–12,
    216; Casablanca Conference, 216–17,
    218–23, 227; Trident Conference, 224–5;
    and the Italian surrender, 233–5; and the
    Aegean, 237, 240–3; Churchill wants
    standstill order in Mediterranean, 237;
    Teheran Conference, 245–7; and
    Yugoslavia, 264, 267–8, 271–3; Italian
    campaign, 276–7; Normandy landings,
    276, 277, 281, 283–6; terms for German
    surrender, 294–9; Ardennes offensive,
    300–1; and capture of Berlin, 302–5;
    objections to chemical and biological
    weapons, 311–12; and de Gaulle, 314,
    317; Pacific war, 319–20; atom bombs,
    320–3, 326, 328, 329–31; Japanese
    surrender terms, 322–5, 329, 331;
    Potsdam Conference, 326, 332, 335–7
United States Strategic Bombing Survey
    (USSBS), 22
US Army Planning Staff, 166
US Congress, 78, 80, 81, 156, 160, 162, 165,
    179, 323
US Joint Strategic Committee, 166
US Navy, 78, 80, 81
US Pacific Fleet, 201
US State Department, 122, 158, 323, 324, 329
Ustase party, 250, 251, 257

V weapons, 307–12, 347
Valiant, 35, 65, 135
Vanguard, Operation, 204
Vansittart, Sir Robert, 17, 19, 59
Vardar river, 88
Vatican, 233, 234
Velebit, General, 252
Veneto, 269

Venezia Division, 255
Venezia Guilia, 271–3
Venice, 267
Versailles Treaty (1919), 5, 13, 18, 58, 290
Vichy France: and the French Fleet, 68; Dakar
    operation, 70; and Iraq, 108–9;
    negotiations with Churchill, 111–21, 341;
    and Syria, 121–5; agreement with Japan,
    147, 148; and Indo-China, 147, 152–5;
    and Madagascar, 201–2; and Indonesia,
    206; and North Africa, 207–13
Vickers, 141
Victor Emmanuel III, King of Italy, 159, 226,
    231–2, 233–6, 237, 250, 345
Vienna, 245, 250, 267, 268, 269, 279, 305,
    306, 347
Vietnam, 154
Vis, 267
Visser't Hooft, Dr Willem-Adolf, 287, 288
Vlieland, C. A., 188–9, 192
Vosges, 317
Vyshinski, Andrei, 247

Walter, J. H., 231
War Cabinet: Norwegian disaster, 25, 27–32,
    35–8; under Churchill, 48; proposed
    Anglo-French union, 59–60; and the
    French Fleet, 65–7; Dakar operation, 70;
    Greek campaign, 88–90, 96; enquiry into
    tank deficiencies, 142; Far Eastern policy,
    149; plans European invasion, 168;
    Dieppe raid, 171–2; and the proposed
    Free Italian movement, 229–30; and the
    Italian surrender, 232; terms for German
    surrender, 294, 295, 296; and the flying
    bombs, 308–10; and de Gaulle, 312
War Office: and invasion of Poland, 15; and
    the Norwegian disaster, 36, 38; Middle
    Eastern campaign, 85; and invasion of
    Greece, 87; edits press communiqués, 92
    North African campaign, 93; and the fall
    of Singapore, 192; proposed Free Italian
    movement, 228–9; and the Italian
    surrender, 232; Normandy landings, 282
Warner, Christopher, 288
Warsaw, 15, 270
Washington, 224, 317
Wavell, General Sir Archibald, 57, 131, 185,
    214, 243, 301; North African campaign,
    82–7, 91–3, 106, 107, 121, 124, 126–8,
    143, 227; Greek campaign, 87–97,
    101–3, 126, 139, 341; attack on Rhodes,
    101; and Iraq, 108–10; and Turkey, 108;
    and Syria, 122–4; dismissal, 127, 128,
    134, 137; ABDA Command, 190–1; and
    the fall of Singapore, 191–5; and threat to
    India, 201, 202; Burma campaign, 202;
    Far Eastern campaign, 204; and the
    proposed Free Italian movement, 229–30;
    Italian campaign, 280

Wavertree by-election (1935), 4
Welles, Sumner, 19, 30, 79
Wesel, 301
West Africa, 69, 112, 115, 211
West Indies, 67, 117
Western Desert, 83, 87, 106, 124, 125, 126–8,
    134–46
Westminster, Bendor, Duke of, 18
Westphal, General, 235–6
Westwood, Joseph, 140
Weygand, General, 48–9, 54, 56, 58, 61,
    111–19, 121, 148, 209
Wheeler-Bennett, J., 287, 292
White, Harry, 297
Wiart, Carton de, 15
Wilfred, Operation, 32, 33–4
Wilhelmina, Queen of Holland, 18
Wilkie, Wendell, 77
Williams, Brigadier Sir Edgar, 286,
    291
Wilson, Sir Arnold, 18
Wilson, General Sir Henry Maitland, 85, 89,
    123, 124, 237–40, 242–5, 260, 261, 264,
    265, 267, 269, 341
Wilson, Sir Horace, 13
Wilson, Woodrow, 9, 290

Wingate, Brigadier Orde, 203
Wiskemann, Elizabeth, 289
Witzleben, General, 288
Wood, Kingsley, 28, 30, 38, 77
Woodward, Sir Llewellyn, 28, 71–3, 121
Woolley, Sir Leonard, 229
Workshop, Operation, 99–102, 103
World Council of Churches, 287, 288
Wright, Sir Michael, 120, 324
Wurm, Bishop of Württemberg, 287

Yalta Agreement, 334, 336, 337
Yalta Conference (1945), 247
Yamamoto, Admiral, 319
Yugoslavia, 232; and the Greek campaign, 88,
    89, 90; joins Axis, 90–1; Germany
    attacks, 93; Balkan Pact, 107; planned
    front, 250; Tito and Mihailovic blunder,
    250–73, 346

Zang, Admiral Jacques, 68
Zeebrugge, 98, 105
Zervas, General Napoleon, 274
Zetland, Marquis of, 197
Zionism, 8, 347
Zipper, Operation, 205–6